Scott Foresman
Science
The Diamond Edition

PEARSON
Scott
Foresman

Editorial Offices: Glenview, Illinois • Parsippany, New Jersey • New York, New York
Sales Offices: Boston, Massachusetts • Duluth, Georgia • Glenview, Illinois •
Coppell, Texas • Sacramento, California • Mesa, Arizona
www.pearsonsuccessnet.com

Series Authors

Dr. Timothy Cooney
Professor of Earth Science and Science Education
University of Northern Iowa (UNI)
Cedar Falls, Iowa

Dr. Jim Cummins
Professor
Department of Curriculum, Teaching, and Learning
The University of Toronto
Toronto, Canada

Dr. James Flood
Distinguished Professor of Literacy and Language
School of Teacher Education
San Diego State University
San Diego, California

Barbara Kay Foots, M. Ed
Science Education Consultant
Houston, Texas

Dr. M. Jenice Goldston
Associate Professor of Science Education
Department of Elementary Education Programs
University of Alabama
Tuscaloosa, Alabama

Dr. Shirley Gholston Key
Associate Professor of Science Education
Instruction and Curriculum Leadership Department
College of Education
University of Memphis
Memphis, Tennessee

Dr. Diane Lapp
Distinguished Professor of Reading and Language Arts in Teacher Education
San Diego State University
San Diego, California

Sheryl A. Mercier
Classroom Teacher
Dunlap Elementary School
Dunlap, California

Karen L. Ostlund, Ph.D.
UTeach Specialist
College of Natural Sciences
The University of Texas at Austin
Austin, Texas

Dr. Nancy Romance
Professor of Science Education & Principal Investigator
NSF/IERI Science IDEAS Project
Charles E. Schmidt College of Science
Florida Atlantic University
Boca Raton, Florida

Dr. William Tate
Chair and Professor of Education and Applied Statistics
Department of Education
Washington University
St. Louis, Missouri

Dr. Kathryn C. Thornton
Former NASA Astronaut Professor
School of Engineering and Applied Science
University of Virginia
Charlottesville, Virginia

Dr. Leon Ukens
Professor Emeritus
Department of Physics, Astronomy, and Geosciences
Towson University
Towson, Maryland

Steve Weinberg
Consultant
Connecticut Center for Advanced Technology
East Hartford, Connecticut

ISBN: 978-0-328-28959-2; 0-328-28959-0 (SVE); 978-0-328-30438-7;
0-328-30438-7 (A); 978-0-328-30439-4; 0-328-30439-5 (B); 978-0-328-30440-0;
0-328-30440-9 (C); 978-0-328-30441-7; 0-328-30441-7 (D)

Consulting Author

Dr. Michael P. Klentschy

Superintendent
El Centro Elementary School District
El Centro, California

Science Content Consultants

Dr. Frederick W. Taylor

Senior Research Scientist
Institute for Geophysics
Jackson School of Geosciences
The University of Texas at Austin
Austin, Texas

Dr. Ruth E. Buskirk

Senior Lecturer
School of Biological Sciences
The University of Texas at Austin
Austin, Texas

Dr. Cliff Frohlich

Senior Research Scientist
Institute for Geophysics
Jackson School of Geosciences
The University of Texas at Austin
Austin, Texas

Brad Armosky

McDonald Observatory
The University of Texas at Austin
Austin, Texas

Content Consultants

Adena Williams Loston, Ph.D.

Chief Education Officer
Office of the Chief Education Officer

Clifford W. Houston, Ph.D.

Deputy Chief Education Officer for Education Programs
Office of the Chief Education Officer

Frank C. Owens

Senior Policy Advisor
Office of the Chief Education Officer

Deborah Brown Biggs

Manager, Education Flight Projects Office
Space Operations Mission Directorate
Education Lead

Erika G. Vick

NASA Liaison to Pearson Scott Foresman
Education Flight Projects Office

William E. Anderson

Partnership Manager for Education
Aeronautics Research Mission
Directorate

Anita Krishnamurthi

Program Planning Specialist
Space Science Education and
Outreach Program

Bonnie J. McClain

Chief of Education
Exploration Systems Mission
Directorate

Diane Clayton Ph.D.

Program Scientist
Earth Science Education

Deborah Rivera

Strategic Alliances Manager
Office of Public Affairs
NASA Headquarters

Douglas D. Peterson

Public Affairs Officer, Astronaut Office
Office of Public Affairs
NASA Johnson Space Center

Nicole Cloutier

Public Affairs Officer, Astronaut Office
Office of Public Affairs
NASA Johnson Space Center

Reviewers

Dr. Maria Aida Alanis
Administrator
Austin ISD
Austin Texas

Melissa Barba
Teacher
Wesley Mathews Elementary
Miami, Florida

Dr. Marcelline Barron
Supervisor/K-12 Math
and Science
Fairfield Public Schools
Fairfield, Connecticut

Jane Bates
Teacher
Hickory Flat Elementary
Canton, Georgia

Denise Bizjack
Teacher
Dr. N. H. Jones Elementary
Ocala, Florida

Latanya D. Bragg
Teacher
Davis Magnet School
Jackson, Mississippi

Richard Burton
Teacher
George Buck Elementary
School 94
Indianapolis, Indiana

Dawn Cabrera
Teacher
E.W.F. Stirrup School
Miami, Florida

Barbara Calabro
Teacher
Compass Rose Foundation
Ft. Myers, Florida

Lucille Calvin
Teacher
Weddington Math &
Science School
Greenville, Mississippi

Patricia Carmichael
Teacher
Teasley Middle School
Canton, Georgia

Martha Cohn
Teacher
An Wang Middle School
Lowell, Massachusetts

Stu Danzinger
Supervisor
Community Consolidated
School District 59
Arlington Heights, Illinois

Esther Draper
Supervisor/Science Specialist
Belair Math Science
Magnet School
Pine Bluff, Arkansas

Sue Esser
Teacher
Loretto Elementary
Jacksonville, Florida

Dr. Richard Fairman
Teacher
Antioch University
Yellow Springs, Ohio

Joan Goldfarb
Teacher
Indialantic Elementary
Indialantic, Florida

Deborah Gomes
Teacher
A J Gomes Elementary
New Bedford, Massachusetts

Sandy Hobart
Teacher
Mims Elementary
Mims, Florida

Tom Hocker
Teacher/Science Coach
Boston Latin Academy
Dorchester, Massachusetts

Shelley Jaques
Science Supervisor
Moore Public Schools
Moore, Oklahoma

Marguerite W. Jones
Teacher
Spearman Elementary
Piedmont, South Carolina

Kelly Kenney
Teacher
Kansas City Missouri
School District
Kansas City, Missouri

Carol Kilbane
Teacher
Riverside Elementary School
Wichita, Kansas

Robert Kolenda
Teacher
Neshaminy School District
Langhorne, Pennsylvania

Karen Lynn Kruse
Teacher
St. Paul the Apostle
Yonkers, New York

Elizabeth Loures
Teacher
Point Fermin
Elementary School
San Pedro, California

Susan MacDougall
Teacher
Brick Community Primary
Learning Center
Brick, New Jersey

Jack Marine
Teacher
Raising Horizons Quest
Charter School
Philadelphia, Pennsylvania

Nicola Micozzi Jr.
Science Coordinator
Plymouth Public Schools
Plymouth, Massachusetts

Paula Monteiro
Teacher
A J Gomes Elementary
New Bedford, Massachusetts

Tracy Newallis
Teacher
Taper Avenue Elementary
San Pedro, California

Dr. Eugene Nicolo
Supervisor, Science K-12
Moorestown School District
Moorestown, New Jersey

Jeffrey Pastrak
School District of Philadelphia
Philadelphia, Pennsylvania

Helen Pedigo
Teacher
Mt. Carmel Elementary
Huntsville Alabama

Becky Peltonen
Teacher
Patterson Elementary School
Panama City, Florida

Sherri Pensler
Teacher/ESOL
Claude Pepper Elementary
Miami, Florida

Virginia Rogliano
Teacher
Bridgeview Elementary
South Charleston, West
Virginia

Debbie Sanders
Teacher
Thunderbolt Elementary
Orange Park, Florida

Grethel Santamarina
Teacher
E.W.F. Stirrup School
Miami, Florida

Migdalia Schneider
Teacher/Bilingual
Lindell School
Long Beach, New York

Susan Shelly
Teacher
Bonita Springs Elementary
Bonita Springs, Florida

Peggy Terry
Teacher
Madison District 151
South Holland, Illinois

Jane M. Thompson
Teacher
Emma Ward Elementary
Lawrenceburg, Kentucky

Martha Todd
Teacher
W. H. Rhodes Elementary
Milton, Florida

Renee Williams
Teacher
Central Elementary
Bloomfield, New Mexico

Myra Wood
Teacher
Madison Street Academy
Ocala, Florida

Marion Zampa
Teacher
Shawnee Mission
School District
Overland Park, Kansas

Science

See learning in a whole new light

Unit A Life Science

How do the different parts of a plant help it live and grow?

Chapter 1 • Plants and How They Grow

Chapter 2 • How Animals Live

How do different animals live, grow, and change?

Unit A Life Science

How are ecosystems different from each other?

Chapter 3 • Where Plants and Animals Live

Chapter 4 • Plants and Animals Living Together

How do plants and animals interact?

Unit B Earth Science

How does water change form?

How does weather follow patterns?

x

Chapter 7 • Rocks and Soil

Why are rocks and soil important resources?

How do forces cause changes on Earth's surface?

Chapter 8 • Changes on Earth

Chapter 9 • Natural Resources

How can people
use natural
resources
responsibly?

Unit C Physical Science

What are the properties of matter?

What are physical and chemical changes in matter?

Chapter 12 • Forces and Motion

How do forces cause motion and get work done?

Unit C Physical Science

How does energy change form?

Chapter 13 • Energy

Chapter 14 • Sound

How does energy produce the sounds we hear?

Unit D Space and Technology

What patterns do the Earth, Sun, Moon, and stars show?

How are the planets in the solar system alike and different?

Chapter 17 • Science in Our Lives

How does technology affect our lives?

How to Read Science

A page like the one below is found near the beginning of each chapter. It shows you how to use a reading skill that will help you understand what you read.

Before Reading

Before you read the chapter, read the Build Background page and think about how to answer the question. Recall what you already know as you answer the question. Work with a partner to make a list of what you already know. Then read the How to Read Science page.

Target Reading Skill
Each page has one target reading skill. The reading skill corresponds with a process skill in the Directed Inquiry activity on the facing page. The reading skill will be useful as you read science.

Real-World Connection
Each page has an example of something you might read. It also connects with the Directed Inquiry activity.

Graphic Organizer
A useful strategy for understanding anything you read is to make a graphic organizer. A graphic organizer can help you think about the information and how parts of it relate to each other. Each reading skill has a graphic organizer.

How to Read Science

Reading Skills

Compare and Contrast
When you **compare** things, you tell how they are alike. When you **contrast** things, you tell how they are different.
- Words and phrases such as *similar, like, all, both,* or *in the same way* are clues that things are being compared.
- Words and phrases such as *different, unlike,* or *in a different way* are clues that things are being contrasted.

Magazine Article

Rock Collectors

Ben and Misha both collect rocks. Ben prefers brightly colored rocks. He is a member of a rock hunters club that goes on collecting trips. Misha has a different way of collecting his favorite kinds of rocks—fossil rocks. His uncle sends Misha fossil rocks from all around the world. Unlike Ben, Misha just has to make a trip to his mailbox to add to his collection.

Apply It!
You can use a graphic organizer as a **model** to show how things compare and contrast.

Different — Alike — Different
Ben — Misha

Use a graphic organizer to show ways that Ben and Misha are alike and different in the way they collect rocks.

197

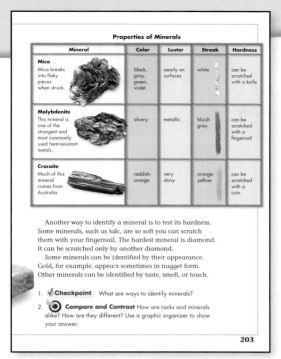

Properties of Minerals

Mineral		Color	Luster	Streak	Hardness
Mica Mica breaks into flaky pieces when struck.		black, gray, green, violet	pearly on surfaces	white	can be scratched with a knife
Molybdenite This mineral is one of the strongest and most commonly used heat-resistant metals.		silvery	metallic	bluish gray	can be scratched with a fingernail
Crocoite Much of this mineral comes from Australia.		reddish-orange	very shiny	orange-yellow	can be scratched with a coin

Another way to identify a mineral is to test its hardness. Some minerals, such as talc, are so soft you can scratch them with your fingernail. The hardest mineral is diamond. It can be scratched only by another diamond.

Some minerals can be identified by their appearance. Gold, for example, appears sometimes in nugget form. Other minerals can be identified by taste, smell, or touch.

1. ✓**Checkpoint** What are ways to identify minerals?

2. **Compare and Contrast** How are rocks and minerals alike? How are they different? Use a graphic organizer to show your answer.

203

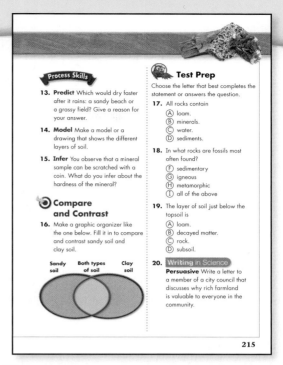

Process Skills

13. **Predict** Which would dry faster after it rains: a sandy beach or a grassy field? Give a reason for your answer.

14. **Model** Make a model or a drawing that shows the different layers of soil.

15. **Infer** You observe that a mineral sample can be scratched with a coin. What do you infer about the hardness of the mineral?

Compare and Contrast

16. Make a graphic organizer like the one below. Fill it in to compare and contrast sandy soil and clay soil.

Sandy soil | Both types of soil | Clay soil

Test Prep

Choose the letter that best completes the statement or answers the question.

17. All rocks contain
   Ⓐ loam.
   Ⓑ minerals.
   Ⓒ water.
   Ⓓ sediments.

18. In what rocks are fossils most often found?
   Ⓕ sedimentary
   Ⓖ igneous
   Ⓗ metamorphic
   Ⓘ all of the above

19. The layer of soil just below the topsoil is
   Ⓐ loam.
   Ⓑ decayed matter.
   Ⓒ rock.
   Ⓓ subsoil.

20. **Writing in Science**
   Persuasive Write a letter to a member of a city council that discusses why rich farmland is valuable to everyone in the community.

215

During Reading

As you read the lesson, use the Checkpoint to check your understanding. Some checkpoints ask you to use the target reading skill.

After Reading

After you have read the chapter, think about what you found out. Exchange ideas with a partner. Compare the list you made before you read the chapter with what you learned by reading it. Answer the questions in the Chapter Review. One question uses the target reading skill.

Graphic Organizers

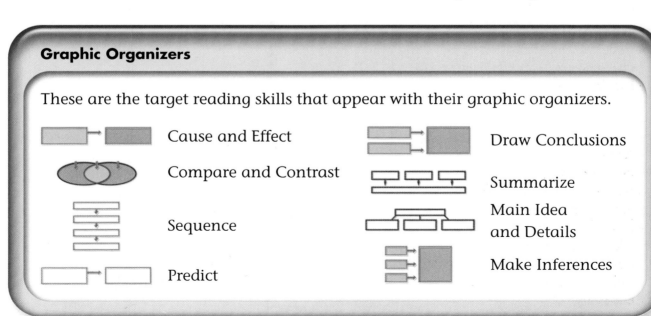

These are the target reading skills that appear with their graphic organizers.

Cause and Effect

Compare and Contrast

Sequence

Predict

Draw Conclusions

Summarize

Main Idea and Details

Make Inferences

Science Process Skills

Investigating Weather

Scientists use process skills when they investigate places or events. You will use these skills when you do the activities in this book. Which process skills might scientists use when they investigate weather?

Observe

A scientist who studies weather observes many things. You use your senses too to find out about other objects, events, or living things.

Classify

Scientists classify clouds according to their properties. When you classify, you arrange or sort objects, events, or living things.

Estimate and Measure

Scientists estimate how much rain will fall. Then they use tools to measure how much rain fell.

Infer
Scientists infer what they think is happening during a storm, based on what they already know.

Predict
Scientists predict how weather will change. Then people know how to get ready for the change.

Make and Use Models
Scientists make and use models such as pictures and maps. Models are like real events in some ways, but are different in other ways.

Make Operational Definitions
Scientists can use what they know to make operational definitions about what they observe during a storm.

Science Process Skills

Form Questions and Hypotheses
Think of a statement that you can test to solve a problem or answer a question about storms or other kinds of weather.

Investigate and Experiment
As scientists observe storms, they investigate and experiment to test a hypothesis.

Identify and Control Variables
As scientists perform an experiment, they identify and control the variables so that they test only one thing at a time.

If you were a scientist, you might want to learn more about storms. What questions might you have about storms? How would you use process skills in your investigation?

Collect Data
Scientists collect data from their observations of weather. They put the data into charts or tables.

Interpret Data
Scientists use the information they collected to solve problems or answer questions.

Communicate
Scientists use words, pictures, charts, and graphs to share information about their investigation.

Using Scientific Methods for Science Inquiry

Scientists use scientific methods as they work. Scientific methods are organized ways to answer questions and solve problems. Scientific methods include the steps shown here. Scientists might not use all the steps. They might not use the steps in this order. You will use scientific methods when you do the **Full Inquiry** activity at the end of each unit. You also will use scientific methods when you do Science Fair Projects.

Ask a question.

You might have a question about something you observe.

What material is best for keeping heat in water?

State your hypothesis.

A hypothesis is a possible answer to your question.

If I wrap the jar in fake fur, then the water will stay warm the longest.

Identify and control variables.

Variables are things that can change. For a fair test, you choose just one variable to change. Keep all other variables the same.

Test other materials. Put the same amount of warm water in other jars that are the same size and shape.

Test your hypothesis.

Make a plan to test your hypothesis. Collect materials and tools. Then follow your plan.

Collect and record your data.

Keep good records of what you do and find out. Use tables and pictures to help.

Interpret your data.

Organize your notes and records to make them clear. Make diagrams, charts, or graphs to help.

State your conclusion.

Your conclusion is a decision you make based on your data. Communicate what you found out. Tell whether or not your data supported your hypothesis.

Fake fur kept the water warm longest. My data supported my hypothesis.

Go further.

Use what you learn. Think of new questions to test or better ways to do a test.

Ask a Question

State Your Hypothesis

Identify and Control Variables

Test Your Hypothesis

Collect and Record Your Data

Interpret Your Data

State Your Conclusion

Go Further

Science Tools

Scientists use many different kinds of tools. Tools can make objects appear larger. They can help you measure volume, temperature, length distance, and mass. Tools can help you figure out amounts and analyze your data. Tools can also help you find the latest scientific information.

You should use **safety goggles** to protect your eyes.

You use a **thermometer** to measure temperature. Many thermometers have both Fahrenheit and Celsius scales. Scientists usually use only the Celsius scale.

You can use a **telescope** to help you see things that are very far away, such as stars and planets.

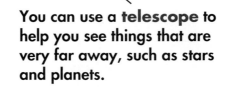

Binoculars make far-away objects appear larger, so you can see more of their details.

A **hand lens** doesn't enlarge things as much as a microscope does, but it is easier to carry.

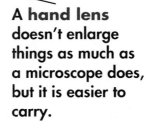

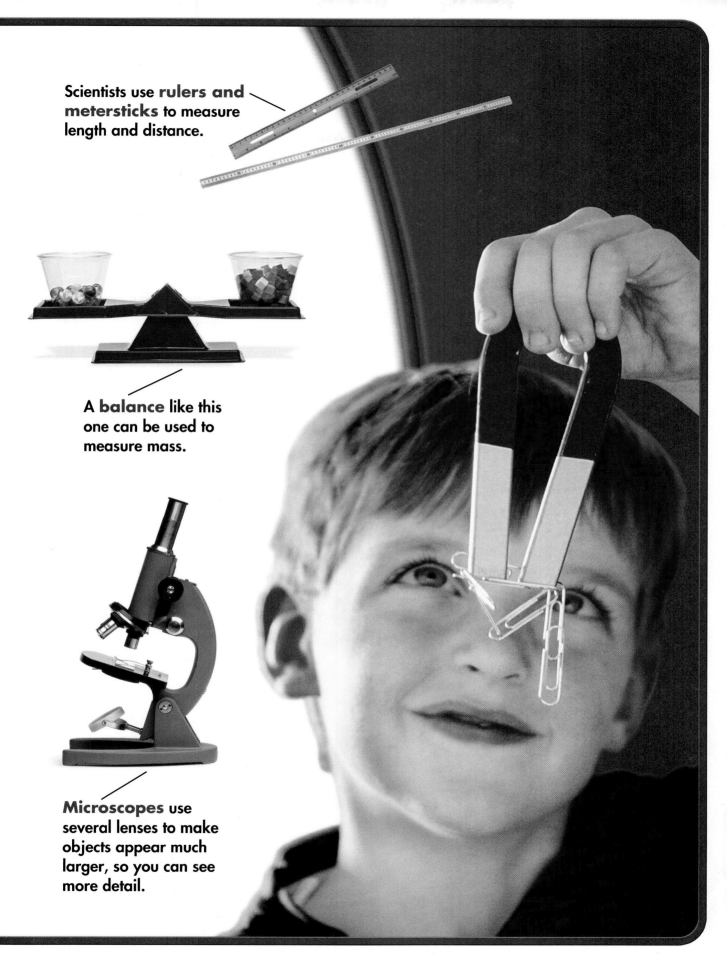

Scientists use **rulers and metersticks** to measure length and distance.

A **balance** like this one can be used to measure mass.

Microscopes use several lenses to make objects appear much larger, so you can see more detail.

Science Tools

Magnets can be used to test if an object is made of certain metals such as iron.

Pictures taken with a **camera** record what something looks like. You can compare pictures of the same object to show how the object might have changed.

A **graduated cylinder** can be used to measure volume, or the amount of space an object takes up.

Calipers can be used to measure the width of an object.

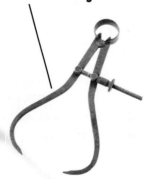

You can figure amounts using a **calculator**.

Scientists use **computers** in many ways, such as collecting, recording, and analyzing data.

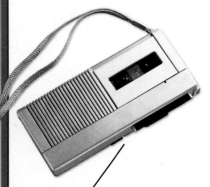

You can talk into a **sound recorder** to record information you want to remember.

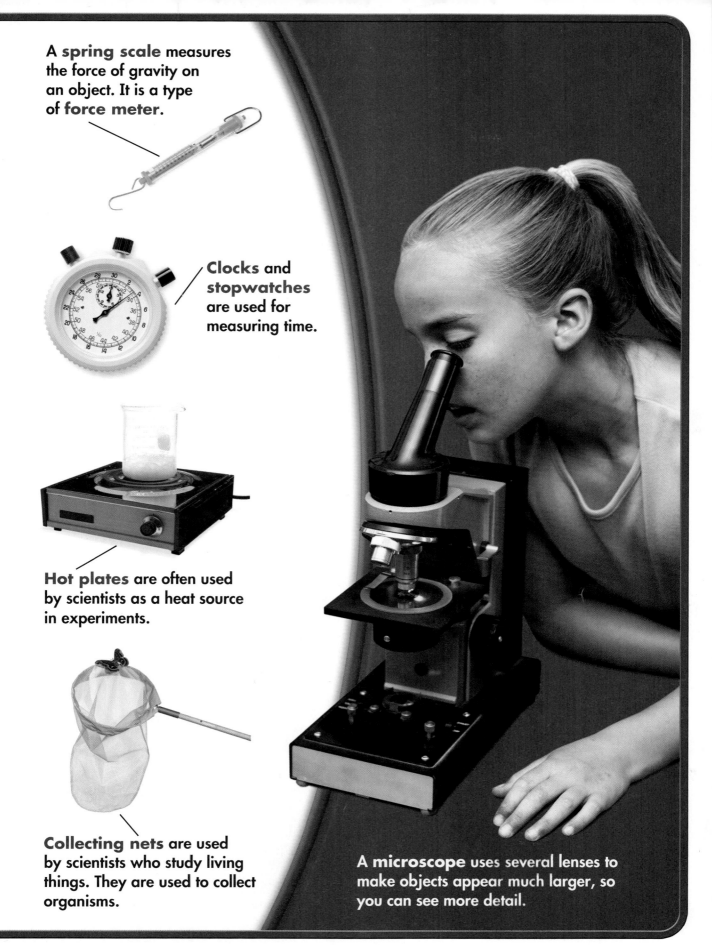

A **spring scale** measures the force of gravity on an object. It is a type of force meter.

Clocks and **stopwatches** are used for measuring time.

Hot plates are often used by scientists as a heat source in experiments.

Collecting nets are used by scientists who study living things. They are used to collect organisms.

A **microscope** uses several lenses to make objects appear much larger, so you can see more detail.

Safety in Science

You need to be careful when doing science activities. This page includes safety tips to remember:

- Listen to your teacher's instructions.

- Read each activity carefully.

- Never taste or smell materials unless your teacher tells you to.

- Wear safety goggles when needed.

- Handle scissors and other equipment carefully.

- Keep your work place neat and clean.

- Clean up spills immediately.

- Tell your teacher immediately about accidents or if you see something that looks unsafe.

- Wash your hands well after every activity.

- Return all materials to their proper places.

Unit A
Life Science

Chapter 1

Plants and How They Grow

online
Student Edition
pearsonsuccessnet.com

1

How do the different parts of a plant help it live and grow?

system

coniferous

pollinate

seed leaf

germinate

2

deciduous

seedling

fossil

extinct

3

Explore How are plants alike and different?

Materials

grass

radish

hand lens

What to Do

1 Observe each plant with a hand lens. Notice the characteristics of their leaves and roots.

2 Look for the places where the leaves grow from the stems of the plants.

3 Look at the roots that grow from the stems of the plants.

root

root

Explain Your Results
Use what you **observed** to explain how the two plants are alike and different.

How to Read Science

Compare and Contrast

Knowing how to compare and contrast can help you understand what you read and the things you **observe.**

- We **compare** when we say how things are alike. We **contrast** when we say how things are different.
- Words and phrases such as *similar, like, all, both,* or *in the same way* are used to compare.
- Words and phrases such as *unlike* or *in a different way* are used to contrast.

Science Article

Plants and Animals

Both plants and animals are living things that need food, air, water, and space to live. Unlike most plants, most animals don't stay in the same place. They move around. Unlike animals, most plants have roots that keep them in the same place.

Plants	Both	Animals
Ways that plants are different from animals	Ways that plants and animals are alike	Ways that animals are different from plants

Apply It!

Make a graphic organizer like the one shown. Use the information from the science article to fill it in.

You Are There!

It's a cool spring day and you are walking along a river in Alaska. Tall trees rise above the river. Why do some have flat, broad leaves, while others have sharp needles? Lots of other kinds of plants are growing here too. Even though they may look different, every plant needs the same things to live and grow. Listen. You hear a splash. An Alaskan brown bear bounds out of the trees into the river. The bear needs certain things too.

AudioText

What are the main parts of a plant?

Most plants have four main parts. These parts are leaves, roots, stems, and flowers. In different kinds of plants, these parts may look similar. They may also look very different.

What All Living Things Need

Most living things, including plants and animals, need food, air, water, and space to live and grow. Animals find and eat plants or other animals to get their food. Unlike animals, plants can make their own food. To make their food, plants need energy from the Sun. Most plants also need soil.

Most plants have four main parts. These parts are leaves, roots, stems, and flowers.

Black-eyed Susans are one of the many plants you might see in a prairie.

1. ✓**Checkpoint** What do plants and animals need to live?

2. **Writing** in Science **Descriptive**
Choose an animal and a plant and describe in your **science journal** what each needs to survive.

Why Plants Need Leaves

A plant's leaves make up its leaf system. A **system** consists of parts that work together. Leaves come in many shapes and sizes. They help green plants because they make food. The food they make is a kind of sugar.

To make food, leaves use air, water, and the energy of sunlight. Carbon dioxide is a gas in air. It enters the plant through tiny holes on the underside of leaves. Water passes from soil through roots and stems and into each leaf. The leaves change the carbon dioxide and water into sugar and oxygen. Oxygen goes out from the plant through the same tiny holes on the lower surface of the leaves. The plant uses the sugar to live and grow.

Gas
Carbon dioxide enters the leaf through tiny holes on its underside.

Water
Water enters the leaf from the roots and stem.

Sugar
The leaves make sugar for food that passes through the stems to the rest of the plant.

Oxygen
Plants make and let out oxygen gas when they make sugar.

Sun
Plants need energy from the Sun to change carbon dioxide and water into sugar and oxygen.

Leaf Veins
Tiny tubes called leaf veins deliver water to the leaf. They also carry sugar made in the leaves to the rest of the plant.

Other Ways Leaves Help Plants

Leaves help plants in other ways. They help plants to balance the amount of water plants take in. If there is too much water in the plant, leaves will let some water out through the tiny holes on their underside. Plants in dry places may have leaves with waxy or fuzzy coatings to help keep water in.

A plant's leaves may also help to protect the plant from being eaten. Leaves might be poisonous, sharp, or tough to chew. Hungry animals will leave the plant alone.

✓ Lesson Checkpoint

1. List the main parts of most plants.

2. How does a leaf help a plant live?

3. **Compare and Contrast** Describe ways that leaves are alike and different. Use a graphic organizer.

Some trees have leaves that look like needles.

A pecan tree leaf is made up of many smaller leaflets that grow across from each other.

This oak leaf is more like the pecan leaves than the needle-like leaves. Yet observe how different it is.

Why do plants need roots and stems?

Along with their leaves, plants need their root and stem systems to live and grow.

How Roots Help Plants

The root system of a plant is often below the ground where you cannot see it. The roots hold the plant in the ground. Roots take in water and materials called minerals from the soil. The roots also store food made by the plant.

Many plants, such as carrots and dandelions, have a large root called a taproot. The taproot grows deep into the soil. The taproot stores food for the plant. Have you ever tasted a carrot or a beet? If your answer is "yes," then you've eaten the taproot of a plant!

A young fir tree has a tangled root system.

Water and minerals travel up the root through tubes to the stem and leaves.

Root hair

Water enters the root through the root hairs.

Growing tip of root

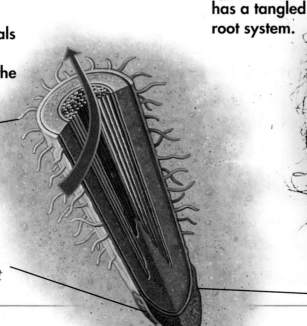

Grasses do not have a taproot.

Roots that We Eat

Beet

Radish

Carrot

Turnip

At the tips of roots are tiny root hairs. Plants take in water through their root hairs. Root branches with their many root hairs grow far into the soil to reach water. Water travels through tubes to the plant's stem and leaves.

On summer days, the root system can be a very busy place. Sunshine and hot air can dry a plant out. The roots must take in water to replace water lost from the plant leaves.

1. ✓**Checkpoint** How do roots help a plant?

2. **Social Studies** in Science Look up the many different ways that people around the world use roots.

How Stems Help Plants

A plant's stems hold up its leaves, flowers, and fruits. Most plant stems have tubes that move water and minerals from the roots of plants to the leaves. Other tubes carry food from the leaves of plants to the stems and roots.

The pictures show some different kinds of stems. Some stems, called stolons, are thin and grow along the surface of the ground. These stems can grow roots and a new plant. Some stems, called vines, grow parts that wrap around objects that support the plant.

Notice how thick cactus stems can be. Cactus stems swell up as they store water. The stems shrink as the plant uses water. Cactus stems also have a thick, waxy covering to help keep them from losing water. This type of stem helps the cactus plant survive in a desert.

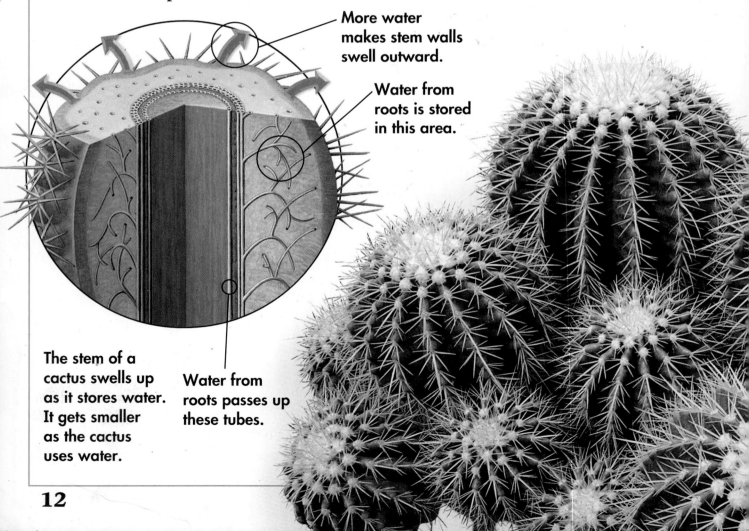

More water makes stem walls swell outward.

Water from roots is stored in this area.

The stem of a cactus swells up as it stores water. It gets smaller as the cactus uses water.

Water from roots passes up these tubes.

Stolons of this strawberry plant are for growing new plants.

Potato

Parts of some stems grow underground. When you eat a potato, you eat a stem part that stored food underground. Underground stems can sprout new stems from buds such as the potato's "eyes." These parts grow upward and become new plants.

Some plants have stems with special features to help them survive. For example, some stems have thorns, spines, or stinging hairs to keep hungry animals from eating them.

Vine

The spines growing out of this cactus stem are a special kind of leaf.

Tree trunk

✓ Lesson Checkpoint

1. How do stems help a plant?

2. How are roots and stems alike and different?

3. **Writing** in Science **Expository**
   Write a paragraph in your **science journal** that describes the special features of a cactus. Explain how these features help the cactus.

13

How are plants grouped?

Plants can be grouped by the kinds of parts they have.

Flowering Plants

An apple tree and a cactus do not look alike, but they both grow flowers with seeds. They belong to different groups of flowering plants. Each group has different kinds of roots, stems, leaves, and flowers. The flowering plants pictured on this page have different types of stems. The dogwood tree has a stiff, woody stem. The dogwood can grow tall. The trillium plants do not have woody stems. They grow low to the ground.

The dogwood tree survives winter because its leaves die and fall off in the fall. The leaves grow back in the spring. A tree that loses and grows leaves like this is a **deciduous** tree. Many flowering plants lose both stems and leaves in the fall. The roots live through winter and the plants grow back from the roots in spring.

Flowering trees and small flowering plants are similar and different.

14

Making Seeds

Flowering plants grow flowers that make seeds. Flowers have parts that make pollen or seeds. Bees, other animals, or wind **pollinate** a flower when they move pollen to the flower part that makes seeds.

After a flower is pollinated, seeds form near the center of the flower. A fruit often grows to surround and protect the seeds.

A flower's petals attract insects and other animals that pollinate the flower.

Pollen sticks to the bodies of bees as bees look for food. They carry this pollen to the part of the flower that makes seeds.

The tip of this part of the flower makes pollen.

Pollen put on the tip of this part helps form seeds down here.

1. ✔**Checkpoint** Describe how a flower makes a seed.

2. **Writing in Science** **Narrative** Write a story in your **science journal** about a flower that invited a bee over for a visit. Be sure to describe the bee's thank-you gift.

Coniferous Trees

Coniferous trees grow cones instead of flowers to make their seeds. Most coniferous trees do not lose all their leaves in the fall. The leaves of most coniferous trees look like needles or brushes. Coniferous trees include pine, fir, spruce, and hemlock.

Two Types of Cones

Coniferous trees make two kinds of cones. They make small pollen cones and large seed cones. Wind blows pollen from the small pollen cones to the large seed cones. When pollen attaches to the seed cone, seeds begin to grow. A seed grows under each scale of the seed cone. When the seeds are ripe, they fall to the ground. If conditions are right, each seed can start growing into a new plant. Over time, the seeds may become trees.

Cones form on branches near the top of conifers.

Seeds are made under the scales of this Douglas fir cone. This cone is about as big as your fist.

Wind blows pollen from these small cones to larger cones on other trees.

Larger cones grow with seeds inside.

Coniferous seeds glide to the ground.

✓ Lesson Checkpoint

1. What are two ways to group plants?

2. Describe two kinds of plant parts that can make seeds.

3. **Writing** in Science **Expository** Write a paragraph in your **science journal** that explains different ways flowers can be pollinated.

17

How do new plants grow?

*Most plants make seeds that grow into new plants.
Sometimes a stem or root grows a new plant.*

Scattering Seeds

When seeds are scattered, they are moved away
from the plant. Then they have more room to grow.

Seeds are scattered in many ways. Some seeds are spread
from one place to another by wind or water. Other seeds are
carried to new places by animals that eat fruit with seeds.
The seeds pass through the animal's body. Then they are
dropped to the ground far from the plant. Some seeds
are carried along when they stick to an animal's fur.

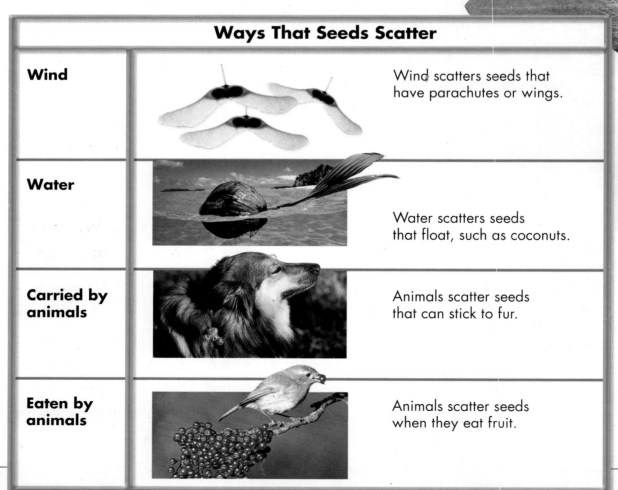

Ways That Seeds Scatter		
Wind		Wind scatters seeds that have parachutes or wings.
Water		Water scatters seeds that float, such as coconuts.
Carried by animals		Animals scatter seeds that can stick to fur.
Eaten by animals		Animals scatter seeds when they eat fruit.

You've probably seen seeds drifting through the air. Wind scatters seeds that are very light. Many of these seeds have special parts that act like tiny wings or parachutes. The seeds can drift for long distances if the wind is strong.

Special Ways of Releasing Seeds

Some types of pine cones need to be heated in a forest fire to release their seeds. The fire also removes other plants around the trees and clears space for the seeds to grow.

Each of these seeds has a tiny parachute. Wind can carry these seeds long distances where they can grow into new plants.

1. ✔ **Checkpoint** What are two ways that animals scatter seeds?

2. **Art** in Science Draw pictures of two groups of seeds. Draw one group of seeds that are scattered by animals. Draw another group of seeds that are scattered by wind. Describe how the parts of these seeds are different.

Germinating and Growing

Seeds have different shapes, sizes, and colors, but they all have the same parts. Every seed has a tiny plant inside it that can grow into a new plant. The seed is covered by a seed coat to protect this tiny plant. Every seed has one **seed leaf** or two seed leaves to provide food for the tiny plant as it grows.

Seeds need air, the right amount of water, and the right temperature to start to grow, or **germinate.** A root grows from the seed and the young plant, or **seedling**, begins to grow. The seedling uses food stored in the seed to grow.

The seedling's stem rises out of the soil. Leaves grow from the stem. The leaves use sunlight to make sugar that the plant uses for food. The seedling can grow into an adult plant that has flowers. The flowers are pollinated and new seeds form. If the seeds germinate, they grow into new plants. Then the cycle begins again.

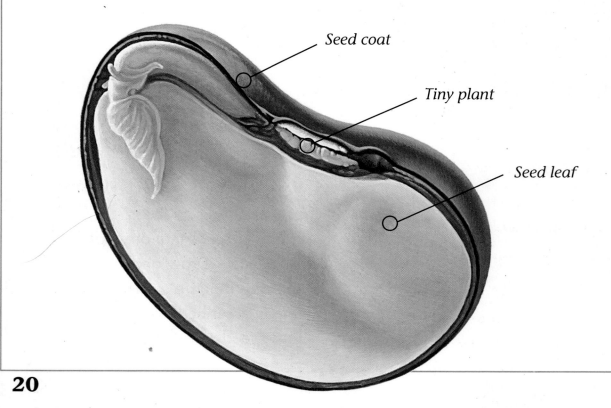

Seed coat

Tiny plant

Seed leaf

Life Cycle of a Plant

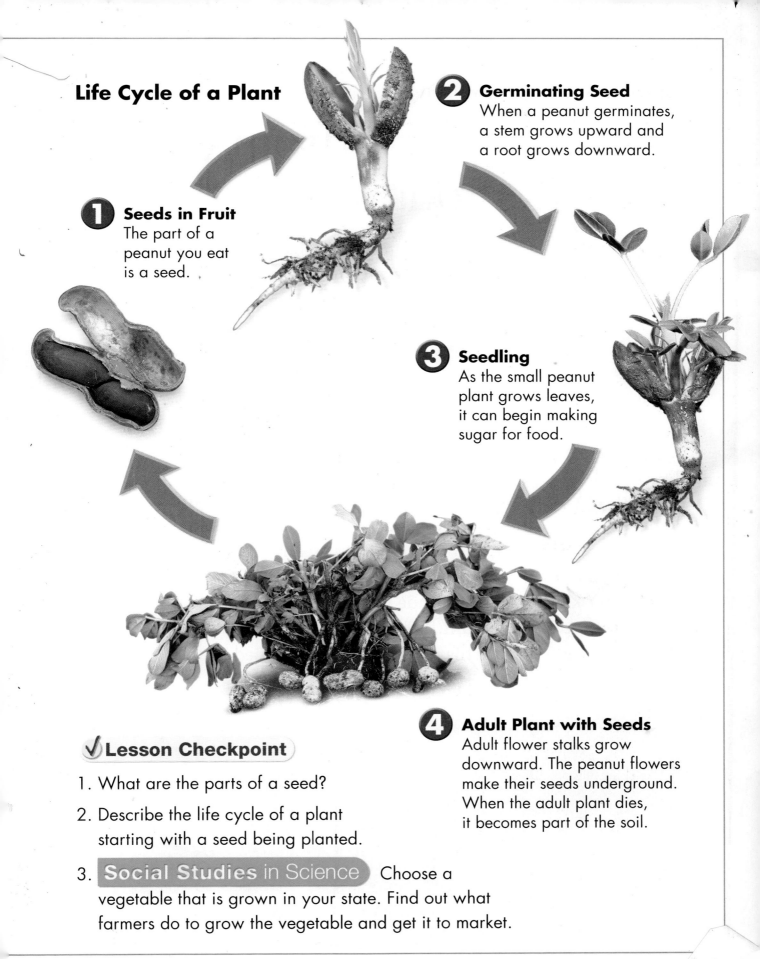

1 **Seeds in Fruit**
The part of a peanut you eat is a seed.

2 **Germinating Seed**
When a peanut germinates, a stem grows upward and a root grows downward.

3 **Seedling**
As the small peanut plant grows leaves, it can begin making sugar for food.

4 **Adult Plant with Seeds**
Adult flower stalks grow downward. The peanut flowers make their seeds underground. When the adult plant dies, it becomes part of the soil.

✔ Lesson Checkpoint

1. What are the parts of a seed?

2. Describe the life cycle of a plant starting with a seed being planted.

3. **Social Studies in Science** Choose a vegetable that is grown in your state. Find out what farmers do to grow the vegetable and get it to market.

Lesson 5

How are plants from the past like today's plants?

Fossils show the kinds of plants that lived long ago. In some ways today's plants are similar to plants from the past that have disappeared.

Plants That Lived Long Ago

We learn about plants that lived long ago by studying fossils. A **fossil** is the remains or mark of a living thing from long ago.

Look at the fern and horsetail fossils in the pictures on page 23. How did they form? Each plant died and was pressed into mud. Next, the plant rotted away. But the mud kept the form of the plant. Over time the mud hardened into rock. The flat imprint of the plant is seen when the rock cracks open.

Another kind of fossil is made when rock replaces the parts that make up a plant. The drawings below show how it might have formed. This rock is called a petrified fossil.

Formation of Petrified Wood

Stump is buried in mud.

Minerals replace wood as time passes.

Rock surrounding the fossil is removed.

Plant Fossils

The fern that made this fossil lived about 350 million years ago.

This fossil shows a kind of fern that is extinct.

This fossil shows a kind of horsetail plant that is extinct.

This log is a fossil trunk of an extinct tree fern.

Petrified wood can form when trees are buried in the ground. Minerals replace wood in the trees. At the same time, water breaks down the wood and carries it away. Over a long period of time, the wood is replaced by stone with exactly the same shape and markings as the original wood.

Many kinds of plants that lived long ago are no longer alive. They are **extinct.** For example, ferns that live today look different from the ferns that lived long ago. Plants related to the extinct ferns and horsetail fossils shown in the photos live on Earth today.

These petrified wood fossils in Arizona look like wood, but they are made of rock.

1. ✔ **Checkpoint** What can scientists learn by studying fossils?

2. **Writing in Science** **Expository** In your **science journal**, write a paragraph that explains how a plant leaf can become a fossil.

Plants Change Over Time

Plant fossils show us that the first plants did not have flowers or cones. Many were like today's ferns and horsetails. As Earth changed over time, however, plants changed too. Trees that made cones appeared. Then plants with flowers appeared. Many of these kinds of plants have completely disappeared.

Magnolias are flowering plants that first appeared when dinosaurs roamed the Earth. The world was warm and wet year-round. Magnolias grew thick leaves that they kept year-round. Their flowers bloomed for months. Magnolias just like this are alive today. Fossils show that the magnolia flower has remained unchanged for 100 million years.

As the Earth changed, so did the magnolias. Some magnolias now are deciduous. They lose their leaves in fall. Their flowers bloom all at once before the leaves appear in the spring. Even so, their leaves and flowers are similar to those of magnolias that lived long ago.

Fossils of magnolia leaves from long ago look similar to today's magnolia leaves.

Flowers of deciduous magnolias bloom all at once in the spring. After flowering, the trees grow new leaves for the summer.

The first magnolia trees were similar to many magnolias alive today. The feathered dinosaur is extinct.

✓ Lesson Checkpoint

1. What is an extinct plant?

2. How do scientists learn about plants that are extinct?

3. **Compare and Contrast** How are extinct magnolias alike and different from magnolias alive today? Use a graphic organizer to show your answer.

Investigate How fast do different kinds of seeds germinate?

Seeds from some kinds of plants germinate faster than seeds from other kinds of plants. Even seeds from just one kind of plant may germinate faster than other seeds from the same kind of plant.

Materials

paper towel and paper plate

waxed paper and masking tape

5 radish seeds

5 corn seeds

5 pinto bean seeds

5 sunflower seeds

cup with water

metric ruler

Process Skills

By **interpreting the data** you **collected** in your chart, you can analyze how different seeds grow.

What to Do

1 Fold a paper towel in half. Fold it again.

2 Make 2 lines to divide the folded towel into 4 parts. Label each part.

3 Put the waxed paper on the plate. Put the folded towel on the waxed paper. Put on the seeds. Wet the towel.

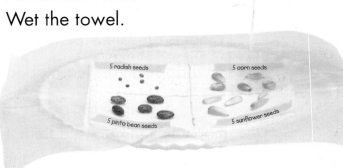

5 radish seeds   5 corn seeds

5 pinto bean seeds   5 sunflower seeds

4 Put the plate in a warm, bright place.

5 **Observe** and record changes for 1 week. Describe or draw the plants as they begin to grow and develop.

After the first day, keep the paper towels moist, but not wet.

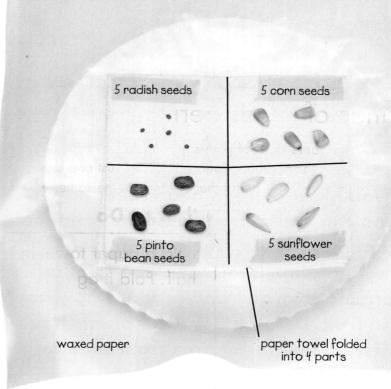

5 radish seeds

5 corn seeds

5 pinto bean seeds

5 sunflower seeds

waxed paper

paper towel folded into 4 parts

Kind of Plant	Description (write or draw)	Day the First of the 5 Seeds Germinated (Day 1, 2, 3, 4, or 5)	Order in Which Different Kinds of Plants Germinated (1st, 2nd, 3rd, or 4th)	Length of Longest Stem on Day 7 (mm)
Radish				
Corn				
Pinto				
Sunflower				

Explain Your Results

1. **Interpret the data** you **collected**. Compare the radish and sunflower seeds. How did they grow and develop differently?
2. Were all the radish plants the same? Explain.

Go Further

Collect more data. Every day count and record the number of each kind of plant that has germinated. Graph your results.

Math in Science

Elapsed Time
from Seed to Fruit

If you plant a green bean seed, how soon can you eat green beans from the plant that grows? The answer is the length of time it takes for the seed to germinate, grow, and produce flowers and fruit. Different kinds of plants have different lengths of time from seed to fruit that is ready to eat.

Green bean

Cucumber

Sweet corn

Tomato

Tools Take It to the Net
pearsonsuccessnet.com

If you plant green bean seeds on May 10, you can start eating green beans 58 days later, on July 7.

Days from planting seeds or seedling to picking ripe fruit	
green bean seeds	58 days
cucumber seeds	55 days
sweet corn seeds	75 days
tomato seedling	59 days

Use the table and calendars to answer the questions.

1 If you plant cucumber seeds on May 21, when could you start eating cucumbers?

2 If sweet corn seeds are planted on May 19, when will the corn be ready to eat?

3 When could you start eating ripe tomatoes if the seedling was planted on May 31?

Lab zone Take-Home Activity

Look at the back of seed packets or go to the library or Internet to search for seed catalogs. Find out how long it takes different kinds of seeds to grow and make fruit. Use a calendar to find what dates the fruit might be ready to pick.

Chapter 1 Review and Test Prep

Use Vocabulary

deciduous (page 14)	**pollinate** (page 15)
coniferous (page 16)	**seed leaf** (page 20)
extinct (page 23)	**seedling** (page 20)
fossil (page 22)	**system** (page 8)
germinate (page 20)	

Use the vocabulary word or words from the list above that best completes each sentence.

1. When conditions are right, a seed will start to grow, or _____.

2. A tree that makes cones is a(n) _____ tree.

3. Bees, wind, and water can _____ flowers.

4. All the leaves and their parts make up a plant's leaf _____.

5. A(n) _____ tree loses all its leaves in the fall.

6. A new plant that has just grown out of the soil is a(n) _____.

7. A new plant uses food stored in a(n) _____.

8. A(n) _____ plant no longer lives on Earth, but a(n) _____ of its remains might be found.

Explain Concepts

9. How do scientists learn about plants that are extinct?

10. Explain why all of a plant's roots and their parts are called a system.

11. What do a plant's leaves need to make sugar?

Process Skills

12. **Classify** Choose one way that plants can be sorted into two groups. Explain how the plants in the two groups are alike and different.

13. **Infer** Bees visit the flowers on apple trees to get food. How might a disease that kills bees affect the number of apples the trees make? Explain your answer.

Compare and Contrast

14. Make a graphic organizer like the one shown below. Fill in the correct information.

| Plants | Both | Animals |

Stay in same place, make own food

Move around, find food

Test Prep

Choose the letter that best completes the statement or answers the question.

15. Before a seed can become a plant, the seed must
- (A) germinate.
- (B) be pollinated.
- (C) make food.
- (D) flower.

16. A cactus stores the most water in its
- (F) roots.
- (G) leaves.
- (H) stems.
- (I) flowers.

17. What fossil is made when minerals replace plant parts, while water breaks the parts down and carries them away?
- (A) imprint
- (B) petrified wood
- (C) extinct fern
- (D) magnolia flower

18. Which of the following is an example of scattering seeds?
- (F) pollen sticking to a bee
- (G) wind blowing pollen
- (H) apples growing on a tree
- (I) burs sticking to a dog's fur

19. Explain why the answer you chose for Question 18 is best. For each of the answers you did not choose, give a reason why it is not the best choice.

20. Writing in Science

Expository Write a paragraph that describes the life cycle of a plant.

Plant Researcher

Do you like plants? Plant researchers study how plants live and grow.

What if food that astronauts need during long space missions runs out? Grow more aboard ship! Dr. Stutte of NASA tests ways to grow wheat aboard the International Space Station. He also tests the ability of plants to clean the air and water that astronauts use.

Growing plants in space is tricky, however. When seeds germinate on Earth roots grow down and stems grow up. In space, there is no up or down. As a plant researcher you might be called upon to solve problems like this one.

Plant researchers look for ways to grow more or stronger plants. Researchers at NASA are studying how plant seeds might grow better in space. Better traits from seeds grown in space could help farmers grow stronger plants on Earth.

Plant researchers have college degrees.

Dr. Gary Stutte

Lab zone **Take-Home Activity**

Draw a machine that would grow cucumbers in space where there is little gravity. Label the parts that supply the plants with water, fertilizer, carbon dioxide, and light. Write a paragraph explaining how it would work.

Chapter 2

How Animals Live

You Will Discover

- ways that animals are grouped.
- how an animal's body and its behavior help it survive.
- how animals grow and change.
- that many animals today resemble animals that lived long ago.

online
Student Edition
pearsonsuccessnet.com

Discovery Channel School
Student DVD
DISCOVERY CHANNEL SCHOOL

How do different animals live, grow, and change?

vertebrate

trait

inherited

migrate

hibernate

34

adaptation

larva

pupa

35

Explore How can you make a model of a backbone?

Materials

pipe cleaner

10 pieces of wagon wheel pasta

9 soft fruit jelly rings

What to Do

1 **Make a model** of a backbone. Bend the end of a pipe cleaner into a knot. String a piece of wagon wheel pasta on the pipe cleaner so the pasta rests on the knot. Next string a jelly ring.

2 Add another wheel and a ring. Keep going until you have used 10 wheels and 9 rings.

3 Bend the other end of the pipe cleaner. Make a knot to hold everything on. Can you bend your model backbone?

Process Skills

Making and using a model can help you understand scientific ideas.

Explain Your Results

How is your **model** different from a real backbone? How is your model like a real backbone?

Reading Skills

TARGET SKILL
Sequence

Sequence is the order in which events take place. Clue words such as *first, next, then,* and *finally* can help you figure out the **sequence** of events. They are marked on the museum display card.

Museum Display Card

Sea Jelly

A sea jelly grows up in stages. First, an adult makes young called larvae. Next, each larva becomes attached to a rock. Then, each larva grows and becomes a polyp. Finally, each polyp grows into a group of young adults.

Apply It!

Make a graphic organizer as a **model** to show the life cycle of the sea jelly. Write each of the four events in the life cycle after your four clue words.

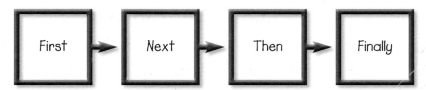

First → Next → Then → Finally

🔊 You Are There!

It's early morning in the forest and the birds are singing. You look down at your feet and notice ants marching by. You stand very still, listening and watching. Suddenly, you spot what looks like two dogs walking through a grassy field in the distance. As you focus your eyes you realize they are not dogs. You've spotted a wolf and her pup! Animals come in many shapes and sizes. Even though they may be different, do animals need the same basic things to live?

How are animals grouped?

All animals have the same basic needs. Animals might be grouped by how they look, where they live, or how they act.

What All Animals Need

Nearly all animals need water, oxygen, food, and shelter to live. Animals can get water from drinking or from the foods they eat. All animals also need the gas oxygen. They get oxygen from the air or from water. Most animals that live on land have lungs to breathe in oxygen. Many animals that live in water, such as fish, breathe with gills.

Animals also need food and shelter. They get their food by eating plants or other animals. Shelters protect animals from the weather and from other animals. While some animals build or seek shelters, others use their own hard shells as their homes.

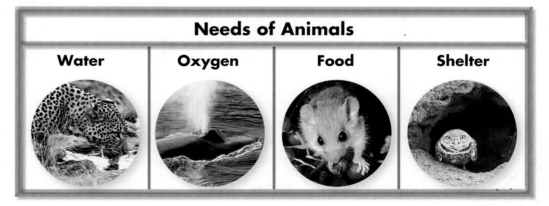

Needs of Animals

Water	Oxygen	Food	Shelter

1. ✓ **Checkpoint** What do all animals need?
2. **Writing in Science** **Descriptive** In your **science journal,** write about how your favorite animal meets its basic needs.

Ways of Grouping Animals

How we group animals depends on what we want to learn about them. Animals can be grouped by where they live or how they act. They also may be grouped by how they look. A body feature passed on to an animal from its parents is called a **trait.** Traits can include things an animal does.

One animal can be placed into different groups. For example, a group of animals that eat mice can include snakes, hawks, and owls. A group of animals that fly can include hawks and owls, but not snakes.

Animals with Backbones

Another way to group animals is by whether or not they have a backbone. An animal with a backbone is called a **vertebrate.** Cats, birds, fish, and snakes all have backbones and other bones in their bodies. Their bones grow as the animals grow. Their bones give them strong support. This allows many vertebrates, such as elephants, to grow very big.

This lynx is a vertebrate.

Groups of Vertebrates

Fish
These vertebrates spend their entire lives in fresh water, ocean water, or both. Most fish have slippery scales and breathe through gills.

Amphibians
Frogs, toads, and salamanders belong to a group called amphibians. Many amphibians spend part of their lives in water and part on land. Most young amphibians live in water. They get oxygen through gills and through their smooth, moist skin. As they grow, most amphibians develop lungs that they use to breathe air.

Reptiles
Snakes, lizards, turtles, crocodiles, and alligators are reptiles. They mostly have dry, scaly skin. These vertebrates breathe air through lungs.

Birds
Birds are vertebrates with feathers and bills that do not have teeth. They breathe air through lungs. Wings and light bones help most birds fly. Their coats of feathers help them stay warm.

Mammals
The vertebrates that you probably know best are called mammals. Mammals have hair at least during part of their lives. The hair keeps them warm. Mammals breathe air through lungs and feed milk to their young.

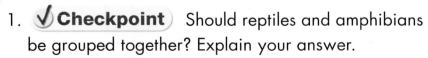

1. ☑ **Checkpoint** Should reptiles and amphibians be grouped together? Explain your answer.

2. **Art** in Science Think about two animals that share some of the same traits. Draw a picture of each animal "in action" using a shared trait.

Animals Without Backbones

Most animals do not have skeletons made of bones inside their bodies. These are the animals without backbones, or invertebrates. Sea stars, butterflies, and spiders are some invertebrates. There are many more kinds of invertebrates than vertebrates, as the chart shows.

A soft sac filled with liquid supports worms and sea jellies. A hard shell supports clams. Insects and other arthropods have a hard covering on the outside of their bodies. These kinds of structures cannot support very big animals. Most invertebrates do not grow as big as most vertebrates.

Many invertebrates are very small. Several million tiny roundworms may live in one square meter of soil. You may not notice many invertebrates, but they live all over Earth.

This dragonfly is an invertebrate.

Kinds of Animals

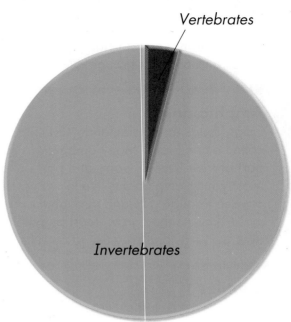

Vertebrates

Invertebrates

The whole circle stands for all kinds of animals. The small piece shows that kinds of vertebrates are only a small part of the total.

Kinds of Invertebrate Animals

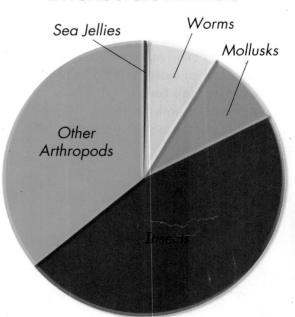

Sea Jellies   *Worms*   *Mollusks*

Other Arthropods

Insects

Most kinds of invertebrates are insects.

Major Kinds of Invertebrate Animals

Sea Jellies	Sea jellies have soft bodies and long, stinging body parts. The body of a sea jelly is made mostly of water. A sea jelly uses its stingers to stun its prey before pulling it into its stomach. Most sea jellies live in the ocean.	
Worms	Worms are animals with long, soft bodies and no legs. You've probably seen an earthworm in the soil. These invertebrates help keep soil healthy.	
Mollusks	Mollusks are animals with soft bodies. Some mollusks include the octopus, squid, clam, and snail. Many mollusks have a hard shell.	
Arthropods	These animals are members of the largest group of invertebrates. They wear their skeletons outside their bodies. The bodies of arthropods are made up of more than one main part and they have legs with joints. Insects, spiders, and crabs are all arthropods.	

✓ **Lesson Checkpoint**

1. If a rattlesnake and a black widow spider both make poison, why are they put in different groups?

2. Explain why most invertebrates are small in size compared to most vertebrates.

3.  There are 5 vertebrates in someone's backyard. There are 20 times as many invertebrates as vertebrates there, too. How many invertebrates are there?

How do animals grow and change?

Different animals have their young in different ways. But all animals grow and change during their life cycle.

Life Cycles

An animal's life starts out as an egg. Sometimes the egg develops into a young animal inside the mother. Then the mother gives birth to a live young. For other animals, the mother lays an egg outside of her body. Then the young develops in the egg and hatches when it is ready.

When some animals hatch or are born, they look like their parents. Many other animals change a lot before they look anything like their parents.

Adult butterflies lay eggs.

1 Egg
This is a close-up view of a very small egg. The picture has been magnified, or made to look bigger.

Life Cycle Stages	
Birth	Animals are born or hatch.
Growth	Animals get bigger.
Development	Animals change into adults.
Reproduction	Animals produce young.
Death	Animals' lives come to an end.

4 **Butterfly**
The adult butterfly comes out of the chrysalis.

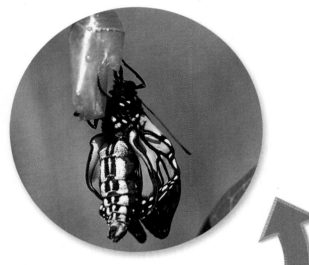

3 **Pupa**
Inside a hard covering, the larva's body changes.

2 **Larva**
The butterfly larva is called a caterpillar.

A Butterfly's Life Cycle

The egg is the first state in the butterfly's life cycle. The tiny egg is hard to see.

A caterpillar hatches from the egg. It is now a **larva.** The larva must eat a lot to survive. It starts munching on the plant where it lives.

The larva grows. It sheds its skin several times. Then the larva spins a covering around itself. A hard covering, or chrysalis, forms. The larva is now called a **pupa.**

The larva's body begins to change when it becomes a pupa. It grows wings and jointed legs. It begins to look like an adult butterfly. Soon it breaks out of the chrysalis. The adult butterfly dries its wings and flies away. After laying eggs, the butterly dies. Its life cycle is complete.

1. **✓ Checkpoint** What is the purpose of the pupa?

2. **Sequence** List the sequence of steps in a butterfly's life cycle. Use the signal words *first, next, then,* and *finally.*

45

Some Vertebrate Life Cycles

Vertebrates have different kinds of life cycles. Some vertebrates, like frogs, go through many changes as they grow and mature. Other vertebrates, like pandas or monkeys, do not change as much.

A Frog's Life Cycle

Just like insects, many amphibians change quite a lot as they become adults. Did you know, for instance, that a very young frog looks and acts a lot like a fish?

Look at how a frog changes during its life cycle. This frog completes all the stages of its life cycle in one summer. All frogs do not develop in the same way. In colder places, a developing frog may dig into the mud during the winter. It will not become an adult frog until the following spring or summer.

A panda cub gets a gentle nudge.

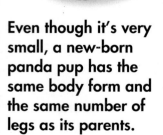

Even though it's very small, a new-born panda pup has the same body form and the same number of legs as its parents.

A Mammal's Life Cycle

Unlike amphibians and insects, young mammals do not change very much as they become adults. Many mammals look like their parents when they are born. Like you, they grow as they get older.

Most mammals develop inside their mother's bodies. When they are born, the babies drink milk from their mothers. They also have hair or fur.

It will be many years before you become an adult. A young rabbit, however, is ready to leave its nest and live on its own when it is less than three weeks old. It will be an adult at about six months.

Frog Life Cycle

② Tadpole
Tadpoles hatch from the frog eggs. Tadpoles live underwater and breathe with gills.

① Eggs
Mother frogs often lay hundreds or thousands of eggs in the water.

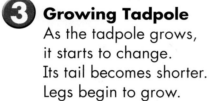

③ Growing Tadpole
As the tadpole grows, it starts to change. Its tail becomes shorter. Legs begin to grow. The back legs grow first.

Before a tadpole becomes an adult frog, it has to grow lungs so it can breathe on land.

④ Adult Frog
The adult frog lives on land and in the water. It will need to return to the water to lay its eggs.

✓ Lesson Checkpoint

1. Before a frog can live on land, how must its body change?

2. How is a mammal's life cycle different from a frog's or a butterfly's life cycle?

3. **Writing in Science** **Expository** Think about how mammals care for their young. In your **science journal,** describe why this kind of care might be helpful for most mammals.

How do adaptations help animals?

Animals have special body parts, features, and ways of doing things that help them survive in their environments.

Adaptations

Animals live in many different places on Earth. An animal needs food, water, oxygen, and shelter. A trait that helps an animal meet its needs in the place where it lives is called an **adaptation.**

The webbed feet of a pelican are an adaptation. They help the pelican swim and survive in the water where it finds its food. Adaptations, such as webbed feet, are **inherited,** or passed on, from parents to their young.

Body parts, such as feet and bills, are important inherited adaptations. There are many different kinds of adaptations. Most kinds, such as body color, differ between members of even closely related groups.

This porcupine skull shows adaptations of a plant-eating animal. Sharp front teeth cut off parts of plants. Flat teeth in the back of the jaw move from side to side, grinding tough plant material.

This hyena skull shows adaptations of a meat-eating animal. Sharp front teeth tear off meat and back teeth shred it.

The bill of a pelican has a pouch that hangs from it. When a pelican swoops into the water for food, the pouch acts like a net to help the bird catch fish.

Adaptations for Getting Food

Animals have many special adaptations for getting food. Prairie dogs and moles have feet that are especially good for digging. Hawks and eagles have feet that can hold tightly onto their food when they swoop down to catch it. Animals may also have the kind of teeth that can handle the foods they eat. Many birds have bills that help them catch and eat their favorite foods. Sometimes you can tell what a bird eats by the shape of its bill.

A long, curved bill helps the flamingo filter food from shallow water.

A short, strong bill helps the cardinal break open seeds.

A small, thin bill helps the warbler pick out insects for food.

1. ✓ **Checkpoint** Give two examples of adaptations and tell how they help the animal survive.

2. **Art** in Science Think about an animal that wades into ponds and spears fish for food. Draw a picture of this animal. Include the special adaptations you think it would need to live and get food.

Adaptations for Protection

The way an animal looks can help it survive. *Camouflage* helps some animals blend into their surroundings. Camouflage helps hide the animals from predators.

Other animals have colors or markings that copy those of a more dangerous animal. This kind of adaptation is called *mimicry*.

The way an animal acts can help it survive. Many animals climb, run, hop, jump, fly, or swim away from danger. Some animals may also use poison to protect themselves. Animals such as skunks and weasels spray a bad-smelling liquid at their enemies. Many animals use body parts such as shells, teeth, claws, hooves, and bills to protect themselves.

A porcupine is covered in quills. These special hairs have sharp hooks on their tips. When the porcupine is scared, special muscles make the quills stand up. Then the porcupine can hit an attacker with its quills. The hooks pierce the attacker's skin and stay attached to it.

Porcupines have loose, barbed quills to protect them from their enemies.

Ways Animals Protect Themselves

Camouflage	Armor	Mimicry	Poison
Animals that can harm or be harmed by this crab spider cannot see it.	Spikes and horns protect this horned lizard.	A harmless hover fly looks like a dangerous hornet.	Lion fish have poisonous spines.
These harlequin shrimp blend in with the bright sea fans.	Pill bugs roll into a ball for defense.	A viceroy butterfly looks like a bad-tasting monarch butterfly.	Monarch butterflies taste bad because of the food they eat.
The fur color of this arctic fox changes with the seasons.	A cassowary has a tough helmet to protect its head as it runs through brush.	This king snake looks similar to the deadly coral snake.	Coral snakes bite with poisonous fangs.

1. ✔ **Checkpoint**   What are some ways that animals protect themselves from their enemies?

2. 🎯 **Sequence** List in the correct sequence what happens when a predator attacks a porcupine. Be sure to use the signal words *first, next,* and *finally* in your list of steps.

51

Behaviors That Help Animals

Behaviors are things that animals do. Animals are born being able to do some things. These behaviors are inherited. You inherit your ability to do many things such as walk and talk.

You do not inherit your ability to read and write. You need to learn these behaviors. You do inherit your ability to learn these behaviors, though.

Baby birds are born knowing how to open their mouths for food.

Monarch butterflies have an instinct to migrate.

Instincts

An instinct is a behavior an animal is born able to do. One instinct is an animal's response to hunger. Baby birds, for example, open their mouths when they sense a parent with food is near. Some animals have an instinct to move, or **migrate,** when the seasons change. Some butterflies migrate thousands of miles to warmer weather to survive the winter.

Other animals have an instinct to **hibernate** during the cold winter months. When animals hibernate, their body systems usually slow down to save energy. Then they don't need as much food to survive.

Bats hibernate during the winter months when food is hard to find.

Learning

Animals learn some behaviors from their parents and other animals. For example, chimpanzees can learn how to use tools like sticks to catch insects to eat. Chimpanzees are not born knowing how to use sticks as tools. They learn how to do this by watching other chimpanzees. Young chimpanzees also learn which foods are safe to eat from their mothers and other adults.

An adult chimp shows a young chimp how to dig for insects.

Some young animals learn hunting behavior from their parents.

✓Lesson Checkpoint

1. Name two types of adaptations having to do with an animal's actions.

2. Why do some animals migrate or hibernate?

3. **Social Studies** in Science
Chimpanzees live in groups and learn how to behave from other chimpanzees. Describe how humans and chimpanzees are alike in the ways that they learn.

53

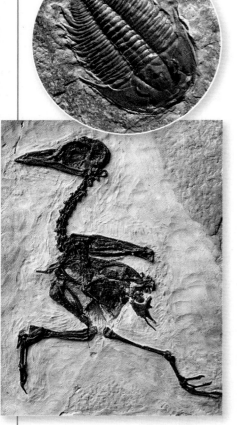

This trilobite fossil is a cast. It shows what the trilobite looked like.

A cast, such as this bird-like dinosaur, is in the shape of the original fossil. It formed when a mold was filled in with rock matter over time.

This fossil cast is of a dinosaur skull about 125 million years old! It looks like the skull of a modern-day crocodile.

How are animals from the past like today's animals?

Fossils show the kinds of animals that lived long ago. Today's animals are similar in some ways to animals of the past that have disappeared.

Animals That Lived Long Ago

Signs of past life are called fossils. Usually only the hard parts of animals become fossils. A fossil is usually not the actual bone or part. Instead, it is rock in the shape of the part.

A space in the shape of an animal in rock is called a fossil mold. Soft earth covers the remains of the animal, which wears away. This leaves a cavity or mold in the shape of the animal's parts. The earth then turns to rock over time. If the mold gets filled in with other rock materials over time, the fossil is called a cast.

Long ago, this spider got trapped in sticky tree sap that hardened into amber.

Unlike the fossil remains of most dinosaur bones, the bones of this fossil saber-toothed tiger are actual bone.

Ancient Insects

Some small animals, or parts of animals, have been found in hardened tree sap called amber. Long ago, an insect might have become trapped in the sticky sap. Soon the sap would have completely covered the insect. Over a long period of time, the sap turned into a hard, yellow or reddish-brown substance called amber. Thin pieces of amber are usually clear enough to see through. What you see is the animal's actual body covering kept together for millions of years.

One other type of fossil is found in tar pits. Saber-toothed tigers and other extinct animals fell into these oily pools many thousands of years ago. The soft parts of their bodies broke down and left only the bones. These fossils are the actual bones of these animals.

1. ✓**Checkpoint** What are some ways that fossils form?

2. **Math in Science** If a modern-day lizard is 10 meters long and a dinosaur skeleton is 3 times as long, how long is the dinosaur skeleton?

How Animals Today Compare to Those of Long Ago

Fossils can tell us how animals have changed over time. Dinosaurs are extinct. An extinct animal is a kind of animal that no longer lives on Earth. As you can see from the pictures, some animals today look like animals of long ago.

Fossils also tell us how Earth has changed over time. The drawing on the next page shows what the Badlands of South Dakota probably looked like more than 65 million years ago. At that time, dinosaurs like *Tyrannosaurus rex* roamed the area. Plant fossils found in layers of rocks near *T. rex* fossils tell scientists that the climate was hot and wet when *T. rex* lived. Plants could grow year-round. That is why you see plants in the drawing of the *T. rex*.

T. rex's habitat has changed a great deal. The photo in the drawing shows what the Badlands look like today. Only animals that are adapted to hot, dry conditions can live there now.

Although this collared lizard is a tiny, modern-day reptile, it resembles dinosaurs of long ago.

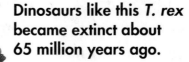

Dinosaurs like this *T. rex* became extinct about 65 million years ago.

Today the Badlands in South Dakota are almost like a desert.

This is one artist's view of how a *T. rex* might have looked. It also shows its habitat.

✓ Lesson Checkpoint

1. Describe four kinds of fossils.

2. What can fossils tell us about extinct animals?

3. **Writing in Science** **Expository** In your **science journal,** write about what might have happened to *T. Rex* when its environment changed.

Comparing Speeds of Fish

There is a great difference in the swimming speeds of fish. Generally, larger fish can swim faster than smaller fish. The bar graph below shows the greatest swimming speeds of six different fish.

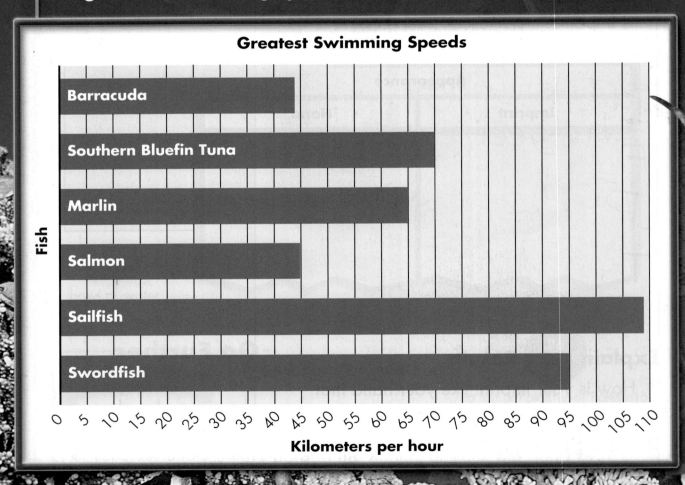

Greatest Swimming Speeds

Fish: Barracuda, Southern Bluefin Tuna, Marlin, Salmon, Sailfish, Swordfish

Kilometers per hour: 0, 5, 10, 15, 20, 25, 30, 35, 40, 45, 50, 55, 60, 65, 70, 75, 80, 85, 90, 95, 100, 105, 110

1. Which of the six fish is the fastest swimmer?
   A. Salmon
   B. Marlin
   C. Barracuda
   D. Sailfish

2. Which of the six fish is the slowest swimmer?
   F. Swordfish
   G. Barracuda
   H. Southern Bluefin Tuna
   I. Marlin

3. Use the data in the graph to list the six fish in order from slowest to fastest.

Lab zone **Take-Home Activity**

Use an almanac, the Internet, or other sources to find the most recent Olympic records for swimming. Make a graph or a chart showing the record times for each swimming event.

61

Chapter 2 Review and Test Prep

Use Vocabulary

adaptation (page 48)	**migrate** (page 52)
hibernate (page 52)	**pupa** (page 45)
inherited (page 48)	**trait** (page 40)
larva (page 45)	**vertebrate** (page 40)

Use the vocabulary word from the list above that best completes each sentence.

1. An animal with a backbone is called a(n) _____.

2. In an early stage of life, when a butterfly eats and grows, it is called a(n) _____.

3. Some animals need much less food to survive when they _____.

4. Something that helps a living thing survive is called a(n) _____.

5. If something passes on from a parent to its offspring, it is _____.

6. The stage in the life cycle of a butterfly during which it changes into an adult is called the _____.

7. Sometimes animals move to another place, or _____, to find better food or shelter.

8. A feature passed on to an animal from its parents is a(n) _____.

Explain Concepts

9. Explain why different animals can be grouped in more than one way.

10. Why does inheriting an adaptation help offspring survive?

11. What is the difference between instinct and learned behavior?

12. Describe the changes a frog goes through during its life cycle.

Process Skills

13. **Infer** If a fossil skull has flat teeth, what do you think this animal probably ate?

14. **Predict** A hawk has feet with sharp claws on them to help it catch small animals to eat. What kind of feet would you predict a bird that swims would have?

Mind Point Quiz Show

 Sequence

15. Use the signal words to put the stages of the life cycle of a frog in the correct sequence.

First

↓

Next

↓

Finally

 ## Test Prep

Choose the letter that best completes the statement or answers the question.

16. Fossils tell us
- (A) about animals that lived in the past.
- (B) about how Earth has changed.
- (C) how today's animals are similar to past life.
- (D) all of the above.

17. The earliest stage in a frog's life cycle is a(n)
- (F) pupa.
- (G) egg.
- (H) chrysalis.
- (I) tadpole.

18. Which of the following is an animal without a backbone, or invertebrate?
- (A) insect
- (B) bird
- (C) mammal
- (D) amphibian

19. Explain why the answer you chose for Question 18 is best. For each of the answers you did not choose, give a reason why it is not the correct choice.

20. **Writing** in Science

Descriptive Suppose a hungry fox comes upon a porcupine. Write a paragraph describing what happens between the two animals.

Paul Sereno: Expert Dinosaur Hunter

Paul Sereno

When he was a boy, Paul Sereno liked to go on nature hikes with his brothers. He brought home insects to add to his collection. Paul went to college to study art. However, while he was in college, Paul decided he wanted to become a paleontologist—a scientist who studies ancient life.

Paleontologists like Dr. Sereno try to find fossils to piece together the story of what life was like long ago. Dr. Sereno and his team have found many new kinds of dinosaurs.

Dr. Sereno's team made a discovery in Africa. A giant claw lying in the desert was the first clue. Dr. Sereno and his team carefully dug for more bones. They found a huge skeleton of a dinosaur. Its skull was long with crocodile-like teeth. Dr. Sereno named the new dinosaur *Suchomimus* which means "crocodile mimic."

It sometimes takes years for paleontologists to make sense of what they find. But their hard work often leads to new discoveries.

Lab zone Take-Home Activity

Using library resources and the Internet, research newly discovered dinosaurs. List them by name, type of dinosaur, and where found.

You Will Discover

- ○ what an ecosystem is.
- ○ different kinds of land ecosystems.
- ○ different kinds of water ecosystems.

Chapter 3

Where Plants and Animals Live

online
Student Edition
pearsonsuccessnet.com

How are ecosystems different from each other?

environment

ecosystem

desert

grassland

66

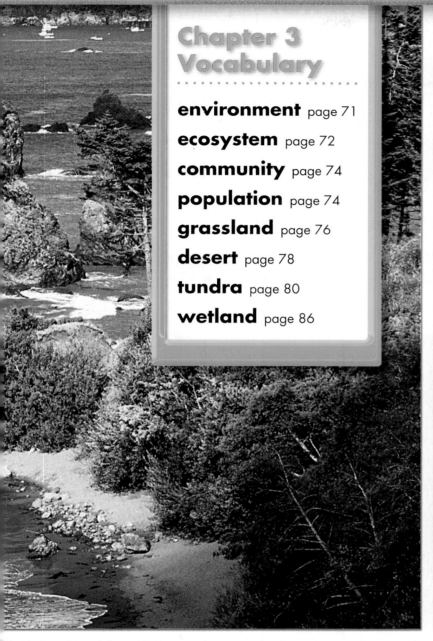

Chapter 3 Vocabulary

population

community

tundra

wetland

67

Explore In which soil do grass seeds grow best?

How will you know in which soil grass seeds *grow best*? Should *grow best* mean the most blades of grass grow, the tallest blades grow, or the greenest blades grow? You decide. **Make an operational definition** of *grow best*. Begin with the words "Grow best means. . . ." Then say what you will observe that will tell you which *grows best*.

Materials

3 paper cups and a pencil

sandy, clay, and loam soils

grass seeds and cup with water

spoon and masking tape

Process Skills

You explained how you would decide in which soil the seeds *grow best.* When you told what you would **observe** to make this decision, you **made an operational definition**.

What to Do

1 Make 4 holes in the bottom of each cup with a pencil. Half fill the cups with soil. Put 2 spoonfuls of water in each cup.

Label the cups.

2 Sprinkle $\frac{1}{2}$ spoonful of grass seeds in each cup. Lightly cover the seeds with more soil. Set the cups in a warm place with bright light.

sandy soil

clay soil

loam soil

3 Add 1 spoonful of water to each cup daily for 2 weeks. **Observe** each cup daily.

Explain Your Results

What is your **operational definition** of *grow best*? In which soil did the seeds *grow best* according to your definition?

How to Read Science

Reading Skills

TARGET SKILL

Main Idea and Details

A number of different things might all be connected to a **main idea**. These are called **details.** Learning to find the **main idea and details** helps you understand what you read. Look at the graphic organizer. The main idea is at the top. The details help support the main idea.

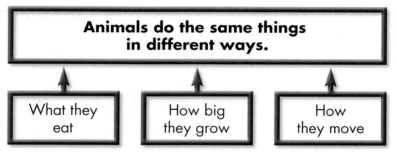

Animals do the same things in different ways.

What they eat	How big they grow	How they move

Science Article

Home Address

Animals live in different places. Some live in forests. Others live in lakes or oceans. Different animals have different body coverings. Some have fur or feathers. Others have scales. The animals' body coverings help them live where they do.

Apply It!

Make a graphic organizer like the one shown above. Use it to help you **make an operational definition** about what you read and what you have observed. Write the main idea at the top. Fill in the missing details that support the main idea from the science article.

🔊 You Are There!

You are standing where the ocean meets the land. You can feel the warm sunlight on your face. You hear the waves rush onto the shore. You wiggle your toes in the cool, damp sand. Birds circle above you. This is a terrific place for you to visit. What makes it a perfect place for certain plants and animals to live?

🔊 AudioText 🔊

What are ecosystems?

Plants and animals meet their needs in the place where they live. Living things depend on other living things and nonliving things around them.

Places for Living Things

Each living thing needs a certain environment. A living thing's **environment** is everything that surrounds it. An environment has living and nonliving parts. The living parts include plants, animals, and other living things. The nonliving parts include sunlight, air, water, and soil.

Sunlight warms the air, water, and soil to the temperature that living things need. Sunlight helps plants make food.

An environment has a climate. Climate is the weather in a place all year. One environment might have cold, wet winters and hot, dry summers. Another environment might be cold and dry all year long.

Water and soil are important parts of an environment. Water falls as rain and snow. The water enters the soil. Soils differ in the way they hold the water. Each type of plant needs a certain amount of water and a certain kind of soil.

1. ✓ **Checkpoint** Name four nonliving things that are part of a plant's or animal's environment.

2. **Art** in Science Draw a picture that shows the things that you need that your environment provides. Write labels on your drawing of what these things are.

71

Parts of an Ecosystem

Living and nonliving parts of an environment act together, or interact. These interacting parts make up an **ecosystem.**

The living parts of an ecosystem depend on nonliving parts. For example, coastal redwood trees need sunlight, soil, and air. They also need a lot of water. There is plenty of rain in winter, but little rain falls in the summer. In summer, the trees get water from fog that rolls in from the ocean.

The living parts of an ecosystem also depend on one another. For example, some sea birds eat fish from the ocean. The birds nest in the redwood trees.

Habitats

The place where a living thing makes its home is its habitat. A habitat has all the things that a plant or animal needs to live. A redwood forest can be a habitat for many plants and animals. There is light, air, water, living space, and pollinators for plants. Animals find food, water, shelter, and living space in the forest. If any of these things is missing, something will change. Some plants and animals may no longer find what they need to live. Plants and animals may die. Animals may move to a different habitat.

Interacting Parts of an Ecosystem	
Living	**Nonliving**
plants	light/heat
animals	air/water
other living things	rocks/soil

The plants, animals, and environment of this coastal ecosystem interact with one another.

This coastal California redwood tree shares its environment with other plants and animals.

Dune grass has tough roots. They help the plant survive in strong wind, bright sunlight, and shifting sand.

1. ✔️Checkpoint What is an ecosystem?

2. 🎯 **Main Idea and Details** Read the caption about the dune grass. Give the main idea. List details that support it.

Groups Within Ecosystems

Coyotes roam the rough brush called chaparral on coastal hillsides in Southern California. All the living things of the same kind that live in the same place at the same time are a **population.** A group of coyotes make up a population.

Coyotes hunt California ground squirrels. The ground squirrels eat plants and live in burrows in the chaparral. All the populations that live together in the same place make up a **community.** The coyotes, ground squirrels, and chaparral plants are part of a community. The populations in a community depend on each other.

A coyote hunts ground squirrels.

Ecosystems Change

Ecosystems change over time. The change starts when one part of the ecosystem changes. This change causes other parts of the ecosystem to change. For example, in one winter the chaparral might get more rain than usual. Plants grow more. Ground squirrels now have more food than usual. This may cause the population of ground squirrels to grow.

The rise in the number of ground squirrels affects the coyotes. The population of coyotes can grow because coyotes find plenty of food.

If a winter has less rain than usual, plants provide less food. Less food supports fewer ground squirrels. As a result, the population of coyotes remains small or decreases.

All the coyotes in one place make up a population.

Fires move quickly through chaparral. This provides space, water, and sunlight for new plants to grow.

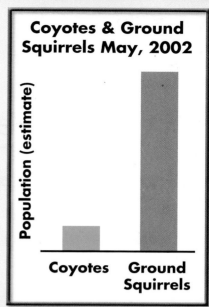

Coyotes & Ground Squirrels May, 2002

Population (estimate)

Coyotes | Ground Squirrels

More food than usual supports a large ground squirrel population.

Coyotes & Ground Squirrels May, 2005

Population (estimate)

Coyotes | Ground Squirrels

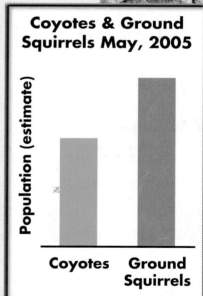

If the ground squirrel population is large, the coyote population might become large too.

✓ Lesson Checkpoint

1. How do coyotes, ground squirrels, and plants interact in their environment?

2. What might happen to plants and animals if there is more rain than usual?

3. **Writing in Science** **Descriptive** Describe a population in your **science journal**. Then describe the community to which your population belongs.

Which ecosystems have few trees?

Different places on Earth have different climates. Some land ecosystems have climates that support only a few trees.

Grassland

Think about looking out over a wide, grassy field. A strong summer breeze makes the tops of the grasses move like waves on the ocean. A **grassland** is a kind of land ecosystem. It has many grasses and flowering plants, but few trees. A climate of cool or cold winters and hot summers supports grasslands. The climate includes little rain, so the soil is dry. Trees cannot grow well in this soil. They need more water. The trees grow mostly in the wetter soil along rivers and creeks.

Many grasses grow well in this kind of habitat. They survive because they have deep roots. These roots help the plants in many ways. When grazing animals, fire, or the cold winters kill the plants above ground, the roots survive. Deep roots also help the plants find water in the dry, hot summers.

Some grasslands get more rain than others. Tall-grass prairies grow in the wetter eastern parts of the Midwest. Short-grass prairies grow farther west where less rain falls.

Climate in the Kansas Grassland		
Average Temperature (°C)		Average Yearly Rainfall (cm)
Summer	Winter	
20	2	90

Map Fact
This is the Konza Prairie in Kansas. Like other parts of the Midwestern United States, it is grassland.

Winters are cool or cold in the grasslands. Deep roots help the plants store food for winter.

Many kinds of insects, such as this grasshopper, live in grasslands.

Once huge herds of bison roamed the grasslands. Now, only a few herds remain.

1. ✅ **Checkpoint** What is a grassland?

2. 🎯 **Main Idea and Details** Tell the main idea about grasslands. Give supporting details.

Desert—A Surprising Ecosystem

A **desert** is an ecosystem that gets very little rain. Days are often hot, but the nights are cool or even cold. Many people think of deserts as nothing but sand. However, most desert ecosystems are full of life. Desert plants and animals can live with little rainfall. Some plants, including cactuses, store water in their leaves or stems.

During the day, you might see a lizard warming itself on a rock. But many desert animals rest out of sight during the hottest time of day. Some stay in underground tunnels. Others find a shady spot under a plant. At night the desert comes alive. Animals come out of their hiding places to search for food.

Climate in a Desert		
Average Temperature (°C)		Average Yearly Rainfall (cm)
Summer	Winter	30
30	10	

Yucca plants provide shade and cover for small animals like snakes and lizards. Small birds eat the fruits.

This sidewinder rattlesnake usually hunts at night. It kills small animals for food.

This desert bobcat warms itself on a sunny rock in winter. At night, it hunts for birds and other small animals.

Map Fact

Joshua Tree National Park is a desert ecosystem in southern California. Joshua trees are a kind of yucca plant, which grows only about 6 centimeters a year. More than 78 kinds of birds nest in the park.

1. **✓Checkpoint** Why do certain plants do well in deserts?

2. **Writing in Science** **Expository**
   Write a newspaper article about desert animals. Explain why they are active at night.

Tundra—Land of Long Winters

The **tundra** is a cold, dry, land ecosystem. It is in the very northern part of the world. Parts of Alaska are tundra. Winters there are long and cold. Snow falls and cold winds blow. Summers are short and cool. The snow melts in summer, but the soil below the surface does not become soft. It stays frozen all year.

Summer days are very long in the tundra. In some places, the summer Sun shines 24 hours a day. Winter days are very short. Some places get no sunlight at all in winter.

Many plants cannot grow in this climate. For example, few trees grow in the tundra. Their roots cannot grow in frozen soil. Small plants grow here instead. These include grasses and wildflowers.

In summer, the melting snow forms ponds in the tundra. Many ducks, geese, and swans nest near these ponds. Other birds also nest in the tundra. In summer, there are millions of insects for them to eat. Most tundra birds travel to warmer places during winter.

Climate in the Tundra		
Average Temperature (°C)		Average Yearly Rainfall (cm)
Summer	Winter	
6	30° below 0	10

Caribou travel in large herds. In winter, they find food by digging through the snow with their front hooves.

What type of plant is missing in this tundra? Trees! Their roots cannot grow into the frozen soil. Grasses and wild flowers grow close to the ground.

Lichens grow in clumps close to the ground. It is the main winter food of caribou.

Wolves usually travel in groups, or packs, to hunt for food. They hunt caribou, hares, and lemmings. Other large hunters include brown bears and golden eagles.

✓ Lesson Checkpoint

1. What is the coldest land ecosystem?

2. List three kinds of land ecosystems.

3. **Math** in Science   A day is 24 hours long. Nome, Alaska, has about 21 hours of daylight on July 4. How many hours of darkness does it have? Nome has 4 hours of daylight on January 1. How many hours of darkness does it have then?

What are some forest ecosystems?

There are ecosystems that have different kinds of thick forests. Each kind of forest ecosystem has its own plants and animals.

Coniferous and Deciduous Forests

Coniferous forests grow mainly in northern North America, Europe, and Asia. They grow where summers are warm and dry. Winters are cold and snowy. Spruce, fir, and pine are some coniferous trees.

Mosses and lichens can grow under coniferous trees. Few other things grow there. Many animals find food and shelter in coniferous forests.

Climates where deciduous forests grow are generally warmer than climates of coniferous forests. Deciduous forests get rain in summer and snow in winter. Oak, maple, and beech are some deciduous trees. They drop their leaves in the fall. For part of the year, sunlight reaches the forest floor. Many shrubs and other plants can grow there. These plants provide habitats for animals.

1. **✓Checkpoint** How are coniferous and deciduous forests alike and different?

2. **Writing in Science** **Descriptive** Write a short story about walking through an evergreen forest or a deciduous forest. Describe what you see, hear, and feel.

Climate in a Coniferous Forest		
Average Temperature (°C)		Average Yearly Rainfall (cm)
Summer	Winter	50
8	−20	

North American Coniferous Forest

Moose eat twigs, bark, roots, and young stems of woody plants. In summer, they feed on water plants like water lilies.

Many insects and birds live in deciduous forests. Woodpeckers eat beetles that dig into tree trunks.

Climate in a Deciduous Forest		
Average Temperature (°C)		Average Yearly Rainfall (cm)
Summer	Winter	160
25	5	

North American Deciduous Forest

Beavers use their sharp teeth to cut forest trees and branches. They build dams of sticks and mud across streams.

83

Tropical Forests

Where could you find a spider so big that it eats birds? These spiders live in a tropical forest near the equator. The climate in tropical forests can be warm and rainy all year long. Tall trees let little sunlight reach the forest floor. Some of the trees can be 35 meters tall—taller than a ten-story building. Plants such as orchids grow on the trees.

Most animals of the tropical forest live in the trees. Some spend their whole lives there.

Some animals, such as bats, can be found in many different tropical forests. Others live in certain forests and not in others. For example, many kinds of beetles live in only one forest in Brazil. They are found nowhere else. The tropical rainforest has huge numbers of insects. No one has ever named them all.

Woolly monkeys live in South America. They live in trees and eat fruits, leaves, seeds, and some insects.

Rainbow lorikeets live in the tropical forests of eastern Asia and Australia. These noisy birds eat nectar, flowers, seeds, and fruit.

Climate in a Rainforest		
Average Temperature (°C)		Average Yearly Rainfall (cm)
Summer	Winter	
25	25	300

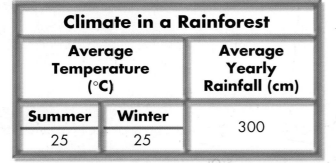

These red stinkbugs live in tropical forests.

Venomous snakes, such as this palm viper, live in tropical forests. Most snakes eat frogs, lizards, and other small animals.

✔ Lesson Checkpoint

1. What kind of climate can tropical forests have?

2. List three kinds of forests.

3. **Writing** in Science **Descriptive** Write a paragraph in your **science journal** describing how climate affects different kinds of forests.

What are water ecosystems?

Water ecosystems can have fresh water, salt water, or both.

Florida Everglades

Freshwater Ecosystems

Freshwater ecosystems include lakes, ponds, rivers, and streams. Lakes and ponds are water surrounded by land. Rivers and streams are moving water. Rain or melting snow supplies water for most lakes and rivers. Springs that flow from underground supply water for others. Many plants and animals live in lakes and rivers.

The Everglades in south Florida is a large wetland. A **wetland** is low land that is covered by water at least part of the year. Water flows very slowly through the Everglades south to Florida Bay. This "river of grass" is very wide. But its water is very shallow. Trees, grasses, and water plants live there. Animals such as fish, bears, and birds live there, too.

Many large Florida springs are the winter homes of manatees. These slow-moving mammals eat water plants.

Alligators have sharp teeth and strong jaws. They eat fish, birds, and anything else they can catch.

Map Fact

There are hundreds of springs that empty into lakes and rivers in Florida. Weeki Wachee Spring in central Florida supplies the water for the Weeki Wachee River, shown here.

1. ✓**Checkpoint** Name four kinds of freshwater ecosystems.

2. **Technology in Science** Use the Internet to find out about the plants and animals that live in the Everglades. Make a list of these plants and animals.

Saltwater Ecosystems

Oceans cover much of Earth's surface. There is salt in ocean water. The ocean is shallow along the shore. Clams, crabs, kelp, fish, and coral live here. Otters, seals, and sea birds swim and dive for fish.

The ocean gets very deep, but most life is in the top 200 meters of water. Very small animals feed on tiny algae that make food. Large fish and whales also live here. The deep ocean is dark and cold, and it has little food. Few animals live here.

Many rivers flow into the ocean. Fresh water from the rivers can mix with salt water from the ocean. Wetlands called salt marshes can form in these areas. Plants and animals here are able to live in salty water and soil. Many plants grow in salt marshes. Some tiny animals in the muddy marsh are too small to see with just your eye. Many kinds of fishes, crabs, and other ocean animals begin their lives in salt marshes.

Life in the Oceans	
Kinds of Living Things	275,000 kinds
Longest Animal	Blue Whale, 33 meters
Longest Fish	Whale Shark, 12 meters
Fastest Ocean Animal	Sailfish, 30 meters per second

This reef cuttlefish can squirt a jet of water out of its body. This helps it escape from an enemy.

A coral is an animal about the size of an ant. It builds a hard, rocky skeleton around itself for protection. Millions of corals build a coral reef.

Map Fact

The Great Barrier Reef is a huge coral reef. It is along the eastern coast of Australia. Australia is in the southern Pacific Ocean.

Australian Great Barrier Reef

✓ **Lesson Checkpoint**

1. Where do most corals live?

2. Where is most life found in the oceans?

3. **Writing** in Science **Narrative** Find out about an animal that lives in salty water. Then write a story in your **science journal** about that animal. Title your story (Name of your animal)—This Is Your Life!

89

Guided Inquiry

Investigate How can you show that mold needs food?

You have learned that animals of each ecosystem find the food they need where they live. In this activity you will show that in order to stay alive and grow, mold must get the food it needs. If it is in an "ecosystem" without the food it needs, it will not grow.

Materials

gloves   moldy strawberry

hand lens

bread slice
(without preservatives)

foil square

2 plastic bags

dropper   cup with water

Process Skills

You **interpret data** when you use data from an investigation to answer a question.

What to Do

1 **Observe** the mold on the strawberry. Draw what the mold looks like.

Be careful!

Wear gloves.

2 Lightly rub some mold off the strawberry onto the bread. Do the same for the foil.

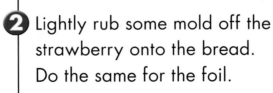

3 Put the bread in a bag. Put the foil in another bag. Use a dropper to add 10 drops of water to the 2 spots where the mold was rubbed.

4 Seal the bags. Put them in a warm, dark place.

After you seal the bags, do not reopen them.

5 After 4 days, observe the bags. Draw pictures of any mold growing in the bags.

Mold gets the energy needed for growth from the bread.

Drawings of Observations		
Mold on Strawberry	Mold on Bread	Mold on Foil

Explain Your Results

1. In which bag did mold grow?
2. **Interpret Data** Which has the food that mold needs to grow, the bread or the foil? Explain.

Go Further

Does mold need light to grow? Investigate. Use a camera to keep a record.

91

How do plants and animals interact?

consumer

producer

herbivore

98

Chapter 4 Vocabulary

decomposer

decay

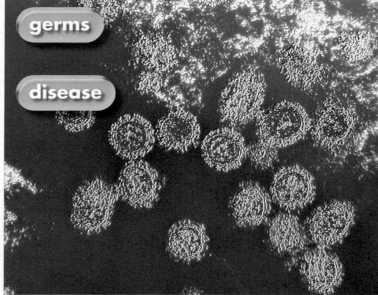

germs

disease

omnivore

carnivore   predator

competition   prey

Explore How do pill bugs stay safe?

Materials

plastic jar

soil, dead leaves, lettuce

cup with water

spoon

4 pill bugs

cheesecloth

rubber band

What to Do

1 Make a habitat for pill bugs.

2 Use the spoon to gently put pill bugs into the habitat. Add 3 spoonfuls of water. Cover the jar.

Notice how a pill bug can roll into a ball. In a ball, its hard body covering helps protect its soft belly. A pill bug also may hide in dark places to avoid enemies.

cheesecloth

rubber band

lettuce

dead leaves

layer of soil

3 **Observe** the pill bugs for 5 minutes each day for one week. Describe what they do.

Explain Your Results

1. **Infer** How might rolling into a ball help a pill bug stay safe?

2. Why might pill bugs need lettuce or other plants in their habitat?

How to Read Science

Draw Conclusions

A good reader can put together facts and then build a new idea, or a conclusion. The conclusion should make sense and be supported by the facts. You might use a graphic organizer to show a conclusion.

Science Article

What's on the Menu

Shrews need food to be active. They find a lot of pill bugs to eat under rotting logs. One type of spider eats only such bugs. Toads, lizards, and birds eat pill bugs, too.

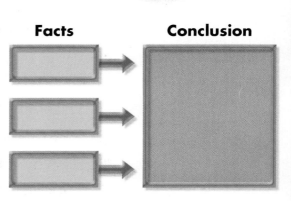

Apply It!

Make a graphic organizer like the one shown. Fill it in with three facts from the paragraph above. Then **infer** a conclusion. Show how the facts led to the conclusion.

Facts   **Conclusion**

🔊 You Are There!

You are floating in clear ocean water. You look down through a face mask. You see a school of small fish. They swim left, right, up, and down. They all move together. Suddenly the school turns. You blink with surprise. When you look again, the school is gone! Where did the fish go? Why were they swimming together like that?

🔊 AudioText 🔊

Lesson 1

How do living things interact?

Living things may affect each other when they interact. The interactions can be helpful, harmful, or neither.

Ways Living Things Interact

Living things interact in different ways. Their interactions may help them survive. Study the examples in the chart. Those living in groups help each other. One kind of living thing might help another kind without being helped in return. Or different kinds might help each other.

Ways Living Things Interact		
Helping in Groups	Members of a herd protect each other.	
One Kind Helping Another	A tree helps a flower get light.	
Two Kinds Helping Each Other	While it drinks flower nectar, an insect spreads pollen among the flowers.	

1. ✓**Checkpoint** List three ways in which living things might interact.

2. **Writing in Science** **Narrative** In your **science journal** describe a day during which you helped as a member of a group. Describe how the group helped you.

One bee may find flowers. Then it will fly back to the beehive and move in a certain way. This "dance" tells the other bees where the flowers are.

Living in Groups

Animals that live together might all help protect the group from predators. Together, the animals may be safer than each animal alone. For example, prairie dogs live in groups. Coyotes and golden eagles eat them. Coyotes hunt on the ground. Eagles hunt from the sky. Prairie dogs take turns standing watch at their burrow openings. If any prairie dog senses danger, it whistles. At this sound, the whole group runs and hides. All the prairie dogs stay hidden until the danger has passed.

One Kind of Living Thing Helping Another Kind

Notice the barnacles on the whale. Some barnacles swim through the ocean and attach to the skin of a whale. A barnacle usually spends its whole life attached to the same whale.

The barnacle opens and closes its shell to catch food as the whale moves through the water. The barnacles do not harm the whales. They don't help the whales either. In this partnership, only one partner is helped— the barnacle.

A grown barnacle is about 5 cm wide. It grabs food from the water that the whale swims through.

Helping One Another

Some kinds of living things help each other. The moth seen here shares its life with only one kind of yucca plant.

The moth helps the yucca by carrying pollen from another yucca. The yucca helps the moth by giving it a habitat and food for its young. The moth lays her eggs in the flower pods. Each larva hatches in the pods and eats some of the seeds the flower pod makes.

The cleaner fish is another example. Several kinds of small fish clean larger fish. They eat pests off the big fish. The cleaner fish gets a meal. The other fish gets clean and stays healthy.

A yucca moth provides a ball of sticky pollen from another yucca. In exchange it lays its eggs in the flower.

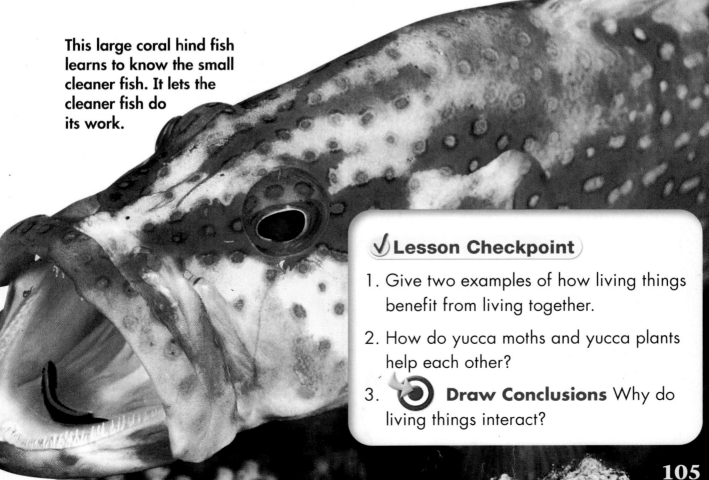

This large coral hind fish learns to know the small cleaner fish. It lets the cleaner fish do its work.

✓ Lesson Checkpoint

1. Give two examples of how living things benefit from living together.

2. How do yucca moths and yucca plants help each other?

3. **Draw Conclusions** Why do living things interact?

105

How do living things get energy?

Plants get energy from the sun. Animals get energy from plants or from other animals that eat plants.

Sources of Energy

Green plants make their own food. A living thing that makes its own food is a **producer.** Producers use energy from sunlight to make food out of matter from the air and soil.

Many living things cannot make their own food. They must get their energy from food that they eat. A living thing that eats food is a **consumer.**

Kinds of Consumers

Some consumers eat plants, others eat animals, and some eat both. A consumer that eats only plants is an **herbivore.** A consumer that eats only animals is a **carnivore.** A consumer that eats both plants and animals is an **omnivore.**

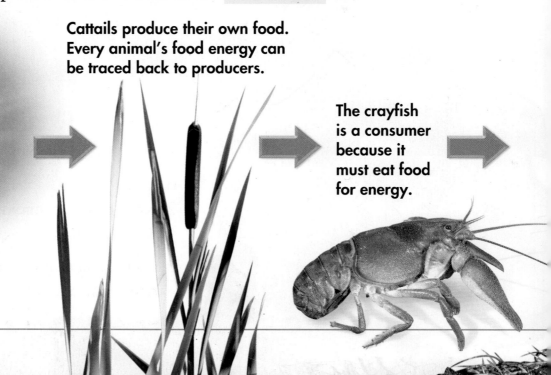

Cattails produce their own food. Every animal's food energy can be traced back to producers.

The crayfish is a consumer because it must eat food for energy.

Sunlight provides all the energy for an ecosystem.

Sheep are herbivores. They eat only plants.

A wolf is a carnivore. It eats only meat.

A bear is an omnivore. It eats both plants and animals.

Food Chains

Energy passes to living things within food chains. Food chains are groups of producers and consumers that interact in a special way. A consumer eats a producer. The producer passes energy to that consumer. That consumer may then become **prey** for another consumer. Prey is any animal that is hunted by others for food.

The prey passes energy on to a **predator.** A predator is a consumer that hunts for food. In this way, energy can move from a producer to a predator. As each living thing uses food energy, some energy is given off as heat.

The raccoon is an omnivore. It eats crayfish, other animals, and plants.

✓Checkpoint

1. Trace the transfer of energy through a food chain that includes raccoons, crayfish, cattails, and sunlight.

2. **Art in Science** Draw a food chain that shows how grass, a cow, and a person drinking milk are connected.

Energy in a Food Web

A food chain is simple. Energy moves from one type of living thing to another. Real life is not so simple. Energy often moves in many different ways. It might transfer from one kind of producer to many kinds of consumers. One kind of consumer might be prey for more than one kind of predator.

Energy flow in a community forms a web. A food web is made up of more than one food chain. Food webs tie a community together. Each part of a web affects other parts.

An example of a food web is found on the Great Plains. Prairie grasses grow there. They are producers. Energy flows from the grasses to the animals that eat them. These animals include prairie dogs and mice. Prairie dogs are prey for ferrets and golden eagles. Ferrets are prey for badgers. So energy can flow through the food web from grasses to golden eagles and badgers.

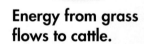

Energy from grass flows to cattle.

Energy from grass flows to prairie dogs.

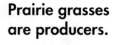

Prairie grasses are producers.

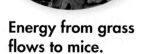

Energy from grass flows to mice.

A Changing Food Web

If one part of a food web is removed, other parts change. For example, prairie dogs once built large colonies on the grassy plains. Then cattle began to feed on these same plains. This reduced the habitat for prairie dogs. Many prairie dogs also became sick and died. As a result, the number of prairie dogs was reduced.

Removing one part of the food web caused a number of things to happen. The cattle had more food, but ferrets had less. With fewer prairie dogs to eat, ferrets no longer had the food they needed. Ferrets began to die out.

This, in turn, affected predators of ferrets, such as badgers. Now badgers had to look for other food. Golden eagles and foxes also hunt prairie dogs. They too had to get more food energy from other kinds of prey, such as mice. All this can happen when one part of a food web is removed.

Ferrets eat mostly prairie dogs. Energy flows to the ferrets.

Badgers eat ferrets. Energy flows to the badgers.

Golden eagles eat prairie dogs and mice. Energy from these animals flows to the eagles.

✓ Lesson Checkpoint

1. How did reducing the number of prairie dogs affect ferrets?

2. How does the loss of prairie dogs affect eagles and foxes?

3. **Draw Conclusions** Tell what happens when a food chain is broken.

109

The young trees in this forest compete for sunlight and room to grow.

This male bower bird competes with other males to attract females to its nest.

Many different animals compete for water in dry places.

How do living things compete?

Maybe you have tried to fit under an umbrella with another person to stay dry. You had to compete with the person for shelter. Living things often compete with one another. Usually they compete for food, water, and room to live.

Competing for Resources

Picture yourself in a dark, cool forest. The treetops form a roof high above you. Few small trees are growing. Why? They struggle to get enough energy from sunlight to grow. The small trees are in **competition** with one another. When two or more living things need the same resources, they are in competition. Since the tall trees in this forest get most of the sunlight, the small trees compete for the light that is left.

Living things compete for many kinds of resources besides light. These resources include food, water, and living space. The winners in these competitions survive. The losers might not survive.

SciLinks Take It to the Net
pearsonsuccessnet.com
keyword: competition
code: g3p110

Predators and Prey

Many predators may compete for the same prey. Faster, stronger ones might catch more food. For example, some hunting birds may get more food by stealing prey caught by the other birds. Predators with greater ability are more likely to survive and reproduce. They pass these valuable traits on to their young.

Different types of predators may compete with each other. Lions and hyenas might want the same prey, for example. The lions hunt and kill the prey. Then the hyenas fight the lions and try to steal it.

Animals that are prey also compete. Deer that are stronger or healthier than others are more likely to protect themselves. They are better able to escape from predators.

The lions have killed the prey. But the hyenas are not afraid to compete for as much of this food as they can get.

✓ **Checkpoint**

1. What do living things compete for?

2. **Writing** in Science **Expository**
Write a short paragraph in your **science journal** explaining why living things compete.

111

Other Kinds of Competition

Some living things compete for space. Purple loosestrife is a plant that was brought to the United States. Animals here do not eat it, and it spreads easily. Purple loosestrife takes space away from other plants. Some plants are crowded out completely.

Animals and humans can compete for space. People move to places where animals live. People may see coyotes in their backyards or flocks of sea gulls on their beaches.

Living things may compete for oxygen. Algae are like plants. They provide oxygen and food for fish and other living things. If too many algae grow, some do not get enough sunlight. These algae die. Many tiny consumers of dead algae grow and use up oxygen in the water. Fish and other living things compete for the oxygen that is left.

A Competition Cycle

Lemmings are small mammals that live in the tundra. When there is plenty of grass for them to eat, the lemming population can grow quickly. Then there is less food available because so many lemmings are eating it.

After three years, too many lemmings are competing for the food. Many leave to find food elsewhere. The lemming population becomes smaller. Then the grass can grow back. The competition cycle begins again.

Purple loosestrife competes with other plants for space.

Sea gulls compete with humans for living space.

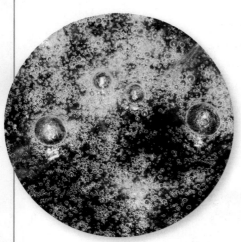

If too many algae grow, there is less oxygen for fish and other living things.

Competition between these lemmings for food can follow a cycle over time.

A Competition Cycle

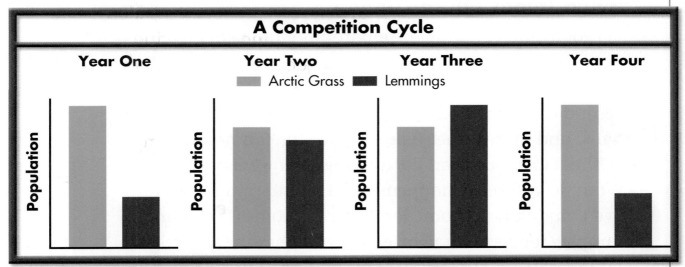

Year One **Year Two** **Year Three** **Year Four**

Arctic Grass   Lemmings

Population   Population   Population   Population

There is plenty of arctic grass for lemmings to eat.

The population of lemmings grows. The amount of grass goes down.

The population of lemmings grows. There is not enough food. Many lemmings leave or die.

With fewer lemmings, the grass grows back. Once again there is enough food.

✓ Lesson Checkpoint

1. Why do living things compete with one another?

2. What kind of living thing usually survives in a competition?

3. **Draw Conclusions** Explain the pattern of change in the lemming population over time.

113

How do environments change?

Plants and animals can change their environment. Natural events, such as fire, can change the environment too. These changes affect plants and animals that live in the environment. Changes often occur in patterns.

Living Things Cause Change

People often change the environment to better suit their needs, but they are not the only ones. For example, when a beaver builds a dam, many changes occur. Water backs up behind the dam. Then a new wetland habitat grows. Fish, birds, and many other types of animals can now live there.

The dams, however, flood places that were once dry. What do you think happens to the living things that once lived on dry land? Some look for new homes. They might compete for space in nearby places. Others may not survive.

Beavers change the environment when they build their homes and dams of sticks and mud.

This place was once a grassy meadow. How has this beaver dam changed it?

Natural Events Cause Change

Natural events also change environments. For example, hurricanes can change coastlines. They wash away beaches and knock down trees. They can cause terrible floods.

Floods change environments too. They kill plants and wash away birds' nests. Floods spread thick blankets of mud. They also carry rich soil from one place to other places.

Too little water also causes changes. Little rain falls during a drought. Plants die from lack of water. If animals cannot find enough water, then they may die or move to other places.

The Mississippi River sometimes floods. The floodwater carries rich soil down the river. When floodwater drains off the land, it leaves behind a layer of soil.

High winds and water will change this environment.

Few plants, animals, or humans can live in a drought area.

✓ Checkpoint

1. Describe ways that living things and natural events can cause an environment to change.

2. **Writing in Science** **Descriptive**
Write a paragraph or a poem in your **science journal** about one change you have seen in your environment.

Living Things Return

On May 18, 1980, the volcano Mt. St. Helens erupted in the State of Washington. This eruption was huge. Winds carried clouds of ash around the world.

The blast changed the local environment. It knocked over trees. It burned whole forests. Rivers of mud covered large areas.

There were few signs of life after the eruption. Over time, however, wind carried the seeds of grasses, flowers, and trees to the mountain. New plants began to grow. Soon spiders and beetles arrived. Birds returned to live in the standing dead trees. Each new change allowed more kinds of plants and the animals that depend on them to live there again. Today, even elk live on Mt. St. Helens. The mountain is filled with life once more.

In September 2004, Mt. St. Helens rumbled to life again. An active volcano can bring sudden change at any time.

Mt. St. Helens erupts.

Fires also change environments. Fires happen often in forests and grasslands. Lightning may strike a tree. A burning branch falls to the ground. Then a fire creeps along the forest floor. It removes small plants competing for space to grow. However, the plants that do not burn will have more living space. Also, ash from fires is good for the soil. It helps plants to grow.

Eruptions and fires are examples of events that cause change. The changes often kill plants and destroy animal homes. The changes, however, may improve habitats for other plants and animals.

✓ Checkpoint

1. Explain how fire is a change that can improve growing conditions for plants.

2. **Art** in Science Draw a forest before a fire. Then draw the forest on fire. Finally, draw the forest five years later.

Ground fires kill plants but help new plants grow.

This young pine grows fast in an area cleaned by fire.

This burnt stump gives a spruce seedling a place to grow.

Very few plants remained after the volcano erupted.

New life has returned to the mountain.

117

Many years will go by before these Douglas fir seedlings become full-grown trees.

Smaller trees compete for sunlight because they are shaded by tall trees.

Map Fact
Forests of tall coniferous trees grow in the temperate rain forest along the coast of the State of Washington.

Patterns of Change

Living things change together. These changes often happen in patterns. Let's look at one growth pattern.

Douglas fir trees grow in cool, misty forests in the northwestern United States. Squirrels often knock the cones from the trees. The seeds from the cones sprout on the forest floor. The seedlings compete for sunlight and other resources. A few survive and grow into giant trees. Some of these giants grow old, die, and fall.

Mushrooms and other decomposers feed on the dead trees. A **decomposer** is a living thing that breaks down waste and living things that have died. This action is called **decay.** Decay returns certain materials to the soil. Decomposers cause the dead trees to slowly crumble into the soil.

Western hemlock trees live in the same forest. Seeds from their cones can land on the decaying Douglas fir logs. The decaying logs supply things that help young seedlings to grow. Also, light reaches logs in the open where the giant trees once stood. The hemlock seeds sprout and grow quickly.

SciLinks Take It to the Net
pearsonsuccessnet.com
keyword: decomposer
code: g3p118

In time, the hemlocks become tall trees. They provide homes for squirrels, spotted owls, and other animals.

When the older hemlocks are near the end of their lives, carpenter ants and decomposers go to work. The ants build nests in the decaying tree trunks. The old trunks fall to the ground. They decay and become part of the soil.

The life cycles of the trees are connected. The changes occur in a pattern that happens over and over again.

These mushrooms are decomposers. They find this dead log a good food source.

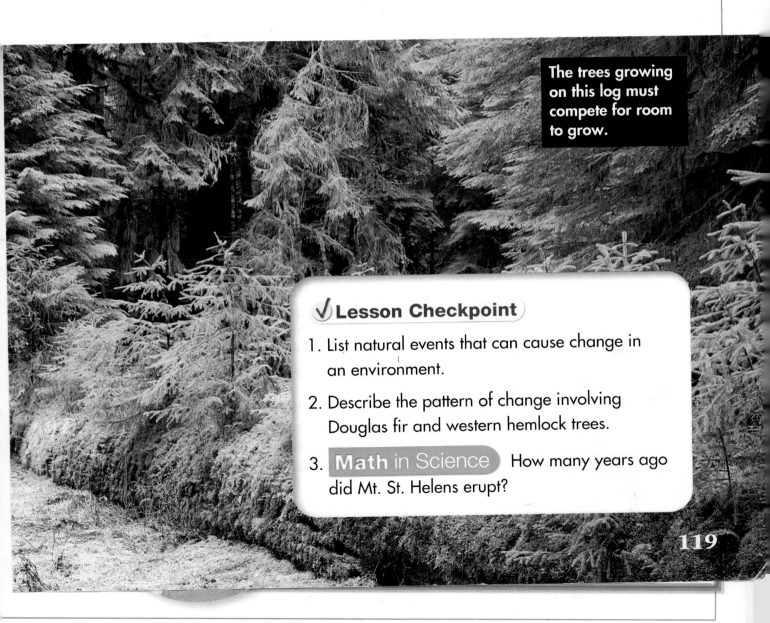

The trees growing on this log must compete for room to grow.

✓ Lesson Checkpoint

1. List natural events that can cause change in an environment.

2. Describe the pattern of change involving Douglas fir and western hemlock trees.

3. **Math in Science** How many years ago did Mt. St. Helens erupt?

119

Healthful Foods

To be sure you are getting all the vitamins, minerals, and other nutrients your body needs, you must eat a variety of healthful foods. This variety includes whole grains, fruits, and vegetables, as well as nuts, fish, eggs, dairy foods, and meats. Your body also needs a good amount of water each day.

To be kept healthful, food should be stored carefully. Fresh fruits and vegetables should be washed and kept in a cool place. Fish, eggs, dairy foods, and meats must be wrapped and kept cold. Using food while it is still fresh is also important.

Cooks and others who handle food must have clean hands and clean tools. Their tools include knives and cutting boards as well as mixers, bowls, spoons, and forks.

Drinking juice is a healthful choice.

Dairy products help bones grow strong.

Vegetables such as carrots and broccoli make good snacks.

Eat fruit, such as grapes, every day.

Fish contain materials your body needs to grow.

From Food to Energy

What happens to food after you eat it? The body's digestive system goes to work. It breaks foods down into a form that our bodies can use to live and grow. These are the main parts of the digestive system.

Food goes down a long tube to reach your stomach. Your intestines also are tubes, all curled up. The small intestine is longer, but narrower, than the large intestine.

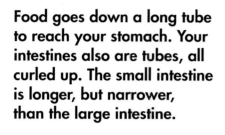

Mouth
Teeth break food into pieces. The tongue mixes food with saliva so you can swallow it.

Small Intestine
Most digestion happens here. More juices break down food. Food particles pass through the intestine walls and into the bloodstream.

Stomach
Muscles mix food with digestive juices. Food becomes a sticky paste.

Large Intestine
Water passes into the bloodstream. Some food parts are not digested. These form solid waste, which passes out of the body.

✓ Lesson Checkpoint

1. How can you be sure of getting all the nutrients you need?

2. Write the steps that show how an apple changes from the time you eat it until the time you can use its energy.

3. **Health** in Science   Interview a person who cooks. Find out how that person chooses and takes care of food.

How can people stay healthy?

People want to be as healthy as possible. There are many things they can do to help keep their bodies healthy.

Exercise

Safe, regular exercise is important. People in good shape have the energy to work, play, and feel good. Exercise helps keep bodies healthy.

Some people get exercise by biking or swimming. They may play basketball or soccer. But exercise does not have to be a sport. House and yardwork can be exercise too.

When you rest, your heart beats about ninety times per minute. It beats faster when you exercise.

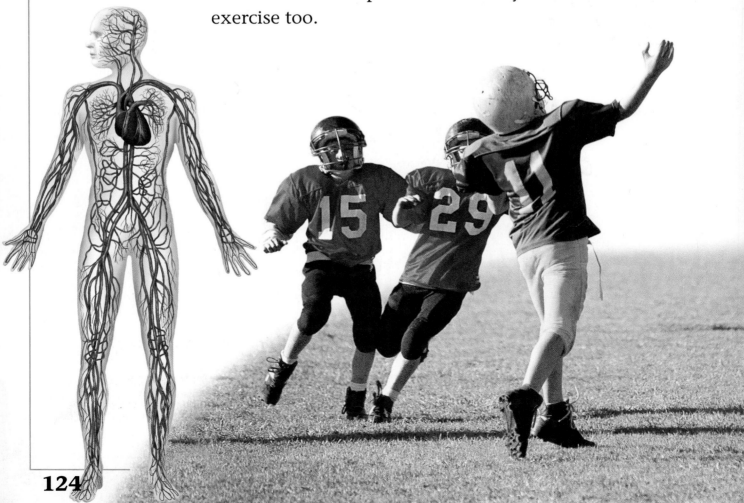

124

Exercise keeps a person's lungs, heart, and muscles strong. Your lungs are part of your respiratory system. They put oxygen from the air you breathe into your blood. Your heart and blood vessels are part of your circulatory system. The heart pumps blood through blood vessels. Blood carries oxygen and other materials to your muscles. Blood carries wastes away from your muscles. Exercise helps your systems work together well.

People who feel good about themselves take care of their bodies. They eat a variety of good foods. They get enough exercise and rest. They avoid things that are unhealthy.

When you breathe in, air goes down a long tube called the windpipe. The windpipe divides into two tubes. Each tube leads to a spongy lung.

The proper equipment keeps these young football players safe.

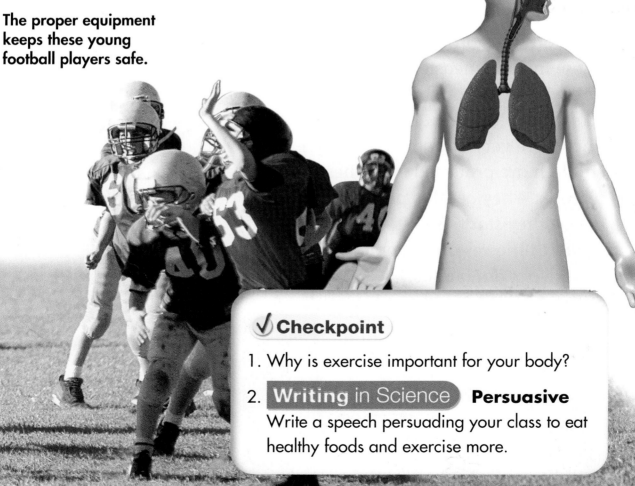

✓ **Checkpoint**

1. Why is exercise important for your body?

2. **Writing** in Science **Persuasive**
Write a speech persuading your class to eat healthy foods and exercise more.

Avoiding Germs

Lin is sneezing. Shauna is coughing. Aidan has a runny nose and teary eyes. Several of their classmates are at home, sick with the flu. What are causing these illnesses? Germs.

Germs are very small living things or particles. Examples include bacteria and viruses. Many germs can make people ill. The pictures show germs that can cause disease. A **disease** is a condition in which the body or a part of the body does not work properly. You may have had one or more diseases such as the flu, chicken pox, or strep throat.

There are many other diseases that you have probably not had. These include measles, mumps, and whooping cough. Years ago, many people caught these illnesses. They were very dangerous. Today, children are protected from these diseases. They get this protection before they start school.

Most illnesses that people get are not dangerous. Still, no one likes to be sick. Everyone can help to stop the spread of germs.

This picture shows the virus that causes the flu. This picture was taken through a special, very powerful microscope.

Microscopes are used to observe things that are very small.

The germs shown below cause whooping cough.

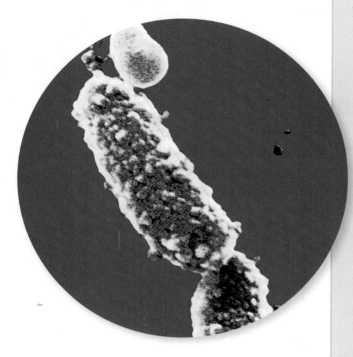

Stopping the Spread of Germs

People can help stop the spread of germs by remembering some simple rules.

- Stay home from school and work when you are ill.
- Wash your hands often, especially after using the restroom and before and after working with food.
- Cover your nose and mouth when you sneeze or cough. Wash your hands if you sneeze or cough into them.
- Clean and cover cuts and scrapes.

Wash your hands often with soap and warm water so that you don't spread germs.

The germs that cause strep throat look like tiny beads.

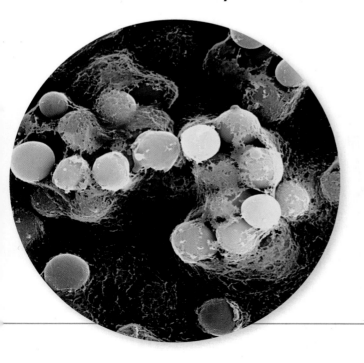

✔ Lesson Checkpoint

1. How do your respiratory and circulatory systems work together?

2. Make a list of things you can do to stop the spread of germs.

3. **Technology** in Science
   Choose an illness to research. Find out its causes and possible cure. Use the Internet or other technology to help in your research.

Investigate What can happen in a place without predators?

Without predators, a population of prey can starve. In this activity, your teacher will pick some students to be deer. All live in a place without predators. The deer pretend to eat the same kind of food (unpopped popcorn).

Materials

unpopped popcorn

What to Do

1 If you are picked to be a deer, line up on the side of the marked area. This is where you find food.

2 **Round A** When told, cross the area one deer at a time. Collect 5 pieces of food (unpopped popcorn) to "stay alive." Do not take more than 5 pieces.

Round	Number of Deer Alive at End of Round
Round A	
Round B	
Round C	
Round D	
Round E	

The number of rounds will depend on the number of deer and the amount of food supplied.

Record how many deer are alive at the end of each round. After each round your teacher will add food.

3 If you survive, you reproduce. Pick another student to join for the next round.

4 **Round B** Cross again and collect 5 more pieces of food.

Process Skills

You can use the **data** you **collect** during an investigation to help make an **inference**.

Deer line up here.

area where deer find food

5 Repeat until "starvation" begins. Make a bar graph to show the **data** you **collected**.

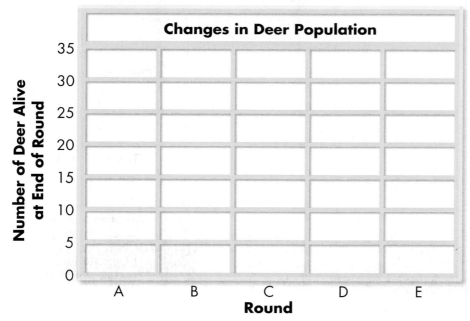

Changes in Deer Population

Number of Deer Alive at End of Round

35
30
25
20
15
10
5
0

A   B   C   D   E

Round

Explain Your Results

1. While there was plenty of food, how did the number of deer change? What finally happened?

2. **Infer** What can happen in a place without predators?

Go Further

What might happen if predators were added? Make a plan to answer this or a question of your own.

Health
By the Numbers

You have learned how important it is to choose the right foods for good health. It is also important to know how many Calories you need and how many are in the foods you eat.

Smiley Flakes
Serving Size 1 cup (30 grams)
Calories: 110
Total Fat: 2 grams
Cholesterol: 0 grams
Sodium: 210 milligrams
Carbohydrates: 23 grams
Fiber: 1 gram
Sugar: 1 gram

Mega Grain
Serving Size 1 cup (30 grams)
Calories: 165
Total Fat: 1 gram
Cholesterol: 0 grams
Sodium: 0 milligrams
Carbohydrates: 39 grams
Fiber: 3 grams
Sugar: 0 grams

Fresh Fruit or Fruit Juice	Serving Size	Calories
Banana slices	1 cup	133
Strawberry halves	1 cup	49
Peach slices	1 cup	66
Orange juice	1 cup	112

Milk Products	Serving Size	Calories
Whole milk	1 cup	146
Reduced-fat milk (2%)	1 cup	122
Low-fat milk (1%)	1 cup	102
Fat-free milk (Skim)	1 cup	83

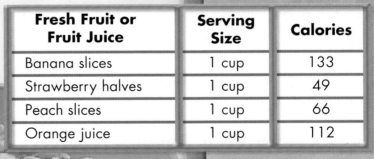

Tools Take It to the Net
pearsonsuccessnet.com

Use the charts and the cereal labels to answer the questions.

1 How many more Calories are in 1 cup of whole milk than in 1 cup of fat-free milk?

2 How many Calories are in the breakfast described below?

1 cup Smiley Flakes

1 cup reduced-fat milk

1 cup strawberry halves

1 cup orange juice

3 Compare the grams of carbohydrates in the two cereals. Which has more? How much more?

4 Suppose you want to eat no more than 2,000 Calories each day. If, for breakfast, you had 1 serving each of Mega Grain, low-fat milk, banana slices, and orange juice, how many Calories would you have left for the rest of the day?

Lab zone Take-Home Activity

For one day, write down everything you eat, including the amount. Also write down the number of Calories for each food you ate. Use labels or a nutrition guide. Find the total number of Calories for the day.

Use Vocabulary

carnivore (page 106)	**germs** (page 126)
competition (page 110)	**herbivore** (page 106)
consumer (page 106)	**omnivore** (page 106)
decomposer (page 118)	**predator** (page 107)
decay (page 118)	**prey** (page 107)
disease (page 126)	**producer** (page 106)

Write the vocabulary word or words from the list above that best completes each sentence.

1. A(n) _____ eats only animals while a(n) _____ eats only plants.

2. Bacteria and viruses are _____, which can cause _____.

3. A(n) _____ is a consumer that hunts another for food.

4. A(n) _____ is a living thing that must eat food to get energy,

5. A(n) _____ makes its own food.

6. _____ happens between living things that have a need for the same resources.

7. A(n) _____ eats both plants and animals.

8. _____ happens when a(n) _____ breaks down a living thing that has died.

9. _____ is an animal that is hunted by others.

Explain Concepts

10. Trace the flow of energy from beginning to end in the following food chain: a ferret eats prairie dogs which eat grasses and other plants.

11. Explain why some plants that are put into a new area can become dangerous weeds.

12. Explain the helpful and harmful effects ground fires have on plants in a forest community.

13. Describe ways to stay healthy.

Process Skills

14. **Classify** the following living things as producers or consumers: prairie dog, whale, purple loosestrife, barnacle, Douglas fir.

15. Predict The lemming population keeps growing. There are just enough resources. Predict what might happen to the lemmings if their population grows more.

16. Interpret Data You collect data in a field next to a stream. You trap and count 16 field mice and 10 rabbits. A beaver dam floods the field. You trap and count 7 field mice and 4 rabbits. Interpret this data.

 Draw Conclusions

17. Make a graphic organizer like this one. Fill it in with three facts about whales and whale barnacles from the chapter. Then write a conclusion based on those facts.

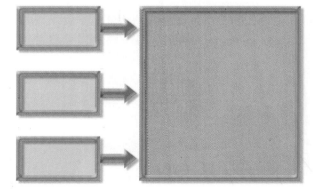

Facts   **Conclusion**

 Test Prep

Choose the letter that best answers the question.

18. Which living thing helps the second living thing in the pair to survive?
- Ⓐ barnacle–crayfish
- Ⓑ yucca moth–whale
- Ⓒ Douglas fir tree–western hemlock tree
- Ⓓ raccoon–cattail

19. Which of the following is true?
- Ⓐ Your lungs are a part of your circulatory system.
- Ⓑ Exercise maintains health.
- Ⓒ Washing your hands after coughing into them spreads germs.
- Ⓓ Nutrients pass through the walls of the intestine into the stomach.

20. **Writing in Science**
Expository Write a short paragraph describing how yucca moths and the yucca plant interact.

Moon Trees

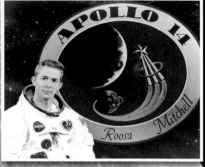

Astronaut Stuart Roosa took seeds with him into space.

Did you know there might be Moon trees growing where you live? You may be asking yourself, "What do Moon trees look like? Did they come from the Moon? Where are they growing on Earth?"

Well, Moon trees did not come from the Moon. They are trees grown from seeds that traveled to the Moon and back on the Apollo 14 mission in 1971.

Astronaut Stuart Roosa took the seeds into space. Astronaut Roosa worked for the U.S. Forest Service fighting forest fires before he joined NASA. He loved forests and wanted to protect them. He took seeds of pine, sycamore, redwood, Douglas fir, and sweet gum into space to honor the U.S. Forest Service.

A third-grade class in Indiana made this sign for their Moon tree. Astronaut Roosa's son, Col. Christopher Roosa, visited the tree with the students and their teacher.

MOON TREE

THIS SYCAMORE WAS GROWN FROM A
SEED THAT TRAVELED TO THE
MOON AND BACK ON
APOLLO XIV JANUARY 1971.
PRESENTED TO CAMP KOCH IN 1976
REDEDICATED APRIL 10, 2003

"LONG MAY OUR MOON TREE LIVE"

When the seeds were brought back to Earth, scientists examined them to see if space travel had changed them in any way. Then they were planted. No one knew what the trees would look like or even if they would grow.

The Moon trees grew until they were big enough to plant outside. People all over the world began to learn about the Moon trees. They wanted one of their own. In 1975 and 1976, the little trees were sent to places around the world. Most Moon trees were sent to schools, parks, and public buildings.

Today you can find a Moon tree growing near the Liberty Bell in Philadelphia. Another grows at the White House. Let NASA know if you find that a Moon tree is growing where you live.

You can see this Moon tree at the NASA Goddard Space Flight Center in Maryland.

Lab zone Take-Home Activity

Space travel might have had what effect on the Moon tree seeds and the way they would grow? Write a paragraph.

Germinating Seeds

Seeds need the right conditions to germinate and grow.

Idea: Use plastic cups, potting soil, and bean seeds to find out how well seeds germinate and grow with different amounts of water.

Growing Mealworms

When mealworm eggs hatch, they look nothing like their parents.

Idea: Use mealworms and a habitat to observe and record the different stages in their life cycle.

Selecting a Habitat

Different plants and animals need different habitats to survive.

Idea: Select a plant or an animal and make a habitat in which it can survive.

A Food Chain Model

Living things are connected by their need for food.

Idea: Choose a food chain and use paper chains with names or pictures to show the connections among the living things.

Using Scientific Methods

1. Ask a question.
2. State a hypothesis.
3. Identify/control variables.
4. Test your hypothesis.
5. Collect and record your data.
6. Interpret your data.
7. State your conclusion.
8. Go further.

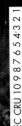

EC CRU 10 9 8 7 6 5 4 3 2 1

Unit B

Earth Science

You Will Discover

○ why all living things need water.
○ how much water Earth has.
○ how water changes phase.
○ how water is cleaned.

Chapter 5
Water

online
Student Edition
pearsonsuccessnet.com

How does water change form?

wetland

water cycle

water vapor

groundwater

evaporation

146

Chapter 5 Vocabulary

precipitation

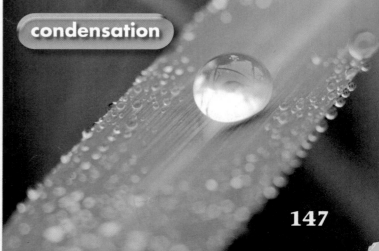

condensation

Explore Where is Earth's water?

What if all of Earth's water would fit in a bottle?

Materials

2 L plastic bottle filled with water

4 cups

dropper and masking tape

funnel and graduated cylinder (or measuring cup)

What to Do

1 Label the 4 cups.

Earth's Water	Amount of Water (total = 2200 mL)
Atmosphere (fresh water)	about $\frac{1}{2}$ drop
Lakes, rivers, streams (fresh water)	about 4 drops
Groundwater (fresh water)	13 mL
Icecaps and glaciers (fresh water)	47 mL
Oceans and seas (salt water)	2139 mL

2 Look at the chart. Find the amount of water shown for the atmosphere. Take out that amount of water from the bottle. Put it in the atmosphere cup.

Hold the bottle with both hands.

3 Repeat for the other places water is found. Use the graduated cylinder when needed.

4 Label the bottle *oceans and seas*.

Explain Your Results

Infer Why should people use fresh water wisely?

How to Read Science

Cause and Effect

A **cause** makes something happen. An **effect** is what happens. Science writers often use clue words and phrases such as *because, so, since,* and *as a result* to signal cause and effect. The following example will help you **infer** why people should use fresh water wisely.

Science Article

Clean Streams

Factories make things for people. They often use water that gets dirty. Dumping this water into streams can harm wildlife and our water supply. As a result, the government makes laws to reduce the harm done. These laws help keep our environment clean.

Apply It!

Make a graphic organizer like the one shown. Then use it to list three causes and an effect from the science article.

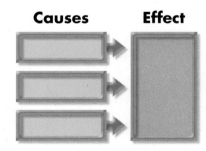

Causes   Effect

149

Bright sunlight gives way to rain clouds. Little splashes of water appear on the lake. Suddenly rain is pouring down all around you. Your face and clothes are quickly soaked. Too bad you don't have the waterproof feathers of a duck. Getting wet can be a bother, but what makes water so important?

Why is water important?

You could go without sweets or TV if you had to. But you can't give up water. You could not live more than a few days without it.

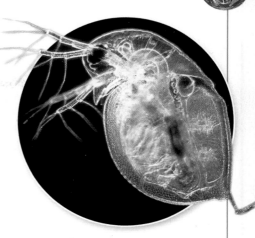

Daphnia are very tiny. This picture was taken through a microscope.

Living Things and Water

Living things from big trees to small snails need water to survive and grow. Green plants need water to make food. Fish and other animals need oxygen in water to breathe.

Water makes up about two-thirds of your body. Water is busy helping every part of your body. For example, water helps digest food into small particles. Water in your blood carries materials to every part of your body. Water also carries wastes away from every part.

Water helps keep your body at the correct temperature. What if the air temperature turns cold? Water in your body tends to hold onto its heat, keeping you warm. If your body heats up, you might sweat. The water in sweat carries heat away from your body.

Some organisms must spend their whole lives in water. Many of these creatures are very small. Daphnia, for example, are less than 1.5 mm long. Daphnia live mostly in ponds and lakes.

1. **✓Checkpoint** How does water help you live?
2. **Health in Science** Why is it important to drink water, especially after you exercise?

The Uses of Water

People use water in many ways. Lakes, rivers, and oceans supply us with fish and shellfish. Farmers use water to help make crops grow. Some of this water falls from the sky. But some flows through pipes to fields.

People use the power of moving water to make electricity. They build dams and power stations across rivers. Rushing water turns giant wheels inside turbines. Turbines help make electricity. This electricity can travel long distances through wires.

We also use water for transportation and enjoyment. Large ships carry goods from one place to another. Some people row on ponds or sail across oceans. Others go tubing, or swimming, or canoeing. People can have fun in the water.

Most plants take in water through their roots to grow.

1. ✓**Checkpoint** List three ways that people use water.

2. ↻ **Cause and Effect** What would happen if we did not protect our supply of fresh water?

152

Drinking

People need to drink water. All animals need water too. This impala slurps up a drink. The tiny bird on its horn will have some too.

Food

Water provides food. People get animals from the sea. Some fish live near the bottom of the sea. Others can be seen from boats. Boats bring back seaweed as well as fish. Seaweed is food for people and animals.

Crops and Farms

In many parts of the world, farmers irrigate land. They bring water to it. The water lets farmers grow crops in many places where no crops grew before. One third of water used in the U.S. is for irrigation.

Industry

Factories use water in many different ways. Water is used to clean foods and the insides of buildings. It is used to make paper and steel. Most of the water used in manufacturing is later put back into rivers and streams.

Electricity

Water is used to make electricity. Moving water or steam can turn large turbines. Turbines are special engines that help make power. Electric power can be used for light, heat, and to run machines.

The Planet of Water

You could call Earth "the blue planet." That's because about three fourths, or 75 percent, of Earth's surface is covered with water.

Most of Earth's water is salty ocean water. Some of the salt in ocean water comes from rock on the ocean floor. Other salt is washed off the land into the oceans. The salt mixes with the water. You cannot drink, wash clothes, or water plants with ocean water. You cannot use this water to make products in factories.

Water is found in many places. Some water moves downward into the ground. Some is frozen into ice. Some water is found in the air as an invisible gas called **water vapor.** Clouds are made of water vapor that has changed to tiny drops of liquid water.

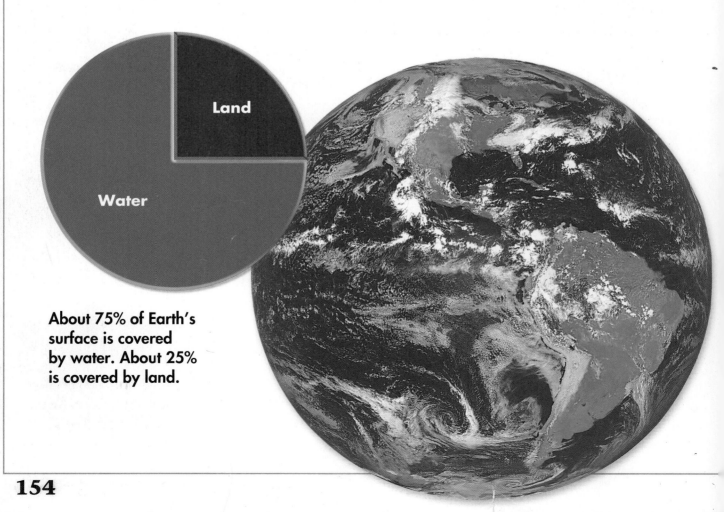

About 75% of Earth's surface is covered by water. About 25% is covered by land.

Fresh Water

There is little salt in fresh water. We need fresh water to drink. A very small amount of the water on Earth is fresh water. Most of this water is frozen as ice near the North and South Poles.

Many lakes, rivers, and streams supply fresh water. Streams run together to form rivers. Rivers can flow into and out of lakes.

Some of the fresh water we use comes from underground. Water seeps down slowly through the soil. It collects in spaces between underground rocks. This water is called **groundwater.** People dig wells to bring groundwater to the surface.

In some places, the top level of the groundwater is very close to Earth's surface. If water soaks the ground at least part of the year, the place is called a **wetland.**

Wetlands are homes for many animals. They also help prevent floods by soaking up extra water. Some water in wetlands seeps down through soil. This helps refill the groundwater supply.

A spring is a stream of groundwater that flows out of the ground.

Fresh water is frozen in huge chunks of ice. This iceberg is near Antarctica.

Small streams can flow together to form larger streams and rivers.

✔ Lesson Checkpoint

1. Why is fresh water important?

2. What are four sources of fresh water?

3. **Writing in Science** **Descriptive** In your **science journal**, write a paragraph about a time you spent near water. What did you see? What did you hear? What did you feel?

SciLinks Take It to the Net
pearsonsuccessnet.com : keyword: wetland
code: g3p155 **155**

Lesson 2

How do forms of water change?

Follow a particle of water for a year. One day the particle is rushing down a mountain stream. Later, it is frozen in pond ice. Later still, it is drifting high in the air. On its journey, water goes through many changes.

Forms Water Can Have

Cold weather can freeze water from a liquid to a solid. In some places, the weather is below 0 degrees Celsius all year long. In other places, the weather is cold just part of the year. In these places, water may freeze only when the weather is very cold.

When water freezes, it takes up more space. The water in the bottle on the right has frozen. It pushes out the sides of the bottle and out of its top.

Warm temperatures in the spring and summer keep the water in this marsh in its liquid form. What is the temperature in this marsh in degrees Fahrenheit? in degrees Celsius?

Water can also become a gas called water vapor. The process of a liquid becoming a gas is called **evaporation.** The Sun's energy evaporates surface water. Then the water becomes water vapor in the air. You cannot see water vapor, but sometimes you can feel its effects on hot summer days. On these days water leaves your skin as sweat. But sweat cannot easily evaporate if there is a lot of water vapor in the air. So you feel "sticky" from the sweat.

Water vapor in the air can turn back into a liquid. This process is called **condensation.** When the air cools, condensation turns invisible water vapor back into drops of water. Small droplets form clouds and fog. Large drops that form on plants are dew.

Cold temperatures in the winter cause the water in the marsh to freeze. What is the temperature in this marsh in degrees Fahrenheit? in degrees Celsius?

Water vapor in air condenses as dew-drops on plants.

1. ✓**Checkpoint** What are the three forms of water?

2. **Math in Science** What is the difference between the temperature of the marsh in spring and in winter? Give your answer in °F and °C.

How Water Moves Around Earth

There is only a certain amount of water on Earth. It must be used again and again. The movement of water from Earth's surface into the air and back again is the **water cycle.** The water cycle gives us a constant supply of fresh water.

Water changes form or state as it moves through the water cycle. The Sun's energy and winds cause water to evaporate and become water vapor.

Rain is just one form of precipitation.

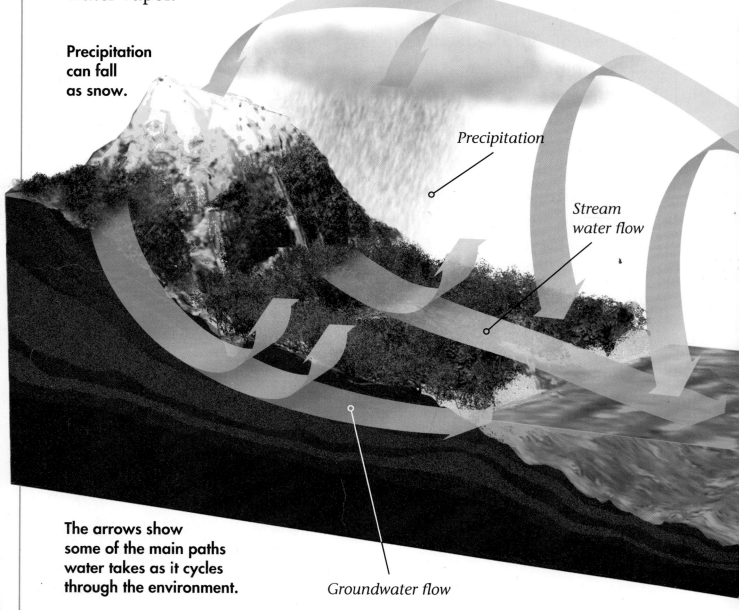

Precipitation can fall as snow.

Precipitation

Stream water flow

The arrows show some of the main paths water takes as it cycles through the environment.

Groundwater flow

Water vapor rises into cooler air, cools, and turns into water droplets or ice crystals. This process is called condensation. These water particles collect and form clouds.

When water particles in clouds grow in size and weight, they fall faster. Water that falls to Earth is called **precipitation.** Precipitation might be rain, snow, sleet, or hail. The form of precipitation depends on the temperature at the Earth's surface.

Some precipitation seeps into the ground. There it becomes groundwater. Other precipitation falls onto streams, rivers, lakes, and oceans. Water that flows across Earth's surface is constantly moving downstream toward the ocean. A lot of ground water reaches the surface in lower areas where there are streams and rivers. This surface water evaporates. In this way, the water cycle continues all the time—everywhere.

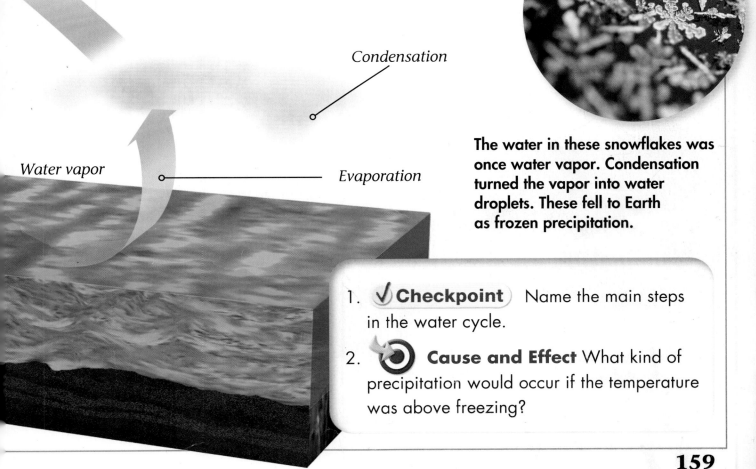

Condensation

Water vapor

Evaporation

The water in these snowflakes was once water vapor. Condensation turned the vapor into water droplets. These fell to Earth as frozen precipitation.

1. ✔**Checkpoint** Name the main steps in the water cycle.

2. **Cause and Effect** What kind of precipitation would occur if the temperature was above freezing?

Ways to Clean Water

People need clean water. Water may contain germs that make people sick. It may contain dirt or salt that can harm machines. These things can make the water taste and smell bad. The water that people use is cleaned to remove these things.

In some places, people get water from their own wells. They must filter the water to remove dirt and chemicals.

In cities, people do not need to clean their own water. The water for most cities is cleaned in one place. First, the water is sent through pipes to a water-treatment area. There, several things may happen.

This filter cleans only the water that comes out of this faucet.

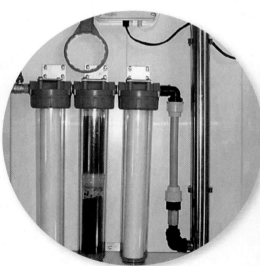

This kind of filter cleans all the water that comes into this building.

Chemicals may be added to the water. Some chemicals kill germs. Others, such as fluoride, help make teeth strong.

In some treatment plants, the water is sprayed into the air. This makes the water taste and smell better. Often, the water is stored in big tanks for a while. Tiny pieces of dirt sink to the bottom of the tank. Finally, the water is pumped through a filter. Even more dirt is removed.

The water now is clean. It can be pumped all over the city. Homes and businesses will have clean, fresh water to use.

Map Fact

The city of Chicago has two of the largest water-cleaning plants in the world. These clean between one and two billion gallons of water a day. People who live in and around Chicago use this water.

A water-cleaning plant in Chicago

✓ **Lesson Checkpoint**

1. What properties of water allow the water cycle to take place?

2. Why must water be cleaned?

3. **Writing in Science** **Expository** Explain in your **science journal** what happens to the water in a puddle on a hot day. Include at least two steps of the water cycle.

Chapter 5 Review and Test Prep

Use Vocabulary

condensation (page 157)	**water cycle** (page 158)
evaporation (page 157)	**water vapor** (page 154)
groundwater (page 155)	**wetland** (page 155)
precipitation (page 159)	

Use the vocabulary word from the list above that best completes each sentence.

1. _____ happens when water changes into water vapor and rises into the air.

2. An area where water soaks the ground for at least part of the year is called a(n) _____.

3. The _____ moves water from Earth's surface into the air and back again.

4. When water evaporates, it turns into an invisible gas called _____.

5. Water that falls from clouds in the form of rain, snow, sleet, or ice is called _____.

6. _____ occurs when water vapor changes back into water droplets.

7. Fresh water found under the ground is _____.

Explain Concepts

8. Explain why all living things need water.

9. Describe where water is found on the Earth.

10. Why is most of Earth's water salt water?

11. Describe the changes that water goes through in the water cycle.

Process Skills

12. **Infer** Why is it important that poisonous materials do not leak into the ground?

13. **Predict** What might happen to a glass bottle if it is filled with water, capped tightly, and put in the freezer?

Cause and Effect

14. Make a graphic organizer like the one shown below. Fill in the correct effect.

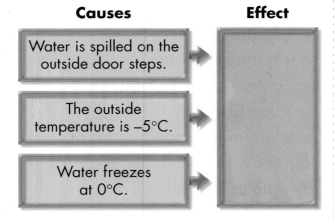

Causes	Effect
Water is spilled on the outside door steps.	
The outside temperature is –5°C.	
Water freezes at 0°C.	

Test Prep

Choose the letter that best completes the statement or answers the question.

15. About 75 percent of Earth's surface is covered by

   Ⓐ air.   Ⓑ water.
   Ⓒ plants.   Ⓓ animals.

16. The step in the water cycle in which water forms water vapor in the air is called

   Ⓕ evaporation.
   Ⓖ condensation.
   Ⓗ precipitation.
   Ⓘ groundwater.

17. When the temperature of water falls below 0 degrees Celsius, the water will

   Ⓐ evaporate.
   Ⓑ shrink.
   Ⓒ freeze.
   Ⓓ condense.

18. Wetlands help refill the groundwater supply when

   Ⓕ water evaporates.
   Ⓖ water seeps down into the ground.
   Ⓗ the winds blow.
   Ⓘ water freezes.

19. Explain why the answer you chose for Question 17 is best. For each of the answers you did not choose, give a reason why it is not the best choice.

20. **Writing** in Science

Persuasive Practice writing a letter to the editor of your town newspaper. Explain why you think it is important for everyone in your town to conserve water, rather than waste it.

How does weather follow patterns?

You Are There!

You are playing outside on a sunny day. Suddenly you hear a loud rumble in the sky. You look up. Huge black clouds are moving toward you. You see a flash of lightning in the distance. Uh-oh! Here comes a big change in the weather. What caused it? Time to get to safety.

AudioText

These cumulus clouds look a little like balls of cotton. You see these on sunny days.

These are very high, thin cirrus clouds. They are made of tiny ice crystals. You see these clouds on sunny days too.

What makes up weather?

Weather changes all the time. Measuring weather helps people predict weather accurately.

Parts of Weather

What will the weather be like this weekend? Will it be sunny or rainy? **Weather** is what the air is like outside. It includes the kinds of clouds in the sky and the kind and amount of water in the air. It also includes the temperature of the air and how the wind is blowing.

Clouds are made of water droplets in the air. Different kinds of clouds form in different weather. Because of this, clouds can help predict what will happen to the weather. Some kinds of clouds form in sunny weather. Others form in rainy or stormy weather.

Look at clouds on a warm, bright day. The clouds are white and fluffy. On a stormy day, clouds are dark.

1. ✔**Checkpoint** How do clouds look on stormy days?

2. **Writing in Science** **Narrative** Write a paragraph in your **science journal** that tells what the weather would be like on a perfect day for you. Explain why you like this weather.

175

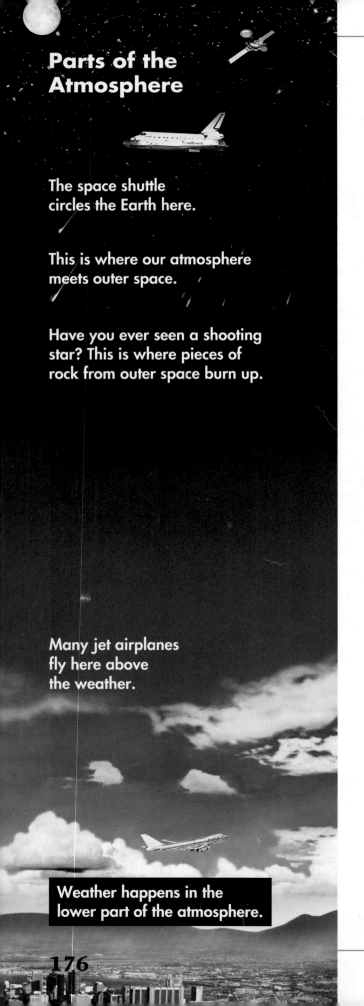

Parts of the Atmosphere

The space shuttle circles the Earth here.

This is where our atmosphere meets outer space.

Have you ever seen a shooting star? This is where pieces of rock from outer space burn up.

Many jet airplanes fly here above the weather.

Weather happens in the lower part of the atmosphere.

The Atmosphere

The **atmosphere** is the blanket of air that surrounds Earth. This air is made up of gases that have no color, taste, or odor. The temperature is different in different parts of the atmosphere. Weather happens in the lower part of the atmosphere.

The atmosphere has weight, so it presses down on Earth. This pressing down is called air pressure. When the air presses down a lot, the air pressure is high. When it presses less, the air pressure is low.

Describing Weather

You may say the weather is too hot today. Someone else might not agree. That person might like the weather. Words like *hot* mean different things to different people. But 34° Celsius (93° Fahrenheit) means just one thing. It is a fact that describes the temperature of the air. Scientists use special tools to help them describe and measure the weather.

Measuring and Predicting

Scientists can measure air pressure with a tool called a barometer. Scientists use measurements of air pressure to predict changes in weather. Weather reports often describe air pressure. Low air pressure often means that weather will be cloudy or rainy. High air pressure often means skies will be clear.

A tool called an anemometer measures wind speed. A wind vane shows the direction of the wind.

Scientists use hygrometers to measure how much water vapor is in the air. The amount of water vapor in the air is called humidity. The humidity is low when air is dry. The humidity is high when air has more water in it. Rain gauges measure liquid water. They show how much rain has fallen.

Weather tools or instruments help scientists learn more about weather. They also help scientists predict what the weather will be like.

1. ✓**Checkpoint** How do tools help scientists describe the weather?

2. 🎯**Make Inferences** High pressure is moving into an area. Use this observation and what you know about air pressure to predict the weather change.

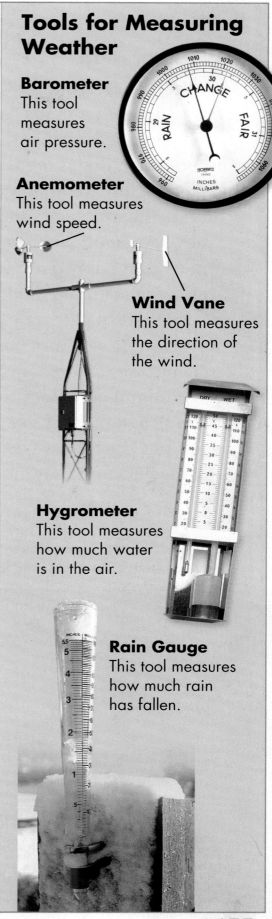

Tools for Measuring Weather

Barometer
This tool measures air pressure.

Anemometer
This tool measures wind speed.

Wind Vane
This tool measures the direction of the wind.

Hygrometer
This tool measures how much water is in the air.

Rain Gauge
This tool measures how much rain has fallen.

Weather Map

Weather tools gather weather data. Scientists show this data on weather maps. Weather maps show data for a large area. They show temperatures and storms. Some maps give information about areas of high and low air pressure.

Look at the weather map below. It shows the United States. The numbers show the temperatures in different cities. The small pictures show what the weather is like. You can probably guess what some pictures mean. The key shows the meaning of all the pictures.

Weather satellites gather weather data from all over the world. These satellites move high above the Earth. They can take pictures of large areas of the planet. They send these pictures and data back to scientists on Earth.

Information from satellites is very useful to scientists. For example, they can see storm clouds form and can tell the direction that the storms are moving.

This weather map uses pictures to interpret data that weather tools have gathered. What can you learn from this weather map?

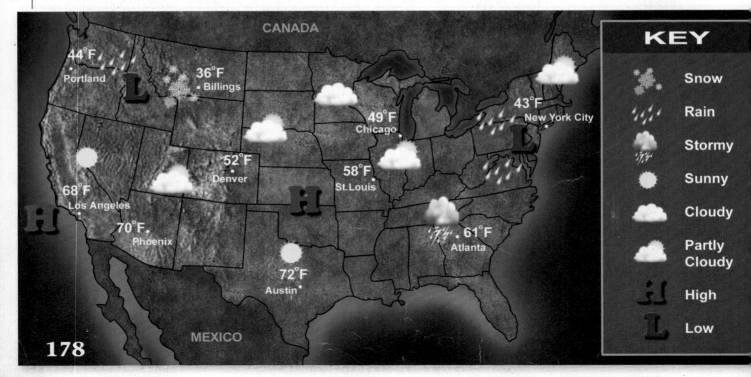

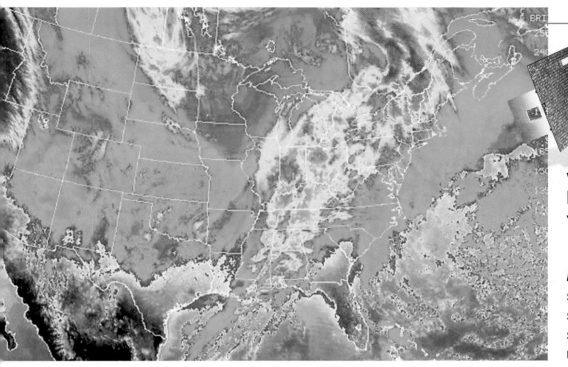

Weather satellites like this one gather weather data.

Maps made from satellite data can show the direction storm clouds are moving.

Pollution Alerts

Weather news may include smog and ozone pollution alerts. In many cities, cars and trucks help cause these alerts. The gases that leave their engines are called exhaust. On some days, a lot of exhaust stays in the air. The Sun's rays can turn that air into smog and ozone. On days with little wind, the smog and ozone do not move away.

Smog and ground-level ozone can be harmful to health. They can make people cough. Some people might not be able to breathe easily. During air pollution alerts, some people must stay inside.

The Sun's rays strike the exhaust from gasoline burned in cars and trucks. This causes smog.

**Lesson Checkpoint**

1. What can weather maps show?

2. What is one effect that humans can have on weather?

3. **Make Inferences** If there is a smog alert, what can you infer about the weather?

Western Washington State has a pattern of cool, wet winters.

Eastern Washington State has a pattern of cold, dry winters.

How are weather patterns different?

Patterns of weather vary from place to place. People must protect themselves during severe weather.

Weather Patterns

Changes in weather follow patterns. Weather patterns depend on the Sun, water, and the location.

Places near oceans have different weather patterns than places far from oceans. Washington State is by the Pacific Ocean. In winter, warm, moist air from over the ocean moves over the land. There are clouds in the air. Rain falls over the western valleys.

As the clouds move east, they rise up the side of the Cascade Mountains. The clouds get colder, and snow falls. Western Washington State has a pattern of cool, wet winters.

After the air has crossed the mountains, the air does not have much moisture. Little rain or snow falls. Eastern Washington State has a pattern of cold, dry winters.

Winter in Washington State		
Locations	Average Temperature	Average Rainfall (cm)
West	5°C (41°F)	30
East	−2°C (28°F)	6

All deserts are dry. Some deserts are cold, while others are hot. Each desert has its own weather pattern.

North America has four large desert regions. The Sonoran Desert is in the southern part of Arizona and California. This desert receives some winter rain from storms that reach it from the Pacific Ocean. But most rain falls in short, heavy downpours during the hot summer. The average rainfall during the summer is 5 centimeters (2 inches). The moist air for this rain comes from the Gulf of California.

The saguaro cactus is adapted to live in the desert. The wide, shallow roots of the cactus soak up the rain. The cactus stores the water for later use.

In the hot summer the saguaro cactus stores water from storms.

Winter rain causes spring wildflowers to bloom in the Sonoran Desert.

1. ✓**Checkpoint** What do weather patterns depend on?

2. **Make Inferences** Moist air from the Gulf of California causes storms in the Sonoran Desert in summer. What weather does moist air from the Gulf of Mexico cause in the Midwest in summer?

Seasons in the Sonoran Desert		
Season	**Average Temperature**	**Average Rainfall (cm)**
Fall	16°C (61°F)	2
Winter	12°C (54°F)	2
Spring	24°C (75°F)	1
Summer	29°C (84°F)	5

A satellite high above Earth took this picture of the swirling winds of a hurricane.

Dangerous Storms

Thunderstorms can be dangerous. Lightning can strike people or objects. People should find shelter during thunderstorms.

A **hurricane** is a huge storm. Hurricanes form over oceans. They have winds of at least 119 kilometers (74 miles) per hour. Heavy rains, strong winds, and huge waves cause damage. Waves can lift boats out of the water and flip them over. People usually know about hurricanes before they strike.

A **tornado** is a spinning, funnel-shaped, column of air that touches the ground. Tornadoes are much smaller than hurricanes. However, their winds are stronger. Tornadoes form beneath thunderstorm clouds. They can form suddenly and without warning. When a tornado starts, people must go to safe places. They must stay away from windows.

Sudden heavy rains can cause floods. Very high waves can cause floods too. Water from flooding can block roads and damage homes. People usually have some warning that an area may flood. Then they must move to higher ground.

A **blizzard** is a winter storm. Blizzards have low temperatures and lots of blowing snow. People can get lost or stuck in the snow. They can also get too cold to move to warm shelter.

Radio and television stations send out storm safety information. The National Weather Service puts out watches and warnings. These warn people about dangerous storms. A *watch* means that a storm could happen where you live. A *warning* means that a storm is already in or near your area. Everyone who hears a warning should take action to stay safe.

Hurricanes do damage when they move over land.

Students head for home when a winter storm watch warns of a blizzard.

Most tornadoes do damage along a narrow path.

✓ Lesson Checkpoint

1. What part of the State of Washington has a wet and snowy weather pattern in winter?

2. What does a severe thunderstorm warning mean? What should people do in response?

3. **Writing in Science** **Descriptive** In your **science journal** write about a storm that happened near your home. Tell how people prepared themselves or didn't before the storm came.

Heavy rains caused a flood that blocks this road.

183

Chapter 6 Review and Test Prep

Use Vocabulary

atmosphere (page 176)	**tornado** (page 182)
blizzard (page 183)	**weather** (page 175)
hurricane (page 182)	

Use the vocabulary word from the list above that best completes each sentence.

1. A(n) _____ is a spinning column of air that touches the ground and happens quickly.

2. Temperature, wind speed, and clouds are parts of the _____.

3. A(n) _____ is a huge, strong storm that forms over the warm ocean.

4. A winter storm with low temperatures, strong winds, and lots of blowing snow is a(n) _____.

5. The _____ is made up of gases that surround Earth.

Explain Concepts

6. Why is weather important?

7. If you had tools for measuring parts of the weather, what information could you collect?

8. List some clues that indicate a change in the weather.

9. Give an example of a weather pattern and describe it in detail.

10. How does the National Weather Service help people stay safe?

11. Use the chart below to tell which city has warmer average temperatures in July. Which city has the biggest difference between the average high and average low?

	Birmingham, Alabama	Santa Fe, New Mexico
Average High in July	33°C (91°F)	29°C (85°F)
Average Low in July	21°C (70°F)	12°C (53°F)

Process Skills

12. **Predict** It is a rainy day, but the air pressure is getting higher. How might the weather change?

13. **Infer** How might weather be different if water never evaporated? Explain your answer.

Make Inferences

14. Copy the table below. Fill in the missing inference.

Facts	Inference
Earth has become slightly warmer over the past 100 years.	
Many places get more or less rain than before.	

 Test Prep

Choose the letter that best completes the statement or answers the question.

15. What kind of winter weather would a city near the ocean in the western U.S. most likely have?

- Ⓐ warm and rainy
- Ⓑ warm and snowy
- Ⓒ cold and snowy
- Ⓓ cool and rainy

16. A severe thunderstorm watch means

- Ⓕ a severe thunderstorm is in the area.
- Ⓖ a tornado is in the area.
- Ⓗ flooding could happen soon.
- Ⓘ a thunderstorm might happen.

17. If a tornado forms, people should

- Ⓐ go to safe places.
- Ⓑ move to higher ground.
- Ⓒ close windows.
- Ⓓ drive to another city.

18. Most smog and ozone in cities are caused by

- Ⓕ acid rain.
- Ⓖ forest fires.
- Ⓗ carbon dioxide.
- Ⓘ burning gasoline.

19. Explain why the answer you chose for Question 15 is best. For each of the answers you did not choose, give a reason why it is not the best choice.

20. Writing in Science

Expository Write a paragraph that describes both helpful and harmful effects that the weather can have on people.

189

Studying Clouds From
SPACE

You know that NASA studies space. NASA also studies Earth's clouds from space. NASA satellites orbit Earth and use different tools or instruments to collect information about clouds and other parts of the Earth system, including weather. Some of the tools measure the amount of sunlight that bounces off clouds. Other tools measure how much heat is trapped by clouds and how much escapes into space.

Cumulus

Cirrus

Cumulonimbus

Stratus

Clouds are an important part of weather patterns. They are part of the water cycle. They interact with the gases that trap heat and warm Earth. NASA scientists are studying how clouds affect Earth's climate.

Many schools are helping NASA study clouds. Students and teachers at these schools observe and measure clouds and other weather conditions. They are given special times to take their measurements. These are the same times when NASA satellites are recording information for their area.

Cirrostratus

Altocumulus

Lab zone Take-Home Activity

Record your own observations of clouds and the temperature at the time of day you observed them. Collect this data for a week. Organize data into a chart. Decide if the kinds and amounts of clouds affected the temperature.

Air Traffic Controller

You are in the control tower at an airport. You can see all the planes and runways. Computers tell you the height, speed, and course of all aircraft.

As an air traffic controller, you make sure planes take off and land safely. You give pilots directions so they can keep their planes a safe distance from other planes. You also give them information about weather patterns. Pilots need to know about any storms. They also must know about sudden changes in the speed or direction of the wind. They need to know what the weather is like near the airport. Is it foggy, snowing, or rainy? Is it clear? The information you give pilots helps keep them and their passengers safe.

People who become air traffic controllers usually have four years of college. Then they must take tests to make sure they would make good air traffic controllers.

Lab zone Take-Home Activity

Suppose you are watching planes as they approach an airport. Describe the information that you need to give the pilots.

EC CRU 10 9 8 7 6 5 4 3 2 1

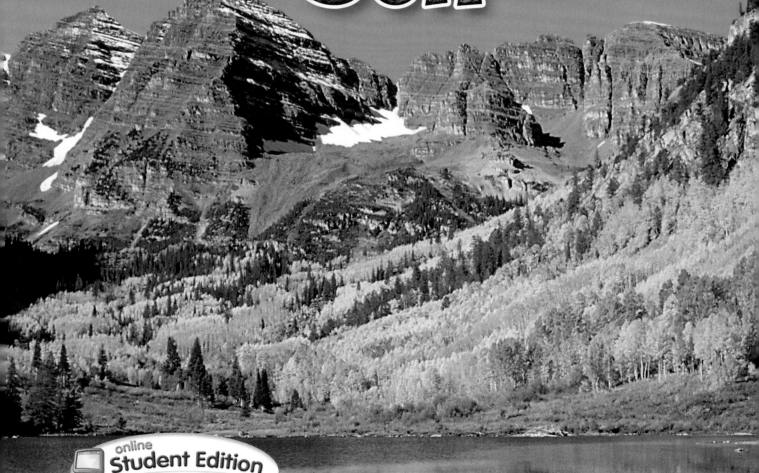

Chapter 7
Rocks and Soil

You Will Discover

- how to tell one kind of rock from another.
- how rocks are formed.
- what soil is made of.
- why soil is important.

online
Student Edition
pearsonsuccessnet.com

193

What are some kinds of rocks and soils?

rock

igneous rock

sedimentary rock

metamorphic rock

194

loam

soil

mineral

decay

The slow breaking down of the remains of living things in soil

nutrient

Material in soil that plants need to grow

195

You Are There!

Be careful as you climb on the rocks. It's a good thing you have on hiking boots. They will help you climb. Can you see that some of the rocks have sharp edges? Some look rough. Others look smooth. There are differences in color. What are rocks made of and where do they come from?

AudioText

Lesson 1

How do rocks form?

Rocks are everywhere. Some are as large as a mountain. Others are smaller than a grain of sand. Minerals make up rock. Rock forms in different ways.

Rocks

Earth consists of mostly different kinds of rocks. **Rock** is natural, solid, nonliving material made of one or more minerals. A **mineral** is a natural material that forms from nonliving matter.

You can tell rocks apart by looking at their physical properties. The physical properties of rocks include color, what minerals they are made of, and texture.

The rocks you see here range in color from gray to brown. Sometimes the minerals are so small that they aren't easy to see. Texture is the size of the bits of minerals, or grains, that make up the rock. Some rocks may have grains that are big enough to see. These different sizes of minerals make rocks feel smooth, rough, or bumpy.

1. ✓**Checkpoint** What are some physical properties of rocks?

2. **Compare and Contrast** How are the rocks shown in the pictures alike? How are they different?

Rock Groups

Rocks can be placed into three main groups. Rocks in each group formed in a certain way. Each group contains many kinds of rocks.

Igneous rock forms from a very hot mixture of melted minerals and gases. This mixture may cool slowly below ground until it hardens. Then the mineral grains may be large. If the rock cools quickly above ground or on the ocean floor, the grains may be too small to see.

Another group of rocks form from sediments, which are tiny bits of rock, sand, shells and other materials. Sediments settle to the bottom of rivers, lakes, and oceans. Over thousands of years, the sediments are pressed together and cemented into **sedimentary rock.** Sedimentary rock forms in layers—one layer at a time.

Fossils of extinct plants and animals can be found in sedimentary rocks. Their bodies were buried in sand and mud that hardened into rock. Fossils in sedimentary rock can show the history of life over time.

Fossils in Sedimentary Rock

Crinoids were ancient animals that looked like plants.

Trilobites were like modern crabs.

Ammonites looked similar to today's snails.

Igneous rock can come from volcanoes.

Metamorphic rock is rock that has been changed by heat and pressure. Shale is a sedimentary rock. Heat and pressure underground change the minerals in the shale. The shale becomes slate, a metamorphic rock. Granite is an igneous rock. It can be changed into gneiss, a metamorphic rock.

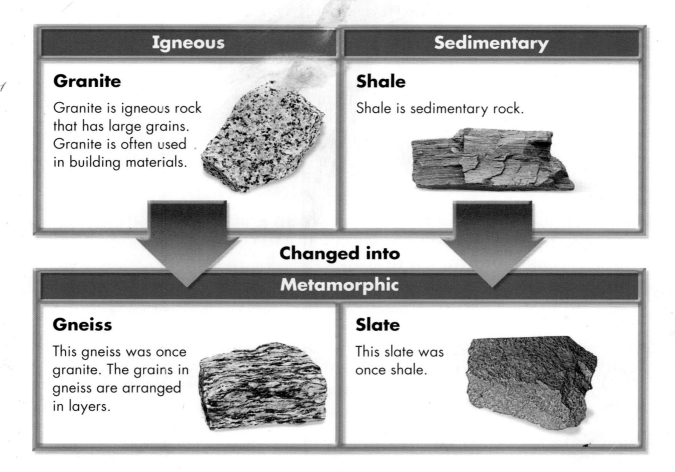

Igneous

Granite

Granite is igneous rock that has large grains. Granite is often used in building materials.

Sedimentary

Shale

Shale is sedimentary rock.

Changed into

Metamorphic

Gneiss

This gneiss was once granite. The grains in gneiss are arranged in layers.

Slate

This slate was once shale.

✓ Lesson Checkpoint

1. How is igneous rock that forms above ground different from igneous rock that forms below ground?

2. Describe clues, found in sedimentary rock, which show that living things have changed over time.

3. **Writing in Science** **Expository** List facts in your **science journal** about the three kinds of rocks. Then write a paragraph describing each of the three kinds.

Lesson 2

What are minerals?

Minerals are the most common solid material found on Earth. Gold and silver are rare minerals. Rock salt and quartz are common minerals.

Identifying Minerals

Color is a property you notice easily about a mineral. But some minerals can be found in different colors. For example, the mineral quartz can be pink, purple, yellow, brown, white, or black. Other minerals always have the same color.

A better way to identify a mineral is by the color in its powder form. When you rub a mineral across a rough surface, it may leave a streak mark or powder. The color of these effects are always the same even if two pieces of the mineral are different colors.

Luster is a property that shows how a mineral reflects light. Minerals can be metallic, pearly, silky, greasy, glassy, or dull.

The mineral magnetite has the property of magnetism. Objects that contain iron are pulled to the magnetite.

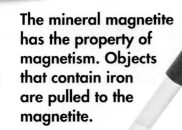

Vinegar fizzes on limestone that contains the mineral calcite. The fizzing happens because the vinegar reacts with the calcite. The reaction gives off carbon dioxide.

Properties of Minerals

Mineral	Color	Luster	Streak	Hardness
Mica Mica breaks into flaky pieces when struck.	black, gray, green, violet	pearly on surfaces	white	can be scratched with a knife
Molybdenite This mineral is one of the strongest and most commonly used heat-resistant metals.	silvery	metallic	bluish gray	can be scratched with a fingernail
Crocoite Much of this mineral comes from Australia.	reddish-orange	very shiny	orange-yellow	can be scratched with a coin

Another way to identify a mineral is to test its hardness. Some minerals, such as talc, are so soft you can scratch them with your fingernail. The hardest mineral is diamond. It can be scratched only by another diamond.

Some minerals can be identified by their appearance. Gold, for example, appears sometimes in nugget form. Other minerals can be identified by taste, smell, or touch.

1. ✓**Checkpoint** What are ways to identify minerals?

2. 🎯 **Compare and Contrast** How are rocks and minerals alike? How are they different? Use a graphic organizer to show your answer.

How the Body Uses Minerals

These are some ways that the body uses minerals.

Mineral	How Used
Calcium	Helps form bones and teeth and helps cause muscles to contract
Chromium	Helps change digested food into energy
Copper	Helps form skin and other tissues
Iron	Carries oxygen in blood to all parts of the body
Potassium	Helps nerves and muscles work
Phosphorus	Helps release energy and form bones and teeth
Sodium	Helps control water levels and carry messages through nerves

How We Use Minerals

It is almost impossible to go through a day without using minerals. The cavity-fighting fluoride in your toothpaste came from the mineral fluorite. The glass you look through in your window came from the minerals quartz, soda ash, and limestone. The salt in your food is the mineral halite. The metal in your spoon is a mineral. Even the graphite that you write with in your pencil is a mineral. Almost everything we use is made from minerals or contains minerals.

Minerals Keep Us Healthy

People also need minerals to keep their bodies healthy and full of energy. Many of these minerals are found in plants. Green leafy vegetables, such as spinach, contain calcium. Iron is found in fruit and green vegetables. Sodium in vegetables such as celery, and potassium in fruits work together to help transmit nerve impulses and control muscles. Almost everything we eat has some minerals in it.

✓ Lesson Checkpoint

1. What is a mineral?
2. Why are minerals important to your health?
3. **Writing in Science** **Expository** In your **science journal** list five things you did today that used minerals. Use a chart with two columns. Head the first column, *Activity*. Head the second, *Mineral*.

Other Ways We Use Minerals

Halite

The mineral halite is crushed and then ground up. We use it to flavor and preserve food. (We know this mineral as table salt.)

Copper

The mineral copper is found in igneous rock. The rocks are mined from the ground. When the rocks are crushed and heated, the copper becomes separated from the rock. Then, the copper can be made into objects such as pots and pans.

Fluorite

The mineral fluorite is found in many rocks, such as granite. The rocks are crushed and the fluorite is separated out. Then, it is used to make many products such as toothpaste.

Lead

Lead is found in a mineral known as galena. The rocks are crushed and heated to produce lead. Lead is put into aprons such as the ones shown to protect people while X-ray pictures are taken.

Iron

Iron is a mineral found in the rock called hematite. The rocks are crushed and heated. Then, iron in the melted material is separated out. Iron is mixed with other materials to make steel. Steel is used for many tools and machines.

Earthworms mix up the topsoil as they dig through it. That improves the soil.

We depend on topsoil to grow our food.

Soil must pack down hard and stay firm so that houses built on it don't shift.

Why is soil important?

Soil is an important part of the system that supports all life on land. Soil and parts of soil have different properties.

Parts of Soil

Soil is the thin layer of loose material that covers most of Earth's land. Soil is not simply dirt. Natural processes develop soil over a long period of time. It takes hundreds of years for nature to rebuild lost topsoil. Soil has the material plants need to grow.

Squeeze a handful of soil and see that it's more than bits of rock. Soil might clump together because it holds water and material that was once living.

Living things in soil break down the remains of plants and animals. This process is called **decay.** Decay releases things plants need in order to grow. Each of these things is a **nutrient.** Some minerals also release nutrients. Water and nutrients support most plants on land, including crops. When you think about it, soil is more valuable than gold!

Soil Layers

Soil is organized into layers. Different places have layers of different thicknesses and color.

Topsoil

Topsoil is the top layer. Topsoil includes rock particles mixed with the dark products of decay. The decayed parts of plant and animal remains are called humus. Humus contains much of what plants need to grow.

Subsoil

Subsoil is under topsoil. It is often lighter in color than topsoil. It doesn't have as much humus as topsoil. Subsoil includes pieces of broken rocks. Tree roots grow into the subsoil. Water from precipitation may be in this layer.

Bedrock

As this rock breaks down, it provides raw material for making new soil.

1. ✓**Checkpoint** What is soil made of?

2. **Math in Science** Suppose it takes 1,500 years for 1 centimeter of soil to form in a certain place. How long would it take for 2 centimeters of soil to form? Show your work.

Comparing Soils

Soil is not the same everywhere. Soil near your home may be different than soil at your school. The kind of soil depends in part on the types of rock particles that help make up the soil. Sand, silt, and clay are the three main types of particles found in soil. They differ in size. Sand particles are the largest. Clay particles are the smallest.

Sand
Large spaces in sand allow water to easily pass through. Roots of many plants in sandy soil may not have time to soak up the water. Sandy soil feels rough and gritty.

Silt
The medium-sized particles in silt are more closely packed together. Although water passes through silt, silty soil also holds water well.

About Loam
Loam is good soil for growing plants. The graph shows the amount of each ingredient in loam.
- Sand, Silt, Clay
- Air
- Water
- Humus

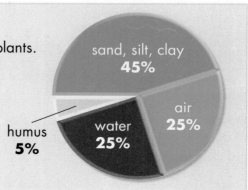

sand, silt, clay
45%

air
25%

water
25%

humus
5%

All soil has the same four ingredients. Weathered rocks containing minerals make up most of the soil. Humus makes up another part. Humus is made up of decaying plants and animals. Humus is a very important part of soil. Air and water fill in the spaces between particles of rock and humus.

Most soils are a mixture of sand, silt, and clay. Soils with this mixture are called **loam.** Loam also contains humus, which has many minerals and other nutrients. Loam soil with its minerals, humus, air, and water is a very good mixture for growing most plants. Loam soils hold onto water loosely enough for plant roots to soak it up.

Clay
Clay particles are the smallest. Water passes slowly into clay. Once clay absorbs water, the particles hold tightly together. Very wet clay feels smooth and sticky.

✓ Lesson Checkpoint

1. Explain the importance of soil.

2. Compare the ability of sand, silt, and clay to hold water.

3. Social Studies in Science Find information about states that have many large farms. Find out which fruits, vegetables, and grains grow in each area.

Chapter 7 Review and Test Prep

Use Vocabulary

decay (page 206)	**mineral** (page 199)
igneous rock (page 200)	**nutrient** (page 206)
loam (page 209)	**rock** (page 199)
metamorphic rock (page 201)	**sedimentary rock** (page 200)
	soil (page 206)

Use the vocabulary word from the list above that best completes each sentence.

1. Rock made up of layers of sediment that have hardened is _____.

2. Most of the land is covered with a thin layer of loose material called _____.

3. A(n) _____ is a natural material that makes up rock.

4. When living things _____, they break down, or rot.

5. Soil that is a mixture of sand, silt, clay, minerals, and decayed matter is called _____.

6. Any kind of solid, nonliving material found on Earth and made of minerals is a(n) _____.

7. Each type of small particle that plants take into their roots is a(n) _____, found in good growing soil.

8. Rock that has changed to another type of rock by heat and pressure is _____.

9. Rock that forms when melted Earth materials cool and harden is _____.

Explain Concepts

10. What is one way that sedimentary rock forms?

11. Explain why a bone is not considered a mineral.

12. Describe the layers of soil from top to bottom.

13. Predict Which would dry faster after it rains: a sandy beach or a grassy field? Give a reason for your answer.

14. Model Make a model or a drawing that shows the different layers of soil.

15. Infer You observe that a mineral sample can be scratched with a coin. What do you infer about the hardness of the mineral?

Compare and Contrast

16. Make a graphic organizer like the one below. Fill it in to compare and contrast sandy soil and clay soil.

Sandy soil	Both types of soil	Clay soil

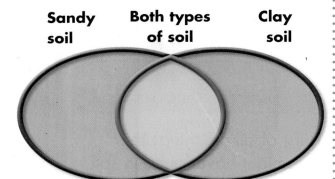

Test Prep

Choose the letter that best completes the statement or answers the question.

17. All rocks contain
- (A) loam.
- (B) minerals.
- (C) water.
- (D) sediments.

18. In what rocks are fossils most often found?
- (F) sedimentary
- (G) igneous
- (H) metamorphic
- (I) all of the above

19. The layer of soil just below the topsoil is
- (A) loam.
- (B) decayed matter.
- (C) rock.
- (D) subsoil.

20. Writing in Science
Persuasive Write a letter to a member of a city council that discusses why rich farmland is valuable to everyone in the community.

217

NASA
Biography

Dr. Elissa R. Levine

Dr. Levine is a Soil Scientist for NASA's Goddard Space Flight Center. She has

How do forces cause changes on Earth's surface?

magma

lava

landform

mantle

crust

core

218

weathering

erosion

Explore How do some mountains form?

Materials

clay

waxed paper

What to Do

1 Make a **model** of one way mountains can form. First, make flat layers of clay. Then, stack the layers on waxed paper.

2 Next, push on the ends of the clay. Keep the clay on the waxed paper.

surface of the Earth

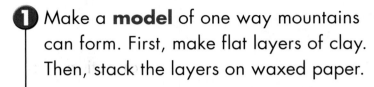

Push!

Push!

layers of rock

In real life this change would be too slow to see.

Do not change what you record just because your results are different from those of someone else.

3 Finally, record what happens to your model. Make a sketch or diagram.

Explain Your Results

1. This model shows a way some mountains form. Think about the layers of rock in this type of mountain. Do you think the layers will be mostly tilted or mostly level? Explain.

2. Compare and contrast your model and a real mountain. How does **using the model** help you learn about real mountains?

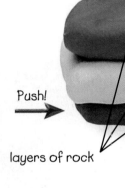

Process Skills

When scientists **use a model** to help learn about a real thing, they compare and contrast the model and the real thing.

How to Read Science

 Sequence

A **sequence** is a series of actions that take place in a certain order.

- A writer might use clue words such as *first, then, next,* and *finally* to show a sequence.

- An artist might use numbers and labels in a drawing to show a sequence.

Science Article

Eruption

How does a volcano erupt? First, pressure and heat melt rock within the Earth. This material is magma, a hot, thick liquid mixed with gases. Then, some of the material rises through cracks in the rock above it. Next, the liquid rock and gases build up pressure on the rock at the surface. Finally, the pressure gets so great that liquid rock, gases, and bits of rock come out of the ground.

Apply It!

Make a sequence to **model** how a volcano forms. Place information you read into a graphic organizer like this one.

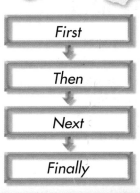

First
↓
Then
↓
Next
↓
Finally

221

You Are There!

What is that billowing cloud on the horizon? What is making that rumbling sound? Is there a storm forming over there? No, it's a volcano erupting! The cloud above the volcano rises miles high. The Sun disappears behind the huge plume of smoke and ash. What force could cause such a tremendous change?

AudioText 🔊

What are Earth's layers?

Mantle

Crust

Core

If you could remove a big chunk of Earth, you would see that it is made up of layers.

Earth's Layers

Earth can be divided into three main layers. You live on the outer layer of Earth—the **crust.** Earth's crust is made of different kinds of rock. The thickness of the crust varies from place to place. Its thickness under the continents is about 37 kilometers (23 miles). That may seem pretty thick. If you compare all the Earth to a peach, however, the Earth's crust would be just the skin.

Beneath the crust lies the **mantle.** Earth's mantle is made of very hot igneous and metamorphic rock. It may flow like oozing toothpaste.

The **core** is the innermost layer of Earth. It is made of metal. The core is hot enough to melt. The center of the core is packed together so tightly, however, that it remains mostly solid. The much larger outer part of the core is a very hot, dense liquid.

1. ✓**Checkpoint** What is Earth's core like?

2. **Writing in Science** **Expository** Compare Earth's layers to the parts of a peach. Make a labeled drawing in your **science journal**. Then, write a paragraph that compares the two.

223

Shapes on Earth's Surface

Does the land near you have mountains, hills, and valleys? Each is an example of a **landform.** Landforms are the solid features formed on Earth's crust. Other features include bodies of water.

Many forces shape landforms. These forces come from above and below Earth's crust. Moving water, though, is the main force. For example, rivers can act like saws. Pebbles and sand in the moving water slowly cut through rock. Flooding rivers deposit pebbles, sand, and silt on their banks. These processes help shape valleys. Notice how many of the landforms below were shaped by water.

Glacier
A glacier is a large, moving body of ice. It forms in cold places where snow and ice pile up year after year. It slowly moves downhill.

Valley
A valley is a low, narrow area on the crust. Some valleys are formed by rivers, while others are formed by glaciers.

Plateau
A plateau is a plain that is higher than the land around it.

Ocean
The ocean is the salt water that covers almost three-fourths of Earth's surface.

Coast
The coast is land next to the ocean, which helps to shape the coastline.

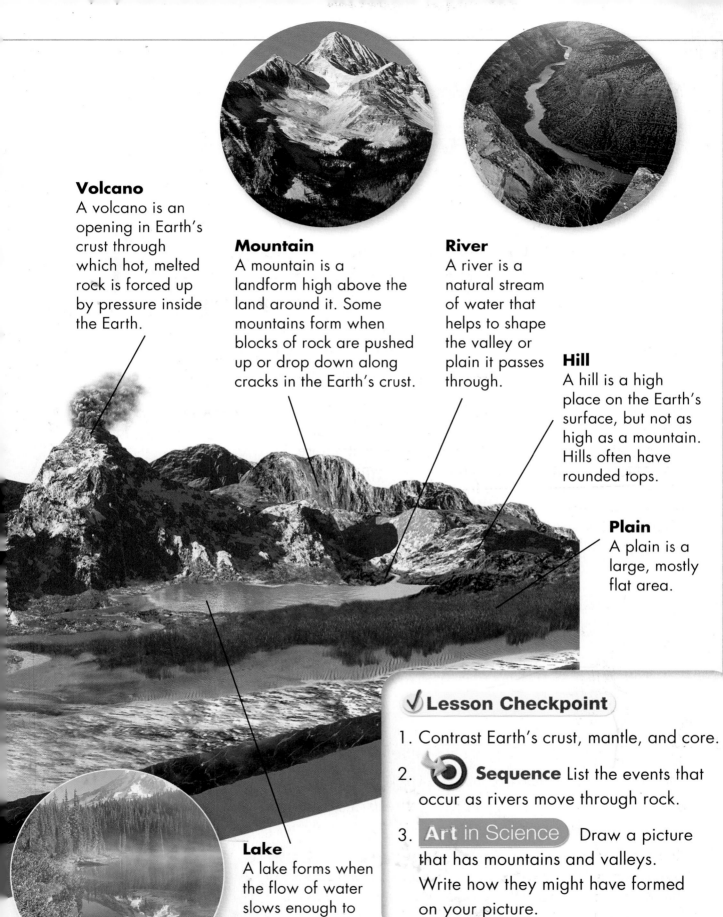

Volcano
A volcano is an opening in Earth's crust through which hot, melted rock is forced up by pressure inside the Earth.

Mountain
A mountain is a landform high above the land around it. Some mountains form when blocks of rock are pushed up or drop down along cracks in the Earth's crust.

River
A river is a natural stream of water that helps to shape the valley or plain it passes through.

Hill
A hill is a high place on the Earth's surface, but not as high as a mountain. Hills often have rounded tops.

Plain
A plain is a large, mostly flat area.

Lake
A lake forms when the flow of water slows enough to fill an area.

✔**Lesson Checkpoint**

1. Contrast Earth's crust, mantle, and core.

2. **Sequence** List the events that occur as rivers move through rock.

3. **Art in Science** Draw a picture that has mountains and valleys. Write how they might have formed on your picture.

225

Lesson 2

What are volcanoes and earthquakes?

Volcanoes and earthquakes cause rapid and sometimes dangerous changes in the landscape.

How Do Volcanoes Form?

Volcanoes begin deep within the mantle where **magma** forms. Magma is hot, pasty rock that moves within the mantle. Magma close to the suface melts and flows easily because the pressure is less. Magma can gush out of weak spots in the crust, aided by the pressure of gases it contains. A volcano is an opening out of which this hot material erupts.

An eruption is like opening a can of shaken soda. Bubbles of gas separate from the liquid and force the liquid out. Material that erupts from a volcano contains ash, cinders, and hot, molten rock called **lava.** As lava cools and hardens, it becomes igneous rock. That's brand-new crust! If the rock builds to great heights, a mountain or island forms.

Volcanoes

Magma collects in large pockets called magma chambers. As magma leaves the chamber, it moves up a tunnel or central vent. Sometimes, magma escapes from the central vent and erupts from side vents. Most magma, however, erupts at the top of the volcano through a bowl-shaped crater.

The red hot lava from this volcano hisses as it meets the cool water.

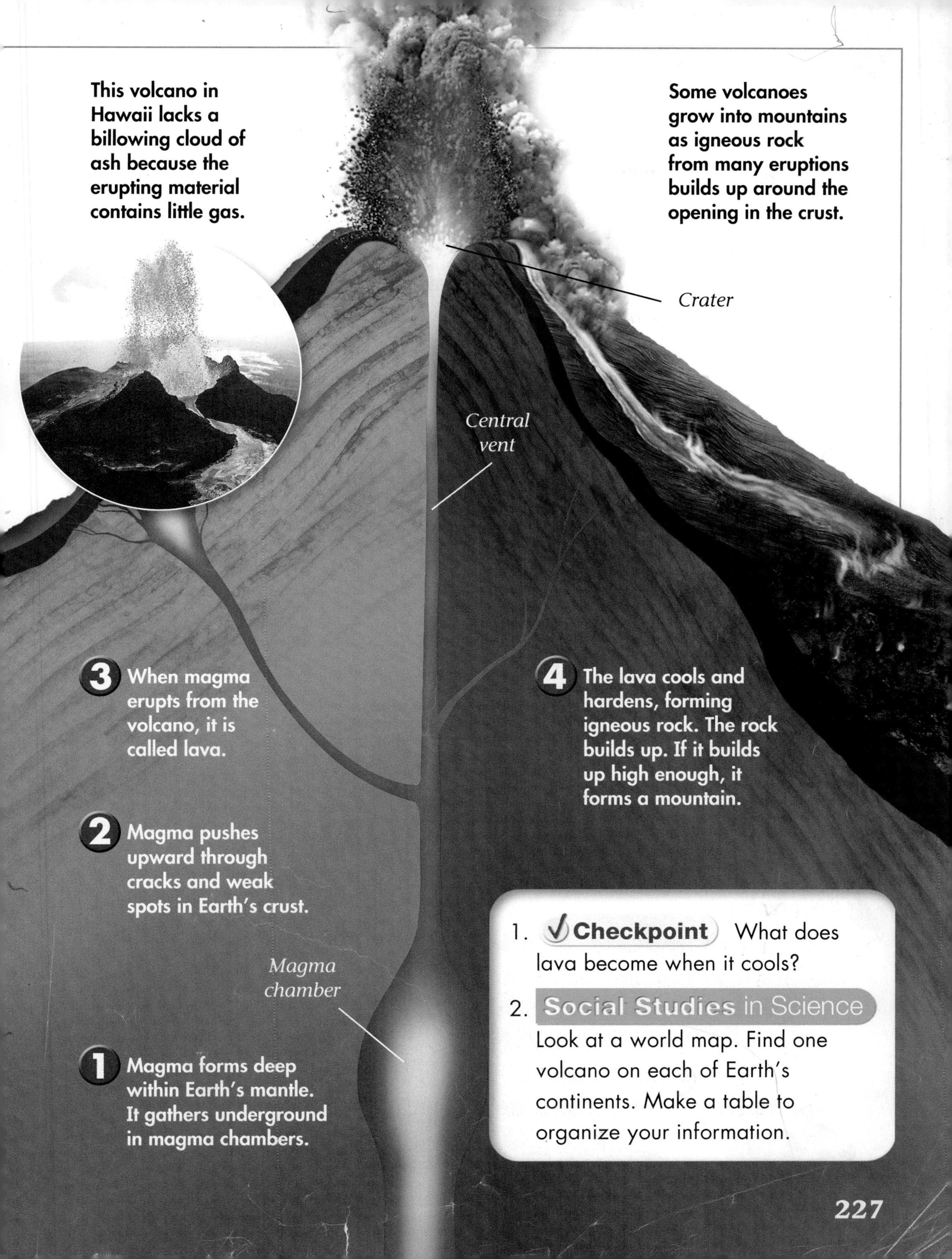

This volcano in Hawaii lacks a billowing cloud of ash because the erupting material contains little gas.

Some volcanoes grow into mountains as igneous rock from many eruptions builds up around the opening in the crust.

Crater

Central vent

3 When magma erupts from the volcano, it is called lava.

4 The lava cools and hardens, forming igneous rock. The rock builds up. If it builds up high enough, it forms a mountain.

2 Magma pushes upward through cracks and weak spots in Earth's crust.

Magma chamber

1 Magma forms deep within Earth's mantle. It gathers underground in magma chambers.

1. ✓ **Checkpoint** What does lava become when it cools?

2. **Social Studies** in Science
Look at a world map. Find one volcano on each of Earth's continents. Make a table to organize your information.

Earthquakes

Have you ever built a play house out of flimsy cardboard? A sudden bump sends vibrations through the house and it can fall over. In a similar way, sudden shifts between parts of Earth's crust cause the ground to vibrate in all directions. This shaking is an earthquake. Most earthquakes happen along faults. A fault is a large crack in the Earth's crust.

The vibrations of an earthquake move as waves through the Earth. Waves move back and forth and up and down along Earth's surface. These waves can cause cracks in the Earth's surface. Rubble can pile up in areas where the crust moved.

The 15-second Loma Prieta earthquake in 1989 destroyed this road in Oakland, California.

Earthquake Damage

The damage an earthquake causes depends on how close the earthquake is to the surface and how long the crust shakes. Also, the closer an earthquake is to a city or town, the more damage it can cause to buildings, bridges, and underground pipes.

An earthquake can cause landslides. Landslides are just what you might think they are. They are downhill movements of rocks and earth. The loose surface of the land slides down a slope.

Landslides can happen on the ocean floor or on land. Undersea landslides can form giant waves. Landslides on hills and mountains can ruin homes and destroy roads. They can bury large areas.

Vibrations from an earthquake cause cracks such as this one.

Parts of this parking garage snapped during a 1994 earthquake.

✔ Lesson Checkpoint

1. Compare and contrast magma and lava.

2. Where do most earthquakes happen? Why?

3. **Sequence** Use a graphic organizer to show the steps in the eruption of a volcano.

Loose soil and rock slid down this hillside during a landslide.

The growing roots of this tree in Arizona are helping to break the rock apart.

What are weathering and erosion?

Weathering and erosion are forces that change the surface of the Earth.

Weathering

Landforms change constantly. For this to happen, rocks in landforms must first break apart. **Weathering** is any action that breaks rocks into smaller pieces.

Weathering changes can be very slow. Some may take less than a year. Others might take centuries. Weathering goes on all the time.

Plants sometimes cause weathering. Their roots can grow into cracks in rocks. As the roots grow, they can split and break up the rocks.

Water can soak through soil. The water changes the minerals in rock below the soil. The rock is weakened and it begins to break apart.

While in a glacier, this rock became smaller and smoother as forces acted upon it.

When water freezes and thaws, it can cause weathering. Water can get into cracks in rocks. When water freezes, it expands, or grows larger. The ice pushes against the sides of the cracks. Over the years, the rocks may break apart.

Ice weathers rocks in another way. A glacier is a huge amount of ice that moves slowly over Earth's crust. As a glacier moves, it carries rocks with it. The rocks and ice scrape against the ground. The huge force of this action grinds valleys wide and smooth. When a glacier melts, weathered rocks of all sizes are left on the ground.

1. ✓ **Checkpoint** Describe weathering, giving three examples.

2. **Math in Science** Look at the pictures of rocks on this page. How much bigger is a boulder than a cobble? How much smaller is a sand grain than a pebble? How many sand grains could you line up along a meter stick?

Sizes of Rocks

Weathering breaks rocks into smaller and smaller pieces. Water wears many rocks to a smooth and rounded shape. The following lists the order of size from largest to smallest.

Boulder 300 mm

Cobble 100 mm

Pebble 30 mm

Sand 1 mm

Silt Each is a tiny speck!

Clay You need a microscope to see clay particles!

231

It took millions of years for waves carrying sand and pebbles to carve a hole in this cliff.

This island formed as sand settled from moving water. Waves will continue to shape it.

The whole side of this hill has moved down.

Erosion

Sometimes weathered material stays in place. Sometimes it is picked up and slowly or quickly carried to other places. The movement of weathered material is **erosion.** Water, wind, gravity, and glaciers can cause erosion.

Erosion by Water and Wind

Water causes erosion in many places. Rainwater can carry away soil from farm fields. Waves cause erosion along shorelines. Rivers carry bits of rock from place to place. Sand and mud flow over a river's banks during a flood.

New islands can form as a result of erosion. This happens when rivers carry rock and bits of soil to the ocean. These particles build up over time. Some form islands just off the coast. Wind and waves continue to shape these islands.

Erosion by wind is common in dry regions, such as deserts. Wind can carry dry sand and soil to other places. Few tall plants grow in deserts, so there is little to stop the particles from blowing around. The particles bump into rocks and break off tiny grains. Over time, more grains are broken off. The rocks slowly change.

Erosion by Gravity and Living Things

Gravity can cause erosion. Gravity pulls rocks and soil downhill. This material moves slowly on gentle slopes. Weathered material can move quickly on steep slopes. A mudflow is the quick movement of very wet soil. A rockslide is the quick movement of rocks down a slope.

Living things can cause erosion. Ground squirrels tunnel through soil. Worms mix and move soil. Ants move soil to make underground nests. Erosion continues as water and air move through the tunnels.

Map Fact
Water erosion shaped these rocks in Bryce Canyon in Utah. The shapes that look like creatures are called "hoodoos."

Rain and melting snow carved out these rock columns.

✓ Lesson Checkpoint

1. How are weathering and erosion different? How are they alike?

2. How does most erosion happen in dry regions?

3. **Writing in Science** **Expository**
   Use the photos on page 232 and this page to explain in your **science journal** how water is causing erosion.

233

Chapter 8 Review and Test Prep

Use Vocabulary

core (page 223)	**lava** (page 226)
crust (page 223)	**magma** (page 226)
erosion (page 232)	**mantle** (page 223)
landform (page 224)	**weathering** (page 230)

Use the vocabulary word from the box above that best completes each sentence.

1. Hot, molten rock on Earth's surface is _____.

2. Earth's _____ is the innermost layer of the planet.

3. A hill, a mountain, and a valley are each a(n) _____.

4. The thinnest layer of Earth is the _____.

5. Hot, molten rock that forms deep underground is _____.

6. Magma forms in Earth's thickest layer, which is called the _____.

7. The breaking of rocks into smaller pieces is _____.

8. The moving of weathered materials is _____.

Explain Concepts

9. Which is a better model of Earth's layers, a raw egg or a hard-boiled egg? Explain your choice.

10. Explain how weathering and erosion change Earth's landforms.

11. How do volcanoes change Earth's surface?

12. Compare and contrast erosion that wind causes and erosion that water causes.

Process Skills

13. **Classify** Classify each of the following as either weathering or erosion.
    - Ⓐ a river carrying silt flooding its banks
    - Ⓑ water freezing in the crack of a cliff
    - Ⓒ mud sliding down a hill

14. **Model** Make a series of four drawings to show how a volcano builds up over time.

15. Infer A fault lies between a town with a few buildings and a city with many skyscrapers. The town is 10 miles from the fault. The city is 5 miles from the fault. Infer which area might have the most damage in an earthquake.

 **Sequence**

16. Make a graphic organizer like the one below. Fill in the spaces to show the steps that water may take to weather rocks.

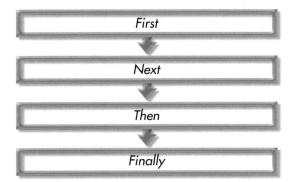

| First |
| Next |
| Then |
| Finally |

 Test Prep

Choose the letter that best completes the statement or answers the question.

17. Why is Earth's core solid when it is hot enough to melt?

(A) It is in the middle of the planet.
(B) It is smaller than the mantle.
(C) It is made of igneous rocks.
(D) It is under great pressure.

18. What makes water a powerful cause of weathering?

(F) It is a liquid.
(G) It takes up more space when it freezes.
(H) It evaporates.
(I) It rains all the time.

19. Why is erosion by wind so effective in deserts?

(A) Deserts are very moist.
(B) Deserts are very dry.
(C) Deserts are landforms.
(D) Deserts do not have living things.

20. Writing in Science

Narrative Think of being in San Francisco in 1906. That year, a violent earthquake shook the city. Write a paragraph about your experience in this earthquake. Tell what happened during the earthquake and in the week following it.

How can people use natural resources responsibly?

natural resource

renewable resource

nonrenewable resource

242

conservation

recycle

243

You Are There!

You are walking through a lush, green forest. A soft cushion of needles keeps your footsteps silent. You smell the trees. You hear chipmunks twittering in the branches. Birds dart back and forth. This is a beautiful place. But the trees may soon be cut down for lumber and paper. Can we keep our forests and still have the products we need?

AudioText

Lesson 1

What are resources?

Everything we use comes from materials found on Earth. Some of these materials can be replaced, but others cannot. Some resources are never used up.

Resources That Can Be Replaced

The things we need come from natural resources. A **natural resource** is an important material from the Earth that living things need.

Trees are a natural resource. People cut down trees for wood. Wood is used to build new houses. Wood chips are turned into pulp. Pulp is made into paper. Paper products include boxes, newspapers, and books.

People can plant new trees to replace those cut down. If the new trees get the sunlight, air, and water they need, they can grow big enough to be cut down. A resource that can be replaced in a fairly short time is called a **renewable resource.** Trees are a renewable resource.

These logs at a lumber or paper mill came from trees.

Lumber mills saw tree trunks into boards that are used to build new houses.

1. **✔Checkpoint** What makes some resources renewable?

2. **Writing in Science** **Expository** In your **science journal** make a table with two columns. Title one column *Wood.* Title the other *Paper.* Use the table to list things found in your home made from each. Then, write two paragraphs about how your family uses wood and paper products.

Resources That Cannot Be Replaced

Many natural resources come from below the ground. Miners dig into the ground to get rocks called ores. Ores contain metals and other minerals that people use. Copper, iron, and aluminum are some useful metals. Hematite is an ore that contains the metal iron.

Steel is made from iron. Steel is used to make nails, cars, and many other products. There is only so much iron ore in the ground. Once we use it up, it cannot be replaced. A resource that cannot be replaced is a **nonrenewable resource.**

Coal is a nonrenewable resource. Like oil and natural gas, coal is a fuel. When it is burned it releases useful energy. The energy from these fuels can be used to heat buildings. The energy can power cars and planes. We can get more fuel by digging more of these materials from the ground. But supplies of these fuels are limited.

Using Resources	
Resource	**Uses**
Oil	Gasoline, paint, plastic, shampoo
Coal	Electricity, heat, paint thinner, insecticides
Iron ore	Machines, bicycles, autos, buildings

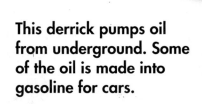

This derrick pumps oil from underground. Some of the oil is made into gasoline for cars.

When we use up an ore, mineral, or fuel resource in one place, we must find them in a new place. Mining and drilling can leave permanent marks, such as the open pit mine in the picture. Getting natural resources from Earth can change its surface.

Hematite is an ore that contains iron.

An Endless Supply of Resources

Some natural resources are not used up. Plants need sunlight, air, and water to grow. We need air to breathe and water to drink. These resources are not used up. Sunlight, air, and water are resources that are always available on Earth.

This coal formed in the Earth from plants that lived millions of years ago.

A huge crane loads coal into a dump truck at a mine.

✔Lesson Checkpoint

1. List two nonrenewable resources.

2. Why is coal a nonrenewable resource?

3. **Compare and Contrast**
   How are renewable and nonrenewable resources alike? How are they different?

Dirty water is piped into a wetland in Florida. It will become clean enough to be piped back into a river.

Water from homes is filtered through sand in ponds like these. Farmers use the recycled water for their orange trees.

How can we protect our resources?

We must protect natural resources by not using them up or damaging them.

Using Resources Responsibly

When people walk instead of riding in a car, they save fuel. When they choose products that have less packaging, they save paper and plastic. There is less garbage. Saving in these ways is called conservation. **Conservation** is the wise use of natural resources so that people do not waste them or use them up.

Conserving Water

You can conserve water by using less of it. You can turn off the water while brushing your teeth and take shorter showers.

One way that communities conserve water is to clean used water. Wetlands can clean used water. First, the dirty water is piped into wetlands. Soil filters out harmful particles. Then, plants and tiny living things break down the particles. Finally, the water is clean enough to flow back into a river and be used again.

Conserving Soil

Soil needs protection from erosion. Some farmers plant crops around hills instead of up and down the hills. The curved rows of plants hold back rainwater. Soil soaks up water instead of being washed away. Farmers also plant trees by fields to keep soil from blowing away.

As people in cities need more room, they often build new houses on nearby farmland. Buildings and roads cover the soil. There is less farmland. Landfills may also take up famland space.

We can conserve soil in our own yards. We can put yard clippings and leaves where they decay instead of sending them to a landfill. The decayed material turns into compost. You can add compost to garden soil for fertilizer.

We could allow these leaves to decay into compost. Then they would add nutrients to soil.

Contour plowing keeps soil from washing away.

1. ✓ **Checkpoint** Describe ways people can conserve water.

2. **Writing in Science** **Expository** Research ways to make a compost pile that will become fertilizer. In your **science journal** write a paragraph to explain it.

Using Up Land Space for Trash

Everything we use is made from natural resources. For example, plastic milk jugs are made from oil. Food cans are made from metals such as steel and tin. When we no longer need these products, we throw them away. They become trash. The trouble with our trash is that it never really goes away. A truck often hauls trash to a landfill. A landfill is a large area in which trash is buried. Trash rests on top of a liner so that pollution does not leak into groundwater. Once in place, we no longer have to see, smell, or worry about our garbage making us sick. But it still exists and the landfills continue to grow.

We put more than two hundred million tons of trash each year into landfills like this one.

What is in a Year's Worth of My Trash?	
Materials	**Mass (in kilograms)**
Paper	250
Plastic	80
Metal (steel cans)	40
Metal (aluminum cans)	10
Glass	40
Food scraps	80

Landfills are filling up and closing down. The number of landfills has fallen from 8,000 in 1988 to less than 2,000 today. Our need for land in which to bury our trash continues to grow. Most people, however, would rather see land used for other purposes.

One way we are reducing the need for landfill space is by burning garbage in special furnaces. Burning garbage also gives off energy that can heat buildings and generate electricity. However, the smoke from the burning must be cleaned. If the smoke is not cleaned, it can harm the air we breathe. Special smoke cleaners are expensive.

Another way we are lessening the need for landfill space is by reducing the amount of trash we make. If we were not doing this, we would have needed 100 new landfill areas. What are ways we are reducing the amount of trash we make?

These are objects we use every day. Can some of these materials be used again?

✓ Lesson Checkpoint

1. Where does most garbage go after it is taken from your home?

2. What are some ways to save landfill space?

3. **Math in Science** If you throw away 2 kilograms of trash each day, how much trash would you throw away in a year?

253

What are ways to use resources again?

Many things can be used more than once. Old materials can be used to make new things. Reusing and recycling conserves land, keeping it from becoming landfill space.

Using Resources Again

When you reuse things, you conserve resources. For example, you can reuse cloth napkins, but not paper ones. You can reuse empty jars to store leftover food. Or you can give toys and clothes you have outgrown to others to use.

Another way to conserve resources is to recycle things that contain useful material. You **recycle** when you change something so that it can be used again. The useful resources that went into making objects can then be made into new products. Many of these new products are made from recycled metal, glass, plastic, or paper.

Sort Glass
Recycled glass bottles and jars are separated by color. They are broken into small pieces.

Ship to Glass Company
Pieces of glass are put into boxes. The boxes are shipped to a glass reprocessing company.

Let's follow the process used to recycle things that contain glass. Workers at the recycling plant sort glass by color. Common colors are clear, brown, and green. The bottles and jars are then broken into pieces called shards. Shards are shipped to glass companies. Glass shards must be passed under a magnet to remove metal caps and rings. Shards are then crushed into grain-sized particles called cullet. The cullet is cleaned and dried. Now the cullet is ready to be turned into new glass things. It is melted in furnaces and blown by machines into glass bottles and jars. Some is flattened into windowpanes. If glass is recycled, it can be used over and over again.

1. ✓**Checkpoint** What are the four main types of materials that are recycled?

2. **Compare and Contrast** How is recycling glass the same as recycling water? How does recycling glass differ from recycling water?

100-watt light bulb

Food can

Glass bottle

It takes more energy to make new steel cans and glass bottles than to recycle them. Recycling one soup can may save enough energy to light a 100-watt bulb for about half an hour. Recycling one glass bottle saves enough energy for four hours of light.

❸ Process Crushed Glass
Glass bits are crushed into grain-sized particles. They are cleaned and dried.

❹ Make New Glass Bottles
The bits are melted and reformed into glass bottles or jars.

Using Recycled Materials

Reusing and recycling are not new ideas. Your great-grandparents might have bought flour in cloth sacks. They cleaned the empty sacks, cut them, and sewed them into rags, towels, and even clothing!

Today, recycling is easier than ever. Many communities collect items to be recycled when they collect the regular garbage. Places such as movie theaters and office buildings have special containers for bottles and cans. Grocery stores collect used plastic shopping bags that can be recycled.

Conserving recycled material requires buying or using products that include it. For example, you can shop for products made out of recycled material. Your next sleeping bag might include stuffing made out of shredded plastic bottles. Your next sweater might be knit out of yarn recycled from old garments. Or you can play on playgrounds that have a surface made out of shredded car tires.

This park bench was made from recycled plastic. It will last for about 50 years.

This wall is made of old tires and aluminum cans held together with mud and straw.

A reused plastic barrel makes a terrific flower pot.

This playhouse was made from recycled plastic milk bottles.

The Three *R's*

What's a good way to remember what you've learned to protect natural resources? Just think about the three *R's*—reduce, reuse, and recycle. *Reduce* the amount of resources you use and the trash you make. *Reuse* old things in new ways. *Recycle* everything you can. Every time you practice one of the three *R's*, you are helping to care for Earth.

Stuffing in this sleeping bag and yarn in this sweater are from recycled materials.

✓ **Lesson Checkpoint**

1. Why is it important to recycle?

2. What are the three *R's*?

3. **Art in Science** Draw or make a model showing how you might reuse something in an unusual way.

Investigate Where are some freshwater resources?

When it rains, some water soaks into the ground. This water collects in aquifers, layers of underground rock, gravel, and sand. People drill wells to get this water. People also get water from lakes and rivers.

Materials

safety goggles

container and gravel

paper cups and water

metric ruler

pencil and tape

spray nozzle and piece of nylon

plastic bag

Process Skills

When you **collect data**, you can make and use a table or a chart to help record your **observations**.

What to Do

❶ Make the **model** of an aquifer shown below.

❷ Slowly add water until the lake is 1.5 cm deep.

Use a pencil to poke 5 small holes in the bottom of a cup.

❸ Make it rain. Hold the cup with holes over the land. Move the cup as your partner pours a cup of water into your cup. **Observe** the water level.

5 cm

Water above ground forms lakes and rivers.

land

lake

water level

gravel

1.5 cm

You are modeling the effect on an aquifer of a year of heavy rains.

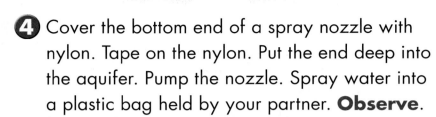

4 Cover the bottom end of a spray nozzle with nylon. Tape on the nylon. Put the end deep into the aquifer. Pump the nozzle. Spray water into a plastic bag held by your partner. **Observe**.

water between rocks

Wear safety goggles!

You are modeling the effect of very heavy pumping.

5 Record your observations in a chart. Make and label a sketch or diagram of your model.

	Observations		
	Changes in Height of Water Table (increased, decreased, no change)	**Changes in Depth of Lake** (increased, decreased, no change)	**Explanation of Your Observations** (How do you know? Why do you think so?)
Rain			
Pumping			

Explain Your Results

1. **Infer** Think about a real aquifer. How might rain and pumping from wells affect the water level?

2. What problems might be caused by too much pumping? How might the problems be solved?

Go Further

Change your model. Show how pollution could enter the aquifer.

Recycling

Almost everything we throw away can be recycled. But we do a better job recycling some things than other things.

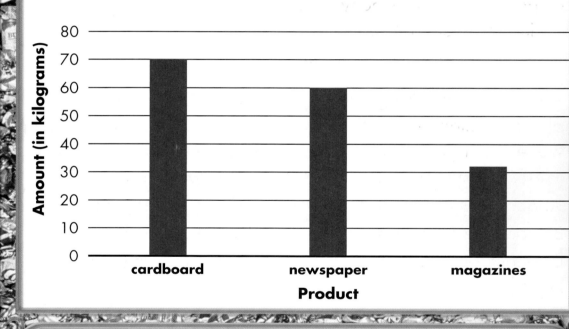

Amount of Paper Products Recycled for Every 100 Kilograms

Amount (in kilograms)

80
70
60
50
40
30
20
10
0

cardboard   newspaper   magazines

Product

The bar graph shows how much of three different paper products we recycle. We recycle 70 kilograms of cardboard boxes from every 100 kilograms we make. We recycle 60 kilograms of newspapers from every 100 kilograms we make. But we recycle only 32 kilograms of magazines from every 100 kilograms we make.

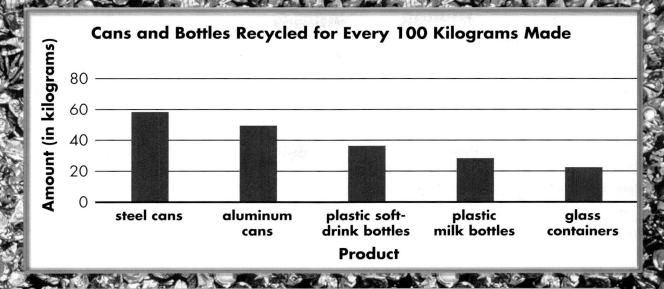

Cans and Bottles Recycled for Every 100 Kilograms Made

Amount (in kilograms)

80
60
40
20
0

steel cans | aluminum cans | plastic soft-drink bottles | plastic milk bottles | glass containers

Product

This bar graph shows how many kilograms of cans and bottles we recycle from every 100 kilograms we make.

Use the graph to answer the questions.

1 About how many kilograms of glass containers do we recycle from every 100 kilograms made?

A. about 58 kilograms

B. about 32 kilograms

C. about 28 kilograms

D. about 22 kilograms

2 Which container is recycled most?

F. steel cans

G. aluminum cans

H. plastic soft drink bottles

I. plastic milk bottles

3 From every 100 kilograms of aluminum cans we make, about how many kilograms do we **not** recycle?

A. about 50 kilograms

B. about 20 kilograms

C. about 80 kilograms

D. about 100 kilograms

Lab zone Take-Home Activity

Recycling 1 glass jar saves enough energy to run a TV for 3 hours. Find how many glass jars you have in your kitchen. How many hours of TV-watching in your home would recycling the jars pay for in energy savings?

Chapter 9 Review and Test Prep

Use Vocabulary

conservation (page 250)	**recycle** (page 254)
natural resource (page 247)	**renewable resource** (page 247)
nonrenewable resource (page 248)	

Use the term from the list above that best completes each sentence.

1. Trees, iron ore, water, and air are each a _____.

2. A natural resource that can be replaced in a fairly short period of time is a _____.

3. When we change something so it can be used again, we _____ it.

4. A resource that cannot be replaced once it is used up is a _____.

5. The saving and wise use of Earth's resources is called _____.

Explain Concepts

6. Explain the difference between a renewable resource like trees and a nonrenewable resource like iron ore.

7. What is the difference between a limited resource like iron ore and a limitless resource like air?

8. What are ways to conserve soil?

9. How is making compost out of yard wastes and food scraps one solution to the garbage problem?

10. Why is conserving natural resources important to everyone?

11. Why should people try to buy products made from recycled materials?

Process Skills

12. We get milk from cows and wool to make clothing from sheep. **Infer** whether milk and wool are renewable or nonrenewable resources. Explain your answer.

13. Copy the table below on a sheet of paper. Then **classify** each kind of trash as paper, plastic, or metal.

Trash	Classification
Milk carton	
Soft-drink can	
Magazine	
Laundry detergent bottle	

Compare and Constrast

14. Make a graphic organizer like the one below. Write in each part ways to show how reusing and recycling are similar and different.

Reusing   **Both** Reusing/ Recycling   Recycling

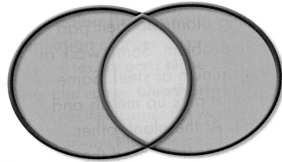

Test Prep

Choose the letter that best completes the statement or answers the question.

15. Which of the following is a renewable resource?
  (A) coal   (B) oil
  (C) aluminum   (D) sunlight

16. Which of the following does NOT conserve soil?
  (F) planting different crops
  (G) planting trees along the edges of fields
  (H) plowing up and down hillsides
  (I) adding compost to soil

17. Which of the following is a nonrenewable resource?
  (A) soil
  (B) iron ore
  (C) water
  (D) trees

18. Many power plants use coal to make electricity. Which of the following is a way you could help conserve coal?
  (F) Ride a bicycle instead of riding in a car.
  (G) Leave the television on when going outside.
  (H) Turn off lights when leaving a room.
  (I) Plant a flower garden using compost.

19. Explain why the answer you selected for Question 18 is best. For each of the answers you do not select, give a reason why it is not the best choice.

20. **Writing** in Science
Narrative Write a story about a person who saw how natural resources were not being protected and did something about it.

263

(D) Evaporation changes water vapor to liquid water.

265

267

269

271

Unit B Wrap-Up

Lab Zone Full Inquiry

Discovery CHANNEL SCHOOL

Science Fair Projects

Full Inquiry

Using Scientific Methods

1. Ask a question.
2. State your hypothesis.
3. Identify/control variables.
4. Test your hypothesis.
5. Collect and record your data.
6. Interpret your data.
7. State your conclusion.
8. Go further.

Predicting Weather

Weather patterns help people predict the weather, but predictions can be wrong.

Idea: Compare your observations of the weather with weather forecasts from TV and radio stations, and newspapers to see how accurate they are.

Comparing Soils

Soils have different amounts of sand, silt, clay, and humus.

Idea: Use a hand lens to compare soil samples in your area.

An Earthquake Model

Most earthquakes happen along breaks in Earth's crust.

Idea: Use clay, heavy cardboard, and objects to model what happens to Earth's crust, roads, and other objects during an earthquake.

Recycling

Recycling conserves landfill space and resources.

Idea: Use information about your community's recycling program to make a display with examples of what can be recycled and ways to sort it.

Unit C

Physical Science

Chapter 10
Matter and Its Properties

You Will Discover

- how to observe and describe matter.
- the different states of matter.
- ways to measure different properties of matter.

online
Student Edition
pearsonsuccessnet.com

Discovery Channel School
Student DVD

 DISCOVERY CHANNEL SCHOOL

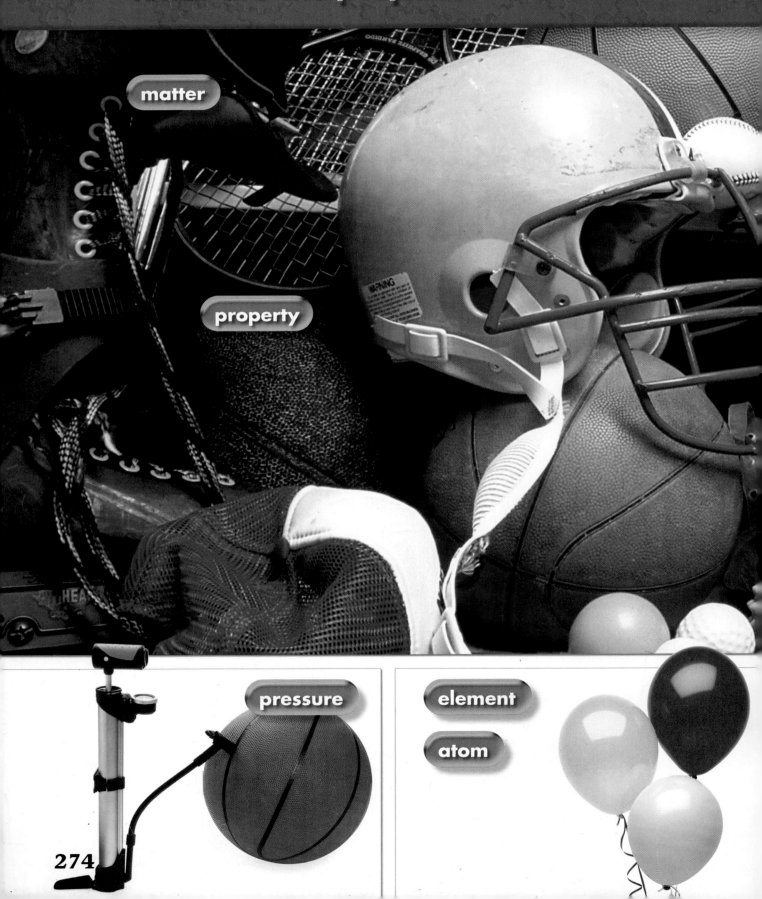

What are the properties of matter?

matter

property

pressure

element

atom

Chapter 10 Vocabulary

periodic table

Periodic Table of Elements

State at Room Temperature
= Solid   = Liquid   = Gas

density

buoyancy

mass

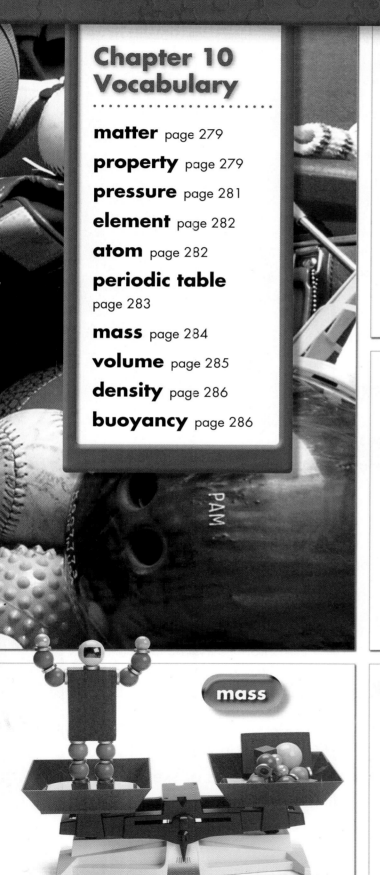

volume

Explore Which material has a surprising property?

Materials

safety goggles

resealable plastic bag

water

tub

3 sharpened pencils

What to Do

1 Put water in the plastic bag.

What do you think would happen if you push a pencil into the bag?

2 Slowly push a pencil into the bag. **Observe**. Based on your observations, **infer** why the result occurred.

Discuss the results with other students. Think about their explanations.

3 Based on your observations, **predict** what will happen if you push the pencil point out the other side. Try it.

Push 2 more pencils into the bag. See if you get the same results.

Seal bag!

half full

Hold over tub!

Process Skills

When you made your **prediction**, you used what you had just **observed** to help **infer** what would happen.

Explain Your Results

Compare your **prediction** in step 3 with your **observation**. Draw diagrams or sketches to show your prediction and your result.

Reading Skills

Cause and Effect

- A **cause** makes something change. An **effect** is the change you **observe**. Sometimes science writers use clue words and phrases such as *because, so, since,* and *as a result* to signal cause and effect.

- With careful **observations**, you might **predict** an effect that a certain cause will have.

Science Article

The Matter with Juice

Justin poured some juice from a bottle into a glass. Because juice is a liquid, its shape changed when it was in the glass. He decided to measure how much juice he had, so he poured it into a measuring cup. Then he decided to make a solid, so he put the juice into a mold and put sticks in it. He put the mold in the freezer. As a result, he had a frozen juice bar!

Apply It!

Make a graphic organizer like the one shown. Then use it to list two **causes** and two **effects** from the science article.

Causes   **Effects**

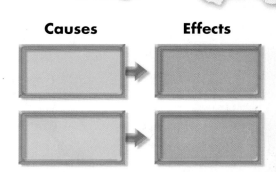

You Are There!

You walk into a room and see all these objects.
Wow! It's a sports-lover's dream! You look around for
the item you need for your favorite game. How do
you find it among all of this stuff? Well, you
look for certain colors, sizes, and shapes.
Let's see now . . . Ah! There it is. What
makes it different from all the rest?

AudioText

How can we describe matter?

Everything you can see, smell, or touch is matter. Many things that you cannot see, smell, or touch are matter too.

A World of Matter

All of the objects you see around you are made of matter. **Matter** is anything that takes up space and has mass. You can feel the mass of objects as weight when you pick them up. When you blow up a balloon, you see that even air takes up space.

A **property** is something about matter that you can observe with one or more of your senses. A ball looks round and feels smooth or bumpy. It could be hard or soft. The sound of it bouncing off the floor tells you more about the ball's properties. For other kinds of matter, such as a flower, your sense of smell tells you about other properties.

These balls, the hockey puck, the baseball mitt, and the air inside the tennis ball are matter.

1. **Checkpoint** What is *matter*?

2. **Writing in Science** **Expository** Draw two columns titled *Object* and *Properties*. Fill in the box with the properties of some things you see. Choose one object and write a paragraph using the information in the Properties column. Exchange your paragraph with a classmate. Try to guess each other's object.

States of Matter

All the matter around you is a solid, a liquid, or a gas. Each kind of matter is made of very small particles. These particles are so small that you cannot see them, even under a magnifying lens. The particles always move. In some kinds of matter they just jiggle. In other kinds they slide past one another or bounce around.

Solids

The bowling ball is a solid. You can put it over a small opening to a large container. But the ball won't change shape and fall through the opening. Like other solids, the ball keeps its shape. The particles of a bowling ball, or any other solid, are held tightly together. They jiggle or vibrate very fast. However, they stay firmly in place.

Liquids

Look at the orange juice being poured into a glass. The juice is a liquid. It will take the shape of the glass into which it is being poured. The particles of orange juice, or any other liquid, are loosely held together. The particles can flow past one another. If you pour the orange juice from the glass into another container, the juice will change shape again. However, the juice will take up the same amount of space in the new container.

Orange juice is a liquid. The particles of juice are loosely held together.

A bowling ball is a solid. The particles of the ball are firmly held together.

Gases

The air being pumped into the basketball is a gas. When you pump air into a ball, the air fills the space. Like other gases, air has no shape. The tiny gas particles are not held together. They bounce off one another as they move freely. Unlike solids and liquids, the amount of space that air takes up changes. The air spreads out, or expands, to fill whatever space is available.

As air is pumped into a ball, the air at first expands. It starts to push against the inside of the ball. This pushing is called **pressure**. As the ball is filled, the air becomes more compact. It presses together. You can feel the pressure by pushing on the ball before and after air is added.

1. ✔**Checkpoint** What are three states of matter?

2. **Cause and Effect** How does melting ice into water, and then letting the water evaporate, change the state of the ice?

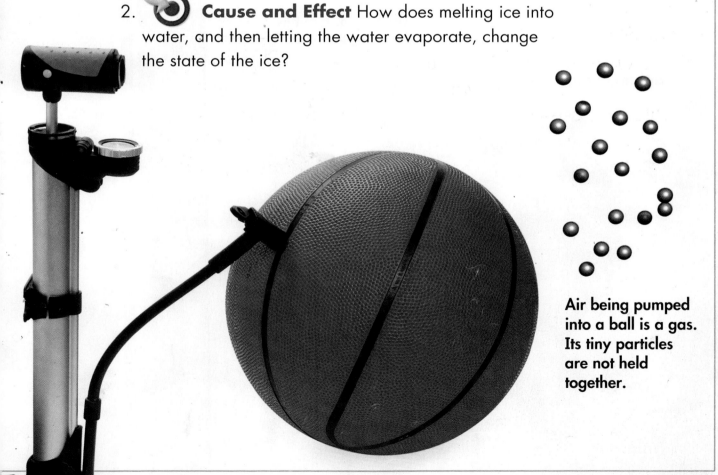

Air being pumped into a ball is a gas. Its tiny particles are not held together.

Parts of Matter

Suppose you could break a chunk of gold into smaller and smaller pieces. Each piece of gold is still the matter we call gold. Gold is an element. An **element** is matter made of a single type of particle too small to see. A chunk of gold is made only of particles of gold.

Most matter, however, is made out of many types of particles combined together in different ways. The smallest particle of an element that has the properties of that element is an **atom.** Gold is made up of atoms of gold. Clay, however, is made up of different kinds of atoms. These atoms act together to give clay its properties.

A particle of clay is made of different kinds of atoms. The atoms act together to give clay its properties.

Clay pots are made of particles of clay.

The helium that fills these balloons is an element.

282

Science experiments show that there are more than 100 different elements. Scientists arrange these elements in a **periodic table** of the elements. Elements are arranged based on their properties. Examples include how they respond to heat and other elements. This table is shown below.

Empedocles

Empedocles [em PÉD uh KLEEZ] lived in ancient Greece. He and others thought that earth, air, fire, and water were the four elements that made up all matter.

Periodic Table of Elements

State at Room Temperature
= Solid   = Liquid   = Gas

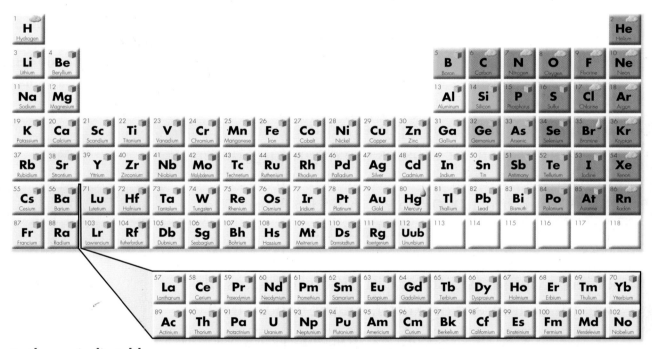

In the periodic table, elements in the same column have similar properties.

✓ **Lesson Checkpoint**

1. Explain why most objects you observe are not elements.

2. What about elements is used to arrange them in the periodic table of the elements?

3. **Social Studies in Science** Use library resources to find out about atoms. Find out who first used the word *atom*.

Lesson 2

How are properties of matter measured?

You can observe many properties of matter through your senses. You also can use tools to measure some properties of matter.

Tools for Measuring Mass

One property of matter is mass. An object's **mass** is the amount of matter it has. Solids, liquids, and gases all have mass. A balance is a tool to measure mass. The balance shown has two pans at the same level. The mass of the toy on left the is the same as the mass of the toy's pieces on the right.

A metric unit for mass is the gram (g). Larger amounts of matter are measured in kilograms (kg). There are 1,000 grams in a kilogram. The mass of a baseball bat is about 1 kg.

An object's mass is the same everywhere. An object's weight is different in different places. Its weight is different on Earth, on the Moon, and in space. The scales in doctors' offices and grocery stores measure weight.

A balance measures mass, or the amount of matter an object has. The whole toy has the same mass as its parts.

This table shows the mass of some common objects.

Mass of Common Objects	
paper clip	1 g
dime	2 g
pencil	5 g
mug	400 g
stapler	500 g

Tools for Measuring Volume

Another property of matter is volume. An object's **volume** is the amount of space that the object takes up. Solids, liquids, and gases all have volume. To measure the volume of a liquid, you might use a measuring cup or a graduated cylinder.

The basic metric unit for measuring liquid volume is the liter (L). A measuring cup might show marks for smaller parts of a liter called milliliters (mL). There are 1,000 milliliters in a liter.

Solids also have volume. You can measure the volume of a solid such as a rock, using water. A rock will keep its shape in water. But it pushes water out of its way. Put some water in a measuring cup. Record the level of the water. Slide the rock into the water. Record the new water level. Subtract the two levels to find how much water the rock pushed aside.

The volume of the water in this measuring cup is 500 mL.

The volume of the milk in this jug is about 2 L.

The volume of the orange juice in this bottle is about 1 L.

The volume of the water in this water bottle is about 500 mL.

1. ✔️**Checkpoint** How are an object's mass and weight different?

2. 🎯 **Cause and Effect** What effect would cutting a piece of wood in half have on the total mass of the wood?

Measuring Density

Density is another property of solids, liquids, and gases. **Density** is a measure of the amount of matter in a certain amount of space. The bowling ball and the rubber ball shown are the same size. They have the same volume. The bowling ball is harder to lift. It has more mass in the same amount of space. The bowling ball has greater density.

You can study the density of an object by observing how it floats in a liquid or a gas. This property is **buoyancy.** For example, rocks have little buoyancy in water. They sink. Rocks have a higher density than water. A balloon filled with helium is buoyant in air. A helium balloon floats upward. Helium has a lower density than air.

This ball is the same size as the bowling ball. How could you tell which has more matter in it?

How do you compare the density of solid objects? To do this, you need to measure the mass and the volume of the objects. If the objects have the same volume, the object that has the greater mass has greater density.

Knowing the density of matter helps scientists tell different kinds of matter apart.

Pennies

Marbles

Paper boat

Cork

These objects differ in their density compared to water. Predict which objects will sink and which will float.

An object will float in water if it has less density than water. It will sink if it has greater density than water.

1. ✔ **Checkpoint** What is *density*?

2. **Writing in Science** **Expository** Write a paragraph in your **science journal** that explains how to tell which of two liquids has less density.

Tools for Measuring Other Properties

Size is another property that can be measured. Length, for example, is the distance from one end of an object to the other end. Metric rulers and tapes are used to measure length. The basic metric unit of length is the meter. Shorter lengths are measured in centimeters (cm) or millimeters (mm). There are 100 cm in a meter. There are 1,000 mm in a meter. Much longer distances are measured in kilometers. There are 1,000 meters in a kilometer.

Other tools and units can be used to measure the volume of solid objects. A cubic unit is a cube that is used to measure volume. To find the volume of a box, you can find how many cubes of one size would fit inside the box. A cube that measures 1 centimeter on each side has a volume of 1 cubic centimeter. If 12 of these cubes fit inside a box and fill it up, the volume of the box is 12 cubic centimeters.

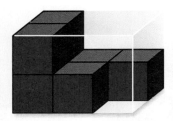

1 cubic unit

Fill the box with cubes to find its volume.

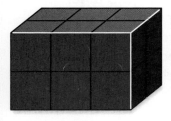

12 cubes fill the box. The volume is 12 cubic units.

The tape measures the length of this model airplane's wingspan in centimeters. How long is the wingspan?

A hand lens makes this pillbug much easier to see.

The lens lets you see small units on the ruler clearly in order to measure with accuracy.

Some objects are too small to see easily. For instance, you may need a hand lens or magnifying glass to observe and measure the properties of a pillbug. If you put a metric ruler under the lens, you can more easily measure the length of the pillbug.

✓**Lesson Checkpoint**

1. Describe how you would measure the volume of a liquid.

2. How could you measure the volume of a box?

3. **Math** in Science   What is the basic metric unit for length? What units are used to measure shorter lengths?

Use Vocabulary

atom (page 282)	**periodic table** (page 283)
buoyancy (page 286)	**pressure** (page 281)
density (page 286)	**property** (page 279)
element (page 282)	**volume** (page 285)
mass (page 284)	
matter (page 279)	

Use the vocabulary word from the list above that best completes each sentence.

1. An object's _____ is the amount of matter it has.

2. When you see that a ball is red, you are observing a(n) _____ of the ball.

3. Each of the tiny particles that make up an element is called a(n) _____ .

4. A measuring cup is used to find a liquid's _____.

5. A balloon gets larger when air is blown into it because of air _____.

6. An object that floats in water has _____ in water.

7. Anything that takes up space and has weight is _____.

8. Elements are arranged in a(n) _____ based on their properties.

9. An object's _____ is a measure of the amount of matter the object has in a certain amount of space.

10. Matter that has only one kind of atom is a(n) _____.

Explain Concepts

11. List the two properties of matter that are needed to measure density and explain why you need to measure both.

12. List the following metric units from the smallest to the largest: meter, millimeter, kilometer, centimeter.

Process Skills

13. **Predict** You pour juice from a tall, narrow glass into a short, wide glass. What happens to the volume of the juice?

14. **Infer** An object falls into a pond and sinks. What do you know about the density of the object?

Cause and Effect

15. Carrie and her friends wanted to play soccer. Their ball was too soft, so they needed to use a pump. Explain how the pump changed the ball so they could play with it. Use a graphic organizer to show all the causes and their effects.

Causes		Effects
	➡	
	➡	

Test Prep

Choose the letter that best completes the statement or answers the question.

16. How many states of matter can we observe?

ⓐ 1   ⓑ 2
ⓒ 3   ⓓ 5

17. Which tool is used to observe the visible properties of a tiny object?

Ⓕ balance
Ⓖ metric ruler
Ⓗ graduated cylinder
Ⓘ hand lens

18. If you weigh an object and then break it into two pieces, the sum of the weights of its pieces will be

Ⓐ less than the weight of the object.
Ⓑ equal to the weight of the object.
Ⓒ greater than the weight of the object.
Ⓓ half the weight of the object.

19. About how many different elements are there?

Ⓕ 3   Ⓖ 5
Ⓗ 100   Ⓘ 500

20. **Writing in Science**

Expository Make a chart that shows what tools and metric units are used for measuring mass, volume, and length.

Measurement	Tool	Unit
mass		
volume		
length		

Write a paragraph that tells what the chart shows.

Chemist

Do you like to cook? When you cook you use chemistry. Chemistry is the study of substances and how they change. You might not want to eat all the ingredients separately. After they are mixed and baked, however, they change. Then they taste just right.

Chemists also study the properties of substances. Some materials mix together easily. Sugar dissolves in water quickly. Other substances do not mix together well. Dr. John Pojman is a chemist. He directs experiments that are done in space where gravity won't interfere.

Dr. Pojman and other scientists are developing experiments to find out more about the ways that liquids mix together.

Chemists earn a degree in chemistry. Then they work for companies that make food, plastics, and medicine. Many chemists work for NASA.

Dr. John Pojman does experiments with fluids in low-gravity conditions.

Lab zone Take-Home Activity

Plastics are made from different substances. Each type of plastic has different properties. Find objects around your home that are made of plastic and list their properties.

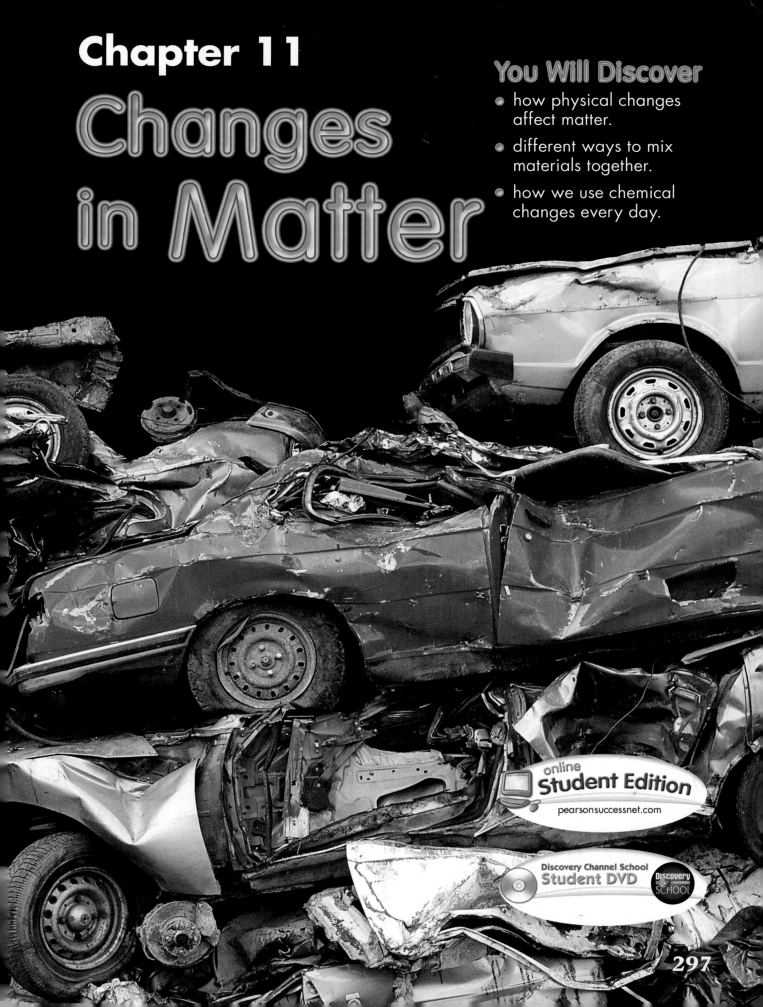

Chapter 11
Changes in Matter

You Will Discover

- how physical changes affect matter.
- different ways to mix materials together.
- how we use chemical changes every day.

online
Student Edition
pearsonsuccessnet.com

Discovery Channel School
Student DVD
DISCOVERY SCHOOL

What are physical and chemical changes in matter?

physical change

solution

mixture

298

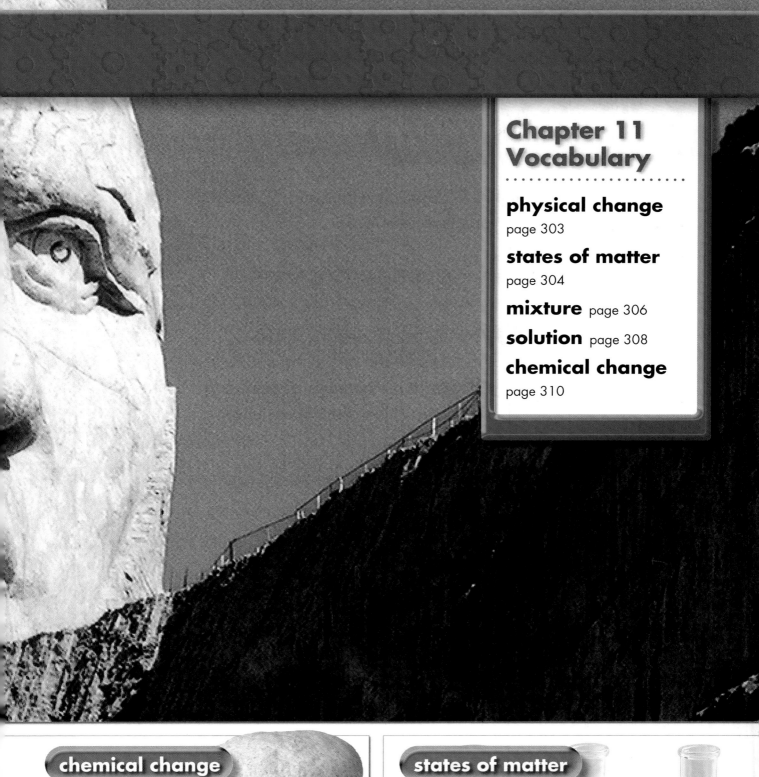

Chapter 11 Vocabulary

chemical change

states of matter

299

You Are There!

You stand at the base of the great mountain. The noise of heavy equipment fills your ears. Dust sticks in your nose and throat. You look up at the top of the mountain—and can hardly believe your eyes! A huge face of stone stares out over the distant land. Amazing! What kinds of changes are happening to that mountain?

AudioText

Lesson 1

What are physical changes in matter?

Physical properties such as size, weight, color, and position can change. Materials can also change state.

Making a Physical Change

The people in the picture are carving a statue of the Native American leader Crazy Horse out of this mountain. They are chiseling, hammering, and even blasting rock to bits. The bits of rock look different than the mountain. But each bit is still the same kind of rock as the whole mountain. The people are making a physical change to the mountain.

Matter goes through a **physical change** when it changes the way it looks without becoming a new kind of matter.

Cutting fruit into pieces causes a physical change. The pieces are made of the same kind of matter as the whole fruit.

1. ✓**Checkpoint** Describe a physical change in matter and explain why it is a physical change.

2. **Technology** in Science Use the Internet to find out more about the Crazy Horse Memorial project. Who started it? When did it begin? How long will it take to finish?

303

Some Ways to Cause Physical Change

There are lots of ways to cause physical change in matter. The pictures show some of them.

States of matter are the forms that matter can take—solid, liquid, and gas. Matter can change from one state to another. But if the state changes, it remains the same kind of matter. For example, when liquid water freezes, it becomes ice. Ice is a solid. However, when ice melts, you can see that it is still water. Ice and water are the same kind of matter.

A change in temperature can cause matter to change state. For example, water evaporates quickly when heated to 100°C (212°F). That means the water changes from a liquid into a gas. Even though you cannot see the gas, a physical change has happened. The water particles are still water. But the particles are so far apart in the air that you cannot see them. Even though the water has changed state, it has not become a new kind of matter.

Water also changes state when it is cooled. Above 0°C (32°F), the particles of liquid water slide past one another. At 0°C, liquid water changes to solid ice. Each water particle slows down and vibrates very fast in place.

You make a physical change when you fold clothes.

When you cut paper you are making a physical change.

And what happens when you hold an ice cube in your hand? The heat from your hand makes the water particles move faster. They no longer vibrate in place. They move freely, flowing as liquid water. You feel it dripping through your fingers. But no matter how many physical changes you make, the amount and kind of matter remain the same.

In ice, water particles vibrate in place.

You can make a sculpture of water only when it's in a solid state.

In liquid water, the water particles slide past one another.

Some water has evaporated. The water particles in the gas called water vapor are far apart.

✓ **Lesson Checkpoint**

1. List ways that you can make physical changes in matter.

2. What physical changes happen to water as it freezes?

3. **Cause and Effect** Make a graphic organizer like the one on page 301. Fill it with ways to cause physical changes to a piece of paper. Describe the effects each change would have on the paper.

305

Lesson 2

What are some ways to combine matter?

Many kinds of matter can be combined. Sometimes you can separate substances from the combination.

The different coins in this mixture can easily be separated.

Mixtures

Each single coin on this page is made up of matter. So what happens when you put all these different pieces of matter together? You get a mixture. A **mixture** is made of two or more kinds of matter that are placed together. The amounts of each kind of matter do not have to be the same. For example, there may be more quarters than pennies in the coin mixture. But it's still a mixture. In fact, each coin is a mixture. Two or more metals are melted together to form each type of coin.

What parts make up this mixture?

What is important about a mixture is that each kind of matter in it does not change into another substance. Each kind of matter can also be separated from every other kind in the mixture.

Some mixtures are very easy to separate. For example, you can separate sand grains and marbles because of their size. You could put the mixture into a strainer with fairly small holes. The marbles are too big to go through the holes of the strainer, but the sand pours right through.

You can also separate sand and iron pieces if you use a magnet. The magnet pulls the iron out of the mixture. The sand remains behind.

How does a magnet help separate the parts of this sand-iron mixture?

1. ✔**Checkpoint** Give three reasons why a bowl of different kinds of beans is a mixture.

2. **Social Studies** in Science Find out what metals are melted together to make a penny, a nickel, a dime, and a quarter.

A strainer helps separate the parts of this marble-sand mixture.

Has this ever
happened to you?
Why does the gas
explode from the can?

Solutions

Have you ever mixed lemonade powder into water to make lemonade? After you stir the powder into the water, the powder seems to disappear. But it doesn't go away. It dissolves. This means the particles of powder become so tiny that you cannot see them. The particles spread out in the water.

When a substance dissolves in another substance, a **solution** forms. A solution is a kind of mixture. But you may not be able to see the particles in a solution. You can't see the particles of powder in the lemonade. But you know the powder is there if you taste the solution.

You use all kinds of solutions. Soda is a solution of carbon dioxide gas and other substances dissolved in water. Shake a can of soda and the gas separates quickly from the water. In a closed can, the separated gas has no place to go. Pressure builds. When you open the can, the gas escapes.

Straining doesn't separate the salt from salt water. But if you boil away the water, the salt is left behind.

Separating Parts of Solutions

Since a solution is a kind of mixture, you can separate its parts. Think about a pitcher of salt water. How can you separate the salt from the water? You can try pouring the salt water through a strainer. That helped separate the marble-sand mixture. But the salt particles in salt water are too tiny to be trapped by a strainer. If you taste the water that runs through the strainer, it's still salty.

What if you heat the salt water? The water evaporates quickly. The salt is left behind. The same thing happens with lemonade. If the water evaporates, the substances in the powder stay behind.

These "disappearing acts" are physical changes. The changes may make the substance look different. But each is still the same substance in the same amount.

Some substances, like lemonade mix, will dissolve in water.

Some substances, like these small stones, will not dissolve in water.

✓ Lesson Checkpoint

1. What makes ocean water a mixture?

2. What makes ocean water a solution?

3. **Writing in Science** **Descriptive** In your **science journal,** describe some things for a mixture. What do you think will happen when you mix them? Be sure to name the parts of your mixture.

Lesson 3

What are chemical changes in matter?

Some changes in matter can produce new kinds of matter. We use these changes all the time.

Forming Different Materials

Mmmmm . . . there's nothing like the smell of fresh, warm bread. It tastes so good right out of the oven. But you wouldn't want to eat it before it was baked. A bowl of flour, baking powder, and eggs wouldn't taste very good.

In a **chemical change,** one kind of matter changes into a different kind of matter. A chemical change happens when bread is baked. The batter is a mixture of ingredients. But the heat of the oven causes chemical changes to happen. Then a new substance, bread, is formed.

A chemical change happens when eggs cook. They can never change back into the same form as raw eggs.

Baking bread produces a chemical change. You cannot get the ingredients back because a new substance is formed.

Remember that after water freezes into ice, the ice can melt back to water. Each change is a physical change. The water and ice are the same material. But what about the materials that make up the bread? Can you ever separate them from the bread? Probably not. Materials that have gone through a chemical change usually cannot be changed back to the original kind of matter.

Sometimes a chemical change can happen quickly. For example, fire can burn wood in minutes. Other times, a chemical change happens slowly. Think about an iron chain that's left outside. Aided by water, the iron slowly combines with oxygen gas from the air. Then the iron and oxygen change to rust. The rust is now a different kind of matter, and it will not change back into iron and oxygen gas.

Rusting is a slow chemical change.

Burning is a fast chemical change. When the sticks burn, the wood changes to gases and ashes. Some of the gases and ashes make up smoke.

1. ✔**Checkpoint** How do you know that burning wood is a chemical change?

2. **Cause and Effect** Let's say you paint an iron door the color of iron rust. Meanwhile, the bread you are baking turns a rust color on top. Which is a physical change? Which is a chemical change? Explain.

Using Chemical Changes

We use chemical changes every day. From eating pizza to watching a fireworks show, chemical changes are part of our lives.

Chemical changes start in your mouth the moment you begin to chew a piece of food. Then more changes happen as the food goes through your body. It's a good thing too. Chemical changes give your body the material it needs for energy and growth.

Chemical changes also help move us from place to place. Gasoline burning is a chemical change that releases the energy that the car's engine uses.

Chemical changes make many things in life easier to do. For example, laundry soap often has additives that cause chemical changes which break down stains. Without these changes, clothes might keep getting dirtier and dirtier.

Many soaps cause chemical changes that break down dirt and grime.

Burning gasoline in cars is a chemical change.

Chemical changes in batteries release electricity that appliances use.

You rely on the ability of many kinds of material to undergo chemical changes. When you turn the switch on your CD player, for example, chemicals will combine inside batteries. New substances will form. The chemical change will make a small amount of electricity to help you hear your favorite music.

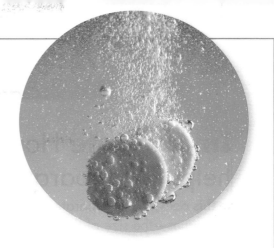

A chemical change between the water and the tablets causes the bubbles.

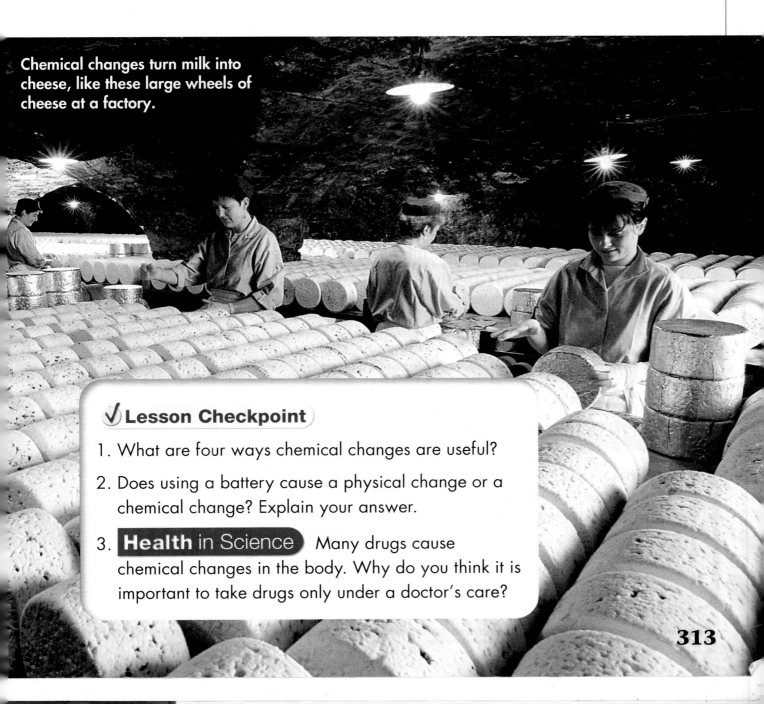

Chemical changes turn milk into cheese, like these large wheels of cheese at a factory.

✓ Lesson Checkpoint

1. What are four ways chemical changes are useful?

2. Does using a battery cause a physical change or a chemical change? Explain your answer.

3. **Health in Science** Many drugs cause chemical changes in the body. Why do you think it is important to take drugs only under a doctor's care?

313

Chapter 11 Review and Test Prep

Use Vocabulary

chemical change (page 310)	**solution** (page 308)
mixture (page 306)	**states of matter** (page 304)
physical change (page 303)	

Use the vocabulary term from the list above that best completes each sentence.

1. A change in which the matter does not turn into a new kind of matter is called a _____.

2. Salt water is a _____ because one substance dissolves in another.

3. A _____ is two or more substances combined without changing any kind of matter.

4. A change in which one kind of matter is changed into another kind of matter is called a _____.

5. Solids, liquids, and gases are _____.

Explain Concepts

6. Explain why chopping wood is a physical change but burning wood is a chemical change.

7. Describe three different ways to cause a physical change.

Process Skills

8. **Infer** why a puddle of water can be on the sidewalk one day and be gone the next.

9. **Predict** what kind of a mixture you would have if you mix sugar and water.

10. **Predict** A dog dish of water is left outside during the night. The temperature will be −3°C during the night. What will happen to the water?

11. **Infer** Think of an egg frying in a pan. Does the frying produce a physical change or a chemical change? Give a reason for your answer.

12. **Draw Conclusions** When sugar is heated for a long time, it forms a solid black substance. What kind of change takes place? Explain your answer.

13. **Sequence** Put these steps in the correct order: ashes, paper, burning paper.

Cause and Effect

14. Make graphic organizers like the ones shown below. Fill in the correct cause and effect.

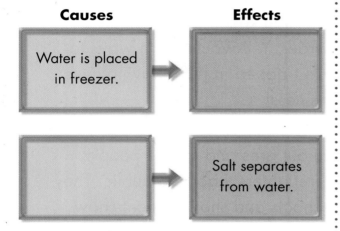

Causes	Effects
Water is placed in freezer.	
	Salt separates from water.

Test Prep

Choose the letter that best completes the statement or answers the question.

15. Which of the following is a chemical change?

Ⓐ Water freezes.
Ⓑ Wire bends.
Ⓒ Paper is cut.
Ⓓ Wood burns.

16. A fruit salad is an example of a

Ⓕ change in state.
Ⓖ mixture.
Ⓗ solution.
Ⓘ chemical change.

17. What happens in a physical change?

Ⓐ The kind of matter remains the same.
Ⓑ The kind of matter changes to another kind.
Ⓒ Some of the matter changes to another kind.
Ⓓ The amount of matter changes.

18. In salt water

Ⓕ the parts become new kinds of matter.
Ⓖ the amount of each part is the same.
Ⓗ the parts cannot be separated.
Ⓘ the parts are mixed together in a solution.

19. Explain why the answer you chose for Question 18 is best. For each of the answers you did not choose, give a reason.

20. **Writing in Science**

Descriptive Write a paragraph describing what you see when you arrive at a forest fire. Include a description of chemical changes taking place.

319

This firefighter is teaching students about safety.

Firefighter

Each year fires kill people and destroy property. As a firefighter, you would work to prevent and control these disasters. You would drive and operate special trucks. You would assist in keeping them clean and in working order. You would learn ways to rescue people trapped in fires. Saving lives is serious business!

But not all of a firefighter's time is spent putting out fires and saving people. Sometimes firefighters teach the public. They might visit schools and show students how to be safe from fire at home. They also must train a lot and keep in good health.

You have to graduate from high school to become a firefighter. Then, if you can pass a physical and written test, you can go to firefighter training. Some firefighters go to college and study fire science. They learn a lot about how fires get started and how they spread.

Lab zone Take-Home Activity

On a piece of paper, design escape routes from each area of your house. Record the time it takes to move from each area through the proper exit.

Chapter 12

Forces and Motion

You Will Discover

- different ways to describe position and motion.
- how force affects motion.
- how simple machines work.

online
Student Edition
pearsonsuccessnet.com

How do forces cause motion and get work done?

position

motion

speed

relative position

gravity

Chapter 12 Vocabulary

force

friction

magnetism

work

323

Explore How can you describe motion?

Materials

2 balls

metric ruler

books or wooden blocks

2 long books

If you wish, you can use cardboard or wood to build your ramps.

What to Do

1 Make 2 ramps. Let go of a ball from the top of each ramp at the same time.

2 books

1 book

ball A

ramp A (higher ramp)

long books

ball B

ramp B (lower ramp)

2 **Observe** how each ball moves down the ramp. Does its speed increase or decrease? Which reaches the bottom first?

3 **Communicate** After each ball reaches the bottom, does its speed increase or decrease?

Explain Your Results

1. Which ball moved faster? Describe the location of each ball when it stops moving. Which was farther from the ramp?

2. **Communicate** Compare how a ball's speed changes before and after reaching the bottom of a ramp. Describe the 2 types of motion that you **observed**.

Process Skills

After the activity, you were able to **communicate** the 2 types of motion you **observed**.

How to Read Science

Summarize

When you **summarize** an article, you **communicate** all the information in just one or two sentences. Summarizing helps you remember what you read.

- Sometimes the summary is a sentence at the beginning or at the end of an article.
- Sometimes there is no written summary. Then you think about the pieces of information and summarize them.

Science Article

A World of Motion

Look around. Do you see anything moving? What about the second hand on the clock? Cars may be rolling by outside. Is anyone walking along the sidewalk? No doubt, we live in a world of motion.

Apply It!

Study the graphic organizer below.

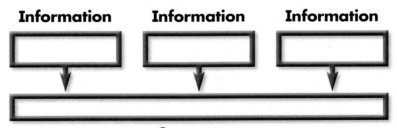

Make a graphic organizer like the one above. Write three details and the **summary** of the science article.

You Are There!

Here it comes—the wave you have been waiting for. You paddle quickly to get going. Then you stand up on your surfboard just as the monster wave arrives. Suddenly—whoosh! You're riding the wave. You're moving fast. The water crashes all around, but you keep your balance as you slice through the water. What a ride! Can you explain where you've been, where you've ended up, and how you got there?

Lesson 1

What happens when things change position?

An object is in motion when its position changes. The speed and direction of an object's motion can also change. An object's position and motion depend on what you compare it with.

When Things Move

Can you tell when something is moving? Think about dropping a spinning top onto a hilly sidewalk. You can tell it has moved because its location has changed. It was in your hand. Now it's on the sidewalk spinning. If an object is in a different location, its **position** has changed.

A spinning top has circular motion. What else moves like a top?

Watch the top move down the sloping sidewalk in a certain direction. It is in **motion** as its position changes. It also moves in circles around a central point. The spin has given the top circular motion. You have made your top move down, then forward, and round and round as well.

1. **✓Checkpoint** How can you tell something is in motion?

2. **Writing in Science** **Descriptive** Write a paragraph in your **science journal** describing different kinds of motion you have observed.

Ways of Looking at an Object's Position

Have you ever gotten lost trying to get somewhere? Finding your way can be confusing. As you change position, things around you stay in place. For example, as you walk along, the water fountain is in front of you. Then you walk past. The water fountain is behind you. The fountain seems to be moving away. The position, direction, and movement of an object often depend on how a person looks at it.

Sometimes a map can help. A map is a drawing of a place. Objects marked on a map are not real, of course. They are models of things. A map models the position of objects in relation to each other. Maps work because the objects on the map are fixed in place.

Suppose you visit the school shown in the map below. Can you describe a trip to the lunch room using position terms? Position terms include words like *forward, left, right,* and *behind.*

The arrows on the school map show a path from a classroom to the lunch room.

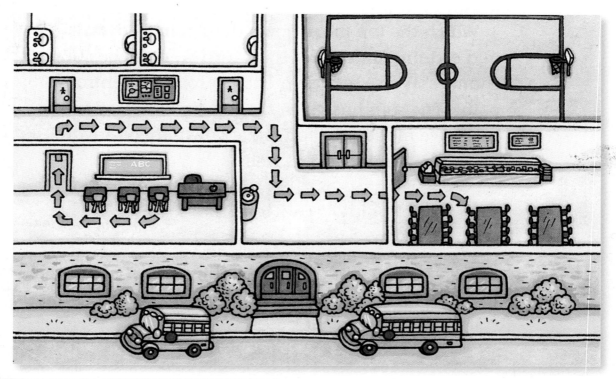

Positions of Moving Objects

The position of each object on a map is relative to other objects. *Relative* can mean that one thing depends on another thing for its meaning.

What is the position of car 64 in the picture? You would say its relative position is in front of the other cars. **Relative position** is the position of one object compared with the position of other objects.

But what about cars that aren't in the picture? Some might be in front of car 64. You would say car 64 is behind those cars. So the position of car 64 depends on the position of the other cars. The relative position of car 64 changes depending on the position of cars around it.

Will car 64 win the race? Only if its relative position when it crosses the finish line is in front of the other cars.

Look at the train moving down the track. The locomotive is in front of the cars it is pulling. Could the train cars move in front of the locomotive? They could if the train started moving backward. The direction of their motion changes the relative position of objects.

1. ✓**Checkpoint** In what ways can the relative position of an object change?

2. **Social Studies** in Science
   Describe a trip to the lunch room of your school. Use position words.

When the locomotive is pulling the train cars, it is in front of them. When it's pushing the train cars, the locomotive is behind them.

How Fast Things Move

How fast does a jet plane fly? How fast does a caterpillar move? **Speed** is the rate, or how fast, an object changes its position. When things change position, they do so at a certain rate of speed.

Speed can be very fast. A jet plane moves fast. The two arms of the tuning fork are moving back and forth so fast they are just a blur. Did you ever see a meteor flash across the sky? It moves so fast that if you blink, you might miss it.

Speed can also be very slow. Some things have such a slow speed that you can't even see them move. The flowers in the picture have moved to face the light. If you turn the plant around, the flowers will slowly move back to face the light. The thick, syrupy honey is another slow mover. It moves slowly from the scoop down into the jar.

The arms of the tuning fork move back and forth very fast as they vibrate.

Constant Speed

Sometimes moving objects do not change how fast or slow they move. They are moving at a constant speed. Objects that move at a constant speed change position at the same rate. For example, suppose a car is moving steadily on a road at 35 miles an hour. It is moving at constant speed. Its speed, or rate, stays the same.

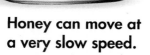

Honey can move at a very slow speed.

These flowers slowly change position as they grow toward the light. This motion is too slow to see.

Variable Speed

If you were in one of the bumper cars, you could change the direction of the car's motion. You could move forward, backward, to the side, or in a circle. You could also change the speed of the bumper car. You might try to bump into another car. You can cover the distance between you and the other car in less time by going faster. Maybe you can get away before the other car can bump into you!

The bumper cars move at a variable speed. Variable means that it changes. An object moving at a variable speed changes speed as it moves.

The bumper cars can move in different directions. They also can move at different speeds.

✓ Lesson Checkpoint

1. List at least three different ways objects can move.

2. What are four kinds of speed?

3. **Summarize** Write a sentence that summarizes what relative position is.

Lesson 2

How does force affect motion?

Forces act on objects to change their motion. A force can involve two or more objects that contact each other. Other kinds of forces can act on an object without touching it.

The Causes of Motion

Did you push or pull on a door today? A **force** is any push or pull. A force can change an object's position or the direction of its motion.

Most of the forces you use are contact forces. When you push or pull an object, you must contact, or touch, the object. For example, the force from a baseball bat, can change the direction and the speed of a ball. If the bat doesn't make contact with the ball, these changes cannot occur.

How much an object changes its direction and speed depends on how much force is used. If you push harder on a moving shopping cart, it will move faster. If a larger force acts on an object, the object will have a greater change in motion.

If the bat makes contact with enough force, the ball's change in speed and direction could take it out of the ballpark.

This shopping cart needs little force to start it moving, but wait until it's full!

Effects of Mass and Friction

How an object moves also depends on how much mass it has. When you start shopping, your cart is empty. You don't need to use much force to push it. As you fill the cart with groceries, it gains mass. You have to use more force to make it move.

As you push your cart along, its wheels rub against the floor. This causes friction. **Friction** is a contact force that goes against motion. Friction can cause a moving object to slow down or stop.

The amount of friction between two objects depends on their surfaces. Pushing a cart over smooth tiles is pretty easy. You need more force to push the cart across a bumpy parking lot. The smooth tile produces less friction on the wheels than the parking lot.

Sometimes friction is a helpful force. Think about a time you were skating or sledding and wanted to slow down or stop. What did you do? If you dragged your foot on the ground, you used friction to slow you down.

1. ✓**Checkpoint** What is a force?

2. **Writing** in Science

   Narrative Make a two-column chart in your **science journal**. Head the first column, *Forces.* Head the second column, *Change.* Fill in the chart with different forces that you have used today. Include how the forces changed the position or speed of objects.

The greater mass of more carts causes you to use more force to get them going.

Motion and Combined Forces

You have learned that pushes, pulls, and friction change the motion of objects. Now, think about pulling on a rope in a game of tug-of-war. Your team's pull is a force in one direction. The pull of the other team is a force in the opposite direction. If the forces are equal, the rope does not move.

How can you win the game? If more people join your team, you can pull with greater force. The pulls of everyone on your team combine to move the rope in your direction. But what if even more people join the other team? Their pulls combine to move the rope in their direction. The rope will move in the direction of the stronger force.

The pulls of the two teams oppose each other. The team pulling with the greater force moves the rope in their direction.

The forces the cyclists are applying to their bikes overcome friction. These forces keep the bikes moving forward.

By shifting his weight, the rider can make the turn without losing speed.

Many forces can cause a bicycle to change its motion. What forces do you use when you ride a bike? Your legs push on the pedals. You shift your weight and push the handlebars to turn. Friction between the bicycle tires and the ground slows your motion. When you go uphill, you have to pedal with more force. Going downhill, you speed up. You use the brakes to slow down. As you move, wind pushes against you. You keep pedaling to keep moving forward.

Each force has its own amount and acts in its own direction. All the forces combine to keep the bicycle going forward safely.

What a workout!

The road produces less friction than the dirt path.

1. ✓ **Checkpoint** What two things about forces are important when forces are combined?

2. **Math in Science** If two pulling forces applied to an object are in the same direction, would the forces be added together or subtracted?

Gravity and Magnetism

The forces you have learned about so far need objects to be touching or in contact. Another kind of force is a non-contact force. A non-contact force is a push or pull that can affect an object without touching it. **Gravity** is a non-contact force that pulls objects toward each other. These skydivers, for instance, are being pulled toward Earth by gravity. Without the force of gravity, they would all float away. Gravity pulls you and everything else on Earth toward Earth's center.

Gravity pulls the skydivers toward the ground.

Gravity pulls the bobsled down the hill. The sled speeds up quickly because the slippery ice surface causes little friction.

SciLinks Take It to the Net
pearsonsuccessnet.com   keyword: gravity
code: g3p336

The amount that gravity pulls on an object is its weight. An object's weight depends on where it is. Since the Moon has less gravity than Earth, for instance, you weigh less on the Moon. The pull of gravity is also less the farther you are from the center of Earth. So you weigh a little less on a mountaintop than you do at the base of the mountain.

The pull of gravity on an object depends on how much matter is in it. Objects with more matter have more mass. So the pull of gravity is greater if the object it is pulling has more mass. Even if the pull of gravity on an object changes, the object's mass remains the same.

Magnetism is another non-contact force. Magnets pull on, or attract, certain kinds of metal such as iron. For example, a strongly magnetic bar might pull a steel paper clip from halfway across your desk. Steel is a metal that has iron in it. Magnets do not attract wood, plastic, paper, or other objects that do not contain these metals.

A magnet does not affect a crayon because the crayon lacks metal that the magnet can attract.

✓ **Lesson Checkpoint**

1. What are three contact forces?

2. What are two non-contact forces?

3. **Math in Science** Denver, Colorado, is more than 1 kilometer above sea level. How would your weight in Denver compare to your weight on an ocean beach? How would your mass compare in both places?

Magnetism attracts these paperclips because they contain iron.

The soccer player applies force to change the direction of the soccer ball. Is work being done?

The snowball appears stuck, despite all the pushing. Is work being done?

Lesson 3

How do simple machines affect work?

Work is done when a force moves an object. Simple machines help you do work more easily.

Work

Have you done any work today? In science *work* has a special meaning. You do **work** when you use a force to move an object. You do work when you move a shopping cart, rake leaves, or carry out the trash. But work can be fun too. You do work when you pedal a bike or kick a soccer ball. The amount of work you do depends on how far you move an object and the mass of the object you move.

Work is NOT done when the position of an object does not change. Imagine pushing a big ball of snow with all the force you can. If the snowball does not move, no work is done. The football players are pushing against each other with as much force as they can. But the players are not moving in the direction they are pushing. No work is being done because none of the players moved.

How much work can you do in one day? To answer this, you would need to add up the amount of pushing and pulling you do. You would also need to measure the distance those pushes and pulls moved things. And you must measure the mass of the objects you moved.

Suppose you put a library book back on its shelf. That would be a certain amount of work. What if you put the book on a shelf that is twice as high? You do twice as much work. What if you move two books to the first shelf? Again you did twice as much work as you did the first time.

When Work Is Done	
Activity	**Work**
Thinking about a math problem	No
Turning a jump rope	Yes
Holding a puppy	No
Lifting a puppy	Yes
Pulling on a locked door	No
Opening an unlocked door	Yes
Trying to scoop rock-hard ice cream	No

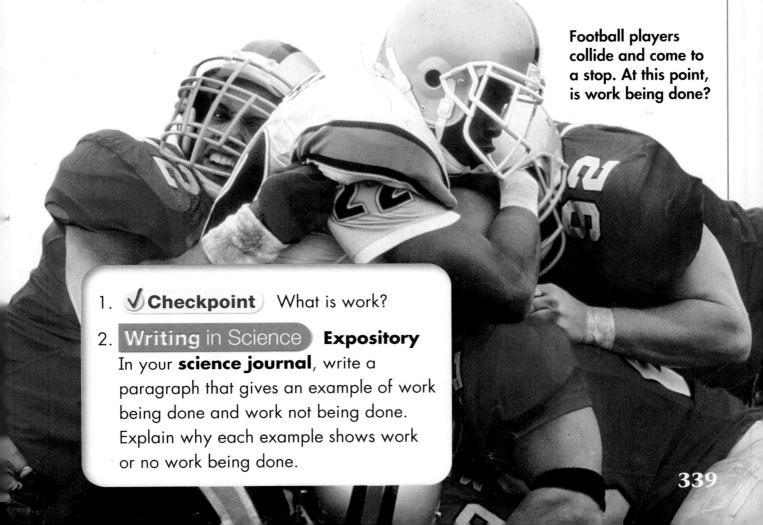

Football players collide and come to a stop. At this point, is work being done?

1. ✓ **Checkpoint** What is work?

2. **Writing in Science** **Expository**
In your **science journal**, write a paragraph that gives an example of work being done and work not being done. Explain why each example shows work or no work being done.

Instead of lifting the cart, the mover pushes the cart up a ramp.

The axe head is a wedge that separates the wood of the log.

Some Simple Machines

Making work easier is the reason for many inventions. Machines don't actually lessen the amount of work that is done. Machines help make work easier. Six kinds of simple machines help you do just that.

Inclined Plane

Look at the man pushing a cart up the ramp. Without the ramp, he would have to lift the cart straight up off the ground high enough to place it in the truck. That would take a great deal of effort. He is using a simple machine called an inclined plane. An inclined plane, or a ramp, is a slanting surface that connects a lower level to a higher level. The mover pushes the cart with less force over a longer distance. He still has the same amount of work to do, but it takes less effort to do it.

Wedge

Wedges are used to split, cut, or fasten things. A wedge is a simple machine made up of two slanted sides that end in a sharp edge. They act as a pair of inclined planes working together. When work is done with a wedge, the wedge moves through the material being worked on. The material separates as it slides up the sides of the wedge. A knife cutting through a pie, and a nail moving through a piece of wood are wedges.

A screw is an inclined plane wrapped around a center post.

This slide is an inclined plane wrapped around a center post. It is a kind of screw!

Screw

A screw is an inclined plane wrapped around a center post. A good example of how a screw looks is the spiral slide in the picture. Do you see how the slide wraps around the center post?

The slide is similar to a screw you use with a screwdriver. Screws can be used to hold things together, and to raise and lower things. When you open a jar, the lid raises if you turn it one way and lowers if you turn it the other way. The jar lid is a screw.

Lever

A seesaw is an example of a simple machine known as a lever. A lever is a stiff bar that rests on a support. A lever is used to lift and move things. If you push down on one side of the bar, you can raise an object on the other side.

A seesaw is a lever that rests on a support.

support

1. ✔ **Checkpoint** What is an inclined plane?

2. 🎯 **Summarize** State briefly how using an inclined plane makes work easier.

More Simple Machines

Wheel and Axle

When you turn a doorknob to open a door, you are using a simple machine called a wheel and axle. The knob is a wheel and the post that attaches to its center is an axle. You would use less force to turn the doorknob a far distance than to turn the axle attached to the knob a shorter distance. This makes opening the door easier, although the work is the same.

A Ferris wheel and merry-go-round use a huge wheel and axle too. Instead of turning the wheel, however, the motor in these rides turns the axle. The distance over which the motor turns the axle is small. But the distance the axle turns the wheel is great. The force applied to the axle to do this must be great. The people on the ride are having fun. They probably are not thinking about the simple machine at work.

What kind of simple machine are the Ferris wheel and merry-go-round?

Pulley

Sailors pull sails to where the sails can fill with wind and push the sailing ship. But the sailors have to move the sails in directions that are uncomfortable for them. Simple machines called pulleys can help them. A pulley changes the direction of motion of an object to which a force is applied. The sail is attached to a pulley. The pulley has a grooved wheel that turns on an axle. The sailors can pull on the rope to turn the grooved wheel. As they pull the rope toward them, the sail is pulled in the proper direction. Now they are ready to hit the high seas!

Pulleys, like those on the boat above, help workers reposition heavy sails.

✓ Lesson Checkpoint

1. How do you know when a simple machine has done work?

2. What simple machine has a grooved wheel, an axle, and a rope?

3. **Summarize** Write a sentence that summarizes how simple machines are useful.

Investigate How much force will you use?

An overpass is an inclined plane.

Materials

string and paperback book

long book

2 books

meter ruler

spring scale

What to Do

1 Tie string around the paperback book.

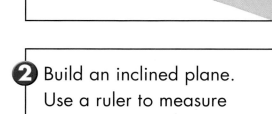

2 Build an inclined plane. Use a ruler to measure its height.

3 Hook a spring scale under the string. Hold the spring scale and lift the book straight up to the height of the inclined plane.

Pull straight up.

The force of gravity pulls the book down. The scale measures the force you used to overcome gravity.

4 **Observe** the reading on the scale. Record.

Process Skills

Before you **predict**, think about what you **observed** and about what you already know.

5 **Predict** what the scale will read when you pull the book up the inclined plane. Record.

6 Holding the scale, pull the book up the inclined plane. Observe the reading on the scale.

If you wish you can construct your ramp out of cardboard or wood.

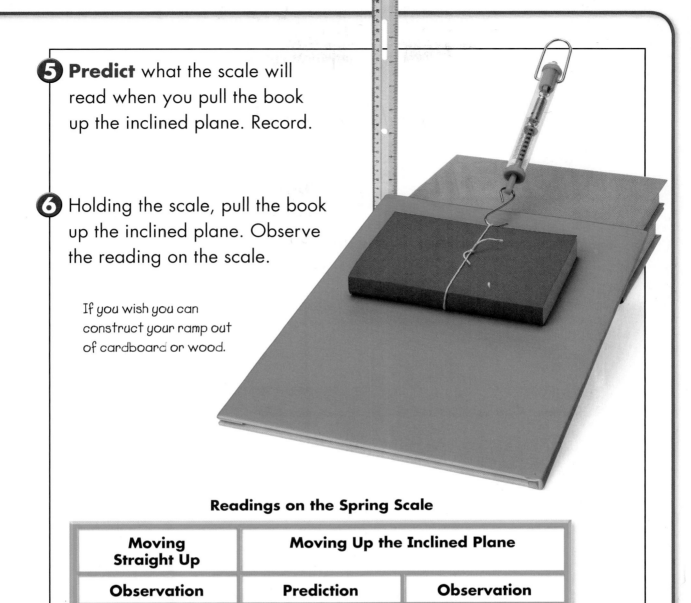

Readings on the Spring Scale

Moving Straight Up	Moving Up the Inclined Plane	
Observation	Prediction	Observation

Explain Your Results

1. What information did you use to make your **prediction**?

2. Compare your **observations**.

3. **Infer** How do you think the steepness of the ramp affected the amount of force needed to pull the book up the ramp.

Go Further

Use your data to predict what would happen to the force if you changed the steepness of the ramp. Make a plan to test your prediction.

Chapter 12 Review and Test Prep

Use Vocabulary

force (page 332)	**motion** (page 327)
friction (page 333)	**position** (page 327)
gravity (page 336)	**relative position** (page 329)
magnetism (page 337)	**speed** (page 330)
	work (page 338)

Use the vocabulary term from the list above that best matches each statement.

1. If an object is in a different location, it has changed _____.

2. An object is in _____ if its position is changing.

3. A force that slows down a moving object is _____.

4. A push or a pull is a _____.

5. How fast an object changes position is its _____.

6. A change in position of one object compared to another object is its _____.

7. The non-contact force of _____ pulls any two objects toward each other.

8. The non-contact force of _____ pulls objects that contain iron.

9. If you use force to move an object, you have done _____.

Explain Concepts

10. Explain how you can tell that an object is in motion.

11. A train is moving 435 kilometers (270 miles) per hour. A plane is flying 965 kilometers (600 miles) per hour. How much faster is the plane moving than the train?

12. Write a paragraph about a simple machine you have used and how it helped you do work.

Process Skills

13. **Infer** what would happen to a thrown baseball if gravity and air friction did not affect it.

14. **Predict** how much more work you would do lifting two identical books compared to lifting just one.

 Summarize

15. Make a graphic organizer like the one below. Fill in the summary.

Work is the force it takes to move an object a certain distance.	The amount of force it takes to move an object is called effort.	Machines change the amount of effort it takes to move an object.

 Test Prep

Choose the letter that best completes the statement or answers the question.

16. Friction is a
- (A) moving object.
- (B) contact force.
- (C) gravitational force.
- (D) magnetic force.

17. What machine is an inclined plane wrapped around a center post?
- (F) lever
- (G) pulley
- (H) wedge
- (I) screw

18. Which of the following describes a constant speed?
- (A) fast, slow, fast
- (B) slow, slower, slowest
- (C) fast, faster, fastest
- (D) fast, fast, fast

19. Explain why the answer you chose for Question 18 is best. For each of the answers you did not choose, give a reason why it is not the best choice.

20. **Writing in Science**
Descriptive Choose one of the skydivers on page 336 and describe the position of that person. Hint: You can use position words such as *to the left of, across from,* and *to the right of.*

Exercising in Space

Do you like to exercise? Running, playing ball, and bicycling are exercises that have motion, speed, and force. But you don't have to be moving to exercise your muscles. Pushing against a wall may not do any work, but the pushing force you use exercises your muscles.

On Earth, the force of gravity helps you exercise. That's because every time you lift your legs or arms, you have to lift them against the force of gravity. So, you have to give your arms and legs force, and that's good exercise. Suppose you are an astronaut aboard the Space Shuttle or the International Space Station. You do not feel the tug of gravity. The very high speed it takes to stay in orbit around the Earth is the reason. It reduces the effect of gravity to zero. You float around the cabin. This makes exercising in space harder than on Earth. Imagine trying to push against a wall on the shuttle. It just sends you off in another direction!

Astronauts have to wear weights on the treadmill used in space.

The cycle machine exercises the heart, legs, and arms.

Without exercise, your muscles and bones get weaker. Astronauts in space must exercise every day to keep their muscles and bones healthy.

Special exercise machines had to be built for space. One kind of machine is like an exercise bicycle. Another machine is like a treadmill. The third kind of machine is like a rowing machine that pushes and pulls on muscles. Astronauts have to be strapped to the machines so they don't float away. Then they put on weights so they can exercise their muscles.

Information learned about muscles and bones in space has helped people on Earth know more about keeping healthy. Many gyms on Earth have exercise machines based on those designed for space. This is just another example of how things developed for use in space can help us here on Earth.

Muscles and bones are made stronger by using the resistance machine.

Lab zone Take-Home Activity

On a piece of paper, design a machine, using pulleys and levers, that allows you to exercise one or more parts of your body.

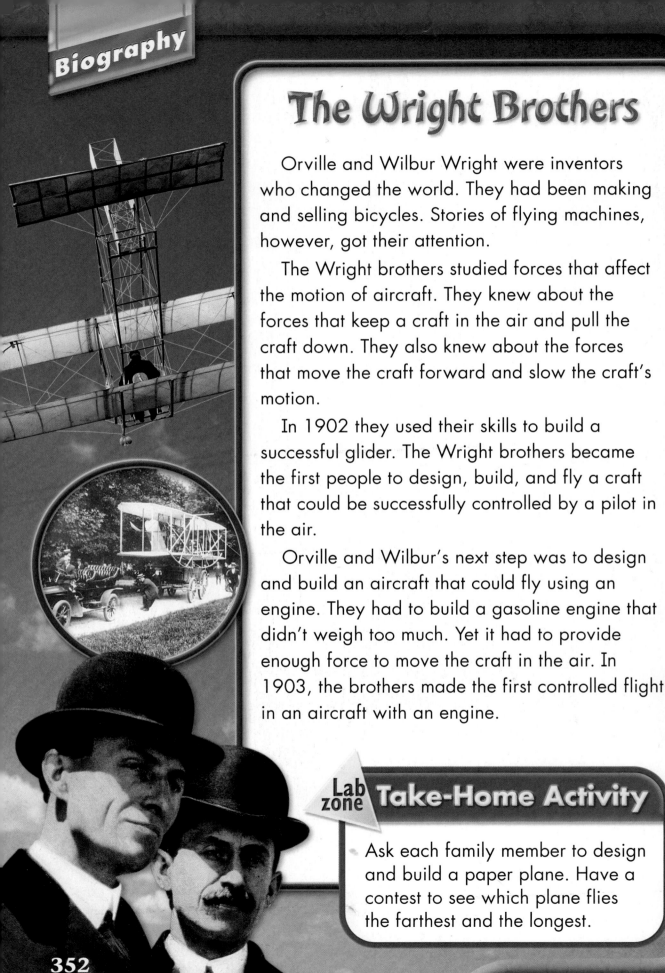

The Wright Brothers

Orville and Wilbur Wright were inventors who changed the world. They had been making and selling bicycles. Stories of flying machines, however, got their attention.

The Wright brothers studied forces that affect the motion of aircraft. They knew about the forces that keep a craft in the air and pull the craft down. They also knew about the forces that move the craft forward and slow the craft's motion.

In 1902 they used their skills to build a successful glider. The Wright brothers became the first people to design, build, and fly a craft that could be successfully controlled by a pilot in the air.

Orville and Wilbur's next step was to design and build an aircraft that could fly using an engine. They had to build a gasoline engine that didn't weigh too much. Yet it had to provide enough force to move the craft in the air. In 1903, the brothers made the first controlled flight in an aircraft with an engine.

Lab zone Take-Home Activity

Ask each family member to design and build a paper plane. Have a contest to see which plane flies the farthest and the longest.

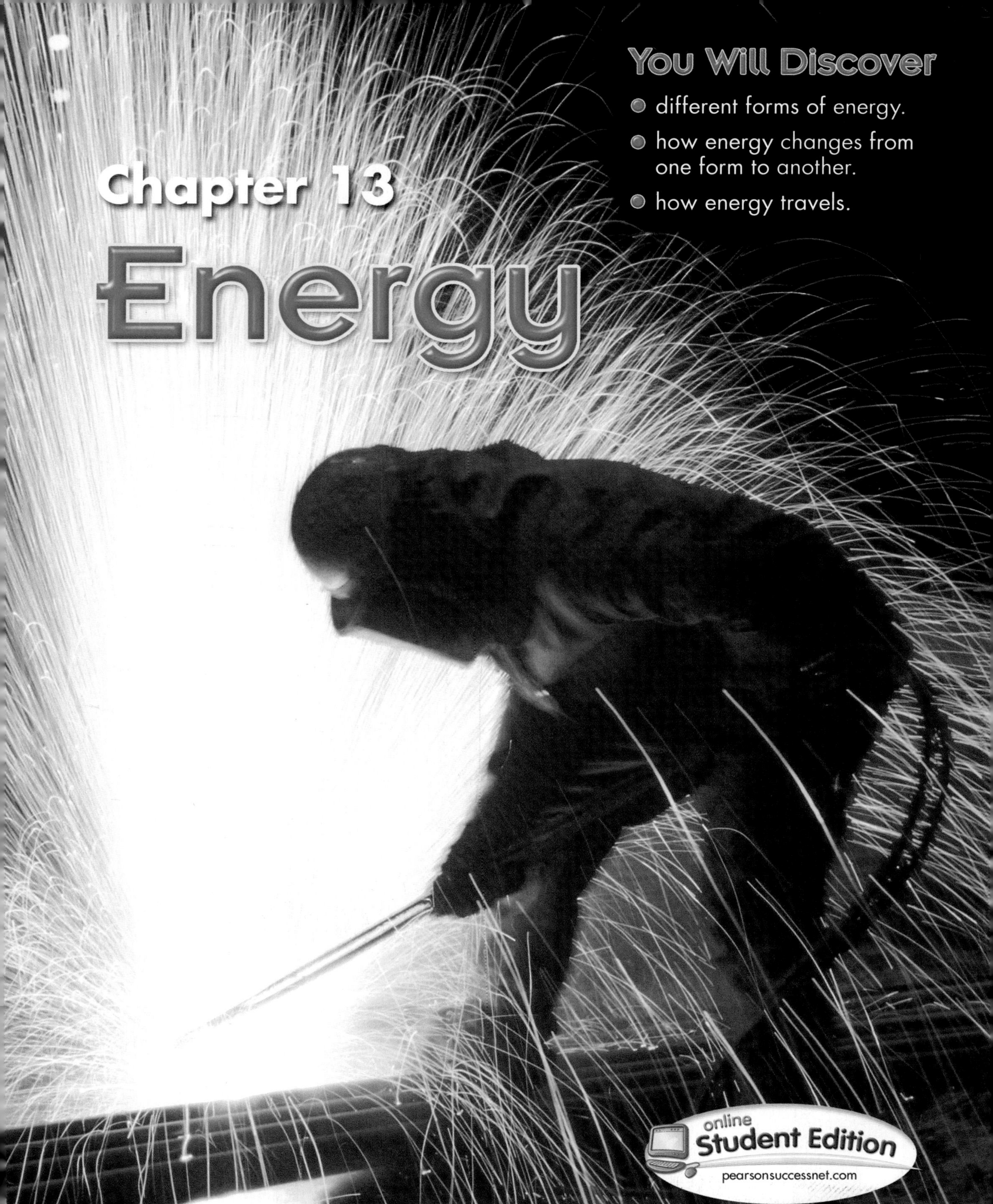

Chapter 13 Energy

You Will Discover

- different forms of energy.
- how energy changes from one form to another.
- how energy travels.

online Student Edition
pearsonsuccessnet.com

🔊 You Are There!

The Sun is shining brightly, but the air outside is cold. You stomp your feet and rub your hands together to warm them. You're looking forward to going inside and warming up. Maybe you'll listen to some music or play a DVD. How many different forms of energy will you use by the end of the day?

Lesson 1

What is energy?

The main source of energy on Earth is the Sun. Energy takes many forms. Energy can be stored and can change form.

Energy

Energy is the ability to do work or to cause change. Remember that work is done when a force makes an object move. You already know about the effects of the Sun's energy. Its warmth makes Earth a place in which we can live. The Sun's light energy makes plants grow. The Sun's energy also causes winds to blow and water to move through the water cycle.

We use many forms of energy in addition to the forms that come directly from the Sun. Electrical energy runs just about everything in this kitchen. Sound energy comes out of your CD player. Chemical energy in fuel runs the engine of a car. The energy of the car's motion gets you to the store. How do all these forms of energy come about?

How many things in this kitchen use energy?

1. ✔**Checkpoint** What are two forms of energy that Earth gets from the Sun?

2. **Writing in Science** **Descriptive** Write a paragraph in your **science journal** about the forms of energy you observe or use on your way to school.

Stored Energy

As you stand ready to jump, run, or ski, your body has stored energy that makes movement possible. Stored energy is **potential energy.** Potential energy changes into another kind of energy if you use it to do work or cause a change.

Oil, coal, natural gas, and gasoline, also have potential energy. The energy stored in these fuels started as sunlight. Long ago, plants used energy from sunlight to make food. After the plants died, they changed into a fossil fuel. When we burn a fuel, we release its potential energy. We use the energy to do work.

Every time you use batteries, you also release potential energy. The stored energy in food, fuels, and batteries is chemical energy.

Position or height stores another kind of potential energy. This energy is gained from gravity. A skier standing at the top of a hill has potential energy of position.

The standing skier has potential energy.

Gasoline contains the stored energy of living things that died long ago.

Batteries store energy as chemical energy.

Energy of Motion

Potential energy can change to kinetic energy. **Kinetic energy** is the energy of motion. A car can move when the potential energy stored in gasoline changes to kinetic energy. Look at the picture of the standing skier. When he pushes off, he goes down the hill. He's in motion. Potential energy the skier had at the top of the hill changes to kinetic energy. The force of gravity pulls him down the hill.

Many sources of energy are renewable. After a day of skiing, the skier can replace the energy he used by eating food. The skier can climb the hill again. You have learned that some sources of energy are not renewable. We cannot easily replace gasoline, natural gas, and other fossil fuels.

WHOOSH!

As the skier slides down the hill, potential energy changes to kinetic energy.

✓ Lesson Checkpoint

1. What are two kinds of potential energy?

2. Give two examples of potential energy and kinetic energy that you see every day.

3. **Main Idea and Details** Use a graphic organizer. What is the main idea of the paragraph at the top of this page? What details support it?

Lesson 2

How does energy change form?

Energy comes in different forms. Energy can change from one form to another. When energy changes form, some energy is given off as heat. People change energy into forms they can easily use, such as electricity.

Living things, such as this tarsier, change chemical energy stored in food to energy of motion and heat.

Changing Forms of Energy

Energy changes into more useful forms all the time. For example, your body stores potential energy as chemical energy. The chemical energy stored in your body changes to kinetic energy as you move.

Using Energy

You can't use the kinetic energy of your moving arm to make a light bulb burn bright. But you can use this kinetic energy to flip a light switch. This, in turn, helps change electrical energy to light energy. Most light bulbs also get hot. Some of the electrical energy changes to a kind of energy felt as heat. Energy cannot change completely from one form to another. Some energy is always given off in the form of heat.

Electrical energy changes to kinetic energy as the cable car moves along the track.

Forms of Energy

Chemical	Motion	Electrical	Light	Thermal

This energy holds the particles of matter together, such as in food. Eating food is the way we get energy.	This is the energy of moving objects. The moving parts in our machines and playground equipment have this form of energy.	This energy can pass through wires. This form of energy can change into forms that run appliances in our homes.	We see the Sun's energy in this form. Plants make food with light energy. We also change other forms of energy into light so we can see.	This form of energy makes particles of matter move faster. We feel this energy as heat.

People also use machines to change forms of energy. The cable car in the picture changes electrical energy to energy of motion. The electric toothbrush in the picture stays in a base that has an electric cord that plugs into an outlet. The electrical energy is stored as chemical energy in the toothbrush's battery. The chemical energy changes back to electrical energy and then to energy of motion when the toothbrush is turned on.

Chemical energy changes to electrical energy, which changes to energy of motion as the toothbrush moves.

1. ✓**Checkpoint** What form of energy do living things change into mechanical energy and thermal energy?

2. **Math** in Science Food energy is measured in Calories. John eats 2,000 Calories in food in a day. How many Calories does he eat in a week?

Ways That Energy Travels

Energy can travel from one place to another. A moving object, such as a baseball, carries energy. You feel the energy when you try to catch the ball. You can tell how much energy the ball has by how hard it hits your hand.

Energy can also travel as waves. Have you ever seen waves of water? These waves carry energy as the baseball does. These waves of energy have the same shape as the waves of a moving rope. Look at the rope on the next page. How would you describe it? Notice that parts of the rope take turns going from side to side. Energy causes this effect as it travels from one end of the rope to the other. The rope itself does not travel forward. Light and certain other forms of kinetic energy move as waves.

Waves in water can be as small as the ripples in the bucket below. Waves caused by hurricanes can be huge. How big the wave is depends on how much energy it carries.

Ocean waves carry energy.

PLOP!

The energy from the falling drop moves in waves across the water. As the waves move away from the source, they lose strength.

Parts of a Wave

You can measure the amount of energy that a wave carries. Look again at the waving rope. One way to measure a wave's energy is by measuring the distance from the midpoint of the wave. The bottom of the wave is called a *trough*. The top of the wave is called a *crest*. Waves with greater distance from the midpoint have more energy. Waves with lesser distance have less energy.

Another way to measure a wave's energy is by measuring the length of the wave. The length of a wave can be the distance from the top of one crest to the top of the next crest. Shorter waves have more energy. Longer waves have less energy.

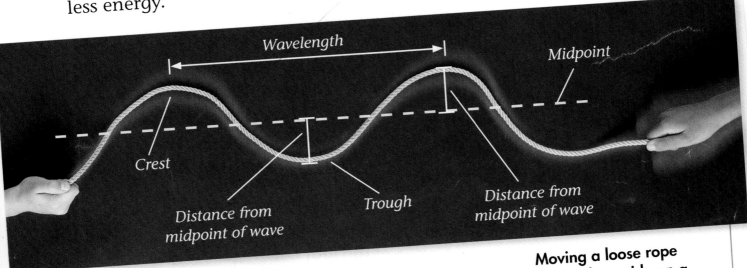

Wavelength

Midpoint

Crest

Distance from midpoint of wave

Trough

Distance from midpoint of wave

Moving a loose rope from side-to-side on a table makes energy move forward along the rope in the form of waves. The rope itself does not travel forward.

✓ **Lesson Checkpoint**

1. Name two types of energy that travel in waves.

2. What happens to energy as it travels away from the source?

3. **Main Idea and Details** Read the paragraph at the top of this page. Use a graphic organizer. What is the main idea? What are the supporting details?

365

Lesson 3

What is heat energy?

Matter contains thermal energy. Thermal e̶n̶e̶r̶g̶y̶

Effects of Heat on Matter

Heat energy affects matter. Think about a cup of liquid water. At 0°C (32°F) water has too little thermal energy to stay in its liquid state. At 0°C, water is a solid called ice.

What happens when you add heat to ice? When the temperature of the air is above 0°C, ice melts. It becomes a liquid.

You can measure the effect of heat on matter. For example, you could record the time ice takes to melt. Look at the stack of ice cubes in the pictures. At 9 A.M. you put the ice cubes in a warm place. At 9:15 A.M. what do you observe? Heat has moved from the air into the ice. You can measure the amount of ice that has melted. At 9:30 A.M. what do you observe? Record the time when all the ice is melted. Measure the volume of melted ice. Calculate the amount of time it takes for a certain amount of ice to melt at a certain temperature. The time is a rough measure of the change caused by heat energy.

This thermometer shows that the temperature inside and outside is about the same.

The change from ice to liquid water is related to a change in temperature.

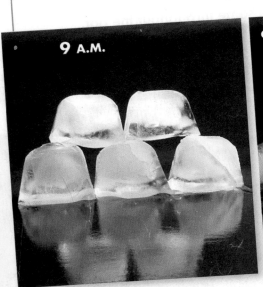

9 A.M.

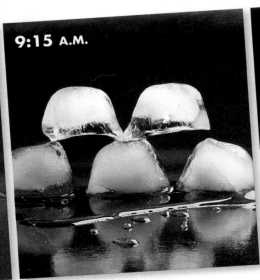

9:15 A.M.

9:30 A.M.

If heat is added to liquid water, it evaporates. It becomes the invisible gas called water vapor. At a temperature of 100°C (212°F), heat makes liquid water boil. Look at the bubbling water. Heat at the bottom of the container makes water expand. Expand means to get bigger. The liquid water expands enough to evaporate. It becomes a hot gas. Bubbles of this gas float to the water's surface. These bubbles break open and release a cloud of hot water droplets.

At 100°C (212°F) heat makes liquid water boil.

Toast Time!
How has heat energy changed this piece of bread?

✓ Lesson Checkpoint

1. What is the main source of heat on Earth?

2. What causes matter to be in a solid, liquid, or gas state?

3. **Writing** in Science
   Descriptive In your **science journal,** write a paragraph that describes how a campfire keeps campers warm on a cold night.

Burning fuels, such as the gas in this gas lamp, can produce light as well as heat.

Electricity in heat lamps makes heat and light. A heat lamp is keeping this meerkat warm.

What is light energy?

Light is a form of energy. We can see some of the ways that light behaves. Light affects some of the properties of matter.

Sources of Light

The Sun is our main source of energy. The Sun's energy travels from the Sun to Earth as waves. The waves have different amounts of energy. We can see or feel the effects of only some of these waves. Light is energy that we can see.

Chemical changes are another source of light. Burning is a chemical change. Candles, campfires, and matches, for instance, give off light as they burn. The lamp in the picture gives off light as the gas burns. The anglerfish's tentacle gives off light too. Chemical changes in the fish's body produce light.

This anglerfish lives deep in the ocean where there is little light. It makes light to attract food.

Electricity is also a source of light. It makes the wire in a light bulb get so hot that it glows and gives off light. Most sources of light are also sources of heat. Heat lamps are used to keep things warm.

The Path of Light

Light travels from its source in straight lines in all directions. Light will continue to travel in this way until it is stopped by an object. Light will not bend or turn corners in order to get around objects. That is why objects that block light's path cause shadows. Shadows are areas behind the objects that are not getting direct light. The length of the shadow depends on the angle of the light. The shadows you have cast may have been taller than you really are!

1. ✓ **Checkpoint** Name three sources of light energy.

2. **Writing** in Science **Narrative** Write a paragraph in your **science journal** telling about the light sources you have seen today. Include what caused the light.

Why do these tables and chairs make shadows in the sunlight?

How Light Changes

You can see through a window and a clear glass of water. These objects do not block all of the light. Most light can pass through objects like these.

If you can see an object, it **reflects** light. This means light bounces in a different direction. Some objects reflect light better than others. A flat, smooth surface reflects light evenly. For example, a mirror reflects light evenly. The light bounces back to your eyes. A smooth lake also reflects light evenly.

What is happening to light in the water droplets in the picture? The droplets **refract**, or bend, the light. Refracted light changes direction. The droplets refract light that bounced off the flowers. The refracted light forms tiny images of the flower. The lens in a telescope refracts light to make big images of objects that looked small. The lenses in your eyes refract light to form images too.

The trees are reflected in the smooth water of the lake.

Each water droplet refracts light. A tiny image of the flower forms.

372

Light refracts because it passes through different materials at different speeds. Light passing through air slows down when it enters water. This causes the straw in the picture to look broken.

Sometimes refraction causes light to separate into its many colors. Then you see a rainbow. Water droplets in the air over a sprinkler refract light this way.

How We See Color

Light is made up of different colors. An object **absorbs**, or takes in, some of the light that hits it. It reflects the rest. Different objects absorb and reflect different colors of light. If an object looks red, it is reflecting red light and absorbing other colors of light. If an object looks white, it is reflecting all the colors of light. If an object looks black, it is absorbing all the colors of light. Dark objects get warmer in sunlight. The light energy they absorb turns to heat.

Water causes light to refract, so the straw looks broken.

✓ Lesson Checkpoint

1. What is the main source of light on Earth?

2. How does a shadow form?

3. **Writing** in Science **Narrative**
   Write a story about light in your **science journal.** Use examples of light being absorbed, reflected, and refracted. Brainstorm with others what your story might include.

Effects of Light

Objects can change light. They can reflect, refract, or absorb it. For instance, in sunlight, this chicken looks mostly white. In turn, light can change objects. How is this green light changing the white chicken?

373

Lesson 5

What is electrical energy?

Matter is made of particles that have electric charges. Electric charges can move as electrical energy through a closed circuit.

Electric Charges

All matter is made up of small particles that have electric charges. An **electric charge** is a tiny amount of energy. Particles have both positive and negative charges. When particles have an equal number of positive and negative charges, they balance each other. The matter has no overall charge. Matter with more negative charges than positive charges has an overall negative charge. Matter with more positive charges than negative charges has an overall positive charge.

A balloon with a balanced charge does not attract the paper pieces.

Lightning is a result of moving electric charges.

374

How Charged Matter Acts

What happens when matter with a negative charge is near matter with a positive charge? The positive and negative charges attract. A negative charge moves toward the positive charge. If you get a shock when you touch someone, negative charges have jumped between you and that person. Lightning is the result of a much bigger jump of charges. Lightning happens when negative electric charges travel within clouds or between clouds and the ground.

The attraction between positive and negative charges can cause objects to stick together. Rubbing a balloon on your hair, for instance, causes the balloon to pick up negative charges. The extra negative charge on the balloon pushes aside the negative charges on one side of a piece of paper. This leaves the side of paper closest to the balloon with a positive charge. The balloon then attracts the positive side of the paper. The paper sticks to the balloon.

Charges that are the same can cause objects to push away from each other. Rubbing two balloons on your hair gives both balloons the same charge. The balloons then push apart.

Rubbing the balloon gives it an electric charge. It attracts objects with the opposite charge. It pushes away objects with the same charge.

1. ✓**Checkpoint** What causes lightning?

2. **Art** in Science Draw a picture of two balloons that shows what happens when one balloon has a positive charge and the other balloon has a negative charge.

Electric Currents and Circuits

Electric current is the movement of electrical energy or electric charge from one place to another. Lightning is an uncontrolled electric current. Lightning can travel in any direction. To be useful, an electric current must travel in a planned way through wires or other materials. This way, electric current can turn on lights or make a CD player work.

Batteries or an outlet that you can plug a cord into are good sources of electrical energy. The path that a controlled electric current flows through is an **electric circuit.** The path must be unbroken for the energy to flow through it. Find the switch in the picture. The switch is on, or closed, so the circuit is unbroken. Electrical energy can flow through the wires of the circuit. If the switch was off, or open, the current could not flow through the circuit.

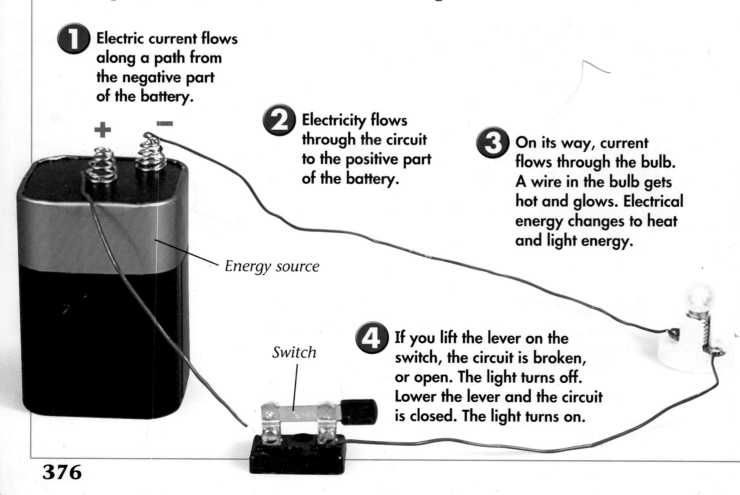

1 Electric current flows along a path from the negative part of the battery.

2 Electricity flows through the circuit to the positive part of the battery.

3 On its way, current flows through the bulb. A wire in the bulb gets hot and glows. Electrical energy changes to heat and light energy.

Energy source

Switch

4 If you lift the lever on the switch, the circuit is broken, or open. The light turns off. Lower the lever and the circuit is closed. The light turns on.

How Electrical Energy Changes Form

	Light	Electricity passes through bulbs of all kinds. Bulbs change electrical energy to light so we can see at night. Some heat is given off.
	Heat	Electricity passes through coils in heaters. Coils change electrical energy to heat so we can be warm in winter, or cook our food.
	Sound	Electricity passes around a magnet. The magnet changes electrical energy to vibrations of plastic discs in headphone speakers. Then we can hear music.
	Magnetic Force	Electricity passes around a huge magnet. The moving electricity makes a magnetic field that attracts metal containing iron to the magnet. The magnet can be used to lift heavy cars.

We rely on electricity for most of our everyday needs. We therefore spend a great deal of effort changing sources of energy into electricity. We change the power of moving water into electricity. We turn the heat of burning coal into electricity. We even turn sunlight into electricity. What happens to electricity once it gets to our homes? Study the table above. Can you imagine not having electricity?

✓ Lesson Checkpoint

1. What is the difference between a controlled and an uncontrolled electric current? Give an example of each.

2. What happens when an electric circuit is open?

3. **Main Idea and Details** Describe the path of electricity through a simple electric circuit.

Investigate Do freshwater ice and saltwater ice melt the same way?

Materials

2 cups and masking tape

water and graduated cylinder (or measuring cup)

spoon and salt

2 thermometers

tub with very warm water (for Day 2)

timer or stopwatch (or clock with a second hand)

Process Skills

By making careful **observations** of ice melting and by **collecting data** and organizing it into a chart, you learned how salt affects the melting of ice.

What to Do

1 Label one cup *fresh water*. Add 100 mL of water.

2 Label the other cup *salt water*. Add 100 mL of water and 1 spoonful of salt. Stir.

3 Place a thermometer in each cup. Your teacher will put the cups in a freezer overnight.

4 After the water is frozen, record the temperature in each cup.

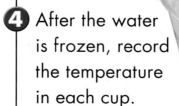

5 Put both cups in a tub of very warm water.
Observe the temperature in each cup until
all the ice in the cup melts.
Record the temperature
every minute.

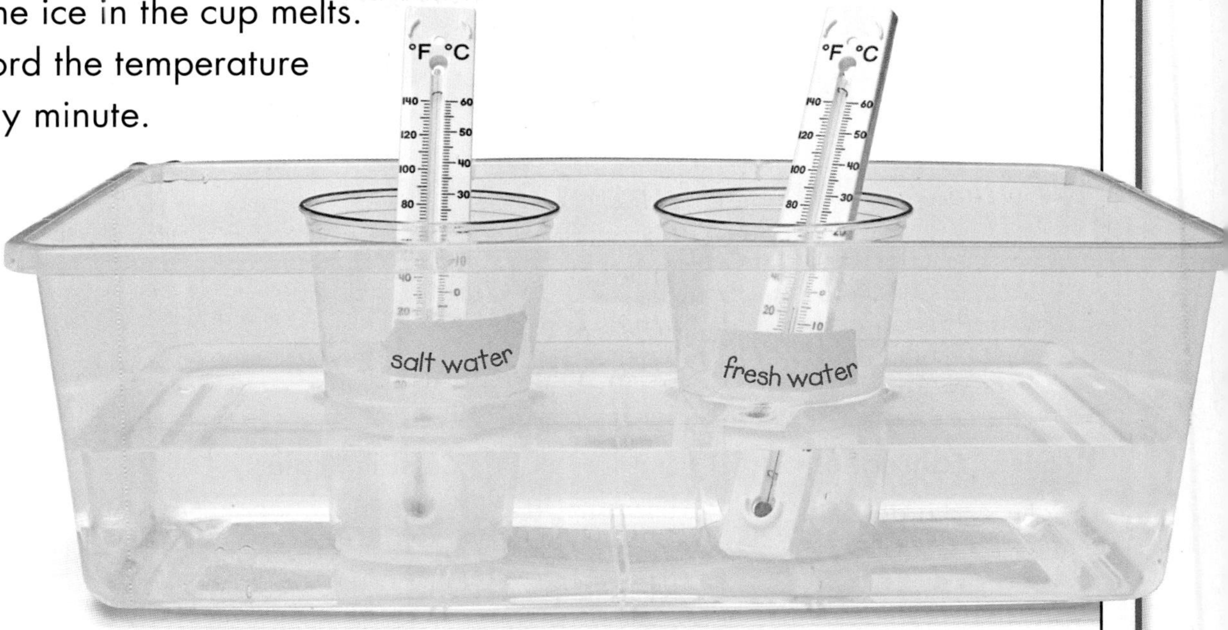

salt water

fresh water

6 Construct a chart or table to help you **collect** your **data**.

Melting Time of Ice

Time (minutes)	Temperature of Salt Water (°C)	Temperature of Fresh Water (°C)
0 (start)		
1		
2		
3		

Make a graph if you think it will better help you interpret the data.

Explain Your Results

1. You put the cups of ice in warm water. This added energy to the frozen water. Heat moved from the warm water to the ice. How did the temperature in each cup change? Look at your chart. Describe the pattern of change.

2. Based on your **observations**, in which cup did the ice finish melting first?

Go Further

How would adding more salt to the water affect how fast the ice would melt? Investigate to find out.

Measuring Temperature

Recording temperature is one way to measure thermal energy. You can use different scales to measure temperature.

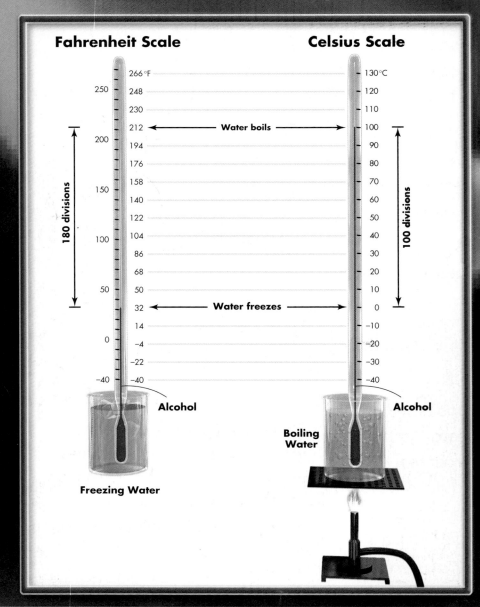

Fahrenheit Scale

Celsius Scale

180 divisions

100 divisions

266°F — Water boils — 130°C

Water boils

Water freezes

Alcohol

Alcohol

Boiling Water

Freezing Water

eTools Take It to the Net
pearsonsuccessnet.com

The Celsius scale is often used in science. The Fahrenheit scale is often used in everyday life, such as reading the temperature outdoors. Sometimes both scales are used.

Degrees Celsius is written °C. So 40°C is read "forty degrees Celsius."

Degrees Fahrenheit is written °F. So 40°F is read "forty degrees Fahrenheit."

1 What is the boiling point of water on the Celsius scale? What is the boiling point on the Fahrenheit scale?

2 What is the freezing point of water on the Celsius scale? What is the freezing point of water on the Fahrenheit scale?

3 About what is the temperature in degrees Fahrenheit when it is 30°C?

Lab zone Take-Home Activity

Watch the weather report on TV. Are temperatures given in degrees Fahrenheit, Celsius, or both? Make a list of three cities talked about in the report. Write down their temperatures in degrees Fahrenheit and in degrees Celsius. You can use the thermometers shown here.

Use Vocabulary

absorb (page 373)	**potential energy** (page 360)
electric charge (page 374)	**reflect** (page 372)
electric circuit (page 376)	**refract** (page 372)
electric current (page 376)	**thermal energy** (page 366)
kinetic energy (page 361)	

Use the term from the list above that best completes each sentence.

1. Energy that has the ability to cause a change is _____.

2. A lens causes light to bend or _____.

3. The energy of motion is _____.

4. Objects _____ light that they take in.

5. The path that a controlled electric current flows through is a(n) _____.

6. Two balloons will push away from each other if they have the same _____.

7. Mirrors work because they _____ light.

8. A(n) _____ is the movement of electrical energy from one place to another.

9. The total energy of all the particles in an object is the amount of _____ the object has.

Explain Concepts

10. Explain how to measure the energy in a wave.

11. Describe how light energy travels.

12. If an object has a temperature of 10°C and the air around it is 20°C, will the object gain or lose heat energy? Explain your answer.

Process Skills

13. **Infer** What would happen to the electric current if the part of the light bulb that glows breaks?

14. **Predict** You are having hot soup for lunch. You put a metal spoon in your soup and leave it for a minute. Predict what will happen to the spoon.

Main Idea and Details

15. Make a graphic organizer like the one shown below. Fill in details that support the main idea.

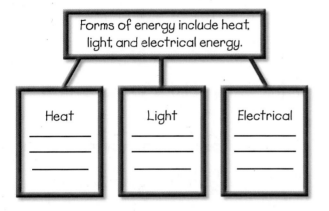

Forms of energy include heat, light, and electrical energy.

Heat	Light	Electrical

Test Prep

Choose the letter that best completes the statement or answers the question.

16. What kind of energy is stored in a battery?

Ⓐ kinetic
Ⓑ light
Ⓒ chemical
Ⓓ thermal

17. What color is an object if it reflects blue?

Ⓕ red
Ⓖ blue
Ⓗ yellow
Ⓘ orange

18. A dark towel that is placed in the sunlight feels warm because it

Ⓐ reflects the Sun's rays.
Ⓑ refracts the Sun's rays.
Ⓒ absorbs the Sun's rays.
Ⓓ allows the Sun's rays to pass through.

19. Explain why the answer you chose for Question 18 is best. For each of the answers you did not choose, give a reason why it is not the best choice.

20. **Writing** in Science

Descriptive Write a paragraph that describes different forms of energy.

Electrical Engineer

You know your house needs electricity to run smoothly. Have you ever thought about how important providing electricity is during space missions?

Barbara Kenny has. She is an electrical engineer who works for NASA on ways to change other kinds of energy into electricity to run spacecraft.

While in orbit, for example, a spacecraft spends part of its time in sunlight. Solar panels gather light and change it to electricity used to run the ship. The spacecraft spends the rest of its time in the shadow of the Earth where there is no sunlight. How does it get electricity then?

Dr. Kenny designs generators that make electricity. One kind uses a heavy wheel called a flywheel. While in sunlight, motors make this wheel spin quickly. The kinetic energy from spinning is used to generate electricity while the spacecraft is in the dark.

Electrical engineers obtain a college degree.

Dr. Barbara Kenny is an engineer who works with forms of energy.

Lab zone Take-Home Activity

If you were an electrical engineer for NASA, what special kind of electrical equipment would you design? How would it be used?

EC CRU 10 9 8 7 6 5 4 3 2 1

Chapter 14
Sound

You Will Discover

- how different kinds of sound are produced.
- how sound energy and matter interact.
- how sound travels through different materials.

online
Student Edition
pearsonsuccessnet.com

How does energy produce the sounds we hear?

vibration

pitch

386

compression wave

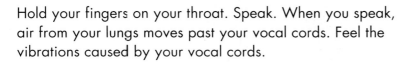
Explore How can you see sound vibrations?

Hold your fingers on your throat. Speak. When you speak, air from your lungs moves past your vocal cords. Feel the vibrations caused by your vocal cords.

Materials

safety goggles

cup

plastic wrap

rubber band

salt

metric ruler

Process Skills

When you make **observations** and show them in a chart, you are **collecting data**.

What to Do

1 Make a vibration viewer.

Be careful!

Wear safety goggles.

Sprinkle a little salt on top.

Tightly cover a cup with plastic wrap. Hold it on with a rubber band.

2 Look down at the cup from 3 cm away. Talk softly and loudly. Use a high pitch and a low pitch. Observe how loudness and pitch affect what the salt does.

Optional: If musical instruments are available, observe the vibrations made as you blow, pluck, or tap a musical instrument. Discuss and compare the ways you change pitch and the ways the vibrations change.

Explain Your Results

Collect Data Make a chart to show what you **observed**.

How to Read Science

TARGET SKILL

Compare and Contrast

When you **compare** things, you tell how they are alike. When you **contrast** things, you tell how they are different.

- Writers sometimes use clue words such as *similar*, *alike*, *all*, *both*, or *in the same way* when they compare things.

- Writers sometimes use clue words such as *different*, *unlike*, or *in a different way* when they contrast things.

You can use what you have already **observed** about how instruments sound to help you compare and contrast.

Advertisement

Sound Machines

All our instruments are alike in one way. Vibrate them and you'll get music! But the sounds and how they are made are very different. How are the sounds alike and different? Come try them out!

Apply It!

The advertisement above asks you to **compare and contrast.** Tell how the sounds of the instruments are alike and different. Use a graphic organizer to compare and contrast.

Different   Alike   Different

◀)) You Are There!

You are in the middle of a huge celebration. Everyone is watching the parade and listening to the marching bands. Thousands of people are in the crowd. Horns are honking. People are cheering. You know that later, after it's dark, the fireworks will make different sounds. What's the reason for all this sound? It's the Fourth of July!

AudioText ◀))

Lesson 1

What causes sounds?

Sounds are all around you. You enjoy some sounds, like music. But other sounds hurt your ears. All sounds are made when matter moves.

Noisemakers like these are sometimes used on New Year's Eve. What kind of sounds do they make?

Suppose you are taking a walk in a city. You might hear the loud sounds of car horns and garbage trucks. You might hear the soft sound of your friend's voice. If you are taking a walk in the country, you might hear the loud sounds of farm tractors. You might also hear cows mooing. In a forest, you might hear the soft sounds of water trickling in a creek and the sounds of birds chirping.

Some of these sounds might be pleasant to you. Others might bother you. Some noises, like the sound of a jet plane taking off, might even hurt your ears. The sounds we hear every day are different. Yet all sounds are alike in some ways.

1. ✓**Checkpoint** Describe some ways that sounds are alike and different.

2. **Writing in Science** **Descriptive** In your **science journal,** write two paragraphs about the sounds you hear every day. Tell why you think the sounds are pleasant or unpleasant.

A tambourine makes sounds when you hit it with your hand or shake it.

The Causes of Sound

Sounds happen when matter moves back and forth very quickly. A back-and-forth movement is called a **vibration.** Sounds happen only when something vibrates.

Suppose you are listening to these instruments being played. You would hear high sounds and low sounds. **Pitch** describes how high or low a sound is. Objects that vibrate slowly make sounds with a low pitch. Objects that vibrate more quickly make sounds with a higher pitch.

When a drum or cymbal is struck, it vibrates and makes a sound. Different sizes and shapes of drums produce sounds with different pitches.

SciLinks
Take It to the Net
pearsonsuccessnet.com

keyword: vibration
code: g3p392

Hitting or Plucking to Make Sound

Percussion instruments make sound when they are hit. Steel drums are played by tapping them with a rubber hammer. Other drums are played with wooden sticks, metal brushes, or the hands.

If you lightly tapped a drum, you would hear a soft sound. If you hit the drum harder, you would hear a louder sound. The harder you hit the drum, the farther the drumhead moves back and forth. The vibrations become stronger. The loudness of the sound depends on the strength of the vibrations.

Stringed instruments make sound when the strings are plucked or when a bow is rubbed across the strings. The pitch of the sound each string makes depends on how long, thick, and tightly stretched it is. The short, thin, and tight strings make faster vibrations. So the sounds they make have higher pitches.

When a musician plucks the harp strings, they vibrate. The vibrations make sound.

This instrument makes sounds when it is hit with a rubber hammer. The vibrations of the blocks make sounds.

1. **✓ Checkpoint** How is sound made?

2. **Compare and Contrast** How are the sounds produced by different strings of a harp alike and different?

Using Air to Make Sound

The sound of your voice also comes from vibrations. You are able to speak and sing because your vocal cords vibrate. When you speak, your vocal cords tighten. They vibrate as air passes between them. The tighter your vocal cords get, the higher the pitch of your voice becomes.

Wind instruments make sounds when air inside them vibrates. You make sounds with a trumpet by blowing into it and vibrating your lips. This makes the air inside the trumpet vibrate also.

You can change the pitch of a trumpet's sound in two ways. One way is to change how your lips vibrate. The other way is to press on the valves of the trumpet. This changes the length of the vibrating air column inside the trumpet.

Place your fingers lightly across your throat. Then hum. Can you feel your vocal cords vibrate?

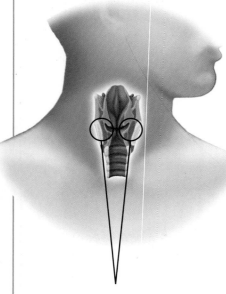

Vocal cords are two pairs of thin tissue in the windpipe.

The trumpet makes sounds when the player blows air into it. The player's lips vibrate against the mouthpiece of the trumpet.

An oboe is also a wind instrument. It has a double reed at the top. A reed is a thin piece of wood. The player blows on the reeds, making them vibrate. This vibration makes the air inside the oboe vibrate and make a sound. Pressing keys on the oboe changes the pitch of the sound.

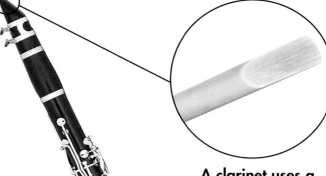

A harmonica has several metal reeds that vibrate when a person blows air across them.

A saxophone has a longer air column than a clarinet. So the sounds it makes have lower pitches than the sounds a clarinet can make.

A clarinet uses a single wooden reed like this one. The reed presses on the player's lower lip and vibrates when the player blows air across it.

This clarinet produces its lowest note when all the holes are covered. Uncovering the last hole makes the air column shorter. Then the pitch of the sound is higher.

✔ **Lesson Checkpoint**

1. What makes the vocal cords vibrate?

2. What are two ways that sounds can be different?

3. **Writing** in Science **Descriptive** Write a paragraph in your **science journal** describing how guitar strings with different lengths make music with different sounds.

395

Sound waves from the jackhammer have a lot of energy. The greatest energy is near the jackhammer.

1. ✔ **Checkpoint** How does sound travel?

2. **Compare and Contrast** How are the sound of a jackhammer and the sound of the little bells alike and how are they different?

397

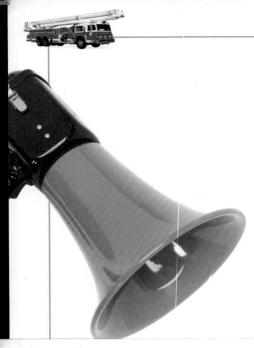

Lesson 2

How does sound travel?

Sound travels through matter. You can hear the sound of a fire engine several blocks away. But if you were on the Moon, you would not be able to hear anything. The Moon has no atmosphere, and sound

The speed of sound through air is about 340 meters per second. You would hear the sound of this bell in less than $\frac{1}{100}$ second if you were 3 m away.

Sound and Matter

Sound travels only through matter. There is no matter between stars and planets in outer space. So there is no sound in space. Sound moves through solids, liquids, and gases. The speed of sound depends on what kind of matter it is traveling through.

Air is made of gases. The particles in gases are farther apart than in liquids and solids. So it takes longer for one gas particle to hit another and move the sound energy along. Particles in liquids are closer together. Water is a liquid. So sound travels more quickly in water than it does in air. Particles in solids are even closer together. Sound travels quickest through a solid.

Echoes

You hear an echo when sound waves strike an object and then bounce back. Ships with sonar equipment send sound waves to the ocean bottom. Equipment measures how long it takes the sound to bounce back. Sound waves travel about 1,530 meters per second in seawater. Scientists can use this to find the depth of the ocean.

The particles in a solid are close together. So sound waves travel quickest in solids. When you use a tin-can telephone, sound waves travel quickly through the string from one can to the other.

Speed of Sound	
Material	**Speed (meters per second)**
Solid—Steel	5,200
Liquid—Seawater	1,530
Gas—Air	340

If you watch fireworks from far away, you see the flash before you hear the sound. That is because light travels much faster than sound.

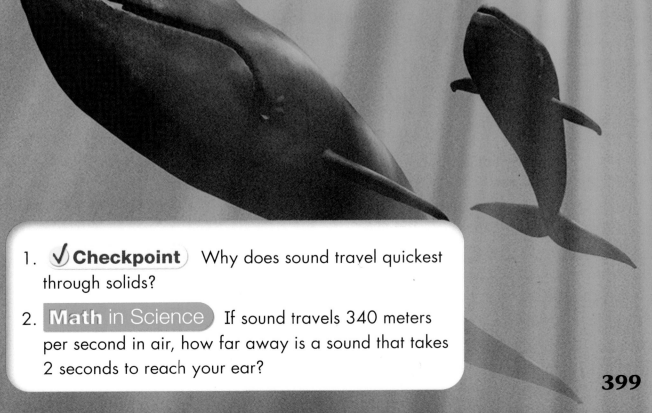

Whales use sounds to communicate with one another underwater. Some whales make sounds that can be heard hundreds of kilometers away!

1. **✓ Checkpoint** Why does sound travel quickest through solids?

2. **Math in Science** If sound travels 340 meters per second in air, how far away is a sound that takes 2 seconds to reach your ear?

The Ear

We hear sounds because of our ears. Our ears receive sound waves. The waves travel along a path toward our brain. The brain receives signals that we recognize as sounds.

Eardrum

Inside the ear, the sound waves hit the eardrum. The eardrum is a thin, skin-like layer stretched across the inside of the ear. When sound hits the eardrum, it begins to vibrate.

Little Bones

Three tiny bones touch the eardrum. When the eardrum vibrates, it makes these bones vibrate. These bones are part of the middle part of the ear.

Outer Ear

The part of the ear that you can see collects sound waves traveling in air.

Humans cannot hear some of the sounds that other animals can hear.

Inner Ear

The inner ear has a part that is shaped like a shell. It is filled with liquid. The movement of the tiny bones makes tiny hairs in the liquid vibrate. The hairs are attached to nerves that carry signals to the brain. This is how we hear.

Zebras make sounds by vibrating their vocal cords, lips, and nostrils.

Many kinds of insects make sounds by rubbing body parts together. This katydid makes chirping sounds by rubbing its wings together.

Most people know the sounds made when animals vibrate their vocal cords. Most have heard a dog's bark or a cow's moo. But not all animals make sounds by using only vocal cords. Woodpeckers use their beaks to tap out sounds on tree trunks. The vibrating wings of bees and mosquitoes make buzzing sounds.

Some bats send out high-pitched clicking sounds that people cannot hear. These sounds bounce off insects and return to the bats' ears. This is how bats find their food.

A male seal can roar loudly at other males. Seals use sound to defend their resources.

✓ Lesson Checkpoint

1. What path do sound waves follow through the ear?

2. How do some insects make sounds?

3. **Art** in Science Draw a picture of a musical instrument or an animal making a sound. Label your drawing to tell how the sound is made and how it travels.

Chimpanzees make many different sounds. They grunt, bark, squeak, scream, and even laugh.

Investigate How well does sound travel through different materials?

Materials

resealable plastic bags

block of wood

water

unsharpened pencil

What to Do

1 Prepare the bags.

Fill a bag with air by blowing into it. Seal tightly.

Fill another bag $\frac{1}{2}$ full with water. Squeeze out any air. Seal tightly.

Put the block of wood into a third bag. Squeeze out any air. Seal tightly.

Process Skills

You **infer** when you use your **observations** to put materials in order from best to poorest carrier of sound.

2 If necessary, roll down the top of the bag to make it puff up. Hold it against your ear. Cover your other ear with your hand. Listen as your partner taps the bag gently with the pencil eraser. Then repeat the test using the bag with water and the bag with wood.

What part of your body is the receiver of sound vibrations?

3 Compare the sounds you heard. Record your **observations**. Which was loudest? Which was softest?

How Well Sound Travels Through Different Materials

Material	Observations (soft, louder, loudest)
air (gas)	
water (liquid)	
wood (solid)	

Explain Your Results

1. Did the tapping seem loudest through air (gas), water (liquid), or wood (solid)?

2. **Infer** Compare how well sound travels through different materials. Arrange the materials in order from the best carrier of sound to the poorest carrier of sound.

Go Further

How can you use a sound recorder to help collect data about the way sound travels through different materials? Make a plan to investigate.

Math in Science

Comparing Speeds of Sound

You know that sound waves travel at different speeds through different types of matter. Sound travels most slowly through gases and most quickly through solids. But what about the same kind of matter? Does sound travel through plastic and through steel at different speeds, even though they are both solids?

The table below shows that sound waves travel at different speeds through different solids. For example, sound travels at 2,680 meters per second through silver. Sound travels almost twice that speed through steel. Out of all the solids in the table, sound travels most slowly through plastic.

Speed of Sound through Solids	
Material	**Speed** (meters per second)
Plastic	1,800
Silver	2,680
Gold	3,240
Copper	3,560
Brick	3,650
Oak wood	3,850
Glass	4,540
Iron	5,130
Steel	5,200

Sound also travels at different speeds through the same material at different temperatures. The table below shows the speed of sound through air at different temperatures. Use the table to answer the questions.

Speed of Sound through Air	
Air Temperature (°C)	Speed (meters per second)
0	332
10	338
20	343
30	349

1 At which temperature do sound waves travel most slowly through air?

A. 0°C   B. 10°C   C. 20°C   D. 30°C

2 How much more quickly do sound waves travel through air at 20°C than at 0°C?

F. 8 $\frac{m}{s}$ G. 11 $\frac{m}{s}$ H. 13 $\frac{m}{s}$ I. 14 $\frac{m}{s}$

3 During which season do you think sound travels most quickly in air?

A. spring   B. summer   C. fall   D. winter

Lab zone Take-Home Activity

Find a very thick book. Hold the book against one ear while someone taps the other side of the book. Do you hear the sound with your ear touching the book before you hear it with your other ear? Explain the difference.

Chapter 14 Review and Test Prep

Use Vocabulary

compression wave (page 396)	**pitch** (page 392)
	vibration (page 392)

Use the term from the list above that best completes each sentence.

1. _____ describes how high or low a sound is.

2. A back-and-forth movement that causes sound is called a _____.

3. A sound wave is a kind of _____.

Explaining Concepts

4. How can guitar strings with different lengths make music that has different sounds?

5. Explain how covering your ears can keep you from hearing a sound.

6. Why does sound travel more slowly through air than it does through water?

7. Explain how people make sounds when they talk.

8. Explain how an oboe makes musical sounds.

Process Skills

9. Infer what happens if you sprinkle confetti on a drumhead and then hit the drum with a drumstick.

10. Suppose you place a rubber band around a book. You place two pencils under the rubber band to hold it up. Then you pluck the rubber band between the pencils. **Predict** how the pitch of the sound will change when the pencils are moved closer together and then farther apart.

11. The loudness of sounds is measured in units called decibels. Sounds with levels between 60 and 84 decibels can be annoying. Sounds above 85 decibels can harm your hearing. Look at the chart below. **Classify** each sound as annoying or harmful.

Sound	Loudness (in decibels)
Jet plane	150
Lawn mower	80
Rock band	110
Vacuum cleaner	70

12. Infer how sonar might be used to protect a ship from going into water that is too shallow.

Compare and Contrast

13. Use a graphic organizer to show how the sounds made by a car horn and a song bird are alike and different.

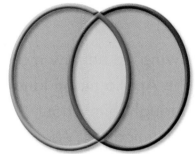

Test Prep

Choose the letter that best completes the statement or answers the question.

14. Which part of the ear collects sound waves?

    Ⓐ eardrum   Ⓑ outer ear
    Ⓒ nerve   Ⓓ bones

15. Hitting a drum harder will make the sound

    Ⓕ louder.
    Ⓖ the same.
    Ⓗ softer.
    Ⓘ lower in pitch.

16. Sound waves travel fastest through

    Ⓐ solids.   Ⓑ liquids.
    Ⓒ air.   Ⓓ gases.

17. A special nerve inside the head carries messages from the ear to the

    Ⓕ eardrum.
    Ⓖ brain.
    Ⓗ tiny bones.
    Ⓘ outer ear.

18. If a guitar string vibrates slowly it will have a pitch that is

    Ⓐ high.
    Ⓑ soft.
    Ⓒ low.
    Ⓓ loud.

19. Which instrument is a percussion instrument?

    Ⓕ harp
    Ⓖ clarinet
    Ⓗ trumpet
    Ⓘ cymbal

20. **Writing** in Science

Narrative Suppose that you are a sound wave. Write a story describing how you were produced, how you traveled, and how you were heard.

Dr. Clifton Horne

If you have been in an airport, you know that planes can make a lot of noise. Some scientists are working on ways to make planes quieter. Clifton Horne, NASA Aerospace Engineer, is doing just that.

Dr. Horne uses many microphones and computers to find the direction to the noise source in a jet plane engine and to find out how to make it quieter. Clifton Horne said, "…in the next 10 years we should be able to … fly on airplanes that people on the ground can see but hardly hear."

While Clifton was growing up he saw many exciting things, such as the Apollo moon landings. He enjoyed hobbies that taught him about astronomy and radio communication. As a result, Clifton decided to become an aerospace engineer.

Dr. Horne says that his English classes, as well as math and science classes, have been very useful in his career. Scientists, including Dr. Horne, spend much time writing and working together in groups. So, the communication skills that Dr. Horne learned in his English classes are very important to him.

Dr. Clifton Horne uses test engines like the one above in the wind tunnel at NASA's Ames Research Center.

Lab zone Take-Home Activity

People use sound to communicate, to entertain, and to warn of danger. Research a career in industries where sound is important.

Unit C Test Talk

Use Information from Text and Graphics

Information in text, pictures, and diagrams can help you answer test questions. Read the text and study the graphics. Then answer the questions.

The diagrams show how the particles in solids, liquids, and gases are connected. The captions explain how the particles in solids, liquids, and gases are connected and how they move.

The particles of a solid are firmly connected. They jiggle in place.

The particles of a liquid are loosely connected. They flow past one another.

Gas particles are not connected. They bounce off one another and move freely.

Use What You Know

To answer the questions, find the information in the captions and the graphics. Read each question and decide which answer choice is best.

1. A solid has particles that are
- Ⓐ loosely connected.
- Ⓑ not connected.
- Ⓒ firmly connected.
- Ⓓ connected in pairs.

2. A liquid has particles that
- Ⓕ stay in place.
- Ⓖ flow past one another.
- Ⓗ move freely.
- Ⓘ move in pairs.

3. Which statement describes gas particles?
- Ⓐ They are packed closer together than liquid particles.
- Ⓑ They are firmly connected.
- Ⓒ They are connected in groups.
- Ⓓ They are farther apart than solid or liquid particles.

409

Unit C Wrap-Up

Chapter 10

What are the properties of matter?

- Matter takes up space, has mass, and has other properties that can be observed.
- Mass, volume, density, and length are some properties of matter that can be measured.

Chapter 11

What are physical and chemical changes in matter?

- Matter can change in its size, shape, or state during a physical change.
- During a chemical change, matter changes into new kinds of matter.

Chapter 12

How do forces cause motion and get work done?

- Forces cause a change in motion and work to be done by changing an object's speed or direction.
- Contact forces change motion only by touching objects. The forces of gravity and magnetism can change an object's motion without touching it.

Chapter 13

How does energy change form?

- Potential energy can change to kinetic energy and kinetic energy can change to potential energy.
- Energy can transfer between the forms of light, electrical, thermal, sound, chemical, mechanical, and magnetic energy.

Chapter 14

How does energy produce the sounds we hear?

- Sound is produced by the energy of vibrating matter traveling as compression waves.
- The pitch of a sound depends on how fast an object vibrates.

Performance Assessment
Identify Electric Charges

Use a wool cloth and balloons to show what happens when objects have different charges. What happens when you move two balloons with no charge toward each other? How can you make a balloon negatively charged? What happens when you move a negatively charged balloon toward a balloon with no charge?

Read More About Physical Science!

Look for books like these in the library.

Experiment How does energy affect the distance a toy car travels?

When you pull back a pullback car, you wind it up. You give it potential energy. When you let it go, the potential energy changes to kinetic energy as the car begins to move. In this activity, you will find out how a car's potential energy affects the distance the car can travel.

Materials

meterstick

pullback toy car

masking tape

Ask a question.

How does a car's potential energy affect the distance it can travel?

State a hypothesis.

If a pullback car's potential energy is greater, then will the distance it travels increase, decrease, or remain about the same? Write your **hypothesis**.

Identify and control variables.

You will change the potential energy your toy car has just before it begins to move. You do this by changing the distance you pull the car back. You will measure the distance the car travels. Everything else must stay the same.

Process Skills

The basis of an **experiment** is a **hypothesis**, a testable **prediction** that helps guide the experiment.

Test your hypothesis.

1 Make a starting line with masking tape.

2 Put down another piece of tape and mark it at 0, 5, 10, 15, 20, 25, and 30 cm.

Using Scientific Methods

1. Ask a question.
2. State a hypothesis.
3. Identify/control variables.
4. Test your hypothesis.
5. Collect and record your data.
6. Interpret your data.
7. State your conclusion.
8. Go further.

Comparing Density

Matter that has less density than water has buoyancy—it will float in water.

Idea: Compare the density of objects with that of water. Use a container of water and a variety of objects.

Separating Mixtures

The best way to separate a mixture depends on the kinds of matter in the mixture.

Idea: Use a variety of mixtures. Demonstrate the best way to separate each mixture.

Changing Potential to Kinetic Energy

Energy can be stored as potential energy and released as kinetic energy.

Idea: Use a wind-up toy to show how the amount of potential energy affects the distance the toy can travel.

Making Sounds

Sounds vary depending on the way matter vibrates.

Idea: Show how sound changes. Stretch rubber bands of varied sizes across the opening of a box.

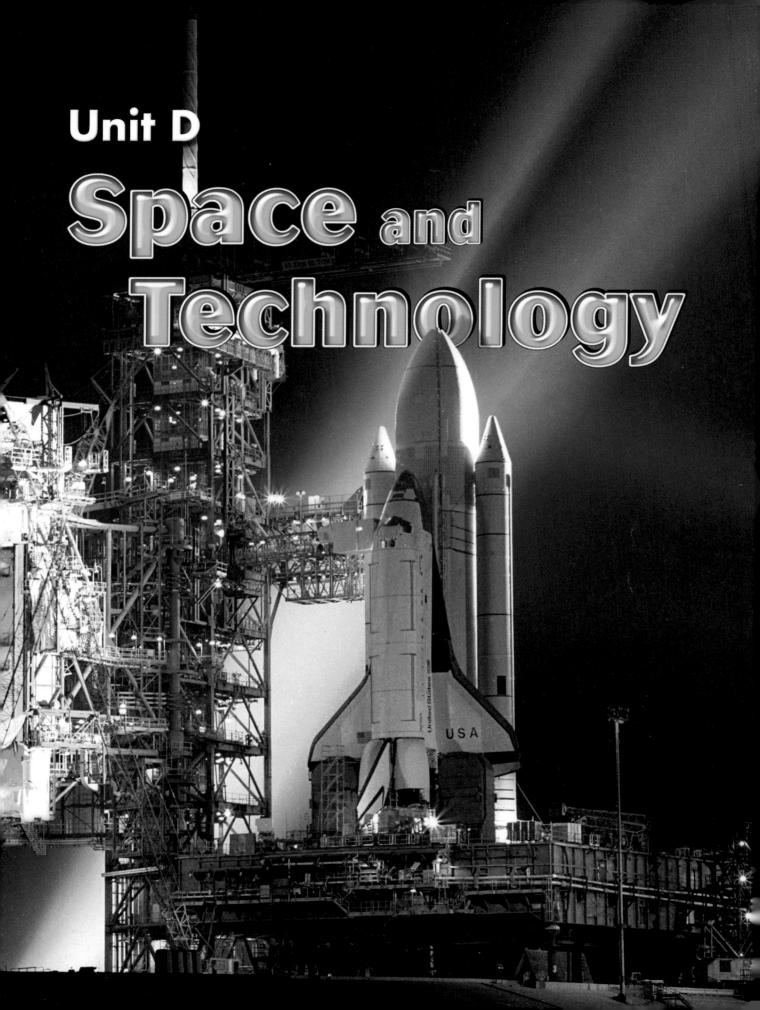

Unit D
Space and Technology

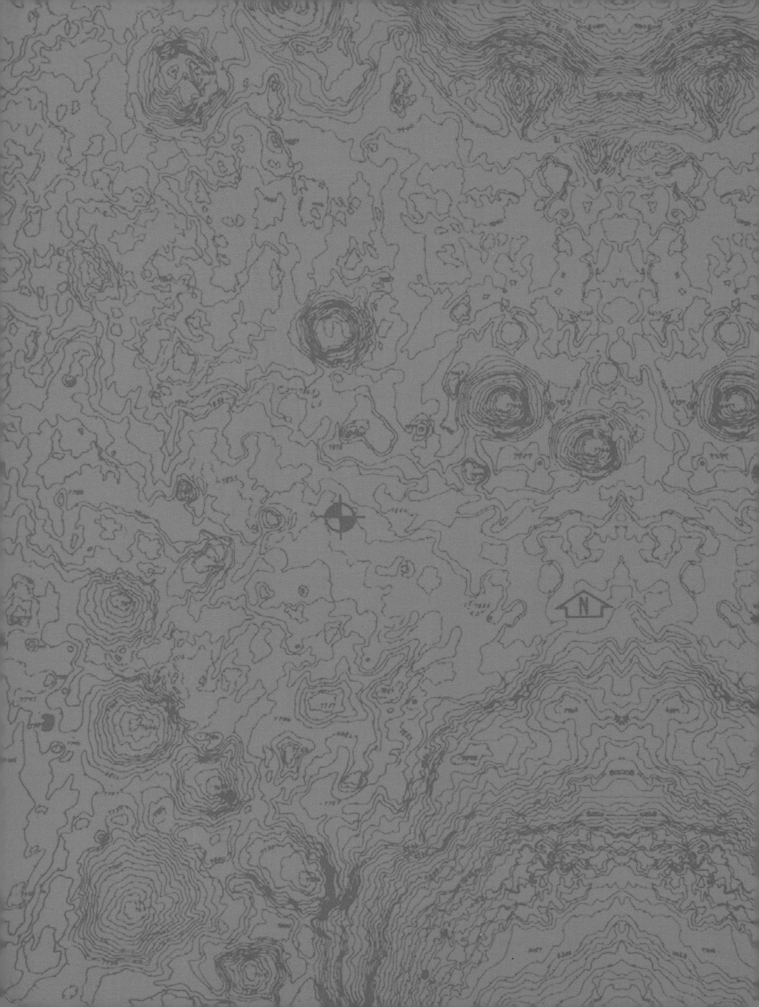

Chapter 15
Patterns in the Sky

You Will Discover

- what causes day, night, shadows, and seasons.
- why the Moon's shape seems to change.
- what tools help people study stars.

online
Student Edition
pearsonsuccessnet.com

What patterns do the Earth, Sun, Moon, and stars show?

star

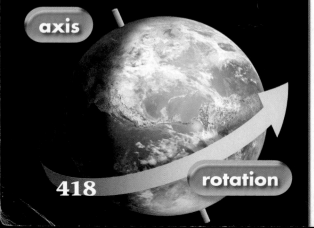

axis

rotation

418

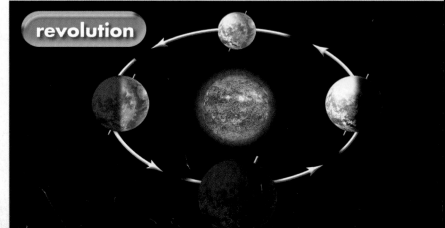

revolution

Chapter 15 Vocabulary

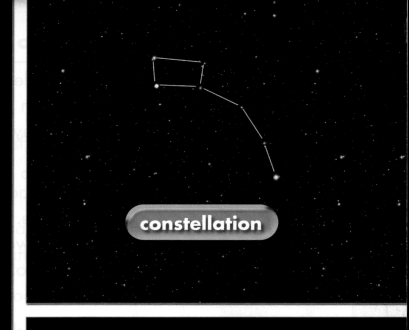

constellation

phase

lunar eclipse

telescope

419

You Are There!

You are floating in space outside the Space Shuttle. The Sun has just risen above the curve of the Earth. Look how bright the Sun is in the blackness all around! Sunlight shimmers on the ocean far below. It's another amazing sunrise. What are these patterns of movement, light, and darkness that you have seen on your space journey?

AudioText

What are some patterns that repeat every day?

Every day there is light during the day followed by darkness at night. If the day is sunny, you might notice shadows. Day, night, and shadows are caused by light from the Sun and the movement of Earth.

The Sun

You see the Sun in the sky on a sunny day. The Sun is in the sky on cloudy days too. The Sun is a **star**—a giant ball of hot, glowing gases. If you think of a plate that is almost round, the Sun would be in its center. Earth would be between the center and the plate's edge. The Sun is the main source of light and energy for Earth.

Earth is very small compared to the Sun. Like the Sun, Earth is shaped like a ball. Unlike the Sun, Earth does not glow or make its own light. The half of Earth's curved surface facing the Sun is lit by sunlight. The half of Earth's surface facing away from the Sun is not lit by sunlight and is dark.

1. ✓**Checkpoint** What star is the source of light on Earth?

2. **Sequence** Describe a pattern on Earth that happens every day.

Earth Spins

If you stand outside, you do not feel as if you are moving. But you are. Earth is always moving. One way it moves is that it spins around an imaginary line. The ends of the line would stick out of Earth at the North Pole and at the South Pole. This imaginary line around which Earth spins is its **axis.** Find Earth's axis in the drawing below. If you could look down at the North Pole, you would see the Earth turns in a counterclockwise direction. This is the opposite direction to the way the hands of a clock move. We could also say that Earth turns from west to east.

Daytime begins when the Sun first appears over the horizon. Although the Sun looks like it rises, it actually stays in the same place. As Earth rotates, this part of Earth is just beginning to face the Sun.

Half of Earth faces the Sun and receives sunlight as Earth spins on its axis.

Day and Night

Earth makes one complete spin on its axis, or **rotation,** every 24 hours. During this time, half of Earth faces the Sun. That half of Earth has day. The half of Earth that is not facing the Sun has night. As Earth spins, or rotates, a different part of Earth faces the Sun.

Earth rotates at the same speed every day of the year. You may have noticed that the number of hours of sunlight and darkness changes during the year. But if you add the hours of sunlight and darkness for one day together, you will find they equal 24 hours.

Things are not always as they seem. For instance, the Sun appears to rise in the east. It seems to move across the sky and set in the west. You might think that the Sun moves around Earth. But the Sun only appears to move across the sky. Actually Earth is moving.

The path that the Sun appears to take across the sky is predictable. We can tell ahead of time when the Sun will rise and set.

1. ✓**Checkpoint** What is Earth's axis?

2. **Writing** in Science) **Expository** Write a paragraph in your **science journal** that explains how spinning on the Earth's axis causes day and night.

As Earth rotates on its axis, the half of Earth that was in darkness begins to receive sunlight.

Around noon the Sun is at its highest point in the sky.

As Earth continues to rotate, the Sun appears to set in the west. Daytime ends when the Sun disappears below the horizon.

Lesson 2

What patterns repeat every year?

Earth's tilt and movement around the Sun cause the seasons. The amount of light and heat Earth receives during different seasons causes seasonal patterns.

Earth Moves Around the Sun

You know that Earth rotates on its axis. Earth also moves, or revolves, around the Sun. Find Earth's axis in each part of the diagram. Earth's axis is not straight up and down. It is tilted.

Earth makes one **revolution** when it makes one complete trip around the Sun. One revolution takes one year. As Earth revolves around the Sun, Earth's tilted axis always points in the same direction in space.

Earth's Position During the Year
The part of Earth pointed toward the Sun receives the most direct sunlight and has warmer temperatures.

In this diagram sizes are not true to scale.

June
The northern half of Earth tilts more toward the Sun. The northern half gets more direct sunlight than the southern half. It is summer in the northern half and winter in the southern half of Earth.

In some places on its path around the Sun, the northern half of Earth is tilted toward the Sun. In other places along its path, the southern half of Earth tilts toward the Sun. The part of Earth that is tilted toward the Sun receives the most direct rays of the Sun and is heated the most. That part of Earth also spends more hours in daylight than in darkness during each 24 hours.

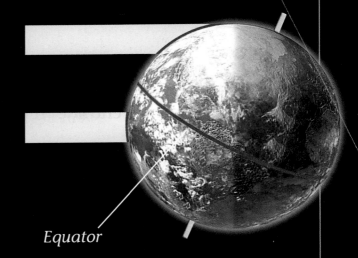

Equator

Direct rays near the equator cover less area. The equator is the imaginary line that separates the north and south halves of the Earth. The rays here are more concentrated. They heat Earth more than rays that strike at an angle.

March
The northern and southern halves of Earth get about the same amounts of sunlight. Neither pole points toward the Sun or away from it. The northern half is getting warmer, but the southern half is getting cooler.

December
The northern half of Earth tilts away from the Sun. This tilt causes the northern half of Earth to receive less sunlight and have colder temperatures than the southern half. It is winter in the north, but summer in the south.

September
As in March, neither end of the axis points toward the Sun or away from the Sun. The northern half of Earth is getting cooler, but the southern half is getting warmer.

1. ✓**Checkpoint** What does Earth revolve around?

2. **Sequence** Describe the pattern of temperature changes during the year in the northern half of Earth. Why does this happen?

Why does the Moon's shape change?

The Moon revolves around Earth while Earth revolves around the Sun. These movements and light from the Sun cause the Moon to appear different throughout a month.

The Moon and Earth

Did you ever see a full moon rise above the horizon or a half-moon set below it?

Like Earth, the Moon rotates and revolves. It rotates on its axis and revolves around Earth. Unlike Earth, the Moon takes about 27 Earth days to complete one rotation. The Moon completes one revolution of Earth in almost the same time.

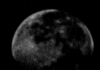

Can you describe how the Earth and Moon move in space?

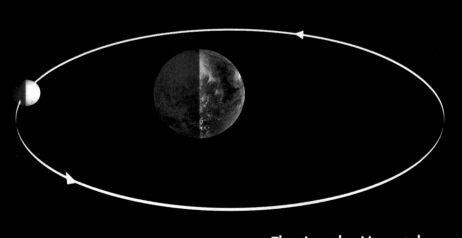

The time the Moon takes to rotate and revolve once is about the same.

This photo taken from space shows that the Moon is small compared to Earth.

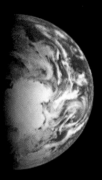

The Moon is the closest natural object to Earth. It is 384,000 kilometers (239,000 miles) away. The Moon also is the brightest object in the night sky, but it does not make light. The light you see from the Moon is light from the Sun that shines on the Moon and bounces off.

Notice the sunlight hitting half of Earth and half of the Moon in the picture. Sometimes you can even see the Moon during the day. It does not look as bright as it does at night. Sunlight that reflects off the Moon is only a little brighter than sunlight that passes through the daytime atmosphere. Sometimes you cannot see the Moon at night.

Did you know that we always see the same side of the Moon? We never see the other side from Earth. A spacecraft took the first pictures of the Moon's far side in 1959.

1. ✓ **Checkpoint** What are two ways the moon moves? How do these movements affect the appearance of the Moon?

2. **Math** in Science About how many days does it take for the Moon to revolve around the Earth 4 times?

The Moon and the Sun

On some nights, the Moon looks like a circle of bright light in the night sky. Other nights, you cannot see any part of the Moon, even if the sky is clear. In between these two times, you can see different amounts of the Moon. How the Moon looks in the sky changes a little each day. The pattern of changes is predictable. And the entire pattern repeats itself about every four weeks or 29 1/2 days.

Each different way that the Moon looks is a **phase** of the Moon. Find some of these phases on the next page. Notice that you can see more and more of the Moon until you see a full Moon. Then you see less and less of the Moon. When you cannot see the Moon at all, the phase is known as a new Moon.

Lunar Eclipse

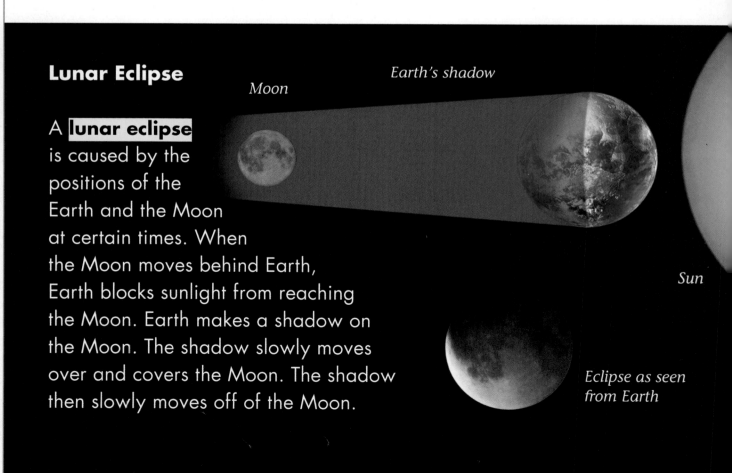

Moon

Earth's shadow

Sun

Eclipse as seen from Earth

A **lunar eclipse** is caused by the positions of the Earth and the Moon at certain times. When the Moon moves behind Earth, Earth blocks sunlight from reaching the Moon. Earth makes a shadow on the Moon. The shadow slowly moves over and covers the Moon. The shadow then slowly moves off of the Moon.

SciLinks Take It to the Net
pearsonsuccessnet.com | keyword: lunar eclipse
code: g3p434

The Lunar Cycle

The pictures show some of the changes in the Moon's appearance along its path around Earth. Half of the Moon is always lit by sunlight. The lit half of the Moon cannot always be seen from Earth. The movements of Earth and the Moon cause different amounts of the lit half of the Moon to be seen from Earth. The amount of the Moon that can be seen from Earth is a phase of the Moon.

New Moon Phase
None of the Moon appears lit.

First Quarter Phase
About a week after the New Moon, the Moon looks like a half circle.

Full Moon Phase
About two weeks after the New Moon, you see all of the lit half of the Moon. It looks like a circle.

Third Quarter Phase
Three-fourths of the Moon's cycle is complete. In about a week, there will be a New Moon phase again.

✓ Lesson Checkpoint

1. How much of the Moon is lit by sunlight?

2. What position of Earth causes a lunar eclipse?

3.  **Sequence** Describe the pattern of the phases of the Moon starting with a New Moon.

Lesson 4

What are star patterns?

Stars appear to move in the night sky. Telescopes make studying patterns of stars easier.

Stars and the Telescope

Think about being outside on a clear, dark night. You see thousands of twinkling stars. You notice that some stars are brighter than others and are easier to see. They all look so small in the sky because they are trillions of miles away. But some of the stars are actually larger than the Sun. Other stars are smaller. The stars that are the farthest away are the dimmest and the hardest to see. You cannot see many stars at all without certain tools to help you.

The camper in the picture is using binoculars to see the stars more clearly. Binoculars and the **telescope** are tools that magnify objects that are far away. They make objects look larger and easier to see. If you use a telescope, you can see many more stars than with your eyes alone.

Find the huge mirror inside the Keck telescope in Hawaii. Telescopes help people see stars that they cannot see with their eyes alone.

436

Scientists use different kinds of telescopes. The telescope on page 436 and telescopes you might use are similar. These telescopes use tubes, mirrors that make light reflect, and lenses that bend light or refract it. All these parts help bring as much light as possible into the telescope. The result is a larger and clearer view of objects in the sky. Other kinds of telescopes do not collect light. They collect other kinds of waves, such as radio waves.

Binoculars make far-away objects appear larger, brighter, and easier to see.

1. **✓Checkpoint** What are two tools that can help you see stars?

2. **Art** in Science Draw a picture of some star patterns that you have seen.

Patterns of Stars

Have you ever spent time looking at stars? You might notice that some groups of stars seem to make patterns or shapes. A group of stars that makes a pattern is a **constellation.** You can imagine lines drawn between stars. Find the lines drawn in the pictures of the stars on page 439. Many people see two cups with handles. These patterns are the Big Dipper and the Little Dipper. The Big Dipper is a part of the constellation Ursa Major (the Big Bear). The stars of the Little Dipper make up the constellation Ursa Minor (the Little Bear).

People living in ancient times saw the shapes of animals, people, and objects in star patterns. They made up stories about the constellations and gave them names. Some of these names are still used today. You might have heard of the constellation Orion. When people living in ancient Greece saw the stars of Orion, they saw a hunter.

The stars that make up a constellation look like they are close together in space. They really are very far apart. Some of the stars are much farther from Earth than others. If you looked at the same stars from far away in space, they would not make the same pattern.

How Stars Seem to Move

The picture on the right shows how stars appear to move across the sky at night. Like the Sun, stars really do not move this way. They look like they move across the sky because Earth rotates on its axis. The stars look like they revolve around the North Star. The patterns of stars also change with Earth's seasons. As Earth revolves around the Sun, constellations are in different parts of the night sky. Notice that the Big Dipper and the Little Dipper are in different positions in the sky.

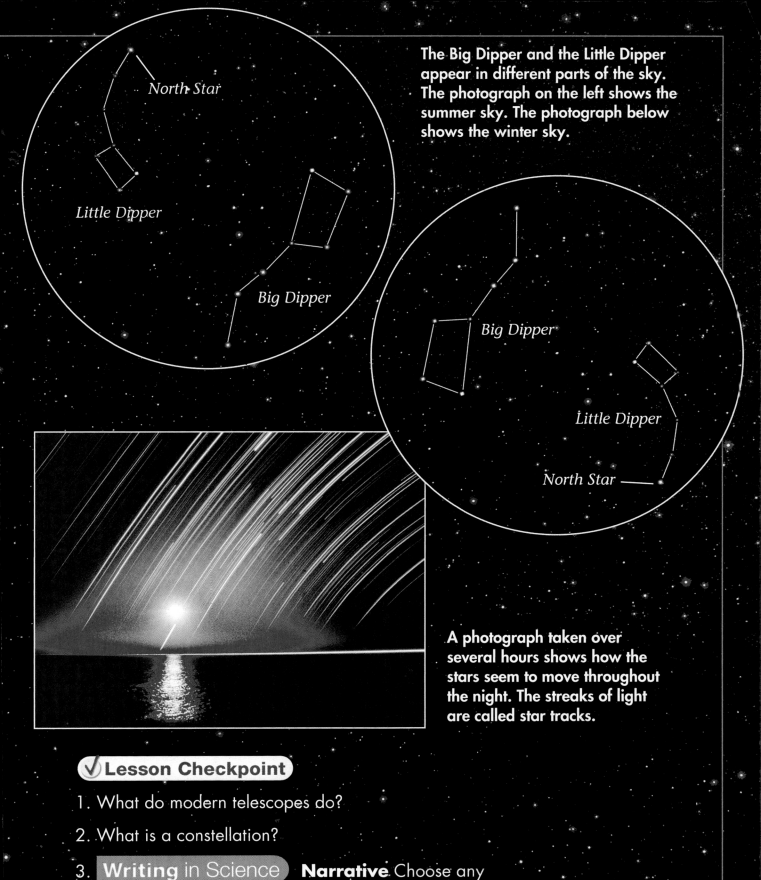

North Star

Little Dipper

Big Dipper

The Big Dipper and the Little Dipper appear in different parts of the sky. The photograph on the left shows the summer sky. The photograph below shows the winter sky.

Big Dipper

Little Dipper

North Star

A photograph taken over several hours shows how the stars seem to move throughout the night. The streaks of light are called star tracks.

✓ Lesson Checkpoint

1. What do modern telescopes do?

2. What is a constellation?

3. **Writing** in Science **Narrative** Choose any constellation and write a story in your **science journal** about the constellation.

Investigate When is the Big Dipper not the Big Dipper?

A constellation is a pattern of stars people see from Earth. Viewed from a faraway part of the universe, the same pattern might not be seen.

Materials

Pattern for a Big Dipper Model and Drawing of the Big Dipper

7 straws and 7 pieces of foil

metric ruler

scissors, tape, and clay

What to Do

1 Use the Pattern for a Big Dipper Model. Label the straws from A to F. Cut each to the correct length.

2 Make a foil ball around one end of each straw.

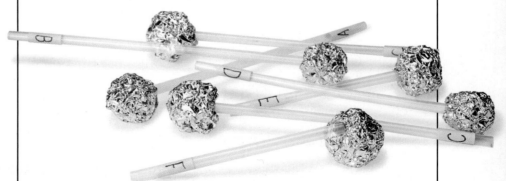

3 Put each straw on top of its letter on the Pattern for a Big Dipper Model. Use a small ball of clay to make each straw stand up.

Process Skills

Some **models** can be used as tools to help make and test **predictions** and get new understandings.

4 **Observe** from the front, 2 steps back. Identify the pattern you see.

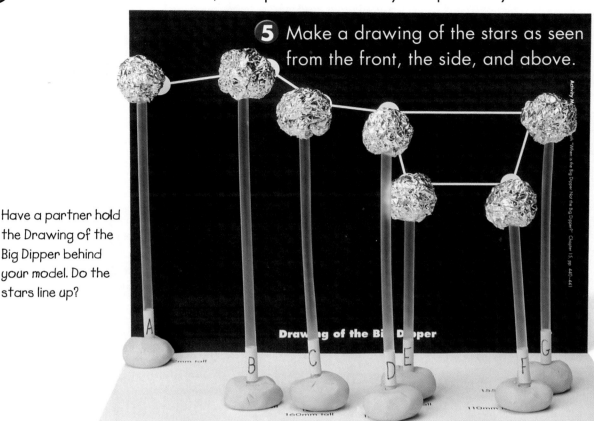

5 Make a drawing of the stars as seen from the front, the side, and above.

Have a partner hold the Drawing of the Big Dipper behind your model. Do the stars line up?

Drawing of the Big Dipper

Pattern for the Big Dipper Model

Sketches or Drawings of Big Dipper Model		
View from Front	**View from Side**	**View from Above**

Explain Your Results

1. **Observe** Does your Big Dipper **model** look like the Big Dipper from all directions? Explain.

2. **Infer** If you were a space traveler, could you see all the familiar constellations? Explain.

Go Further

Do constellations change as they "move" across the night sky? Can different ones be seen in different seasons? Find out.

Comparing Times of Sunrises and Sunsets

As Earth revolves around the Sun, the amount of sunlight hitting different parts of Earth changes each day. The Sun looks like it rises above the horizon and sets below the horizon at different times. In the northern half of Earth, the Sun rises a little earlier and sets a little later each day from January to late June. The days slowly have more daylight hours and fewer hours of darkness. The pattern is reversed in the southern half of Earth.

eTools Take It to the Net
pearsonsuccessnet.com

The chart below shows the pattern in the times of sunrise and sunset for four days during the year.

Sunrise and Sunset Standard Times for a City in the Northern Half of Earth		
Date	Sunrise	Sunset
March 21	5:52 A.M.	6:05 P.M.
June 21	5:16 A.M.	8:29 P.M.
September 21	6:38 A.M.	6:49 P.M.
December 21	7:15 A.M.	4:23 P.M.

Comparing Times

Use the chart to answer the following questions.

1. How many hours and minutes of daylight are there on March 21?

2. Which day has the most hours of daylight?

3. Which day has the fewest hours of daylight?

4. During which month would the southern half of the Earth have its longest day? Explain.

Lab zone Take-Home Activity

Find the times of sunrise and sunset in your area daily for the next week. Compare the times and decide if the days are getting longer or shorter.

Chapter 15 Review and Test Prep

Use Vocabulary

axis (page 424)	**revolution** (page 428)
constellation (page 438)	**rotation** (page 424)
lunar eclipse (page 434)	**star** (page 423)
phase (page 434)	**telescope** (page 436)

Use the vocabulary word from the list above that best completes each sentence.

1. A(n) _____ is a giant ball of hot, glowing gases.

2. Earth spins on its _____.

3. Earth makes one complete _____ every 24 hours.

4. Earth makes one complete _____ around the Sun every year.

5. A(n) _____ of the Moon is the way the moon looks in the sky.

6. A(n) _____ happens when Earth's shadow moves across the Moon.

7. A(n) _____ magnifies objects that are far away.

8. The Big Dipper is part of a(n) _____.

Explain Concepts

9. Explain what causes the phases of the Moon.

10. Explain what causes constellations to move across the sky at night.

11. On March 1, sunrise is at 6:25 A.M. and sunset is at 5:42 P.M. On March 30, sunrise is at 5:36 A.M. and sunset is at 6:15 P.M. Which day has the most daylight?

Process Skills

12. **Infer** What would happen to daytime and nighttime if Earth did not spin on its axis?

13. **Infer** You notice that the shadow made by a pole outside your window has been getting longer. What does this tell you about the time of day? Explain your answer.

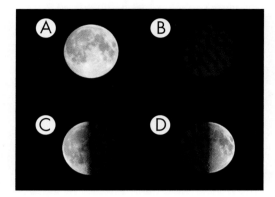

14. Draw the images of the Moon phases in the boxes below in the order that they would appear in the sky. Start with picture B.

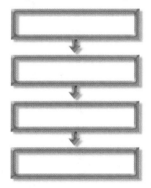

 Test Prep

Choose the letter that best completes the statement or answers the question.

15. A Full Moon can be seen about once every
(A) night.
(B) month.
(C) season.
(D) year.

16. You can see many more stars if you use a
(F) calendar.
(G) microscope.
(H) telescope.
(I) hand lens.

17. What season does the southern half of Earth have if Earth's north axis is tilted toward the Sun?
(A) spring
(B) summer
(C) fall
(D) winter

18. Which of the following is closest to Earth?
(F) Moon
(G) Sun
(H) stars
(I) constellations

19. Explain why the answer you chose for Question 18 is best. For each of the answers you did not choose, give a reason why it is not the best choice.

20. **Writing in Science**
Expository Write a paragraph that describes the patterns of light and temperatures in different seasons.

445

The Hubble Space Telescope

You can use a telescope to make stars and other objects in space easier to see. Imagine how many stars you could see with a telescope 13.2 meters (43.5 feet) long and 4.2 meters (14 feet) wide. Imagine it weighing 11,000 kilograms (24,000 pounds)—about the size of a school bus. You would not be taking it over to a friend's house to look at stars. A telescope this size would not fit in a car, but it did fit in a Space Shuttle.

In 1990, NASA launched the Hubble Space Telescope. The Hubble stays in space about 600 kilometers (375 miles) above Earth. It revolves around Earth every 97 minutes.

The Hubble collects information from space and sends it to scientists on Earth every day. It provides detailed images of Mars and Pluto. It helps scientists understand more about Uranus and Neptune. The Hubble also has helped scientists learn about objects outside our solar system. It provides information about black holes, quasars, and the birth and death of stars.

An astronaut works on the Hubble Space Telescope.

The Hubble Telescope was made in a way that makes it easy to repair and update. Since it has been launched, astronauts have made missions to the Hubble to keep it working well. During space walks, astronauts have replaced parts that have worn out. Astronauts also have added parts so that the Hubble always has the newest technology. Each servicing mission adds four to five years to the working life of the Hubble.

This image of the ant nebula, a dying star, was taken by the Hubble Space Telescope.

The solar panels provide power to the telescope.

Lab zone Take-Home Activity

If you have Internet access at home or at the library, go to the NASA Web site (http://hubblesite. org) and look at images from the Hubble.

Galileo
1564–1642

Galileo was born in Italy in 1564. He studied medicine and mathematics at a university in Italy. He later became the head of the math department at another university.

Galileo became known for inventing science tools and experimenting. One of the tools he is most famous for is a better telescope. When he heard that someone had invented a tool that could magnify objects, he went to work to improve the telescope. Galileo soon had a telescope that could magnify objects twenty times.

Galileo pointed his telescope toward space and made many discoveries. He found that the Moon has craters. Galileo saw four moons revolving around Jupiter and different phases of Venus.

Galileo used his observations to show that Earth revolves around the Sun. Most people during that time believed that the Sun revolved around Earth. Galileo's experiments and observations challenged beliefs of the time and added to the knowledge of science.

Lab zone Take-Home Activity

Look up the work of Galileo. Describe other observations he made. Tell what his experiments led him to say about patterns in the sky.

Chapter 16
The Solar System

You Will Discover

- how the Sun makes heat and light.
- how the planets move in space.
- what is special about each planet.

online
Student Edition
pearsonsuccessnet.com

Web Games
Take It to the Net
pearsonsuccessnet.com

Explore How can you make a distance model of the solar system?

Materials

metric ruler
and meterstick

adding machine tape

scissors

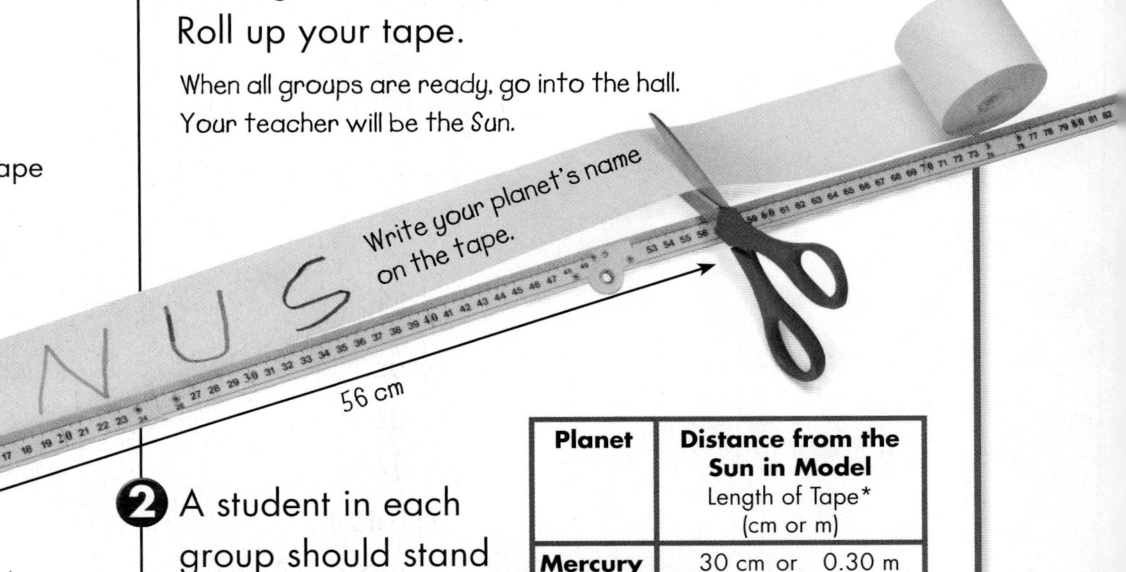

The chart shows distance in cm and m. Select the easier one to use. Select a ruler or a meterstick for your measuring tool.

What to Do

Your teacher will help you select a planet.

1 The chart shows the distance your planet is from the sun in the model. **Measure** and cut adding machine tape to the correct length. Roll up your tape.

When all groups are ready, go into the hall. Your teacher will be the Sun.

Write your planet's name on the tape.

VENUS

56 cm

2 A student in each group should stand by the Sun and hold the free end of the tape. Another student should walk down the hall, unrolling the tape.

Planet	Distance from the Sun in Model Length of Tape* (cm or m)
Mercury	30 cm or 0.30 m
Venus	56 cm or 0.56 m
Earth	77 cm or 0.77 m
Mars	120 cm or 1.2 m
Jupiter	400 cm or 4 m
Saturn	740 cm or 7.4 m
Uranus	1500 cm or 15 m
Neptune	2300 cm or 23 m

*Scale: 1 cm = about 1,940,000 km

3 Compare the distances to the planets.

Process Skills

Your class **measured** the adding machine tape using two standard units, centimeters and meters.

Explain Your Results

Based on your **model**, would it be harder to travel to Mars or Neptune? Explain.

Reading Skills

Compare and Contrast

When you **compare** things, you tell how they are alike.
When you **contrast** things, you tell how they are different.

- Clue words and phrases such as *similar, like, both, all, unlike, in the same way* or *in a different way* may signal *comparing* or *contrasting.*

- **Measuring** is one way to compare and contrast objects.

Science Article

Venus

Earth

Venus and Earth

Venus and Earth are both inner planets. Venus is the second planet from the Sun. Earth is the third planet from the Sun. Both planets are made of rock. Like Earth, Venus has no rings. Unlike Earth, which has one moon, Venus has no moons. Earth is the only planet known to have living things.

Apply It!

Use a graphic organizer to **compare and contrast** Venus and Earth.

Different	Alike	Different
How is Venus different?	How are Earth and Venus alike?	How is Earth different?

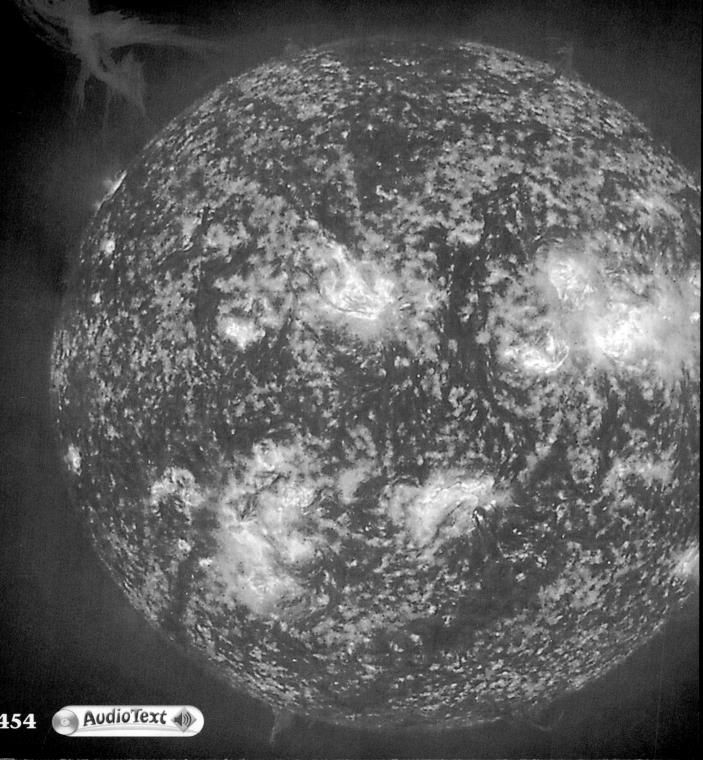

You Are There!

Don't look at it! The Sun has a great amount of energy. You should never look directly at it. The Sun is the fiery center of our solar system. This huge ball of energy holds our solar system together. But what's going on underneath its surface?

What are the parts of the solar system?

The solar system includes the Sun and other objects that travel around it. The Sun gives off energy that moves out in all directions through space.

The Sun

The Sun is a ball of hot, glowing gases called plasma. It is a star. The Sun looks larger and brighter than stars you see at night because it is a lot closer to Earth. The other stars in the sky look small because they are so far away.

How big is the Sun? In a word—huge! It is 109 times as wide as Earth, or wider than the length of 15,000,000 football fields! In fact, the Sun is large enough to hold one million Earths inside it!

The temperature on the surface of the Sun is 5,500°C. The center is millions of degrees hot. It's so hot that gas particles that have a positive charge collide and join. This releases a lot of energy. Energy that travels from the Sun through space includes sunlight.

1. ✔️**Checkpoint** Why is the Sun so bright and hot?

2. **Art** in Science Draw a tiny circle to represent Earth. Then use information from this page to decide how big to draw the Sun.

The Sun is much nearer to Earth than other stars.

How Objects In the Solar System Move

You live on the planet Earth. A planet is a large, ball-shaped body that revolves, or travels, around the Sun. Find Earth and the seven other planets in the drawing. Many of these planets have moons. The Sun, the eight planets and their moons, and other objects that revolve around the Sun make up the solar system. The Sun is the center of the solar system.

The path an object takes as it revolves around the Sun is its orbit. Planets travel in an orbit that is a slight oval shape. The strong pull of the Sun's gravity holds the planets in their orbits.

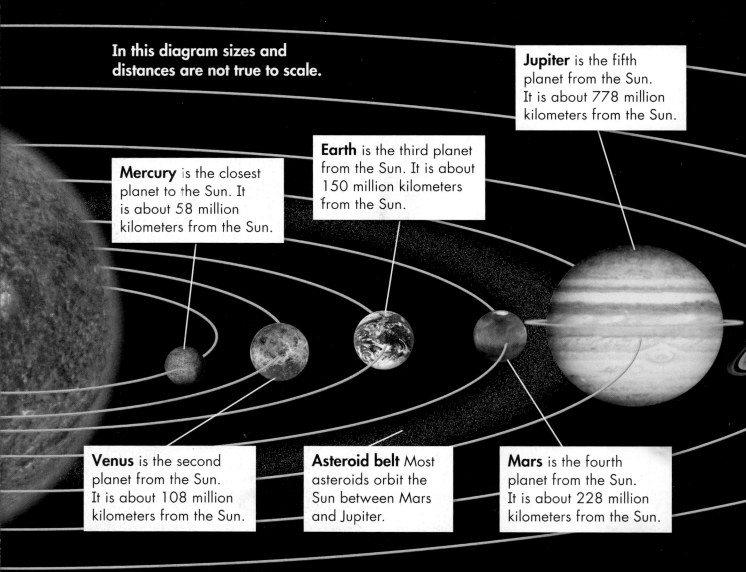

In this diagram sizes and distances are not true to scale.

Jupiter is the fifth planet from the Sun. It is about 778 million kilometers from the Sun.

Earth is the third planet from the Sun. It is about 150 million kilometers from the Sun.

Mercury is the closest planet to the Sun. It is about 58 million kilometers from the Sun.

Venus is the second planet from the Sun. It is about 108 million kilometers from the Sun.

Asteroid belt Most asteroids orbit the Sun between Mars and Jupiter.

Mars is the fourth planet from the Sun. It is about 228 million kilometers from the Sun.

SciLinks Take It to the Net pearsonsuccessnet.com keyword: planet code: g3p456

The planets are divided into inner and outer planets based on their distances from the Sun. The four inner planets are Mercury, Venus, Earth, and Mars. The outer planets are Jupiter, Saturn, Uranus, and Neptune. Compare the distances of the planets from the Sun.

An **asteroid** is a small chunk of rock that orbits the Sun. Thousands of asteroids are found in the asteroid belt between Mars and Jupiter.

✓ Lesson Checkpoint

1. What makes up the solar system?
2. How do objects in the solar system move?
3. **Math** in Science How much farther from the Sun is Venus compared to Mercury?

Saturn is the sixth planet from the Sun. It is about 1 billion, 400 million kilometers from the Sun.

Uranus is the seventh planet from the Sun. It is about 3 billion kilometers from the Sun.

Neptune is the eighth planet from the Sun. It is over 4 billion, 500 million kilometers from the Sun.

What are the planets?

Each of the planets in our solar system has special features. They are different sizes. Some are rocky. Some are made of gases. Some have many moons. Some have no moons.

The Inner Planets

The inner planets—Mercury, Venus, Earth, and Mars—are alike in some ways. They are the planets closest to the Sun. They are rocky planets. But they have many differences too.

Look at the surface of Mercury below. It has many craters like those on our Moon. Mercury is also dry and very hot. That's because it is the closest planet to the Sun. Mercury is the smallest planet. It is less than half the size of Earth. It has no atmosphere. In 59 Earth days, Mercury rotates once. Mercury takes 88 Earth days to revolve around the Sun one time. It has no moons.

Venus, like Mercury, is a very hot, rocky planet. It has craters, mountains, and valleys. It has an atmosphere and is covered by thick clouds that trap a lot of heat. Venus takes 225 Earth days to revolve around the Sun. It takes 243 Earth days for Venus to rotate one time. Venus is larger than Mercury. It is a little smaller than Earth. Venus has no moons.

Venus

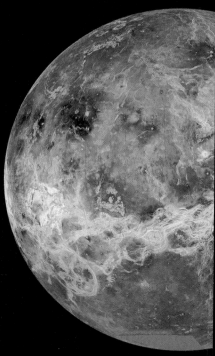

No atmosphere hides the craters of Mercury, seen below. Volcanoes and wide lava fields cover Venus, seen above without its cloud cover.

Mercury

Earth

Mars

Oceans of liquid water make Earth the "blue planet." Rust in the soil of Mars makes it the "red planet."

Find the planet that looks like a blue, white, and brown marble. You found the third planet from the Sun—Earth. The swirling white clouds are part of its atmosphere. Our planet is slightly larger than Venus. One Earth year lasts $365\frac{1}{4}$ days. That means it takes 365 days and 6 hours for Earth to revolve around the Sun one time. Its day, or rotation, lasts 24 hours. Earth has one moon.

Mars is the next farthest planet from the Sun. Mars is called the "red planet" because it has a reddish-orange surface. Mars has a very thin atmosphere. It has volcanoes and deep canyons. Mars is about half the size of Earth. One year on Mars is equal to 687 Earth days, or almost two Earth years. One day on Mars lasts 25 Earth hours. That's very close to a day on Earth. Mars has two moons.

1. **✓Checkpoint** Which of the planets are inner planets?

2. **⟲ Compare and Contrast** How do the sizes of the four inner planets compare?

Earth Supports Life

From space you can see that Earth is very different from the other planets. Blue water covers almost three fourths of Earth's surface. You also can see white clouds in the atmosphere, the solid land of the continents and, the white ice caps.

What you cannot see from space is that Earth is the only planet in the solar system that can support a wide variety of living things. Earth has the mild temperatures, liquid water, and atmosphere that living things need. Its atmosphere contains the right amounts of oxygen and carbon dioxide. The atmosphere also absorbs most of the rays of light that can harm living things. Earth's gravity holds the atmosphere close to Earth.

Extremes on Earth	
Highest place	Mount Everest in Nepal and China 8850 meters (29, 035 feet)
Lowest place	Dead Sea between Israel and Jordan 400 meters (1, 300 feet) below sea level
Hottest place	El Azizia in Libya once measured 57.8°C (136°F)
Coldest place	Antarctica once measured −89°C (−129°F)
Driest place	Possibly Atacama Desert in Chile 0.76 mm (0.03 inches) of rain a year
Wettest place	Possibly Lloro, Columbia 13,299 mm (523.6 inches) of rain a year

The coldest place on Earth is Antarctica.

The hottest place in the United States is Death Valley, California. A very hot 57°C (134°F) has been recorded there.

The Sun is the main source of energy for Earth. Sunlight warms Earth. It also provides energy for plants to grow. However, about one half of the Sun's light that comes toward Earth does not reach Earth's surface. The atmosphere absorbs one fifth. One third more is reflected off the ground and clouds. Much of the reflected light is scattered by gases in the atmosphere. This makes the sky look blue.

Earth's rocky surface, both on land and under the oceans, is broken up into sections called plates. The plates constantly move. Earthquakes and volcanoes often happen where the plates meet. In some places the plates move apart from each other. In other places the plates collide or slide past each other. The moving plates cause the Earth's surface to keep changing.

1. ✔ **Checkpoint** What makes life on Earth possible?

2. **Writing** in Science **Descriptive** Brainstorm with a partner why the surface of Earth keeps changing. Write your explanation in your **science journal**.

Jupiter and Saturn, Two Gas Giants

The outer planets are much farther apart than the inner planets are. Unlike the rocky inner planets, most of the outer planets are huge and made mostly of gas. They are called gas giants. Their surfaces are not solid. They have deep atmospheres with thick layers of clouds and strong winds. Gas giants also have rings around them. The two largest gas giants are Jupiter and Saturn.

Jupiter is the fifth planet from the Sun and the largest planet in the solar system. It is over 11 times the size of Earth. It takes almost 12 Earth years for Jupiter to revolve around the Sun one time. Jupiter rotates in only 10 Earth hours. Jupiter is covered with thick layers of clouds that reflect sunlight. Bands of clouds, strong winds, and storms make the planet look like it does in the picture. Jupiter has more than 60 moons, but only four are as large or larger than Earth's Moon. Jupiter's rings are hard to see.

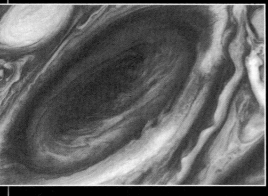

Jupiter's Great Red Spot is actually a huge storm. This storm is always present but it changes in size.

The asteroid belt is between the orbits of Mars and Jupiter. Some asteroids are hundreds of kilometers wide. Most are less than 1 kilometer wide.

Saturn's rings are very bright and easy to see with a telescope. Gravity holds the rings in orbit around Saturn.

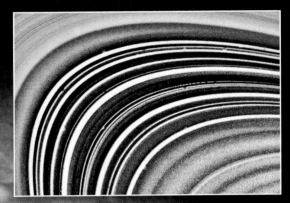

Saturn is the sixth planet from the Sun and the second largest planet. Saturn's most famous feature is its rings. They are made of chunks of ice and rock that circle the planet. Saturn takes 29 Earth years to make one revolution around the Sun. Saturn rotates in about 11 Earth hours. Saturn has at least 30 moons.

1. ✓**Checkpoint** In what ways are Jupiter and Saturn alike?

2. **Technology** in Science Scientists use the Hubble Telescope to learn about the planets. Use the Internet or other resources to find out more about the Hubble Telescope.

463

Uranus and Neptune

Like Jupiter and Saturn, Neptune and Uranus are gas giants. Uranus is the seventh planet from the Sun. It is smaller than Saturn or Jupiter but about 4 times the size of Earth. It takes Uranus 84 Earth years to revolve around the Sun just one time. However, Uranus rotates in just 17 Earth hours. Uranus is unlike other planets because it rotates on its side. It has 26 moons.

Neptune is the eighth planet from the Sun. It is only slightly smaller than Uranus. Neptune is so far away from the Sun that its orbit around the Sun takes 165 Earth years. Like the other gas giants, Neptune has strong winds and storms. Neptune looks light blue and has rings that are hard to see. Neptune takes about 16 Earth hours to rotate one time. It has at least 13 moons.

Like other gas giants, Uranus is surrounded by rings.

One of Pluto's moons (shown in the right-hand corner) is named Charon.

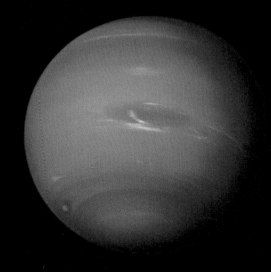

The weather on Neptune constantly changes. Light cloud-like bands appear and disappear. Storms are seen as dark spots.

Pluto, a Dwarf Planet

A small, cold, rocky object called Pluto orbits far from the Sun. Until 2006, Pluto was described as the ninth planet in the solar system. But many scientists think that Pluto should never have been called a planet. Pluto has a very unusual orbit. Sometimes Pluto is closer to the Sun than Neptune is. Pluto's orbit is at an angle to the orbits of the eight planets. Pluto is smaller than Earth's Moon. In August of 2006, scientists decided to put Pluto into a different category. It is now called a dwarf planet.

Other objects similar to Pluto have been discovered. Some are bigger than Pluto. Scientists think there are many more objects beyond Neptune's orbit.

✓ Lesson Checkpoint

1. Which of the planets are outer planets?

2. What small, ball-shaped object orbits the Sun and is now called a dwarf planet?

3. Compare and Contrast On a two column chart list the ways that the inner planets and the gas giants are alike and different.

Investigate How can a planet's distance from the Sun affect its surface temperature?

A planet's temperature can be affected by its atmosphere, its surface, and other factors. How does a planet's distance from the Sun affect its surface temperature?

Materials

metric ruler

lamp and 3 thermometers

books

What to Do

1 **Make a model** of the Sun and the planets. Place a lamp, books, a metric ruler, and thermometers as shown.

Be careful!

The light bulb and parts of the lamp will get hot!

The thermometers that are different distances from the light bulb stand for planets that are different distances from the Sun.

Remove ruler before turning on the lamp!

large books

The lamp stands for the Sun.

Process Skills

You can use a **model** to help you make accurate **inferences**.

2 Turn on the lamp.

3 Make a data chart like this one. **Collect** the **data** you need to complete the chart.

4 Wait 15 minutes. Turn off the lamp. Parts of the lamp will be hot!

5 Record the temperature of each thermometer. Make a line graph of your data.

Effect of Distance on Temperature

Distance from Light Bulb (cm)	Temperature after 15 Minutes (°C)
7 cm	
14 cm	
28 cm	

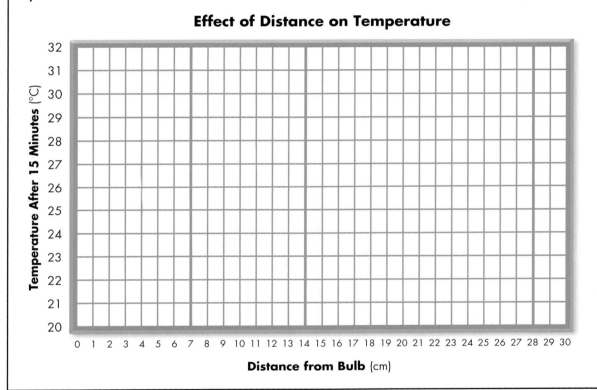

Effect of Distance on Temperature

Temperature After 15 Minutes (°C)

Distance from Bulb (cm)

Explain Your Results

1. Which thermometer showed the highest temperature? Which showed the lowest temperature?

2. **Infer** Think about your **model**. How does a planet's distance from the Sun affect its surface temperature?

Go Further

What do you think happens to the temperature on the side of the planet not facing the Sun? Make a plan using a model to help investigate.

Math in Science

Patterns in Planets

The distance of a planet from the Sun affects the time needed to revolve around the Sun.

The first column in the chart below lists the outer planets in the order of their distances from the Sun, from the nearest to farthest. The second column gives the length of time each planet takes to complete one orbit.

The Outer Planets

Planet	Revolution Time
Jupiter	12 Earth years
Saturn	29 Earth years
Uranus	84 Earth years
Neptune	165 Earth years

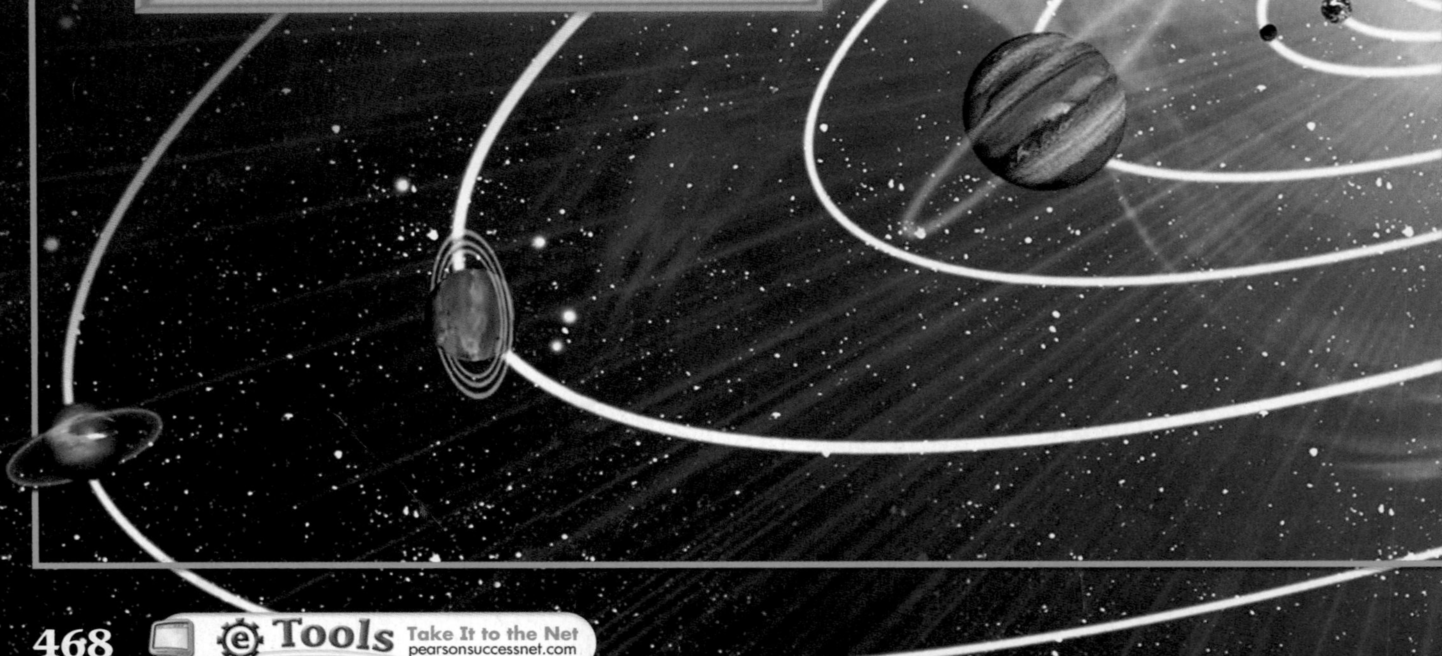

Use the chart to answer the questions.

1 Which of the outer planets takes the shortest time to revolve around the Sun?

    A. Jupiter   B. Saturn   C. Neptune   D. Uranus

2 How much longer is the revolution time of the outer planet farthest from the Sun than that of the outer planet closest to the Sun?

    F. 17 Earth years   G. 83 Earth years

    H. 81 Earth years   I. 153 Earth years

3 What pattern do you see about the distance of a planet from the Sun and the planet's revolution time?

    A. Planets closer to the Sun take longer to revolve around the Sun.

    B. Planets farther from the Sun take longer to revolve around the Sun.

    C. Planets farther from the Sun take a shorter time to revolve around the Sun.

    D. The chart shows no pattern.

Lab zone Take-Home Activity

Choose two charts of information about things in newspapers and magazines. Write down what patterns you see in the tables.

Use Vocabulary

asteroid (page 457)	**planet** (page 456)
orbit (page 456)	**solar system** (page 456)

Use the vocabulary term from the list above that best completes each sentence.

1. A(n) _____ is a large, ball-shaped body that revolves around the Sun.

2. The path a planet takes to revolve around the Sun is its _____.

3. The Sun, eight planets and their moons, and other objects that orbit the Sun make up the _____.

4. A(n) _____ is a small chunk of rock that orbits the Sun.

Explain Concepts

5. Explain why some stars seem so much brighter in the night sky than other stars.

6. Explain how energy is released from the Sun.

7. Explain why the four outer planets are called gas giants.

8. If you were traveling from the inner planet farthest from the Sun to the closest outer planet, what would you see in orbit? Explain your answer.

9. Why is Mars called the Red Planet?

10. Use the chart below to find a pattern in the number of moons and the size of the planets. How does the size of a planet seem to be related to the number of moons a planet has?

Planets and Moons		
Planet	**Distance Through Planet's Center**	**Number of Moons**
Mercury	4,900 kilometers	0
Venus	12,000 kilometers	0
Earth	12,750 kilometers	1
Mars	6,800 kilometers	2
Jupiter	143,000 kilometers	more than 60
Saturn	120,000 kilometers	more than 30
Uranus	51,000 kilometers	26
Neptune	49,000 kilometers	at least 13

11. Write a paragraph explaining how Pluto is different from the eight planets.

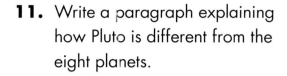

12. Predict where Earth will be in its orbit around the Sun exactly one year from now.

13. Model Make a model to show the orbits of the planets around the Sun.

Compare and Contrast

14. Reread the information about the inner and outer planets. Make a chart that compares and contrasts information about the eight planets.

Test Prep

Choose the letter that best completes the statement or answers the question.

15. Which planet is an inner planet?
- Ⓐ Uranus
- Ⓑ Venus
- Ⓒ Neptune
- Ⓓ Jupiter

16. What do all of the gas giants have?
- Ⓕ oxygen
- Ⓖ rocky surfaces
- Ⓗ liquid water
- Ⓘ rings

17. Which is the only planet that supports many living things?
- Ⓐ Earth
- Ⓑ Mars
- Ⓒ Venus
- Ⓓ Mercury

18. Which object has an unusual orbit and is called a dwarf planet?
- Ⓕ Jupiter
- Ⓖ Mercury
- Ⓗ Pluto
- Ⓘ Uranus

19. Explain why the answer you chose for Question 18 is best. For each of the answers you did not choose, give a reason why it is not the best choice.

20. **Writing** in Science

Persuasive Choose a planet that you would like others to visit. Then write a travel brochure that tries to persuade them that it would be a great place to spend a vacation.

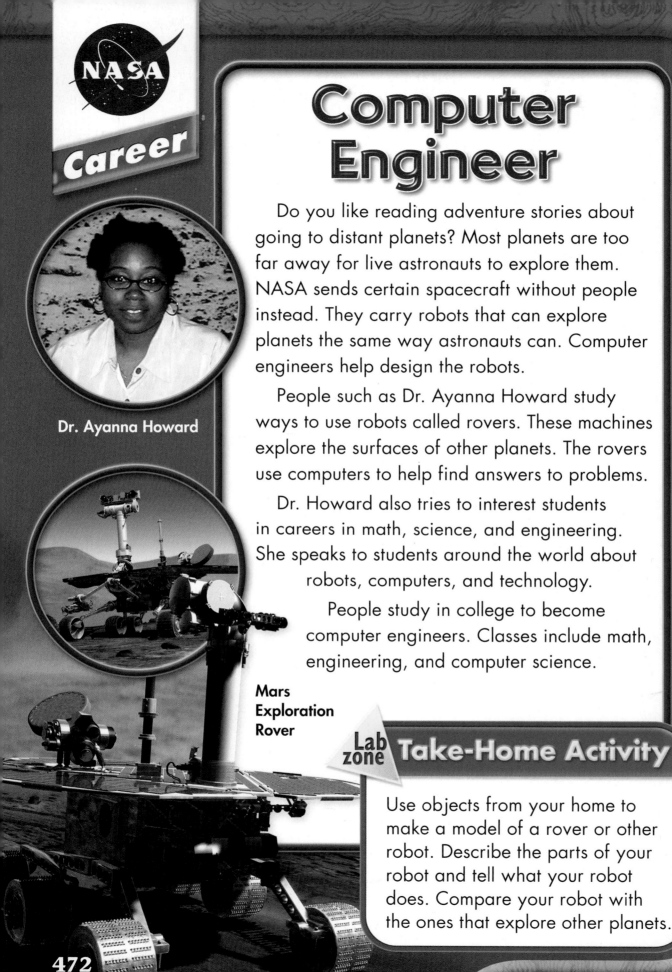

Computer Engineer

Dr. Ayanna Howard

Do you like reading adventure stories about going to distant planets? Most planets are too far away for live astronauts to explore them. NASA sends certain spacecraft without people instead. They carry robots that can explore planets the same way astronauts can. Computer engineers help design the robots.

People such as Dr. Ayanna Howard study ways to use robots called rovers. These machines explore the surfaces of other planets. The rovers use computers to help find answers to problems.

Dr. Howard also tries to interest students in careers in math, science, and engineering. She speaks to students around the world about robots, computers, and technology.

People study in college to become computer engineers. Classes include math, engineering, and computer science.

Mars Exploration Rover

Lab zone Take-Home Activity

Use objects from your home to make a model of a rover or other robot. Describe the parts of your robot and tell what your robot does. Compare your robot with the ones that explore other planets.

Chapter 17
Science in Our Lives

You Will Discover

- ways we use science and technology every day.
- ways we use technology to solve problems.

Discovery Channel School
Student DVD
DISCOVERY CHANNEL SCHOOL

online
Student Edition
pearsonsuccessnet.com

How does technology affect our lives?

technology

invention

tool

474

Chapter 17 Vocabulary

computer

Explore Which transport system works best?

Materials

Possible Water
Transport Systems

newspaper

plastic tube

funnel

empty cup and
cup with water

Process Skills

When you **predict**, you use what you have **observed** and what you already know to help tell what will happen.

What to Do

1 Examine *Possible Water Transport Systems.* **Predict** which of these systems will always work? Which will never work? Which will trap some water?

2 Test your predictions. Set up each system.

3 For each system, pour a half cup of water in the funnel. Have a group member hold the tube in place. **Observe** how well the water flows through the system.

Put down newspaper before you begin.

Repeat each test. This will help make your results more reliable.

Explain Your Results

1. In what direction does water flow best through a system?

2. Examine the different designs, your **predictions**, and your results. Find a rule that explains the results you **observed**.

How to Read Science

Sequence

A **sequence** is a series of actions that happen in a certain order.

- Sometimes writers use clue words such as *first, then, next,* and *finally* to signal a sequence.

- When a sequence has a repeating pattern, you can **predict** what comes next.

Newspaper Article

The Wright Brothers Fly!

Kitty Hawk, North Carolina–December 17, 1903. Today, Wilbur and Orville Wright flew their powered airplane. How did they do it? At first, the Wrights watched how birds control their flight. Then they flew kites

to test their ideas. Next they built gliders to find the right wing shape. Finally, they built an airplane with an engine. The flying machine, called *Flyer I,* became the world's first powered airplane.

Apply It!

Make a graphic organizer like the one shown. Fill it in to show the **sequence** of events that led to the Wright brother's historic first flight.

First,
↓
Then,
↓
Next,
↓
Finally,

What a beautiful bridge! The arches seem perfectly lined up. It's hard to believe this structure was built by the ancient Romans over 2,000 years ago. The bottom part was used as a road. But the top part was made to carry something completely different. This bridge was part of an amazing system designed to bring water from mountain springs to Roman cities. The ancient Romans, like other people, used technology to solve problems.

Lesson 1

How does technology affect our lives?

Science helps people understand the way the world works. Technology helps people apply this understanding to solve problems and improve their lives.

Finding New Ways

People have always asked questions about the world around them. As they learned new things, they began to use this knowledge. They used it to solve problems and form new ideas. People invented tools to help. A **tool** helps to do work more easily. Tools, in turn, helped people think of new ways of doing things. In other words, they used technology. **Technology** is the use of knowledge to design new tools and new ways to do things. A tool can be as simple as a sewing needle. A tool can be as complicated as a computer.

The invention and use of arches was important technology in ancient Rome. An **invention** is something made for the first time. The Romans needed to get water to their cities. They figured out that an arch with a central stone could support a lot of weight. They used these arches for building bridges and for carrying water to the cities.

The keystone, or central stone wedged at the top, keeps the stones of the arch in place.

1. ✓**Checkpoint** What is technology?

2. **Art** in Science Draw a picture in your **science journal** of two kinds of technology that were not around 100 years ago.

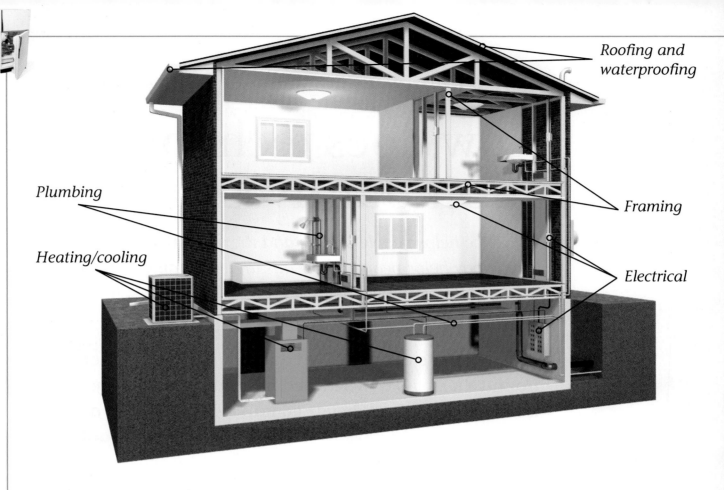

Roofing and waterproofing

Framing

Electrical

Plumbing

Heating/cooling

Technology in Your Home

Technology found in a house or apartment is more than a loose bunch of inventions. Different parts of buildings work together as systems, which interact.

For example, when you flush the toilet, you use the plumbing system. This system is made of faucets, drains, sinks, and pipes linked together. Some water in the system passes through a water heater. The electrical system is connected to it. Electricity heats the water. You wouldn't like to take a shower if these systems didn't interact, would you?

In a similar way, the heating and cooling system is made up of many parts that work together. The furnace in some systems burns fuel. Others use electricity. No matter what energy source is used, the heating system needs the electrical system to turn it on and off. In these ways, technology systems interact and work together.

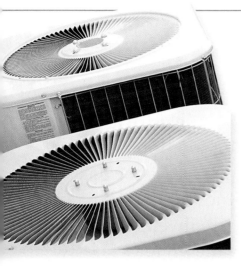

These air conditioning units are part of the cooling system. This system keeps us comfortable during hot summers.

What technology do you see in the frame of the house shown here? Boards are not placed just any old way. House designers know that placing the boards in certain patterns makes the building sturdy. To create the form of something, you need to plan it out in a skillful way.

Now look closely at the particle boards that form part of the wall. They are made of wood chips that have been pressed and glued together. Such wood chips used to be burned. That caused air pollution. New technology now turns those chips into strong boards for buildings.

Particle board is a technology that solves two problems at once. It provides a strong building material and uses waste wood chips that would otherwise be burned.

1. ✓ **Checkpoint** Explain how some technology systems work together in a house.

2. **Writing in Science**
Expository In your **science journal** write a paragraph about two technology systems you would expect to find in a kitchen.

Technology Yesterday, Today, and Tomorrow

A kitchen in the early 1800s did not have electricity. So there was no refrigerator or freezer to keep things cold. People had to chop wood to burn in a stove to cook their food. Preparing meals could take most of the day.

Every few years brought more and more inventions and ideas. Ice boxes made of wood and metal, for example, held blocks of ice that kept food cold. Food could be kept longer without spoiling. Ice boxes were a fantastic technology—until electric refrigerators came along.

Technology has made today's kitchens change in many ways since the 1800s. Microwave ovens cook food in minutes. Electric dishwashers replace the chore of washing dishes by hand.

What do you do with leftovers? Plastic bowls with an airtight seal were invented in 1947.

The non-stick coating on this pan was invented in 1954. How did that make cooking easier?

To hear music not long ago, you played a record with wavy grooves scratched into it. While it spun, a metal needle was dragged along the groove. A machine read the vibrations in the needle. The machine then translated the vibrations into sound. In an audio CD player, a special beam of light now reads the computer-coded plastic discs. A computer translates the information to sound.

This CD player uses a light beam to read and play back the music stored on compact discs.

It's hard to imagine how technology will affect the homes of tomorrow. Some people think that computers will soon run the entire home. Perhaps computer chips in each package of food will tell the oven how to cook it. Refrigerators might be connected to the Internet. The refrigerator could order food over the Internet when food supplies are running low.

Will these and other ideas come true? Probably some of them will. One thing is for sure. As long as people continue to learn, technology will change. Who knows what exciting things are in store?

This DVD player uses a light beam to play back movies recorded on plastic discs.

✓ Lesson Checkpoint

1. Why was the invention of the arch important technology in ancient Rome?

2. Explain the need for systems in order for technology to work in the home.

3. **Social Studies** in Science How is a modern kitchen different from a kitchen in the early 1800s?

No more getting lost! Signals from satellites track the exact location of this car.

Satellites with special cameras provide images with many kinds of information.

What are some new technologies?

Modern technology includes tools that allow us to go far beyond what we can normally see and hear.

Tools for Extending Our Senses

People on ships once had to figure out where they were by looking at stars. Now people can use a Global Positioning System (GPS). This system relies on signals from satellites. A ship's GPS computer uses the signals to figure out the ship's location.

What if you were hiking in a forest? You could use a GPS receiver the size of a cell phone to find your way. Some cars have GPS. Farmers may use GPS on their tractors to locate crops that need their attention.

Cameras in satellites can also make pictures using the infrared light that growing things give off. These satellites track crops, forests, and grasslands over time. Infrared pictures show where plants are too dry or are not growing well. Infrared pictures can also show detailed weather patterns. Forecasters use the pictures to observe and predict the weather.

Tools for Processing Information

A **computer** stores, processes, and sends electronic information incredibly fast! For instance, a computer can rapidly turn countless bits of information about the weather into a weather forecast.

Computer technology is everywhere. A digital watch tells time with a computer chip. Calculators, cameras, and cars all use computer chips.

Optical fibers are making computer networks better. These fibers are thin strands of bendable glass that use light to carry information. The fibers are replacing wires in computer, telephone, and cable television systems. Optical fibers do not get hot like wires. They take up less space. Also, a single fiber can carry more data than hundreds of wires twisted into a fat cable.

Copper wires are being replaced in communication systems by optical fibers.

Small wireless phones are replacing bulky phones fixed in place.

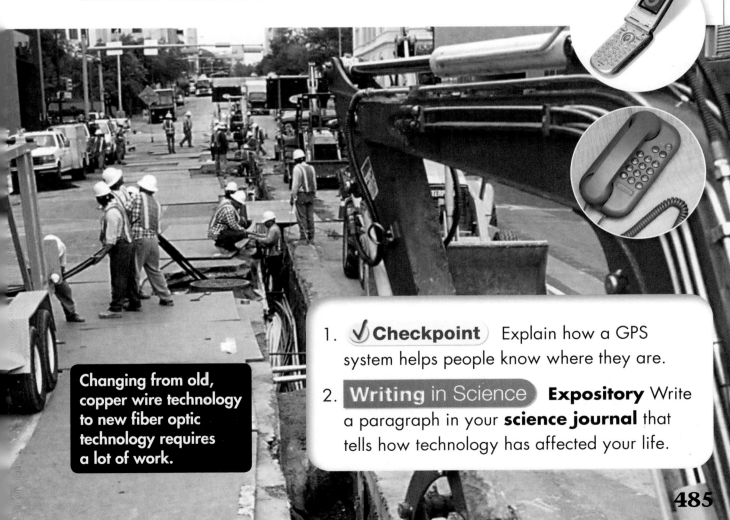

Changing from old, copper wire technology to new fiber optic technology requires a lot of work.

1. ✓**Checkpoint** Explain how a GPS system helps people know where they are.

2. **Writing** in Science **Expository** Write a paragraph in your **science journal** that tells how technology has affected your life.

Tools for Transporting Materials

Roads are a very important part of our lives. We travel on them to go to work and school. We follow them to pick up and deliver goods. We use them to visit friends and family or just to see the sights.

Fast, safe highways are now in place. Some people call the National Highway System the greatest wonder of the modern world. This system includes all the major highways that go from one state to another. About 80 million trucks carry the nation's supplies on over 260,000 kilometers (160,000 miles) of national highways. About 120 million cars carry passengers from place to place.

The United States began to build the National Highway System so that military vehicles like this one could move quickly over great distances.

Did you ever wonder how complex highway systems are designed? That's the job of highway engineers.

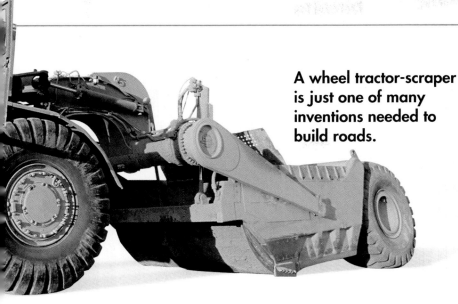

A wheel tractor-scraper is just one of many inventions needed to build roads.

Trains began to transport goods on railroads long before trucks began to transport goods on freeways.

Planes are now the fastest way to carry cargo. Cargo planes can carry loads that weigh 100,000 kg.

Big tools are needed for building big highways. First, earthmoving machines like the tractor-scraper in the picture lay out the new road. Then workers lay down sand, crushed stone, and concrete or asphalt. Finally, workers paint markings and put up traffic signs.

Roads are not the only pathways over which people and things move. People and freight use railroads and planes such as the ones shown.

The first transportation system in the United States was the nation's rivers. Today, boats push barges loaded with freight over the same rivers. Technology will always help get people and things from place to place.

1. ✓**Checkpoint** Why is a modern roadway system important?

2. **Technology** in Science Use the Internet to view maps of the National Highway System. Then plan a trip across the country using the maps.

Using powerful tugboats has improved our nation's river transportation system.

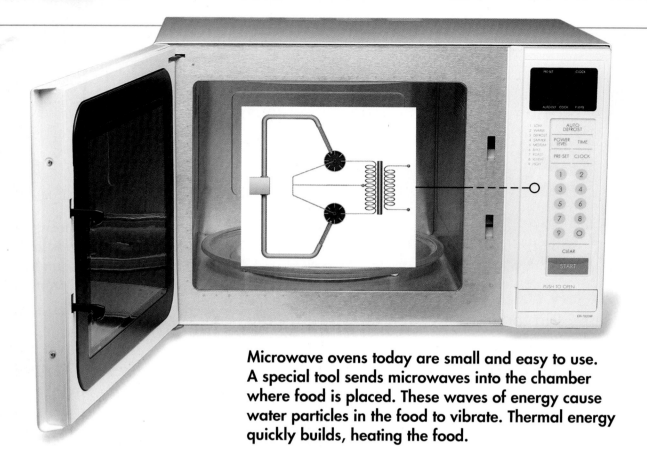

Microwave ovens today are small and easy to use. A special tool sends microwaves into the chamber where food is placed. These waves of energy cause water particles in the food to vibrate. Thermal energy quickly builds, heating the food.

Unexpected Uses

Sometimes technology becomes useful in unplanned ways. For example, back in 1946 Percy Spencer was working to improve radar. He was testing a light bulb that used microwave energy. Microwaves are a form of radiation, like visible light and invisible radio waves.

One day Spencer stood near the tube. He noticed that a candy bar in his pocket melted. Curious, he put popcorn kernels near the microwave energy. They rapidly popped into fluffy pieces.

Spencer realized that if microwaves could quickly cook popcorn, they could quickly cook other foods, too. He made a drawing that led to the first microwave oven. Technology that was first designed for radar is a great help to those who eat in a hurry!

This design by Percy Spencer explains how the first microwave oven would work. The first oven weighed 750 pounds and cost $5,000.

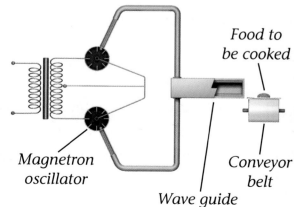

Food to be cooked

Magnetron oscillator

Wave guide

Conveyor belt

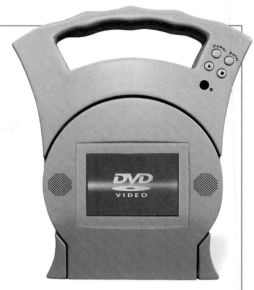

Will you watch TV today? Television sets and computers started out using glass tubes to display the picture. But these tubes cannot be made to be very big. Glass is heavy and breaks easily in big screens. Now TV screens are huge. How could this happen? New technology makes the difference. In 1970, James Fergason invented the first modern LCD screen. LCD stands for liquid crystal display. Electricity causes each fluid crystal to act like the shutter in a camera. The crystals either block the light or allow the light to pass through. This causes an image on the screen. Screens using these crystals do not need heavy glass. They are light in weight. They are also flat, as the picture shows.

DVD players that you can carry show movies on tiny LCD screens.

✓ Lesson Checkpoint

1. What did Percy Spencer accidentally discover that microwaves could do?

2. What does a computer do?

3. **Writing** in Science Why was it important for Percy Spencer to keep asking questions after his candy bar melted? Answer this question in a paragraph in your **science journal.**

A screen made of glass is shaped like a box. But this LCD screen is flat. Computers using LCD screens do not take up a lot of desk space.

Lesson 3

How does technology help us get energy?

Technology has changed the way we get energy. But most of the energy sources we use today cause problems for the environment. We can use technology to develop cleaner energy sources.

Mills used to grind grain into flour. Others drove machinery that made things.

Using Energy

Plop in a DVD, pop some popcorn in the microwave, and you're set to watch a movie. But be sure everything is plugged in! Today we take our electrical energy for granted. In the past it wasn't so easy.

Before engines and electricity, people relied on wind and water as sources of energy. Water-powered mills like the one shown were built next to rivers. The force of flowing water turned a big wheel. At a sawmill, for instance, the wheel turned a series of rods, gears, and belts. This caused saws to cut wood.

Moving water makes the parts in this lawn sprinkler spray water in different directions.

The force of water runs a modern lawn sprinkler. Study the diagram shown. First, the hose sends water into the sprinkler. The moving water has kinetic energy to do work. Water then turns a waterwheel. Next, the waterwheel turns wheel and axle gears. The gears slowly rock the spray arm back and forth. Finally, water from the spray arm waters the lawn.

Windmills were also used to do work. As you might guess, windmills use the energy of moving air instead of water as a power source. The windmill in the picture is still used today. The turning blades move gears in a small box. The gears move a rod up and down. This pumps water from under the ground.

There are good and bad things connected with using windmills and water mills. They do not pollute the air or water. However, water mills can only work along a river. Both wind and water are renewable energy resources. But they don't supply enough power for all our needs.

1. ✔**Checkpoint** What renewable sources of energy have people used for centuries to generate power?

2. **Sequence** Use a graphic organizer and describe the steps of how a modern water sprinkler works.

Windmills like this one use wind energy to pump water.

491

Producing Electricity

We still use waterwheel technology inside hydroelectric power dams. These dams are built on rivers that back up behind the dam to form reservoirs. Study the diagram. The deep water stores potential energy. To release this energy to do work, gates let water rush into the power station. The kinetic energy of the flowing water then spins the blades of waterwheels in turbines. The spinning axle of each turbine drives a generator to make electricity. The electricity is used for power in cities.

Hydroelectric power does not produce much pollution. Since it depends on water, it also is a renewable energy source. But dams can affect fish that travel up the rivers on which the dams are built. The large lake behind the dam floods land, which then changes the environment. There also is a danger of more flooding if a dam breaks.

Generators like this one in a hydroelectric dam change the energy of flowing water into electricity.

Below each generator, the energy of moving water becomes the energy of moving blades in a turbine.

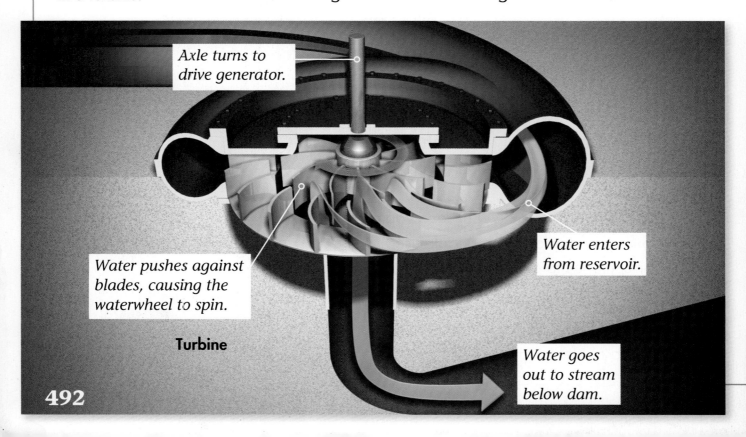

Axle turns to drive generator.

Water pushes against blades, causing the waterwheel to spin.

Water enters from reservoir.

Turbine

Water goes out to stream below dam.

Another way to change energy into electricity is by burning coal, oil, or natural gas. The heat from burning this fuel is used to boil water. Boiling water makes steam. Pressure from steam turns wheels of turbines that drive electricity generators.

This technology is a solution to the problem of producing enough electricity for everyone. But this is an example of how technology can create problems too. Burning fuel for electric generators can pollute the air. Burning fuels to move cars also pollutes the air. People are working on ways to use technology to make cars and generators that pollute less.

Map Fact

Herbert Hoover Dam sits on the Colorado River that divides Arizona and Nevada. It was completed in 1936. Hoover Dam is one of the largest dams in the world.

1. ✔ **Checkpoint** How are cars a helpful and a harmful example of technology?

2. **Social Studies** in Science Use the library to learn more about how Hoover Dam on the Colorado River was built.

Future Sources of Energy

Our energy needs seem to keep growing. How will we meet these needs in the future? Many people are working to answer that question.

Solar energy is one answer. This energy comes directly from the Sun's rays. Panels, like the ones in the picture, gather the Sun's rays. Each panel has lots of small solar cells spread across it. The cells work together to provide enough power to be useful. Solar energy is a major source of electricity in desert areas where there are many days of sunshine.

New technology is making solar energy cheaper to use. Many people put panels on the roofs of their houses. Instead of making electricity, however, they make hot water. First, water runs through small tubes. Next, the energy of the Sun's rays is changed into heat when the panels absorb the rays. Then the heat warms the water in the tubes. Finally, the heated water flows into a container that stores the hot water until it's time to take a shower.

Solar panels concentrate the Sun's rays. This energy is changed into electricity.

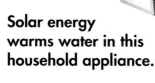

Solar energy warms water in this household appliance.

Wind rotates the arms of these windmills to generate electricity.

Wind energy also holds promise. Thousands of windmills like the ones above have already been set up in areas where the wind blows strong and often. To change enough kinetic energy of wind into electrical energy, the blades must be huge. Some blade wheels are wider than a football field is long! Computer technology can sense changing wind conditions. Motors then make shifts in the direction and angle of the blades. Doing this makes the most use of the wind for making the most electricity. These wind farms produce a lot of electricity for the surrounding community.

1. ✓**Checkpoint** What two renewable energy resources might meet more of our energy needs in the future?

2. **Sequence** List the steps that lead from the energy of sunshine in solar panels to the energy of hot water in a water tank. Use a graphic organizer.

Technology Time Line

Throughout human history, people have made discoveries and inventions to improve their lives.

312 B.C.
Rome completes the first aqueducts. Aqueducts brought water to Roman cities.

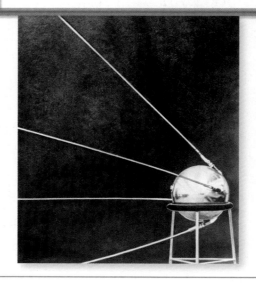

3500 B.C.
People connect wooden planks with other pieces of wood to make wheels.

1608
Dutch eyeglass maker Hans Leppershey places lenses in a tube and makes the first telescope. The famous scientist Galileo soon improves this tool and makes important discoveries about space.

1957
The Soviet Union launches the first artificial satellite, called *Sputnik 1*. It is only about the size of a basketball but this new piece of technology starts an international race for space.

1948
Opening of the Mount Palomar Observatory in California. It allows scientists to collect new data about our galaxy and beyond. Until 1976 it is the world's largest single-mirror telescope.

1903
Orville and Wilbur Wright invent the powered airplane. The first flight lasts only 12 seconds but it sparks a whole new wave of inventions that build the airline industry.

1876
Alexander Graham Bell invents the telephone. Imagine what life would be like without telephones.

2004
Spirit, the Mars expedition rover, prepares to drill into a rock. Will manned expeditions to Mars be soon to come?

1969
Astronauts Neil Armstrong and Edwin Aldrin land on the surface of the Moon. The *Apollo 11* astronauts bring moon rocks back to Earth for further study.

✔ Lesson Checkpoint

1. What changes in technology have changed the way we get energy?

2. What must we do in order to continue to use non-renewable fuel resources for energy?

3. **Math in Science** Figure the time in years between the Wright's flight, the launch of *Sputnik 1,* and the first Moon landing. How does this show how fast technology is changing?

Investigate How does a GPS device find your location?

GPS, the Global Positioning System, can tell you your location anywhere on the globe—if you have a GPS device. The Global Positioning System uses GPS satellites to help find your location. In this activity, you solve a problem: How does a GPS device find a location?

Materials

Location of
GPS Satellites over
North America

metric ruler

3 circle patterns

What to Do

1 **Make a model** of how a GPS device finds your location. The GPS device learns you are 2,500 km from satellite A. On this map 5 cm stands for 2,500 km. So, use a circle pattern to draw a circle around satellite A with a 5 cm radius.

Satellite	Actual Distance from Your Location (km)	Distance on Map from Your Location (cm)
A	2,500 km	5 cm
B	1,500 km	3 cm
C	2,000 km	4 cm

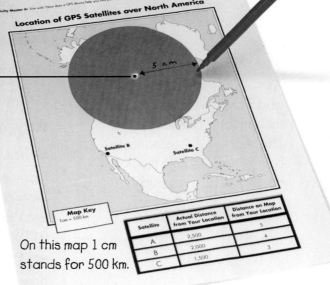

Satellite A

The 5 cm circle shows all the places that are 2,500 km from satellite A. Because you are 2,500 km from satellite A, you must be somewhere on this 5 cm circle.

On this map 1 cm stands for 500 km.

2 Repeat step 1 for satellites B and C. Use the distances shown in the chart to make 2 more circles. Your location must be on each of these circles too.

3 Your location is the spot where all the circles meet. Mark an **X** on the map to record your location.

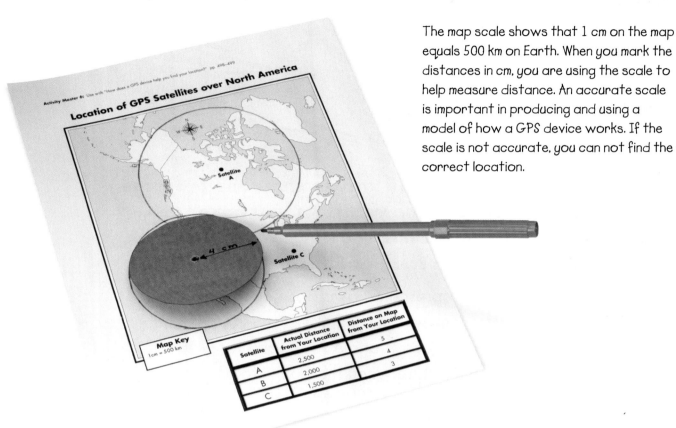

The map scale shows that 1 cm on the map equals 500 km on Earth. When you mark the distances in cm, you are using the scale to help measure distance. An accurate scale is important in producing and using a model of how a GPS device works. If the scale is not accurate, you can not find the correct location.

Location of GPS Satellites over North America

Activity Master 6: Use with "How does a GPS device help you find your location?" pp. 498-499

• Satellite A

• Satellite C

4 cm

Map Key
1 cm = 500 km

Satellite	Actual Distance from Your Location	Distance on Map from Your Location
A	2,500	5
B	2,000	4
C	1,500	3

The data for this activity includes the satellite locations, your distance from each satellite, the circles you made, and the **X** you made to show your position.

Explain Your Results

1. You needed to know your distance from more than 2 satellites in order to find your location. **Infer** why at least 3 satellites were needed.

2. Describe the scale on this map and tell how you used it to **measure** distance. Why was the scale important in this **model** of how a GPS device finds a location?

Go Further

What would happen if the three satellites were in different places? Use a map to find a new GPS location, or investigate other questions you may have.

Technology
Through the Years

Using a time line is a good way to show the progress of technology through the years. As you have seen, a time line is a number line showing events that took place during a certain span of time.

Any number can be represented as a position on a number line. The position of a number on a number line is important. Since 0.5 is halfway between 0 and 1, the point for 0.5 (or 1/2) should be halfway between the points for 0 and 1. Notice where 0.25 and 0.75 are placed.

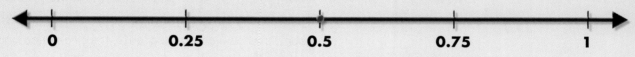

Since 25 is one fourth of 100, the point for 25 should be one fourth of the distance from 0 to 100.

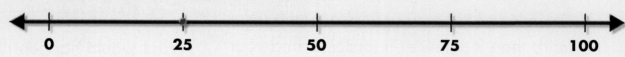

In the same way, on a time line, the point for the year 1950 should be halfway between the points for the years 1900 and 2000. 1925 would be one fourth of that distance. 1975 would be three fourths of the distance from 1900 to 2000.

| 1900 | 1925 | 1950 | 1975 | 2000 |

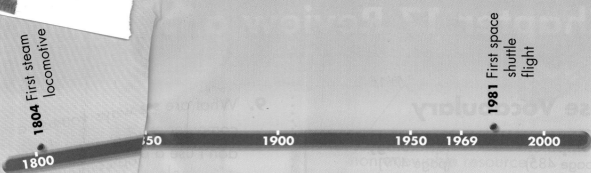

1804 First steam locomotive

1981 First space shuttle flight

1800 | 1850 | 1900 | 1950 | 1969 | 2000

On grid paper, copy the time line above. Count grid squares to place the given points correctly. For each event in the table below, mark a point on your time line. Label each point with the year and the event above the line. The first event is already on the line you copied.

Transportation Technology

	Event		Year	Event
1	First steam locomotive	6	1956	Beginning of National Highway system
2	First railroad tracks laid across the U.S.	7	1969	First moon-landing by astronauts
	First gasoline-powered automobile	8	1981	First space shuttle flight
3	First gasoline-powered airplane	9	1999	First hot-air balloon flight around the world
34	First diesel train in the U.S.	10	2004	First privately-funded space flight

17.

Lab zone Take-Home Activity

Make a time line that shows how technology has changed over the years. You might choose computers, space travel, or buildings. Use library resources to find important dates and events. Choose what events you want to show.

Science Teacher

Dr. Michelle Thaller

Ms. Doris Daou

Are you excited about science? How would you like to get students, teachers, and the public excited about science too? Michelle Thaller and Doris Daou, for instance, are Astronomers and Teachers for NASA. They promote the exciting work NASA is doing to help people study space.

Dr. Thaller and Ms. Daou help schoolteachers use NASA materials in their lessons. They appear on television shows. They speak to thousands of students every year. One area of study they teach audiences about is the use of special telescopes. For instance, following Earth in its orbit around the Sun is the Spitzer Space Telescope. Using infrared technology, it takes pictures of stars and solar systems that hide behind vast clouds of gas and dust.

Science teachers go to college and learn about life, earth, physical, and space science. They train in schools like yours to gain experience in teaching students like you.

Lab zone Take-Home Activity

Find out more about how infrared telescopes work. Describe the difference between pictures taken with visible light and with infrared rays.

Spitzer Space Telescope

Unit D Test Talk

Test-Taking Strategies

Find Important Words

Choose the Right Answer

Use Information from Text and Graphics

▶ Write Your Answer

Write Your Answer

To answer the following test questions, you need to write your answer. Read the passage and then answer the questions.

The Sun and other stars appear to move across the sky because Earth is moving. Earth rotates, or spins, on its axis. One complete spin, or rotation, takes 24 hours. This rotation and light from the Sun cause the patterns of day, night, and shadows.

Earth also revolves or moves in an orbit around the Sun. One complete trip around the Sun is one revolution. One revolution takes one year. Earth's axis always points in the same direction. As a result, sometimes the northern half of Earth is tilted toward the Sun and receives the most direct sunlight. Sometimes the southern half of Earth is tilted toward the Sun. Earth's tilt and movement around the Sun causes the patterns of seasons.

The Sun is the star at the center of our solar system. Mercury, Venus, Mars, Jupiter, Saturn, Uranus, and Neptune are other planets besides Earth that orbit the Sun. These and other objects that revolve around the Sun make up the solar system.

Use What You Know

To write your answer to each question, you need to read the passage and the test question carefully. Write your answers in complete sentences. Then read your answer to make sure it is complete, correct, and focused.

1. What causes the patterns of day, night, and shadows?

2. What are two ways that Earth moves?

3. Explain how Earth's tilt and revolution cause seasons.

4. What are the names of the planets in our solar system?

Unit D Wrap-Up

Chapter 15

What patterns do the Earth, Sun, Moon, and stars show?

- Earth's revolution around the Sun and rotation on a tilted axis cause the patterns of day, night, shadows, seasons, and the movement of stars across the sky.

- Light from the Sun and the revolution of the Moon around Earth cause the patterns of the phases of the Moon and eclipses.

Chapter 16

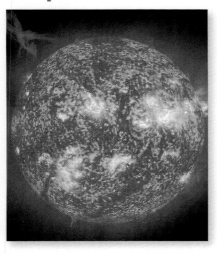

How are the planets in the solar system alike and different?

- The planets in the solar system all rotate on an axis and revolve around the Sun in orbits. The planets are different sizes, different distances from the Sun, and take different amounts of time to rotate and revolve.

- Each planet in the solar system has special features that make it different from the other planets.

Chapter 17

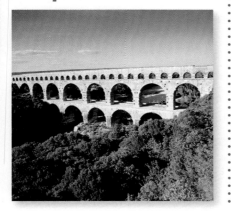

How does technology affect our lives?

- Technology applies the knowledge gained from science to solve problems and improve our lives.

- Technology helps us to get energy to do work and to develop cleaner energy sources.

Performance Assessment

Model a Solar System

Use a large sheet of paper and colored markers to make a model of a solar system that has a star, three planets, and one moon. Describe the parts of the solar system and the patterns your model shows. What is at the center of your model? How are the planets alike and different?

Read More About Space and Technology!

Look for books like these in the library.

Lab zone Full Inquiry

Experiment How does the speed of a meteorite affect the crater it makes?

Materials

safety goggles

copier paper box lid

spoon, marble,
cup with flour

metric ruler and
meterstick

calculator or
computer (optional)

Process Skills

In an **experiment**, you **identify** the independent and dependent **variables**. You **control** other variables.

Ask a question.

How does the speed of a meteorite affect the size of the crater it makes?

State a hypothesis.

If a meteorite is moving faster, then will it make a crater with a width that is smaller than, larger than, or about the same size as a crater made by a slower meteorite? Write your **hypothesis**.

Identify and control variables.

The marble is a **model** of a meteorite. The flour is a model of the surface the meteorite hits. Use the same marble and the same amount of flour in all tests. These are **controlled variables**.

> Controlled variables are things you need to keep the same if you want a fair test.

The variable you change is the height from which you drop the marble. A marble dropped from a greater height will be moving faster when it hits the flour pile.

> The variable you change is the independent variable.

The variable you will measure is the width of the crater.

> The variable you measure is the dependent variable.

> What are the controlled, independent, and dependent variables?

More Lab Activities Take It to the Net
pearsonsuccessnet.com

Test your hypothesis.

1 In the center of the box lid, make a flat pile of flour.

Be careful!

Follow safety rules. Wear safety goggles. If you cannot safely drop a marble from 1.5 meters, explore ways to solve this problem with your teacher.

2 Place the empty flour cup on the floor. Stand above the cup. Close one eye. Aim down at the cup. Drop a marble into the cup. Practice until the marble lands in the cup every time. Then try dropping the marble from 1.5 m above the cup.

3 Now it is time to make your crater. Drop the marble from a height of 0.5 m (50 cm). Hit the center of the flour pile. Measure the width of the crater.

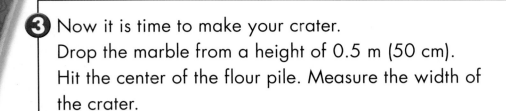

Select a tool to measure the width of the crater in millimeters.

4 Remove the marble. Push the pile back together. Repeat steps 3 and 4 twice.

5 Repeat steps 4 and 5, but drop the marble from 1 m and 1.5 m.

When you repeat your observations and measurements, you can improve their accuracy. Record accurately. Do not change your results because others have different results. Similar investigations seldom turn out exactly the same. However, similar results are expected. Accurate records help scientists learn why there are differences in repeated experiments.

Collect and record your data.

	Crater Width (mm)		
	Marble dropped from a height of 0.5 m	Marble dropped from a height of 1 m	Marble dropped from a height of 1.5 m
Trial 1			
Trial 2			
Trial 3			
Average			

Your teacher may ask you to use a calculator or a computer with the right software. These tools can help you find the averages and help you graph your data.

Interpret your data.

Make a bar graph. Study your chart and graph.
What patterns do you see in your data?

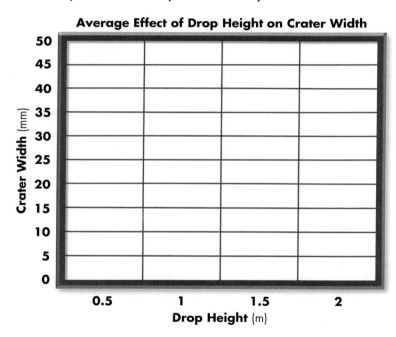

Discuss your observations with others.

State your conclusion.

Describe your results. Compare your hypothesis with your results.
Communicate your conclusion.
Explain the effect of drop height on crater width.

Go Further

Interpret your data to predict the effect of dropping the marble from other heights. Use your model system to check your prediction.

Science Fair Projects

Using Scientific Methods

1. Ask a question.
2. State your hypothesis.
3. Identify/control variables.
4. Test your hypothesis.
5. Collect and record your data.
6. Interpret your data.
7. State your conclusion.
8. Go further.

Observing Patterns of Daylight

The Sun appears to rise in the east and set in the west.

Idea: Use a calendar and a watch with a second hand to observe and record the time the Sun rises and sets every day for two months.

Planet-Size Models

One way that planets in the solar system are different is their size.

Idea: Use a metric ruler and posterboard to make models that demonstrate the size of the Sun and each of the planets.

Inventing

People use their knowledge to design new tools and new ways to do things that solve problems and improve their lives.

Idea: Use your knowledge to invent a tool or a way to do something to make a job easier.

EC CRU I0 9 8 7 6 5 4 3 2 1

Metric and Customary Measurement

The metric system is the measurement system most commonly used in science. Metric units are sometimes called SI units. SI stands for International System because these units are used around the world.

These prefixes are used in the metric system:

kilo- means *thousand*
1 kilometer equals 1,000 meters
centi- means *hundredths*
100 centimeters equals 1 meter
milli- means one-*thousandth*
1,000 millimeters equals 1 meter

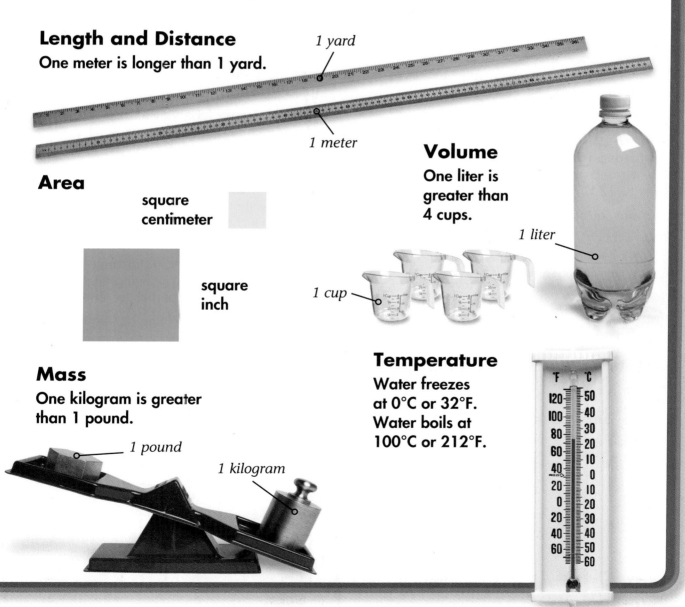

Length and Distance
One meter is longer than 1 yard.

1 yard

1 meter

Area

square centimeter

square inch

Volume
One liter is greater than 4 cups.

1 liter

1 cup

Mass
One kilogram is greater than 1 pound.

1 pound

1 kilogram

Temperature
Water freezes at 0°C or 32°F.
Water boils at 100°C or 212°F.

Glossary

The glossary uses letters and signs to show how words are pronounced. The mark ′ is placed after a syllable with a primary or heavy accent. The mark ′ is placed after a syllable with a secondary or lighter accent.

To hear these words pronounced, listen to the AudioText CD.

Pronunciation Key

a	in hat	ō	in open	sh	in she
ā	in age	ȯ	in all	th	in thin
â	in care	ô	in order	ŦH	in then
ä	in far	oi	in oil	zh	in measure
e	in let	ou	in out	ə	= a in about
ē	in equal	u	in cup	ə	= e in taken
ėr	in term	u̇	in put	ə	= i in pencil
i	in it	ü	in rule	ə	= o in lemon
ī	in ice	ch	in child	ə	= u in circus
o	in hot	ng	in long		

A

absorb (ab sôrb′) to take in (p. 373)

adaptation (ad′ ap tā′ shən) trait that helps a living thing survive in its environment (p. 48)

asteroid (as′tə roid′) a small chunk of rock that orbits around the Sun (p. 457)

atmosphere (at′mə sfir) the blanket of air and gases that surround the Earth (p. 176)

atom (at′əm) one of the tiny particles that make up all of matter (p. 282)

axis (ak′sis) an imaginary line around which Earth spins (p. 424)

B

blizzard (bliz′ərd) a winter storm with very low temperatures, strong winds, heavy snowfall, and blowing snow (p. 183)

buoyancy (boi′ən sē) force exerted on an object that is immersed in a gas or liquid that tends to make it float (p. 286)

C

carnivore (kär′nə vôr) living things that hunt other animals for food (p. 106)

cause (kȯz) why something happens (p. 277, 311)

change of state (chānj uv stāt) physical change that takes place when matter changes from one state to another (p. 304)

chemical change (kem′ə kəl chānj) a change that causes one kind of matter to become a different kind of matter (p. 311)

classifying (klas′ə fī′ing) to arrange or sort objects, events, or living things according to their properties (p. 244)

collecting data (kə lek′ ting dā′ tə) to gather observations and measurements into graphs, tables or charts (p. 26)

communicating (kə myü′ nə kāt′ ing) using words, pictures, charts, graphs, and diagrams to share information (p. 324)

community (kəm myü′ nə tē) all the populations that live together in the same place (p. 74)

compare (kəm pâr′) to show how things are alike (p. 5, 245, 389, 453)

competition (kom′ pə tish′ən) struggle that happens when two or more living things need the same resource (p. 110)

compression wave (kəm presh′ən wāv) wave that has spaces where particles are squeezed together and spaces where particles are spread apart (p. 396)

computer (kəm pyü′ tər) tool which stores, processes, and gets electronic information (p. 485)

conclusion (kən klü′ zhən) decision reached after considering facts and details (p. 101)

condensation (kon′ den sā′ shən) the changing of a gas into a liquid (p. 157)

coniferous tree (kō nif′ər əs trē) a tree that produces seeds in cones (p. 16)

conservation (kon′ sər vā′ shən) wise use of natural resources (p. 250)

constellation (kon′ stə lā′ shən) a group of stars that make a pattern (p. 438)

consumer (kən sü′ mər) living things that eat food (p. 106)

contrast (kən trast′) to show how things are different (p. 5, 245, 389, 453)

core (kôr) the innermost layer of Earth (p. 223)

crust (krust) the outermost layer of Earth (p. 223)

decay (di kā′) to break down, or rot (p. 118, 206)

deciduous (di sij′ü əs) loses leaves in fall and grows new ones in spring (p. 14)

decomposer (dē′kəm pō′zər) a living thing that breaks down waste and things that have died (p. 118)

density (den′sə tē) measure of the amount of matter in a certain amount of space (p. 286)

desert (dez′ərt) an ecosystem that gets less than 25 cm of rainfall a year (p. 78)

details (di tālz′) individual pieces of information that support a main idea (p. 69, 357)

disease (də zēz′) the name we give an illness (p. 126)

dwarf planet (dwôrf plan′it) small, ball-shaped object that revolves around the Sun (p. 465)

earthquake (ėrth′kwāk′) a shaking of Earth's crust caused by sudden, shifting movements in the crust (p. 228)

ecosystem (ē′kō sis′təm) all the living and nonliving things that interact with each other in a given area (p. 72)

effect (ə fekt′) what happens as the result of a cause (p. 149, 277)

electric charge (i lek′trik chärj) tiny amount of energy in the particles of matter (p. 374)

electric circuit (i lek′trik sėr′kit) the path that a controlled electric current flows through (p. 376)

electric current (i lek′trik kėr′ənt) the movement of an electric charge from one place to another (p. 376)

element (el′ə mənt) matter that has only one kind of atom (p. 282)

energy (en′ ər jē) the ability to do work or to cause a change (p. 359)

environment (en vī′rən mənt) everything that surrounds a living thing (p. 71)

equator (i kwā′ tər) the imaginary line that separates the north and south halves of Earth (p. 429)

erosion (i rō′ zhən) the movement of weathered materials (p. 232)

estimating and measuring (es′tə māt ing and mezh′ər ing) to tell what you think an object's measurements are and then to measure it in units (p. 210)

evaporation (i vap′ ə rā′ shən) the changing of a liquid into a gas (p. 157)

experiment (ek sper′ə ment) to formulate and test a hypothesis using a scientific method (p. 140)

explore (ek splôr′) to study a scientific idea in a hands-on manner (p. 36)

extinct (ek stingkt′) no longer lives on Earth (p. 23)

food chain (füd chān) the movement of energy from one type of living thing to another (p. 108)

food web (füd web) the flow of energy between food chains which ties a community together (p. 108)

force (fôrs) a push or a pull (p. 332)

forming questions and hypotheses (fôrm′ing kwes′chənz and hī poth′ə sēz′) to think of how you can solve a problem or answer a question (p. 140)

fossil (fos′ əl) remains or mark of a living thing from long ago (p. 22)

friction (frik′ shən) a contact force that opposes the motion of an object (p. 333)

gas (gas) the form of matter which has no shape, has particles that are not connected to each other, and takes up whatever space is available (p. 281)

germinate (jėr′ mə nāt) begins to grow (p. 20)

germs (jėrmz) small living things that include bacteria and viruses, many of which can cause illness (p. 126)

grassland (gras′ land′) land ecosystem that has many grasses and few trees (p. 76)

gravity (grav′ə tē) a non-contact force that pulls objects toward each other (p. 336)

groundwater (ground′ wȯ′ tər) water that has slowly made its way through soil and then collects in spaces between underground rock; it is brought to the surface by digging wells (p. 155)

habitat (hab′ə tat) the place where a living thing makes its home (p. 72)

heat (hēt) the transfer of thermal energy from one piece of matter to another (p. 366)

herbivore (ėr′bə vôr) living things that eat only plants (p. 106)

hibernate (hī′bər nāt) to spend winter resting; body systems slow down in order to save energy (p. 52)

hurricane (hėr′ə kān) a huge, strong storm that forms over the ocean (p. 182)

identifying and controlling variables (ī den′tə fī ing and kən trōl′ ing vâr′ē ə bəlz) to change one thing, but keep all the other factors the same (p. 40)

igneous rock (ig′nē əs rok′) rock that forms when melted earth materials cool and harden (p. 200)

inclined plane (in klīnd′ plān) a slanting surface that connects a lower level to a higher level (p. 340)

inference (in′fər əns) a conclusion based on facts, experiences, observations, or knowledge (p. 173)

inferring (in fėr′ ing) to draw a conclusion or make a reasonable guess based on what you have learned or what you know (p. 100)

inherited (in her′it əd) passed on from parent to offspring (p. 48)

interpreting data (in tėr′prit ing dā′tə) to use the information you have collected to solve problems or answer questions (p. 26)

invention (in ven′ shən) something that has been made for the first time (p. 479)

investigate (in ves′ tə gāt) to solve a problem or answer a question by following an existing procedure or an original one (p. 26)

investigating and experimenting (in ves′ tə gāt ing and ek sper′ə ment ing) to plan and do an investigation to test a hypothesis or solve a problem (p. 508)

kinetic energy (ki net′ik en′ər jē) energy of motion (p. 361)

landform (land′ fôrm) a natural feature on the surface of Earth's crust (p. 224)

larva (lär′ və) stage in an insect's life after it hatches from the egg (p. 45)

lava (lä′ və) hot, molten rock on Earth's surface (p. 226)

lever (lev′ər) a simple machine used to lift and move things (p. 341)

life cycle (līf sī′kəl) the stages through which an organism passes between birth and death (p. 44)

light (līt) a form of energy that can be seen (p. 370)

liquid (lik′wid) matter that does not have a definite shape but takes up a definite amount of space (p. 280)

loam (lōm) soil that contains a mixture of humus and mineral materials of sand, silt, and clay (p. 209)

lunar eclipse (lü′nər i klips′) Earth's shadow moving across the Moon (p. 434)

magma (mag′mə) hot, molten rock that forms deep underground (p. 226)

magnetic (mag net′ik) having the property to pull on, or attract, metals that have iron in them (p. 337)

magnetism (mag′nə tiz′əm) a non-contact force that pulls objects containing iron (p. 337)

main idea (mān ī dē′ə) what a paragraph is about; the most important idea (p. 69, 357)

making operational definitions (māk′ ing op′ə rā′ shən əl def′ə nish′ənz) to define or describe an object or event based on your own experience (p. 68)

making and using models (māk′ ing and yüz′ ing mod′lz) to make a model from materials or to make a sketch or a diagram (p. 36)

mantle (man′tl) the middle layer of Earth (p. 223)

mass (mas) amount of matter (p. 284)

matter (mat′ər) anything that takes up space and has mass (p. 279)

metamorphic rock (met′ ə môr′ fik rok′) rock that forms when existing rock is changed by heat and pressure (p. 200)

microscopic (mī′krə skop′ ik) not able to be seen without a microscope (p. 126)

migrate (mī′ grāt) to move to another place to find better climate, food, or a mate (p. 52)

mineral (min′ ər əl) natural material that forms from nonliving matter (p. 199)

mixture (miks′ chər) two or more kinds of matter that are placed together but can be easily separated (p. 306)

Moon (mün) the natural satellite that orbits around Earth (p. 432)

Moon phase (mün fāz) the way the Moon looks because of the amount of the lit side of the Moon that can be seen from Earth at the same time (p. 434)

motion (mō′shən) a change in the position of an object (p. 327)

natural resources (nach′ ər əl ri sôrs′əz) natural materials, such as soil, wood, water, air, oil, or minerals, that living things need (p. 247)

nonrenewable resources (non ri nü′ə bəl ri sôrs′ əz) resource that cannot be replaced once it is used up (p. 248)

nutrient (nü′ trē ənt) thing plants need in order to grow (p. 206)

observing (əb zėrv′ ing) using your senses to find out about objects, events, or living things (p. 4)

omnivore (om′ nə vôr′) living things that eat plants and other animals for food (p. 106)

orbit (ôr′ bit) the path of any object in space that revolves around another object in space (p. 456)

organ (ôr′ gən) a structure containing different tissues that are organized to carry out a specific function of the body such as a stomach, intestine, etc. (p. 123)

periodic table (pir′ē od′ik tā′bəl) an arrangement of elements based on their properties (p. 283)

physical change (fiz′ ə kəl chānj) a change that makes matter look different without becoming a new substance (p. 303)

pitch (pich) how high or low a sound is (p. 392)

planet (plan′it) a large, ball-shaped body of matter that revolves, or travels, around any star (p. 456)

pollinate (pol′ ə nāt) move pollen from the part of a flower that makes pollen to the part of a flower that makes seeds (p. 15)

pollution (pə lü′ shən) waste materials that make the environment dirty (p. 124)

population (pop′ yə lā′ shən) all the living things of the same kind that live in the same place at the same time (p. 74)

position (pə zish′ ən) the location of an object (p. 327)

potential energy (pə ten′shəl en′ ər jē) the energy something has because of its position (p. 360)

precipitation (pri sip′ə tā′ shən) water that falls to Earth as rain, hail, sleet, or snow (p. 159)

predator (pred′ə tər) a consumer that hunts other animals for food (p. 107)

predicting (pri dikt′ ing) to tell what you think will happen (p. 162)

pressure (presh′ər) force per unit area that is applied to a substance (p. 281)

prey (prā) any animal that is hunted by others for food (p. 107)

producer (prə dü′sər) living things that make their own food (p. 106)

property (prop′ər tē) something about matter that you can observe with one or more of your senses (p. 279)

pulley (pul′ē) a machine that changes the direction of motion of an object to which a force is applied (p. 343)

pupa (pyü′pə) stage in an insect's life between larva and adult (p. 45)

recycle (rē sī′kəl) treat or process something so it can be used again (p. 254)

reflect (ri flekt′) to bounce off of (p. 372)

refract (ri frakt′) to bend (p. 372)

relative position (rel′ə tiv pə zish′ən) a change in an object's position compared to another object (p. 329)

renewable resource (ri nü′ ə bəl ri sôrs′) resource that is endless like sunlight, or that is naturally replaced in a fairly short time, such as trees (p. 247)

resource (ri sôrs′) See Natural Resources, Renewable Resources, Nonrenewable Resources

revolution (rev′ə lü′ shən) one complete trip around the Sun (p. 428)

rock (rok) natural, solid, nonliving material made of one or more minerals (p. 199)

rotation (rō tā′ shən) one complete spin on an axis (p. 425)

scientific method (sī′ən tif′ik meth′əd) organized ways of finding answers and solving problems (p. xxvi)

sedimentary rock (sed′ə men′tər ē rok′) rock that forms when small pieces of earth materials collect and become bound together (p. 200)

seed leaf (sēd lēf) part of a seed that has stored food (p. 20)

seedling (sēd′ ling) a new, small plant that grows from a seed (p. 20)

sequence (sē′kwəns) the order in which events take place (p. 37, 221, 421, 477)

soil (soil) the part of Earth's surface consisting of humus and weathered rock in which plants grow (p. 206)

solar system (sō′lər sis′təm) the Sun, eight planets and their moons, dwarf planets, and other objects that revolve around the Sun (p. 456)

solid (sol′id) matter that has a definite shape and takes up a definite amount of space (p. 280)

solution (sə lü′shən) a mixture in which one or more substances dissolves in another (p. 308)

speed (spēd) the rate at which an object changes position (p. 330)

star (stär) a massive ball of hot gases that produces its own light (p. 423)

states of matter (stāts uv mat′ər) the forms of matter – solid, liquid, and gas (p. 304)

summarize (sum′ə rīz′) to cover the main ideas or details in a sentence or two (p. 325)

Sun (sun) our star; a huge ball of hot, glowing gases (p. 424)

system (sis′təm) a set of parts that interact with one another (p. 8)

technology (tek nol′ə jē) the use of science knowledge to invent tools and new ways of doing things (p. 479)

telescope (tel′ə skōp) a tool that gathers lots of light and magnifies objects that are far away and makes faint stars easier to see (p. 436)

thermal energy (thėr′məl en′ər jē) the total kinetic energy of all the particles that make up matter (p. 366)

tool (tül) an object used to do work (p. 479)

tornado (tôr nā′ dō) a rotating column of air that touches the ground and causes damage with its high winds (p. 182)

trait (trāt) a feature passed on to a living thing from its parents (p. 40)

tundra (tun′drə) land ecosystem that is cold and dry (p. 80)

vertebrate (vėr′tə brit) animal with a backbone (p. 40)

vibration (vī brā′shən) a very quick back-and-forth movement (p. 392)

volcano (vol kā′nō) an opening in the Earth's crust from which hot, melted material erupts (p. 226)

volume (vol′yəm) amount of space matter takes up (p. 285)

water cycle (wȯ′tər sī′kəl) the movement of water from Earth's surface into the air and back again (p. 158)

water vapor (wȯ′tər vā′pər) water in the form of an invisible gas in the air (p. 154)

weather (weℓH′ər) what it is like outside including temperature, wind, clouds, and precipitation (p. 175)

weathering (weℓH′ər ing) any process that changes rocks by breaking them into smaller pieces (p. 230)

wetland (wet′land′) low land ecosystem that is covered by water at least part of the time during the year; marshes and swamps are wetlands (p. 86)

wheel and axle (wēl and ak′səl) a simple machine made of a wheel and a rod joined to the center of the wheel (p. 342)

work (wėrk) what happens when a force moves an object over a distance (p. 338)

Index

This index lists the pages on which topics appear in this book. Page numbers after a *p* refer to a photograph or drawing. Page numbers after a *c* refer to a chart, graph, or diagram.

Earth, p424, 424–425, p425, 453, p456, 457, 458, p458
axis of, 424
changes from erosion, 232–233
extremes on, c460, p461
fossils and, 56
Hubble Space Telescope and, 446
layers of, 223–225
life on, 460–461, p460–461
lunar eclipse and, 434
Moon and, 432–433
plates on, 461
rotation of, 425, 459
seasons and, 428–429, p428–429
shapes on surface of, 224, p224, p225
size of, 459
water on, 148, 154, p154

Earthquake, 228, p228
damage from, 229, p229
measuring, c236, 236–237

Earthworm, p206

Echo, 399

Eclipse, p419, 434, p434

Ecosystem, 71–75
desert, p78, 78–79, p79
forest, 82–83, p83
freshwater, 86, p86, p87
grasslands, 76–77, p77
groups within, 74, p75
parts of, 72, c72
saltwater, 88, p89
tropical forest, 84, p85
tundra, p80, 80–81, p81
water, 86–89

Egg
animal growth and, 44
butterfly, p44
frog, p46

Electrical energy, 359, c363, 367, p374, 374–377, p375, p376, c377

Electrical Engineer, 384

Electric charge, p354–355, 374–375

Electric circuit, p355, p376, 376–377, c377

Electric current, p355, 376, p376, 376–377, c377

Electricity, p370
form changed by, c377
in home, 480, p480
light from, 371
past and present technology and, 482
producing, p492, 492–493, p493
in space missions, 384
water for, 152, p153

Element, p274, 282, p282, 283, p283

Energy, 354, 357, p357, 359, p359
changing form by, 362–363
electrical, p374, 374–377, p375, p376, c377
from food, 123
in food web, 108
forms of, c363
from fuels, 248
future sources of, 494–495, p494–495
heat, p366, 366–369, p367, p368, p369
light, 370–373
for living things, 106–109
of motion, 361
for new and recycled goods, p255
sound and, 386, 398

sources of, 490
technology and, 490–495
travel of, 364–365, p364–365
in waves, 365

Environment, 71
of California redwood tree, p73
change in, 114–117
clean, p121
healthy for people, 120–123
living things return to, 116
patterns of change in, 118–119

Epedocles, p283

Equator, 429

Erosion, p219, 232–233, p233, 234–235

Eruption, 221, p221

Estimating and Measuring, 172, 210, 211, 269, 290, 291, 414, 452

Evaporation, p146, 157, 158, p159, 309, 369

Everglades, 86, p86

Evergreen trees. See Coniferous trees

Exercise, p124, 124–125

Exercising in Space, 350–351, p350–351

Exhaust, 179

Experiment. See Full Inquiry, Experiment

Experimenting. See Investigating and Experimenting

Explore. See Directed Inquiry, Explore

Credits

Photographs

Every effort has been made to secure permission and provide appropriate credit for photographic material. The publisher deeply regrets any omission and pledges to correct errors called to its attention in subsequent editions.

Unless otherwise acknowledged, all photographs are the property of Scott Foresman, a division of Pearson Education.

Photo locators denoted as follows: Top (T), Center (C), Bottom (B), Left (L), Right (R), Background (Bkgd).

Cover: ©Flip Nicklin/Minden Pictures, ©David Nardini/Getty Images.

Front Matter: iii Daniel J. Cox/Natural Exposures, (T) Getty Images; v ©Frans Lanting/Minden Pictures; vi ©DK Images; vii (R) ©Randy M. Ury/Corbis, (L) ©Breck P. Kent/Animals Animals/Earth Scenes; viii ©Jack Dykinga/Getty Images; xi ©Douglas Peebles/Corbis; xii ©Lloyd Cluff/Corbis; xv ©RNT Productions/Corbis; xxii ©Timothy O'Keefe/Index Stock Imagery; xxiii Getty Images; xxiv ©Robert Sullivan/AFP/Getty Images; xxix Getty Images; xxv ©Frank Greenaway/DK Images; xxviii (BL) Getty Images, (CL) ©Dave King/DK Images; xxx ©Comstock Inc.

Unit Dividers: Unit A (Bkgd) Getty Images, (CC) Digital Vision; Unit B (Bkgd) ©Kim Heacox/Getty Images, (BC) Getty Images; Unit C (Bkgd) ©Lester Lefkowitz/Getty Images; Unit D (Bkgd) Corbis

Chapter 1: 1 (B) ©Wolfgang Kaehler/Corbis, (T, C) Getty Images; 2 (T) ©John Warden/Index Stock Imagery, (BL) DK Images, (BL) Getty Images, (BR) ©Nigel Cattlin/Photo Researchers, Inc.; 3 (BL) ©Nigel Cattlin/Holt Studios, (BC) Neg./Transparency no. K13073. Courtesy Dept. of Library Services/American Museum of Natural History; 5 (CR) ©Stone/Getty Images, (Bkgd) ©John Warden/Index Stock Imagery; 6 ©John Warden/Index Stock Imagery; 7 (BR) ©Jim Steinberg/Photo Researchers, Inc., (TR) ©Photographer's Choice/Getty Images; 8 ©DK Images; 9 (CR, TR, BR) ©DK Images, (TC) Getty Images; 10 (R) Silver Burdett Ginn, (TL) Getty Images; 11 ©DK Images; 12 ©Lou Jacobs Jr./Grant Heilman Photography; 13 (TR) ©George Bernard/NHPA Limited, (TR) ©DK Images, (CR) ©TH Foto-Werbung/Photo Researchers, Inc., (TR) ©Niall Benvie/Corbis, (BR) ©The Garden Picture Library/Alamy Images; 14 (BL) ©Stone/Getty Images, (BR) ©Jeff Lepore/Photo Researchers, Inc., (TL) ©Peter Smithers/Corbis; 15 (BR) ©DK Images, (TL) Getty Images; 16 (B) ©Carolina Biological/Visuals Unlimited, (TL) Getty Images; 17 (CL) ©M & C Photography/Peter Arnold, Inc., (TR) ©Brad Mogen/Visuals Unlimited, (TC) ©Pat O'Hara/Corbis, (CR) ©Wally Eberhart/Visuals Unlimited, (BR) ©DK Images; 18 (BC) ©Darryl Torckler/Getty Images, (CR) ©Brian Gordon Green/NGS Image Collection, (BC) ©John Poutier/Maxx Images, Inc., (BC) ©Jorg & Petra Wegner/Animals Animals/Earth Scenes, (TL) ©DK Images; 19 (L) ©DK Images, (CR) ©Steve Bloom Images/Alamy Images; 21 (CL) ©DK Images, (CR) Nigel Cattlin/Holt Studios, (BC) ©Kenneth W. Fink/Photo Researchers, Inc., (BC) ©Nigel Cattlin/Photo Researchers, Inc.; 23 (TR) ©Dr. E. R. Degginger/Color-Pic, Inc., (CL) ©John Cancalosi/Peter Arnold, Inc., (TL) Neg./Transparency no. K13073. Courtesy Dept. of Library Services/American Museum of Natural History, (BR) ©David Muench/Muench Photography, Inc, (CR) ©James L. Amos/Corbis; 24 (BL) ©The Natural History Museum, London, (BR, TL) ©DK Images; 26 ©Ed Young/Corbis; 28 (TR) ©Dennis MacDonald/PhotoEdit, (CR) ©Inga Spence/Visuals Unlimited, (CR) ©Steven Emery/Index Stock Imagery, (BR) ©Comstock Inc.; 31 (TL) DK Images, (TR) ©Kenneth W. Fink/Photo Researchers, Inc.; 32 (Bkgd) ©MSFC/NASA, (TL, BR) NASA.

Chapter 2: 33 (B) ©Barbara Von Hoffmann/Animals Animals/Earth Scenes, (Bkgd) ©David Harrison/Index Stock Imagery; 34 (BL) ©David L. Shirk/Animals Animals/Earth Scenes, (CR) ©Tom Brakefield/Corbis, (BR) ©Jeff L. Lepore/Photo Researchers, Inc.; 35 (BL, BR) ©Brad Mogen/Visuals Unlimited; 37 (C) ©David Stover/ImageState, (Bkgd) ©Tom Brakefield/Corbis; 38 Tom Brakefield/Corbis; 39 (BR) ©Tom Vezo/Nature Picture Library, (BC) ©Zefa/Masterfile Corporation, (BL) ©Taxi/Getty Images, (BC) ©Natural Visions/Alamy Images, (TR) ©Frans Lanting/Minden Pictures; 40 (B) ©Tom Brakefield/Bruce Coleman Inc., (TL) ©Randy M. Ury/Corbis; 41 (CR) ©DK Images, (BC) ©Jim Brandenburg/Minden Pictures, (CR) ©Frans Lanting/Minden Pictures, (CR) Getty Images, (TR) ©Ken Lucas/Visuals Unlimited; 42 (BL) Jupiter Images, (TL) ©David Aubrey/Corbis, (TR) ©Danny Lehman/Corbis, (TR) ©Robert Pickett/Corbis, (CR) ©The Image Bank/Getty Images, (BR) ©Brian Rogers/Visuals Unlimited; 44 (TL, TR) ©DK Images, (BR) ©Charles Melton/Visuals Unlimited; 45 (B) ©Brad Mogen/Visuals Unlimited, (T) ©Dick Scott/Visuals Unlimited; 46 (CL) ©Bettmann/Corbis, (BR) ©Keren Su/China Span/Alamy Images, (TL) ©Zefa/Masterfile Corporation; 47 (TR) ©Carolina Biological Supply Company/Phototake, (CL, BL) ©DK Images, (BR) ©Breck P. Kent/Animals Animals/Earth Scenes, (BR) ©Randy M. Ury/Corbis; 48 (BR) ©DK Images, (TR) ©Ken Lucas/Visuals Unlimited, (TL) ©Tony Evans/Timelapse Library/Getty Images; 49 (CL) ©Frans Lanting/Minden Pictures, (TR) ©Kevin Schafer/Corbis, (CR) ©Gary W. Carter/Corbis, (BR) ©DK Images; 50 ©Vittoriano Rastelli/Corbis, (TL) ©Photodisc Green/Getty Images; 51 (TC) ©Rod Planck/Photo Researchers, Inc., (CC) ©James Robinson/Animals Animals/Earth Scenes, (TL) ©Michael Quinton/Minden Pictures, (TR) ©Chris Newbert/Minden Pictures, (CL) ©The Image Bank/Getty Images, (BL) ©Rolf Kopfle/Bruce Coleman Inc., (BC) ©Tim Laman/NGS Image Collection, (BC) ©Suzanne L. & Joseph T. Collins/Photo Researchers, Inc., (CC) ©Steve E. Ross/Photo Researchers, Inc., (TC) ©Ken Wilson/Papilio/Corbis, (CR) ©David Aubrey/Corbis, (BR) ©E. R. Degginger/Bruce Coleman, Inc., (BL) ©Rick & Nora Bowers/Visuals Unlimited; 52 (TR) ©DK Images, (CR) ©George Grall/NGS Image Collection, (BR) ©Jeff L. Lepore/Photo Researchers, Inc., (TL) ©Eric and David Hosking/Corbis, (TL) ©Photodisc Blue/Getty Images; 53 (T) ©Gerry Ellis/Minden Pictures, (B) ©Terry W. Eggers/Corbis; 54 (TL) ©James L. Amos/Photo Researchers, Inc., (B) ©DK Images, (CL) ©Layne Kennedy/Corbis; 55 (TL) ©DK Images, (TR) ©Breck P. Kent/Animals Animals/Earth Scenes; 56 (R) ©Breck P. Kent/Animals Animals/Earth Scenes, (B) Senekenberg Nature Museum, (TL) Colin Keates/Courtesy of the Natural History Museum, London/©DK Images; 57 ©Ross M. Horowitz/Getty Images; 58 ©Larry L. Miller/Photo Researchers, Inc.; 60 Digital Vision; 61 ©Masa Ushioda/Visual & Written/Bruce Coleman, Inc.; 63 ©DK Images; 64 (TL) ©Dutheil Didier/SYGMA/Corbis, (BL) ©Reuters/Corbis.

Chapter 3: 65 (Bkgd) Getty Images, (T) ©Photodisc Green/Getty Images; 66 (T) ©Mark E. Gibson Stock Photography, (BL) ©J. Eastcott/Y. Eastcott Film/NGS Image Collection, (BR) ©Enzo & Paolo Ragazzini/Corbis; 67 (BL) ©Andy Binns/Ecoscene, (BR) ©Jim Zipp/Photo Researchers, Inc., (CR) ©Alan Carey/Photo Researchers, Inc., (TR) ©Steve Kaufman/Corbis; 69 ©Mark E. Gibson Stock Photography; 70 ©Mark E. Gibson Stock Photography; 71 ©Siede Preis/Getty Images; 72 Getty Images; 73 (Bkgd) ©Melissa Farlow/Aurora & Quanta Productions, (TC) ©DK Images, (BC) ©Kurt Stier/Corbis; 74 (CL) ©Royalty-Free/Corbis, (BL) ©Alan Carey/Photo Researchers, Inc.; 75 (CR) ©Joseph Van Os/Getty Images, (L) ©Kennan Ward/Corbis, (BR) Darren Bennett/Animals Animals/Earth Scenes; 76 ©OSF/Animals Animals/Earth Scenes; 77 (T) ©Enzo & Paolo Ragazzini/Corbis, (BL) ©Jason Edwards/NGS Image Collection, (BR) Steve Kaufman/Corbis; 78 (BL) ©Jack Dykinga/Getty Images, (BR) Jerry Young/©DK Images, (TL) ©DK Images; 79 (Bkgd) ©J. Eastcott/Y. Eastcott Film/NGS Image Collection, (TL) Daniel J. Cox/Natural Exposures; 80 (BL) Daniel J. Cox/Natural Exposures, (TL) ©Ed Reschke/Peter Arnold, Inc.; 81 (L) ©Andy Binns/Ecoscene, (TR, CR, CR) Daniel J. Cox/Natural Exposures; 82 ©Tim Laman/NGS Image Collection; 83 (TR) ©Michio Hoshino/Minden Pictures, (TL, BR) ©Jim Brandenburg/Minden Pictures, (BL) ©Jay Dickman/Corbis, (CR) ©David Ulmer/Stock Boston; 84 (CR) ©Roy Toft/NGS Image Collection, (TR) ©Claus Meyer/Minden Pictures, (BR) ©Ken Preston-Mafham/Animals Animals/Earth Scenes, (TL) Alamy; 85 (BL) ©Michael & Patricia Fogden/Minden Pictures, (T) ©Tui De Roy/Minden Pictures; 86 (B) Daniel J. Cox/Natural Exposures, (TR) ©Jim Zipp/Photo Researchers, Inc., (TL) ©Roy Toft/NGS Image Collection; 87 (Bkgd) Daniel J. Cox/Natural Exposures, (TR) ©Joseph H. Bailey/NGS Image Collection; 88 (TL) ©Medford Taylor/NGS Image Collection, (BR) ©Fred Bavendam/Peter Arnold, Inc.; 89 (TR) ©Mick Turner/PhotoLibrary, (Bkgd) ©Royalty-Free/Corbis; 90 Getty Images; 95 ©Ken Preston-Mafham/Animals Animals/Earth Scenes; 96 ©Bettmann/Corbis.

Chapter 4: 97 ©M. Colbeck/OSF/Animals Animals/Earth Scenes; 98 (T) ©Stephen Frink/Corbis, (BL) ©Carol Havens/Corbis, (BR) ©K. H. Haenel/Zefa/Masterfile Corporation; 99 (BL) ©D. Robert and Lorri Franz/Corbis, (TR) ©Jim Brandenburg/Minden Pictures, (CR) ©Dr. Gopal Murti/Photo Researchers, Inc., (BR) ©Gerald Hinde/ABPL/Animals Animals/Earth Scenes; 101 (CR) ©Richard Walters/Visuals Unlimited, (Bkgd) ©Stephen Frink/Corbis, (BR) ©Bob Marsh/Papilio/Corbis, (CC) ©David Boag/Alamy Images; 102 ©Stephen Frink/Corbis; 103 (CR) Brand X Pictures, (BR) ©Patti Murray/Earth Scenes/Maxx Images, Inc., (CR) ©Laura Sivell/Papilio/Corbis, (TR) Getty Images; 104 (B) ©Richard Kolar/Animals Animals/Earth Scenes, (T) ©Rick Raymond/Index Stock Imagery; 105 (T) ©Michael & Patricia Fogden/Corbis, (B) ©B. Jones/M. Shimlock/Photo Researchers, Inc.; 106 (BL) ©Chase Swift/Corbis, (BC) ©Carol Havens/Corbis, (BR) ©Frank Blackburn/Ecoscene/Corbis, (TL) ©Hope Ryden/NGS Image Collection; 107 (B) ©D. Robert and Lorri Franz/Corbis, (TL) ©K. H. Haenel/Zefa/Masterfile Corporation, (CL) ©Randy Wells/Corbis, (BL) ©Danny Lehman/Corbis; 108 (TL, BL) Getty Images, (BR) ©Yva Momatiuk/John Eastcott/Minden Pictures, (BC) ©Naturfoto Honal/Corbis, (CC) ©Kevin R. Morris/Corbis; 109 (C) Minden Pictures, (CR) ©Claudia Adams/Alamy Images, (BL) ©Tom Brakefield/Corbis; 110 (T) ©Gerry Ellis/Minden Pictures, (CL) ©Michael & Patricia Fogden/Corbis, (BL) ©Martin Harvey/Photo Researchers, Inc., (TL) ©Photodisc Green/Getty Images; 111 ©Gerald Hinde/ABPL/Animals Animals/Earth Scenes; 112 (T) ©DK Images, (CL) ©Raymond Gehman/Corbis, (BL) ©Scott Camazine/Photo

The NATIONAL GEOGRAPHIC SOCIETY

100 YEARS OF ADVENTURE AND DISCOVERY

The NATIONAL GEOGRAPHIC SOCIETY

100 YEARS OF ADVENTURE AND DISCOVERY

C. D. B. BRYAN

HARRY N. ABRAMS, INC. PUBLISHERS

Page 1: Lightning dances across the mountains behind Tucson, Arizona.

Pages 2–3: African elephants find drink and sanctuary in Namibia's Etosha National Park.

Pages 4–5: The gaping crater of Washington State's Mount St. Helens a year after the May 18, 1980, eruption.

Pages 6–7: The face behind the mask of an Asaro Valley, Papua New Guinea,"Mudman."

Pages 8–9: A frog-eating bat swoops down at a poisonous toad.

Pages 10–11: Afghan horsemen play the national sport, *buz kashi*, a wild version of polo.

Pages 12–13: The roof of the world: the Himalayas in Nepal.

This page: Four large mullet in Japan's Izu Oceanic Park.

Overleaf: The Great Pyramids at Giza, Egypt.

Editor, First Edition: Edith Pavese
Editor, Updated and Enlarged Edition: Robert Morton
Editorial Assistant, Updated and Enlarged Edition: Nola Butler
Art Director: Samuel N. Antupit
Designer, Updated and Enlarged Edition: Liz Trovato

Library of Congress Cataloging-in-Publication Data
Bryan, C. D. B. (Courtlandt Dixon Barnes)
   The National Geographic Society : 100 years of adventure and discovery / C.D.B. Bryan.
      p.   cm.
   Includes bibliographical references and index.
   ISBN 0–8109–3696–8 (clothbound)
   1. National Geographic Society (U.S.)   I. Title.
G3.N37B79   1997
910'.6'073—dc21   97–10714
ISBN 0–7922–7080–0(NGS)/ISBN 0–7922–7081–9 (NGS: deluxe ed.)

Printed and bound in Japan

Harry N. Abrams, Inc.
100 Fifth Avenue
New York, N.Y. 10011
www.abramsbooks.com

Contents

Introduction

Writing this book could not have been anything but fun. To have the opportunity to explore nearly one hundred years of the National Geographic Society's history is like becoming a child again—a child who, confined indoors on a languorous, rainy, endless summer afternoon, discovers in the attic of a rented beach cottage the elaborate illustrated family albums of a somewhat eccentric, always fascinating, and truly remarkable clan.

Since its founding in 1888, the Society has been offering "a window on the world" to millions of its members. Before color photography, before movies and television, the familiar *National Geographic Magazine* provided—through riveting eyewitness accounts and dazzling photographs—the primary means by which generations of armchair explorers first discovered the distant wonders, exotic customs, and strange people throughout our world. A century of exploding scientific knowledge and expanding ecological awareness is reflected in the pages of the Magazine, as are a hundred years of American intellectual curiosity and the Society's sometimes rose-colored political attitudes and reporting. Books, articles, and films disseminate the results of diverse scientific researches. And its Explorers Hall displays its heroes' memorabilia.

What are five-score years of the Society's journal but nearly twenty-dozen memory-crowded scrapbooks in which stirring adventures, awesome disasters, breakthrough discoveries, and daring explorations have been carefully recorded? How can one not feel affection for a Society that has played so significant a role in the dreams of so many millions?

Where else but in the pages of the *Geographic* might one read the entirely serious late-nineteenth-century report of a man who proposed attaching hydrogen-inflated balloons to himself so that he might bound across the frozen Arctic wastes to reach the North Pole?

Where else but at the Society could one browse unrestrained through the correspondence of one of this nation's legendary editors—Gilbert Hovey Grosvenor—and discover that two of his Salem forebears had been hanged as witches? Or learn that a French Ambassador had awarded him the Legion of Honor for having done so much to "vulgarize geography"? Or find such a gem of dismissal as this terse Grosvenor note written in 1930 to an editor about a man seeking Society support: "Mr. Graves, this man is a windbag! He can

Opposite: Bradford and Barbara Washburn map the heart of Grand Canyon, a monumental seven-year task completed in 1970.

19

use more words & say less than a Tibetan prayer wheel. I wouldn't answer him further."

During the year and a half I lived and worked among the men and women of the National Geographic Society, I was able to interview them freely. I read their articles and books, pored over their photographs, paintings, and films. I attended their lectures and press conferences, sat in on their division meetings, and first suffered and then appreciated their researchers' meticulous dedication to facts. I lunched with them, laughed with them, shared their visions and their stories. There really is nothing like the National Geographic Society in the world.

Where else could one find a nineteenth-century English explorer's account of his adventures in Africa as charming as this excerpt taken from a January 1899 *National Geographic Magazine* report, "Lloyd's Journey Across the Great Pygmy Forest":

> ...I reached the Belgian frontier post of M'beni on October 1, and then entered the great dark forest. Altogether I was twenty days walking through its gloomy shades...At one little place in the middle of the forest...I came upon a great number of pygmies who...told me that, unknown to myself, they had been watching me for five days, peering through the growth of the primeval forest at our caravan. They appeared to be very frightened, and even when speaking covered their faces. I slept at this village, and in the morning I asked the chief to allow me to photograph the dwarfs. He brought ten or fifteen of them together, and I was enabled to secure a snapshot. I could not give a time exposure, as the pygmies would not stand still. Then with great difficulty I tried to measure them, and I found not one of them over four feet in height... Their arms and chests were splendidly developed, as much so as in a good specimen of an Englishman.

Albert B. Lloyd, one of those Englishmen who hitherto seemed to have existed only in our comic imaginations, continued his journey down the Belgian Congo's (now Zaire) Aruwimi River, where, he wrote,

> Personally I was received most kindly by these cannibals. They are, it is true, warlike and fierce, but open and straightforward. I did not find them to be of the usual cringing type, but manly fellows who treated one as an equal. I had no difficulty with them whatever. At one place I put together the bicycle I had with me, and, at the suggestion of these people, rode round their village in the middle of a forest. The scene was remarkable, as thousands of men, women, and children turned out, dancing and yelling, to see what they described as a European riding a snake.

How could there not be a special satisfaction in having the chance to read, firsthand, explorer Robert E. Peary's 1909 account of becoming the first to reach the North Pole; or Hiram Bingham's discoveries in 1912 at Machu Picchu; or Richard E. Byrd's 1926 and 1930 articles on being the first to fly over the North and South Poles; or the Army balloonists' 1935 daring, record-setting ascent into the stratosphere? Or Barry C. Bishop's sense of accomplishment upon his successful ascent of Everest in 1963 despite the loss of his toes?

How could there not be a thrill in sharing, even vicariously, Matthew Stirling's excitement in 1939 at unearthing in the Mexican jungle a colossal and mysterious twenty-ton stone head? Or Jacques Cousteau's exhilaration diving with Aqua-Lungs to sunken ships in the 1950s? Or Jane Goodall's pleasure in a baby chimp's affection in the 1960s? Or Louis and Mary Leakey's excitement with their discoveries during the 1960s and 1970s of our early ancestor's fossils and footsteps in East Africa? Or Robert D. Ballard's awe in the 1980s upon seeing the huge, rusting, sunken remains of the once-grand luxury liner *Titanic*, lost in a collision with an iceberg nearly three-quarters of a century before. In spirit and support, the Society was with them all.

Members visiting the Geographic's marble and glass headquarters in Washington, D.C., rarely get beyond Explorers Hall on the first floor. Visitors on their way back from viewing one of Peary's heavy sledges or the patched, taffeta American flag he wore wrapped around his body during his dash to the Pole, might see Society staff passing through the lobby or waiting at the elevators—the men, conservatively dressed in jackets and ties, politely stepping aside to let equally properly-dressed women staff members enter the elevators first. But the staff's deceptive appearance would give no hint of the adventures they have experienced and the stories they have to tell. Tales of bandit raids and angry mobs, of walking away from airplane and helicopter crashes, of being flung from boats into icy rapids, of having cameras bitten by crocodiles or retrieved only through tugs-of-war with venomous sea snakes, of surviving shark bites, capricious imprisonments, and mysterious fevers.

Where else but at the Society would one learn of freelance photographer Alan Root, who, while on assignment in Mzima Springs, Kenya, in 1974, was attacked by a bull hippopotamus. "The next thing I knew," Root said, "he had my right leg in his mouth. The hippo then shook me like a rat." After skin grafts, treatment for gangrene, and a month's convalescence in a Nairobi hospital, Root recovered.

Where else might a guest be privy to such amusing anecdotes as the one told me by former Geographic staffer Edwards Park, who, upon learning he was being sent on assignment to Machu Picchu, had sought Illustrations Editor Kip Ross' advice and was told, "Watch out for snakes." Ted Park, hating snakes, pressed Ross for details and learned that Ross, while riding mule back up to the high ridge upon which the lost city of the Incas had been built, had heard little rustling noises in the grass along the trail and asked his guide, "Pedro, what is that?"

"Señor," the guide said, "that is a fer-de-lance."

"Oh my God," Ross said. The fer-de-lance, he knew, was a species of large, extremely dangerous pit viper that infests those parts. Ross and the guide rode together in silence for a few minutes then Ross asked, "Pedro, what happens if I get bitten by a fer-de-lance? What do I do?"

Pedro thought for a moment and answered, "Señor, you *compose* yourself."

With annual receipts in excess of $350 million, with nearly eleven million members in 170 out of the 174 nations that now exist, the National Geographic Society is the largest non-profit scientific and educational membership institution in the world. Why has the Geographic been so successful?

National Geographic Editor Wilbur E. Garrett asked himself that same question in 1983. "I believe it is primarily because we still fill the same need felt by that small group of thoughtful men who gave us our start almost a century ago," he wrote, "—a need to address the insatiable human curiosity to know what makes this world tick."

Within the pages of this centennial volume that celebrates the National Geographic's insatiable curiosity with the world around it, it is my hope that readers may gain some insight into what makes the Society "tick" as well.

"A Society for the Increase and Diffusion of Geographical Knowledge"

Washington, D.C., January 10, 1888.

Dear Sir:

You are invited to be present at a meeting to be held in the Assembly Hall of the Cosmos Club, on Friday evening, January 13, at 8 o'clock P.M., for the purpose of considering the advisability of organizing a society for the increase and diffusion of geographical knowledge.

Very respectfully, yours,

Gardiner G. Hubbard.
A.W. Greely,
   Chief Signal Officer, U.S.A.
J.R. Bartlett,
   Commander, U.S N.

Henry Mitchell,
   U.S. Coast and Geod. Survey.
Henry Gannett,
   U.S. Geol. Survey.
A.H. Thompson,
   U.S. Geol. Survey
And Others.

O n January 13, 1888, a damp, chilly Friday evening in the nation's capital, thirty-three gentlemen made their way by foot, on horseback, or by elegant private carriages through the fog to the Cosmos Club, a club notable over the preceding decade for its ability to draw upon Washington's scientific élite for its members. The thirty-three gentlemen—bearded, mustached, in heavy dark suits with high stiff collars and somber four-in-hand ties tucked into waistcoats crossed by thick gold chains—had been invited to gather at the clubhouse, situated on Lafayette Square diagonally across from the White House, that evening at eight to consider "the advisability of organizing a society for the increase and diffusion of geographical knowledge."

They were geographers, explorers, military officers, lawyers, meteorologists, cartographers, naturalists, bankers, educators, biologists, engineers, geodesists, topographers, inventors. As one of their own put it, they were the "first explorers of the Grand Canyon and the Yellowstone, those who had carried the American flag farthest north, who had measured the altitude of our famous mountains, traced the windings of our coasts and rivers, determined the distribution of flora and fauna, enlightened us in the customs of the aborigines, and marked out the path of storm and flood."

There was the prematurely aged Brigadier General Adolphus Washington Greely, Chief Signal Officer of the United States Army, who seven years earlier as a thirty-seven-year-old lieutenant with no Arctic experience had led an expedition of men farther north than any had gone before and become stranded. Not rescued until 1884, only Greely and six of the original twenty-five men were found still alive.

There was the heroic, pain-wracked geologist and explorer John Wesley Powell, who lost his right arm in the bloody Battle of Shiloh and seven years

Preceding spread: *Responding to an invitation to organize "a society for the increase and diffusion of geographical knowledge," thirty-three men gathered at Washington's Cosmos Club on January 13, 1888. Within its first year the Society's fledgling* National Geographic Magazine *began publication. Artist Stanley Meltzoff based his painting of the Society's founding fathers' historic meeting on individual portraits. (See key opposite.)*

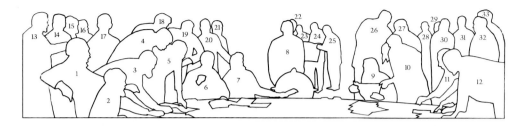

later, in 1869, led the first expedition down the Colorado River through the Grand Canyon in boats—a hazardous, remarkable journey of some 900 miles.

There was brisk, assertive lawyer-capitalist Gardiner Greene Hubbard, friend and adviser to presidents, statesmen, and scientists, financer and promoter of his son-in-law Alexander Graham Bell's experiments and subsequently trustee of the Bell Telephone Company. (Though not a founder himself, Bell was one of the Society's 165 original members.)

There was the dashing student of Russian affairs George Kennan, who, during his eleven-week crossing of Siberia, had, he reported in *Tent Life in Siberia*, "changed dogs, reindeer, or horses more than two hundred and sixty times and had made a distance of five thousand seven hundred and fourteen miles, nearly all of it in one sleigh." There was Henry Gannett, the distinguished chief geographer of the U.S. Geological Survey and a pioneer mapmaker of Colorado and Wyoming's Rocky Mountains in addition to other parts of those states. And there was tenacious O. H. Tittmann, leader of numerous surveying expeditions to the opening frontiers, who in 1900 would be appointed Superintendent of the U.S. Coast and Geodetic Survey.

There was naturalist William H. Dall, pioneer explorer of Alaska; geologist Robert Muldrow II, who would measure Mount McKinley; and meteorologist Edward E. Hayden, who had lost his leg in a landslide.

There was the noted physician and naturalist C. Hart Merriam, who had shortly before been made Chief of the U.S. Biological Survey; and stolid, persevering Navy Commodore George W. Melville, chief engineer on a relief expedition ship that four years earlier had finally broken through the ice to retrieve the by-then near-starved and frozen, half-crazed Greely.

As they gathered on that foggy, wintry evening in the nation's capital, it is, perhaps, an interesting comment on those times that so momentous an assembly of notable men had been achieved in response to an invitation issued but three days before. Washington was smaller then, its population only about a third of what it is now. That January 1888 marked the last year of Grover Cleveland's first presidential term; the year William II would become Kaiser of Germany; the year Van Gogh would paint *The Night Café* and Toulouse-Lautrec, *Cirque Fernando: The Equestrienne*; the year Tchaikovsky's Fifth Symphony and Rimsky-Korsakov's *Sheherazade* would premier in St. Petersburg; the year Oscar Wilde would publish *The Happy Prince and Other Tales* and "Jack the Ripper" would murder at least six women in London; the year George Eastman in America would introduce the Kodak box camera, Thomas Edison refine the phonograph, and Hiram Maxim produce the first satisfactory fully automatic machine gun.

Now as Melville and Greely, Hubbard and Powell, Kennan and Gannett, Tittmann and Merriam, Dall and Muldrow and Hayden and the others collected about the huge, round mahogany table in the Cosmos Club's Assembly

Hall with its dim portraits, its gas-lit chandeliers, and its large standing globe with so much of its landmasses and oceans as yet unexplored, they agreed unhesitatingly about the necessity of a geographic society in Washington, D.C., the center then not only of the nation's politics but also its science.

Warmed by after-dinner coffee, brandy, and the blazing hardwood fire, they readily approved passage of the resolution offered by the U.S. Geological Survey's A. H. Thompson that the Society be organized "on as broad and liberal a basis in regard to qualifications for membership as is consistent with its own well-being and the dignity of the science it represents." A nine-man committee was appointed to prepare a draft constitution and plan of organization, both to be presented at the second meeting, to be held the following week, and the National Geographic Society was born.

Two weeks later the founders of the Society would elect Gardiner Greene Hubbard to lead them. In his introductory speech, Hubbard would tell them that he was "not a scientific man," nor could he "claim to any special knowledge that would entitle [him] to be called a 'Geographer.' "

"I owe the honor of my election as President of the National Geographic Society," Hubbard continued, "simply to the fact that I am one of those who desire to further the prosecution of geographic research. I possess only the same general interest in the subject of geography that should be felt by every educated man."

"By my election," Hubbard declared, "you notify the public that the membership of our Society will not be confined to professional geographers, but will include that large number who, like myself, desire to promote special researches by others, and to diffuse the knowledge so gained, among men, so that we may all know more of the world upon which we live."

Hubbard's opening oratorical humility was not lost on his audience. Although he was not a scientist himself, no one in that room was unaware that Hubbard had long had a keen interest in science, eagerly promoted science, and had many friends in the scientific community. Nor would any present question Hubbard's assumption that his interests were those "that should be felt by every educated man," for the educated man of that time was committed to science.

Eventually, Hubbard's basic egalitarian ideal—*to increase and diffuse* what would become *geographical* knowledge (defined only in its broadest, least-binding sense) with any interested citizen—became the fundamental tenet which would both guide the National Geographic Society's policies and provide the essential explanation for the Magazine's astounding popularity throughout the next hundred years. At that time, however, Hubbard was only reflecting late-nineteenth-century America's love affair with science.

If, in the 1880s, this was a nation staggering under the onerous burden of strangling monopolies, tariff favoritism, political patronage, corrupt city bosses, ruthless robber barons, economic depressions, federal troops and hired thugs called out to combat strikes by fledgling national labor unions, child-labor abuses, despairing farmers, and such vast waves of immigration that in some major cities fewer than half the population was American-born, it was also a nation of exhilarating optimism, unbridled energy, boundless ambition, insatiable curiosity, and a passionate belief in science's ability to provide the cure for society's ills.

One need look no further than the Society's remarkable, self-educated

Opposite: *First President of the National Geographic Society, Gardiner Greene Hubbard, and his wife Gertrude McCurdy Hubbard, on the veranda at Twin Oaks, their Washington, D.C., summer home.*
"By my election," declared Hubbard in his February 17, 1888, introductory speech to the new Society's assembled members, "you notify the public that the membership of our Society will not be confined to professional geographers, but will include that large number who, like myself, desire to promote special researches by others, and to diffuse the knowledge so gained, among men, so that we may all know more of the world upon which we live."

Geologist and explorer John Wesley Powell, one of the Society's founders, speaks with a Paiute Indian in this 1873 photograph taken on the Kaibab Plateau on the north rim of the Grand Canyon in northern Arizona. Powell, who lost his right arm in the Civil War Battle of Shiloh, in 1869 led the first expedition in boats down the Colorado River through the Grand Canyon.

geologist and anthropologist W J McGee to find a spokesman for that era's awesome confidence in science. For it was McGee, one of the *National Geographic Magazine*'s earliest editors, who would rhapsodize in 1898:

> In truth, America has become a nation of science. There is no industry, from agriculture to architecture, that is not shaped by research and its results; there is not one of our fifteen millions of families that does not enjoy the benefits of scientific advancement; there is no law in our statutes, no motive in our conduct, that has not been made juster by the straightforward and unselfish habit of thought fostered by scientific methods.
>
> —From "Fifty Years of American Science," *Atlantic Monthly*, September 1898

The Society's first magazine, published in October 1888, was a slim, tall, octavo-sized scientific brochure with a somewhat forbidding-looking terra-cotta-colored cover. An "Announcement" published in its opening pages articulated the Society's aims:

> The "National Geographic Society" has been organized "to increase and diffuse geographic knowledge," and the publication of a Magazine has been determined upon as one means of accomplishing these purposes.
>
> It will contain memoirs, essays, notes, correspondence, reviews, etc., relating to Geographic matters. As it is not intended to be simply the organ of the Society, its pages will be open to all persons interested in Geography, in the hope that it may become a channel of intercommunication, stimulate geographic investigation and prove an acceptable medium for the publication of results....
>
> As it is hoped to diffuse as well as to increase knowledge, due prominence will be given to the educational aspect of geographic matters, and efforts will be made to stimulate an interest in original sources of information.
>
> In addition to organizing, holding regular fortnightly meetings for presenting scientific and popular communications, and entering upon the publication of a Magazine, considerable progress has been made in the preparation of a Physical Atlas of the United States.
>
> The Society...has at present an active membership of about two hundred persons. But there is no limitation to the number of members, and it will welcome both leaders and followers in geographic science, in order to better accomplish the objects of its organization.

Over the years, the earliest volumes of the Magazine have been unfairly criticized for being "dreadfully scientific, suitable for diffusing geographic knowledge among those who already had it and scaring off the rest." Consistently, the example given to buttress such censure is W J McGee's scholarly Vol. I, No. 1, article "The Classification of Geographic Forms by Genesis." ("...The second great category of geologic processes," McGee wrote, "comprehends the erosion and deposition inaugurated by the initial deformation of the terrestrial surface.") But buried within that first issue's pages was Everett Hayden's report of The Great Storm of March 11–14, 1888.

Certainly this article on the now notorious "Great Blizzard" was scientific; certainly it contained meteorological charts with isobars, isotherms, and arrows whose feathers indicated the force of the winds; and certainly one had to wade through much of the text before learning that the storm dumped forty inches of snow over the northeastern United States, brought freezing temperatures and seventy mph winds. But the text also included a compelling account of the gallant efforts by which the New York pilot boat No. 3, *Charles H. Marshall*, survived the violence and long duration of the storm (see p. 30).

(see p. 30).

When, seven months after the first issue, the second *National Geographic Magazine* appeared, in April 1889, its lead piece, "Africa, its Past and Future," by Society President Gardiner G. Hubbard, was notable for its unromantic depiction of the African continent's geography:

> ...a vast, ill-formed triangle, with few good harbors, without navigable rivers for ocean-vessels, lying mainly in the torrid zone. A fringe of low scorched land, reeking with malaria, extends in unbroken monotony all along the coast, threatening death to the adventurous explorer....

And its brutal assessment of the dangers an "adventurous explorer" risks:

> Some [travelers] who have entered [Africa] from the Atlantic or Pacific coasts have been lost in its wilds, and two or three years after have emerged on the opposite coast; others have passed from the coast, and have never been heard from. Zanzibar has been a favorite starting-point for the lake region of Central Africa. Stanley started from Zanzibar on his search for Livingstone with two white men, but returned alone. Cameron set out by the same path with two companions, but, upon reaching the lake region, he was alone. Keith Johnson, two or three years ago, started with two Europeans: within a couple of months he was gone. Probably every second man, stricken down by fever or accident, has left his bones to bleach along the road.

Hubbard's subsequent argument against the "sinister effects" of the slave trade and slavery—"the great curse of Africa," he called it—may have been somewhat weakened by his assertion that the Negro's "temper and disposition...make him a most useful slave. He can endure continuous hard labor, live on little, has a cheerful disposition, and rarely rises against his master." Still, Hubbard's observation on the slave trade was remarkable for its forthright journalism.

Of the four to five million slaves estimated by Hubbard to have been imported to America (even the larger of the two figures was believed by Hubbard to be an underestimate) he wrote, "12½ per cent were lost on the passage, one-third more in the 'process of seasoning;' so that, out of 100 shipped from Africa, not more than 50 lived to be effective laborers." And Hubbard unflinchingly provided eyewitness accounts by those familiar with the problem:

> [The explorer] Cameron says that Alrez, a Portuguese trader, owned 500 slaves, and that to obtain them, ten villages, having each from 100 to 200 souls, were destroyed; and of those not taken, some perished in the flames, others of want, or were killed by wild beasts. Cameron says, "I do not hesitate to affirm that the worst Arabs are angels of mercy in comparison to the Portuguese and their agents. If I had not seen it, I could not believe that there could exist men so brutal and cruel, and with such gayety of heart." Livingstone says, "I can consign most disagreeable recollections to oblivion, but the slavery scenes come back unbidden, and make me start up at night horrified by their vividness."

That sort of judgmental reporting would not last long in the Magazine; even over the next ten years one has to search hard to find it.

By the turn of the century, straightforward, unfettered journalism had disappeared from the Magazine almost entirely and would reappear only inter-

Founder Adolphus Washington Greely aboard the Thetis *about two weeks after founders George W. Melville and Winfield Scott Schley, of Schley's relief expedition, reached Greely's Greenland camp on June 22, 1884, and found the explorer more dead than alive.*

Greely, later to become a member of the Society's Board of Managers and one of its first vice presidents, had led his twenty-four-man Lady Franklin Bay Expedition into the Arctic in 1881 for purposes of scientific study and exploration—especially an attempt to push north. In 1882 four of Greely's men, before rejoining Greely's party, did reach latitude 83° 24' N—four miles farther north than any rival expedition had gone before but still 440 miles short of the Pole. In late summer 1883, after promised supply and relief ships failed to arrive, Greely led his expedition 500 miles south to Cape Sabine, which they reached after fifty-one days of difficult travel. By June 1884, when Greely and his party were finally rescued, only seven of the original twenty-five were still alive.

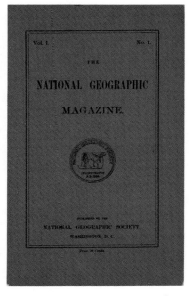

The cover of the first National Geographic Magazine. *Membership numbered 165.*

"FIGHTING FOR LIFE AGAINST THE STORM"

When [the *Charles H. Marshall* was] about 18 miles S.E. from the lightship, a dense fog shut in, and it was decided to remain outside and ride out the storm. The wind hauled to the eastward toward midnight, and at 3 A.M. it looked so threatening in the N.W. that a fourth reef was taken in the mainsail and the foresail was treble-reefed. In half an hour the wind died out completely, and the vessel lay in the trough of a heavy S.E. sea, that was threatening every moment to engulf her. She was then about 12 miles E.S.E. from Sandy Hook lightship, and in twenty minutes the gale struck her with such force from N.W. that she was thrown on her beam ends; she instantly righted again, however, but in two hours was so covered with ice that she looked like a small iceberg. By 8 A.M. the wind had increased to a hurricane, the little vessel pitching and tossing in a terrific cross-sea, and only by the united efforts of the entire crew was it possible to partially lower and lash down the foresail and fore-staysail. No one but those on board can realize the danger she was in from the huge breaking seas that rolled down upon her; the snow and rain came with such force that it was impossible to look to windward, and the vessel was lying broadside to wind and sea. A drag was rigged with a heavy log, anchor, and hawser, to keep her head to sea and break the force of the waves, but it had little effect, and it was evident that something must be done to save the vessel. Three oil bags were made of duck, half filled with oakum saturated with oil, and hung over the side forward, amidships, and on the weather quarter. It is admitted that this is all that saved the boat and the lives of all on board, for the oil prevented the seas from breaking, and they swept past as heavy rolling swells. Another drag was rigged and launched, although not without great exertion and danger, and this helped a little. Heavy iron bolts had to be put in the oil bags to keep them in the water, and there the little vessel lay, fighting for life against the storm, refilling the oil bags every half hour, and fearing every instant that some passing vessel would run her down, as it was impossible to see a hundred feet in any direction. The boat looked like a wreck; she was covered with ice and it seemed impossible for her to remain afloat until daylight. The oil bags were replenished every half hour during the night, all hands taking turn about to go on deck and fill them, crawling along the deck on hands and knees and secured with a rope in case of being washed overboard. Just before midnight a heavy sea struck the boat and sent her over on her side; everything movable was thrown to leeward, and the water rushed down the forward hatch. But again she righted, and the fight went on. The morning of the 13th, it was still blowing with hurricane force, the wind shrieking past in terrific squalls. It cleared up a little towards evening, and she wore around to head to the northward and eastward, but not without having her deck swept by a heavy sea. It moderated and cleared up the next day, and after five hours of hard work the vessel was cleared of ice, and sail set for home. She had been driven 100 miles before the storm, fighting every inch of the way, her crew without a chance to sleep, frostbitten, clothes drenched and no dry ones to put on, food and fuel giving out, but they brought her into port without the loss of a spar or a sail, and she took her station on the bar as usual.

—From Everett Hayden's report of The Great Storm of March 11–14, 1888, which appeared in the first issue of the Magazine, October 1888

mittently until its eighty-ninth year, by which time Gilbert H. Grosvenor's grandson, Gilbert M. Grosvenor, was occupying the editor's desk.

Vol. I, No. 3, published in July 1889, contained "The Rivers and Valleys of Pennsylvania," inaugurating what would be one hundred years of the Magazine's coverage of the states; and Vol. I, No. 4, appeared three months later with "Across Nicaragua with Transit and Machéte" by R. E. Peary, a young naval civil engineer who would later gain fame in less temperate climes.

Peary's description of the brutal hardships involved in clearing the Nicaraguan jungles in order that engineers might take transit sightings and determine elevations for the then-proposed trans-Nicaraguan canal, closed with this surprisingly eloquent passage:

> After the day's work comes the dinner, the table graced with wild hog, or turkey, or venison, or all. After dinner the smoke, then the day's notes are worked up and duplicated and all hands get into their nets. For a moment the countless nocturnal noises of the great forest, enlivened perhaps by the scream of a tiger, or the deep, muffled roar of a puma, fall upon drowsy ears, then follows the sleep that always accompanies hard work and good health, till the bull-voiced howling monkeys set the forest echoing with their announcement of the breaking dawn.

Two years later the Society published in its April 1891 issue "Summary of Reports on the Mt. St. Elias Expedition," which, although jointly sponsored with the U.S. Geological Survey, was the Society's first "venture in exploration."

Under Society sponsorship, an expeditionary force of ten men, led by the geologist Israel C. Russell, had explored Mount St. Elias, the highest point on the boundary between Alaska and Canada, discovered Mount Logan (subsequently determined to be, at 19,524 feet, North America's second-highest peak), and a huge frozen river of ice they named Hubbard Glacier after the Society's first president.

"In several ways, this first expedition set a pattern for the Society's 200 explorations and researches that have followed over the years," Melvin M. Payne, the National Geographic's now-retired Chairman of the Board of Trustees, would write in 1963. "It triumphed over the forces of nature. It added to man's knowledge of his world. And it established a tradition of close cooperation between the National Geographic Society and agencies of the United States Government."

In addition, Russell's first-person adventure-narrative in the following month's *Geographic* established the pattern for reporting explorations:

> Darkness settled and rain fell in torrents, beating through our little tent. We rolled ourselves in blankets, determined to rest in spite of the storm. Avalanches, already numerous, became more frequent. A crash told of tons of ice and rock sliding down on the glacier. Another roar was followed by another, another, and still another. It seemed as if pandemonium reigned on the mountains.
>
> Looking out, I saw rocks as large as one's head bounding within a few feet of our tent. One struck the alpenstock to which the ridgerope was fastened. Our tent "went by the board," and the rain poured in. Before we could gather our soaked blankets, mud and stones flowed in upon them. We retreated to the edge of the glacier and pitched our tent again. Wet and cold, we sought to wear the night away. Sleep was impossible.

—From *Great Adventures with National Geographic*

As this December 27, 1888, Annual Report of the Treasurer shows, the National Geographic Society's total assets at the end of its first year were $626.70.

By January 1896 the erratically issued *National Geographic Magazine* became a monthly. In the hopes of increasing its disappointing circulation the Board of Managers offered copies at 25 cents each through newsstands and began to accept advertising. The Magazine's terra-cotta cover was discarded in favor of a buff cover, with the contents, editors, authors, and the legend "An Illustrated Monthly" superimposed upon a latitudinal and longitudinal lined globe.

The January 1896 issue contained Hubbard's article "Russia in Europe" in which he did for the Russian peasant what he had done for the African Negro:

> The peasants wear the same clothes night and day…and are required by their priests to bathe every Saturday evening….They lead idle, listless lives in winter, and when winter ends are little inclined to work….
>
> We can scarcely comprehend such a people or such a life and are not surprised to learn that they resort to cards and drink as the only relief from the dullness of the interminable winter. They never hurry, for time is not money.

One relief from the dullness of Washington's interminable winter was the Society's lecture series; although to Hubbard and his contemporaries, the increase and diffusion of geographical knowledge was serious business. For, as WJ McGee had dourly reported to the Board of Managers: "In choosing popular speakers on current topics, preference is given either to actual explorers or original investigators who are known to treat geography as a branch of science, and such speakers arrange and present their matter freely, save that *the excessive use of picture and anecdote is discouraged*—the object is to instruct as well as entertain." [Author's italics.]

McGee's admonition to the lecturers was assumed to relate to the *Geographic* as well. And yet an article in the next issue "The Recent Earthquake Wave on the Coast of Japan" by geographer Eliza Ruhamah Scidmore, an Associate Editor of the Magazine and the only woman then to serve on the Board—with its photographs of a floating corpse, splintered houses and beached, demasted ships—ignored McGee's caveat entirely:

> The barometer gave no warning, no indication of any unusual conditions on June 15, and the occurrence of thirteen light earthquake shocks during the day excited no comment. Rain had fallen in the morning and afternoon, and with a temperature of 80° to 90° the damp atmosphere was very oppressive. The villagers on that remote coast adhered to the old calendar in observing their local fêtes and holidays, and on that fifth day of the fifth moon had been celebrating the Girls' Festival. Rain had driven them indoors with the darkness, and nearly all were in their houses at eight o'clock, when, with …a roar, and the crash and crackling of timbers, they were suddenly engulfed in the swirling waters. Only a few survivors on all that length of coast saw the advancing wave, one of them telling that the water first receded some 600 yards from ghastly white sands and then the Wave stood like a black wall 80 feet in height, with phosphorescent lights gleaming along its crest. Others, hearing a distant roar, saw a dark shadow seaward and ran to high ground, crying "*Tsunami! tsunami!*" Some who ran to the upper stories of their houses for safety were drowned, crushed, or imprisoned there, only a few breaking through the roofs or escaping after the water subsided….Ships and junks were carried one and two miles inland, left on hilltops, treetops, and in the midst of fields uninjured or mixed up with the ruins of houses, the rest engulfed or swept seaward….Many survivors, swept away by the waters, were cast ashore on out-lying islands, or

Opposite: "*As the rain became heavier, the avalanches, already alarmingly numerous, became more and more frequent….It seemed as if pandemonium reigned on the mountains…. Looking out, I saw rocks as large as one's head bounding past within a few feet of our tent.*"

Thus reported Society founder Israel C. Russell on the thundering avalanche that clipped his tent on Marvine Glacier in Alaska during the first expedition organized by the Society. Russell's joint Society–U.S. Geological Survey team then pressed on across ice fields and treacherous passes toward Mount St. Elias, mapped several hundred square miles of the region and discovered and named Mount Logan, Canada's highest peak (a fact then unknown to them).

Russell's first-person account, "An Expedition to Mount St. Elias, Alaska," appeared in the May 1891 issue of the National Geographic Magazine *and set the pattern for reporting future explorations.*

seized bits of wreckage and kept afloat. On the open coast the wave came and withdrew within five minutes, while in long inlets the waters boiled and surged for nearly a half hour before subsiding. The best swimmers were helpless in the first swirl of water, and nearly all the bodies recovered were frightfully battered and mutilated, rolled over and driven against rocks, struck by and crushed between timbers. The force of the wave cut down groves of large pine trees to short stumps, snapped thick granite posts of temple gates and carried the stone cross-beams 300 yards away. Many people were lost through running back to save others or to save their valuables.

One loyal schoolmaster carried the emperor's portrait to a place of safety before seeking out his own family. A half-demented soldier, retired since the late war and continually brooding on a possible attack by the enemy, became convinced that the first cannonading sound was from a hostile fleet, and, seizing his sword, ran down to the beach to meet the foe.

And immediately following a turgid piece on "The Economic Aspects of Soil Erosion" in the October issue, there appeared a report on the Nansen Polar expedition which began:

> On the 17th day of June, 1896, as some of the men of the English Jackson and Harmsworth expedition, in Franz Josef land, were looking out over the ice they discovered a weird figure advancing towards them, with long straggling hair and beard and garments covered with grease and blood stains, who proved to be none other than Dr Fridtjof Nansen, who fifteen months previous had left his ship, the *Fram*, at 83° 59' north latitude and 102° 27' east longitude in order to push on with sleds, boats, and dogs towards the Pole. In a shelter some distance off was Dr Nansen's companion, Lieutenant Johansen.

But perhaps more surprising still was the appearance in the November 1896 *Geographic* of a photograph of a half-nude Zulu bride and bridegroom in their wedding finery, both staring full face into the camera—the groom with obvious courage and pride, the bride looking somewhat less stoic. He is holding her hand as if they were sealing their troth with a handshake. It is a nice photograph, even a tender photograph, and the reader must have wondered what to make of its accompanying text: "These people are of a dark bronze hue, and have good athletic figures. They possess some excellent traits, but are horribly cruel when once they have smelled blood."

Despite its facelift, despite running its first photographic bare-breasted woman, despite becoming "An Illustrated Monthly," and despite its occasional more popular than technical journalistic reporting, the Magazine was still being edited by committee and its determinedly academic approach to geography remained essentially unchanged. Circulation rose only slightly.

Gardiner Greene Hubbard died in 1897, and his son-in-law Alexander Graham Bell was, as Bell would later recount, "forced to become president of the [National Geographic Society] in order to save it." Bell, after considerable persuasion, accepted the presidency in January 1898.

Alexander Graham Bell was a stout, fifty-one-year-old, bearded bear of a man, a daring, innovative, somewhat disorganized, eccentric genius with a childlike enthusiasm for and fascination with the world around him. It was

This 1896 Japanese print depicts the earthquake-generated wave that struck the coast of Japan on June 15 of that year. Eliza Ruhama Scidmore's report on the devastating eighty-foot-high, phosphorescent-crested Sanriku tsunami appeared in the September 1896 National Geographic.

through his work with the deaf that Bell, then twenty-five years old, met Gardiner Greene Hubbard in Northampton, Massachusetts, in 1872. Hubbard's then-fifteen-year-old daughter, Mabel, had been left totally deaf from a severe attack of scarlet fever ten years before. Hubbard had sought Bell's advice on improving her speech. Bell became Mabel Hubbard's teacher, they fell in love, and five years later—only after Bell felt he had proved himself through his invention of the telephone—they married.

For their first two years of marriage, the Bells' worst quarrels were over the inventor's preference for working late at night when the quiet gave him peace. Bell would not retire until four o'clock in the morning, after making sure his wife and children were shielded from moonlight. (Bell's one superstitious fear, his biographer Robert V. Bruce disclosed, was having moonlight fall on himself or others while asleep.)

In early 1892, the insatiably curious Bell reported to Mabel that after an evening spent reading Jules Verne he had turned to "my usual night reading, Johnson's Encyclopedia. Find this makes splendid reading matter for night. Articles not too long—constant change in the subjects of thought—always learning something I have not known before—provocative of thought—constant variety."

During the first year of Bell's presidency of the National Geographic Society, he seems to have been too absorbed in his experimental work on flying machines to give the Magazine much time or thought. And by Bell's first anniversary as President, membership had increased only from 1,140 to 1,400, a dismayed Board was faced with the Society's $2,000 debt, and the Magazine was on the brink of bankruptcy.

Bell was not discouraged. He approached the Board and outlined his plan. In effect he told them, "Geography is a fascinating subject, and it can be made interesting. Let's hire a promising young man to put some life into the magazine and promote the membership. I will pay his salary. Secondly, let's abandon our unsuccessful campaign to increase circulation by newsstand sales. Our journal should go to *members*, people who believe in our work and want to help." Bell recognized that the lure was not the Magazine, but *membership* in a society that made it possible, as Ishbel Ross would later write in a 1938 *Scribner's* article, for "the janitor, plumber, and loneliest lighthouse keeper [to] share with kings and scientists the fun of sending an expedition to Peru or an explorer to the South Pole."

Bell's first step was to search out a full-time editor, someone who would devote his entire time to the editorial work required by the Magazine and the promotion of Society membership. Up to now these duties had been carried out by a committee whose distinguished members performed their work without pay. As Bell was to write later, "But in starting out to make a magazine that would support the Society, instead of the Society being burdened with the magazine, a man was of the first necessity; if we did not get the right man the whole plan would be a failure...."

He already had a young man in mind.

Among the noted scholars and scientists invited to lecture before the Society in 1897 was the distinguished historian Professor Edwin A. Grosvenor, who, before accepting his appointment at Amherst College, had been a professor of history at Robert College in Constantinople for twenty-three years. While a guest in the Bells' Washington home, Professor Grosvenor had spoken glowingly of his identical twin sons, Gilbert and Edwin. The Bells' attractive teen-age daughter Elsie had listened with interest and when later that spring Mrs. Grosvenor invited Elsie and her sister, Daisy, to attend the twins' graduation from Amherst, the girls accepted.

Throughout their years as students and until they graduated and separated, their father, as if to accentuate their twin-ness, insisted that Edwin and Gilbert dress alike; if one of the boys were to come down to dinner wearing a tie different from that of the other, he would be sent immediately upstairs to change to a tie that was the same (see p. 39).

Gilbert Grosvenor so enjoyed being an identical twin that he felt it was "next to a wife...the greatest favor the Lord can give a man."

That summer following the Grosvenor boys' graduation from Amherst, Elsie, who had no difficulty in telling the twins apart, found herself attracted to Gilbert. Aware that her father was searching for a "promising young man," she reminded him about the twin sons of his friend Professor Grosvenor. Perhaps one of them might be interested in working in Washington?

"Dr. Bell, who greatly admired my father, embraced the idea as his own," Gilbert H. Grosvenor later wrote. "Soon he was at his desk, writing to his friend. Would either of the twins, Edwin and Gilbert, be interested in a job that might be 'a stepping stone to something better?'"

Bell then sent a brief personal note to each of the twins along with a copy of the letter he had written their father. Bell's offer appealed strongly to young Gilbert Grosvenor who, from early childhood, had been interested in editing and writing, and had helped with the proofs and layout of his father's erudite two-volume 1895 *Constantinople*, according to Grosvenor, the first scholarly work to be profusely illustrated with photographs. Authors and editors were common visitors in the Grosvenor household, and young Bert eagerly took part in their literary discussions. But he wanted to make sure that Edwin was genuine in his denial of having any interest in running a magazine. Edwin was sincere. He was interested in the law and recommended that Gilbert follow his heart, take the job, and be near the young lady in Washington.

At that time, Gilbert Grosvenor was studying for his master of arts degree and was in his second year of teaching at the Englewood Academy for Boys in New Jersey. Hired as an instructor in French, German, Latin, college algebra, chemistry, public speaking, and debating, Grosvenor would later recall, "Compared with this program, a job as editor seemed very easy."

He wrote Dr. Bell that the editing job did interest him and was invited to a meeting at Bell's home. Present also were the inventor's wife and his daughter Elsie.

Bell showed Gilbert copies of some of the leading magazines of that period—*Harper's Weekly, McClure's, Munsey's, The Century*, among others—and asked Grosvenor, "Can you create a geographic magazine as popular as these, one that will support the Society instead of the Society being burdened with the magazine?"

"Yes, I believe I can," Grosvenor replied, "but I must proceed slowly and feel my way."

Aware that Dr. Bell expected quick results, Grosvenor found he had to emphasize repeatedly that the Magazine would have to go through a period of evolution; and because of the magnitude of the task, Dr. Bell should not expect it to become a success overnight.

The article that accompanied this November 1896 National Geographic *photograph "ZULU BRIDE AND BRIDE-GROOM" (the first bare-breasted natives to appear in the* National Geographic*) reported, "These people are of a dark bronze hue, and have good athletic figures. They possess some excellent traits, but are horribly cruel when once they have smelled blood."*

The twins Edwin Prescott Grosvenor and Gilbert Hovey Grosvenor (about ten years old) with their elder brother, Asa Waters Grosvenor (right to left), photographed in their home near today's Istanbul, Turkey. The twins, born in what was then Constantinople in 1875, lived there until 1890 while their father, Edwin A. Grosvenor, taught history at Robert College. "Before the future president of your Society went to America," later wrote Maynard Owen Williams, for many years chief of the Geographic's foreign staff, "his eyes were focused on scenes of many lands and his ears tuned to the babel of tongues then spoken on Galata Bridge....

"His nurse was an Armenian, Kurdish porters toiled up the cobbled paths carrying provisions to his home. Albanians, Bulgarians, and Greeks were his classmates....

"Little wonder that geography seemed to Gilbert Grosvenor a dramatic series of living pictures, rather than mere dots on a chart."

Bell accepted Grosvenor's cautions then proposed something that immediately made Grosvenor wary: Some years earlier, Dr. Bell and Gardiner Hubbard had spent $87,000 in a vain attempt to establish a magazine called *Science*, which had failed after two unprofitable years. Bell told the young man he was willing to back the *National Geographic Magazine* with funds equal to those poured into *Science*.

Much to the relief of Mrs. Bell, who was not in the least happy at the thought of her husband losing a vast sum in a magazine again, Grosvenor firmly told Dr. Bell he would accept the job only if the inventor limited his gift to a $100 monthly salary—a figure even less than Grosvenor had been earning as a teacher.

"I knew that sheer weight of money would not accomplish what he wanted," Grosvenor would later write of that fateful meeting with Bell. "I also realized that, despite Dr. Bell's good will, a youth of 23 was not prepared to administer so large a sum. Older men, men unwilling to experiment, inevitably would push me aside, and I would have little opportunity to create and to try new ideas. Yet, without imagination and a new approach, there could be no hope for the magazine."

Dr. Bell reluctantly accepted Grosvenor's conditions and the meeting was concluded. In the brief moment that Elsie had alone with Gilbert by the door before he departed, she whispered, "I told Papa you had the talent he sought and would like to come to Washington!"

On April Fool's Day, 1899, Bell brought Gilbert H. Grosvenor to the Society's headquarters opposite the United States Treasury building. The "headquarters" Grosvenor later wrote, was but "half of one small room (the other half occupied by the American Forestry Association), two rickety chairs, a small table, a litter of papers and ledgers, and six enormous boxes crammed with *Geographics* returned by the newsstands."

Bell looked about the room. "No desk!" Bell exclaimed. "I'll send you mine."

That afternoon deliverymen brought Grosvenor a handsome rolltop desk made of Circassian walnut. When he sat down before it, Grosvenor was looking at the only visible property of the National Geographic Society. The treasury was not just empty; the Society was nearly $2,000 in debt.

Poor in funds though the Society may have been, it was extraordinarily rich for its most recently acquired asset: Gilbert Hovey Grosvenor, its first full-time employee.* However, it was not, as Dr. Bell's letter had proposed, with the title of Managing Editor, but as Assistant Editor that Grosvenor was hired—and only for three months with the understanding that a more permanent engagement would be made at the end of that time if the appointment was satisfactory to the Society's Editorial Committee.

John Hyde was Editor of the Magazine. And although Hyde was employed as statistician to the U.S. Department of Agriculture, he clearly had considerably more influence over the selection of the materials and editing of the Magazine than Grosvenor edited *Geographic* histories would have one believe.

During his first few days at the *Geographic*, Dr. Bell took pains to introduce Grosvenor to his distinguished colleagues of the Society, all men consid-

---

There was, in addition to Grosvenor, one part-time Assistant Secretary, a clerk who, Grosvenor later recalled, "had just had a baby—his first—and about every half hour he'd go out and drink to its health."

THE GROSVENOR TWINS AS COLLEGE SPORTS: GAME, SET, AND MATCHED

Neckties were at the root of some of the social games the twins played at college. In those days of dance cards young men would not be permitted to sign up for more than one dance with a young lady or else their attentions might appear unseemly. Gilbert would arrive at the dance in a black dress tie, Edwin in white. If one of the twins had been granted a dance with a young lady whom the other desired, they would swap ties and the girl would not only be unaware of the difference, she would be rather pleased with herself for noticing that the color of the necktie was the key to the twin's identity. But as the October 7, 1900, *Boston Sunday Post* article on the twins reported:

"The only hitch came when both preferred to dance with the same partner, and then it was a contest of wits, and each was unscrupulous in stealing marches on the other. This necessitated carrying an extra necktie to use when an exchange was refused."

There were those times, however, as in college athletics, when dressing alike was demanded by fashion. And, as the Boston newspaper article concluded:

"Even in the college sports the twins had their opportunity. Both were exceptional tennis players, and so even was their relative ability that in contests against each other victories were evenly distributed. But it was as partners in doubles that the boys made their reputation, and so skilful were they that they won the college championship and represented Amherst in doubles

Edwin P. Grosvenor (left) and Gilbert H. Grosvenor (right) shown with fellow members of the Amherst College Class of 1897 elected to Phi Beta Kappa in April 1896.

in the intercollegiate tournament at New Haven. Dressed alike in tennis shirts, duck trousers and white canvas shoes, they were more indistinguishable than ever. One excelled in service and the other in net play, and their college mates used to assert that they took advantage of this to have one serve for both, since neither opponents nor spectators could tell the difference. This charge they always repudiated, but it was a standing joke among their friends..."

39

41

47

weeks before Bell left. "I can't help feeling that Mr. Hyde wants to retain the editorship after all, and thought that if he could get someone else in my place, he would be sure to stay in. I do not like to suspect him, but when he tells Mr. Bell he loves me like a son, and with the same breath that I am lacking in business ability and weak in proof-reading and hence do not deserve any increase in salary (not in these words, but to that effect), it is funny to say the least.... My position was referred to the Executive Committee, by the Board, with the unanimous recommendation that I receive a good promotion. The Executive Committee is comprised of [Henry] Gannett, [John] Hyde and [Alfred J.] Henry, and I shall hear from them today what they propose...." Six weeks later, on July 27, 1900, the Executive Committee offered Grosvenor his same job; he was given neither a promotion nor a raise.

Grosvenor's father, aware of the young editor's continuing problems with Gannett and Hyde, was counselling his son that troublesome summer in Washington, "Just be patient, be patient." But Grosvenor wrote his father that he would resign in the fall if the ideas of the Executive Committee and Mc-Clure prevailed.

Grosvenor had not wanted to bother Dr. Bell with his difficulties, but on August 6, 1900, knowing the inventor was preparing to return to Washington, he wrote that the battle with the Executive Committee was Bell's, too, and that soon he would have to face it again. "Naturally I am very much distressed with the committee," Grosvenor wrote, "but as I firmly believe that they are working not against me personally...but against your plans for the Society and for their individual interests, I do not intend to get out of their way, as they plainly hint they want me to."

An unexpected dividend to the Executive Committee's opposition to the young editor was that it angered Elsie Bell enough in late August for her to write Grosvenor that she would be glad to marry him, if he hadn't changed his mind. By return mail Grosvenor assured Elsie that he hadn't.

Dr. Bell telegraphed his congratulations, and shortly thereafter Mrs. Bell wrote Gilbert Grosvenor's mother:

> Of course, Elsie would not have written to Gilbert as she did at this time without Mr. Bell's and my full approval. We feel that Gilbert has proved his mettle in this summer's trials and deserves the reward Elsie wants to give him. He has certainly had a hard summer—meeting treachery where he expected loyal help and friendship—but I doubt whether Elsie would have been as sure of her own mind if all her love and sympathy had not been aroused by her indignation at the attacks upon him. So perhaps after all, Mr. Hyde has unwittingly done Gilbert a great service, and his late troubles are blessings in disguise.

Upon his return to Washington in September, Dr. Bell called together a meeting of the scientists, professionals, explorers, and businessmen who comprised the Society's Board of Managers. The Executive Committee did not have the support of this distinguished group; and in a resolution passed by the Board of Managers on September 14, 1900, they made a point of praising Grosvenor's work, unanimously reaffirmed his permanent status with the Society, named him Managing Editor, and increased his salary to $2,000 a year—the additional $800 to be paid by the Society beginning January 1, 1901.

Hyde was given the title of Editor-in-Chief but remained without pay.

The following day Grosvenor wrote his father:

...the resolutions...are, I think, all one would wish....Gannett and Hyde were thunderstruck and neither went to the meeting....But as Henry said when recording [the resolution], "they did it because of my work and because they believed in me and not because I was to be Mr. Bell's son-in-law." And I am going to think that true or mostly true.

"I had interpreted the title Managing Editor as the controlling man in the organization," Grosvenor later said. "And from that time on, I was the chief executive of the office, being responsible for the Magazine, the makeup of the Magazine, and the responsibility of increasing the membership of the Society."

Convinced that the rift between himself and the Executive Committee had been mended, Gilbert joined Elsie in London. They were married on October 23, 1900—the anniversary of his parents' wedding—and immediately set out on their honeymoon tour of Europe. On their way to Constantinople, the young couple had reached Vienna, when Grosvenor found himself worrying about the Magazine. Instinct warned him that something was wrong. He and Elsie returned to Washington, arriving early in December 1900.

Something indeed was wrong: in Grosvenor's absence the Executive Committee had arranged to have the Magazine printed not as it had been at Judd & Detweiler in Washington, but at McClure, Phillips & Company in New York. Evidently, Dr. Bell, who had gone abroad at the same time as the young Grosvenors but had returned before them, had participated in the lengthy discussions preceding the move and had opposed neither the negotiations, nor the contract when it was signed. Grosvenor confronted Bell with the New York printing bill for the January 1901 issue, pointing out that not only was the charge twice as expensive as the previous Washington bill, but that McClure, Phillips had failed to acquire for the *Geographic* either new members, new advertising, or revenues. Bell responded, "Well, Bert, the Board made you the Managing Editor. You are responsible now."

As Managing Editor Grosvenor was responsible; furthermore, he had the authority to act. He immediately went to New York. However, both the January and February 1901 issues were printed there before he could reverse the Executive Committee's actions and return the printing to Washington. But return it he did and "knew," he later wrote, "I had saved something more important than dollars: [I had saved] Dr. Bell's original plan to enlist members who would help us create a great educational institution."

In what with hindsight can be seen as the pivotal point in the young Magazine's history, Grosvenor had overturned the Executive Committee's decision, overruled his father-in-law's concurrence, and convinced the Board of Managers not only of the need to retain the Magazine's link with the Society through membership-subscription, but also to eventually disregard every one of McClure's suggestions. From that point on the National Geographic Society was run by Gilbert Hovey Grosvenor and not the other way around.

Grosvenor, offered the job less than two years earlier as "a stepping stone to something better," was to become the driving force behind the National Geographic Society for the next sixty-six years. Under his leadership the *Geographic* was transformed from an irregular, often dowdy technical journal with a circulation of a few hundred, into a glossy, color-packed popular publication with a circulation at the time of Grosvenor's death of over 5,000,000—large enough for one month's edition to make a stack twenty-five miles tall.

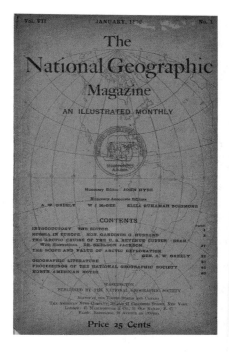

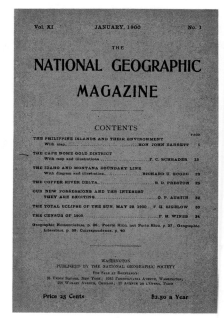

Top: *In January 1896, the erratically issued* National Geographic Magazine *became a monthly, and its forbidding terra-cotta cover was discarded in favor of the one shown here.*

Above: *By the end of 1900 the* National Geographic Magazine's *cover had changed for the third time, and circulation had risen to more than 2,200.*

"The Most Cherished of Geographical Prizes"

*"The Pole at last!!! The prize of 3 centuries, my dream &
ambition for 23 years.* **Mine** *at last. I cannot bring myself to
realize it. It all seems so simple..."*
—From Robert E. Peary's diary, April 6, 1909

*"So we arrived and were able to plant our flag at the geo-
graphical South Pole. God be thanked!"*
—From Roald Amundsen's diary, December 15, 1911

I n the annals of Polar exploration probably no man was more obsessed with
attaining the Polar prize than America's Robert E. Peary. In 1880, when
Peary was twenty-four years old, he had written to his mother, "I shall not
be satisfied that I have done my best until my name is known from one end of
the world to the other." The following year Peary entered the Navy as a civil
engineer and began a tour in Nicaragua surveying sites for the proposed Atlan-
tic-Pacific canal route across that country. While in Nicaragua, Peary chanced
to come across an account by Adolf Erik, Baron Nordenskjöld, of his 1879 voyage through the Northeast Passage across the top of Europe and Asia to the Pacific Ocean. Peary immediately recognized that Arctic exploration had
potential, that, as L.P. Kirwin wrote in *A History of Polar Exploration*, it could
be Peary's "avenue to fame, an avenue leading to the most cherished of all geographical prizes, the North Geographical Pole."

In April 1891, before departing on his 1891–92 Greenland expedition,
Peary addressed a gathering of Society members. "At the end of [his] talk,"
Benton McKaye later recalled in a letter written to Gilbert Hovey Grosvenor,

President Hubbard, striding across the stage, picked up a large American
flag, unfurled it, and stood facing Peary, to whom he addressed a brief
speech of encouragement, then spoke these final words: *"Now take this flag
and place it as far north on this planet as you possibly can!"*

Peary gripped the flag and made his bow, while we of the audience
roared forth a bon voyage for this start of Peary's career as an explorer.

During this 1891–92 Greenland expedition Peary walked some 600 miles
across the mile-high ice cap and back again from what would be subsequently
named Peary Land. On the way, he made many valuable scientific observations,
established that Greenland was an island and not continental land reaching
the Pole, and so enhanced his reputation that he became a popular lecturer,
earning most of the money to finance future expeditions.

During the 1890s, Peary returned four more times to Greenland, perfect-
ing the techniques that would enable him to reach the Pole. In 1898, three
years after the Norwegian Fridtjof Nansen reached a record 86° 12′N, 229.5
miles from the Pole, Peary made a brief effort, losing eight of his toes. In 1900,

Preceding spread: *An icy bath befell
one of the Steger 1986 Polar expedition's sled dogs when it slipped into a
narrow lead. However, as the* Geographic *noted in its September 1986
"North to the Pole" report, "Bred for
hardship and well insulated by their
thick coats, the dogs easily withstood
such common mishaps. But had a
sled gone through the ice, the expedition would have ended immediately."*

Opposite: *"Eyes intent on a long-
sought goal, Comdr. Robert E. Peary
reached the North Pole over the ice on
April 6, 1909—a feat never accomplished before or since," wrote the*
Geographic *of this photograph in its
1888–1946 Index. But on May 1, 1986,
the Steger International Polar Expedition's five men and one woman
arrived at the North Pole, the first dogsled expedition to make it to the top
of the world without resupply since
Peary's triumph seventy-seven years
before.*

Overleaf: *Crowded with sled dogs,
walrus blubber, and seventy tons of
whale meat, the 186-foot ship* Roosevelt *carrying Peary north for his dash
to the pole contained a "choking
stench" that its captain, Bob Bartlett,
never forgot.*

·53·

Italian Navy Lt. Umberto Cagni of the Duke of the Abruzzi's expedition penetrated twenty-two miles closer to the Pole than had Nansen. Peary made a brief try in 1901, and again in 1902, but fell far short at 84° 17'N. Finally, in 1906 on his fourth try, Peary reached 87° 6'N, 175 miles from the Pole and attained the record for "farthest north."

On the evening of December 15, 1906, at the annual white tie banquet of the National Geographic Society, attended by 400 members, various foreign dignitaries, U.S. government officials, and other distinguished guests, President Theodore Roosevelt presented the Society's first Hubbard Medal to guest of honor Commander Robert E. Peary. There was prolonged applause as Peary rose to his crippled feet to accept. Peary, his penetrating ice-blue eyes sparkling over his walrus mustache and hatchet nose, looked with intense personal satisfaction about the room then down at the gold medal. On one side was the seal of the Society, and on the reverse a map of the Arctic upon which was inscribed: "The Hubbard Medal, awarded by the National Geographic Society to Robert E. Peary for arctic exploration. Farthest north, 87° 6'. December 15, 1906." A blue sapphire star marked the northernmost point Peary had attained.

Peary looked back up at the President and the Society's officers and guests, and as the room quieted down he began to speak:

> ...The true explorer does his work not for any hope of rewards or honor, but because the thing he has set himself to do is a part of his very being, and must be accomplished for the sake of accomplishment, and he counts lightly hardships, risks, obstacles, if only they do not bar him from his goal.
>
> To me, the final and complete solution of the Polar mystery, which has engaged the best thought and interest of the best men of the most vigorous and enlightened nations of the world for more than three centuries, and today quickens the pulse of every man or woman whose veins hold red blood, is the thing which *should* be done for the honor and credit of this country, the thing which it is intended that *I* should do, and the thing that *I must do* [author's italics].

The National Geographic Society awarded Peary $1,000, its first grant, and the Peary Arctic Club of New York built and outfitted a ship for him. In July 1908, not quite a year and a half after receiving the Hubbard Medal, Peary left New York in the middle of a heatwave and two months later his expedition's ship, *Roosevelt*, rounded the northeastern tip of Ellesmere Island in the Arctic Ocean and punched through the ice to 82° 30'N, the northernmost point reached by a ship under its own power. As the ice closed in about the *Roosevelt*, supplies were off-loaded at a quickly built igloo village and, five months later, sledged ninety miles to the Cape Columbia base camp established at the northern tip of Ellesmere Island, 413 nautical miles from the Pole.

Peary's polar team consisted of 24 men and 133 dogs. Seventeen of the men were Eskimos; the remaining seven were Peary, the leader; Robert A. Bartlett, the *Roosevelt*'s captain; Dr. John W. Goodsell, a surgeon; Ross Marvin, a civil engineer; George Borup and Donald MacMillan, two young Arctic enthu-

"ESKIMO SEXTETTE. MAIN DECK, ROOSEVELT" was the caption given this photograph, presented to the Society by Mrs. Josephine Peary, the explorer's widow.

Above: *"ENTERING THE PLANE FOR THE FLIGHT TO THE POLE"* was the title for this photograph of Lt. Cmdr. Richard E. Byrd at Spitsbergen, with Pilot Floyd Bennett at his left and Lt. G.O. Noville at his right, when it appeared in the September 1926 Geographic. The caption of this photograph, which appeared as part of Byrd's article *"The First Flight to the North Pole,"* went on to point out that the parkas worn by the men had been carried 500 miles by dogsled from Nome to Fairbanks, Alaska, and were made of *"reindeer skin with an inner parka of squirrel skin."* Their boots and gloves were of reindeer skin, too, but their trousers were *"of polar-bear skin with the fur outside...."*

Right: *"The dog sledge must give way to the aircraft; the old school has passed,"* Lt. Cmdr. Richard E. Byrd told a National Geographic audience in 1926 upon returning from his epic first flight over the North Pole. This romanticized 1926 painting by N.C. Wyeth of Byrd's trimotor Josephine Ford *flying toward the North Pole hangs in Hubbard Memorial Hall, the Society's first headquarters building.*

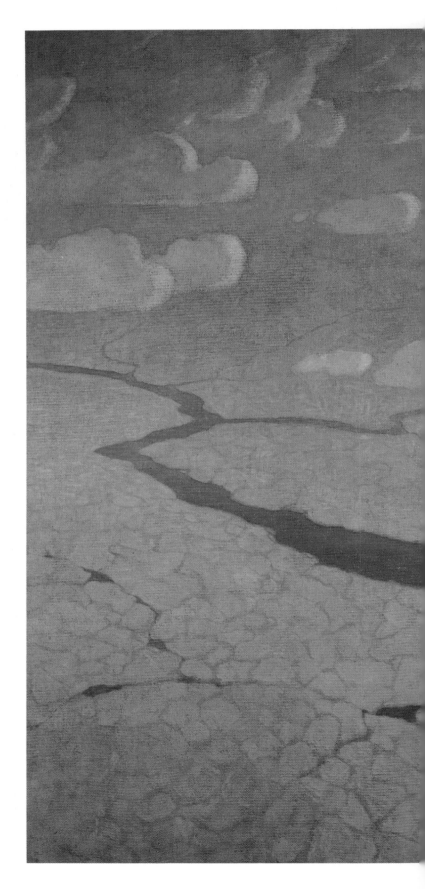

On the fifth march a rise in temperature to 15° below reduced the friction of our sledges. The dogs seemed to catch our spirit. They tossed their heads and yelped as they ran with tight-curled tails.

I had now made my five marches and on April 6 was in time for a hasty noon observation: 89° 57'. Three nautical miles from the magic 90°. With the Pole practically in sight, I was suddenly too weary to take the last steps. I turned in for a nap, then pushed on with two Eskimos and a light sledge for another ten miles and made another observation.

I was now beyond the Pole.

"The Pole at last!!! The prize of 3 centuries, my dream & ambition for 23 years. *Mine* at last," Peary wrote in his diary. "I cannot bring myself to realize it. It all seems so simple...."

Peary, Matthew Henson, and the Eskimos Ootah, Egingwah, Seegloo, and Ooqueah remained at the North Pole thirty more hours in "side trips taking [latitude] observations and photographs, planting flags, depositing records," Peary wrote. "The weather was flawless: minimum temperature 33° below, maximum 12° below. On the afternoon of April 7, we double-fed the dogs, repaired the sledges for the last time, discarded spare clothing, and started back...."

Sixteen days later, having force-marched the old trail in perfect weather, Peary arrived at the Cape Columbia base camp; after sleeping for two days and making two more marches he boarded the *Roosevelt*. There he learned that Ross Marvin, who had turned back with his support party on March 25, had drowned in a big lead en route to Cape Columbia. His death, Peary wrote, "was a bitter flavor in the cup of our success."

On Sunday night, September 5, 1909, the *Roosevelt*, delayed by the absence of its captain, who was out on the Greenland icecap, next by sea ice, and then by a stop to take the Eskimos home, reached Indian Harbor, Labrador. The following morning Peary and Bartlett rowed ashore for their first opportunity to send messages. Peary's cables went to *The New York Times*, to the Associated Press, to the Secretary of the Peary Arctic Club, and the following to his wife: HAVE MADE GOOD AT LAST. I HAVE THE D.O.P.* AM WELL. LOVE....

"This was the news the world had been waiting to hear for 300 years," Peary later wrote, "the discovery of the top of the earth."

On September 8, Peary sent the following telegram to President William Howard Taft:

HAVE HONOR TO PLACE NORTH POLE AT YOUR DISPOSAL.

The President wired Peary in reply:

THANKS FOR YOUR GENEROUS OFFER. I DO NOT KNOW EXACTLY WHAT I COULD DO WITH IT. I CONGRATULATE YOU SINCERELY ON HAVING ACHIEVED, AFTER THE GREATEST EFFORT, THE OBJECT OF YOUR TRIP, AND I SINCERELY HOPE THAT YOUR OBSERVATIONS WILL CONTRIBUTE SUBSTANTIALLY TO SCIENTIFIC KNOWLEDGE. YOU HAVE ADDED LUSTRE TO THE NAME "AMERICAN."

* *The New York Times*, upon learning of Peary's cable to his wife, asked her what "D.O.P." meant. She replied, "Damned Old Pole."

◀

Beneath a twilit, autumnal sky, stately emperor penguins surveyed their bleak and unforgiving Antarctic kingdom.

Opposite: *Expedition photographer Herbert G. Ponting's photograph of an ice cave frames Scott's ship* Terra Nova, *which in 1913 sailed back without him.*

If the President's response seems somewhat muted, one explanation might be that Taft had received the following telegram from Copenhagen only four days before:

> I HAVE THE HONOR TO REPORT TO THE CHIEF MAGISTRATE OF THE UNITED STATES THAT I HAVE RETURNED HAVING REACHED THE NORTH POLE.
>
> FREDERICK A. COOK

Over the years the controversy has continued to rage as to whether or not Cook beat Peary—or whether either Cook or Peary even made it to the Pole. Both men were asked to submit their records and observations to a group of National Geographic scientists for verification. Peary did; Cook would not.

As recently as December 1983, CBS television aired "Cook and Peary: the Race to the Pole," a drama purporting to prove that Cook—by all accounts a charming man—had reached the Pole a year before Peary, but had been denied his claim by a vicious and paranoid Robert E. Peary. It was further suggested that the National Geographic Society had taken part in perpetrating a fraud upon the American public. Letters from members asked what really happened. Gilbert M. Grosvenor in the Magazine's March 1984 President's page responded that the CBS program was "blatant distortion of the historical record, vilifying an honest hero and exonerating a man whose life was characterized by grand frauds."

Grosvenor recounted some of Cook's deceptions: that he had published another man's life work as his own, that his false claim to have climbed Mount McKinley had resulted in his expulsion from the Explorers Club, of which he had been a founder and President, that he had served a prison sentence as a result of his part in an oil-stock swindle. Grosvenor also cited the lack of any evidence or witnesses that Cook had, in fact, reached the Pole, then concluded:

> Peary's claim is backed by astronomical observations made by others as well as himself, by soundings taken through the ice, and by the testimony of his companions, including Eskimos. Even his severest critics cannot deny he came close to his goal, and his supporters have no doubt that he made it. It is small wonder that he felt his life's achievement had been stolen by a con man.

Perhaps the best evaluation of the controversy can be found in an aphorism popular during that era: "Cook was a gentleman and a liar; Peary was neither."

The seduction of the Poles for explorers was—and is still—their inaccessibility, the challenge of getting there, but most of all getting there first. Norway's Roald Amundsen, the restless, driven, consummate professional, who was the first to traverse, and thereby prove the existence of the Northwest Passage, was in Norway in September 1909, preparing an expedition to the North Pole when news of Peary's accomplishment reached him. Amundsen immediately and secretly switched plans. Nine months later, when already at sea, he turned his ship southward, in order to make an attempt on the South Pole. On September 13, the *Times* of London announced that Captain Robert Falcon Scott of the Royal Navy was arranging his own expedition to the South Pole that "will, it is hoped, start in August next." Not quite two years later both Scott and Amundsen were in Antarctica about to set out on a race that was to

Above: *"Alone in a hut beneath the Antarctic ice, Byrd spent four bitter winter months in 1934. He had moved to the advance station to make weather observations, but fumes from a defective stove soon made him ill. Realizing his comrades would risk their lives to save him if they knew his peril, he sometimes crawled on hands and knees to make regular radio reports. Finally alerted by his faltering signals, three men broke through the polar night and rescued him." Caption from the April 1962 Geographic tribute "The Nation Honors Admiral Richard E. Byrd."*

Right: *Richard E. Byrd's triumphant May 9, 1926, flight over the North Pole was seconded three years later when, on November 28, 1929, he and three companions flew their Ford trimotor from their Little America Antarctic base to the South Pole and back. Byrd's broadcasts, originating from his unearthly Antarctic base, were as thrilling to a previous generation as were the first transmissions from astronauts on the moon.*

be both remarkable and glorious, terrible and tragic, a race which, though won by the best man, ironically saw the vanquished emerge the hero.

On October 19, 1911—a dull, foggy day with a maliciously shifting wind—Amundsen and his finely honed Norwegian team set off from their Bay of Whales base camp on the Ross Ice Shelf for the perilous 1,244-mile trip by ski and sledge to the Pole. Eleven days later and sixty miles farther from the Pole, Scott and his ill-prepared party left their Cape Evans winter camp above McMurdo Sound on foot behind two impractical motorized sledges and nine ponies unsuited for the Antarctic temperatures. The race for the South Pole—one of the last classic expeditions with men and animals and no outside support—had begun.

Not quite two months later, at a little after three in the afternoon, on December 14, 1911, Amundsen, together with his four companions, was standing at the South Pole under clear skies and in calm air and a temperature of −7.6°F.

In his diary Amundsen simply noted, "So we arrived and were able to plant our flag at the geographical South Pole. God be thanked!"

Just over a month later, on January 15, 1912, Scott's exhausted and frostbitten party arrived and first found one of Amundsen's black flags marking a miles-wide circle enclosing the Pole, which they mistook for his mark at the Pole itself. It mattered little, the flag was proof the race had been lost. As Scott despondently noted in his diary:

> The Pole. Yes, but under very different circumstances from those expected. ...Great God! this is an awful place and terrible enough for us to have laboured to it without the reward of priority.

The next morning members of Scott's assault team saw, in the distance, a black speck which upon investigation turned out to be Amundsen's tent with the Norwegian flag and one from Amundsen's ship, *Fram*, flapping and trembling over their goal. But disappointment at not being first made Scott's achievement of reaching the Pole a hollow one. None of Scott's party survived the agony, the hunger, the exhaustion of the storm-ridden, freezing two-month walk back toward the base camp. The glory Scott had sought in his lifetime came to him only in his death when his diaries, found seven months later with his body, were published. Amundsen had won the Pole, but Scott's carefully edited diaries made him the legend. As his biographer Roland Huntford noted in *The Last Place on Earth*, Scott's achievement was to perpetuate the romantic myth of explorer as martyr and, in a wider sense, to glorify suffering and self-sacrifice as ends in themselves."

Two years after Scott's death, World War One began and the age of Polar exploration, as typified by Amundsen and Peary, was near its end. Within a decade, radios, airplanes, and powerful motorized tracked vehicles began to replace dogs, sledges, and Polar adventurers isolated from the rest of the world.

In 1926, not long after Lt. Cmdr. Richard E. Byrd and his co-pilot, Floyd Bennett, guided by a sun compass invented by the Society's chief cartographer

"Navy icebreaker Atka," *shown in a February 1965* Geographic *article, "smashes through frozen Antarctic seas, sculptured by raging winds into* *fantastic crags. She keeps channels open in the summer season (September to March) to support Americans quartered at the bottom of the world."*

Above: *This wind-tattered flag shown at the Amundsen-Scott South Pole Station on March 22, 1957, flies at half-mast in honor of Richard E. Byrd, who had died just eleven days before.*

Right: *The sun seems to skip rather than to rise or set in this six-exposure photograph taken over the course of three hours in November 1957 by* Geographic *staffer Thomas J. Abercrombie, the first civilian photographer to reach the South Pole Station.*

Above: *"Waddling through the snows
...a gentoo penguin wears a radio
backpack that provides monitoring biologists with data on blood flow and
pressure,"* explained the caption of
this November 1971 *"Antarctica's
Nearer Side"* **Geographic** *photograph.
"This project—helping man understand penguin physiology and
adaptation to a harsh environment—
is part of the multi-nation Antarctic
research program that began with the
1957—58 International Geophysical
Year [IGY]."*

The crossing of Antarctica: Sir Vivian Fuchs' great motorized Polar trek of 2,158 bleak wind-lashed miles from Shackleton Base at the edge of the Weddell Sea over hidden crevasses and iron-hard sastrugi across the South Pole to Scott Base at McMurdo Sound marked the completion by the British Commonwealth Trans-Antarctic Expedition of 1957–1958 of what Antarctic pioneer and Hubbard Medal winner Ernest H. Shackleton had called "the last great Polar journey that can be made."

Albert H. Bumstead, had been the first to fly to the North Pole and back, Byrd told a National Geographic audience, "The dog sledge must give way to the aircraft; the old school has passed."

With the North Pole behind him—and an unsuccessful attempt the following year at beating Charles Lindbergh in becoming the first to cross the Atlantic non-stop for the $25,000 Orteig prize—Byrd turned his attention to the Antarctic, which remained one of the world's great mysteries.

At 3:29 A.M., on November 28, 1929, at Little America, the Byrd expedition's Antarctic headquarters near Amundsen's former base camp overlooking the Bay of Whales, Byrd and three companions, pilot Bernt Balchen, co-pilot Harold June, and cameraman Capt. Ashley McKinley, climbed aboard a stripped down, high wing Ford trimotor airplane for an attempt to fly to the South Pole. Byrd had named the aircraft the *Floyd Bennett* after his beloved companion, who had been badly injured in a trial flight for their transatlantic endeavor and then, the following year, while on a rescue mission in Canada, had contracted pneumonia and died. Byrd and Bennett had planned the South Polar flight together. "Fate had sidetracked him," Byrd wrote, "but he was not forgotten." Byrd brought a stone from Bennett's grave with which he would weight the American flag he planned to drop at the Pole.

With the *Floyd Bennett*'s engines running hot and smooth, the cumbersome, heavily loaded, trimotor wallowed on its skis across the packed snow, gradually picking up speed until it fought its way into the air.

Byrd later said in his story published in *Great Adventures*,

> As the skis left the snow I saw my shipmates on the ground jumping, shouting, throwing their hats in the air, wild with joy that we were off for the Pole. We circled, emerged from clouds into sunshine....Snow-covered peaks 100 miles away glittered like fire in the sun's reflection.
>
> What we faced far surpassed the demands of a simple flight of 800 miles to the Pole. For hundreds of miles we would fly over a barren, rolling surface, then climb a mountain rampart thousands of feet high and continue across a 10,000-foot plateau....Now we began to climb. Before us, beyond the great mountains, lay uncertainty.
>
> McKinley struggled with his camera, I navigated, June sent radio messages, fed gas from cans to tanks, and cranked his movie camera. We were heading for Heiberg Glacier, the plane near its absolute ceiling. Amundsen had reported the high point of the pass as 10,500 feet. Peaks towered on both sides. To our right stretched a wider glacier. Should we tackle Heiberg, altitude known but with air currents around those peaks that might dash us to the ice, or should we try the unknown glacier? We had to choose quickly—we were heading into the mountains at more than a mile a minute. We chose the unknown glacier.
>
> Bernt Balchen fought for altitude while air currents tossed the plane about like a cork in a washtub. Suddenly the wheel turned loosely in his hands; the ailerons failed to respond. Above the engines' roar Bernt shouted, "It's drop 200 or go back!"
>
> "A bag of food overboard!" I yelled. McKinley shoved a 150-pound bag of emergency rations out the two-foot trapdoor.

"The situation looked distinctly uncomfortable," Fuchs wrote after a snow bridge collapsed under his Sno-Cat's weight.

"The End of the Beginning"

HEBARD
WINCHESTER
& OGDEN AVS.

> *"The year 1905 marked the turning point in the Society's fortunes, the 'end of the beginning....'"*
> —Gilbert H. Grosvenor

"At the outgoing of the old and the incoming of the new century," President William McKinley wrote in his 1900 Annual Message to Congress, "you begin the last session of the Fifty-sixth Congress with evidences on every hand of individual and national prosperity and with proof of the growing strength and increasing power for good of Republican institutions."

In turn-of-the-century America there were only forty-five states; the population was 75,994,575; the average wage of workers in manufacturing industries was 22 cents an hour; automobiles cost about $1,500 each; the bus and the truck had not yet been invented; there were fewer than one hundred and fifty miles of paved road in the entire nation; one out of fifty-six persons owned a telephone; there was no such thing as a radio, or an electric refrigerator; the average yearly teacher's salary in a public school was $325; sixty percent of the population was rural; more people worked on farms than in any other occupation, and, as McKinley had suggested in his annual address, life in the United States was pretty good—though short. (The life-expectancy of the average white male was 46.6 years, of the non-white male 32.5 years.)

In 1900, the Boxers rose up against the Christian missionaries in China, Colette wrote her first *Claudine* novel, Conrad wrote *Lord Jim*, Dreiser *Sister Carrie*, Sigmund Freud published his *Interpretation of Dreams*, and Nietzsche died. Picasso painted *Le Moulin de la Galette*, Cézanne his *Self Portrait with Beret*, Monet his *Pool of Water Lilies*, and Sargent *The Sitwell Family*. Puccini's opera *Tosca* premiered in Rome, the first Browning revolvers were manufactured, the Canadian R. A. Fessenden transmitted human speech over radio waves, the first flight of a Zeppelin occurred, the cakewalk was the dance of the hour, and a revolution then occurring in American magazine publishing saw periodicals splitting into two camps, camps divided by illustration methods and price.

From the latter part of the nineteenth century through the first decade of the twentieth, of all the methods by which ideas were readily disseminated—and, at that time, those means were principally newspapers, magazines, lecture platforms, church pulpits, theater stages, and the graphic arts—none underwent so dramatic an increase in effectiveness as did magazines.

It had always been difficult to make a clear-cut distinction based on content between newspapers and magazines. And in the 1880s and 1890s, with the advent of the newspaper Sunday "supplements" and special Saturday editions—which in essence were weekly magazines containing signed literary

Preceding spread: *Delegates participating in the Eighth International Geographic Congress aboard a Chicago horse-drawn sightseeing coach. Gilbert H. Grosvenor found this 1904 Congress, meeting in the United States for the first time, "an eye-opener." The editor (hat on knee) sits on the top deck facing his wife, Elsie.*

pieces by leading writers—the difference became even more difficult to perceive. Although the introduction of the newspaper supplements had little impact on the major "quality" magazines like *Scribner's Magazine, Lippincott's, The Century,* and *Harper's,* the lesser magazines retaliated by competing directly with the newspapers by publishing breaking news stories and covering the latest controversy and events. This competition resulted in many of the magazines dropping their cover prices to 10 and 15 cents. [Information based on *A History of American Magazines* by Frank Luther Mott.]

Furthermore, the emergence of a vast, educated, ambitious middle class (generated by the increasingly sophisticated, expanding public-school systems and the easier access to colleges and universities) had created a market for an increasing number of periodicals tailored to fit its specific needs.

Among the thousands of magazines founded between 1885 and 1905—the formative years of the *National Geographic*—there were scores of specialty periodicals such as *American Anthropologist, Astrophysical Journal, Popular Astronomy, Terrestrial Magnetism, American Geologist, Journal of Geology, Physical Review, Journal of Physical Chemistry, Journal of Analytical and Applied Chemistry, Aquarium, Biological Bulletin, American Museum Journal,* and *Plant World.* Approximately 3,300 periodicals were published in America in 1885; twenty years later there were about 6,000. During those same two decades almost *11,000* different magazines had been launched [according to Mott]; and the 6,000 magazines being published at the end of that period is less a reflection of the near-doubling of the number of periodicals available than an indication of how many periodicals during that same period had failed. With this in mind, the decision of the fledgling *National Geographic*'s young editor, Gilbert H. Grosvenor, to ignore—if not violate—every single recommendation made by S. S. McClure, the publisher of one of that era's most successful magazines, can be seen as either self-confidence bordering on arrogance or as devotion to the highest personal convictions. Be that as it may, at the turn of the century the *National Geographic* was only one of about 5,500 magazines being published in America—and one of the very, very few that would survive.

It survived because, during the revolution occurring in magazine publishing, brought about by the introduction of the new, cheaper halftone method of reproducing photographs, the *National Geographic*'s young Assistant Editor allied himself and his Magazine with the winning side.

Initially certain publishers resisted the halftone illustrations. They felt that dot-patterned photographic reproductions looked "trashy" compared with the fine-line steel engravings. But, halftone soon took over the field and one of the major reasons for this was economic: a full-page steel engraving cost $100, whereas a halftone could be purchased for less than $20.

"In those days many publications scorned photographic illustrations," Gilbert Grosvenor recalled. "The famous and successful editor of *The Century* [Richard Watson Gilder] had gone so far as to predict in print that 'people will tire of photographic reproduction, and those magazines will find most favor which lead in original art.' This same editor once told me that he—and the public!—considered our halftone photoengravings 'vulgar' and preferred steel engravings costing $100 a plate."

Other innovative editors recognized the promise low-priced illustrations held and, like Grosvenor, ignored the criticism of editors like *The Century*'s Gilder and took advantage of the new techniques that made it possible to ac-

This previously unpublished photograph of Elsie Bell Grosvenor was taken by her husband, Gilbert H. Grosvenor, in 1901, a year after their marriage.

quire a Levy-process halftone for between $7 and $8 for a full-page plate.

"It was like striking gold in my own backyard when I found Government agencies would lend me plates from their publications," Grosvenor wrote. "I illustrated numerous articles in this way."

Any magazine editor could have had these same photoengravings, but they were not interested. Grosvenor—recalling both Alexander Graham Bell's earlier advice about the material available from the government's nearby scientific agencies at no cost and the success of his father's liberally illustrated, scholarly book on Constantinople, which, with its 230 photoengravings, had been highly praised and sold well—never wavered in his confidence that photographic illustrations were a valuable asset to the Magazine.

During this period Grosvenor had been using the Society's popular and income-producing lecture series as "a barometer of public opinion concerning good geographic subject matter for The Magazine." He would place himself in Washington's 1,200-seat Columbia Theater where the lectures were presented, in a position from which he could observe both the audience and the speaker. Attendance during technical lectures on the more mundane geologic and geographic topics would average no more than twenty. In 1902, however, on the night of the lecture about the disastrous volcanic explosion of Mont Pelée on the island of Martinique, the Columbia Theater was jammed.

Mont Pelée had exploded at 7:50 A.M. on May 8, 1902, with a deafening roar heard hundreds of miles away. In less than three minutes the city of St. Pierre, its neighboring homes, and seventeen out of eighteen ships in the harbor had been destroyed by the superheated steam and flaming gases from the volcano's split belly, and 30,000 men, women, and children were killed.

Second Engineer Charles Evans of the *Roraima*, anchored off St. Pierre and the only ship to survive, was to report:

> "I was standing at the ship's rail, looking at the mountain. Suddenly it seemed to explode. An immense dark cloud shot up, blacking out the sky. Then a second cloud, even larger than the first, burst from the side of the volcano and rushed down on the city. Its speed was unbelievable. Flames spurted up wherever it touched. A huge wall of hot ashes filled the air, coming toward us *against* the wind....
>
> "Rope and bedding on the *Roraima* caught fire. I turned to run below and was burned on the back. The shock of the explosion hit like a hurricane; I could get no air to breathe. Then an enormous wave struck our port quarter. We keeled over so far the bridge went under and water poured into the hold through the fiddlers."
>
> —From *Great Adventures with National Geographic*

Although the lecturer had photographs of the Mont Pelée disaster, he had thought them too grisly to show—or perhaps he was mindful of Associate Editor W J McGee's admonition that "the excessive use of picture and anecdote is discouraged." In any case, it was precisely the *lack* of pictorial illustration during this particular Society lecture that convinced Grosvenor that McGee's thinking was in error, for in the course of the lecture Grosvenor overheard two young women behind him complain, "Why doesn't he show exciting photographs? That's what we want."

The two young ladies' frustration over the lack of photographs, Grosvenor later recalled, "helped to confirm my belief that The Magazine should use pictures—realistic ones replete with human interest...the character the Geo-

Left: *Elsie and Gilbert Grosvenor swing their children Mabel, Melville, and Gertrude on a broom handle at Beinn Bhreagh, the Bell estate near Baddeck, Nova Scotia.*

Bottom left: *Summers at Baddeck were not all play; in a tent pitched in a sylvan glade Grosvenor diligently edited the Magazine's articles—despite occasional interruptions from his children (Gertrude and Melville, in this instance) and his inventor father-in-law.*

Above: *The joy young Melville Bell Grosvenor felt in his grandfather's company glows from this photograph. "I would look forward to the trip to Nova Scotia all year long," Melville later recalled. "[My grandfather] was such a vibrant person. He had a wonderful way with children."*

graphic should take gradually became clear: lucid, concise writing; material of general, not academic, interest; an abundance of pictures. Yet pictures were hard to find, and so were good articles....in those days we had to solicit [material]. So I spent much time seeking contributors in Government departments and also in the Cosmos Club, which had then, as now, a large membership among scientists."

Most of the *Geographic*'s contributors up to that point had been connected with the various government bureaus and departments. And although the Magazine had begun to publish its now familiar "travelogue" pieces—S. P. Langley's "Diary of a Voyage from San Francisco to Tahiti and Return..." had appeared in December 1901; Congressman Ebenezer J. Hill's "A Trip through Siberia" ran in February 1902—the Magazine continued to reflect a markedly Washingtonian point of view. The Pelée eruption, however, provided Grosvenor with a deluge of material of more national interest.

On May 14, 1902, six days after the eruption, the National Geographic Society dispatched three of its members "on a special expedition to Martinique and St. Vincent to investigate the volcanic conditions of the West Indian regions." They were Robert T. Hill, of the U.S. Geological Survey; Israel C. Russell, who twelve years earlier had led the Society's Mount St. Elias expeditions; and Commander C. E. Borchgrevink, an Antarctic explorer who had studied Erebus and Terror, the southernmost volcanoes of this earth. The June 1902 *Geographic* reported:

> The expedition is the most important and best equipped commission ever sent out to study actual volcanic action. Results of great scientific and practical consequence may be expected to flow from their work. On their return to the United States they will report the results of their observations to the Society. This report, forming a series of illustrated articles, will be published in full in the journal of the Society, the *National Geographic Magazine*.

The June issue, with its announcement of the expedition, an article on the 1883 eruption of Krakatoa excerpted from a British author's book, a short essay by Grosvenor on volcanoes in general with a map showing their distribution, a report on "Magnetic Disturbance Caused by the Explosion of Mont Pelée," a map on the volcanic islands of the West Indies, and a piece by the noted author Lafcadio Hearn on "The Island and People of Martinique," also carried a preliminary report by the expedition that contained the following Associated Press account of Professor Angelo Heilprin's* ascent of Mont Pelée:

> "Saturday morning [May 31] Professor Heilprin determined to attempt the ascent to the top of the crater....The volcano was very active, but amid a thousand dangers Professor Heilprin reached the summit and looked down into the huge crater....He saw a huge cinder cone in the center of the crater. The opening of the crater itself is a vast crevice 500 feet long and 150 feet wide.
>
> "While Professor Heilprin was on the summit of the volcano several violent explosions of steam and cinder-laden vapor took place, and again and again his life was in danger. Ashes fell about him in such quantities at times as to completely obscure his vision. One particularly violent explosion of mud covered the Professor from head to foot with the hideous viscid

"IT IS NO EASY MATTER TO BRING DOWN ONE OF THESE STURDY FLYERS WHEN THE WIND IS BLOWING HARD," the Geographic *noted beneath this photograph of Melville (right) at Baddeck helping Alexander Graham Bell and others haul to earth one of the inventor's giant tetrahedral kites.*

*Heilprin, who became a member of the National Geographic Society's Board of Managers, was also President of the Geographical Society of Philadelphia.

86

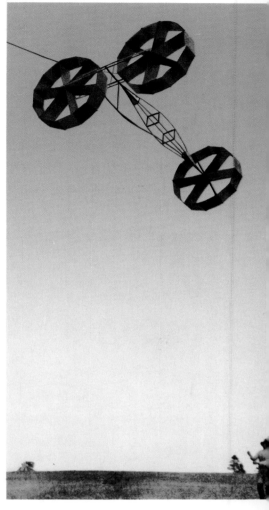

"...I have been continuously at work upon experiments relating to kites. Why, I do not know, excepting perhaps because of the intimate connection of the subject with the flying-machine problem," Bell reported in a 1903 address to the National Academy of Sciences in Washington, D.C. In the course of his pioneer studies into developing a stable flying machine capable of taking off at slow speeds, Bell experimented with a multitude of kite shapes and styles.

and semi-solid matter. He still persisted in his study and observations, however, and twice more was showered with mud. He learned, as had been suspected, that there were three separate vents through which steam issued."

The June issue was simply a warm-up for the July 1902 issue, which carried on its cover the title "MARTINIQUE NUMBER."

This issue contained a forty-four-page report by Robert T. Hill on the explosion of Mont Pelée on Martinique, ten pages on "Volcanic Rocks of Martinique and St Vincent," three pages of "Chemical Discussion of Analyses of Volcanic Ejecta from Martinique and St Vincent," and two pages on "Reports of Vessels as to the Range of Volcanic Dust." This last included the following account:

> From the log of the steamship *Louisianian*, Captain D. Edwards, Liverpool to Trinidad, April 25 to May 9, 1902:
>
> "Arrived in Carlisle Bay, Barbados, May 7, at 11 a.m. (Martinique N.W., 140 miles), the weather being fine and clear. Between 1 and 3 p.m. reports as of heavy artillery firing were heard, and shortly afterward a dense black cloud appeared in the west, in the direction of St Vincent (W. 100 miles), and gradually moved E.S.E. At 4 p.m. the whole sky was overcast, except a low arch to the northward. At 4.30 light showers of dust began to fall, and it was so dark that lights had to be burned on the ships and ashore. At 5.30 we departed for Trinidad (Port of Spain), the weather being so dark that we could not distinguish a large mooring buoy at a distance of 40 yards. At this time the dust was pouring down and speedily covered the decks to the depth of a quarter of an inch...."
>
> Log of ship *Lena*, Nibbs, master, Barbados to New York:
>
> "While at Barbados a heavy rain of volcanic dust fell from Mount Soufrière (W., 100 miles) on the decks and awnings of the vessel. Seven tons of same were thrown into the hold for ballast...."

Most important of all, the July 1902 issue carried a dozen photographs graphically depicting the destruction caused by the volcano's eruptions.

In February 1903, Gilbert H. Grosvenor was given the title Editor, with full authority to try his own ideas for the development of the Magazine. (He was also appointed the Society's Director, with control of all business and membership affairs.) Not long after, Grosvenor sought Bell's counsel about publishing photographs of Filipino women working in the fields, naked from the waist up. Since, as Grosvenor later recalled, "the women dressed, or perhaps I should say undressed, in this fashion...the pictures were a true reflection of the customs of the times in those islands."

Bell advised the young editor to print them and agreed with Grosvenor that prudery should not influence the decision.

The photograph, one of four illustrations for a May 1903 article on "American Development of the Philippines" was captioned "Primitive Agriculture. Tagbanua Women Harvesting Rice, Calaminanes Islands." As Tom Buckley, in his *New York Times Magazine* article "With the National Geographic On Its Endless, Cloudless Voyage," said of the response to the *Geographic*'s publication of that photograph, " So unquestionably genteel was the magazine, and so patently pure its anthropological interest, that even at a time when nice people called a leg a limb it never occurred to anyone to accuse Grosvenor of impropriety."

Above: "*PRIMITIVE AGRICULTURE. TAGBANUA WOMEN HARVESTING RICE, CALAMINANES ISLANDS,*" *was the caption for this photograph in the May 1903 Magazine.*
When the young editor sought the inventor's counsel about publishing photographs of half-naked Philippine Island natives, Alexander Graham Bell advised Grosvenor that prudery should not influence the decision. Grosvenor agreed and later defended publication on the grounds that "the pictures were a true reflection of the ... times in those islands."

Opposite, top: *A tranquil street scene in St. Pierre, Martinique, before the devastating 1902 eruption. Mont Pelée is seen looming in the background.*

Opposite, bottom: "*7:50 A.M., May 8, 1902: Blotting out the sky, churning down Pelée's slope at 100 miles an hour, superheated steam and ash from the volcano's belly smash the city, snuff out its life, roar across ships in the harbor where terrified seamen leap for cover. Only one vessel in 18 stays afloat as the wall of death engulfs them." This caption accompanied Paul Calle's painting for "Mont Pelée: Volcano that Killed a City" (a rewrite for the Society's 1963 book Great Adventures of Robert T. Hill's 1902 article "Volcanic Disturbances in the West Indies").*

The Society's first headquarters building: Gardiner Greene Hubbard Memorial Hall, completed in 1903.

On October 24, 1903, shortly after moving into the new building at the corner of 16th and M Streets, N.W., and two weeks after Grosvenor had requested "a desk phone on the basis of 1000 calls at $72," the Editor wrote the Chesapeake and Potomac Telephone Company to complain.

"Gentlemen:

A great deal of the telephoning from this office is with the Government Departments; on several occasions I have called up certain individuals in the War Department for instance and 'Central' has given me the Department but has then informed me that the line of the individual desired is busy. We have then been informed that the message has been charged to our number though no connection was made...."

It would have been about this time, too, that Grosvenor's seven guiding principles for editing the Magazine began to evolve, principles that reflected, in current *Geographic* Editor Wilbur E. Garrett's words, Grosvenor's "own cultured background, thoughtful personality, and Victorian courtesy to create a different, but highly successful, form of journalism." It would be these principles that would shape both the strengths and the weaknesses of the Magazine over the next fifty years. In a report subsequently made to his Board of Trustees (successors to the Society's Board of Managers), Grosvenor stated these principles as follows:

1. The first principle is absolute accuracy. Nothing must be printed which is not strictly according to fact....
2. Abundance of beautiful, instructive, and artistic illustrations.
3. Everything printed in the Magazine must have permanent value....
4. All personalities and notes of a trivial character are avoided.
5. Nothing of a partisan or controversial character is printed.
6. Only what is of a kindly nature is printed about any country or people, everything unpleasant or unduly critical being avoided.
7. The contents of each number is planned with a view of being timely....

"Fortunately," wrote Frederick G. Vosburgh, Grosvenor's associate of many years and Editor of the Magazine from 1967 through 1970, "some of these points—notably numbers 5 and 6—had a certain built-in elasticity, and the Editor determined the amount of stretch. There was never any doubt about that, or his editorial courage."

Grosvenor's editorial courage was strengthened by an incident that occurred early in his editorship. A paper was submitted to the Magazine by the distinguished Harvard geographer William Morris Davis, which Grosvenor found "exceedingly hard to digest." Nevertheless he passed it on to Alexander Graham Bell, who admitted that he, too, thought the paper difficult to understand, but because of the high academic stature of its author, Bell suggested Grosvenor go ahead and print it.

"With many misgivings, I printed the article," Grosvenor later wrote. "Soon letters of protest from educators deluged us, among them a letter from G. Stanley Hall, President of Clark University, one of the most ardent supporters of our project, who swore that if that article was to be the kind of geography we published, we had better discontinue our efforts.

"From that day," Grosvenor continued, "no sentence has found space in the National Geographic that could not be readily understood."

Recalling the sort of editor Gilbert Hovey Grosvenor was, Vosburgh wrote:

Gilbert Grosvenor had no patience with murky thinking. "What does this mean?" he would pencil sternly beside a paragraph long on pretentious words but short on clarity of thought.

Bombast bored him. "Come down off your soapbox," he said firmly to writers carried away by their opinions to the point of speechifying in print. "Stick to the facts. Our readers can be trusted to form their own opinions."

"People like to learn," he once observed, "but dislike the feeling of being taught."

Use a long word when a short one would do as well, and the manuscript would come back from his paper-piled office with the offending word circled and labeled: "This is a jawbreaker."

Qualify a statement with the lazy phrase "is said to" and you would be called into his presence and informed: "The *National Geographic Magazine* does not publish hearsay. Either it is a fact or it is not. Find out."

If you came to consider yourself an expert on a field of science or a country and affected esoteric terms or high flown language, Gilbert Grosvenor would puncture your inflated ego and bring you down to earth. Snobbish use of foreign words without translation was, and is, similarly taboo, on the grounds that no one knows every language and it is our business to make ourselves understood.

Once he spelled it out for me patiently: "If you don't tell the people, they won't know."

This mild-seeming gentleman of courtly manners had the soul and heart of a fighter. Those who challenged his plans and principles struck steel beneath the velvet....

On April 26, 1902, the cornerstone of the Society's new headquarters, Hubbard Memorial Hall, had been laid at the corner of 16th and M Streets in Washington. By October 1903, the National Geographic Society had moved out of its rented office in the Corcoran Building and into its new headquarters paid for by the Hubbard and Bell families. By then Dr. Bell had already resigned the presidency of the Society—after telling his son-in-law, "Bert, you are competent to paddle your own canoe." Bell wanted to devote himself to his scientific research, which, at that time, was concentrated upon tetrahedral kites.

In June 1903, the *National Geographic Magazine* had run thirty-two pages of text and seventy-nine photographs of Bell's experimental kites in an issue devoted primarily to "The Tetrahedral Principle in Kite Structure." Four years earlier, in April 1899, Bell had addressed the National Academy of Sciences in Washington on the subject of "Kites with Radial Wings." Since that time, Bell had written for the *Geographic*, he had been "continuously at work upon experiments relating to kites. Why, I do not know, excepting perhaps because of the intimate connection of the subject with the flying-machine problem."

Bell's piece continued:

> We are all of us interested in aerial locomotion; and I am sure that no one who has observed with attention the flight of birds can doubt for one moment the possibility of aerial flight by bodies specifically heavier than the air. In the words of an old writer, "We cannot consider as impossible that which has already been accomplished."
>
> I have had the feeling that a properly constructed flying-machine should be capable of being flown as a kite; and, conversely, that a properly constructed kite should be capable of use as a flying-machine when driven by its own propellers. I am not so sure, however, of the truth of the former proposition as I am of the latter.

On December 17, 1903, six months after Bell's article appeared in the *National Geographic*, Wilbur and Orville Wright realized one of man's oldest dreams when they achieved the world's first successful controlled, powered, manned, heavier-than-air flight, with Orville at the controls of their Wright Flyer. This epoch-making 120-foot flight lasted only twelve seconds, but aviation was born.

The new Society headquarters in Hubbard Hall "bulked as large as a palace" in young Gilbert Grosvenor's mind, and he "resolved that we would prove worthy of so splendid a headquarters. Zestfully I attacked the myriad problems that beset a lone editor. Sometimes, however, those problems seemed insurmountable...."

Hubbard Memorial Hall with a bust of Gardiner Greene Hubbard in the foreground.

One such problem occurred in December 1904, when the printer called Grosvenor to say he needed eleven more pages for the January issue and the young Editor did not have a decent manuscript available, nor did he feel in the mood to come up with eleven pages of copy himself. By coincidence, on his desk lay that day's mail, and on top was a large, bulky envelope bearing foreign stamps. Still brooding about how to fill the January issue, Grosvenor listlessly opened the envelope then looked "with mounting excitement at the enclosures that tumbled out."

Before him lay fifty photographs of the mysterious city of Lhasa in Tibet, taken by the explorers Tsybikoff and Norzunoff for the Imperial Russian Geographical Society, which was offering them free to the *National Geographic*. These photographs—among the first ever taken of the Tibetan capital—were so extraordinary that Grosvenor quickly chose eleven of them and told the printer to fill the Magazine's empty pages with the photographs of Tibet. Then, expecting to be fired for stuffing the pages of a serious magazine with scenic photographs accompanied only by captions, Grosvenor went to the club "for a holiday," and later went home and told his wife what he had done.

Even in that era of trumpeted "illustrated" magazines, for Grosvenor to have used that many nontechnical photographs to support a basically textless piece was more than daring, it was heresy. But, as Grosvenor told Elsie, it wasn't just using the photographs that worried him, it was that he had paid for the halftone plates out of the Society's meager bank account.

Grosvenor's anxiety was swiftly dispelled when, upon the January issue's publication, Society members stopped him on the street to congratulate him on the Magazine and to say how much they had enjoyed "the first photographs of romantic Lhasa."

The National Geographic Society flag with its three stripes—blue representing the sky, brown the earth, and green the ocean—was designed by Gilbert Grosvenor's wife, Elsie, for the 1903 Ziegler Polar Expedition.

As Grosvenor later recalled, Elsie "asked me...what my idea was, and I said I would like a flag that was recognizable. In Washington we'd been watching parade after parade with notables and nine-tenths of the flags were so complicated, having a seal with the motto around it, that the bystander from the sidewalk couldn't tell what it was—what state.

"I just asked Mrs. Grosvenor if she would please design something that was readable from the sidewalk; and so she hit upon these three stripes, and then she thought she'd put 'National Geographic Society' in big letters on it so that everybody could read what's on the flag. You see my idea: a flag that is not readable fails in the purpose for which flags exist. A flag is supposed to tell the observer who is assembled with it."

"Our members liked the pictures better than the manuscripts we had been feeding them," Grosvenor recalled in 1951. "They showed their pleasure by sending in many new members. The incident taught me that what I liked, the average man would like, that is that I am a common average American. That was how the *National Geographic Magazine* started on its rather remarkable career of printing many pictures, and later more *color* pictures, than any other publication in the world."

The success of the Tibet photographs lulled Grosvenor into thinking his role as Editor would be easier; all he needed to do was to "fill our pages with pictures." But it was as difficult to come up with good photographs of geographic interest as it was to find good manuscripts. "The only photographs that seemed obtainable then were of mountains and scenery," he later complained. But luck, again, was with him.

The following month, in February 1905, Grosvenor's cousin William Howard Taft, then Secretary of War, told him that in April the War Department would be publishing the first "Census Report of the Philippines" and that the report would be illustrated with numerous photographs. If Grosvenor would inform Society members of this interesting publication, Taft told the young Editor, the National Geographic Society could help both the government and the people of the Philippines.

Grosvenor's interest had been pricked the moment his cousin had mentioned "photographs." "That word had become as musical to my ear as the jingle of a cash register to a businessman," Grosvenor wrote.

Taft had the Census Director lend Grosvenor the copper plates of any of the photographs contained in the report that Grosvenor wished to reprint, and Grosvenor chose thirty-two full-page plates containing 138 photographs in all for the April 1905 issue.

To have obtained such photographs on its own, the Society would have had to pay several thousand dollars, plus at least another $350 to engrave that many photographic plates, and, as Grosvenor later pointed out, it was "money The Society did not have at the time."

The April 1905 "A Revelation of the Filipinos" issue was such a success and brought in so many new members that Grosvenor had to reprint the issue.

The time seemed right for a determined membership campaign. Grosvenor hired additional clerical help and boldly began spending money in an all-out membership drive. By September, membership in the Society had soared to 10,000, triple the membership of the year before. The Magazine was doing so well that that same month Grosvenor was able to inform the Board of Managers that the Society would finish the year not only in the black but with a surplus of $3,500. In recognition of this milestone, Grosvenor introduced the following resolution to the Board:

> *Resolved:* That the National Geographic Society, through its Board of Managers, thank Dr. Bell for his generous subscription to the work of The Society from 1899 to 1904, and inform Dr. Bell that The Society is now on such a substantial basis that it can relieve him of his subscription for 1905.

Now, for the first time since April 1, 1899, Bell would no longer be called upon to donate the $100 per month toward Gilbert Grosvenor's salary. "Elsie and I were jubilant," Grosvenor would later recall. "At last her generous father had seen his dream realized: a geographic magazine that would support the

Society. His total gift to establish the magazine was $6,900 instead of the $87,000 he had offered in 1899."

That same month, membership nominations were coming in in such numbers that Grosvenor asked if Dr. Bell's secretary might be able to come into the Society offices to help. As the two young men were working together, Grosvenor asked the secretary if he knew of anyone who might like to work at the Geographic permanently, and "one morning," Grosvenor later recalled, "this splendid looking young man—very husky—came in. He handed me his card and I looked at it—John Oliver La Gorce." He continued:

> The word "John" appealed to me very much. It was a most honored name in the Bible. The name "Oliver" was one of the magic names of chivalry. I didn't know at the time what "La Gorce" stood for, but I soon found that his father was a colonel of artillery in a very distinguished French family. I also learned that his mother was Irish, and I thought the combination of Irish and French would be very suitable. He was sure to be a good mixer, and practical.
>
> So I asked Mr. La Gorce if he would like the job, explaining—as Dr. Bell had explained to me in offering a job—that it might be a steppingstone to something better. He said, yes, he would like it. We made no contract. I never asked him for a reference.
>
> A few days after, Dr. Alexander Graham Bell came down to call. He was received by Mr. La Gorce, and he came into my office and asked, "Who is that fine young fellow you have out there? What a gracious manner he has." I introduced them, and it was a mutual admiration society.

La Gorce remained at the Society for the next fifty-two years and retired as President and Editor on January 8, 1957, two years after having been awarded the Grosvenor Medal "for Outstanding Service to the Increase and Diffusion of Geographic Knowledge for Fifty Years, 1905–1955."

The year Grosvenor hired La Gorce, he also decided that the Society should hold an annual banquet. Grosvenor knew that not only would Washington members enjoy such a function, but if he were able to convince a nationally known figure to serve as the banquet's principal speaker, the Society's reputation would be enhanced. Grosvenor felt an ideal choice would be the Secretary of War, his cousin William Howard Taft. Although Taft's bulk was a clear indication of his love for eating, Grosvenor could not be sure that banquet fare and the tug of familial kinship would provide Taft reason enough to accept, so the young Editor was not beyond exercising a little manipulation. Knowing that Taft's wife enjoyed social evenings, Grosvenor made sure to invite the Secretary in the presence of Mrs. Taft.

"Why, what a nice suggestion!" Mrs. Taft responded. "We would be delighted to attend."

Grosvenor had his banquet speaker; Mrs. Taft had her social evening; the Secretary of War came up with a commendable address; and the Society's first annual banquet was a success.

By the end of that year, membership in the Society had grown from 3,662 to 11,479, and "the year 1905," Grosvenor would later recall, "marked the turning point in the Society's fortunes, the 'end of the beginning.' " The National Geographic Society's paid staff numbered nine people: Gilbert Hovey Grosvenor, Editor and Director; John Oliver La Gorce, Assistant Secretary; and an Assistant Treasurer, a Librarian, four clerks, and a janitor.

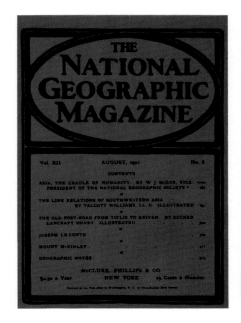

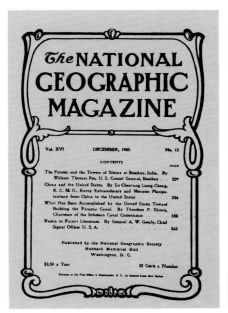

In 1901, the design of the National Geographic Magazine's *cover changed a fourth time to the style shown at top. That design remained until 1904, when the heavy, dark frame and oval border around the contents and title were discarded in favor of a lighter "art nouveau" look below. This fifth design lasted until 1910.*

At the end of 1905, the circulation of the Magazine *was 11,479.*

95

"Lord, that's enough now. Please stop it."

"Lord, that's enough now. Please stop it."
—a tearful 16-year-old girl standing with her mother in their violently heaving
front yard during Alaska's 8.5 magnitude earthquake on Good Friday, March 27,
1964

"VANCOUVER! VANCOUVER! This is it...."
—the last words of geologist David Johnston, at 8:32 A.M. on May 18, 1980, six
miles from Mount St. Helens

For several weeks early in that spring of 1980, *National Geographic* Assistant Editor Rowe Findley had been working on a prospective Magazine article about the national forests. On March 21, a Forest Service friend telephoned Findley at the Society's headquarters to tell him that earthquakes were shaking Washington State's 9,677-foot-high Mount St. Helens, the restless Cascade Range volcano that dominated Gifford Pinchot National Forest. When Findley began researching the mountain, he came upon Drs. Dwight Crandell and Donal Mullineaux's paper "Potential Hazards From Future Eruptions of Mount St. Helens." Mount St. Helens, Findley read, had been the most active of the Cascade volcanoes during the mid-nineteenth century, and, the authors predicted, was due for another eruption before the end of this one.

By March 26, the quakes had grown in strength and force and, as Findley later wrote, "the dormant volcano was stirring and stretching." He booked a flight out early Friday, March 28. By the time he arrived, intermittent plumes of smoke and ash were rising two miles above the peak, dusting its northeast slope sooty gray. It was, Findley noted, "the start of a geologic event—the first volcanic eruption in the contiguous 48 states since California's Lassen, another Cascade peak, shut down in 1917 after a three-year run."

Journalists, geologists, crackpots, and the curious, drawn by the restive volcano, poured into nearby communities eager to bear witness to the potentially cataclysmic drama. The volcano, however, like a supremely confident old performer, refused to heed any curtain time but its own.

Through the remainder of March and all of April the mountain, Findley wrote, still did not "fully awake. A second crater appeared beside the first, then the two merged into a single bowl 1,700 feet across and 850 feet deep. But the eruption level, geologists said, remained 'low-energy mode.' "

Findley spent time during the week between May 11 and May 18 with his new friends Reid Blackburn, a twenty-seven-year-old photographer on loan to the *National Geographic* from the Vancouver *Columbian,* and eighty-four-year-old Harry Truman, whose refusal to leave his Spirit Lake lodge five miles from the volcano's peak had captured media attention.

On May 15 and 16, clouds closed in, making the mountain nearly invisible. On Saturday, May 17, the sun shone but the mountain, Findley wrote, "drowses

Preceding spread: *On January 23, 1973, a volcano was born when a fissure opened in the earth on the outskirts of Vestmannaeyjar, the only town and port of Iceland's Heimaey Island. Within twenty-four hours, ships and planes evacuated most of the island's 5,300 people; and over the next weeks the deep advancing lava and falling ash buried much of the port city while adding about one square mile of new territory to the island. Today Eldfell, as the new volcano was christened, looms over Vestmannaeyjar and, as the Society reported in its 1983 Book Service volume* Exploring Our Living Planet, *"local teenagers are said to find Eldfell's warm crater an ideal trysting place."*

Opposite: *St. Pierre, Martinique, shortly after the May 8, 1902, eruption of Mont Pelée, whose explosion, heard hundreds of miles away, released a cloud of superheated steam and gases that destroyed the city in less than three minutes and left 30,000 dead in its ruins.*

Sunday, May 18, 1980: Photographer Gary Rosenquist, in the right place at the wrong time, snapped this extraordinary sequence of Washington's Mount St. Helens blowing the top 1,300 feet of its crest in a massive eruption that left scores of people dead or missing.

"Some two million birds, fish, and animals perished in the May 18 explosion," noted the Geographic in its January 1981 "Eruption of Mount St. Helens" report, "and more than 150 miles of trout and salmon streams and 26 lakes were destroyed. The forests near the mountain were simply removed—uprooted, shredded, or blown away by sandblasting winds of hurricane force...."

on. The north-face bulge continues—swelling five feet a day; other signs say that nothing is about to happen." Findley drove to Cougar, a timber-industry settlement twelve miles southwest of Mount St. Helens.

"Sunday, May 18. First sun finds the mountain still drowsing," wrote Findley (in his January 1981 article titled "St. Helens: Mountain With a Deathwish"):

Because it is drowsing, I decide not to watch it today, a decision that soon will seem like the quintessence of wisdom. Because it is drowsing, others—campers, hikers, photographers, a few timber cutters—will be drawn in, or at least feel no need to hurry out. Their regrets will soon be compressed into a few terrible seconds before oblivion.

Ten megatons of TNT. More than 5,000 times the amount dropped in the great raid on Dresden, Germany, in 1945. Made up mostly of carbon dioxide and water vapor, innocuous except when under the terrible pressure and heat of a volcano's insides and then suddenly released.

That 5.0 quake does it. The entire mountainside falls as the gases explode out with a roar heard 200 miles away. The incredible blast rolls north, northwest, and northeast at aircraft speeds. In one continuous thunderous sweep, it scythes down giants of the forest, clear-cutting 200 square miles in all....Within three miles of the summit, the trees simply vanish—transported through the air for unknown distances.

Then comes the ash—fiery, hot, blanketing, suffocating—and a hail of boulders and ice. The multichrome, three-dimensional world of trees, hill, and sky becomes a monotone of powdery gray ash, heating downed logs and automobile tires till they smolder and blaze, blotting out horizons and perceptions of depth. Rolling in the wake, the abrasive, searing dust in mere minutes clouds over the same 200 square miles and beyond, falling on the earth by inches and then by feet.

The failed north wall of the mountain has become a massive sled of earth, crashing irresistibly downslope until it banks up against the steep far wall of the North Toutle Valley. This is the moment of burial for Harry Truman and his lodge, as well as for some twenty summer homes at a site called the Village, a mile down the valley.

The eruption's main force now nozzles upward, and the light-eating pillar of ash quickly carries to 30,000 feet, to 40,000, to 50,000, to 60,000. ...The top curls over and anvils out and flares and streams broadly eastward on the winds.

The shining Sunday morning turns forebodingly gray and to a blackness in which a hand cannot be seen in front of an eye.

In the eerie gray and black, relieved only by jabs of lightning, filled with thunder and abrading winds, a thousand desperate acts of search and salvation are under way.

Psychological shock waves of unbelief quickly roll across the Pacific Northwest. In Vancouver and Portland, in Kelso and Longview, and in a hundred other cities and towns, the towering dark cloud is ominously visible.

A phone call...sends me outside to gaze at the spectacle. As soon as I can, I get airborne for a better look and recoil from accepting what I see.

The whole top of the mountain is gone.

Lofty, near-symmetrical Mount St. Helens is no more. Where it had towered, there now squats an ugly, flat-topped, truncated abomination. From its center rises a broad unremitting explosion of ash, turning blue-gray in the overspreading shadow of its ever-widening cloud. In the far deepening gloom, orange lightning flashes like the flicking of serpents' tongues. From the foot of the awesome mountain there spreads a ground-veiling pall.

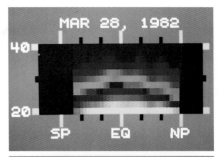

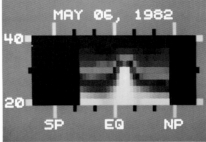

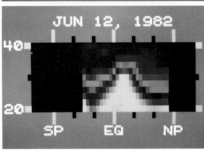

Above: "*Comparable in ash output, the Mexican and U.S. volcanoes had very different impacts. Mount St. Helens' predominantly lateral blast laid waste an area of...approximately 232 square miles. El Chichón's scorched earth was only a quarter that, but... atmospheric conditions together with the force of the blast enabled it to penetrate that cold-air barrier and enter the stratosphere....Computer profiles of satellite data taken over Europe document the cloud's spread through the stratosphere....*"

Opposite: "*Colossal plume of natural air pollutants, the largest in the Northern Hemisphere since the eruption of Alaska's Mount Katmai in 1912, El Chichón's April 4 [1982] explosion is seen as a bright circular puff over Mexico's isthmus in this weather-satellite image.*"

Overleaf: *Masked against El Chichón's abrasive ash, residents of San Cristóbal de las Casas, nearly sixty miles southeast of the volcano, clear their streets at noon.*

Somewhere down there lies Coldwater I [a U.S. Geological Survey Camp], above the rushing waters of Coldwater Creek and the valley I had left in verdant beauty only 40 hours before.

Reid Blackburn at Coldwater I, eight miles from the blast, had time to fire four frames of film and dash for his car before being caught in the burning, suffocating ash. Harry Truman and his lodge, buried under hundreds of feet of ash and debris, became part of the mountain he had always said was a part of him. They were two of the dozens who lost their lives when Mount St. Helens erupted.

The whole top of the mountain, as Findley had noted, was indeed gone; the explosion blew away almost a cubic mile of its summit, reducing its elevation from 9,677 feet to 8,364 feet.

Two years later, in March and April 1982, a small, 4,134-foot-high volcano, El Chichón in the Mexican state of Chiapas, was blown apart in a series of violent eruptions that hurled 500 million metric tons of ashes, dust, and gases into the atmosphere. El Chichón, half the size of Mount St. Helens, filled the air with at least ten times the amount of debris, and, although the official death toll was 187, unofficial estimates of the number of victims ran into the thousands.

And on November 13, 1985—two months after a massive offshore earthquake sent seismic waves racing more than 350 kilometers east toward Mexico City, destroying buildings and killing possibly as many as 30,000 people—a minor eruption of the 17,822-foot-high volcano Nevado del Ruiz, 3,200 kilometers to the south, melted part of its ice cap, triggering a murderous mudslide that killed some 20,000 persons in Armero, thirty miles from its peak. There, in that once-busy agricultural center, the mudslides struck after 11 P.M. when most were asleep, entombing them in mud nearly ten feet deep.

Mexico City's quake occurred on September 19, 1985, at 7:18 A.M., when a huge slab of the earth's crust moved twelve miles beneath the ocean's surface.

"Seismic waves a thousand times more powerful than the atomic bomb that leveled Hiroshima fanned out toward Mexico City, in pulses traveling 25,000 kilometers an hour (15,500 mph) and registering 8.1 on the Richter scale," wrote *Geographic* senior editorial staff member Allen A. Boraiko. "So violent was the earthquake that tall buildings trembled in Texas, water sloshed in Colorado pools, and the entire Earth vibrated like a struck bell."

When we look at photographs taken of the earth by the astronauts and see our lovely, cloud-traced, blue sphere floating serenely through the star-studded, black velvet canopy of space, the image our planet projects is one of deceptive tranquillity. Within those clouds lurk violent, thunderous forces unleashing havoc upon an earth whose fragile crust is constantly grinding and trembling and threatening to explode beneath our feet.

As Kendrick Frazier, a former editor of *Science News* magazine, pointed out in his book *The Violent Face of Nature*, at any given time 1,800 thunder-

Workers in front of the fallen wooden cupola of the Santa Rosa Courthouse, damaged in the San Francisco earthquake of April 18–19, 1906. Some fifty miles north of San Francisco, Santa Rosa suffered greater earthquake damage for its size than any other town in the area.

storms are churning across the expanse of our planet; 100 lightning bolts strike its surface each second; in late summer, of the fifty or so hurricanes and typhoons that are spawned each year, one—and maybe more—is moving toward a populated coastline. Half a billion people live on floodplains that supply food for a third of the world's population. Rampaging waters somewhere are inundating peoples' homes and croplands.

More than fourteen thousand earth tremors, strong enough to jiggle seismograph needles, shake our planet each week. Twice a day an earthquake will somewhere damage buildings; from fifteen to twenty times a year an earthquake will occur with enough force to result in widespread death and destruction. "And all the while," Frazier adds, "there are 516 active volcanoes waiting to spring loose their violence. An eruption begins somewhere every 15 days."

In the summer of 1927, when Secretary of Commerce Herbert Hoover, in his capacity as director of relief operations, looked upon the devastation caused by the overflowing Mississippi River, he said, "We are humble before such an outburst of the forces of Nature and the futility of man in their control." Hoover called it "the greatest peace-time disaster in our history."

The *National Geographic* was there to report on "The Great Mississippi Flood of 1927," just as it has been there to cover nearly all the other great disasters that have shaken our planet since the Society's founding. In fact, starting with its first issue's report on The Great Storm of March 11–14, 1888, accounts of floods, blizzards, famines, droughts, hurricanes, pestilences, avalanches, earthquakes, and volcanic eruptions, photographed in vivid detail and written up with gusto, have figured prominently in the Magazine's pages.

Nowhere is the *Geographic's* reporting more moving than in the accounts of starving children. And famine cares not where it takes its victims, whether in flood-stricken Bangladesh as the Magazine's Steve Raymer reported in 1975:

> The scene is chilling, horrifying. Several thousand starving Bengalis wait patiently, it seems, to die in a refugee camp in Rangpur, one of the remotest districts in the poor, desperate land of Bangladesh.
>
> There is only enough food on hand from the United States and Canada to provide each with a daily cup of flour, but no powdered milk. Many are too weak to eat, or to swat at the flies swarming around the kitchen.
>
> I see a child—a naked skeleton—waiting for his meager ration; his withered body bears the telltale signs of advanced malnutrition. Others like him sit almost lifeless in their filth. A woman clad in rags clutches an infant so thin his ribs look like a birdcage beneath his peeling skin. I see a tear in the mother's eye.

Or, as Melville Chater wrote in the Magazine in 1919, the famine finds its victims in Armenia:

> As we neared Igdir our interpreter, a cheery, affable young Armenian... turned to us from the front seat and inquired with just a trace of the showman's manner:
>
> "What you like to see, gentlemens?"

Alaska's March 27, 1964, Good Friday earthquake dropped buildings and pavements as much as thirty feet in downtown Anchorage. Two days later, troops patrol the area and survey the devastation caused by the strongest quake in North America since 1899.

"Conditions," snapped the doctor.

"You like best conditions of dyings or deads? Dyings is easy to see everywhere in the streets. But I know where many deads are, too—in what houses—if you like."

"Drive on," I said hastily. "We'll decide later."

The town of Igdir, with its local and near-by populations of 30,000 Armenians, 20,000 Tatars and 15,000 Yezidis, revealed some squalid streets with but a few people seated disconsolately here and there as we drove in. Throughout those tortuous, sun-beaten byways no children played and no animals roamed. The air was heavy with dreadful silence, such as hangs over plague-smitten communities.

We found the children, such as they were, inhabiting an orphanage wherein one sickened at putridity's horrible odor, and were informed that there were neither medicines nor disinfectants wherewith to allay the condition of the many little sick-beds.

Sick? Say, rather, the bed-ridden—a word which more justly describes those tiny, withered up, crone-like creatures, upon whose faces the skin stretched to a drumhead's tightness: whose peering eyes show terror and anguish, as if Death's presence were already perceptible to them, and who lay there at Famine's climax of physical exhaustion....

"They'll all die," was the brusque observation of the doctor, who had taken one glimpse and gone out. "We can't do them any good. Silly business, anyway, to come out here in a broken-down car."

"We will now see conditions of the deads?" inquired our interpreter, sweetly....

Further on in his Armenia piece Chater tells of coming upon "fifty wizened children [sitting] about a long board" in an open space "eating the American Committee's daily dole of boiled rice. This was accomplished at a gulp," he reported. Then, he added:

> ...the children scattered, searching the ground as I had seen others do beside our car at Alexandropol. Soon one was chewing a straw, another the paring of a horse's hoof, a third a captured beetle.
>
> One seven-year-old girl crouched by herself, cracking something between two stones and licking her fingers. The doctor bent over, examining the object. He asked with peculiar sharpness, "Where did she get that—that bone?"
>
> The child looked up with a scared, guilty glance; then her answer came through the interpreter, who said in a low voice, "Yonder in the graveyard."
>
> I am not sure that we preserved our composure.

If the weather or political oppression doesn't cause the drought that creates the famines, there are the locust plagues such as the one Ethiopia suffered in 1958, in which the insects devoured 167,000 tons of grain—enough to feed a million people for a year.

In his stunning and disturbing July 1977 article, "The Rat, Lapdog of the Devil," Thomas Y. Canby noted that rats had caused the Bombay plague epidemic of 1898 which killed 12½ million Indians, and that during the Black Plague of the Middle Ages, the rat, host for the plague-carrying flea, had caused an estimated 25 million deaths. "In a world haunted by threat of famine," Canby continued, "[rats] will destroy approximately a fifth of all food crops planted. In India their depredations will deprive a hungry people of enough grain to fill a freight train stretching more than 3,000 miles."

The average rat, Canby pointed out, can

wriggle through a hole no larger than a quarter;
scale a brick wall as though it had rungs;
swim half a mile and tread water for three days;
gnaw through lead pipes and cinder blocks with chisel teeth that exert
   an incredible 24,000 pounds per square inch;
survive being flushed down a toilet, and enter buildings by the same
   route;
multiply so rapidly that a pair could have 15,000 descendants in a year's
   life span;
plummet five stories to the ground and scurry off unharmed.

"This year in the United States alone," Canby continued, "rats will bite thousands of humans, inflicting disease, despair, terror. They will destroy perhaps a billion dollars worth of property, excluding innumerable 'fires of undetermined origin' they will cause by gnawing insulation from electrical wiring."

That's the bad news. The good news is that "in laboratories the rat has contributed more to the cure of human illness than any other animal." Furthermore, the author pointed out, the rat, when deep-fried in coconut oil, has "the pleasing gaminess of squirrel or rabbit."

Of all the natural disasters that can befall man none are more dramatic than earthquakes—themselves, in many cases, the cause of volcanic explosions. The magnitude of an earthquake is measured on the scale developed in the 1930s and 1940s by Charles F. Richter and Beno Gutenberg of the California Institute of Technology. The Richter scale is not geometric but *logarithmic*. Each increase of 1 in the scale represents an increase of 32 times in the force of the tremor, and ten times in the size of the seismic wave measured by the seismograph. Therefore, an earthquake such as the one that struck San Francisco in 1906, which measured 8.3 on the Richter Scale, is not twice as powerful as one of, say, a 4.1 magnitude, but a *million* times more powerful.

Between 1970 and 1980, twenty-one earthquakes of a 6.3 magnitude or higher occurred, killing close to 960,000 people.

On March 27, 1964, an earthquake measuring 8.5 struck Alaska—the strongest quake to hit the North American continent in this century. Bill Graves reported on the damage for the July 1964 Magazine:

> It began years before that fatal Good Friday of March 27, 1964. Deep in the earth, perhaps 12 miles beneath the region north of Prince William Sound, fearful and little-understood forces were at work on the earth's crust, twisting and straining the great layers of rock as a truck strains its laminated springs going over a bump. Eventually, at a point called the focus, the rock gave way, snapping and shifting in an instant with the force of 12,000 Hiroshima-size atomic explosions.
>
> The devastation spread with terrible speed in an arc 500 miles long.... Crackling through the earth at thousands of miles an hour, the shock wave sliced, churned, and ruptured the land like some enormous disk harrow drawn over the surface. Highways billowed with the upward thrust of the shock, great concrete slabs overlapping one another like shingles set awry.

◄ ───────────────────────────────────────

After leaving 250 dead in the Caribbean, Hurricane Allen's 190-mph winds and ferocious seas lashed Corpus Christi, Texas, in August 1980.

As Gilbert Hovey Grosvenor's editorial policies evolved with the new century, the *National Geographic* evolved too, moving increasingly toward its maturity as a popular magazine of catholic interests, reflecting Grosvenor's confidence that "what I liked, the average man would like..."

Bell's articles on the construction of kites were followed by articles on topics as varied as geographical distribution of insanity in the United States, immigration, the "Proportion of Children in the United States," the San Francisco earthquake, Polar exploration, eugenics, American industries, "Queer Methods of Travel in Curious Corners of the World," "Children of the World," and so on.

Two articles, indicative of the enlarging sphere of interest, appeared in the July 1905 issue and are worth noting: the first, "The Purple Veil: A Romance of the Sea," was signed "H. A. L."—the last initial standing for, readers learned the following year, "Largelamb." H.A. Largelamb's "The Purple Veil" opens:

> Off the New England coast a curious object is often found floating on the water, somewhat resembling a lady's veil of gigantic size and of a violet or purple color....In 1871 the late Prof. Spencer F. Baird had the opportunity of examining one of these objects at sea, and he found it to present the appearance "of a continuous sheet of a purplish-brown color, 20 or 30 feet in length and 4 or 5 feet in width, composed of a mucous substance, which was perfectly transparent...." On examining the substance with a magnifying glass...it was obvious that the purple veil, as a whole, was the egg-mass of a fish.

What fish? The *Lophius piscatorius*, the author tells us, "variously known as the 'Goose-fish,' the 'All-mouth,' or the 'Angler,' one of the most remarkable fishes in existence." And one of God's ugliest, too, a fact irrelevant to Largelamb, who explains the "Goose-fish" name as having derived from its

> "having been known to swallow live geese," a statement almost incredible; but a reputable fisherman told the late G. Brown Goode that "he once saw a struggle in the water, and found that a Goose-fish had swallowed the head and neck of a large loon, which had pulled it to the surface and was trying to escape."

Largelamb provides additional accounts of goosefish stomachs having been opened to reveal within "seven wild ducks," "large gulls," and on a third

Preceding spread: Answering President Woodrow Wilson's call for a show of support to alert the nation to defense needs before the U.S. entered World War One, 150 employees of the National Geographic—the women in white, the men in straw hats—march up Pennsylvania Avenue, Washington, D.C., behind Society President Gilbert H. Grosvenor, his wife, Elsie, and Society Assistant Secretary George W. Hutchison in the Preparedness Parade organized for Flag Day, June 14, 1916.

occasion "six coots in a fresh condition," all of which leads H.A.L. to conclude: "The fish is a most voracious, carnivorous animal—indeed omnivorous—and quite indiscriminate in its diet."

"The Purple Veil" marked H. A. Largelamb's first appearance in the *Geographic*, but not the first appearance of "The Purple Veil"'s famous author; the byline "H. A. Largelamb" is an anagram: unscramble the letters and you get none other than the ubiquitous A. Graham Bell.

The second article of note that July 1905 was written by the Honorable Eki Hioki, First Secretary of the Japanese Legation, one of the earliest publications of a foreign power's point of view in the *National Geographic*. In "The Purpose of the Anglo-Japanese Alliance," Hioki concluded:

> Instead of Japan coveting the possessions of the United States in the Pacific, Japan welcomes the United States as a neighbor....
>
> For the same reason that Japan does not menace the United States politically Japan does not threaten the United States commercially....There never has been, is not now, or ever will be a strong commercial rivalry between Japan and the United States....The United States will not be swamped by the products of the loom and the forge of Japan....

Although Grosvenor had recognized early in his editorship the value of "beautiful, and instructive" illustrations—the eruption of Mont Pelée, the Lhasa, Tibet, and Philippine Census Report photographs, for example, had been resounding successes—those early illustrations still tended to be of *places* and *things* rather than people; on those occasions when people were shown, they were usually posed in native costume. However, the January 1905 *Geographic* article "Our Immigration During 1904" contained photographs that were eloquent despite the poses. The article was, a member of the Society's Book Service would write in 1981 in *Images of the World*, "illustrated by lineups at Ellis Island: weary old men, a young black man, a barefoot woman wearing a babushka. In photos they are what they would become in poetry—the tired, the poor, the huddled masses yearning to breathe free."

There was still the sense, however, that Grosvenor's recognition of such eloquence might have been more accidental than intentional. But just as the *Geographic* began to move toward "exotic natives in colorful costumes," it began to move away from the "Marine Hydrographic Surveys of the Coasts of the World" type of article. In its place came the first-person-narrated "adventure," as in this excerpt from the March 1906 article "Morocco, 'the Land of the Extreme West'":

> We had gathered in the drawing-room directly after dinner, when we were startled by loud screams from the servants' quarters. Followed by my stepson, Mr. Cromwell Varley, whose wife and two daughters, just home from school at Geneva, completed, with [my wife] Mrs. Perdicaris, our family circle, I rushed down a passage leading to the servants' hall, where I came upon a crowd of armed natives.
>
> Even then we did not realize our danger, but thought...that they, like ourselves, had rushed in to learn the cause of the uproar....
>
> As I turned to inquire of these natives who crowded about me as to what had occurred, I saw some of our European servants already bound and helpless and, at the same moment. we ourselves were assailed by these intruders, who struck us with their rifles. At the same instant our hands were roughly twisted and bound behind our backs with stout palmetto cords that cut like knives.

Author Ion Perdicaris relates how he, his family, and servants are forced out of the house where they are held under guard by the rifle-toting invaders, while

a little apart stood their leader, a man of fine presence, attired in the handsome dress worn by the native gentry. One of my men was reproaching this personage bitterly for this unprovoked aggression.

The leader of the mountaineers raised his hand and, in low but emphatic tones, declared that if no rescue were attempted nor any disturbance made, no harm would befall us and in a few weeks we should be safely back among our people, adding, "I am Raisuli! the Raisuli!"—this...being his clan appellation, since this chereef, or native nobleman, is known among his own followers as Mulai Ahmed ben Mohammed, the Raisuli.

On hearing him declare his name I felt at once that the affair was possibly more serious than I had hitherto anticipated....

Raisuli had indeed been reported to be on the warpath for some time past, but...no one imagined he would attack any one in the immediate neighborhood of Tangier....

Approaching him, bound as I was and in evening dress, I said to him in Arabic, "I know you by name, Raisuli, and I accept your safe conduct, but we cannot go with you thus. We must have our overcoats, hats, and boots."

"Which of your servants shall I have released to return to the house for what you require?" replied Raisuli.

I selected Bourzin, the younger of the guards, on duty that evening....

The tame photographs accompanying Perdicaris' article—"A Group of Camels Passed on the Way to Tsarradan. The Site of Our Captivity," "A Waterwheel Driven by a Donkey on the Road to Tsarradan. Raisuli's Stronghold. Notice the earthen jars and the blindfolded animal," "Moorish Women at the Spinning-wheel Waited on by a Slave"—gave no hint of the international furor the Perdicaris incident had caused. Text and illustration were still separate entities; all they had in common was locale. But the captivity of Perdicaris was serious enough to prompt President Theodore Roosevelt to instruct his Secretary of State to cable, "WE WANT PERDICARIS ALIVE OR RAISULI DEAD." Perdicaris had been freed by the time his article appeared and, four months later, in July 1906, the *Geographic*'s cover proclaimed:

"Photographing Wild Game with Flashlight and Camera"

By Hon. George Shiras, Third
Member of Congress 1903–1905

With a Series of 70 Illustrations of Wild Game—
Deer, Elk, Bull Moose, Raccoon, Porcupine
Wild Cat, Herons, Ducks, Snowy Owl,
Pelicans, Birds in Flight, etc.

"In 1906 George Shiras 3rd, a member of Congress and scion of a prominent family, walked into my office with a box full of extraordinary flashlight photographs of wild animals," Grosvenor later wrote. "He had invented the technique for making such pictures, and an exhibit of his work had won gold medals at Paris and St. Louis Expositions."

"With mounting excitement I sorted the photographs into two piles, one towering, the other small," Grosvenor continued. "Mr. Shiras had been able to interest a leading New York publication in only three of his pictures, so he was astounded when told I intended to print every photograph in the large pile. And I did—74 of them on 50 pages with only four pages of text, in the July issue." Shiras' text contained a description of how he had mounted two cameras, focused at between thirty and forty feet on the bow of a light fourteen-foot boat. Above the cameras was a powerful lamp. Shiras would float down along the edge of the streams or lake "jacklighting" the wildlife, in order to get close enough to photograph them. "There is no sound or sign of life," he wrote, "only the slowly gaining light...."

"When these extraordinary pictures of wildlife appeared, letters poured in demanding more natural history," Grosvenor reported. "But two distinguished geographers on the Board resigned, stating emphatically that 'wandering off into nature is not geography.' They also criticized me for 'turning the magazine into a picture book.'"

By the end of 1906, the Magazine's circulation had risen to 19,237, a figure Grosvenor felt warranted a campaign for additional advertising, "a task I assigned to John Oliver La Gorce," Grosvenor later recalled. "I gave him a free hand except for policy rules that I imposed, among them a firm ban on liquor, beer, wine, and patent medicine advertisements. The magazine even then was widely used in schools. Also, I decided it would benefit both advertisers and readers if ads were printed separately from pictures and text."

By 1908, more than half of the *National Geographic*'s pages were photographs. Referring to one particular article, Thomas Barbour's August 1908 "Further Notes on Dutch New Guinea," a Society editor noted in *Images of the World* how the Magazine had begun to show not only how people lived,

In each case, Grosvenor, with the full support of the Board of Managers, was able to hold his power intact. In 1910, upon Moore's retirement, Henry Gannett was elected President of the Society. "Mr. Gannett was a foremost geographer of the time, and everybody had great regard for him," Grosvenor recalled. "One member of the Board got up after Mr. Gannett was elected, and said, 'Thank the Lord we now have as the head of The Society a *real* scientist.' Mr. Moore...had been chief of the Weather Bureau for a long time and considered himself a very great scientist. But he was a politician...and was not regarded as a scientist by the meteorologists.* When this was said of the new president, Mr. Moore got his hat and got up immediately and he left the meeting. He resigned a few days later from the Board. One member of the Board thought [Moore behaved the way he did because it was his desire] to get on the payroll of the National Geographic. By that time the Society was 'roaring' we were getting members so fast."

The first series of hand-tinted illustrations appeared in the November 1910 issue of the *Geographic*—"color paintings," Grosvenor called them: twenty-four hand-tinted color pictures made from black-and-white photographs of "Scenes in Korea and China" taken by wealthy New Yorker William W. Chapin, who had made his fortune investing in Kodak during its early days. Color film had not yet been perfected, and Chapin had a Japanese artist color his photographs based on careful notes he had kept on the costumes and backgrounds he had photographed.

One photograph showed a rear-view of a Korean farmer wearing a large woven straw hat and a loose-hay cape to ward off rain. "This and other photographs in a twenty-four-page spread caused a sensation when they appeared," readers of a *Geographic* history later learned. A reader today would be less impressed by the photographs of heavily laden coolies, Buddhist nuns, shackled prisoners, and shy Manchu women strolling along a Peking street—especially since the reader would want more information about the subjects than captions such as "Manchu Women: Peking, China" provided. Even the text seemed distant, removed, with lines like: "The street scenes of Seoul offer great variety for the kodak; the burden-bearers of both sexes furnishing a constant change of scene; most of them being willing victims, entirely satisfied with a small tip."

Each color page cost four times the amount of a black-and-white page to reproduce and Grosvenor had been tempted to publish only a few color photographs at a time throughout the year to spread the expense; but he decided that doing so would spoil the effect of the series. The membership's excited response to Chapin's hand-tinted photographs and the leap in advertising revenue convinced Grosvenor that the impact of color was worth the expense. The problem, however, was that the development of color photography still lagged behind Grosvenor's enthusiasm for printing it.

"By 1910," Grosvenor was later to write, "income was sufficient for me to start a photographic laboratory. Soon the *National Geographic* began pioneering in the use of color photographs made by the Lumière Autochrome process, and later by other processes—Agfacolor, Finlay, Dufay. As each improvement became available, the magazine put it to superlative use."

*Nor, presumably, was Moore regarded as a scientist by the politicians. The day before William Howard Taft's March 4, 1909, inauguration as President, Moore sent him a telegram assuring Taft of fair weather. The morning of the inauguration enough snow fell on the capital to interrupt all traffic.

In 1910, Queen Victoria's son, King Edward VII, died and was succeeded by George V; Japan annexed Korea; China abolished slavery and Congress passed the Mann Act (prohibiting the transportation of women across state lines for immoral purposes); Halley's Comet was observed; and Mark Twain, Leo Tolstoy, and Julia Ward Howe died. Cézanne, Van Gogh, and Matisse had paintings shown in Roger Fry's Post-Impressionist exhibition in London. Prince Albert I founded the Musée Océanographique in Monaco; the ballet for Stravinsky's "The Firebird" was performed in Paris; and the dance craze sweeping Europe and America was the South American tango. Barney Oldfield drove a Benz racer 133 mph at Daytona; Henri Farman flew approximately 300 miles in eight and a quarter hours; the "weekend" was becoming popular in the United States; on Broadway Marie Dressler was singing "Heaven Will Protect the Working Girl" (someone had to; by 1910 there were 7.5 million women and girls employed outside the home); and Society membership would reach 74,018.

The January 1910 issue of the *Geographic* contained a report on the Society's annual banquet, on December 15, 1909, and the presentation of a special gold medal to Commander Robert E. Peary for his discovery of the North Pole.

Beginning with its February issue, the Society adopted the cover design longtime readers of the Magazine remember with affection to this day: the yellow border with the four globes representing views of the four hemispheres imbedded in a gray "grosgrain ribbon," with acorns and oak and laurel leaves.

One of the most powerful pieces from this era was "Race Prejudice in the Far East" by Melville E. Stone, General Manager of the Associated Press, which appeared in the December 1910 issue. Stone argued that rather than accept that the Oriental mind was "unfathomable," he still had "some respect for Cicero's idea that there is a 'common bond' uniting all of the children of men. And whatever our ignorance of, or indifference for, the Orientals in the past, it is well to note that conditions, both for us and for them, have entirely changed within the last decade."

Stone provided examples from his own personal observation of the failure of Europeans to accept the Asian:

> At the Bengal Club at Calcutta last year a member in perfectly good standing innocently invited a Eurasian gentleman...to dine with him. It became known that the invitation had been extended, and a storm of opposition broke among the members. The matter was finally adjusted by setting aside the ladies' department of the club, and there the offending member and his unfortunate guest dined alone. The next day the member was called before the board of governors and notified that another like breach of the rules would result in his expulsion.

At a Government House ball in Calcutta, white men dance with native princesses, but according to Lady Minto, wife of the Viceroy of India, Stone reported, "No white woman would think of dancing with a native; it would certainly result in ostracism." But the most horrendous example given Stone was provided by a Japanese Harvard graduate, then a minister of the Japanese crown:

> "When [Commodore] Perry came here [in 1853] and Townsend Harris (of blessed memory) followed him and made the first treaty with Japan, it was stipulated that we (the Japanese) should give them ground for their legation and their consulates' compounds. We did so. Yokohama was then an unimportant place, a native fishing village. It was the natural port of Tokio,

Thomas Barbour's photograph, published in 1908, "MEN OF TOBADI VILLAGE, HUMBOLDT BAY [NEW GUINEA]" *was captioned:* "Fond of ornaments, they wear boars' tusks in their noses, feathers in their hair, and in their ears almost anything. The boys, who are not yet full members of the tribe, have their hair cut as the picture shows. This is done by scraping the head with a splinter of shell from the giant clam (Tridacna). It is indeed a bloody operation."—From "Further Notes on Dutch New Guinea," August 1908 issue

The National Geographic's *first color series: William W. Chapin's photographs—"Peasant in Rain-coat and Hat: Seoul, Korea" (above) and "The Manchu Family Airing: Peking, China" (opposite, bottom)—published in November 1910, "marked a turning point for the magazine," Gilbert H. Grosvenor wrote in 1963. "Returning from the Orient, Mr. Chapin offered me his entire collection of black and whites, most of which a Japanese artist had tinted by hand. Determined to introduce new features into* National Geographic, *I printed 24 pages of color in one number; no editor had ever run so much before. The issue created a sensation and brought in hundreds of new members."*

"Dancing Girls" (opposite, top) appeared in November 1911 in a second color series titled "Glimpses of Japan."

but as we had no foreign trade that meant nothing. We gave them ground in Yokohama for their consulate. Merchants and traders followed, and we gave them ground also for their shops. The British and the Russians and other European nations came in and we gave them like concessions....

"Well, as time went on the village grew into a city....Sir Harry Parks, the British minister, asked for ground in Yokohama for a race-track. We cautiously suggested that horse-racing was said to be wicked by the European missionaries. But he insisted and we gave him the ground. Then we were asked for ground for a social club for the foreigners, and we gave them a plot on the sea front, the finest piece of land in the city.

"Later they wanted to play cricket and football, and finally golf. Well, we gave them ground for this. As the city grew, this cricket-field was so surrounded by buildings that it was practically in the center of town. Understand, all of this ground was donated. Last year we suggested that we could use the cricket-field, and we offered to give in place of it a field in the suburbs. As railways had been built meanwhile, the new field would be even more accessible than the old one was when we gave it. The foreigners demurred, and proposed that we buy the old field and with the purchase-money they would secure a new one. Finally, we compromised by paying for their improvements and furnishing them a new field with like improvements free of cost.

"The question of taxation arose. Yokohama had grown to be a city of 300,000 inhabitants, with millions of dollars invested in buildings owned by foreigners. We asked no taxes on the ground we had donated to them, but we did think it fair that they should pay taxes on their buildings. They said no, that everywhere in the West the buildings went with the ground. We submitted the question to the Americans, but they dodged the issue, saying they would do whatever the others did. Then, under the law of extra-territoriality, we were compelled to leave the decision to the British consul, and he decided against us. The case has now gone to The Hague Court.

"Finally, when I tell you that in the light of this history no native Japanese gentleman has ever been permitted to enter the club-house or the grand-stand of the race-track or to play upon the cricket-field, perhaps you will understand why there is some feeling against foreigners in Yokohama."

In June 1911, as a supplement to its regular issue, the *Geographic* offered an eight-foot-long, seven-inch-wide, panoramic photographic view of the Canadian Rockies. "It remains to this day," Grosvenor recalled in 1957, "one of the most marvelous mountain views ever photographed. Twenty peaks, passes, canyons and other features were distinctly captioned on the supplement." On March 29, 1912, Robert Falcon Scott, leader of the British Antarctic Expedition, made his last diary entry and died on his return from the South Pole. In September 1912, "Head-Hunters of Northern Luzon," a piece by Secretary of the Interior of the Philippine Islands Dean C. Worcester, was accompanied by Charles Martin's photographs—one of which was a grisly full-page picture of "An Unlucky Ifugao Head-Hunter Who Lost His Own Head and Thereby Brought Disgrace Upon His Family and Village." The headless victim, trussed like a turkey with his wings folded over his chest, is being carried off on some men's shoulders. The text, with its description of the ceremony surrounding the triumphant warriors' return with the victim's head, was equally grim.

In 1913, construction was begun on the Society's new administration building next to Hubbard Hall; that year Gilbert H. Grosvenor bought a hundred-acre farm in Bethesda, Maryland, and discovered his love for birds.

The June 1913 issue contained fifty color plates of "Fifty Common Birds of Farm and Orchard."

Charles Martin (above at left) *was an Army sergeant assigned to the staff of Dean C. Worcester, Secretary of the Interior of the Philippine Islands, when his photographs caught Grosvenor's eye.*

Martin's grisly photograph (opposite, bottom right) *accompanying Worcester's 1912 article* "Head Hunters of Northern Luzon" *was titled* "An Unlucky Ifugao Head-Hunter Who Lost His Own Head and Thereby Brought Disgrace Upon His Family and Village." *The two other arresting Martin photographs from that era, Kalinga Province chiefs listening to a phonograph* (opposite, top) *and Luzon natives smoking tobacco* (opposite, bottom left) *had not previously been published.*

In 1915 Charles Martin was hired to become the Society's photographic laboratory chief.

Gilbert H. Grosvenor later recalled, "My twin brother, Edwin Prescott Grosvenor, had told me that the U.S. Department of Agriculture's edition of 100,000 copies of a circular, *Fifty Common Birds of Farm and Orchard*, had been exhausted in two weeks and that the Department was not able to supply thousands of applications for it. I borrowed the color plates and republished the bulletin, with credit to the authors, in the *National Geographic Magazine*. Our members liked it immensely."

The first Lumière Autochrome appeared in July 1914, a single photograph of "A Ghent Flower Garden." The caption explained that the photograph had been taken at the last exhibition held in the Horticultural Hall at the World's Fair Grounds in Ghent, the "Flower Garden of Belgium," and went on to conclude, "The picture makes one wonder which the more to admire—the beauty of the flowers or the power of the camera to interpret the luxuriant colors so faithfully." Lumière Autochrome, the first commercial process in color photography, was developed in France and marketed beginning in 1907. The Ghent flower garden color photographic reproduction was significant for its technological achievement, not its subject matter. It would still be years before the novelty of color photography in a popular magazine would fade.

On June 28, 1914, Archduke Franz Ferdinand, heir to the throne of Franz Josef of Austria-Hungary, was assassinated by a Serbian nationalist at Sarajevo; on July 28, Austria-Hungary declared war on Serbia; Russia ordered full mobilization; on August 1, Germany declared war on Russia; on August 3, Germany declared war on France and invaded Belgium and Luxembourg; on August 4, England declared war on Germany; and within weeks Montenegro and Japan joined the Allies (England, France, Belgium, Russia, Serbia), and the Ottoman Empire, or what little was left of it, joined the Central Powers (Germany and Austria-Hungary).

While non-*National Geographic* readers were scurrying through sadly out-of-date atlases trying to follow the action, Society members received their August *Geographic*s containing a "Map of the New Balkan States and Central Europe" and the explanation:

> The eyes of the civilized world are now focused upon Europe and the stupendous war there beginning. Therefore the map accompanying this issue of the *National Geographic Magazine* is particularly timely. It contains the most complete and up-to-date data about central Europe, including the boundaries of southern Europe as reformed by the Balkan wars and as determined by the London Conference.
>
> This map will prove of much value to the members of the Society who wish to follow the series of military campaigns that it is feared will be without parallel in history.

Distribution of the map was a publishing coup arranged the year before by Gilbert Grosvenor when he and his wife had been caught in Edinburgh. "We couldn't get any money for three days—the banks were all closed because they expected a European war," Grosvenor later recalled. "We called the Secretary of the Royal Geographical Society. I asked him what he thought about a war. 'Oh,' he said, 'We'll never have a European war. Never.' That was 1913."

Grosvenor, aware of the growing tensions and the talk of war, ordered an updated map of central Europe from commercial cartographers upon his return. "We had several hundred thousand of them printed," he said, "and they were waiting in the cellar until the war started in 1914. Within a week we dis-

"My camera recorded splendors of Tsarist Russia when my wife, parents, and I travelled to Moscow in 1913," wrote Gilbert H. Grosvenor, shown (right) in 1913 by Baddeck Bay in Nova Scotia, examining his Speed Graphic camera, newly purchased that same year in London. Its shutter speed of 1/500 of a second was a far cry from that of the 4A Folding Kodak with which he recorded the Moscow scenes "The Cathedral of St Basil's" (opposite, top) and "A Poor Man's Funeral Procession in Moscow" (opposite, bottom). Grosvenor had his St. Basil's photograph hand-tinted by his own instructions for inclusion in his November 1914 article "Young Russia: The Land of Unlimited Possibilities."

tributed that map of central Europe to our members. Of course, it helped very much to get more members."

The United States may, at that time, have been militarily neutral, but the *Geographic* made its sympathies clear with articles such as Arthur Stanley Riggs' long (100 pages), copiously illustrated (seventy-three black-and-white and sixteen color photographs) "The Beauties of France" (November 1915) that ran along with an editorial, "The World's Debt to France." The September 1914 issue's "Belgium: The Innocent Bystander," with its photograph of slain horses in a shelled-out village street, was followed by "Belgium's Plight" in May 1917, the month after the United States entered the war.

The November 1914 *Geographic* carried Gilbert H. Grosvenor's own "Young Russia: The Land of Unlimited Possibilities," for which he had provided both the stunning, "candid" hand-tinted photographs and a text that decried the illiteracy rate and censorship. Grosvenor reported:

> There are conditions in Russia which a visitor from the land of free schools, free speech, and a free press finds it difficult to understand; the deplorable rarity of good schools, making it a sore trial for a poor man to get his son educated; the arrival of his American newspaper, with often half a page stamped out by the censor in ink so black that it is impossible to decipher a single letter; the timidity, nay fear, of some people of being overheard when talking frankly on political subjects....

He also pointed out the "devoutness of the people," the nation's resources, that Russia's siding with the Union during our Civil War had perhaps prevented England's intervention in behalf of the Confederates, and that "the progress of the times...has set to work forces that inevitably will spell the doom of illiteracy and ignorance and make Russia in fact the land of unlimited possibilities."

While the war raged in Europe, the *National Geographic* published articles on "The France of Today" and "The German Nation," "Hungary: A Land of Shepherd Kings," "Glimpses of Holland" and "Partitioned Poland," "Armenia

130

World War One Geographic *photographic coverage included:* (far right) *"BANDAGING A WOUNDED DOG...With a heroism that makes them akin to their masters, these gallant animals carry succor to the helpless and the dying who lie in no-man's land between the trenches. Heartless indeed must be the sharpshooter who can make a target of one of these dumb messengers of mercy"* (May 1917); (near right) *the membership-supported twenty-bed special* National Geographic Society Ward *in the American Ambulance Hospital at Neuilly, France* (July 1917). *It was published with the note* "Suppose He Were Your Boy!" *above a donation form that members could clip out and send in; and* (below) *this classroom scene showing the* National Geographic Magazine *being used to help foreign-born soldiers at Camp Kearny, California, learn English* (August 1918).

A photograph of munitions workers was titled "Munitions Manufacturing Is No Respecter of Age," with the caption underneath: "Many of the women of France who are doing their bit in the production of large-caliber shells for the big guns at the front have completed their allotted threescore years and ten, yet they gladly give the closing days of their lives 'for France.' In many cases their labor is all that they have left to give, for grandsons, sons, and husbands already have been sacrificed on the firing line."

Ex-President William Howard Taft contributed "A Poisoned World"—a reference to how "the minds of a great people…have been poisoned into the conviction that it is their highest duty to subordinate every consideration of humanity to the exaltation and the development of military force…" And Major General John J. Pershing wrote "Stand By The Soldier."

The October 1917 *Geographic* was a special issue containing full-color depictions of 1,197 different flags and standards of the world's nations and private organizations—including the National Geographic—resulting in what the *Geographic*'s Editor called "the most expensive, instructive, and beautiful number of its magazine in the history of periodical literature."

The National Geographic Society and its now more than 625,000 members were off to war, and readers were invited to contribute to a National Geographic Ward in the American Ambulance Hospital in Neuilly, France, and treated to articles like "The Life Story of an American Airman in France," "Plain Tales from the Trenches," a new National Geographic Society "Map of the Western Theatre of War," and "Hospital Heroes Convict the 'Cootie.'"

The war ended on November 11, 1918, and the entire next month's issue was given over to Edwin A. Grosvenor's lavishly illustrated, remarkable article, "The Races of Europe: The Graphic Epitome of a Never-ceasing Human Drama. The Aspirations, Failures, Achievements, and Conflicts of the Polyglot People of the Most Densely Populated Continent."

The following year the entire March issue was devoted to another single subject: the noble dog. The lead article in that issue, "Mankind's Best Friend: Companion of His Solitude, Advance Guard in the Hunt, and Ally of the Trenches," was followed by "Our Common Dogs" and "The Sagacity and Courage of Dogs: Instances of the Remarkable Intelligence and Unselfish Devotion of Man's Best Friend among Dumb Animals."

As 1919 drew to a close, Theodore Roosevelt was dead, President Wilson presided over the first League of Nations meeting in Paris—although the United States Senate was later to vote against America's joining. The Third International was founded in Moscow, the Hapsburg dynasty exiled from Austria, the German fleet scuttled at Scapa Flow, and the peace treaty signed at Versailles. Sherwood Anderson published *Winesburg, Ohio*; James Branch Cabell, *Jurgen*; Hermann Hesse, *Demian*; W. Somerset Maugham, *The Moon and Sixpence*; and Carl Sandburg won a special Pulitzer award in poetry for *Cornhuskers*. Walter Gropius founded and built the Bauhaus in Weimar, Germany. Jazz arrived in Europe, Jack Dempsey knocked out Jess Willard to win the world heavyweight boxing championship, and the "Black Sox" scandal stunned professional baseball. The U.S. House of Representatives was considering limiting immigration, Lady Astor was elected to Parliament, American Oliver Smith perfected the mechanical rabbit, paving the way for modern greyhound racing, and National Geographic Society membership reached 668,174.

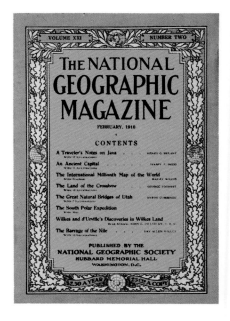

The February 1910 issue was the first to carry the distinctive acorn, oak, and laurel wreath cover. The border, however, was buff—as was the interior box containing the table of contents.

The cover design continued to change and, by 1920, the table of contents box was white.

In 1910, the Magazine's circulation was 74,018 and, by 1920, it increased nearly ten-fold to 713,208.

"Ruins, Lost Cities, and Bones"

"...I laid considerable emphasis on the fact that the map making...ought to be completed at once, while the same topographer was available and willing to undertake the work. His work is purely geographical...you replied that you were not interested in that so much as you were in the ruins, the lost cities, and the bones."

—From a letter written March 18, 1912, by Hiram Bingham to Gilbert H. Grosvenor, Esq.

Above: *Hiram Bingham in front of the main tent at his Machu Picchu expedition camp in 1912.*

Opposite: *Archeologist, historian, and statesman, Bingham, here seen helping paddle a primitive ferry in Peru, later became Governor of Connecticut and a U.S. Senator.*

Preceding spread: *The lost city of the Incas, Machu Picchu, lay hidden amid Peru's misty peaks for three centuries, until its discovery in 1911 by Hiram Bingham, who then led three National Geographic–Yale University expeditions to the site, in 1912, 1914, and 1915.*

The long, mutually beneficial relationship between the National Geographic Society and Hiram Bingham, who was to discover Machu Picchu, did not get off to a good start. In 1908, three years before Bingham found the lost city of the Incas, his wife forwarded photographs and two of his articles to *Geographic* Editor Gilbert Hovey Grosvenor, who flatly rejected them explaining, "We have on hand a number of articles on South America and therefore cannot find room for them."

When, however, Bingham's book *The Journal of an Expedition Across Venezuela and Colombia* was published the following year, 1909, Grosvenor thought it "splendid" and asked whether Bingham could send him "an article of about 4500 words describing the least known section which you traversed with as large a selection of photographs as possible." Grosvenor offered "$25 for the article and $1.50 for each photograph used."

"I scarcely know what to say," Bingham wrote back. Portions of the book and "some of the pictures...the very ones which you say you found particularly interesting," he pointed out, had already been rejected by Grosvenor nine months before. Bingham continued, "As you did not find those articles desirable (although they contained the very cream of my first trip) I do not believe that you would find anything that I might write on this last trip, worth printing or paying for."

Bingham's letter was forwarded to Grosvenor, by then summering at Baddeck, Nova Scotia. Grosvenor immediately replied, "It is very strange, but I haven't the remotest recollection of the articles you state Mrs. Bingham sent me...." He promised to "look the matter up as soon as I return to Washington." If he did look up the matter, there is no record of any action taken, and correspondence between the thirty-three-year-old *Geographic* Editor and the thirty-three-year-old Yale University Assistant Professor of Latin American History was, for the time being, dropped.

During the summer of 1911, Bingham was a few days out of Cuzco, Peru, on a winding jungle trail alongside the turbulent rapids of the Urubamba River. "Cliffs rose 2,000 feet, and above soared snow-capped Andean peaks," Bingham later recalled.

Bingham was sure he had found the legendary Vilcabamba, the last stronghold of the Inca ruler who, it was believed, had sought refuge there when he fled the Spanish in 1537. Bingham made a sketch map of what he had found, then continued up the Urubamba to Vitos on the Vilcabamba in search of other rumored Inca cities before returning to New Haven, Connecticut, to tell his sponsors what he had found.

On February 23, 1912, after several conversations with Gilbert Grosvenor, Bingham had written asking for a letter from Society President Henry Gannett and another from Grosvenor himself, expressing support and interest in Bingham's work. "The stronger the credentials which you can give me," Bingham wrote, "the better able I shall be to persuade...[the politicians in Lima] that our object is scientific and not commercial." Grosvenor wrote back in mid-March, "We find there is considerable feeling that the work is archaeologic and not sufficiently geographic, and I am afraid that we shall have to give up our plans for the present. I will write you again later. I am most interested in your work, and am doing all I can to put the proposition through."

Bingham was stunned.

March 18, 1912.

My dear Grosvenor:—

Your letter is very disappointing. I planned the work with especial emphasis on the archaeological side because I gathered from my conversation with you that you were particularly interested in that field. You will remember that in my first conversation with you in your office I laid considerable emphasis on the fact that the map making begun by the Yale Peruvian Expedition ought to be completed at once, while the same topographer was available and willing to undertake the work. His work is purely geographical. You remember that you replied that you were not interested in that so much as you were in the ruins, the lost cities, and the bones. Accordingly it was in an effort to meet your interest in the matter that the plans were drawn up with so much emphasis on the archaeological side of things. If you wish to present the matter to your Committee in another way, or if you would like to have me alter my plans so as to devote more time to the work of archaeological [crossed through with *geographical* written above] exploration, including geology, physiography, topography and natural history, I shall be very glad to do so....

[And]...if I can get the money for the archaeological end of things, [I] would like to do exclusive [crossed through with *extensive* written above] excavating near Cuzco, and reconnoissance [sic] excavating in the ruins discovered last time.

If you still think that it will be necessary to abandon any idea of coöperation for the present year, I shall appreciate it if you will let me know as soon as possible.

I am extremely grateful for your interest in our work and I realize that you are doing all you can to put the proposition through. I hope you will be successful.

Faithfully yours,

s/Hiram Bingham

At Gilbert H. Grosvenor's urging, the National Geographic Society finally agreed to support Bingham's return to Machu Picchu and announced in its April 1912 Magazine that it had subscribed $10,000 "to the Peruvian expedition of 1912, to which the friends of Yale University have made an equal grant." The $10,000 to Bingham was the Society's first archeological grant.

149

A Love Affair with Automobiles, Airplanes, and Autochromes

By January 1920, the 18th Amendment to the Constitution of the United States was in effect. But Prohibition had no impact on the Magazine's income, since advertisements for liquor, beer, and wine had always been forbidden in its pages.

America in the 1920s was poised between the naïve idealism of youth and a post-war world-weariness. The Senate's vote against our country joining the League of Nations was symptomatic of the nation's eagerness to disengage from Europe's traumas.

"America's present need," presidential candidate Warren G. Harding said in 1920, "is not heroics but healing; not nostrums but normalcy; not revolution but restoration…not surgery but serenity." Harding spoke for the middle-aged; but when F. Scott Fitzgerald wrote, "The uncertainties of 1919 were over. America was going on the greatest, gaudiest spree in history," he was speaking for the Jazz Age young, who didn't want problems; they wanted excitement.

Despite a business slump at the beginning of the decade—in 1921, for the first time since Gilbert H. Grosvenor's employment, membership in the Society actually declined*—what ensued was the most spectacular economic boom this country has ever seen; that boom was followed, however, by an equally spectacular bust.

Between the latter part of October and the middle of November 1929, stocks declined more than $30 billion in paper value (over 40 percent of their total value in previous trading) and on October 29, 1929, "Black Tuesday," stock values plunged $14 billion during that one day alone. Still, while the party lasted, the '20s were great fun.

Bobbed-haired flappers "charlestoned" in short skirts, cloche hats, silk stockings rolled down below their knees; baggy-trousered young men with hip flasks in their pockets strummed ukuleles and serenaded their ladies with tunes like "Barney Google" (with his goo-goo-googley eyes), "Baby Face" ("you've got the cutest little baby face"), "Runnin' Wild" ("lost control/ Runnin' wild, mighty bold"), and ("Your lips tell me no, no, but..!") "There's Yes Yes in Your Eyes."

Great sports writers like Grantland Rice, Paul Gallico, Damon Runyon, and Ring Lardner wrote about great sports heroes like Babe Ruth, Lou Gehrig,

_____
* *Circulation fell off 65,867, to 647,341.*

Preceding spread: *"TEN OF A KIND TAKING THE TWIN PEAKS' GRADE ON HIGH AT SAN FRANCISCO"* began the National Geographic's *caption when this Chandler Motor Car Co. press release photograph made its way into the October 1923 issue on the automobile industry. "A San Francisco distributer decided to show the world what his cars could do on heartbreaking hills," the caption went on to explain. "Ten owners, one a woman, came to the scratch at the foot of the hill and not a gear was shifted after the start. The power of the American-built motor represents an outstanding engineering achievement."*

162

Bill Tilden, Johnny Weissmuller, Jack Dempsey, Gene Tunney; they immortalized Knute Rockne's "Four Horsemen" and horse racing's Man O'War. The '20s were not all glitter, however; it was also the decade of the St. Valentine's Day Massacre, the divorce of fifty-one-year-old millionaire Edward ("Daddy") Browning and Frances ("Peaches") Browning, his fifteen-year-old schoolgirl bride, Leopold and Loeb's "thrill murder" of fourteen-year-old Bobby Franks, of Floyd Collins trapped in a Kentucky cavern, and Rudolph Valentino's death.

But more than anything else, the '20s were the era of America's love affair with the automobile. As one writer has observed:

> In the '20s the automobile created the greatest revolution in American life ever caused by a single device....It decentralized cities and created huge, sprawling suburbs, took families off for Sunday outings and decreased church attendance. It gave hard-working Americans an escape to fun and new sights, reasserted their independence and saddled them with debt (by 1925, three of every four cars were bought on the installment plan).
>
> —From *This Fabulous Century, 1920–1930*

And, inevitably, this love affair was lavishly and exuberantly reflected in the pages of the *National Geographic:* In October 1923, the Magazine devoted 79 pages and 76 illustrations to staff writer William Joseph Showalter's "The Automobile Industry: An American Art That Has Revolutionized Methods in Manufacturing and Transformed Transportation."

Not surprisingly, *Geographic* contributors tried to outdo each other by taking their cars where none had gone before—and did so, as in Melvin A. Hall's "By Motor Through the East Coast and Batak Highlands of Sumatra"—with predictably exotic results:

> After an hour of unavailing labor, Joseph and I abandoned the effort to extricate the machine, and as darkness was rapidly falling we...decided to desert the car and attempt to flounder through the mud to the nearest native village. It was a desperate decision, but the only alternative was a night in the car....
>
> About a mile beyond where the car was entombed we came to...half a dozen natives....I was surprised at finding human beings there, and, feeling consequent misgivings over the security of our abandoned car and luggage, I asked the man in charge if he or one of his men would, for a suitable consideration, spend the night in an automobile...to guard it from being molested during my absence. To my astonishment he promptly refused, and, asking the question in turn of his men, met with immediate negatives.
>
> I could not account for their unwillingness. The cushions of the tonneau would surely afford as comfortable quarters as any they were accustomed to; it could not be the storm of which men of the highlands were afraid; and the reward I had offered, though small enough, was probably equivalent to about a week's income.
>
> Then it occurred to me that they were afraid of the automobile itself, and I hastened to assure them that it was not only dry and comfortable, but quite safe; that I had locked it up, and that it could not move until I myself released it.
>
> "Oh, it is not that," said the spokesman, with an air of having slept in automobiles most of his life.
>
> "Well, what is it then?" I was both curious and a trifle annoyed.
>
> "Tigers."

A car pauses for the photograph "MOTORING THROUGH THE FAMOUS WAWONA TUNNEL TREE, MARIPOSA GROVE, CALIFORNIA," from the October 1923 Magazine.

"Tigers?"

"Yes, indeed," said Joseph nervously, translating. "He say plenty of tigers here come down sure and eat him up!"

"But not in the automobile," I objected.

"Oh, no; tiger first take him out."

"By Motor Through the East Coast and Batak Highlands of Sumatra" was followed in January 1924 by "The Conquest of the Sahara by Automobile" and its June 1926 Citroën Central African Expedition sequel: "Through the Deserts and Jungles of Africa by Motor: Caterpillar Cars Make 15,000-Mile Trip from Algeria to Madagascar in Nine Months" (caterpillar-tracked ten-horsepower forerunners of the vehicles used for the marvelous Citroën-Haardt Trans-Asiatic Expedition of the next decade).

In February 1925, the Magazine published Felix Shay's "Cairo to Cape Town, Overland: An Adventurous Journey of 135 Days, Made by an American Man and His Wife, Through the Length of the African Continent." Shay's piece contained such wonderful lines as "With evening came relief. A gentle breeze blew from the Nile and we sat on the earth terrace in front of the hotel from dinner until midnight, drinking lemon squashes and whiskeys-and-sodas" and "Each night we heard the sob and boom of the tom-toms lasting into the dawn."

Six months after Shay's journey from Cairo to Cape Town appeared, the Magazine ran Major F. A.C. Forbes-Leith's "From England to India by Automobile: An 8,527-mile Trip Through Ten Countries, from London to Quetta, Requires Five and a Half Months."

By 1929 *Geographic* readers tiring of automobile adventures could cross Madagascar "by Boat, Auto, Railroad, and Filanzana," or travel from Buenos Aires to Washington by horse—"A Solitary Journey of Two and a Half Years, Through Eleven American Republics, Covers 9,600 Miles of Mountain and Plain, Desert and Jungle."

There was even an "African Queen"-like report by Frank J. Magee, R.N.V.R., on "Transporting a Navy Through the Jungles of Africa in War Time," which Gilbert Grosvenor introduced, saying, "No single achievement during the World War was distinguished by more bizarre features than the successfully executed undertaking of 28 daring men who transported a 'ready-made' navy overland through the wilds of Africa to destroy an enemy flotilla in control of Lake Tanganyika."

But if during the '20s the *Geographic* was having a love affair with the automobile, it was a mere passing fancy compared to the ardor with which its editors embraced the airplane! During that decade thirty different aviation articles appeared in the Magazine. Brigadier General William (Billy) Mitchell celebrated the future of the airplane and airship in the Magazine's issue of March 1921; Richard Byrd reported his flight with Floyd Bennett across the North Pole in September 1926, the South Pole in August 1930, and across the Atlantic in September 1927. Byrd's transatlantic achievement, accomplished with a four-man crew in his trimotor Fokker *America,* had been overshadowed, however, by Charles Lindbergh's historic solo crossing in his single-engine Ryan monoplane *Spirit of St. Louis* just thirty-three days before.

The story of the flight of Sir Ross Smith, his brother Keith, and two crew members from London to Australia appeared in March 1921. "The aëroplane

is the nearest thing to animate life that man has created," Ross Smith declared. An account of Lindbergh's flight in the *Spirit of St. Louis* from Washington, D.C., on a tour of thirteen Latin American countries and back appeared in May 1928.

The July 1924 issue was entirely devoted to aviation and featured "America from the Air," containing aerial photographs of this country (no such views had been printed before), and "The Non-Stop Flight Across America," U. S. Army Air Service Lt. John A. Macready's personal account of the successful completion of the first non-stop coast-to-coast flight across the United States he and Lt. Oakley G. Kelly had made in a large, single-engine, high-winged Fokker *T-2*.

Kelly piloted the plane on takeoff from Mitchel Field on Long Island and Macready landed it at Rockwell Field in San Diego. During the slightly less than 27-hour flight through blinding rainstorms, the darkness of night, and narrow mountain passes, the pilots exchanged places five times—a difficult and hazardous maneuver requiring one man to fly the plane from the near-

"No single achievement during the World War was distinguished by more bizarre features," wrote Gilbert H. Grosvenor in the October 1922 Geographic of this successful effort by twenty-eight men of the British Navy to carry "overland through the wilds of Africa" a small ready-made flotilla.

166

blind rear controls within the fuselage (there was visibility only to the sides) while the other abandoned the open cockpit:

> On the completion of six hours at the controls in the front cockpit the pilot would signal energetically, by shaking the wheel, for the pilot in the rear to take the controls, and when satisfied that everything was functioning satisfactorily, would open the small door to his rear, pull out the back of the pilot's seat, and drop it on the floor through this hole, together with the parachute and cushion.
> Lifting up one side of his hinged seat, he would crawl through this small door and back through the narrow passageway paralleling the gas tank to the rear pilot. By yelling in a very loud voice, the pilots could converse in the rear....
> After placing the plane in a safe flying attitude, the change at the wheel was made by the active pilot quickly stepping out and forward and the new pilot sliding in from the rear.
> Crawling up over the wires through the tunnel and into the front seat, the pilot on duty took the controls and flew the plane, the other pilot placing the parachute cushion and seat back in position.

Royal Italian Air Force Commander Francesco de Pinedo covered 60,000 miles and six continents by seaplane and, in September 1928, jubilantly wrote, "Sindbad, tied to a roc's foot, flew over no stranger sights than I."

And where airplanes went, so did cameras: for the October 1927 issue, American aviators would "Hurdle the High Andes, Brave Brazilian Jungles, and Follow Smoking Volcanoes to Map New Sky Paths Around South America" in "How Latin America Looks from the Air."

How things looked from the air captured the imagination of Gilbert H. Grosvenor and suddenly every other picture caption seemed to be of one place after another "seen from the air," or "as it looks from the air," or "looking down on," or "viewed from above," or "an airplane view of...." These aerial photographs, of course, were in black and white; but the decade of the 1920s saw the *Geographic*'s picture-minded Editor turn increasingly to color.

As John Oliver La Gorce had stated in a 1915 Society promotional pamphlet designed to attract advertising:

> When, in the judgement of the editor, it is impracticable to create the real atmosphere of a far-away country in black and white, then it is produced in color or photogravure at great expense, so that the readers, young and old, may readily understand the actual conditions without drawing unduly on their imaginations.

Two new employees, Charles Martin and Franklin L. Fisher, had been hired by the Society in 1915 to supervise the Magazine's increasingly sophisticated use of photography. Martin had been put in charge of the Society's new darkrooms and laboratory and Fisher was made chief of the Illustrations Department. By 1920, Gilbert Grosvenor was confident enough in the future of color photography to enlarge the darkrooms and install the first color laboratory in American publishing; but because few magazines in the early 1920s printed color photographs, the vast majority of professional photographers did not find it worth the expense and time it took to learn the process. Therefore the few photographers with any experience in making Lumière Autochromes were eagerly sought out by the *Geographic*. And Editor Grosvenor, aware that the key to his Magazine's progress was the continuing improvement of photo-

Above: *"MEMBERS OF THE NATIONAL GEOGRAPHIC SOCIETY ARRIVING TO RECEIVE TICKETS FOR THE LINDBERGH RECEPTION."* Long before the announced hour, members gathered before the Society's headquarters, Hubbard Hall, to obtain tickets. There were requests for 30,000 but only 6,000 members could be accommodated at the Washington Auditorium ceremony, where, on November 14, 1927, Charles Lindbergh was awarded the Hubbard Medal by President Calvin Coolidge. "Disappointment of many was regrettable, but inevitable," the Geographic noted.

Opposite: Crowds eagerly mob Lindbergh and his Spirit of St. Louis at the Croydon Aërodrome, England, June 6, 1927, more than two weeks after his thrilling New York-to-Paris nonstop solo flight. He had flown to England from Brussels, Belgium.

168

graphic quality, was constantly encouraging his small photographic staff to try even harder. As he wrote to Maynard Owen Williams in France in 1926:

> The art of taking photographs in color requires the technique of an engineer, the artistic ability of a great painter, and the news interest of a daily-newspaper photographer, so if you do not strike 100 with every photographic attempt in colors, I hope you will not be discouraged. I am much pleased with the increasing quality shown by all your pictures.

Meanwhile Illustrations Editor Franklin Fisher, who had been combing the United States and Europe for photographers able to provide color plates for the Magazine, was eventually able to assemble a small group of freelancers drawn primarily from the artistic ranks and independently wealthy hobbyists.

The post-war era of color photography commenced in March 1921 with Helen Messinger Murdoch's eight Autochromes of India and Ceylon that accompanied Sir Ross Smith's "From London to Australia by Aëroplane"; her work never appeared in the *Geographic* again.

Two whose work did reappear were Fred Payne Clatworthy, who specialized in photographing the American West, and Franklin Price Knott, who had been a painter of miniatures until he succumbed, in his words, to "the magic of autochromes."

In his March 1928 "Artist Adventures on the Island of Bali" Knott wrote:

> By color photography, millions who read this magazine may glimpse the glories of Nature—God's own great studio. Like an artist's brush, now the camera catches every tint and shade from Arizona desert or Alpine sunset to the gorgeous panoply of Indian rajah courts and the bronze beauty of jungle maids asplash in lotus pools.

Knott spoke for the frustrations of all that period's color photographers with their heavy, cumbersome, forbidding-looking equipment when, referring to his thwarted attempts to capture those shy bronze maids asplash in Bali, he wrote:

> There was one girl in particular on that island, a veritable Venus—straight, slim-limbed, graceful as a deer. Often I got fleeting glimpses of her. Sometimes she would be bathing with other girls in a wayside pool, or walking sedately to the temple with an offering of fruit or flowers. Time and again I sought to take her picture, but caught only the flash of her dazzling smile as she flitted swiftly away.

In order to achieve better coverage of Europe, Franklin Fisher contracted with European photographers Gervais Courtellemont in France, Hans Hildenbrand and Wilhelm Tobien in Germany, Gustav Heurlin in Sweden, and Luigi Pellerano in Italy. As a rule these men would process their Autochromes in the field and send the fragile plates packed in padded crates by steamer to New York. Some of them never saw the National Geographic's Washington offices throughout their careers. These photographers, working independently of each other, produced, as Priit Vesilind noted in his thesis on color photography at the Geographic, perhaps the only complete photographic record of Europe prior to World War Two.

Additional personnel had by now been added to the Society staff. Maynard Owen Williams (1919), Edwin L. Wisherd (1919), Clifton Adams (1922), and W. Robert Moore (1927) had joined Laboratory Chief Charles Martin in Washington and, like their European counterparts, were systematically assembling a color photographic record of pre-war America. Of the 1,818 Autochromes that

Above: *Justification for publishing M. Stéphane Passet's shocking May 1922 Autochrome "A MONGOLIAN WOMAN CONDEMNED TO DIE OF STARVATION" was that it, too, provided "true reflection of the customs of the time."*

Opposite: *Ever since Gilbert H. Grosvenor's 1903 decision to publish the photograph of two half-naked Filipino women working in a field, barebreasted native women have been a National Geographic staple.*
Franklin Price Knott's Autochromes of Balinese maidens for the March 1928 issue were captioned (opposite, top) "EVEN THE CAMERA COULDN'T COAX A SMILE FROM THIS RESERVED AND DIGNIFIED DAUGHTER OF THE EAST" and (opposite, bottom), with perhaps an odd attempt at ethnographic detachment, "BALI HAS NO BLONDES."

"That was in '26. Now here I am again in the spring of '29."

"I have felt for several years that in your desire to save The Society money you have been too earnest to purchase your photographic material at the minimum amount that the contributor will accept," Gilbert H. Grosvenor scolded Fisher in an October 27, 1928, memo. Grosvenor's long, alternately congratulatory and chiding letter continued:

> We have discussed this matter repeatedly, and in each case where you have, at my request, increased the honorarium you originally set, whether it was Clatworthy or Courtellemont or Sakamoto, immediate improvement has been obtained in the quality and number of the photographs submitted. By this increased expenditure, the Magazine has derived material far exceeding in value the amount of the advance in cost which I authorized.

Grosvenor reminded Fisher of the original low payment for Clatworthy's Autochromes, pointing out that the price came out to "$10 per page," and that the photographer "was urged to submit another series." Grosvenor's letter continued:

> Several years passed and [Clatworthy] submitted nothing. Finally he called one day and I inquired why he had not sent in any photographs, and he replied that the amount of the honorarium you offered him would not pay his expenses. I therefore made him an offer of $1,000 for a series of 16 full-page negatives satisfactory to us, and within a few months he submitted a remarkable series that we printed in our June 1928 number, entitled "Photographing the West in Colors."
>
> This series of Clatworthy cost us $62.50 per original picture. The sum paid was enough to enable Clatworthy to recoup his actual expenses in making the pictures, but it was not sufficient to enable him to make a financial profit. I consider, however, that it was a fair price, as the great reputation he obtained from this series increases the popular demand for his lectures and the fees he obtains from these lectures.
>
> From The Society's point of view, an expenditure of $62.50 per page, which expense is distributed through an edition of 1,200,000 copies, is almost negligible. So this was an excellent investment for the National Geographic Society.
>
> In the purchase of photographs and other material for the Magazine, we must not lose sight of the fact that advertisers consider space in the Magazine of sufficient value to pay $2,500 for one page, one insertion, and they pay many dollars additional for preparation of their copy. Space so valuable to advertisers is even more valuable to the National Geographic Society.
>
> Common business reasoning, therefore, indicates that the National Geographic Magazine can pay several times $62.50 for a page illustration, as every page of our Magazine is an advertisement of the National Geographic Society's product. An attempt to save a few dollars on the purchase price of pictures is a suicidal policy, as this policy prevents us from obtaining material that we must have, if the National Geographic Society is to exist.

From "Human Emotion Recorded by Photography" (October 1920) to "Through Java in Pursuit of Color" (September 1929) articles celebrating both photography and the photographers appeared in the *Geographic* of that decade. And so, of course, did articles on birds, from "The Crow, Bird Citizen of Every Land: A Feathered Rogue Who Has Many Fascinating Traits and Many Admirable Qualities Despite His Marauding Propensities" (April 1920) to "The Eagle in Action: An Intimate Study of the Eyrie Life of America's National Bird" (May 1929).

There were articles on "The Hairnet Industry in North China" (September 1923); an American woman's trip by houseboat in China—marvelously titled "Ho for the Soochow Ho" (June 1927); and "Stalking the Dragon Lizard on the Island of Komodo" (August 1927); followed by "Mickey the Beaver" (December 1928).

In September 1921 the Magazine published "Our Greatest National Monument: The National Geographic Society Completes Its Explorations in the Valley of Ten Thousand Smokes." Archeologist Neil M. Judd's articles on the riddle of New Mexico's Pueblo Bonito prehistoric ruin ran in 1922; and explorer-botanist Joseph F. Rock's series of adventures in China and Tibet began in 1924.

In 1922, the Society expanded its publishing efforts when it printed *The Valley of Ten Thousand Smokes* in book form as well. In his foreword to the book, Gilbert Grosvenor reemphasized the role of the membership, with his explanation that the expeditions had been:

> ...financed by the 750,000 members of the National Geographic Society, each of whom, millionaire and college professor, captain of industry and clerk, had an equal share in its support. Every member of the organization may thus derive considerable satisfaction that he or she has assisted to bring about such important additions to our knowledge of the young and active planet upon which we live.

Unfortunately, volcanoes were not the only forces active on our young planet in the 1920s and as that decade drew to a close, no article quite so captured the spirit and the innocence of the *Geographic* of this period as did Lincoln Eyre's December 1928 article, "Renascent Germany." Scores of brown-shirted, swastika armband-wearing, *"Sieg Heil!"*-saluting marchers in short pants appeared in a photograph captioned "Members of the National Socialist Party Parade at Nuremberg." And that illustration was followed by one showing little schoolboys in dark uniforms marching in a street; it is captioned "Green as Goslings Now, but Practice Makes the Goose Step Perfect."

The next year Hitler appointed Heinrich Himmler Reichsfuhrer S.S.; Trotsky was expelled from the Soviet Union; Warren Harding's Secretary of the Interior was convicted of accepting a $100,000 bribe in the Teapot Dome scandal; and Herbert C. Hoover took office as the thirty-first President of the United States. Also in 1929, William Faulkner published *The Sound and the Fury,* Hemingway *A Farewell to Arms,* Thomas Wolfe *Look Homeward, Angel,* and Erich Maria Remarque *All Quiet on the Western Front.* Marc Chagall painted *The Milkmaid;* Disney released *Steamboat Willie,* his first musical Mickey Mouse cartoon; and "talkies" killed off silent films. The German *Graf Zeppelin* airship flew 19,500 miles around the world in 20 days, 4 hours, and 14 minutes (and its commander, Dr. Hugo Eckener, received a special medal of honor from the Society for the feat). Kodak introduced 16 mm color film; the U.S. stock exchange collapsed; the world economic crisis began; and the 5th Earl of Rosebery died a happy man at the age of eighty-two after having gained his three lifetime wishes: he had married the richest heiress in England, won the Derby (three times), and become Prime Minister.

As the decade ended, membership in the National Geographic Society reached 1,212,173. The following year, 1930, 34,810 new members would join, bringing the total membership to 1,246,983. It would not be until 1946 that the Society would again meet and then surpass that membership figure.

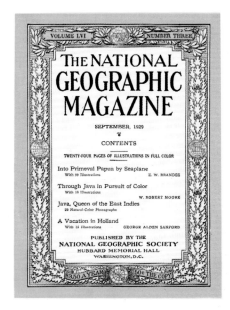

By the end of 1930, membership in the Society had reached 1,246,983. Not until World War Two had ended would membership reach that level again.

"Something lost behind the Ranges. Lost and waiting for you. Go!"

> *"Till a voice, as bad as Conscience, rang interminable changes*
>   *On one everlasting Whisper day and night repeated—so:*
> *'Something hidden. Go and find it. Go and look behind the*
>   *Ranges—*
> *'Something lost behind the Ranges. Lost and waiting for you.*
>   *Go!'"*
>
> —From Rudyard Kipling's "The Explorer" (1898)

> *"...a task, any task, undertaken in an adventurous spirit*
> *acquires the merit of romance."*
>
> —Joseph Conrad, *A Personal Record* (1912)

Throughout the history of the National Geographic, men and women have heeded what Kipling called "a voice, as bad as Conscience." Some, like Theodore Roosevelt, followed it into the wilds of Africa; others, like Greely, Peary, and Steger, fought their way through Arctic wastes in an attempt to reach the Pole. Charles and Anne Morrow Lindbergh flew 29,000 miles through the worst possible conditions in a small, single-engine seaplane to search for safe commercial airline routes; and Robin Lee Graham, Tim Severin, and Thor Heyerdahl, seeking something within themselves, put to sea in fragile boats. But during the first third of this century, as adventurers and explorers fanned out across this globe, only the moon seemed more forbidding, mysterious, and "lost behind the Ranges" than China. And although seventy China-related articles appeared in the *Geographic* between 1900 and 1935, none quite so captured the imagination of the Magazine's readers as those written by two very different kinds of men—Maynard Owen Williams and Joseph F. Rock.

Williams, a former missionary in China and Syria, was large, gregarious, unaffected, enthusiastic. He joined the *Geographic* in 1919, contributed the text, photographs, or both to ninety Magazine pieces, and was "Mr. Geographic" to a generation of its readers. Among the first journalists to be present at the opening of Tutankhamun's tomb, and to take natural color photographs in the Arctic, Williams was as much at ease in Bulgaria as in Bali. Chief of the *National Geographic*'s foreign staff for more than thirty years, Williams was once asked how he was able to receive the cooperation of difficult people in out-of-the-way places. He responded, "I get around the world by being a nice little lady. I never carry a gun. I tell everyone I am helpless, and that I cannot speak their language."

In 1930, the amiable Maynard Owen Williams was selected to be the Society's sole representative—and the only American—on a motorized expedition across Asia led by France's Georges-Marie Haardt.

Above: *Maynard Owen Williams, shown with an Expedition half-track in the Chinese province of Sinkiang, headed the* National Geographic's *foreign staff for more than thirty years.*

Opposite: *The Expedition's " 'Scarab' nearly came to grief," Williams wrote when a collapsed road left the vehicle teetering forty feet above a gorge in the Himalayas.*

Preceding spread: *Troops outside Farah, Afghanistan, plundered by Genghis Khan, salute the 1931–1932 Citroën-Haardt Trans-Asiatic Expedition as it thunders through en route from the Mediterranean to the Yellow Sea.*

Getting a seven-ton radio car across the Helmand was a ticklish task, shared by our mechanics and the rivermen...led by a picturesque graybeard called "Baba Daria," Father of the River. [He] dubbed [our chief mechanic] "Baba Motor."...

"May my spit cover your faces!" screams Baba Daria.

"What does he say?" asks Baba Motor.

"That the truck is heavier than you said," [replies the translator....]

The expedition pushed on through Afghanistan's Kandahar to Kabul. By late June it had surmounted the Khyber Pass and arrived at Srinagar, then Kashmir's summer capital, 3,445 miles and, counting stops, eighty-one days from Beirut. There, "with the Jhelum on a rampage and the Kashmir Valley a lake, the cars...were stranded..." while "the relief cars from Peiping, which were to meet us in Kashgar, were immobilized...a thousand miles away by an air line which no crow could follow and live."

Expedition leader Georges-Marie Haardt was determined to press on "with two of his seven cars until some definite barrier or lack of time should stop the adventure."

The Pamir Group left Srinagar on July 12 in the two half-tracks, "Golden Scarab" and "Silver Crescent," and reached Bandipur to the north that night.

In the morning...the usual chaos of departure, but with the oddest baggage ever seen. Leather-covered *yakdans* (wooden chests)...small coils of cable on which the porters pounce, only to slink away when they have felt their weight; spare wheels with doughnut tires slung sandwichwise astride half-hidden ponies; axles and gear boxes awkwardly swung between four protesting coolies; cinema tripod, carried upright like a young tree; cameras, sleeping sacks, tool boxes, cases of food, green tents...150 pony loads for our group alone....One porter after another disappears....Servants mount the best ponies and escape before they are detected.

Along the expedition's route waited "grades too steep, hairpin turns too sharp, trails too narrow, underpinning and side walls too infirm." The nine mile "zigzag ascent" from Bandipur Bridge to Tragbal took four and a half hours and was considered "a triumph for the cars."

All around were heavily wooded slopes bathed in morning mist. [Then] an ominous rumble, and...this majestic silence was torn by the roar of a motor. ...a gang of coolies strained the [two] cars around a narrow bend, and on they came, impressive in their slow relentlessness....

Then Williams wrote, "without warning, across the Takla Makan Desert and the Himalayas came the bad news: the China Group definitely stopped in Urumchi; Captain Point a prisoner!"

It was later learned the China Group, under Lt. Cmdr. Victor Point, had crossed the sands of the Gobi and entered Suchow. There they heard reports of an uprising in Sinkiang Province. Despite authorities having closed the "Great Route" to them, Point had continued on and reached the edge of Sinkiang on June 26. A message left by the previous caravan warned of danger; Point, himself, saw "the wreckage of war: horses killed, carts overturned, corpses lining the road and in the ditches, soldiers, women, and children huddled together in utter disorder."

About two weeks later, the China Group was in Turfan when the Governor of Sinkiang Province summoned Point and his party to Urumchi, the provincial capital. Point, unwilling to risk his entire group, left his French members behind and went, with a delegation of Chinese, in one car. Although given a

Opposite: *Maynard Owen Williams was able to persuade a crowd assembled in a Herat bazaar warehouse in Afghanistan to hold perfectly still for the three seconds required for this striking 1931 photograph.*

Asked how he was able to obtain the cooperation of difficult people in out-of-the-way places, Maynard Owen Williams responded, "I get around the world by being a nice little lady. I never carry a gun. I tell everyone I am helpless, and that I cannot speak their language."

"The greatest 'kick' a field man can have is to carry a million and a quarter members up onto a high mountain, show them the world and say, 'It's yours, in a way it could not be without me,'" Maynard Owen Williams wrote Editor Gilbert H. Grosvenor in 1929.

From Urumchi to Peiping [Peking] is 2,300 miles. Two of our caravans had been pillaged. The rebel Ma Chung Ying stood astride the Great Road waiting for us, with tons of our supplies already in his hands. Sand dune and river, desert and rocky defile lay across our path. The cold of the Mongolian plateau was often in our thoughts.

The grueling dash to Peking began: "The tents were seldom pitched," Williams wrote. "Valises and even washbasins were ignored for days at a time. Not only actual cold, but the threat of greater always hung over us. Seldom were we free from fatigue."

They were sheltered by Christian missionaries at short stops before setting off again on the long drives:

Night after night we felt our way ahead over atrocious trails, with a theoretical rest for men and motors from 2 to 5 in the morning. The driver slumped forward over his wheel. His seat-mate, who could doze during the day, watched the temperature dials for water and oil. Whenever a radiator got cold or a bearing stiff, a motor woke with a roar. A hundred fantastic landscapes tossed up by our ranging headlights are now mingled in what some of us feel was reality and others a bad dream.

It was so cold Williams had to suck on his frozen fountain pen to thaw the ink; but he continued taking notes:

We left Sinkiang at Mingshui Pass with a cold early-morning wind at 6,600 feet....After a thirty-hour run without sleep, we passed through a flood of refugees fleeing from Ma Chung Ying and arrived at the gates of Suchow....Meanwhile the rebels under General Ma Chung Ying were near—and coming nearer.

A night attempt to use our wireless brought a colonel down on us. But ...our interpreters...were instructed to lose $29 to him at mah jongg, and the flurry passed.

The following morning permission to leave came....the city gates at last slowly swung open and our cars filed out. Twenty-four hours later Ma Chung Ying's troops entered Suchow.

By then we were at Kaotai [175 miles away] with a bandit's head—one sample from 27 fresh ones—dangling by a cord beside the city gate. We... pushed on.

With the rebel chief Ma Chung Ying in close pursuit, the cars of the Citroën-Haardt Trans-Asiatic Expedition rumbled toward Liangchow following the deeply rutted tracks beneath China's Great Wall, begun twenty-two centuries before. On January 5, 1932, as the *Dàhán*, or Great Cold, approached, the combined Pamir and China groups were halfway between Urumchi and Peking, "but the harder portion lay ahead." They turned toward Ningsia. And then:

North of Ningsia, at midnight, the "Silver Crescent" crashed through thick ice and my camera suddenly went afloat in icy water between my porous leather boots. The headlights were well under water, and still lighted, before I could turn off the current and join my companions by way of a scramble over the roof.

As the car sank lower and lower, Williams and a companion

bridge[d] the watery gap and drag[ged] to safety the heavy trunk of photographic records. Flashlights threw the chaotic scene into wild relief. [One

Above: *The six-year-old Living Buddha of Guya, photographed in 1927 in a Tibetan monastery in a remote corner of north central China by Joseph F. Rock.*

Opposite: *"THE CHIEF DANCER IMPERSONATES THE KING OF HELL" began the caption for this Joseph F. Rock Autochrome published in the November 1928 issue. "With the scepter of death in his right hand," it continued, "the fearsome Yama, the God of the Dead, appears on the steps of the chanting hall and instills fear into the hearts of his Tibetan audience. Later he is joined in the dance by his retinue of demons, the Bawa."*

Botanist-explorer Dr. Joseph F. Rock led two National Geographic Society expeditions (1923–24 and 1927–30) into the remote, unmapped Tibetan borderlands of China and Tibet where no white man had ever been before. Bedeviled by bandits, blasted by blizzards, both a loner and lonely, Rock pushed through desolate defiles and across raging rivers and climbed razor-backed ridges to gather thousands of plants and countless animal and bird specimens. Along the way he sent back reports and photographs that, when published in the National Geographic, gave the world its first look at "the land that time forgot."

Among Rock's submissions was this photograph, which appeared in the November 1928 Magazine with the following caption: "TIBETAN PIPES CALL TO THE DANCE. Monks on the roof of a temple summon the austere Choni lamas to prepare for the ancient pantomime Cham-ngyon-wa. From the 15-foot trumpets are issuing weird, long-drawn notes that can be heard far away in the mountains. These same horns have resounded to the breath of thousands of trumpeters whose very memory is lost in antiquity."

man stood] on the radiator, wielded a piston-like crowbar against the thick ice, the car wallowed lower and lower, finally submerging the entire hood, and after more than an hour of feverish struggle in bitter cold, three other tractors dragged our car, like some submarine monster spewing out water, to the opposite bank. Thirteen hours' delay...and all my [stored] clothing frozen into solid blocks....

In addition to the cold the expedition had to cope with "dust [that] filled our nostrils and mouths. With cold-cracked fingers we scooped out gobs of grit from between our lower teeth and lips. Dust crept through our cylinders as if no air filters were there. Pistons developed unusual wear and oil fouled the spark plugs. While a trifling repair was being made, the water froze about the cylinders."

At Lunghingchang, Chinese officers inspected the group's passports; the army was now becoming more and more evident. In every town uniformed soldiers suspiciously pointed their guns at the half-tracks as they passed.

"Just before nightfall, the 'Silver Crescent' came to a narrow bridge" which the other cars had already crossed. Williams, seated beside the driver, suddenly found himself looking into the barrel of a gun held by a handsome young soldier. "At three or four miles an hour," he wrote, "it took a long time to roll past that swinging rifle barrel." Moments later, as they drove between "chest-high mud walls" lined with troops,

> a salvo of shots rang out. Eleven bullets took effect on "Silver Crescent" and its trailer....
>
> Deploying behind a diagonal bank, we brought our [machine gun] into action.
>
> "Fire high or at a wall," ordered Audouin-Dubreuil [Haardt's second-in-command]....
>
> Four rapid shots. Then a wave of silence. Four more shots. Silence. Four more shots. He had fired twelve cartridges in all when a flag went up over the Chinese headquarters. Men from both sides advanced to a conference, from which Point, bareheaded and laughing, returned.
>
> "This is a terrible country. They had the nerve to call it a 'slight misunderstanding.' "
>
> But after having tea with the officers...both sides agreed to call it that.

Soon after midnight the expedition passed into Inner Mongolia. "The next day a 1919 Dodge, laden with 22 men so deeply coated in dust that they looked like dummies, arrived *en route* to Lunghingchang. Before arriving there, three were killed, the rest stripped of everything."

And then, Maynard Owen Williams wrote:

> At high noon, on February 12, 1932, the Citroën-Haardt Trans-Asiatic Expedition swung into the grounds of the French Legation in Peiping, was welcomed by the élite of many nations, and came into well-earned glory. In 314½ days [the expedition] had blazed a 7,370-mile trail across Asia....

◄ ───

Charles and Anne Morrow Lindbergh in the cockpits of the Lockheed Sirius in which, in 1933, they visited twenty-one countries. Their epic 29,000-mile flight took them to four continents and through arctic cold, blizzards, sandstorms, hurricanes, and tropical heat.

"They were projecting this loop of film over and over again with its brilliant color, and I asked the man if I could examine the film....I put a loupe on it, a magnifying glass, and I saw there were no flecks in it! *Unlike with an Autochrome or a Finlay the white paper and the white shirts had no residual color in them at all! And I wondered,* How in the devil did they get that color?*"*

—Luis Marden, on his first look in 1935 at Eastman Kodak's new Kodachrome 16mm film.

As the Great Depression deepened, magazines fought to avoid going under. *Munsey's* merged with *Argosy, Everybody's* with *Romance,* and even *McClure's*—the magazine Gilbert Hovey Grosvenor had been under such pressure from his Board of Managers to emulate twenty-nine years before—was forced to combine with *Smart Set* in an effort to stay alive. But the *National Geographic,* whose income depended less on advertising revenue than on membership subscription, entered the new decade with the highest circulation in its history.

Still, not even the *Geographic* was immune to outside forces. The membership dipped by 44,362 in 1931, another 168,575 in 1932, and an additional 151,548 in 1933—a loss of 364,485 members in those three years.

Grosvenor was forced to lower salaries of his staff—among them the Society's Foreign Editorial Staff Chief, Maynard Owen Williams, who responded:

April 18, 1933

Dear Dr. Grosvenor:—

I have always felt that when, on occasions of a salary increase, you have said that you announced the increase "with pleasure" that that was no empty phrase. And a sense that such was the case added greatly to the value of the increase.

Since that was true, back there in the halcyon days when we did not appreciate how well off we were, it must have been with a sense of regret that you consented to a necessary reduction of salaries.

In all sincerity, I thanked you for the increases when they came. In all sincerity I thank you for the personal interest and support which, at a time of necessary retrenchment, involves a personal burden and a personal regret to you.

The decrease will call for a change of living, but that should involve no real loss. Sacrifice is a luxury. After so many evidences of *your* interest and support, I cannot but express *my* interest and support in what, because of your personal feelings and sympathy, must be a trying time for you....I hope you don't regard the decreases as in any sense a personal cross. But I hope I'm still enough of a Christian to appreciate a cross, be it mine or yours, and it is a relief to feel that if it is, I'm now having a share in bearing it.

Faithfully yours,

Williams

Preceding spread: *Titled "*STUDENT SMILES FROM FIVE STATES FLASH THROUGH OLD SCROLLWORK GATES AT ASHLEY HALL," *this striking Dufay-color photograph by B. Anthony Stewart of young women in a Charleston, South Carolina, boarding school appeared in the March 1939* National Geographic.

Grosvenor was moved enough to reply that same day:

April 18, 1933

Dear Williams:

I am very much touched by your kind note regarding the salary reductions which it has been necessary to make. Your thoughtful act has eased greatly the aching heart which I have carried as the result of these reductions. Even after the reductions, the salaries of the staff are, I believe, greater than they were in the boom days of 1928.* The National Geographic Society, thanks to the ability and loyalty of the men and women of its organization, has thus far weathered the hurricane of this depression. With trimmed sails we hope to ride it out safely unless some unforeseen cataclysm overwhelms America.

Thank you for your understanding.

Yours faithfully,
Gilbert Grosvenor.

Such flattering communiqués to the "Chief," as Grosvenor was also called by staffers, were not uncommon—especially on the anniversaries of their employment. For sheer adulation, however, no one could surpass those missives sent to Gilbert Grosvenor** by his right-hand man, John Oliver La Gorce, who had named his firstborn son Gilbert Grosvenor La Gorce and had written in 1916:

I wanted to say something to you yesterday but as fat and devil-may-care as I am I couldn't be serious in speaking of it without being a baby— Yesterday was the big double-header—36 on earth but only 11 alive—11 years with you and by your side, absorbing your great broad human viewpoint and your love of your fellows!—You'll never know how you have rolled out many a "petty" kink in my nature and impulse toward others, how often I've stopped to think "Hell no! Grosvenor *wouldn't do that!*"—I owe you a great debt for you have conserved my interests and happiness as your own and I'm ever seeking some way to express it—

This sounds like mush but really it isn't.

The Society's fortunes began to recover in 1934; by 1935, membership had reached more than a million again—in part through the *Geographic*'s continuing celebration of the ordinary: "Hunting for Plants in the Canary Islands," "Our Friend the Frog," "Some Odd Pages from the Annals of the Tulip," along with the long-running series on American cities and states. A Society author, however, points out in *Images of the World* that no matter how rose-colored the lenses, reality sometimes crept in. Referring to the preparation of an article that appeared in November 1934, the author wrote:

In planning for coverage of southern California...illustrations editor Franklin L. Fisher realized that there was one place that needed careful treatment: Hollywood.

Writing to the photographer who had the California assignment, Fisher approved the idea of showing how a movie star was made up. But, he added, be sure to "pick someone with whose name scandal has not been connected. Possibly Joan Crawford might be suitable."

The photographer replied that "the only actress out here who hasn't indulged in scandal seems to be Minnie (Mrs. Mickey) Mouse."

---

*In 1928, Maynard Owen Williams' salary was $7,700 per year; it was raised to $9,000 (less an insurance premium of $272) in 1929.

**Grosvenor, as were the other officers of the Society, was also known by the initials with which he signed his memos. Gilbert Hovey Grosvenor, therefore, was "GHG"; John Oliver La Gorce was "JOL," etc.

Any history of the National Geographic Society is also a history of color photography, for, as Gilbert Hovey Grosvenor wrote in 1963, "In photography—and particularly in the use of color—we have led the way from the first."

The first commercial process in color photography was the Lumière Autochrome, developed in France and marketed in 1907. Although it opened a new world, it required, like the black-and-white photographs of those days, heavy cameras and cumbersome glass plates, and exposures were slow. Franklin Price Knott's Autochrome of a Tunisian carrot peddler ran in the Magazine in September 1916.

The Finlay process photograph, developed in England, appeared in 1930; though grainier than an Autochrome, it offered the increased speed that made it possible for Gilbert H. Grosvenor's son Melville Bell Grosvenor to take the first successful aerial color photographs.

Agfacolor, a German development, allowed exposures of a fifth to a tenth of a second in bright sunlight with lenses set wide open. Although twice as fast as Lumière, Agfacolor was swiftly discarded by the Geographic in favor of the Dufay process, introduced in 1937.

Dufay was only slightly faster than the Finlay process, but it utilized film rather than glass plates—an advantage Geographic photographers in the field, loaded with 150 pounds of cameras, tripods, and glass plates, were quick to appreciate.

Autochromes, Finlays, Agfacolors, and Dufaycolors were all discarded when Kodachrome, introduced by Eastman Kodak in 1936, enabled photographers to capture action in color on 35mm film. In April 1938 the first Kodachromes appeared in the *National Geographic*.

The Autochrome screen (above) *used minute grains of color dyed potato starch. (Autochrome picture,* right)

The Finlay screen (below) *contained 175 lines to the inch. (Finlay picture,* bottom)

206

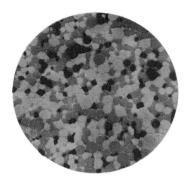

The Agfacolor screen (above) was formed by bits of dyed resin. (Agfacolor picture, left)

The Dufaycolor process ruled screen (below) was made up of parallel and crossed lines. (Dufaycolor picture, right)

Unlike every other photographic process of that time, Kodachrome provided a grainless image with a potential for almost limitless enlargement. (Kodachrome picture, left)

Along with seventy-four human skeletons, jewelry, and an offering stand of silver, shell, and gold, this gilded bull's head with lapis lazuli beard adorned a lyre which lay—its musician's stilled fingers spread over its strings—in the "great death pit" of Ur, the site of royal burial and human sacrifice 5,000 years ago in Iraq. M. E. L. Mallowan's account of the excavation led by C. Leonard Woolley, "New Light on Ancient Ur," appeared in the January 1930 National Geographic.

superlative use," there was evidently some foot-dragging in utilizing Kodachrome, since it did not appear in the *Geographic* until two years after its availability.

There is reason to believe that the first to realize Kodachrome's potential was Luis Marden, who had come to the Geographic the year before in search of a job. Marden, then a twenty-one-year-old journalist for the *Boston Sunday Herald,* was self-educated, quinque-lingual (English, Spanish, Italian, Portuguese, French), and a radio broadcaster. At the suggestion of Kip Ross, then a technical adviser for the E. Leitz Company, Marden had just written *Color Photography With the Miniature Camera,* the first instructional book on that topic; and when he learned the Magazine was looking for photographers Marden wrote the Society that he was "experimenting with color."

The Society responded by inviting Marden to Washington. He appeared in Illustrations Editor Franklin L. Fisher's office with a Leica 35 mm camera slung around his neck. "Do you ever use a Leica in your work?" Marden innocently asked the older man.

"Of course we don't," Fisher replied, in effect. "We don't use toys around here. We do serious photography."

To test Marden's prowess with the color process, Fisher said, "Let's see if he can make a color photograph." He made Marden load Finlay plates in the darkroom, gave him an Ica Juwel camera, a car, and driver, and sent the young man out to look for colorful subjects. "I remember it was the blazing African heat of Washington in July," Marden later recalled:

> …everything was burned and sere. Finally I made one exposure on a tripod of a ship being painted red near Haines Point, with weeping willows. I've never made a better one since. Then I came in and I proceeded to develop the film myself and to register it with the viewing screen. It impressed the hell out of them because plenty of… photographers came around to the *Geographic,* pros of many years standing, but they had never shot color.

In those days professional photographers did not bother to learn the color process because there was no market for it; no magazine other than the *Geographic* regularly printed it, and there were only transparencies, not photographic paper, to enable a photographer to print studio portraits.

In 1935, Kodak released its first Kodachrome as a 16 mm motion-picture film. A year later Marden, by then working at the Magazine exclusively as a photographer, saw a demonstration of the film in the window of a downtown Washington camera store. Marden's recollection continues:

> They were projecting this loop of film over and over again with its brilliant color, and I asked the man if I could examine the film. He gave it to me and I put a loupe on it, a magnifying glass, and I saw *there were no flecks in it*! Unlike with an Autochrome or a Finlay the white paper and the white shirts had no residual color in them at all! And I wondered, *How in the devil did they get that color*?
>
> Of course, anyone with a modicum of technical background could have figured out the only way they could do it would be through superimposed layers—one sensitive to red, one to blue, one to green and so on—but the minute I saw that 16mm film I came rushing back to the Geographic, went to the head of the photo lab, Charles Martin, and I said, "I've seen this new film, it's amazing! If it does come out, it's going to open the door for us, it'll be a photographer's liberation, like being let out of prison."

The liberation would be threefold: First, because the Kodachrome's final image was a dye image only, the resulting picture—unlike every other photographic image of that time, including black-and-white—contained no granules of metallic silver. Marden immediately realized that with Kodachrome one had a *grainless* small image with a potential for almost infinite enlargement. Second, the film was faster. Exposures with Lumière Autochrome require bright sunlight; and although the makers of the Finlay plates boasted that with their process it was possible to take "snapshots"—action photographs— "if there was *any* movement you'd get a blur," Marden explained. Third, since both Autochrome and Finlay used glass plates, photographers had to carry a cumbersome load of equipment.

Marden knew that miniature cameras, roll film, dye images would revolutionize *National Geographic* photography—but *only* if he could convince the Illustrations Division's chief to permit him to use them.

Through friends, Marden managed to acquire two rolls of the new 35mm Kodachrome film before it came on the market. The Geographic did not even own a Leica at this time, so one weekend Marden took his, the two rolls of Kodachrome, and, as he said, "exposed them in every possible way: a macrophotograph of a postage stamp, street scenes, a close-up of a goldfish, a studio portrait..."

That same weekend, Marden also took a photograph of a woman friend horseback riding in Washington's Rock Creek Park, while on horseback himself. Such a feat would have been nearly impossible with the cumbersome Finlay or Autochrome camera equipment. Two weeks later the developed films came back from Eastman Kodak. "They were color transparencies, the same kind you have today; but, of course, the film came back as a whole strip. Kodak was certainly still a long way from cutting them up and mounting them between little cardboard mats." Marden taped the best of the transparencies onto lantern slide glass plates, blacked out everything around them, then asked Franklin Fisher if he would like to see them.

Fisher came down to the small projection room with his assistant and a couple of others. Marden recalled:

> I was only a lowly lab man in the photographic laboratory and I projected them in our small auditorium. They only filled the center of the screen, but still they were about six feet across. I told them you could take Kodachrome fast, it was portable, and reproduce it any size you wanted.... There was dead silence.
>
> Anyone who knew photography would have understood what I was showing them, but these weren't technical people, these were *illustrations* people. It's hard today to realize how astounding these photographs were! They were sharp, they didn't have extraneous color. "See?" I kept saying. "The white shirt? No flecks of color in it. The flesh tones? No red and green in it."
>
> They didn't say much, just asked a few questions, and that was it. I went back to my kennel, the dark room, and I was in there developing prints and I sensed a presence. It was quite dark under the red lights, and I smelled the tobacco of the head of the photo lab. And Charles Martin—he was a very brusque, at times very graceless old man, and he said, "Say Marden...those pictures you made on that new film....Did you make them on your own time?"
>
> I said, "Yes, Mr. Martin. I made those a few weekends ago. Why?"

Even *"The Lion of the Tribe of Judah"* willingly posed for the National Geographic *in his coronation attire.* W. Robert Moore's "natural color photograph" of Haile Selassie, the newly crowned Emperor of Ethiopia, appeared in the Magazine's June 1931 issue.

"This has again been a most interesting voyage," Alan J. Villiers (above), wrote Geographic Illustrations Chief Franklin L. Fisher in 1932 of the grain race from Australia to England by twenty big windjammers, in which Villiers had just captained his square-rigger Parma (left) to victory. "We arrived in Falmouth Bay the other day with a passage of 103 days and a few hours, winning...by four hours (not much in 103 days!)...The voyage was marked by the ferocity of the Cape Horn storms. We...blew out our best sails, washed everything movable overboard, gutted the midships house, and drowned the ship's pig...." A great favorite of the Geographic, Villiers produced more than a score of seafaring articles for the Magazine between 1931 and 1976, as well as for the Book Service publication Men, Ships, and the Sea.

"Well, Mr. Fisher just called up and wanted to know. He said those things will never be worth a damn to the National Geographic."

We were in the gloom of the darkroom, and I don't know if I said, "Do you believe that?" or if we just looked at each other and half-smiled. Being a superb technician, Martin, of all people, knew that that was ridiculous.

Still, Martin did send two separate exposures to the Beck Engraving Company from which they made half-tones. To my knowledge, they were the first half-tones made from a Kodachrome anywhere.

Although the test half-tone engravings were successful, over two and a half years would elapse between Kodachrome's arrival on the market and its first appearance in the *National Geographic Magazine*. As Geographic staffer Priit Vesilind wrote in his thesis on color photography at the Society:

It took a successful field assignment by an established photographer to ignite the *Geographic* on 35mm Kodachrome....

In the summer of 1937, a year after Kodachrome had been available, Bud Wisherd, the assistant chief of the photo lab, requisitioned a dozen more rolls of the film. He mailed five to W. Robert Moore on assignment in Austria, and Marden took the remaining rolls on an expedition in Mexico. But Marden's Mexican Kodachromes were not published until September 1940....Moore's appeared in April 1938....

B. Anthony Stewart may have described Marden's position aptly: "To be new and an originator—that, of all things, is resented. Wait a little before you originate, because you're going to be stepping on people's toes."

Moore, given the privilege of being the *Geographic*'s Kodachrome pioneer, later described [how]...within a few days [he] had shot all of his five rolls of Kodachrome, capturing, among other things, a swirling band of Austrian dancers. "The men swung their partners round and round to the swiftly changing tempo of guitar, mandolin, and wheezy accordion," he later described. "I took pot shots, standing up, and lying down on my stomach in the courtyard. Rough boots kicked up dust, dresses and petticoats swished, the dancers had fun; so did I.

"Routine now, yes, but the dance was one of the first color subjects I had ever shot without having my camera securely anchored to a tripod."

The realization that magazine photography would never be the same hit home at the *Geographic* as Moore's 35mm photographs ran through the processing and editing mill.

"Everyone just went wild over them," remembered B. Anthony Stewart. "The dancing girls, the iridescence of color. It was just something that color photographers had never dreamed of."

"Without doubt," Edwin Wisherd said at his retirement in 1971,[*] "that's the most important thing that has happened in photography during my time here—the development of the 35mm camera and Kodachrome's fast emulsion color film."

In 1938, 3 Lumière Autochromes, 222 Finlays, 69 Dufays, and 18 Agfacolors were published in the Magazine, compared to 62 Kodachromes; the following year, the Magazine published 8 Autochromes, 47 Finlays, 93 Dufays, 11 Agfacolors, and 317 Kodachromes. A revolution in color photography was occurring.

As Melville Bell Grosvenor, by then an Assistant Editor of the *Geographic*, recalled: "Frank Fisher was very old-fashioned in his ideas, but he saw the point instantly. And my father did. And we just threw out our other pictures

---

[*] *Edwin L. (Bud) Wisherd joined the Society Photographic Laboratory in 1919 and, upon Charles Martin's retirement in 1941, replaced Martin as chief.*

"*...it was evident that we had discovered one of the richest and most important fossil fields in all the world,*" Roy Chapman Andrews (above) *wrote in* "*Explorations in the Gobi Desert,*" *for the June 1933 Geographic.* "*The dinosaur eggs alone made it famous, but they were by no means the most important of the thousands of specimens we brought from the Gobi. We were surprised at the universal popular interest that the dinosaur eggs aroused.*"

Opposite: *Roy Chapman Andrews, 1931 Hubbard Medal winner for geographic discoveries in Central Asia, inches out over a Gobi Desert aerie to capture an eaglet.*

from the field—just scrapped them and replaced them as fast as we could with Kodachromes. I'll never forget that—that was really a thrill."

There were other thrills to be found at the *Geographic* in the 1930s, for it was the decade of the great expeditions, the "Glory Years."

The decade had led off with M.E.L. Mallowan's January 1930 "New Light on Ancient Ur" account of one of archeology's great moments—the discovery in Iraq of the "death pits" of Ur, where 5,000 years earlier human sacrifice and royal burials had occurred:

> One of these graves consisted of a shaft dug to a depth of 30 feet below surface level. At the bottom was a single chamber surmounted by a dome… erected over a wooden ceiling which had eventually crashed onto the brick floor, covering up the five occupants. Four were servants and the fifth was a woman, most probably of royal blood…dressed in the brilliant court costume of the period. She wore a headdress of gold ribbons radiating in seven strips from the center of the head, a wealth of gold poplar leaves strung with carnelian and lapis lazuli beads, and around the neck gold chains and carnelian beads.…
>
> The treasures lavished on the dead were remarkable for splendor and number. As we cleared the shaft to the level of the floor, it appeared almost as if we were treading on a carpet of gold.…The [68] women, lying in ordered rows, were decked out after the fashion of the principal occupant of the domed chamber. Hair ribbons of silver or gold were almost invariable and many of the gold ribbons bore marks of exquisitely fine network, the veiling now entirely decayed that had once shrouded the head.
>
> So great was the weight and quantity of jewelry on the heads that the women must have worn wigs that were both large and substantial.…
>
> The six men, perhaps the funeral bodyguard, were ranged in a row against the front wall of the shaft. The women lay in rows across it, and in three corners were buried the principal treasures.

The June 1930 issue contained "The First Airship Flight Around the World," Dr. Hugo Eckener's account of his 19,500-mile, three-week circumnavigation of the globe as commander of the giant German *Graf Zeppelin*, a journey for which he was awarded the Society's Special Gold Medal. In August the Magazine ran Admiral Richard Evelyn Byrd's account of the first conquest of the South Pole by air.

That same year, from the deck of the ocean liner in which he was crossing the Atlantic, Gilbert H. Grosvenor spied the Finnish windjammer *Grace Harwar*. An avid blue-water sailor himself, and one to whom sailing ships "gave a glorious hint of the romance and mystery of the sea," Grosvenor was able to photograph the full-rigged ship as it passed. When he later learned that Australian writer-photographer Alan Villiers had sailed on it when it had carried grain from Australia to England, Grosvenor asked him to contribute sailing pieces to the Magazine. The following year Alan Villiers wrote "Rounding the Horn in a Windjammer," the first of many Villiers articles on sailing to appear in the *Geographic*. It appeared in the February 1931 issue and contained this extract from the diary of Ronald Walker, a young reporter friend of Villiers who had served with him as one of the crew:

> "Great seas come up to meet the ship, thrusting at her, shouldering one another to get at her, like footballers in a mad footer 'scrum.' Up and up they heave, gathering for the blow. You turn to watch them. The wind howls in your face and the sea spits at you spitefully, driving its spray above and

Above: *"SHOCK ABSORBERS SERVE DUAL PURPOSE: Professor [Auguste] Piccard, (right), and his companion of the first flight sat on two cushions and kept certain delicate instruments in two baskets. These baskets and cushions were designed also for head protection against a bump in case of a sudden landing." —From "Ballooning in the Stratosphere," March 1933 issue.*

Opposite: *First woman to fly alone across the Atlantic, Amelia Earhart acknowledges cheers of a crowd upon touchdown at Londonderry, Northern Ireland, on May 21, 1932. The following month, for her accomplishment Earhart received a Special Gold Medal—the first ever awarded to a woman by the Society.*

This photograph of a male and female ivory-billed woodpecker—the first ever of a nesting pair of these rare birds—was taken by ornithology professor Arthur A. Allen for his June 1937 Geographic *article "Hunting With a Microphone The Voices of Vanishing Birds." In this landmark ecologically-aware article in the Magazine, Dr. Allen warned of civilization's inroads on birds such as the trumpeter swan.*

around. A great sea, a liquid mountain of menace, hangs poised above the ship. Up, up, it leaps, shouldering its smaller children aside, the splendid crest whitening where it breaks, lending a touch of color like the plume of a warrior's helmet.

"Down, down, sinks the ship, shuddering already at the impending blow. A hundred lesser blows she has avoided; this mighty one she cannot beat. She writhes like a living thing, in fear and trembling. She heels over heavily; she hovers frighteningly....

"The stars shoot suddenly past the spars—not so bad with them out— careening madly across the sky. The ship receives the blow full, staggering at the impact. A tremor runs through the laboring hull....

"But the shattered sea crest has met its match. The warrior's plume has dropped; the ship rises again, tumbling hundreds of tons of roaring, fighting water from her gushing wash ports. The sea sweeps her furiously end to end, murderously intent upon human prey. Balked of that, it shifts whatever is movable and snarls and hisses at the hatch breakwaters, maddeningly intent at breaking them down....

"But the ship wins. Under her load of hundreds of tons of seething water, she rolls on, recovering her poise, steadying herself to meet the next onslaught, and the next, and the next after that...."

Villiers sadly reports that six days after young Walker made that entry in his diary, he was killed after loosing the three-masted sailing ship's fouled fore upper topgallantsail. While the men on deck heaved to lift the rain-sodden, swollen canvas, the halyards carried away and the yard fell on Walker, below.

In June 1931, William Beebe's "A Round Trip to Davy Jones's Locker" told of his 1930 descent in a heavy steel bathysphere to the depth of 1,426 feet. (Four years later, in 1934, Beebe reached a depth of 3,028 feet—a record that would stand for fifteen years.)

That same month appeared an article announcing the start of the 1931–32 Citroën-Haardt Trans-Asiatic Expedition. With its motor caravan of half-track vehicles, the expedition blazed a 7,370-mile trail across Asia, an overland exploration from the Mediterranean to the Yellow Sea.

Roy Chapman Andrews told of discovering "one of the richest and most important fossil fields in all the world" in his June 1933 piece, "Explorations in the Gobi Desert." Andrews discovered not just dinosaur eggs he estimated to be ninety-five million years old in Mongolia, but also the skulls of tiny rat-size mammals that coexisted with the dinosaurs, and, among others, the thirty-million-year-old bones and "a huge tooth, nearly as large as an apple" from "the giant *Baluchitherium*...the largest land mammal that ever lived upon the earth...an aberrant browsing rhinoceros [that]...stood about 17 feet high at the shoulders and was 24 feet long, and weighed many tons."

For his findings Roy Chapman Andrews in 1931 was presented the Society's Hubbard Medal by its president Gilbert H. Grosvenor, who stated such discoveries "have pushed back the horizons of life upon the earth and filled in gaps in the great ancestral tree of all that breathes."

Alan Villiers appeared again in January 1933 with "The Cape Horn Grain-ship Race," his stirring account of a big square-rigger ship race "Through Raging Gales and Irksome Calms 16,000 Miles, from Australia to England."

Two months later the Magazine published Dr. Auguste Piccard's "Ballooning in the Stratosphere," Piccard's report on his ascent with a companion to 53,152 feet in a spherical aluminum cabin similar in appearance to the bathysphere in which Beebe had descended in the sea. The purpose of his ascent to an altitude of over ten miles, was to study cosmic rays.

In 1934, Anne Morrow Lindbergh became the second woman to be awarded a Society medal. Two years earlier, Amelia Earhart had been presented the Society's Special Gold Medal for the first solo transatlantic flight by a woman. Anne Morrow Lindbergh was awarded the Hubbard Medal for the notable flights she had made in 1931 and 1933 as co-pilot and radio operator on the Charles A. Lindbergh aerial surveys. During their 1933 flight they faced the worst possible flying hazards—blizzards, sandstorms, hurricanes, arctic cold, and tropical heat—while flying their pontoon-equipped Lockheed Sirius to four continents and visiting twenty-one countries. Their 29,000-mile adventure was an incredible feat of flying for that era. And her own account of that trip, laconically titled "Flying Around the North Atlantic," appeared in the Magazine in September 1934.

The following month's issue contained Captain Albert W. Stevens' story of the National Geographic Society–U.S. Army Air Corps Stratosphere Expedition in *Explorer*, the largest free balloon until then ever constructed.

While dazzling heights were being reached in balloons and dazzling distances in aircraft, there was still room in the *Geographic* for old-fashioned adventures such as Henri de Monfreid's November 1937 article "Pearl Fishing in the Red Sea":

> In ten minutes we were outside the island, the mainsail bellying. Night had come and I set the course by the compass....We had to cross the central part of the Red Sea....It was 2 a.m. and all eyes were fixed on the horizon....
>
> With the aid of a night glass I guided us closer and Ali pointed out to me an isolated black point in the sea to the south of the island. It was a za-rug [a small Red Sea sailing craft used by smugglers] moored to... a reef.
>
> Our rifles were quickly loaded with five cartridges each. I had only 50 all told. Then the ax, a jumper bar, and a big iron hammer were put in battle order as if we were going to board....the die had been cast; I could no longer retreat.
>
> We were half a cable's length from the sleeping zarug when the old Sudanese recognized it. I put the helm up, and as the sail fell we drifted to within a few yards of our quarry....I called the usual "Hooooo" as if we were an innocent boat coming there by accident, though this was a very unusual hour to drop anchor.
>
> Meanwhile I had lighted the fuse with my cigarette. The little light from the jet of flame passed unobserved and the black fuse smoked on ominously in the dark.
>
> I plunged the long boat hook into the sea as if about to anchor, but held the bomb under the vital parts of the boat. I carefully counted the seconds up to ten. Then I cried to the nakhoda, who was ready:
>
> "Call your men."
>
> All together we shouted to the men in the zarug to jump into the sea if they could.
>
> The Zaraniks awoke; the breech of a rifle clicked; I continued to count—18, 19....
>
> Then a greenish flame spurted from the center of their boat as the dynamite exploded.
>
> I had held the explosive under the mast, where there are usually no sleepers. The mast crashed down, and a few seconds later stones rained on all sides—the pebble ballast had been blown sky-high....
>
> The zarug sank in a few seconds and men floundered in the water. There were wild shouts. The Sudanese swam heavily by their arms, as they

"Almost within the memory of men still living," Arthur A. Allen (above) *wrote, "four species of North American birds have become extinct. In our museums will be found the dried skins or mounted specimens of the great auk, the Labrador duck, the passenger pigeon, and the heath hen. The Carolina parakeet seems about to follow them...."* Determined to preserve the voices of birds still living, Allen spied on, among others, *"the ivory-billed woodpecker...now perhaps the rarest North American bird,"* and managed to record both its antics and its voice.—From *"Hunting With a Microphone the Voices of Vanishing Birds,"* June 1937 issue

217

"These Marvelous Nether Regions"

> "...the only other place comparable to these marvelous nether regions, must surely be naked space itself, out far beyond the atmosphere, between the stars,...where sunlight has no grip upon the dust and rubbish of planetary air, where the blackness of space, the shining planets, comets, suns, and stars must really be closely akin to the world of life as it appears to the eyes of an awed human being, in the open ocean, one half mile down."
>
> —William Beebe, *Half Mile Down*

William Beebe, writing of that moment on June 6, 1930, when he and Otis Barton first peered out of the portholes of their bathysphere into the murky depths at six hundred feet, noted, "Ever since the beginnings of human history, when first the Phoenicians dared to sail the open sea, thousands upon thousands of human beings had reached the depth at which we were now suspended, and had passed on to lower levels. But all of these were dead, drowned victims of war, tempest, or other Acts of God."

It was not surprising that such a thought had crossed Beebe's mind, for during the last three hundred feet of their bathysphere's descent, he had had good reason to suspect that he and Barton might join them.

Shortly after they had been lowered into the water Beebe heard Barton cry out that their two-ton steel sphere had sprung a leak. Beebe turned his flashlight on the interior of the sphere's 400-pound door and saw a "slow trickle of water beneath it. About a pint had gathered in the bottom. I wiped away the meandering stream and still it came. I knew that the door would fit more tightly the deeper we got, but there remained a shadow of worry as to how much the relaxed pressure of the ascent would allow the door to expand."

The bathysphere was suspended in the waters off Bermuda at the end of a seven-eighths-inch, non-twisting steel cable attached to a seven-ton, steam-powered winch mounted on a barge. The 4-foot-9-inch-diameter steel sphere contained enough oxygen to last the two men eight hours, a rack of carbon dioxide absorber, a searchlight, and a telephone—none of which would do them any good should the door not hold.

After a brief pause at 600 feet, the two men descended again until, as Beebe wrote, " 'Eight hundred feet' came down the [telephone] wire and I called a halt. Half a dozen times in my life I have had hunches so vivid that I could not ignore them, and this was one of the times. Eight hundred feet spelled bottom and I could not escape it."

Five days later, Beebe and Barton were lowered over the side in their bathysphere again. Wrote naturalist Beebe:

Preceding spread: *The onion-shaped portholed dome of Captain Jacques-Yves Cousteau's hangar for his two-man hydro-jet diving saucer, DS-2, was part of Conshelf Two, a submerged colony of four prefabricated steel structures with fish pens and several antishark cages located thirty-six feet beneath the surface of the Red Sea on a coral reef twenty-five miles northeast of Port Sudan, Sudan. Nearby was the Starfish House, shelter for five French oceanauts who lived and worked there for a month in June 1963 without coming to the surface. Conshelf Two was part of Cousteau's long-range research program to test man's ability to build and maintain an underwater village. For more than a decade the National Geographic Society supported Captain Cousteau's underseas studies.*

Opposite: *Dr. William Beebe, oceanographic naturalist, squeezes past the protruding steel bolts that seal the 400-pound door of the bathysphere in which he and Otis Barton descended 3,028 feet in the waters off Bermuda in 1934. That dive, sponsored by the New York Zoological Society and the National Geographic Society, set a depth record that remained unbroken for fifteen years.*

Above: *"Silver Hatchetfish Drifting Through the Abysmal Darkness"* was the June 1931 caption for this painting by Else Bostelmann of the tiny, pop-eyed fish never seen alive until Beebe spied one through the window of the bathysphere during his June 1930 record dive.

Earlier Beebe had written of the moment he and Barton reached 1,426 feet, the deepest point of that 1930 dive: *"There came to me at that instant a...real appreciation of...the whole situation; our barge slowly rolling high overhead in the blazing sunlight,...the long cobweb of cable leading down through the spectrum to our lonely sphere, where, sealed tight, two conscious human beings sat and peered into the abysmal darkness.... isolated as a lost planet in outermost space."—From "A Round Trip to Davy Jones's Locker,"* June 1931 issue

Opposite: *Else Bostelmann's water-color, part of a series in the December 1932* Geographic, *was captioned: "Hawaiian Reefs Present a Sunburst of Color: In the shallows...of the Pacific, great monoliths of coral lift their heads,...seafans enhance the beauty seen through their waving, purple veils; and graceful fish show clashing yet harmonious patterns and colors."*

Jellyfish, large and small, drifted past....Fifteen-inch bonitos darted past in trios and once a small, stodgy triggerfish strayed from his water-logged sargassum shelter to peer in at me....At four hundred feet there came into view the first real deep-sea fish...lanternfish and bronze eels....Pale shrimps drifted by, their transparency almost removing them from vision. ...At five hundred feet...for the first time I saw strange, ghostly dark forms hovering in the distance,—forms which never came nearer, but reappeared at deeper, darker depths....At six hundred feet...I saw my first shrimps with minute but very distinct portholes of lights. Again a great cloud of a body moved in the distance—this time pale, much lighter than the water....

At 1,426 feet on the June 1930 dive, Beebe wrote of "the very deepest point we reached":

> ...There came to me at that instant a tremendous wave of emotion, a real appreciation of what was momentarily almost superhuman, cosmic, of the whole situation; our barge slowly rolling high overhead in the blazing sunlight, like the merest chip in the midst of the ocean, the long cobweb of cable leading down through the spectrum to our lonely sphere, where, sealed tight, two conscious human beings sat and peered into the abysmal darkness as we dangled in mid-water, isolated as a lost planet in outermost space.

Four years later, in 1934, Beebe and Barton returned again to the depths off Bermuda. At 2,100 feet Beebe saw "...ghostly things in every direction." At 2,800: "Here's a telescope-eyed fish." At 3,028: "Long, lacelike things again." His narrative continued:

> A cross swell arose and on deck the crew paid out a bit of cable to ease the strain. We were swinging at 3,028 feet. There were only about a dozen turns of cable left on the reel, and a full half of the drum showed its naked, wooden core. Would we come up?...Through the telephone we learned at this moment we were under pressure of 1,360 pounds to the square inch. Each window held back more than 19 tons of water, while a total of 7,016 tons was piled up in all directions on the bathysphere itself.

Beebe and Barton's descent to a depth of 3,028 feet was a record that would remain unbroken for fifteen years.

Today, more than fifty years later, still only a pitifully small amount of the vast underwater world has been seen. "This world ocean, this vast culture broth and spring of life," James Dugan wrote in the National Geographic's Special Publication *World Beneath the Sea*,

> blankets seven-tenths of the globe and shrouds awesomely spectacular topography. But soundings and electronic magic, rather than personal inspection, have revealed most of the little we know about the grandeur of the depths....
>
> These sketches [made by the stylus of recording sonar] form mere shadows of reality. Most of the underwater canyons, trenches, valleys, mountains, and plains remain a territory not yet invaded by human explorers. And what a territory!
>
> Earth's longest mountain range, the Mid-Oceanic Ridge, meanders between the continental land masses for 35,000 miles through all the oceans. Rising 6,000 to 12,000 feet above the bottom, the pinnacles of the ridge occasionally break through the surface to form islands, such as the Azores

Six-foot sand tiger sharks probe a cave near Japan's Bonin Islands in this photograph made by David Doubilet to accompany Eugenie Clark's August 1981 National Geographic *article* "SHARKS: *Magnificent and Misunderstood.*"

But there was no misunderstanding the sharks' intentions when, during that assignment, Doubilet was lowered in a cage off Dangerous Reef, South Australia, and for the first time in his life was alone with a great white shark:

"I see the shark's head easing out of the murk, a pig-faced beast with an underslung grin," Doubilet wrote in the Society's 1981 Book Service publication Images of the World. "Light dapples his back. Slowly he turns away, scattering the few small fish that hang near my cage. Near its top and on all four sides, the cage has a camera port, a horizontal space 24 inches wide between the bars. I lean out as the shark comes close. The wide-angle 15mm lens takes in all 16 feet of the great white. He makes his turn and passes by the cage again.

"Then I see the eye, silver-dollar size, black, bottomless. It is not the eye of an animal but the porthole of a machine. The shark bangs the cage with his tail. I whirl, my air tank clanging against the metal bars. The shark is gone. Where? Suddenly, he comes again, this time from above, raking his teeth along the yellow floats atop the cage.

"The shark sinks to my eye level. The teeth drop down. He is opening his jaws. I am looking down the animal's throat.

"Now the shark wants a closer look at me—perhaps a taste. He pushes his head into the cage, coming in at the camera port, but...he cannot open his jaws. The shark turns sideways. The pointy nose pushes further in. The dome of my camera housing is one inch from the shark's snout. For the first time, I take my eye from the camera. I'm transfixed. All I can see is the flat black eye.

"Then, inexplicably, the shark is gone, a myth, black-magical animal vanished in a darkening sea."

With the development and perfection of the Aqua-Lung a new, and often rapturous, era of undersea exploration began. Cousteau later wrote of his first tests: "I reached the bottom

other bathyscaphs, both French, had ever operated at that depth). Reaching the depth at which *Thresher* lay was one thing; finding it was another. Four months passed before the *Trieste* could locate *Thresher*'s wreckage. And once there, the bathyscaph was able only to take photographs of the sunken submarine, recover a few pieces, and do no more.

The need to develop submersibles capable of searching large areas was emphasized three years after *Thresher*'s loss when, in January 1966, a U.S. Air Force K-147 refueling a B-52 bomber in flight over Palomares, Spain, suddenly exploded into flames. Fire engulfed the B-52 and it fell out of the sky. On board that bomber, in addition to its crew, were four H-bombs. Three fell on land; the fourth disappeared into the sea off the coast of Spain and sank 2,550 feet to the ocean floor. Though the bomb was unarmed, it was essential that it be recovered. "In the end," James Dugan wrote, "the submarinos *Alvin* and *Aluminaut* provided the key to the suspenseful search."

Alvin, commissioned by the Navy in 1964, was the first and most famous of the new submersibles. The 22-foot-long craft could carry a crew of three, was equipped with an arm-claw, and could travel at a full speed of one-and-a-half knots. Since improved, *Alvin* has been lengthened to 25 feet, been equipped with a second arm-claw, and been given a new pressure hull that enables the tiny submersible to operate at a depth of 13,120 feet. *Alvin* has now made more than 1,700 dives. In 1977, while the *Alvin* scientists were exploring the Galápagos Rift as part of their continuing study of plate tectonics, they were astonished to discover giant clams, bizarre white, thread-like worms, dandelion-shaped creatures never before seen, and long tube worms that defied description.

" 'The crabs were unbelievable!' " said noted underwater photographer Al Giddings. " 'We watched them tiptoe up to the giant tube worms and snip off bites before the worms could retreat into their shelters! Most beautiful was the Rose Garden. There were hundreds of red-plumed tube worms, some nearly as big around as your wrist.' "

"The animals Al described belong to a complex ecosystem," wrote marine botanist Sylvia A. Earle, "all of them heretofore unknown and the most conspicuous—giant tube dwellers—so different that they are being classed as a separate subphylum of animals." Earle, a contributor of numerous articles to the Magazine, continues in the Special Publication *Exploring the Deep Frontier*:

> A significant discovery is that large amounts of hemoglobin—the oxygen-carrying substance in human blood—courses through the bodies of the Galapagos tube worms and accounts for the red color.
>
> The most exciting biological discovery concerning the newfound ecosystem is how it seems to sustain itself. On land, plants derive energy from the sun through photosynthesis. But here, close to the vents, the basic food chain begins instead with sulfur bacteria that obtain their energy from a chemical reaction. Such systems, moreover, may not be so rare in the deep sea, if—as can now be assumed—more vents exist. Later dives in *Alvin* in

◄ ─────────────────────────────────

"A weapon of war? A symbol of authority? On the seabed off Ulu Burun near the Turkish town of Kaş, a diver in 1984 ponders a mace head of stone *from a vessel that sank about 1375 B.C."—From the 1985 Book Service publication* Adventures in Archaeology

Above: *Two-foot-long* Metridium
senile, *sea anemones in the Strait of
Georgia, an inland sea separating
mainland Canada from Vancouver
Island. These most primitive of multicellular animals, photographed by
David Doubilet, thrive in areas of
swift current.*

Right: *This brilliantly colored jellyfish,* Olindias formosa, *was encountered by Anne Levine Doubilet at the
entrance of a cave in Japan's Izu
Oceanic Park at a depth of 130 feet.
The Japanese nickname for it,* hana
gasakurage, *means cherry blossom.*

Above: *This nearly six-foot-tall tree-like coral, an alcyonarian, grows in Izu at a depth of 165 feet. The foliage and trunk of the "tree" are actually a colony of millions of soft-coral animals. And what appear to be leaves are clusters of polyps, opened to feed on current-borne plankton.*

1979 near the tip of Baja California resulted in the discovery of another system, including many groups of organisms similar to those in the Galapagos Rift.

The Baja dives caused even greater excitement when geologists observed chimneys of rock spewing forth black clouds of minerals: iron, copper, zinc, and silver sulfides. "It may be that minerals we find on dry land today were formed by a process such as we witnessed," [scientist-explorer] Robert Ballard commented. "The deep-sea discoveries made during the coming decade should help solve more of the mysteries of earth's origin—and may provide valuable new sources of minerals as well."

The foot-long clams and bright red worms, encased in tubes as long as eight feet, that exist at depths of 9,200 feet around the Pacific vents seem not to exist at the 3,280-foot-deeper vents in the Atlantic. These vents, formed like those in the Pacific as the plates that make up the sea floor slowly spread apart, are home to free-swimming animals such as blind shrimp, an eel-like fish, and a strange six-sided animal that researchers believe is related to an ancient organism known only from Alpine Eocene-era deposits. And from these vents, mineral-rich water spews at temperatures of 662° F—hot enough to melt protective plastic coverings on *Alvin*'s claws. More recently, researchers in *Alvin* discovered off the coast of Oregon colonies of tube worms that feed not off sulfides but methane.

To the layman, *Alvin*'s most dramatic voyage of discovery was not to observe strange new forms of life, but, in 1986, to bear witness to the grim specter of a legendary death. A year earlier, on September 1, 1985, in the North Atlantic, *Argo*, a search vehicle containing video cameras, side-scan sonar, a computerized timing system, and a host of other electronic gear, was being towed behind the U.S. Navy research vessel *Knorr*. Suddenly the first ghostly images of a once-majestic ship were displayed on the *Knorr*'s video screens. "I cannot believe my eyes," Robert Ballard reported in the December 1985 *Geographic*:

> From the abyss two and a half miles beneath the sea the bow of a great vessel emerges in ghostly detail. I have never seen the ship—nor has anyone for 73 years—yet I know nearly every feature of her. She is S.S. *Titanic*, the luxury liner lost after collision with an iceberg in 1912 at a cost of 1,522 lives.
>
> The sea has preserved her well...the lines of the deck's teak planking are visible beneath a thin coating of "snow" formed by remains of marine organisms. Other features stand out in the strobe lights of our towed undersea vehicle. Twin anchor chains run from windlasses...beneath a tangle of cables to hawsepipes near the bow. A ventilator shaft lies open between the chains, and capstan heads stand on either side....

On different camera passes across the field of debris, bottles of wine, bed springs, chamber pots, bits of twisted railing, boiler coal, a metal serving platter all showed up on film. But it wasn't until the return trip, a year later, that *Alvin*, and its pilots, Ralph Hollis and Dudley Foster and Robert Ballard, de-

---

▶

In 1983, diver Doug Osborne, encased in "a submarine you can wear," called WASP, prepared to lift the coral- *encrusted wheel of the* Breadalbane, *a British ship lost in the Arctic 130 years before.*

236

scended 12,500 feet to view the *Titanic* for themselves. "My first direct view of *Titanic* lasted less than two minutes, but the stark sight of her immense black hull towering above the ocean floor will remain forever ingrained in my memory," Ballard wrote in 1986, then added:

> In a way I am sad we found her. After 33 hours of exploring her dismembered hulk, we know her fate, and it is not a pretty sight. Though still impressive in her dimensions, she is no longer the graceful lady that sank a mere five days into her maiden voyage, in 1912....Her beauty has faded, her massive steel plates are dissolving in rivers of rust, and her ornate woodwork has been devoured by an army of countless wood-boring organisms whose hollow calcium tubes now litter her barren shape. After years of gluttony the creatures starved and dropped dead at the table. I have no sympathy for them; they robbed *Titanic* of her last touch of elegance.
>
> *Titanic's* band has long since ceased to play. She is gone, home-ported at last. She will surely never be raised.

As stunning and romantic as was the adventure of seeing the *Titanic* with his own eyes, Ballard recognizes the limitations man's presence imposes:

> The day is fast approaching when that job can be done faster and better without man's physical presence in the sea....Until recently there has been no way of duplicating...man's sophisticated eyes and brain and articulating hands to solve complex problems or perform difficult tasks. Whatever the cost, and the risks, of transporting man into the deep, it has been worth it.

For the previous thirteen years Ballard had spent an average of four months out of the year at sea and logged countless hours crouched beneath the surface in one submersible or another. Many of his dives were made in partnership with the National Geographic Society—exploring the Mid-Atlantic Ridge, descending 20,000 feet into the Cayman Trough, studying the unique forms of life surrounding the warm springs in the Galápagos Rift, and discovering on the East Pacific Rise "black smokers"—hydrothermal vents that spew fluids hot enough to melt lead. "Certainly the dives were exciting," Ballard said, noting that they were "historic achievements, every one of them. But," he added,

> in 13 years I had managed to explore a mere 40 miles of undersea mountain range. There are more than 40,000 miles of such ranges throughout the world's oceans. Did I really want to spend the rest of my life in the hope of exploring another 80 or 100 miles at best?
>
> It seemed to me we had a choice. We could continue indefinitely with manned submersibles, which are limited in the time they can spend below by both their passengers' endurance and their expendable power supply.... [or] we could begin thinking of remotely operated deep-sea vehicles, sophisticated robots that could give man...a "telepresence" in the sea, an extension of his unique senses and capabilities to extreme depths without physically transporting him a foot below the surface.
>
> Through such robots man could remain under the sea for weeks instead of mere hours at a time, extending his reach immeasurably into earth's last great uncharted frontier. Equally important, via live television these machines could bring the wonders of the deep to countless millions rather than to the lucky few who are able to ride in submersibles.

When that happens, those pictures, too, are certain to appear in the *Geographic.*

Above: *One of the most widely used research submersibles ever built, the manned underwater vehicle* Alvin, *laden with instruments and remote-control sensors, has dived more than 1,700 times since being commissioned in 1964.*

Opposite: *The* Alvin's *crewmembers' unexpected 1977 discovery on the sea floor of bright red worms encased in white tubes—some as long as eight feet—clustered near a warm-water vent in the Galápagos Rift prompted scientific study of these oases of life in 1979. But to the layman the most dramatic voyage of discovery was* Alvin's *descent in 1986 to a depth of 12,500 feet to view the sunken remains of the once majestic White Star ocean liner* Titanic, *which sank with a loss of 1,522 lives after its collision with an iceberg on its maiden voyage in 1912.*

Overleaf: *Aboard* Alvin, *shown in this painting by Pierre Mion hovering over* Titanic's *crumpled bow, was Robert D. Ballard, who wrote in the December 1986* National Geographic, *"The stark sight of her immense black hull towering above the ocean floor will remain forever ingrained in my memory."*

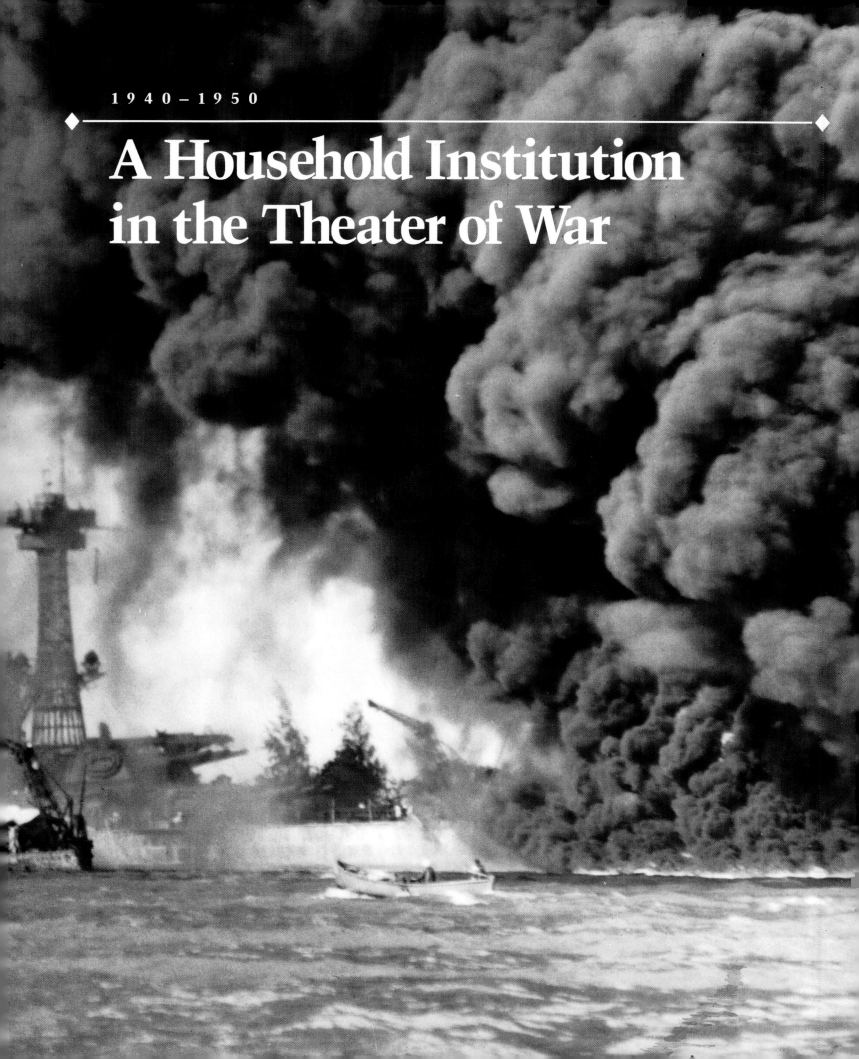

A Household Institution in the Theater of War

On July 26, 1942, the following editorial, "Footnote to Geography," appeared in *The New York Times:*

> For years Americans have been learning geography by the most pleasant method imaginable. They have learned about their own country at first hand and from automobile road maps. They have learned about the far corners of the world from newspaper accounts of famous flights and from the National Geographic Society, which itself seemed always to be sending out a new expedition to find and report on some unknown corner of the planet.
>
> Since the war began we have been learning still more geography, less pleasantly. Laconic military communiqués have told, often in veiled language, what was happening on remote battle fronts. Correspondents have gone with the armies to places remote even in the encyclopedias. And the newspapers have striven mightily to keep up with them for the daily readers.
>
> Inevitably, the newspapers have had to lean on many sources to make intelligible the brief and sometimes cryptic dispatches and communiqués. And chief among those sources is the old reliable National Geographic Society. Not only has it given generously of its information and opened its magnificent geographic library; it has published splendid war maps and it issues daily bulletins to assist the newspapers and news services.
>
> It is highly reassuring, when such place names as Staryi Oskol and Zivotin crop up in the communiqués, to be able to ask somebody what and where they are—and get the right answers. The N. G. S. hasn't failed us yet.

The first map supplement to have appeared in the *National Geographic* was the "Theatre of Military Operations in Luzon," distributed in the June 1899 Magazine, which marked Gilbert H. Grosvenor's first appearance on the masthead as Assistant Editor. The plates for that map had been borrowed from the government. But as the Society's membership and income grew, the young Editor was able to cease borrowing map plates or ordering maps from commercial cartographers and, eventually, as Grosvenor later recalled, "I was able to organize a highly competent research and cartographic staff to design and produce distinctive maps and to contribute original techniques and projections to the science of cartography."

Preceding spread: *Mortally wounded U.S. Navy battleships* West Virginia *and* Tennessee *lie shrouded in smoke after the December 7, 1941, Japanese carrier-plane surprise attack on the U.S. fleet anchored at Pearl Harbor, Hawaii.*

244

In 1916, Albert H. Bumstead, an accomplished mathematician, was appointed the Society's first chief cartographer. And it was under his tutelage that a corps of Geographic mapmakers began turning out the Society's remarkable maps—a production that, perhaps, reached its pinnacle of worldwide distinction during World War Two.

On January 15, 1945, while U.S. forces were recovering from the Battle of the Bulge, *The New York Times*, again in an editorial, saluted the Geographic, this time calling its mapmaking "probably the most ambitious cartographical undertaking on record," adding:

> The maps are to be found at the front, in the air, in our embassies and consulates, in business and newspaper offices, in schools. As a whole they constitute the most comprehensive atlas and gazeteer [sic] ever compiled—no mean achievement at a time like this....The Society deserves thanks for having undertaken voluntarily an important task in education. Its maps not only enable us to follow the war's progress but convince us, as never before, that China, Australia, and Europe are our next-door neighbors.

The *Times* editorial might have mentioned that the Society's maps had found their way into two other very high offices, as well. "One morning, just two weeks after Pearl Harbor, an aide to President Franklin D. Roosevelt called upon me at The Society's headquarters and asked for a map showing a town near Singapore then under Japanese attack," Gilbert H. Grosvenor later wrote.

The aide confided that he had come at the request of the President, who liked to see on a map the location of places in the war news. That morning, however, Mr. Roosevelt had not been able to find the headline-making little town on charts available in the White House. However, we had a map...and [I] gave it to the aide.

That afternoon, I ventured to send President Roosevelt a cabinet containing National Geographic Society maps mounted on rollers. These rollers were so conveniently arranged that the President, while sitting at his desk, could pull down the map of any area in the world that he wished to study....

Within an hour of its arrival at the White House, President Roosevelt had the cabinet mounted directly behind his study chair so that it was within easy reach.... The President's collection of National Geographic maps attracted the attention of more than one distinguished visitor. Prime Minister Winston Churchill was so keenly interested that President Roosevelt telephoned me and asked if The Society would make a duplicate cabinet for him to give Mr. Churchill.

Inscribed "WSC from FDR, Christmas 1943," the case with its maps covering the world was taken by President Roosevelt in his airplane to Cairo and given Mr. Churchill as a personal Christmas gift from the Chief Executive.

National Geographic Society maps, tacked up in kitchens, in dens, in youngsters' bedrooms all over this nation, enabled an entire generation of Americans to chart the daily progress of World War Two. Often, when battlegrounds shifted, that month's issue of the *Geographic*, with uncanny prescience, supplied the appropriate map. When the Germans seized Austria in March 1938, the Society issued a map of "Europe and the Mediterranean" in April. In October 1939, one month after the Nazis invaded Poland and annexed Danzig, and Britain and France declared war on Germany, members received a map of "Central Europe and the Mediterranean, as of September 1, 1939."

"Europe and the Near East" was issued in May 1940 as some 900 vessels of all types and sizes evacuated nearly 350,000 British and French troops from the beaches at Dunkirk. In March 1941 the Society issued a map of the "Indian Ocean Including Australia, New Zealand and Malaysia"; in May, the German battleship *Bismarck* was sunk. In June, the Germans invaded Russia; two months later, Churchill and Roosevelt met and signed the Atlantic Charter. The map of the "Atlantic Ocean," issued in September, covered the seas in which the German U-boat "wolf packs" were operating at peak, and, in time for Pearl Harbor three months later, members received a new "Map of The World."

The "Theater of War in the Pacific Ocean" reached members with the February 1942 issue. That following September, Fleet Admiral Chester W. Nimitz, flying to Henderson Field on Guadalcanal in a B-17, became lost in a driving rainstorm over the Coral Sea. "Studying the big 'Pacific Ocean' map's Solomon Islands inset," Gilbert H. Grosvenor later reported, "the Wartime Commander in Chief of the Pacific Fleet and his ten American and New Zealand aides identified the shore line of San Cristóbal Island in the southeastern Solomons below them. They were thus enabled to put the plane back on its course."

The Pacific Ocean map was followed by a map of "North America" in May 1942; the map of the "Theater of War in Europe, Africa, and Western Asia" in July; "South America" in October; and, in December 1942, "Asia and Adjacent Areas."

Fourteenth Army

U.S. military propaganda intended to mislead the enemy duped the Society as well. Included in its 1944 Insignia and Decorations of the U.S. Armed Forces booklet were twenty-one shoulder sleeve insignia for nonexistent U.S. Army units. Among the fraudulent patches depicted were those for the XXXI Corps, XXXIII Corps, Sixth and Ninth Airborne Divisions; and the Eleventh, Fourteenth, Seventeenth, and Twenty-second Divisions and the Eighteenth and Twenty-first Airborne Divisions—all part of a fake Fourteenth Army's equally fictitious two corps and nineteen divisions.

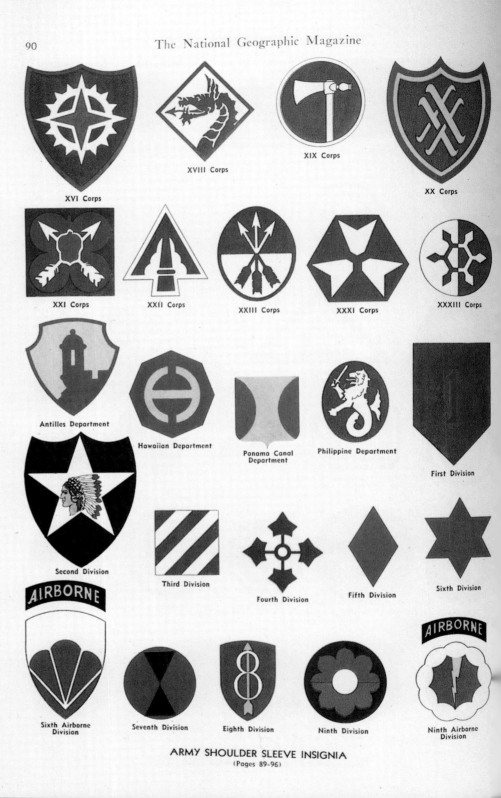

XVI Corps

XVIII Corps

XIX Corps

XX Corps

XXI Corps

XXII Corps

XXIII Corps

XXXI Corps

XXXIII Corps

Antilles Department

Hawaiian Department

Panama Canal Department

Philippine Department

First Division

Second Division

Third Division

Fourth Division

Fifth Division

Sixth Division

Sixth Airborne Division

Seventh Division

Eighth Division

Ninth Division

Ninth Airborne Division

ARMY SHOULDER SLEEVE INSIGNIA
(Pages 89-96)

Tenth Light Division

Eleventh Division

Eleventh Airborne Division

Thirteenth Airborne Division

Fourteenth Division

Seventeenth Division

Seventeenth Airborne Division

Eighteenth Airborne Division

Twenty-first Airborne Division

Twenty-second Division

Twenty-fourth Division

Twenty-sixth Division

Twenty-seventh Division

Twenty-eighth Division

Twenty-ninth Division

Thirtieth Division

Thirty-first Division

Thirty-second Division

Thirty-third Division

Thirty-fourth Division

Thirty-fifth Division

Thirty-sixth Division

Thirty-seventh Division

Thirty-eighth Division

Fortieth Division

Forty-first Division

Forty-second Division

Forty-third Division

Forty-fourth Division

ARMY SHOULDER SLEEVE INSIGNIA
(Pages 89-96)

"GI Joe Shares 'Mess Kit Luck' with Two Young Admirers. The shoulder sleeve insignia identifies him as a member of Lt. Gen. Mark W. Clark's Fifth Army in Italy. Lt. Gen. Lucian K. Truscott, Jr., succeeded General Clark as commander of the Fifth Army," was the caption that ran with this photograph in the Magazine.

By then Lt. Col. Jimmy Doolittle's sixteen carrier-launched B-25s had bombed Tokyo; the Bataan Death March had taken place; Russians and Germans were fighting in the ruins of Stalingrad; and the murder of millions of Jews and political prisoners by the Nazis had begun.

In 1943, the Allied forces in North Africa were placed under General Dwight D. Eisenhower's command; the Japanese were driven off Guadalcanal; U.S. forces landed in New Guinea; and the Allies invaded Sicily, then mainland Italy. Society maps of "Africa" were issued in February, the "Northern and Southern Hemispheres" in April, "Europe and the Near East" in June, and the "Pacific Ocean and the Bay of Bengal" in September, the month Italy surrendered. An updated "World Map" came out that December.

In April 1944, at the suggestion of the United States Army, the Society issued a map of "Japan and Adjacent Regions of Asia and the Pacific Ocean." The center of the map was the heart of Tokyo.

"So highly did the Army Air Forces regard this map of Japan," Gilbert Grosvenor recalled, "that they immediately borrowed the original drawings from The Society and made 5,000 enlargements on sheets 50 by 65 inches for use in over-all planning in the air offensive...."

On June 6, 1944, D-Day, the Allies invaded France; 1,000 transports and gliders dropped paratroopers on Normandy early that morning while 1,000 R.A.F. and 1,400 U.S. bombers provided air support and attacked installations. At 6:30 A.M. assault troops from British, U.S., French, and Polish divisions waded ashore along the sixty-mile-long Carentan-Bayeux-Caen beachline and fought their way inland.

In Italy, Monte Cassino and Rome were occupied by the Allies.

And the following month a National Geographic Society "Map of Germany and Its Approaches" was issued to members. The Army Corps of Engineers made enlargements of this map for use by ground and air forces in Europe and posted copies at road intersections along the Allied forces' routes of advance into Germany.

Lt. Gen. Eugene Reybold, then Chief of Engineers, U.S. Army, wrote Gilbert H. Grosvenor: "Our dependence upon the National Geographic Society for the type of map it issues has, in fact, led us to consider The Society an integral part of our military mapping establishment."

Nine times during a single year the *National Geographic Magazine*'s plates for its big ten-color wall-map supplements had to be put back on the presses to supply the needs of the Army, Navy, and other government agencies.

In August 1944, Allied troops liberated Paris.

In October, as the membership received its map of "Southeast Asia and Pacific Islands From the Indies and the Philippines to the Solomons," General MacArthur returned to the Philippines. That same month the Battle of Leyte Gulf took place—the biggest naval action ever waged. American and Japanese ships fought in three separate engagements: in the Surigao Strait, off Samar and off Cape Engaño. And Japanese naval power suffered a devastating blow.

By February 1945, Manila was recaptured; Corregidor was reoccupied by the first of March. That month's issue had a new map of "The Philippines."

Hitler committed suicide on April 30, 1945; German units began surrendering on May 4, and unconditional surrender was signed three days later, on May 7, 1945. V-E Day was proclaimed the following day.

On August 6, 1945, the United States dropped an atomic bomb on Hiroshima, Japan, population about 350,000. On August 9, a second atomic bomb

Left: *"No Time to Prink in the Mirrorlike Tail Assembly of a Liberator"* stated the unblushing caption for this photograph, and it went on to point out: *"About a third of the country's aircraft workers are women. Many jobs they do as well as men; some they do better. Riveting, a kind of needle point in metals, is one of women's standout operations."— From the August 1944 issue*

Below left: *Wartime gas rationing was absent from this photograph's cheery caption, "Soldiers, WACS, and Government Girls Sight-seeing by Bicycle Make Washington Look Like Amsterdam-on-Potomac."—From the September 1943 issue*

Below: *This photograph of Jane Russell wearing a Dorothy Lamour–type sarong and posed in front of several National Geographic Society maps never appeared in the Magazine.*

was dropped, on Nagasaki, population about 250,000. More than 150,000 Japanese were killed. On August 14, V-J Day, Japan surrendered. The formal surrender ceremony took place on board the U.S.S. *Missouri*, anchored in Tokyo Bay, on September 2, 1945.

In the course of the war the armed services "drew heavily on The Society's collection of 53,000 maps from all over the world," Gilbert Grosvenor later wrote, "many of them large-scale charts of strategic cities, harbors, railroads, air routes, and caravan trails; the vast file of unpublished manuscripts containing geographical data unavailable in print; and our library of some 20,000 travel books. Scores of Government agencies consulted The Society's research departments daily for elusive geographical information needed in war planning."

Even before the Japanese bombed Pearl Harbor the Army and Navy intelligence services were given access to the Society's entire collection of photographs. Although originally taken for "peaceful educational purposes," these photographs provided invaluable documentation of harbors, beaches, industrial sites, bridge crossings, airfields, waterfronts, railroad marshaling yards and other potential targets. Suddenly all those photographs taken over the previous decade showing European sites "as seen from the air" and "an airplane view of" were invaluable when compared with reconnaissance photographs because camouflage and new construction could be readily distinguished. By the war's end over 35,000 prints of National Geographic photographs, selected by the government, had been delivered to the appropriate intelligence agencies.

At its July 2, 1949, convention in Chicago, the Air Force Association presented the National Geographic Society with a Citation of Honor:

> World War II introduced global conflict for the first time in history, and with it the demand for cartographic information to guide American airmen and airplanes to the far corners of the earth and back again.
>
> That the military services could not meet this demand was part of national unpreparedness. That a non-military agency, the National Geographic Society, could help fill the breach was at once a tribute to the significance of this organization and a testimonial to the civilian contribution that made victory possible.
>
> The maps and charts of The Society guided men of the Air Force over the waters of the Atlantic and the ice caps of the Far North; over the islands of the Caribbean and the jungles of South America; helped build the air routes of Africa; went with the men of the Air Force over the Himalayas from India to China; took airmen up the long, hard island route of the Pacific from near defeat in Australia to victory in Japan.
>
> For its ability to meet the emergency requirements of its country, for its invaluable contributions to the Air Force in accomplishing a global mission, the National Geographic Society is awarded this Citation of Honor for outstanding public service.

Despite the fact that scores of editorial and clerical workers had entered the armed services, the *Geographic* continued to print the sort of articles it had run during World War One—timely, informative, chatty, often relentlessly cheerful pieces like: "Lisbon—Gateway to Warring Europe" ("Lisbon is filled with representatives of foreign powers....Some are spies, but the majority are engaged in ordinary commercial work") and "Lend-Lease is a Two-way Benefit" (with a photograph of smiling English school children, spoons raised over bowls of vegetables, or waiting in line for breakfast, plates in hand, captioned "Who Wouldn't Share His Vegetables to Keep These Little Allies Healthy and

Above: *Utah Beach just after D day, June 6, 1944. Landing craft unload tanks, trucks, and supplies on the beach in Normandy, France, as part of the largest invasion armada in history. The following month the Society issued its "Map of Germany and Its Approaches" and the Army Corps of Engineers posted enlarged copies of it at road intersections along the Allied Forces' routes of advance into Germany.*

Left: *"The armed services...drew heavily on The Society's collection of 53,000 maps from all over the world," Grosvenor wrote in his 1957 history of the Society. Chief of Staff General Dwight D. Eisenhower, shown here in his post-war Pentagon office, consults a Society map of Germany like that which traveled with him during his 1945 offensive.*

Smiling!"). And, too, there were the sort of upbeat military service-oriented articles seen before: "QM, the Fighting Storekeeper," "Your Dog Joins Up," "When GI Joes Took London," and "Okinawa, Threshold to Japan," with photographs by a young Lt. David Douglas Duncan, U.S.M.C., who would later gain fame as a photojournalist for his *Time* and *Life* magazine combat photographs of Marines in Korea and Vietnam. (The Okinawa photographs, however, were post-battle.)

In the meantime, the Society's News Service was sending daily news bulletins to hundreds of newspapers with information on the battlefields (a typical bulletin might have discussed the terrain, the flora and fauna of the battle scene and provided a guide to the pronunciation of the more difficult area place names); and the familiar *School Bulletin* was furnishing much the same service for its tens of thousands of teacher and student recipients. Though short of manpower, the Society's "chin up in the face of adversity" was expected by the membership. The Society, in turn, expected no less of its family of members, and in July 1943 the *Geographic* "did something that no other publication would dream of," *Newsweek* reported. "To an experimental block of 100,000 readers Dr. Grosvenor calmly suggested that 1944 dues be paid now so as to lighten year-end billings. Four days later, 2,000 favorable replies had come in. The naturalist-editor wore a pleased smile."

What sort of people were the 1943 Society's 1,199,738 loyal members? In a 1941 Society booklet, under the heading "How National Geographic Family Heads Earn Their Incomes," 529 different categories were listed, among them: dentists and dental surgeons (11,715), executives (13,710), clerks (32,589), barbers (1,557), undertakers (3,000), bartenders (39), politicians (228), senators (159), congressmen (123), college matrons (261), college presidents (456), masseurs (156), poets (15), tropical-fish raisers (3), clergymen (27,843), farmers (36,816), bankers (15,084), philanthropists (9), physicians and surgeons (53,514), road builders (207), lighthouse keepers (126), housewives (39,543), and royalty (114).

And it is perhaps because of the Editor's deliberate effort to make the membership feel that they were all part of one big, happy family that in addition to the thousands of affectionate letters the Magazine received, it also received its share of rebukes: "Don't take us through any more Himalayas or over any more glaciers."

Others were equally blunt:

"Captions poor."

"Text poor."

"Don't care for North and South Pole articles."

"Don't care for prehistoric bones, carvings, or figures."

"Did not care for the Cats."

"Less tiresome discourse."

"Europe, Asia, and Africa do not interest us."

"Authors are not all they should be."

And one that must have cut the Chief to the quick: "Birds—less."

All letters, of praise or rebuke, were answered, although some, such as the reply to the boy who wrote simply, "I am studying the world...send me everything you have," must have given pause.

On February 15, 1942, the Washington *Star*'s Sunday section reported on the preventive measures taken by the Society against air raids in a piece headlined GEOGRAPHIC SOCIETY RAID DRILL EMPTIES BUILDING IN 3 MINUTES and with

" 'Uncle Sam Is a Good Egg,' British School Children Agree. The blackboard tells the story as hungry youngsters take bacon and eggs to frying pans in September, 1941. Then an egg was an event, and it was still in its shell. Not so today; dehydration removes shell and moisture, too."
— From the June 1943 issue

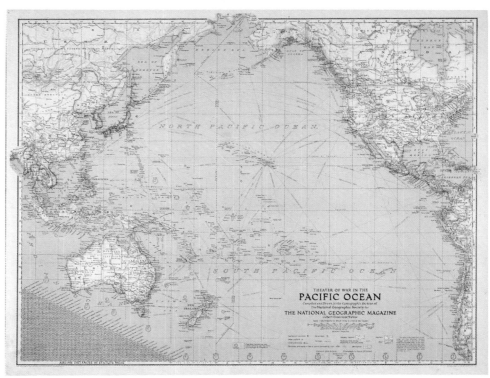

Above: *General Douglas MacArthur receives the Japanese surrender on September 2, 1945, aboard the battleship U.S.S.* Missouri *anchored in Tokyo Bay. Signing for Japan is Major General Yohijiro Umezo.*

Fleet Admiral Chester W. Nimitz, standing farthest left with other senior military and naval officers of the Allied powers, would later write Gilbert H. Grosvenor that the Society had "lent an unexpected but most welcome hand" when the Commander in Chief of the Pacific Fleet was aboard a B-17 flying from Espíritu Santo and became lost in a pouring rainstorm. Nimitz and his companions, with the help of the Society's "Theater of War in the Pacific Ocean" map (right), were able to recognize islands beneath them and landed safely at Guadalcanal's Henderson Field.

the subhead: *226 Employes* [sic] *Fill Evacuation Room; Sand Bags, Pumps Kept in Readiness*. The article went on to say:

> Probably no building in Washington is better prepared to protect its occupants from death or injury in an air raid than the Geographic Society headquarters. The drills going on are part of a well-planned program which the society believes will provide ample protection to its employes if air raids should start.
>
> Charles Althoff, an employe in the shipping department, merely pushed a button and three long blasts blared from seven automobile horns placed at strategic locations. Before the series of three blasts could be repeated, the first employes were filing in the safest room in the building—the cafeteria in the basement.
>
> While the alarm was being sounded again, Dr. Gilbert Grosvenor... reached the evacuation room....
>
> Few things have been missed in making the evacuation room safe from almost anything but a demolition bomb. The society's defense chieftains claim the cafeteria is practically bomb-proof and concussion-proof. Windows on the side next to an alley have been bricked on the outside. Doors leading into the cafeteria have been covered with monk's cloth, and a 16-inch-thick brick wall, 1½ feet higher than the basement windows, has been built along the entire front of the building to prevent bomb fragments from crashing in the windows.
>
> Dozens of big bags full of sand are ready for instant use in barricading three doorways leading from the cafeteria to the kitchen....
>
> A special room has been constructed in another section of the basement for the defense work. Here are located the mechanism which will set the automobile warning horns in operation, as well as all sorts of supplies such as shovels, pick-axes, hoes, radio equipment, bottles of distilled water, asbestos shields and stirrup pumps for fighting fires, flashlights, hundreds of feet of hose and all the other necessary equipment....
>
> Each secretary, stenographer, file clerk and typist has a small canvas bag tacked on the side of her desk. When an alarm sounds, they quickly jam all their important documents into the bag and drop it into large galvanized cans placed in each room. The cans then are picked up by the warden staff and taken to the basement.

The article—illustrated by photographs of a woman employee looking at a stack of sandbags placed in front of the Society headquarters' kitchen door, of Dr. Grosvenor watching a male employee pretending to telephone Society plane spotters on the headquarters' roof, and of the building warden pointing at the sixteen-inch-thick brick wall—then went on to report how the Society's "priceless collection of photographs...are in fireproof vaults on an upper floor," and that the Explorers' Room exhibits were considered safe on the first floor.

However, when air raid drills weren't being held, life in the Society's Washington headquarters continued seemingly undisturbed.

In the fall of 1943 *The New Yorker* magazine published "Geography Unshackled," a three-part profile of Gilbert H. Grosvenor written by Geoffrey T. Hellman. In it, Hellman described the *Geographic*'s Editor as "a kindly, mild-mannered, purposeful, poker-faced, peripatetic man of sixty-seven, endowed with the sprightly air of an inquiring grasshopper, with a clear, pink complexion, and with the mixture of business sagacity, intellectual curiosity, regard for tradition, and tolerance of temperate innovation that is sometimes found in the president of a fairly wealthy college," and told how, "around four or five in the afternoon, just before he leaves for the day, the editor of the *Geographic*,

*"A BIKINI FAMILY SAYS FAREWELL AT
THE GRAVE OF A LOVED ONE" was the
title of a picture illustrating Carl
Markwith's July 1946* National
Geographic *article "Farewell to
Bikini." The Bikinians were being
moved from their atoll so that their
homeland could be used for atomic
tests. "Civilization and the Atomic
Age had come to Bikini," Markwith
wrote, "and they had been in the way."*

who does not touch alcohol or tobacco or accept advertisements for them in his periodical, pours some powdered Ovaltine onto a shoehorn, deposits it in a Lily cup filled with...[warm milk], stirs it with a penholder, and drinks it down with a pleased expression."

Nowhere, perhaps, was life at the Society during this period better captured than in this description of Hellman's:

> The twenty or so editors of the *Geographic*, all of them notably polite individuals who are forever bowing to one another through the sculptured bronze doors of their elevators, move in a leisurely welter of thick rugs, bookshelves stocked with British and American *Who's Who's*, encyclopedias, bound volumes of the *Geographic*, and geographical books published by the Society; interoffice memorandum slips with "Memorandum from Dr. Grosvenor," "Memorandum from Dr. La Gorce," or the like printed at the top; incoming correspondence stamped, in purple ink, "Commendation," "Criticism," or "Suggestions;" and photostatic copies of appreciative letters from generals, admirals, coördinators, and ex-Presidents to whom the Society has presented maps or turned over geographic research, much of it bearing on the war. The editors of the *Geographic* freshen up in rooms where the towels are hung under a hierarchy of name cards; in one room the cards read, from left to right, "Dr. Grosvenor, Dr. La Gorce, Mr. Fisher, Mr. M. B. Grosvenor, Mr. Simpich, Mr. Hildebrand, Mr. Bumstead, Dr. Williams, Mr. Borah, Mr. Riddiford, Mr. Canova, Mr. Vosburgh, Mr. L. J. Canova, Guests, Guests, Mr. Nicholas." For business errands around town, such as trips to the magazine's circulation annex or to its printers, the firm of Judd & Detweiler, the editors have a fleet of five chauffeur-driven cars. They lunch in three private dining rooms, drinking buttermilk, exchanging puns, and ordering excellent à-la-carte meals from menus on which prices are discreetly omitted. One of these dining rooms is reserved for Dr. Grosvenor, and he sometimes eats there alone, like the captain of a ship. This room adjoins a bathroom containing two marble shower baths, which in sticky weather are occasionally patronized not only by Dr. Grosvenor but other of the more important staff members. Next to the private dining rooms is a cafeteria where lesser employees lunch well and inexpensively but without access to as wide a selection of food as is afforded their betters. Here the sexes are segregated, a partition separating the men from the women. "We prefer not to mix 'em up," an officer of the Society once explained. "We feel the men are freer in their own room. If they want to swap a risqué anecdote or two, they can do it." Every now and then, private-dining-room delicacies are displayed, by mistake, in the cafeteria. On one of these occasions, a stenographer, sliding her tray along, pointed to a dish which had captured her fancy. "My goodness, no," said the counter maid. "That's the officers' liver."

Hellman, noting also in his *New Yorker* profile Gilbert Grosvenor's interest in birds, pointed out:

> This war, like the last one, has made the editor of the *Geographic* go easy on birds in his magazine, recent issues of which have featured articles on United States food production, the Alaskan highway, the Coast Guard, Army dogs, convoys, aircraft carriers, women in uniform, and military and naval insignia, but he knows that wars are fleeting affairs compared to birds and he does not propose to wait for the end of the conflict before again doing justice, editorially, to his favorite topic. "The Chief has been begging us to run a series of color photographs on the wrens of Australia for the past three years," a *Geographic* editor recently told an acquaintance. "Everyone conspires to keep him from using these goddam birds. We keep putting him off, but he'll sneak them in any month now."

The first recipient of the Grosvenor Medal was Gilbert H. Grosvenor, to whom it was awarded on May 19, 1949, for "outstanding service to geography as editor of the National Geographic, 1899–1949."

This Selz caricature accompanied Geoffrey T. Hellman's "Geography Unshackled," a three-part profile of Gilbert H. Grosvenor that appeared in The New Yorker in the fall of 1943. Hellman described Grosvenor as "a kindly, mild-mannered, purposeful, poker-faced, peripatetic man of sixty-seven, endowed with the sprightly air of an inquiring grasshopper."

He did. But not until the October 1945 Magazine article "The Fairy Wrens of Australia."

The post-war cartographic staff was kept busy, since the upheavals of World War Two had resulted in the realignment of nations, the redrawing of national boundaries, and the renaming of countries and cities. The remapping of almost the entire face of the globe was required.

The Atomic Age, ushered in by Hiroshima and Nagasaki, was marked in October 1945 by "Your New World of Tomorrow" and in July 1946 by Carl Markwith's "Farewell to Bikini," a piece about moving the native inhabitants of Bikini Atoll in the Ralik Chain of the Marshall Islands to another island so their home could be used for atomic tests. "As good-byes were being called back and forth, I found myself wishing that I could say, as I had each time before, Kim naj drol ilju—'We shall return tomorrow.' I refrained," Markwith wrote, "because there would be no returning for me—nor perhaps for them. Civilization and the Atomic Age had come to Bikini, and they had been in the way."

In January 1947, the Magazine published Melville Bell Grosvenor's "Cuba—American Sugar Bowl," illustrated by forty-two of his color prints, a record for the number of color photographs used in a single story.

"The article, full of hope," the current National Geographic Editor Wilbur E. Garrett wrote in 1984, "gave little hint of the forces and problems even then incubating in Cuba that would soon lead this seemingly semicolonial island nation to become a focus of concern and frustration for United States Latin American policy for decades and even to this day. Yet Cuba was only symptomatic of the postwar storm of change that would toss nations, colonies, and continents like rag dolls in the hands of angry children. Sweeping change was overtaking the map of Africa. Iron, bamboo, and no-name curtains cut off hundreds of millions of people from one another."

No such changes swept over the Geographic; instead it was more of the same: pieces like "Carefree People of the Cameroons," "Weighing the Aga Khan in Diamonds," "'Flying Squirrels,' Nature's Gliders," "Yemen—Southern Arabia's Mountain Wonderland," "First American Ascent of Mount St. Elias," "Rhode Island, Modern City-State," and, in April 1949, an entire issue devoted to "The British Way."

One month later, on May 18, 1949, at the Chevy Chase Club, just outside Washington, in Chevy Chase, Maryland, the Society's trustees honored Gilbert Hovey Grosvenor's fiftieth anniversary as Editor of the National Geographic Magazine with an unofficial dinner attended by those of the staff whose names appeared on the Magazine's masthead, by department heads, and by a few personal friends. The following evening, at the anniversary celebration held in Washington's Constitution Hall, 4,000 guests witnessed the first presentation of a newly designed gold disk with a bas-relief profile of Gilbert H. Grosvenor on one side and signs of the zodiac and a globe on the other. Only an outsider to the Society might think it odd that the first recipient of the new Grosvenor Medal should be Gilbert Hovey Grosvenor himself. Within the Society, however, it raised no more questions than would a monarchy based on the divine right of kings.

"Always accepting praise modestly," Albert W. Atwood wrote in "Gilbert H. Grosvenor's Golden Jubilee" for the Magazine's August 1949 issue, "this generous, gracious, and gentle Editor invariably gives unstinted credit to others. He said at the anniversary celebration in Constitution Hall:

I would not have you exaggerate my part. I realize more keenly than anyone else possibly can that the success of the National Geographic Society, which you generously ascribe so largely to my humble efforts, was brought about by the wise counsel and unswerving support always given me by the distinguished gentlemen of the Board of Trustees and by the faithful and brilliant services of the many remarkably able men and the wonderfully skillful women composing The Society staff...."

Unknown in advance to Dr. Grosvenor, twelve notable leaders of National Geographic Society expeditions had been gathered on the platform to see him receive the medal. Among these expedition leaders were:

Rear Admiral Richard E. Byrd (the first man to fly over the North and South Poles); former U.S. Senator Hiram Bingham (discoverer of the lost Inca city of Machu Picchu); Dr. Dillon Ripley (leader of the Nepal expedition completed only weeks before and future Secretary of the Smithsonian Institution); Dr. Robert F. Griggs (Valley of Ten Thousand Smokes); Maj. Gen. Orvil A. Anderson (*Explorer* balloon stratosphere flights); Dr. Matthew W. Stirling (archeological discoveries in Panama and Mexico; he was present with his wife, Marion); Dr. Maurice Ewing (explorer of the Mid-Atlantic Ridge); and Dr. Arthur A. Allen (who had solved the 163-year-old mystery of the bristle-thighed curlew's nesting place).

A motion picture of the highlights of each of the expeditions, with brief commentaries by their leaders, was shown, and then Trustee and Treasurer of the Society Dr. Robert V. Fleming read a letter of congratulations from President Harry S Truman, which said in part, "Under your direction The Society's magazine has become a household institution in the homes of America and throughout the nations of the world—in short, wherever there is a postal system and wherever geographic knowledge is esteemed."

National Geographic Society Treasurer Fleming then introduced Dr. Charles F. Kettering, former Director of Research and Vice President of General Motors, and a Trustee of the Society, who made the formal presentation of the Grosvenor Medal, which had been created by the Board of Trustees especially for the anniversary celebration.

"Presenting this medal is the most appreciated of all the many pleasures life has brought me," Dr. Kettering said. "If there ever is 'one world,' a copy of the *National Geographic* will be on the center of the table!"

Dr. Kettering presented the medal to Dr. Grosvenor, who, Atwood later reported in the *Geographic*, "held it up for the vast audience to see, in a friendly, unstudied gesture as if to share it with his friends, which brought the crowd to its feet for prolonged cheering.

" 'Every morning when I look into my mirror,' he said, 'I am going to say to my mirror, "You lie." Then I shall take this beautiful medal, look at the idealized Grosvenor face on it which Mrs. [Laura Gardin] Fraser has modeled with fingers of genius, and chuckle to myself! My descendants happily will not know the difference between fact and fiction.'"

A basket of fifty golden roses stood on the speaker's platform. They had been presented to Grosvenor by his National Geographic colleagues. The inscription, "To Our Beloved Chief," Grosvenor told the audience, meant as much to him as "this glorious medal."

The *Geographic*'s circulation at the end of 1949 was 1,831,588; its circulation would continue to climb during the five more years that Gilbert H. Grosvenor would serve as Editor. Its reputation, however, had begun to decline.

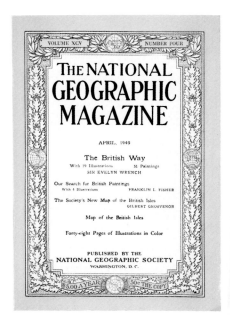

At the end of 1949, the Magazine's circulation was 1,831,588.

"Young Men Put Into the Earth"

"The names have a power, a life, all their own. Even on the coldest days, sunlight makes them warm to the touch. Young men put into the earth, rising out of the earth. You can feel their blood flowing again."

—On the Vietnam Veterans Memorial, in Joel L. Swerdlow's "To Heal a Nation," May 1985

The *National Geographic's* coverage of wars and conflicts during Gilbert Hovey Grosvenor's editorship was determined, for the most part, by how loosely the staff was able to interpret his fifth and sixth editorial guiding principles:

- Nothing of a partisan or controversial character is printed.
- Only what is of a kindly nature is printed about any country or people, everything unpleasant or unduly critical being avoided.

Geographic writers' efforts to produce responsible journalism within the restrictions imposed by Grosvenor's principles were what led, over the years, to accusations that the *Geographic* viewed the world through rose-colored glasses. And the example repeatedly given to support that charge was Douglas Chandler's 1937 article, "Changing Berlin," which in hindsight one now recognizes as appallingly innocent:

> To develop boys and girls in body and mind, and thus insure a sturdy race to defend Germany in the future, is a policy of the present government. ...As a substitute for Scout training, German youngsters now join an institution known as the Hitler Youth organization. Its emblem is the swastika, and its wide activities and political training are enormously popular with all classes.

Curiously enough, Grosvenor's policy had its defenders even in those journalistic camps one would assume most opposed. For instance, on June 21, 1940, *The Detroit News* contained the following editorial:

> How the National Geographic Magazine carries on, month after month, with only an occasional word to suggest its awareness of the war is, on its face, something of a miracle, as publishing goes these days. To write anything now for public consumption which is in no way associated with a war that rocks all mankind is an effort. To assemble any quantity of non-war material that can lure us even momentarily from our dark preoccupation is no mean feat. To be able to get together a periodical on geography, of all things, and leave it out, borders on the supernatural.
>
> It is a policy of the Geographic and we should be grateful to it for trying, and for succeeding so well. And, of course, it is right. There is not much war can do to change physical geography. The Alps will be the Alps when the Caesars return to dust. Old Faithful will spout; the great sea tortoises will waddle ashore on Galopagos [sic]; the Mediterranean will be as

Above: *France, World War One. "An American Ambulance Rolling Through A Ruined Town In France."* — From the May 1917 issue

Opposite: *France, World War One.* The Rampart of Verdun, *drawing by the eminent French artist Lucien Jonas (1880–1947). "Those who held the pass at Thermopylae...Horatius and his comrades at the bridge....First among the immortals of history now stand the defenders of Verdun, who said: 'They shall not pass.'"* —From the April 1918 issue

Preceding spread: *"The names have a power, a life, all their own,"* wrote Joel L. Swerdlow of the Vietnam Memorial. *"Even on the coldest days, sunlight makes them warm to the touch. Young men put into the earth...."* —From "To Heal a Nation," in the May 1985 issue

Above: *London, World War Two. Prime Minister Winston Churchill examines the bomb-shattered ruins of the legislative chamber of Great Britain's House of Commons in 1941, one year after standing before its members to say, "I have nothing to offer but blood, toil, tears and sweat."—From the August 1965 issue*

Opposite: *"December 29, 1940: London's burning. The pall of smoke from 1,500 fires enshrouds her homes, her churches, her dead. But, its golden cross burnished by the flames, St. Paul's dome rides above the searing storm. Like London, St. Paul's was scarred, hit by a bomb two months earlier. Like London, the cathedral would endure."*

blue, and the Sahara the same restless sea of sand. The land will not change, and neither—over much of the earth—will the people who go with it. They will draw their life and sustenance from the nature around them. The races that spring from it will be molded, for good or ill, by necessities imposed on them by nature.

Coverage of World War One had never been anything but supportive of the Allied powers. The *Geographic* took measure of Germany's aspirations and wrote, "Paltry indeed seem the dominions of all the tyrants of the past, who attempted to 'wade through the slaughter' to the throne of world empire, compared with the vaulting ambition of the Hohenzollerns for Prussianizing the earth...."

Bloody World War One battles were hinted at, kept in the distance. "Plain Tales from the Trenches" takes place not along the Somme or in Verdun, but "As Told Over the Tea Table in Blighty—a Soldiers' 'Home' in Paris":

All the long tables are ready for tea. The cloths are blue and white and so are the dishes. The milk pitchers are full to running over, the jam bowls too, and the large plates of fresh, sweet-smelling bread and butter are just where they ought to be. And there's cake—the good kind, full of raisins and currants and nuts. Why, there's even plenty of *sugar*! So, as I tie on my absurd little apron I say to myself that it doesn't look like a war-time tea at all.

But it is, in the fullest sense of the word....

The first three to come to my table are "Kangaroos"—tall and straight, freshly shaven, uniforms brushed and pressed, boots of a dazzling brilliance....a fourth man wearing the same divisional colors on his sleeve joins our group to the gay shout of "Hello, Digger," which is only another name for "mate," you know.

Then: "Where's Barty? Didn't he come along with you?"

The newcomer shakes his head, and when he is asked "Why not?" answers simply, "Dead." To a further question of "When?" he replies, "Monday." And Barty's only requiem from three husky throats is, "He was a good bloke."

The author, Carol K. Corey, temporarily leaves her table in the tea-room. When she returns she finds:

a hot-headed chap storming indignantly: "There you go again, talking about the war. There ought to be a law"—

"That's so," interpolates his neighbor. "What else do we know after three years of it? You pick a nice, new, interesting subject and tell us about it. Why not give us a little lecture on *mud*? That's always interesting to the ladies. They say 'Poor dear' so sweetly that you forget to tell them the one good thing about it, which is that it keeps you warm. I never had a cold till I got here and cleaned it off. And look what a 'beaut' I've got now. I tell you, Missus, the mud's never hurt me. Neither has the war. Why, I used to have asthma somethin' fierce; but now it's all 'partee.' If we get home with all our arms and legs and eyes—or just enough to get on with—this here war's goin' to be a good thing for a lot of us.

"Of course, I ain't sayin' it's pleasant; far from it. There's the route marches and the everlastin' salutin' and the bully beef and the bumps on the ground at night. But there's compensations. Take my case. I had *three* sisters all learning the piano at once, and all of 'em dubs at it. Yeah, it could be worse. Pass the cake, Kid."

"...It could be worse. Pass the cake, Kid" ran in the March 1918 issue. And should the Society membership want some cake for themselves, the April 1918 issue of the *Geographic* asked its members to do without. "...there is a new

opportunity for helping by personal deprivation," the article read, "...opportunity of *pledging himself and his household to eat neither wheat bread, wheat cereals, nor pastry made of wheat flour until the new wheat crop is harvested.*"

Gilbert Hovey Grosvenor remained in place as Editor through World War Two—as did his editorial principles. The January 1944 article, "At Ease in the South Seas," was typical of the conventional homefront morale-boosting articles the *Geographic* was running. Written by Frederick Simpich, Jr., son of longtime *Geographic* Assistant Editor Frederick Simpich, the article told of soldiers' efforts in the South Pacific to keep amused between battles. His piece contained photographs of shirtless GIs sitting around a crate—"Even on Guadalcanal Card Games Have Kibitzers"; their pets—"On Coral Sands, 'Scuttlebutt' the Pup Wears Camouflage on All but Ears"; a sailor dozing in a barnyard bunk—" 'Turn Out and Turn To!' Says This Army Horse Nuzzling a Sleeping Sailor"; and a helmeted soldier posed in his foxhole which has the sign "Beneath These Portals Pass the Fastest Men in the World!" is captioned "Laughs Aimed at Themselves Keep Marines' Morale High in Oft-bombed Guadalcanal."

War was seen as little more than an inconvenience.

"We had an extremely heavy raid one night just before I left London in January, 1941," Harvey Klemmer wrote in "Everyday Life in Wartime England" for the April 1941 *Geographic*:

> Bombs came shrieking down at the rate of one a minute. A number of fires were started, and a good share of the City—London's financial district—was wiped out.
>
> The crash of bombs and the glow of the fires gave us the feeling of living through some sort of medieval nightmare. Few got any sleep that night.
>
> It was almost with dread that I opened my curtains in the morning. But there was no reason for dread, then. The sun was shining brightly. Traffic moved in Berkeley Square as usual. I noticed that an old street sweeper, with whom I had become acquainted, was on the job. The attendants in apartment houses stood on the sidewalk, resplendent in their various uniforms. Models and seamstresses tripped into the gown shop up the street. Large posters in a travel agency window advertised cruises to Australia.
>
> In my own building the valets went about preparing breakfast and laying out clothes. When I went through the lobby, I noticed that one of the porters was very carefully shining the brass about the main entrance.
>
> The difference between that morning and the experiences of the night before is symbolic, to me, of the two kinds of life that now exist in England.

There were even opportunities during the war to have great fun. When Annapolis graduate Melville Bell Grosvenor was invited to take a cruise on a U.S. Navy escort carrier, he grabbed at the chance. Strapped into the rear-seat ball turret of a TBF Avenger torpedo plane, MBG was catapulted off the deck. After a mock-torpedo run on the ship, he wrote,

> Quickly the four planes joined the landing circle, wheeling gracefully around the carrier.

◀ ───

Pacific warfare, World War Two. Aboard the carrier U.S.S. Yorktown, near Truk in April 1944, artist William F. Draper records the York- *town's fight for life against attacking Japanese dive bombers and torpedo planes.*

1949, American and British aircraft made more than two hundred thousand flights into that beleaguered city with supply-carrying planes sometimes landing as often as one every forty-five seconds. More than two million tons of goods were brought in during that period. Post-war Berlin tensions were typified by pieces like "What I Saw Across the Rhine" (January 1947), "Airlift to Berlin" (May 1949), and "Berlin, Island in a Soviet Sea" (November 1951). Such articles were, however, seemingly written with détente in mind.

Gilbert H. Grosvenor and his cartographic department scored a timely triumph when the Magazine's "Roaming Korea South of the Iron Curtain"— containing a map of the Korean peninsula—appeared in June 1950, the month the North Korean Communist forces launched their attack across the Demilitarized Zone that had separated the two countries since the end of World War Two. Korean War reporting, however, remained of the old school: "Our Navy in the Far East," by Arthur W. Radford, and "The GI and the Kids of Korea," by Robert H. Mosier.

The 1956 Hungarian Revolution was covered by "Freedom Flight from Hungary" with Robert F. Sisson's moving photographs of Hungarian families processing through Austrian refugee centers.

And then on August 12, 1961, East German troops and People's Police— giving the excuse that it would keep "revenge-seeking politicians and agents of West German militarism" out of their territory—began construction of that monument to Communism's failure, the Berlin Wall. It was a Saturday night, a Berliner friend of *Geographic* freelancer Howard Sochurek recalled in 1970:

> A million people over there in East Berlin went to bed without any idea of what was going to happen. But I will bet that many of them were planning to get out of Communist Germany. More than three million people had fled the Soviet zone up to that time, and the rate was increasing to about 2,000 a day. You simply took a 20-pfennig train ride to the refugee camp at Marienfelde in West Berlin, since freedom of movement had been guaranteed by the protocols governing the city.
>
> At 2 a.m. on Sunday, tanks and trucks rolled in with East German troops and People's Police. Train service to the West stopped, stations were sealed, and building of the Wall began. A million people woke up in jail....

Not long after, Sochurek was in jail, too. His account of his arrest and that of Jürgen Toft, his East German interpreter, in East Berlin, was chillingly familiar:

> ...at about five o'clock one evening, while Jürgen and I were standing on the Elsenbrücke—a bridge across the Spree River—we were both arrested.
>
> I had been photographing the sunset on the river and the ducks paddling furiously to avoid a large coal barge that was passing by. I had just packed my cameras into their cases and was walking off the bridge when a member of the *Volkspolizei*—People's Police—stepped from a half-concealed guard post under the bridge and called, "*Halt.*"
>
> The uniformed "Vopo" approached and said, "Give me your credentials!"
>
> Jürgen handed over the identity card which every citizen of the GDR must carry, and a letter from the Reisebüro explaining my purpose in East Berlin. I presented my United States passport, complete with the East German visa and the police registration stamp recorded on the day of my arrival.

"You have violated the people's law," the "Vopo" said. "It is forbidden to photograph this port. It is forbidden to photograph the border. It is forbidden to photograph the railroad yard."

Across the street, faces began to appear in the windows of an old, six-story apartment building. They stared down at us—impassive and impersonal. Two sergeants in a dark-green Volga police car drove up. Our "Vopo" had obviously summoned them before he had even halted us.

"This document from the Reisebüro," he now said coldly, "is forged." Jürgen tensed visibly. His face paled. He turned to me and remarked in English, "This is getting serious."

One of the sergeants took our credentials and carried them to a call box across the street. We waited there for an hour until a call was returned.

"You will come with us."

Jürgen and I were instructed to sit in the back of the police car, and we were then driven away.

Sochurek and interpreter Toft were taken to the State Security Service offices in a former SS Headquarters building, up three flights of stairs beneath huge portraits of the German Democratic Republic's then Chairman of the State Council Walter Ulbricht and "Progress Through Work Builds Socialism" banners to a hallway where they were detained for several hours. Finally they were released with the apology that since their arrest had taken place outside of normal business hours, it had taken longer to contact the appropriate authorities.

Sochurek was not unknown to the Magazine's readers; he had already written some of the *Geographic*'s strongest stories on Vietnam—among them "American Special Forces in Action in Vietnam," a piece about the first stages of a revolt against the Republic of Vietnam by 3,000 heavily armed *montagnard* tribesmen in five Special Forces camps. Caught up with American Special Forces Capt. Vernon Gillespie in a war within a war, Sochurek wrote in 1965:

> Frankly, our situation, as I pieced it together, unnerved me. Here we are, I thought, surrounded by Viet Cong who nightly harass the camp with mortar and sniper fire. That isn't enough. The camp itself is indefensible against a large-scale attack. It could be overrun by a full battalion any time the Communists chose to do so—as they had done in July at another camp exactly like Gillespie's. Even that isn't enough. The camp is full of armed montagnards who resent the Government of South Vietnam and the Vietnamese officers on the spot.
>
> In a capsule, I thought, our situation here mirrored the complexity of the problem that the United States faces in Viet Nam.

One does not think of the *Geographic*, with its slow, leisurely, cautious, researched manner of publishing as a journal in which controversial war coverage might emerge. However, the first published photographs of armed American servicemen fighting in Vietnam appeared in Dickey Chapelle's "Helicopter War in South Viet Nam," a November 1962 piece which appeared the year President John F. Kennedy announced that U.S. advisers would fire if fired upon—the same year America's attention was turned not to Vietnam, but to the Cuban missile crisis.

And yet, even a year before Dickey Chapelle's article, W. E. Garrett and Peter T. White had gone to Vietnam to report on how "South Viet Nam Fights the Red Tide." This piece, published three years *before* Congress passed the Gulf of Tonkin Resolution authorizing presidential action in Vietnam and

Opposite: *Saudi Arabia, 1980. "Noontime summons princes and subjects to prayer," began the caption for this photograph of guards laying down their weapons and kneeling with petitioners alongside Prince Salman ibn Abdulaziz, Governor of Riyadh, and member of the Al Saud family, which has ruled the kingdom of Saudi Arabia since its founding in 1932.—From "Saudi Arabia: The Kingdom and Its Power," in the September 1980 issue*

four years before the large-scale commitment of U.S. troops, accurately and eerily warned of what was in store. While Garrett's photographs were, for the most part, of the conventional travelogue variety—Tet celebrants, temple interiors, seaport life, cyclo drivers, beautiful girls in flowing gowns—White's text was conspicuously grim. He wrote of the growing Viet Cong strength: "Quietly and relentlessly—with the world hardly aware of it yet—the rich country in the south was slipping ever deeper into a calculatedly cruel civil war....From dusk to dawn, the Viet Cong ruled nearly half of South Viet Nam."

But it was in the closing paragraphs of his article, with its hints of America's growing involvement and the hopelessness of such an action, that White's prescient appraisal appeared. "You've undoubtedly met the Viet Cong, you know," a South Vietnamese friend tells author White,

> "An elevator boy, or a shopkeeper, or a driver for MAAG. They are everywhere. They collect 'taxes' even in Saigon, by persuasion, or by threats. They give a receipt. If a man takes it to the police station, the Viet Cong kills him. Let the police catch him with it, and he might go to a re-education camp."
> I asked, "What will happen to Viet Nam?"
> "I hope for a miracle to save us," he said. "Otherwise the Viet Cong will get stronger. Will the Americans go home? Maybe they'll let their own soldiers fight. But how could they do better in the swamps and jungles than the French?"
> And what about my six girls, and the eager cadets? [White was asking of the six young women he had met at the Vietnamese-American Association and the cadets he'd spoken with at South Vietnam's Military Academy.]
> "Some will die, some will escape. But most people will have to stay and try to get along. One day you may face those boys across a conference table. Or across a battlefield. As our old primers say: Man is born good, but life makes him bad."

It is estimated that between August 4, 1964, and January 27, 1973, approximately 8,744,000 Americans saw service in Vietnam. Nevertheless, on April 30, 1975, South Vietnam surrendered to the Communists.

In the meantime, however, there had been and would continue to be other wars—wars between Israel and the Arab nations, India and Pakistan, Iran and Iraq, the Soviet Union and Afghanistan; there was continuing violence in Northern Ireland, Central America, and the Far East, where starved, terrified, bedraggled refugees fled Cambodia and its genocidal war in which an estimated one to three million people had been killed. This latter horror was covered in such pieces as Garrett's May 1980 "Thailand: Refuge From Terror" and White's "Kampuchea Wakens From a Nightmare," which appeared in May 1982.

Over the years *Geographic* writers and photographers returned again and again to the Middle East: Joseph Judge's "Israel—The Seventh Day," appeared in December 1972 and quoted a Jerusalem innkeeper who said, "I'm not a deeply religious man. When I was young in Vienna, every time there was a holiday my father would tell me about Jews being killed on this day, or being driven out, or being massacred. Every holiday was the celebration of a tragedy. I said to myself, 'This religion is a dangerous business!' " Several days later, Judge is speaking with a young leader of the Druze sect, who tells him, "At some point a man must say to himself that he cannot hate forever."

Opposite: *Iran, 1984. "The ayatollah speaks....And men listen, go to the front, and earn martyrdom—or return, many with horrible wounds from mines or shrapnel. Rehabilitation centers are well stocked with braces and artificial limbs. This center was a mansion of one of the shah's generals, whose paintings were torn from frames and replaced, here with Khomeini and a poem by a Shiite mystic urging dedication to Allah." —From "Iran Under the Ayatollah," in the July 1985 issue*

*Nicaragua, 1985. "One at a time is
how they usually die in a guerrilla
war..." began the caption for this
December 1985* Geographic *photograph ("NICARAGUA: Nation in
Conflict"). It continued: "Last July
photographer Jim Nachtwey went on
patrol with one of several special
Sandinista battalions charged with
engaging contras in the north. Not far
from San José de Bocay his 200-man
group surprised about 300 rebels,
called in artillery, and attacked....As
the bullets fly overhead, a soldier lies
dying (right), the sole Sandinista
fatality." Nachtwey, a veteran photographer who has covered combat from
Northern Ireland to El Salvador, says
of his work: "It never gets easier. It
only gets harder."*

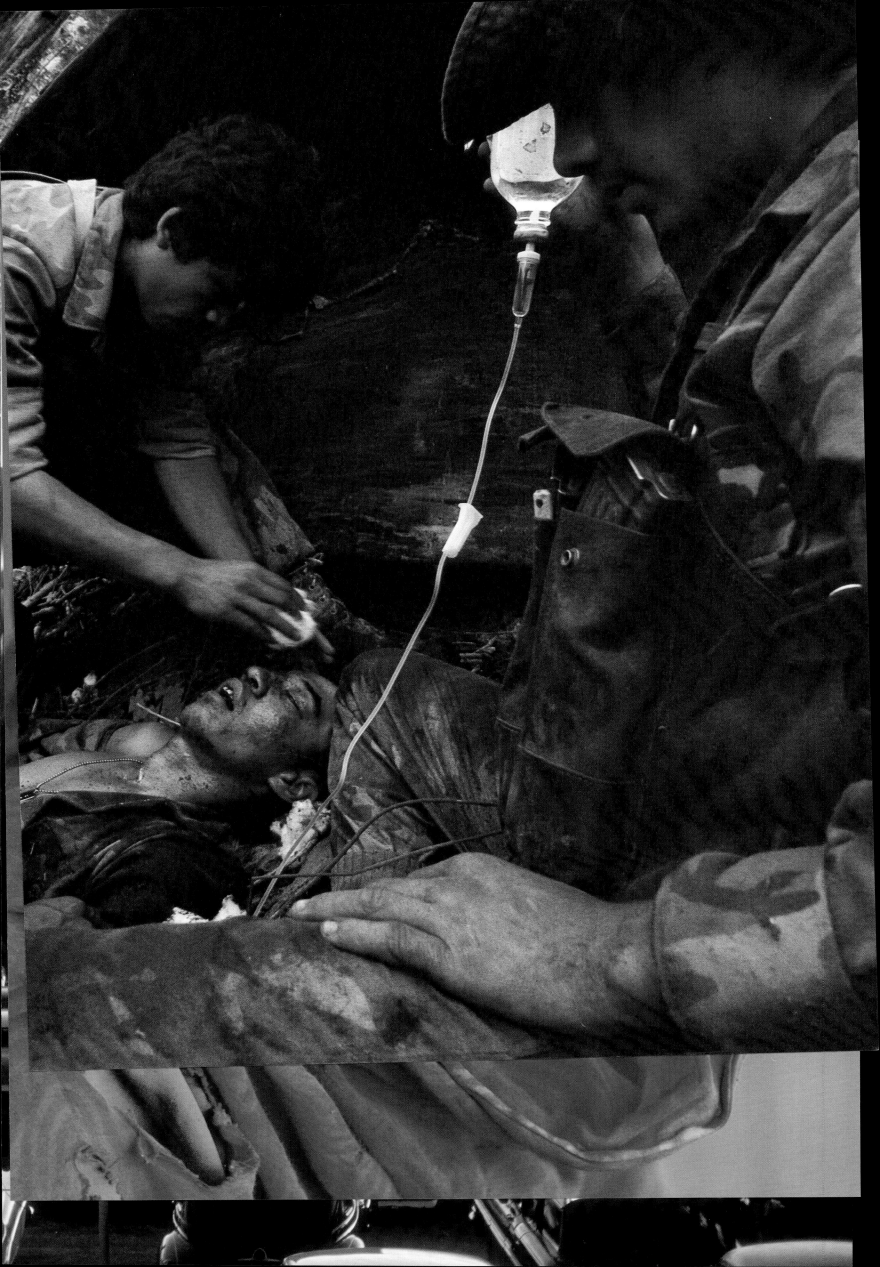

"...they'd go on these expeditions and everybody would be in khaki because that's the color of field uniforms. And they'd come back with the dullest bunch of pictures you ever saw! You couldn't use them editorially because they had no color. So, we decided to have people wear colorful shirts...."
—Melville Bell Grosvenor on the genesis of "The Red Shirt School of Photography"

The 1950s was the decade of the atomic bomb shelter, of Soviet expansionism, the stockpiling of nuclear weapons, and the fear of Communist subversion. In August 1953, nine months after the United States exploded its first H-bomb and obliterated Enewetak in the South Pacific's Marshall Islands, the Soviet Union detonated its first H-bomb in Siberia. By then President Harry S Truman had been succeeded by Dwight D. Eisenhower. It was the time of Senator Estes Kefauver's Special Committee to Investigate Crime hearings; and, on television, a mesmerized nation watched mobster Frank Costello's writhing hands. It was the time, too, of the televised Army–McCarthy hearings, with Boston lawyer Joseph Welch pitted against Joseph McCarthy, the Communist witch-hunting Republican Senator from Wisconsin. What one publication referred to as "a four-year binge of hysteria and character assassination" came to an end when McCarthy attempted to besmirch the reputation of a young man in Welch's law firm and Welch responded, "Until this moment, Senator, I think I never really gauged your cruelty or your recklessness....Let us not assassinate this lad further, Senator. You have done enough. Have you no sense of decency, sir, at long last? Have you left no sense of decency?"

It was the decade of Elvis Presley, of Rock and Roll, of Peggy Lee singing "Fever," Rosemary Clooney "Come On-a My House," and Dick Clark's American Bandstand; it was the decade of Davy Crockett hats, UFOs, the hoola-hoop, of paint-by-number kits of the *Last Supper*, and of seeing how many bodies could be stuffed into phone booths and Volkswagens. It was the decade in which city-dwelling parents of the booming post-war baby population flocked out to the suburbs (1,396,000 brand-new houses were built in 1950, alone; and what was once a Long Island potato farm became, in 1951, a community of 17,447 houses called Levittown). It was the decade of Broadway hit musicals like *West Side Story, My Fair Lady,* and *The Music Man;* books like *The Caine Mutiny, From Here to Eternity, Peyton Place,* and *The Catcher in the Rye.* It was the time when Hollywood, fighting back against the devastating inroads made by television, proclaimed "Movies are better than ever" and proved it with films like *High Noon, The African Queen,* and *The Man With the Golden Arm.* But it was the "foreign flicks" that swept the college campuses—movies such

Preceding spread: *"Movies and motorcars, two American institutions which were born about the same time and grew up over the same years, finally met at the drive-in theater.... Charlton Heston [in* The Ten Commandments *(1956)] spreads Mosaical arms against the evening sky of Salt Lake City, Utah."—From the 1975 National Geographic Society Book Service publication* We Americans

as *The 400 Blows, La Strada, The Seventh Seal, The Lavender Hill Mob, Rashomon,* and *M. Hulot's Holiday, Hiroshima Mon Amour,* and Brigitte Bardot in *And God Created Woman.*

By 1950, Gilbert Hovey Grosvenor had been President of the National Geographic Society for thirty years and first Assistant Editor, then Editor of its Magazine for fifty-one; he was now seventy-five years old. GHG's right-hand man, John Oliver La Gorce, for many years Associate Editor of the Magazine and Vice President of the Society, was seventy-one. Franklin L. Fisher, chief of the Illustrations Division, was sixty-five. J. R. Hildebrand, the Magazine's third-ranking editor, a veteran of the Society for thirty-one years, was sixty-two. Maynard Owen Williams, chief of the foreign editorial staff, was sixty-one.

Lyrics like "Awopbopaloobop-alopbamboom! Tutti-frutti! All rootie!" were not heard in the hallways of the Society. Bermuda shorts were not seen in the ladies' section of the cafeteria. And the sort of ambitious young Turks one might expect to find in organizations the size of the Geographic had yet to be hired.

The Magazine did, however, still reflect some of the forces at work in the world outside the Society's heavy brass doors. "Roaming Korea South of the Iron Curtain," a thirty-two page article by Enzo de Chetelat, with thirty-four illustrations and a map, was published in the June 1950 issue:

> Imagine the United States divided into North and South by a border from east to west at about the latitude of San Francisco, with a Communist curtain over the North and guerrillas raiding the South. Then you will have some idea of the difficulties faced by Korea.

That issue had just been delivered to the Society's membership when, on June 25, the North Koreans launched a massive invasion of the South and by the next month had occupied most of the Korean peninsula. For the second time in five years America was at war.

The October 1950 issue ran "Seeing the Earth from 80 Miles Up," a piece on the testing of captured German V-2 rockets at the White Sands (New Mexico) Proving Ground that was totally innocent of the convulsions the nation's scientific community would go through when the Soviet Union launched its 184-pound *Sputnik* seven years later. The issue also contained "Strife-torn Indochina," one of twenty articles that would appear during the next three decades about Vietnam. The Korean War was touched on again in Robert H. Mosier's "The GI and the Kids of Korea," a May 1953 article subtitled "America's Fighting Men Share Their Food, Clothing, and Shelter with Children of a War-torn Land." It was a piece largely about the heartwarming relationship between a Marine Corps sergeant and his plucky houseboy Kim whose

> father had been killed and his home bombed out, and he had wandered up toward the front in search of work or food or both. He'd been pushed around a good deal, but he wore a grin that looked as if it were stuck on to stay.

"Nevada Learns to Live with the Atom," one of the 1950s' most chilling articles, reflected the nation's major concern: the threat of nuclear war. Despite the resignation implied in its title, and the optimism of its subtitle, "While Blasts Teach Civilians and Soldiers Survival in Atomic War, the Sagebrush State Takes the Spectacular Tests in Stride," the text provided a vivid

289

The spreading mushroom became bright pink. Purple shaded to lavender, orange turned dusty rose, and the hues folded and overlapped in great
rolls and waves of cloud.

Higher and higher the cloud boiled against the bright blue-green of
dawn. On the very summit ice crystals formed, cascading over the rim like
pure-white surf in the sky.

The towering column silhouetted soldiers climbing from the trenches
into the murk of dust. Odors of scorching filled the air, acrid and sharp.
Along the ground it was impossible to see more than 100 feet.

Only above, huge and clear, towered the trademark cloud of atomic explosion, leaning with the wind toward the east, shearing from its stem—a
dirty brownish cloud now topped by pink and gold where the sun hit it
40,000 feet above us.

Within 24 hours this cloud, carrying its invisible spitting radioactive
particles, was to be tracked across Utah, Colorado, Kansas, Missouri, and
into southern Ohio. Airborne and ground teams would follow it with delicate instruments, tracking "fall-out"—the descent of the "hot" particles
back to earth.

Although Matthews mentioned the nervousness of the newsmen and
some of the troops, the basic mood of the piece was *Geographic*-style upbeat:
"The Army is proving that human beings, properly dug in and protected, can
survive atomic blasts at quite close range," he wrote. "Yet such demonstra-
tions by the Department of Defense and the Federal Civil Defense Administration are secondary to the main purpose of the Atomic Energy Commission
in Nevada. Its goal is to provide better weapons to ensure America's security
against attack."

Another reason for the test—a reason made evident more by the photographs than by the text—was to evaluate the impact of an atomic explosion on
civilian structures. Department store-window mannequins were placed fully
clothed in living rooms and kitchens of two wood-frame test houses sited at
different distances from the blast. Plaster babies were tucked into nursery
cribs; dummy drivers were seated behind the steering wheels of cars. The
house nearest to ground zero, Matthews later wrote, had been "crumbled into
matchwood, crushed into the desert, what remained was only wreckage,
charred where it faced the blast."

Six months later the *Geographic* published "Man's New Servant, the
Friendly Atom," a tribute to all the atom's anticipated peacetime benefits,
among them atomic power plants and atomic submarines.

During the early 1950s the Magazine was still running articles like "Our
Home-town Planet, Earth," "Work-hard, Play-hard Michigan," "Playing
3,000 Golf Courses in Fourteen Lands," and "Crickets, Nature's Expert Fid-
dlers." But the real story was what was happening within the *Geographic*—or,
more to the point, what was *not* happening, especially in the Illustrations Division where Franklin L. Fisher remained all-powerful and either unwilling or
unable to see the need for change.

The *National Geographic's* increasing isolation from the mainstream of
both journalistic and photojournalistic efforts during this decade was due to
several factors, among them the fact that the *Geographic* photographers rarely
entered national photojournalism contests. Therefore, they had none of the
healthy stimulation of seeing what other, perhaps more innovative photographers were doing. Another reason was that the *Geographic* had for so long been

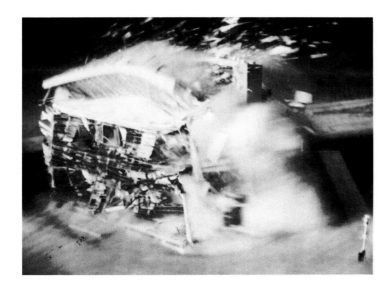

the leading photographic outlet; its staff had grown complacent, confident that they were the best, that outsiders were technically deficient and, therefore, not in the same league as the *Geographic* staff. After all, had not Gilbert H. Grosvenor, on March 6, 1951, received *U.S. Camera*'s Golden Achievement Award for "leadership in the editorial use of color photography"? And had not that citation honored the *Geographic* for having provided "a priceless documentary chapter in the history of color photographic processes"?

There was also the celebration of the *Geographic* by Frank Luther Mott, historian and dean emeritus of the University of Missouri School of Journalism. In his *History of American Magazines*, Mott wrote what Gilbert H. Grosvenor's histories of the *National Geographic* were quick to quote over and over again:

> There is really nothing like it in the world. For more than half a century the *National Geographic Magazine* has not published a single monthly number that has not been interesting and informative, with some measure of value. If it has seemed to some critics too much of a picture book, even they have to admit that in this it is in harmony with its times, and that its pictures are educational to a high degree. By the middle of the twentieth century it had attained the largest monthly circulation in the world at its price, and it had an assured position among the top ten monthly circulations at any price. This is a fabulous record of success, especially since the magazine is founded upon an editorial conviction that rates the intelligence of the popular audience fairly high. The *National Geographic Magazine* has long represented an achievement in editorship and management outstanding in the history of periodicals.

The *U.S. Camera* citation and Mott's laudatory summation were both, of course, the result of the Society's commendable early achievements. The problem with the Society in the 1950s was, however, that its upper echelon of officers was equally entrenched in the past. *Geographic* editors still believed color photographs were interesting as technical achievements, that the act of even being able to take such a photograph provided an end in itself. Therefore, the *Geographic* photographers were still taking color for color's sake, still taking perfectly composed and lighted, professionally challenging photographs—of often boring subjects.

"*National Geographic*'s pictures, with rare exception," Ed Hannigan wrote of that period at the Magazine in a 1962 *U.S. Camera* article, "were all pretty much of the picture postcard type of idealistic beauty, rather than photojournalism." And that picture postcard era reached its culmination in what critics outside the *Geographic* called the "Red Shirt School of Photography"— a reference to the constant use of red shirts, red caps, and red sweaters as props by photographers to brighten up their pictures. (That technique was nothing new; Gervais Courtellement, whose Autochromes had appeared in the *Geographic*s of the 1920s, traveled through Europe, Africa, and Asia with colorful scarves to drape over his models or on nearby fences and walls.)

In fairness to the *Geographic*'s photographers, the emphasis on color came from above: Gilbert H. Grosvenor believed in color; therefore senior editors demanded it, and illustrations editors, reflecting the Chief's views, saw color as being what separated them from lesser, conventional magazines. Color, having become easier to take, was, however, easier to overdo.

Even though Kodachrome was already unnaturally bright, photographers, because of existing imperfect color reproduction methods, splashed the strongest possible colors in their pictures so that they would be more effective in print. One result was that the staff photographers—who were constantly being sent to colorful places to slake what was seen as the public's unquenchable thirst for colorful scenes—would often find themselves needing more color to take advantage of the color film and would resort to placing the people in costume in the photographs. In a *Geographic* article on the modern South, for example, a couple might be dressed in colonial clothing or a mansion's graceful portico might be crowded with Southern belles in antebellum attire. The resulting overposed and artificial photographs were rendered even more ineffective by being jammed together, separated only by hair-thin lines in the Magazine's clumsy, unwieldy layouts.

Former National Geographic Book Service editor Edwards Park relates:

> They tell the story of old Muench, the southwestern photographer, who would go out and set up a tripod in Monument Valley. He'd take a picture with a piece of driftwood in the foreground and those huge monoliths in the background, a lovely sky, the whole thing. He'd shoot that and sell it to *Arizona Highways*. Then he'd snap his fingers and a beautiful girl with a large bosom and something red on would ride into the foreground on a pony and "smile and point at the mountain." Muench would shoot a second picture and sell that photograph to the *Geographic*.

But if one takes into account the context of the times and what the *Geographic* was doing, then the evolution of the "Red Shirt School" is not surprising. The philosophy of the Magazine had always been to increase and diffuse geographic knowledge—and to do so with the brightest possible face. The *Geographic* had not shown the world suffering through the Depression; and only rarely, in their coverage of World War Two, had battle scenes appeared. The photographs we remember from those desperate times were not the *Geographic*'s color photographs because it was never the *Geographic*'s role to provide them. What we do remember are the black-and-white documentary images shot by free-lance photographers with newspaper backgrounds or those who went to work for *Life* magazine; and these photographs were in black and white because that was the way they were shot and appeared out of practical necessity.

Unfortunately for the *Geographic*, during the post-war years and thereafter, black-and-white photographs were increasingly considered the more artistic and creative, while color was considered frivolous and shallow; and that perception also contributed to the *Geographic*'s isolation from the journalistic mainstream. But even if the "Red Shirt School" seems a bit silly *now*, given the kind of magazine the *National Geographic* was *then*, and the sort of article its color photographs were to illustrate, the "Red Shirts" as Melville Grosvenor explained, made perfect sense:

> What happened was that they'd go on these expeditions, and everybody would be in khaki, because that's the color of field uniforms. And they'd come back with the dullest bunch of pictures you ever saw! You couldn't use them editorially because they had no color. So, we decided to have people wear colorful shirts. But some of them went crazy, went to the other extreme for a while. The idea was, if you're going to buy a shirt to wear in the field, why don't you get a lumberman's shirt with plaid colors or something like that? Pictures were just plain monotonous. You might as well be in black-and-white if you're all in khaki or dull green. There's no pep to it. But when a fellow had a red cap on—just a red cap—it would add a little color to the picture.

Although during the 1950s the Geographic's *photographers took advantage of the faster Kodachrome speeds to break away from the more rigidly posed pictures required by the earlier, slower film processes, photographic clichés continued to occur. One particularly popular variant became known as "Smile, and point at the mountain."*

Overleaf: *The "picture-postcard" type of* Geographic *photograph prevalent during the 1950s reached its culmination in what critics outside the Society called the "Red Shirt School of Photography"—a reference to the frequent use by photographers of red shirts, caps, sweaters, or scarfs as props to brighten their pictures.*

The Geographic editors' attempts to appease what they perceived as the membership's unquenchable thirst for colorful scenes resulted in photographers being sent to cover festivals such as the one Jamestown, Virginia, celebrated in 1957 marking the 350th anniversary of its founding (shown above).

In his acceptance speech, Dr. La Gorce said, "Gentlemen, with your continued help I shall do my best to carry forward the high standards of the educational and scientific work of the National Geographic Society and its Magazine." Little more than a year later La Gorce was one of five journalists and editors from the Western Hemisphere to receive an award from Columbia University for furthering friendship between the peoples of the Americas.

For nearly fifty years La Gorce, formerly an expert press telegrapher and one of the Society's original three employees, had worked in the shadow of his mentor, Gilbert H. Grosvenor. A courtly, six-foot-tall, seventy-five-year-old with an erect military bearing, "JOL"—as he was referred to in the office, although he referred to himself as Grosvenor's "man Friday"—was handicapped by a stutter which miraculously disappeared when he made a public address.

Although advertising and promotion were his chief responsibilities, La Gorce occasionally wrote articles for the Magazine—fishing and sea life were his favorite subjects—and he edited the Society's 1952 *Book of Fishes*.

Gilbert Grosvenor was not the only Society officer to have had land features named after him; La Gorce had had a mountain range and a peak named after him in Antarctica and a meteorological station, too. There was, in addition, a Mount La Gorce, La Gorce Lake and La Gorce Glacier in Alaska, an island and a country club and golf course in Miami Beach, Florida, and La Gorce Arch, a rock formation along the Escalante River in Utah.

Visitors to La Gorce's pine-paneled third-floor office would remark on how dark it was, how it was dominated by La Gorce's weapons collection—which included a thirteenth-century Crusader's sword, a Stone Age axe and a World War Two commando dagger.

La Gorce was a man of simple loyalties—and appalling prejudices.

Gilbert H. Grosvenor's loyalties were to the membership of the Society; John Oliver La Gorce's correspondence reveals, as in this telegram sent to GHG on September 21, 1921, that his loyalties were to Gilbert Grosvenor first of all:

> SIXTEEN YEARS AGO TODAY WAS THE MOST FORTUNATE AND HAPPY MILE-STONE OF MY LIFE WHEN I JOINED UP WITH YOU THE BEST LEADER AND FRIEND A MAN COULD HAVE.
>
> J O LAGORCE

Second, his loyalties were to the Society to which he had devoted nearly fifty years; and third, his loyalties were to the membership (so long as it didn't attempt to interfere with that "nonprofit scientific and educational institution's" business of increasing and diffusing geographic knowledge). A 1920 handwritten memorandum from La Gorce to Gilbert H. Grosvenor provides an insight into JOL's attitude toward those members who dared criticize the Magazine's "nude" pictures:

> GHG: In considering the letters received now and then from people who believe it their mission on earth to save man from himself and in spite of himself—in the use of tobacco for example—let us not forget that we get as many letters telling us that the Geographic is corrupting the morals of decent people by publishing so many pictures of nude women. Naturally each is entitled to his own opinion but should the mock modesty of 1/1000 of 1 percent of geographic readers upset the educational work of the book—if not why should the same percentage of hopeless asses force tobacco from our ad pages. I know how broad you are but I want to get a line through on the subject.
>
> JOL

298

Just as La Gorce's and Grosvenor's loyalties differed, so did their prejudices. Gilbert H. Grosvenor, as he once told an interviewer, had "a great sympathy with the idea of combating race prejudice...."

Gilbert H. Grosvenor always said what he thought. John Oliver La Gorce, on the other hand, was more circuitous. It is only through reading his correspondence and memos that one becomes aware that, unless they kept their place, JOL did not like women, blacks, or Jews—though not necessarily in that order.

GHG had always respected women's contributions to science and the arts. There were, after all, precedents: Eliza Scidmore had been on the Magazine's masthead before him, and Ida Tarbell was an Associate Editor in 1901.

"As you know, I have felt for a long time that we should endeavor to develop more women writers for the Magazine," Dr. Grosvenor had written his Assistant Editor, J. R. Hildebrand, in 1949. "Women often see things about the life and ways of people which a man would not notice....Among the educated young women Miss Strider [Personnel Director] has brought to our staff, I am sure there must be some hidden talent. Men are more forward in presenting and asking for assignments than women; perhaps that is one reason why the ladies of our staff have not received as many assignments as the men." Furthermore, GHG's wife, Elsie, an active suffragist, seems to have had enormous influence on him. So La Gorce's attitude toward women in general and lack of appreciation for women on the work force, in particular, seems to represent his views and certainly not those of his Chief who, faced with JOL's intransigence, learned it was easier on occasion simply to bypass La Gorce—an example of which is seen in the parenthetical caveat to the following memo sent on December 2, 1938, by GHG to the editorial staff:

> IT IS INTERESTING TO NOTE THAT OF THE SIX BEST SELLING BOOKS OF FIC-
> TION RECORDED IN THE NEW YORK HERALD TRIBUNE OF NOVEMBER 27, THE
> FIRST, SECOND, THIRD, FIFTH AND SIXTH ARE BY WOMEN; AND OF THE NON
> FICTION BEST SELLERS, THE TWO FIRST IN POPULARITY ARE WRITTEN BY
> WOMEN.
>
> G.H.G.
>
> (TO BE SHOWN TO EACH MEMBER OF THE EDITORIAL STAFF EXCEPTING DR. LA
> GORCE.)

Perhaps no better evidence of La Gorce's attitude toward women can be found than in a letter written by him to GHG occasioned by what La Gorce perceived as a woman staffer's betrayal.

In the fall of 1919, Jessie L. Burrall, a female staffer who had earlier that year contributed the article "Sight-Seeing in School: Taking Twenty Million Children on a Picture Tour of the World," had been made Chief of the Geographic's then-fledgling School Service Division. In September, Miss Burrall had aroused La Gorce's ire by writing him that she was very interested in religious work, and that while traveling for the Society she had been offered the deanship of a college where she would teach religion and would receive, in addition to a $5,000 salary, room, board, and the use of a car.

In a special delivery letter La Gorce sent to Gilbert Grosvenor at his Baddeck summer home, JOL wrote, "I immediately realized why I had always mistrusted her and why, in spite of your constant urging of her qualities, they were always discounted by my somewhat uncanny gift of reading human nature and judging people by what I find...."

"Blooms, Wooden Shoes, and Windmill Say It's Tulip Time in Holland, Michigan" was the caption for this March 1952 photograph from the Geographic. *Not all the members were pleased. "Your photographers have a mania for photographing costumes,"* one wrote. *"I am a nudist and do not care what people wear. I am nevertheless an epicure, and I enjoy reading about the foods of other people."*

Hired by Gilbert Hovey Grosvenor in 1905, John Oliver La Gorce remained at the Society for the next fifty-two years. The photograph at top, showing the Georgia pine paneled and raftered "OFFICE OF JOHN OLIVER LA GORCE, THE ASSOCIATE EDITOR" was published in 1914. Twenty-two years of accumulated clutter and memorabilia later the camera angle was duplicated in this photograph at bottom captioned "IN THIS ROOM JOHN OLIVER LA GORCE 'HAS LABORED WITH LOVE AND CEASELESS ENERGY'" when it appeared in 1936.

"On the office walls...are hung many strange weapons and trophies collected on travels about the world," the caption explained. "Old ships' running lights suspended above his desk lend a tang of the sea, the elephant's foot at the right brings to mind African treks, and many primitive knives, arrowheads, spears, and shields always interest visitors."

JOL pointed out that had not GHG hired her, Miss Burrall "would still be a teacher of geography at $1,500, or $1,800, a year in the back-waters of the Middle West..." and that for her to be "even considering leaving this work..." was "disloyalty pure and simple, showing a very selfish spirit...."

La Gorce's letter continued:

> I will not go into the details of my presentation to her of the fact that instead of being the teacher of 400 pupils, in her present work, she was a teacher of 200,000 teachers and 20,000,000 children and she had her Sunday School Class here in Washington which could occupy her from a religious viewpoint. Further, that there was as much comparison between the countrywide prominence of Chief of the School Service of the National Geographic Society and the Dean of a Jerk-Water College as was between the occupancy of the White House and the management of the Washington Baseball Team.

La Gorce explained that he had told Miss Burrall that GHG was aware that her traveling on behalf of the Society necessitated extra expenses, that he would probably increase her salary, and that she should think it over for a few days. Three days later, continued La Gorce's letter, "she came in, looked me in the eye, and said that she had made her absolute decision on the conviction that her work was *here*, that she would stay, and would not consider for a moment any other proposition made to her."

However, La Gorce wrote, Miss Burrall was next offered a job by "some Baptist Association in New York," and despite JOL's "request and demand that she not disturb you in your rest period" she had telegraphed GHG in Baddeck.

JOL urged GHG to dismiss Miss Burrall, assuring him that there would be no difficulty in finding a replacement. "By this," he added, "I do not mean that we can find a person with all her ability as a worker, a talker, as a social climber, an educational parasite, but we can find a teacher of experience...."

La Gorce's letter ends:

> I know that, with your gentle disposition and unwillingness to hurt anybody's feelings, and Mrs. Grosvenor's interest in the lady, you will probably not wish to take the drastic step I suggest....

JOL was right in his assumption: GHG ignored his request and Miss Burrall remained at the Society until 1920.

JOL's attitude toward Jews is revealed in a 1920 memo he wrote to GHG containing his response to a proposal that the National Geographic Society lend its name to the distribution of films with which the Society had no previous association and which were made and developed primarily for commercial reasons:

> G.H.G.: No one has a keener enjoyment or a more fulsome appreciation of what motion pictures have done for humanity than I, but at the same time the industry is known to be practically in the hands of some of the most unscrupulous men and associations in the country,—mainly Jews who have by a process of elimination and massacre absorbed or done away with the smaller fry, and their business methods have been an unpleasant odor in the commercial nostrils for a long time....

But the most revealing of the La Gorce memos was the one he sent GHG on March 3, 1926, from which the following is extracted:

G.H.G.: May I give you a thought in connection with campaigning for new members in Southern states?

In the matter of the Southern states we have, of course, the danger of negro nominations, but after all that is merely a question of applying thought to the method and at first it will be a trifle more expensive per member, but every other organization in the country is confronted with the same thing and are not afraid to enter the field, so why should we be? I would suggest that we put Boutwell on the job of securing from the N.E.A. or from the Bureau of Education (if we do not have such lists in our files) the names of all negro schools and colleges in the Southern states, and to obtain a list of the faculties. These names could be checked against our membership lists as though they were all nominations, and in the mailing out of nomination letters such names could be omitted by the simple process of putting a tab on the Addressograph card that would trip it through without printing, as in the case of dues.

A second precautionary measure would be to make a special list of all nominations coming from towns where these schools and colleges are and, without giving the name of the nominator, submit the list to some member who we know is white, asking their cooperation in the matter of glancing over the list enclosed and to indicate any names that they know are not of the white race. It will be unnecessary to go into any further detail with any white Southerner, for he, or she, will know why we are making this request and will be only too glad to cooperate. There are few large cities in the South comparatively speaking, and in places of even 30 to 50,000 all white people either know each other, or know who the other fellow is, for that is peculiar to the South....

There is no indication that GHG ever acknowledged JOL's recommendation or that the intricate procedure was ever adopted. Sixteen years later, La Gorce was urging GHG not to run a proposed article on black members of the military because:

I fear it would promptly bring insistent demands from the group of educated Negro agitators who for political reasons have been encouraged and aided by a wellknown source to strike now for social equality in this country....

I do not discount the importance of negro soldiers in the present all-out manpower necessity, but accounts of the Spanish-American and First World Wars do not credit negro soldiers with the sort of courage needed to win battles.

Personally I have always had a kindly feeling for the race, and get along with them because I understand them. We could go as far as to include now and then a picture of Negro troops in training when illustrating appropriate articles, but I'd vote against an article about them.

JOL's prejudices apparently had little effect on GHG and little impact on the Society's policies. His strong personal feelings aside, JOL had made significant contributions to the Society during his tenure: His promotion efforts had increased membership from 10,000 in 1905 to more than two million by the time he became Editor. Advertising, too, had flourished in the Magazine under his direction. In fact, no one since has equaled his advertising record.

Considering that his strength was primarily in promotion and advertising and that he had somewhat limited editorial experience, why was La Gorce made Editor of the Magazine and President of the Society? For several reasons. Chief among them, one suspects, was the feeling that La Gorce *deserved* the recognition as a reward for his lengthy service. A second reason was that he

La Gorce poses at the foot of the stairs beneath his portrait in the clubhouse of Miami Beach's La Gorce Country Club, named in his honor.
La Gorce's Editorship—beginning with Gilbert H. Grosvenor's retirement in 1954, and ending with his own retirement in 1957—was perceived by most of the staff as an interregnum between Grosvenors.

was expected to be an interregnum leader, a custodian, a keeper of the flame. Under GHG's reign, the Society had prospered, and La Gorce was determined to see that during his three years of tenure nothing was changed. The third reason was that in the context of the times La Gorce's prejudices really were not all that surprising. He, like GHG, was ultra-conservative, a product of the Victorian era; but unlike GHG, La Gorce reflected the biases of that earlier time. La Gorce's wartime memo, one should note, was written twelve years before the Supreme Court, in *Brown* v. *Board of Education of Topeka*, would unanimously ban segregation in the public schools.

La Gorce retired on January 8, 1957, after serving less than three years as Editor and President. At the time, GHG presented a resolution to the Board that reflected the close bond and mutual loyalty he and JOL had shared for half a century. In part, GHG said, "With everything the Society has done...he has been identified. Many of our most useful and interesting projects he originated. He labored...to help develop the organization and bring it to the dignified position it now holds in the life of our country."

Just as photography at the *Geographic* was stagnating during the 1950s, so was its writing. The Magazine was still running stories like Jean and Franc Shor's "From Sea to Sahara in French Morocco" with such lines as:

> Morocco is today a neighbor with trouble in its own house. The night we landed in Casablanca terrorists shot up a French cafe a block from our hotel, killing two Frenchmen and wounding three. In Marrakech, as we watched a parade honoring the retiring Resident General, a bomb shattered a French Army unit 50 yards from where we stood. Three soldiers died, 28 were injured. And as we drove from Meknès to Rabat, through Morocco's breadbasket, the horizon was black with smoke from burning grainfields fired by arsonists.

Despite its acknowledgment of the civil disruptions then occurring in French Morocco, the piece swiftly becomes upbeat and positive. A friend at the American Consulate General in Casablanca tells the Shors he thinks their trip from the sea to the Sahara will be no more dangerous than "driving an equal number of miles in American traffic. You and Jean aren't concerned with politics," he says. "You're interested in the land and the people...."

Franc Shor, a member of the *Geographic* staff for twenty-one years and one of its two Associate Editors at the time of his death in 1974, was a legend at the Society. Supreme Court Justice William O. Douglas called Shor "the most traveled man I have ever met." Shor had traveled around the world at least a dozen times; and once said he had been to every country in the world, including some that weren't legally countries when he visited them. Witty, erudite, charming, Shor was the sort of man who, while in Athens for a January 1956 "Athens to Istanbul" *Geographic* piece, would be photographed by Queen Frederika of Greece—who would then ask for and receive a credit line on the photograph when it was published in the Magazine.

Once Shor was forced to bail out of an airplane over China—and took

On assignment in what was then Formosa in 1949, staff writer Frederick G. Vosburgh and companions rode a push car across crude log bridges spanning mountain ravines. "Many people get killed on this railroad?" Vosburgh asked. "Not so many," was the answer.

Although legendary Associate Editor Franc Shor, in fact, came from Dodge City, Kansas, could do rope tricks like Will Rogers, was a magnificent horseman, and, although his mother, in fact, broke horses for the U.S. Cavalry in World War One, many of the *Geographic's* staff still found some of Shor's personal accounts hard to believe.

"So many of Franc Shor's stories you just assumed were lies," Bart McDowell recalled. "Franc would say, 'of course, I speak fluent Chinese'—one of those throwaway lines—and Garrett would say he didn't believe it, that Shor was deluded. And then Shor and Garrett went to China to do the Quemoy-Matsu story ["Life Under Shellfire on Quemoy," March 1959] and some taxi-driver on the street in Hong Kong began to discuss god-knows-what with Shor, and Franc responded in such fluent Chinese the guide said, 'Oh, you come from Chungking!' and suddenly it would turn out that Shor's crazy stories were true!"

nothing with him but his typewriter. He was an "old China hand" who, in order not to be caught short of cash, wore cufflinks made of the gold bars Oriental money-changers recognized as currency wherever one traveled in the days before Chairman Mao.

On one occasion Shor spent five weeks tracing, partly on foot, the path of the first Crusade from France to Jerusalem. On another occasion he trekked across the Gobi desert retracing Marco Polo's journey from Venice to China—"a trip," noted *The New York Times* in Shor's obituary, "that exposed him to fever, bandits, wolves, sandstorms and nearly ended in his death."

"Franc Shor was a great character," Luis Marden recalls. "A great lady's man, a great wine connoisseur—he had a private wine cellar at the Ritz in Paris—a great intellect." It is not inappropriate that Marden speaks of Shor with the fondness one club member feels for another, for the National Geographic in the 1950s was still run very much like a private men's club—although photographer Dean Conger, who joined the Geographic staff in 1959, thought the Society of that period more akin to a Southern plantation. And with reason.

A woman hired by the Society about that time recently said, "One of the first things I noticed when I came here was that all the chauffeurs and the elevator operators were black. They called everybody 'Mr. So-and-so,' and everybody called them by their first names. There was this *noblesse oblige*, a hierarchy that was catered to. I was born and raised in the Midwest and had had no experience with people or places like this. And one day I woke up and suddenly I realized I was living in The South."

There were quite a few women then working at the *Geographic*, but nearly all of them were in secretarial positions. As Anne Chamberlin in her 1963 *Esquire* magazine piece would note, the Society was "considered by many of Washington's best families as a fine, safe place for a post-debutante daughter to put in a few years dabbling in secretarial work before marriage."

However, not all the young women hired in those days were post-debutantes. Legends Editor Carolyn Patterson, who retired in 1986 after nearly thirty-seven years with the Society, came to the National Geographic in 1949 after having served as the first woman police reporter on the *New Orleans State*. Although Miss Strider, the maiden lady Personnel Director then in her mid-fifties, thought Carolyn Patterson overqualified, she hired her as a file clerk but later rebuked her for unladylike behavior—Patterson had been walking too fast in the corridors.

"There was a very, very distinct idea of what ladies did and what ladies did not do here," Carolyn Patterson explained. "In those days we had two dining rooms, one for the men and one for the women and [in] the women's dining room we would lunch in large groups. And in my luncheon group I once asked the single question, 'Has anyone thought of putting a picture on the cover of the *National Geographic*?' Everyone looked terribly shocked that I would even ask the question, and someone reported me to Miss Strider....She called me into her office and said to me, 'The National Geographic is a traditional organization, Mrs. Patterson, and if you don't understand that means keeping the Magazine's cover the way it is, you perhaps do not belong here.' " *

*In July 1942 the American flag had appeared for the first time on the Magazine's cover; cover photographs began appearing regularly in September 1959.

It was precisely because, by the 1950s, the Society had become such a "traditional organization" that the Magazine began to lose the creative impetus that had lifted its circulation from 2,200 in 1900 when Gilbert Hovey Grosvenor became Managing Editor to 2,100,009 in 1954 when he retired. Grosvenor's daring, so instrumental in creating a popular magazine during the previous fifty years, had dissipated with age until all that remained were his Victorian sensibilities. And it was those sensibilities, now entrenched—and, indeed, celebrated—as traditions by his successor, John Oliver La Gorce, that brought about the stagnation of the Magazine, a stagnation evident in its sluggish circulation which increased by but 53,201 during La Gorce's three-year tenure, an average gain of only 17,794 per year.

One long-time Geographic staffer, comparing Gilbert Hovey Grosvenor and John Oliver La Gorce, recalled GHG as "being an enthusiast rather than a professional journalist, and sort of 'inventing the wheel' as he went along," the kind of editor, he continued, who "would lose interest after the first blush of enthusiasm." JOL, on the other hand, was "the phlegmatic ballast of the operation, [the man who] made sure things were spelled correctly, that there weren't any 'typos,' that there was a sense of follow-through and thoroughness…. He was always a good cleaner-upper, but not an innovator in any way.

"Poor old JOL," the staffer said, "stood around like Anthony Eden to GHG's Winston Churchill for all those years, crown prince until he got senile, and then when he finally did get [to be editor], he was never able to do anything with it."

Certainly La Gorce *could* have done things as editor and didn't, not only because, as has been mentioned, he was determined to see that nothing was changed, but also because, if anything, he was even more conservative than his predecessor.

Gilbert M. Grosvenor, who was hired by La Gorce (and told by JOL, "G-Gilbert? the only advice I c-can g-give you is d-don't d-dip your p-pen in the c-company ink well,") recalls one telling incident from that era: "GHG knew what he was doing when he published semi-nude pictures. He 'showed people like they were,'" Gil said, "but he also knew that this was the kind of 'trade-mark' you made. JOL, particularly in the latter years, was a little prudish about that…. There was a case where GHG approved a set of pictures and there was a bare-breasted lady [who]…was apparently very beautiful…Dee Andella [then Printing Production Division chief] had the proofs made. GHG said, 'Yes, these proofs are fine,' and went away, left JOL running the show. JOL looked at the proof and said, 'That's awful!' and he covered her up. So Andella had to go back and put her breasts in shadow or something…GHG came back to town, looked at these final proofs, asked, 'What's going on here? You have ruined this photograph!'…It went back. They made the plate all over again… and that's the way it ran."

If the Magazine was treading water during the La Gorce interregnum, the fact that it did not drown was due to La Gorce's Associate Editor and heir apparent, Melville Bell Grosvenor. In turn brilliantly and imaginatively tutored as a boy by his ebullient grandfather, then strictly dominated and suppressed as an adult by his somewhat distant father, Melville Grosvenor—charged with the kind of enthusiasm and vision one might expect of a man emotionally more Bell than Grosvenor—was impatiently awaiting his turn.

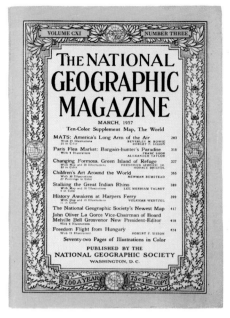

The Geographic *languished under La Gorce. Between January 1954 and his retirement in January 1957 only 53,201 new members joined the Society, bringing its total to 2,144,704. Melville Bell Grosvenor's long-awaited Editorship would change all that.*

"'Why did you want to climb Mount Everest?' This question was asked of George Leigh Mallory, who was with both expeditions toward the summit of the world's highest mountain in 1921 and 1922, and who is now in New York. He plans to go again in 1924, and he gave as the reason for persisting in these repeated attempts to reach the top, 'Because it's there.'"

—The New York Times, March 18, 1923

"Well, we knocked the blighter off!"

—Sir Edmund Hillary, May 29, 1953, returning with Tenzing Norgay from their successful struggle to Everest's 29,028-foot summit, to expedition member George Lowe. As reported in Sir Edmund Hillary's July 1954 *National Geographic* article, "The Conquest of the Summit"

For the April 1891 issue of the Magazine, geologist Israel C. Russell, a founder of the Society, wrote in his "Summary of Reports on the Mt. St. Elias Expedition" that the purpose of the National Geographic Society's first sponsored expedition* was "to study and map...the vicinity of Mt. St. Elias...and, if practicable, to ascend it."

En route to Mount St. Elias, Russell found "a wonderful panorama of snow-covered mountains, glaciers, and icebergs...hoary mountain peaks, each a monarch robed in ermine and bidding defiance to the ceaseless war of the elements."

Russell survived "torrential rains," "blinding snowstorms," "roaring avalanches," "huge grizzly bears," "yawning chasms," "treacherous passes," and was—despite a bout of snowblindness—the first to see and name 19,524-foot-high Mount Logan, the continent's second highest mountain. Russell failed, however, in his attempt to reach Mount St. Elias' 18,008-foot peak.

Since Russell's report, *National Geographic* has been filled with accounts of the world's great mountains scaled or attempted, climbers' triumphs or tragic deaths, expeditions' successes or defeats. Seven years after Russell's attempt, Eliza Ruhamah Scidmore reported on the Italian Duke of the Abruzzi's successful ascent of Mount St. Elias in 1897; and in 1913, Walter Woodburn Hyde wrote this pithy description of his feelings upon having reached the 15,771-foot summit of Mont Blanc:

Do you open your eyes wide in astonishment at the wonderful sight? By no means! You shut them as tight as you can and throw yourself down on the

*The Mount St. Elias expedition was sponsored jointly by the National Geographic Society and the U.S. Geological Survey.

Opposite: *In 1890, a founder of the Society Israel C. Russell and his party crossed the moraines of the Malaspina Glacier in Alaska while on their expedition "to study and map...the vicinity of Mount St. Elias" for the Society's first expedition, sponsored jointly with the U.S. Geological Survey.*

Preceding spread: *First conquest of Antarctica's highest peaks. In December 1966 and January 1967 the unclimbed Sentinel Range of the Ellsworth Mountains, the highest mountains in Antarctica, fell to members of the American Antarctic Mountaineering Expedition. Here expedition leader Nicholas B. Clinch struggles to the top of the Vinson Massif—at 16,860 feet, Antarctica's highest peak.*

"I recall flying around and over the peak...sitting on a gas can by the open door and snapping pictures with a bulky camera—while a rope around my waist let me lean out far enough, and no farther," wrote Bradford Washburn (above) posing with the forty-eight-pound aerial camera with which, in 1936, he photographed Alaska's Mount McKinley on Society-sponsored flights that "resulted in the first complete photographic record of North America's ice-encrusted rooftop."—From Great Adventures with National Geographic

Opposite: *Landing on McKinley's flanks at 10,000 feet, higher than any previous plane, Terris Moore taxis up to Bradford Washburn's 1951 expedition base camp with supplies and mail.*

snow in utter weariness of mind and body, resenting the impertinence of your guides, who urge you to look about.

In 1924, the year after his American lecture tour, George Leigh Mallory, with his partner Andrew Irvine, vanished into the mists on Everest's northeast ridge during his third expedition to the mountain. Before his disappearance, Mallory had expressed a sentiment that all mountain climbers can understand: "Have we vanquished an enemy? None but ourselves."

In 1929, G. H. H. Tate was appalled by the silence on the 9,092-foot summit of South America's Mount Roraima. "One feels oppressed, dwarfed," he noted, "...almost as if one were a trespasser."

That same year explorer-biologist Joseph F. Rock was in China attempting to reach a vantage point from which he might view Minya Konka, "one of the loftiest peaks of western China." Rock wrote in "The Glories of the Minya Konka," for the October 1930 Magazine:

> Our descent [from Chirpin Pass] was very difficult. Men and beasts and loads were many times catapulted...into a snow bank up to our necks....
>
> As the storm continued, to go on the next day was impossible. [My men] were snowblind and were suffering terribly. Fortunately, I had cocaine, with which I made a solution, and this I dropped into their eyes to relieve their pain....To the north, it seemed as if one had entered a different world. There not a tree could be seen: the entire landscape was a bleak waste....
>
> When we reached 15,000 feet we found the snow lay deep...but, fortunately for us, it was frozen, and, as it bore our weight, we advanced cautiously....
>
> And then suddenly, like a white promontory of clouds, we beheld the long-hidden Minya Konka rising 25,600 feet in sublime majesty.
>
> I could not help exclaiming for joy. I marveled at the scenery which I, the first white man ever to stand here, was privileged to see.

In 1933, nine years after Mallory disappeared on Everest's slopes, two especially redesigned British camera-equipped biplanes took off from a landing field near Purnea in Bihar, India, for the 154-mile flight north to Mount Everest in Nepal. In his *National Geographic* account of the journey, "The Aërial Conquest of Everest: Flying Over the World's Highest Mountain Realizes the Objective of Many Heroic Explorers," Lt. Col. L. V. S. Blacker, O.B.E., wrote of clearing Everest's amazing, immaculate crest: "I looked down through the open floor and saw what no man since time began had ever seen before. No words can tell the awfulness of that vision...."

One year later the *Geographic* published Miriam O'Brien Underhill's "Manless Alpine Climbing: The First Woman to Scale the Grépon, the Matterhorn, and Other Famous Peaks Without Masculine Support Relates Her Adventures."

"Non-climbers often ask me how a woman can be strong enough for exertion that would tax an 'athletic young man,' " she wrote. Her answer was "A certain muscular vigor is indispensable, of course...but technique, knowing how to use strength to the best advantage is more important. The greater the technique, the less the power required"—a reply that would appear as relevant today to any climber, male or female.

In 1948, Maynard M. Miller reported on the first American ascent of Mount St. Elias of 1946; Bradford Washburn's account of the first ascent of 20,320-foot Mount McKinley's west buttress, "Mount McKinley Conquered by New Route," appeared in August 1953. (Society staffer Barry C. Bishop,

then a college student, was on that climb, too.) "New Mount McKinley Challenge—Trekking Around the Continent's Highest Peak" by Ned Gillette was his story in the July 1979 issue of the circuit of McKinley.

Asia's Minya Konka (24,900 feet high), Muztagata (24,757), K2 (28,250), Annapurna (26,504), Anyemaqen (20,610), Ama Dablam (22,494) all succumbed to American climbers—but not without loss of life. Despite one of the worst avalanche seasons ever, and despite American Women's Himalayan Expedition members Vera Watson and Alison Chadwick-Onyszkiewicz, both careful and skilled mountaineers, having fallen, roped together, to their deaths, 1978 saw American women reach the summit of Annapurna—the first Americans and the first women to do so.

Still there was Everest.

Between 1921 and 1953 seven major expeditions had attempted to conquer Everest—and failed with awesome loss of life. And then, on March 10, 1953, a British party led by Brigadier Sir John Hunt sallied forth for another attempt. "What manner of mountain is this which for so many years so easily shrugged off all assaults and claimed the lives of at least 16 men?" Hunt asked in the pages of the July 1954 *Geographic*. His explanation followed:

> Other peaks demand more actual climbing. Alaska's Mount McKinley for example, measures 19,000 feet from its lowland base, while Everest rises only about 12,000 above the 17,000-foot Tibetan plateau. Himalayan winds are fierce, but the Scottish Highlands, battered by the North Atlantic's hurricanes, endure gales as terrible. Everest's crags and crevasses test any man's ability but half a dozen Alpine peaks offer technical problems of greater severity. Everest can chill a man to the marrow with summer temperatures down to −40° F. at night; yet on the Greenland icecap and elsewhere explorers have lived through cold worse by 30 or 40 degrees.
>
> What makes Everest murderous is the fact that its cold, its wind, and its climbing difficulties converge upon the mountaineer at altitudes which have already robbed him of resistance. At 28,000 feet a given volume of air breathed contains only a third as much oxygen as at sea level. . . . Above 25,000 feet the climber's heavy legs seem riveted to the ground, his pulse races, his vision blurs, his ice ax sags in his hand like a crowbar. To scoop up snow in a pan for melting looms as a monumental undertaking. In the words of a Himalayan veteran, Frank Smythe: "On Everest it is an effort to cook, an effort to talk, an effort to think, almost too much of an effort to live."

The first assault team of Tom Bourdillon and Charles Evans reached the 28,700-foot South Peak, a mountaineering record, but were forced to descend when Evans' oxygen set failed, leaving them with neither time, oxygen, nor strength to tackle the final ridge. "Now they handed over the expedition's hopes to Hillary and to Tenzing," wrote expedition leader Hunt.

Hillary and Tenzing Norgay reached the summit on May 29, 1953. Almost exactly ten years later the American Mount Everest Expedition, sponsored by the National Geographic Society, with staff man Barry C. Bishop, achieved its historic twin assaults on the summit from the South Col and West Ridge but not before climber Jake Breitenbach died on the mountain. Bishop, Lute Jerstad, Tom Hornbein, and Willi Unsoeld were caught at night on the descent at 28,000 feet with neither oxygen, tents, nor sleeping bags. Bishop and Unsoeld suffered severe frostbite. Bishop lost his toes and parts of

the little fingers of both hands,* Unsoeld lost all but one of his toes.

But of all the mountaineers there is none whose accomplishments inspire more awe among fellow climbers than Reinhold Messner, who, with companion Peter Habeler, first achieved Everest's summit—*without* bottled oxygen, but with the help of Sherpa porters—on the 1978 Austrian expedition.

Two years later Messner attempted Everest without high-altitude porters, without climbers, without bottled oxygen, without a radio, aluminum ladder, or rope.

Messner's only climbing equipment were ski poles, an ice ax, an ice screw and a rock piton "for holding my tent, or even my body, to the ground in case of a severe storm." In "At My Limit," his October 1981 *Geographic* article, Messner wrote, "I was attempting the greatest challenge, to me, in mountaineering—to climb the highest mountain on earth completely on my own."

Before dawn on August 18, 1980, Messner set out from his High Base Camp at 6,500 meters (21,325 feet) and minutes later, he was crossing a snowbridge over a crevasse when,

> Suddenly it went, crumbling into powder and chunks of ice.
> I was falling—falling into the deep. It felt like eternity in slow motion as I bounced back and forth off the crevasse walls. In the next moment I came to a sudden stop. Or had it been minutes?...Blackness surrounded me. "My God! Perhaps I will die down here!"...
> I fumbled with my headlamp. As it flashed on, the walls of ice shimmered a dark blue-green. They were two meters apart where I stood, but nearly joined at the top. The snow platform that had halted my fall was no more than a meter square....I became acutely aware that if the platform collapsed beneath my weight, I would hurtle into the abyss....

With an ice ax in one hand and a ski pole in the other, Messner kicked step after step into the ice until he could escape, then pushed on. At 7 A.M., Messner reached 6,990 meters (22,930 feet) and the saddle of the North Col. Two hours later he was at 7,360 meters:

> "Making good time," I thought, as I climbed over the rolls and bulges that form the lower part of the North Ridge....Snow swirled about my head. Gusts of wind began to sap my energy.
> At 7,500 meters I could feel myself slowing considerably. I must not become exhausted, I told myself. The next two days would be far more strenuous.

Finding a piece of rope left behind by an earlier Japanese ascent, Messner was led to compare large expeditions with multiple climbers and Sherpa high-altitude porters to his own attempt:

> My method...differed immensely. The solo climber, alone against the elements on a Himalayan giant, is like a snail. He carries his home on his back, and moves slowly but steadily upward. No relays. No ferrying up of supplies. No setting up a series of camps higher and higher. No assault team kept well rested for the final push.
> Everything I needed—tent, sleeping bag, stove, fuel, food, climbing equipment—had to go on my back. I would put up my tent for sleep, and then pack it and take it with me the next day. There was no one to carry a second tent, and I was not using oxygen, which could have given me more

---

While on a post-Everest speaking tour, which had brought him to a large midwestern university, Bishop was momentarily at a loss during the question period when a young woman asked, "Other than the loss of the tips of your little fingers and your toes, were any of your other extremities permanently damaged by frostbite?"

The first American to attain Everest's 29,028-foot summit was James W. Whittaker, who reached it with Sherpa Nawang Gombu on May 1, 1963. Four other members of America's first Everest expedition made it to the top as well: Thomas F. Hornbein, William F. Unsoeld, Luther G. Jerstad, and the Society's Barry C. Bishop (above), shown bracing himself against the summit's 70-mph winds while holding the Society flag he carried with him. "If you have to crawl on your hands and knees, you're going to get there," he had told himself.

Opposite: *In 1963, climbers of America's first Everest expedition approach Everest's snow-plumed south summit from Lhotse's slanted face.*

Following spread: *Its back in Tibet, Mount Everest (left), at 29,028 feet, joins Lhotse (center), at 27,890 feet, and Nuptse (right), at 25,850 feet, to form a cradle for the Khumbu Glacier, traditional southern route to Everest's summit.*

strength. The oxygen apparatus is too heavy for an Alpine-style ascent, a single push for the summit. Also my own theories rule out its use. I want to experience the mountain as it really is, and truly understand how my own body and psyche relate to its natural forces. By using an artificial oxygen supply, I feel I would no longer be climbing the mountain towering above me. I would simply be bringing its summit down to me.

Messner made camp the first night at 7,800 meters (25,580 feet). Although his native tongue was German, he found he was talking to himself in Italian, urging himself to eat. "I shoved dried meat, cheese, and bread into my mouth. Just those small movements were exhausting. 'I must begin the cooking,' I told myself. I needed to drink at least four liters of water a day; to dehydrate could be fatal. The tent was fluttering wildly in the wind." Messner scooped snow into his cooking pot to melt and mix with dried tomato soup; he drank that, then two pots of Tibetan herbal salt tea. He dozed off fully clothed, then awoke not knowing "whether it was evening or morning. I didn't want to look at my watch," Messner later wrote. "Deep inside I was frightened. Not only of the present situation. My fear encompassed all my 30 years of climbing mountains: the exhaustion and desperation, and the thundering avalanches. These sensations spread over me and merged into a deepening fear."

The morning of August 19, Messner lightened his load as much as he dared and started off. Within an hour he was wading through knee-deep snow as he closed in on the North Face's steeper slope, which rises toward the Northeast Ridge 455 meters (1,500 feet) below the summit.

Convinced I would be forced to abandon my attempt soon if I had to climb in the deep snow, I searched for an alternate route. The vast snow area of the North Face extended to my right. Several avalanches recently had poured down its flank. With the fresh snow swept away, perhaps the surface would be hard. It was my only chance. Climbing gradually with each step, I began the long crossing to the Great Couloir....Concentrating on each step, I failed to notice the weather turning bad.

By three that afternoon Messner had reached 8,220 meters (26,962 feet) and was exhausted and frustrated by his lack of progress.

I wanted desperately to find a bivouac site. But I could see none.

One hour later, on a snow-covered rock ledge, I managed to pitch my tent. I wanted to photograph myself there. But I hadn't the strength to screw the camera onto the ice ax, put it on automatic, go back ten steps, and wait for the click. Far more important was to prepare something to drink....I measured my pulse while I was melting snow; it was racing—far more than a hundred beats a minute.

What if the fog did not lift by morning? Should I wait? No, that was senseless. At this height there is no recuperation. By the day after tomorrow I would be so weak that I could never advance toward the peak. Tomorrow I had either to go up or go down. There was no other choice.

The morning of August 20 was clear, but clouds were closing in. I strapped my crampons to my boots and took my camera over my shoulder and my ice ax in one hand. Everything else I left in the tent.

Climber Vera Komarkova is reflected in Sherpa Mingma's sunglasses atop the 26,504-foot summit of Annapurna with Sherpa Chewang (at left) and Irene Miller. This first ascent by Americans and women of the world's tenth highest mountain was reported in the March 1979 issue.

At that elevation, over 27,000 feet, Messner was oxygen-starved and hallucinating: "After a short time I missed my rucksack. It was my friend, my partner," he wrote. "I had conversed with it. It had edged me on when I was exhausted. Without it, however, the journey was easier—much easier. Besides, my second companion, the ice ax, was still with me."

Messner's familiarity with the reports of previous British expeditions helped him locate the best route into and up the Great Couloir, a "physically taxing but technically not too difficult" climb until he came to "a snow gully leading to a steep step interspersed with rocks. After a while," he wrote, "soft snow slowed my pace."

> I climbed on hands and knees, like a four-legged animal, sluggish and apathetic. A dark rock wall blocked the path. Something pulled me to the left. Making a small loop, I bypassed the obstacle.
>
> I now stood just below the peak. The fog was thick, and I could hardly orient myself. The next three hours seemed to pass without notice. I climbed instinctively, not consciously. The clouds opened for brief moments, giving fleeting glimpses of the peak against the blue sky.
>
> Suddenly I saw the aluminum tripod! There it was—the blessing of proof, the curse of desecration, on that supreme place of solitude—barely peeking out of the snow, a piece of cloth frozen around the top. The Chinese had anchored it at the highest point in 1975 to make exact measurements.
>
> I sat there like a stone. I had spent every bit of strength to get there. I was empty of feeling. I needed to take several pictures. Each required monumental effort. Patches of blue sky graced me briefly, then clouds closed in once more and swirled about as if the whole earth was pulsating. For the second time I had reached the highest point on earth, and once again I couldn't see anything. This time it simply didn't matter.
>
> I still do not know how I managed to achieve the summit. I only know that I couldn't have gone on any longer. Slowly I rose and began the descent.

In Reinhold Messner's *Geographic* article a final photograph shows him exhausted and dehydrated at his High Base Camp. It was accompanied by the following caption: "First came tears, then the story of the ordeal, told in a flood of memory. Along with Messner's story came the realization that he had pushed himself as far as he could go, learning, as British poet C. Day Lewis wrote,

> *"Those Himalayas of the mind*
> *Are not so easily possessed:*
> *There's more than precipice and storm*
> *Between you and your Everest."*

In October 1986, six years after his triumphant conquest of Mount Everest, Reinhold Messner reached the summit of neighboring Lhotse, the world's fourth highest mountain. He thereby became the first person in history to have reached the summit of all fourteen of the world's mountains whose altitudes are over 8,000 meters (26,246 feet). Known to climbers as the "eight-thousanders," the fourteen are all in the Himalayas. Messner achieved mountaineering's grand slam over a period of sixteen years. He had climbed Lhotse as he had Everest—and the world's twelve other highest peaks—without the use of bottled oxygen.

"Have we vanquished an enemy?" Mallory had asked. His answer, "None but ourselves," is one Reinhold Messner clearly understood.

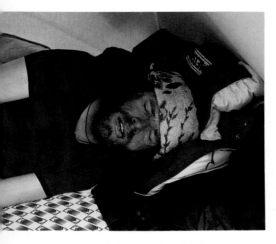

Above: *Alpinist Reinhold Messner, shown recovering from the ordeal, set off from his High Base Camp at 21,325 feet on August 18, 1980, and two and a half days later reached Everest's summit. "I was attempting," he wrote for the October 1981 Geographic, "the greatest challenge, to me, in mountaineering—to climb the highest mountain on earth completely on my own." His accomplishment—without porters, without climbing companions, without a radio, and without bottled oxygen—has been hailed as mountaineering's supreme achievement.*

Right: *Messner had "spent every bit of strength" to get to the top. But now with the aluminum tripod—"the blessing of proof, the curse of desecration"—left anchored to Everest's highest point in 1975 by the Chinese, Messner expended the "monumental effort" to set up his camera and self-timer, then stumbled, dizzy with exhaustion, to the peak.*

Following spread: *"Looking back at Cerro Torre. Photo from just below summit of Fitz Roy after bivouacking on summit snowfield without sleeping bags, standing up most of the night. Before dawn we started moving the last half-hour to the true summit. As we were nearing the top, the first rays of 'alpenglow' hit the peaks.... Cerro Torre, considered the world's most difficult rock spire, is the highest point in the foreground at left.... Behind is the Patagonian Icecap, 200 miles of continuous ice on the border of Chile and Argentina...."—From photographer Galen Rowell's notes to describe this never before published photograph*

"Like a Cluster of Rockets on a Quiet Night"

"Change and resistance, one mellows the other. But back in Jack La Gorce's day he wouldn't change anything. *His whole editorial policy was: Steady as you go, don't upset the apple cart. And I went along with it because that's what he wanted. But I kept all those ideas tucked up in the back of my head—for the day I became editor."*

—Melville Bell Grosvenor, as quoted by Priit Vesilind in his Master of Arts thesis, "National Geographic and Color Photography," December 1977

During the 1954–57 interregnum, there was never any doubt about who would succeed La Gorce. Melville Bell Grosvenor had, in effect, been running the Magazine during those years. So in 1957 when MBG, chafing at La Gorce's conservatism, was finally appointed Editor, one *Geographic* staffer compared Melville's arrival to "a cluster of Fourth of July rockets on a quiet night."

The fireworks were understandable; in one way or another, Melville Grosvenor had been preparing for command of the Geographic ever since 1902, when the five-month-old child, with his father guiding his hand, had affixed a shaky "X" to the dedicatory document which was then sealed and deposited inside the cornerstone of Hubbard Memorial Hall, the Society's new permanent headquarters. Later, with his grandfather Alexander Graham Bell's huge hand gripping his tiny fist, the infant Melville troweled a bit of mortar to help set the cornerstone in place.

Melville's relationship with his grandfather Bell was special to them both. Melville spent his boyhood summer vacations at the Bell home in Baddeck, Nova Scotia, where young Melville basked in his grandfather's love. "Those were wonderful years," he said. "...I learned more from Grandfather than anyone...I was his first grandson and his two sons had died in infancy, so he concentrated all his desire for training a son on me...."

Alexander Graham Bell died in 1922; Melville was then twenty-one years old and a midshipman at the United States Naval Academy. Melville graduated from Annapolis in 1923, served a year as an ensign aboard the battleships *Delaware* and *West Virginia*, resigned his commission in 1924, and began work at the National Geographic.

For the next eighteen years, from 1924 to 1942, Melville wrote and edited picture captions (or "legends" in Geographic parlance); for the following eight years he edited pictures; and from 1950 to 1957 served as an Assistant Editor and later Associate Editor of the Magazine. When he finally became Editor, Melville was fifty-five years old and brimming with ideas—most of which he had presented earlier to his father and La Gorce, only to have them turned down. Still, in the three years following his father's retirement in 1954, Melville had prepared the way for his editorship by hiring young people as full of

Preceding spread: *Melville Bell Grosvenor's decade (1957-1967) as Editor of the Magazine and President of the Society was marked by excitement and innovation. Among the new developments were vivid all-color Magazines, photographs on the covers, expanded research and exploration, the advance into television and expanded book publishing, a 300-page* Atlas of the World, *and the free-floating globes shown here riding a conveyor belt at the Chicago plant of Replogle Globes, Inc., under Melville's and Luther I. Replogle's watchful eyes. Within the first year, more than 120,000 were delivered to National Geographic members in 100 countries.*

ideas as he was—Wilbur E. Garrett, Robert L. Breeden, Thomas J. Abercrombie, and Thomas R. Smith among them.

Almost immediately upon assuming the leadership of the *Geographic*, Melville had to contend with a "palace revolt" within the Illustrations Division. Walter Meayers (Toppy) Edwards, who had started at the *Geographic* as Franklin Fisher's secretary, had simply assumed the Illustrations Editor post vacated in 1953 by Fisher's death; Toppy Edwards reported directly to Melville. Herbert S. Wilburn, Jr., was Assistant Illustrations Editor in charge of color, and Kip Ross was Assistant Illustrations Editor in charge of black-and-white photographs. Under Wilburn and Ross were the picture editors, including Garrett and Breeden.

Although nominally their supervisor, Edwards had little to say about who worked for him. "All of us who were hired in those days were hired by Melville," Garrett explains, "and put under Toppy whether he liked it or not."

Edwards was primarily a picture man. Although he had occasionally written for the Magazine, his chief responsibility for some fifteen years was selecting most of the color pictures for it. Kip Ross's background had been with the Associated Press. He knew journalism, and had done a book on photography, and because he resented having to work under Edwards, constantly undercut and subverted his Illustrations Chief.

Bob Breeden and Bill Garrett were working in black-and-white illustrations under Kip Ross, and urging a modernizing of the Magazine's photographic layout and style. Because Ross was amenable to their tastes, the Magazine's black-and-white pages began to contain more photographs with natural lighting and greater use of white space to create a stronger design. The color sections, however, remained a jumble of miter cuts, hairline rules, and carefully posed set-up shots. And so, as Garrett says, there was a "schism in the Illustrations Division," and

> what made the whole thing intolerable is that there was no layout department. The picture editor was the layout person even if he had no talent at all. It was a totally impossible situation for everybody because it became competitive between the black-and-white picture editors and the color. The color editors would finish the color dummy, so to speak, and then there would be some holes left where the page make-ups went, in which we would then put some black-and-white pictures. And even though Toppy was the head of the department, the black-and-white layouts would go straight to Melville because Kip was much looser. Melville was kind of using the black-and-white department as his experimental lab for make-up and design. It was wonderful because we were allowed freedom. The guys who were on the other side weren't....

The issue came to a head not because of the actions of anyone in the Illustrations Division, but because outsiders from the newly created Book Service Division were brought in: Merle Severy, who had been moved from the staff of the *School Bulletin** to head Book Service, and Howard Paine, a young designer hired by Melville Grosvenor to do layouts for Severy.

**Severy was delighted to be away from the* School Bulletin. *He had written a piece for it that had opened, "If you have a touch of the smuggler in you, then Andorra is the place for you." La Gorce had called Severy into his office and said, "Harumph, Mr. Severy, there are no smugglers among the membership."*

Melville Grosvenor's Leica camera was always at the ready as in this 1959 photograph of the Editor in Cambodia at the great Khmer temple of Angkor Wat. His interest in photography had been encouraged by both his father, Gilbert Hovey Grosvenor, who started Melville taking pictures when he was eleven or twelve years old, and then by his grandfather Alexander Graham Bell, who appointed Melville, at age thirteen, his official photographer of experiments.

BOOK SERVICE

Since 1957, the year MBG created the Book Service Division, nearly fifty separate titles have been mailed out to millions of purchasers. It is difficult to gauge how widespread the influence of these books might be, but Book Service Associate Director Ross S. Bennett tells the following story: In 1962, sophomore Ronald M. Nowak, at Tulane University in New Orleans, read in a Book Service volume titled *Wild Animals of North America* that the red wolf, found in the bayou area of Louisiana and Texas, was fast disappearing. But other books he had read made no mention of the decline. So Nowak decided to investigate. He began writing letters

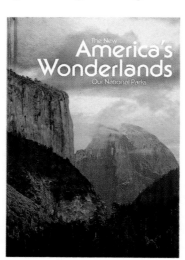

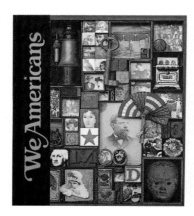

The World in Your Garden

National Geographic Society

asking for information on the red wolf population; he then contacted the United States Fish and Wildlife Service. When his own study confirmed the red wolf's decrease, Nowak helped launch a national campaign that led to a federal effort to save the animal. Nowak went on to become a biologist.

"Years later, when Book Service editors decided to publish a new edition of *Wild Animals* and sought a chief consultant," Bennett reports, "they found their expert right in their own backyard—Ron Nowak, staff mammalogist in Fish and Wildlife's Office of Endangered Species."

Perhaps the Book Service volume closest to Melville Grosvenor's heart was *Men, Ships, and*

the Sea. Melville wanted the book written by someone who had "lived the sea" and wrote of it with passion. He was able to get Alan Villiers, author of many of the most popular *Geographic* seafaring articles, to write the text. Not only was *Men, Ships, and the Sea* one of the first Book Service items that contained material not primarily picked up from the Magazine, it was also an oversized volume—a fact that, Book Service Director Charles O. Hyman recalls, "caused all kinds of hell...Melville was angry because it didn't fit in his bookshelf. He had his bookshelves designed so that they were exactly the height of the Magazine. Merle Severy [the first Director of Book Service] had to sneak into Melville's office with carpenters while MBG was away and raise the bookshelves so *Men, Ships, and the Sea* would fit."

Since 1962, Book Service subjects have "ranged across the spectrum of human interest, from Indians to insects, from national parks to historic shrines, from birds to dogs," says Associate Director Bennett. "Readers have marveled at animal behavior, explored our living planet, discovered Britain and Ireland, journeyed into China, diagrammed the human body, and followed the adventure of archeology. They have watched history come alive in the rise of Western civilization through volumes emphasizing everyday life. ...They have sampled spiritual tolerance in *Great Religions of the World* and rediscovered themselves in *We Americans.*"

Although their painstakingly researched volumes have received wide critical acclaim, the reviews that please Book Service staffers most are ones from young students such as the Brooklyn boy who wrote, "I think your books are wonderful. ...I am 13 years of age and someday I hope to work for the Society along with all of you."

Although Book Service, established in 1957, was new, the Society, of course, had been publishing books for years: *Alaskan Glacier Studies* and *A Book of Monsters* (about insects) had both, for example, been published in 1914, and there had been books on horses (1923), birds (1915, 1918, 1951), and dogs (1919) as well. In 1951, the Society had published *Everyday Life in Ancient Times* with a text by the scholar Edith Hamilton, among others, and *Stalking Birds With Color Camera*. In 1954, Severy, along with Andrew Poggenpohl, had put together *Indians of the Americas*, with a text by Matthew W. Stirling and others. That book, published in 1955, sold 379,152 copies and was such an enormous success that Melville, who wanted to increase the Society's participation in book publishing, felt encouraged enough to establish the Book Service Division.

Until *Indians of the Americas*, the Society's books had been simply a collection of magazine pieces with plates. But when Howard Paine started designing for Severy, the Society's books suddenly began to have a different look— the sort of open-layout-with-lots-of-white-space look that the younger members of the Magazine's Illustrations Division had been clamoring for and couldn't get. The result: resentment.

Severy explains, "The Magazine couldn't get away with the kind of stuff the Book Service did. You couldn't tamper with the Magazine. Psychologically, however, the books were not sacred ground. We'd been allowed to do things with the books because nobody took us seriously—except Melville."

The confrontation occurred after Merle Severy showed Toppy Edwards a copy of his latest book while they were on an airplane en route to a Chicago convention and recommended that Edwards have Howard Paine help with the Magazine layouts. Upon arrival in Chicago, Edwards phoned Garrett in Washington and told him to give the dummy he was working on to Howard Paine to re-do with white space. Garrett had already completed it.

"Is that an order?" Garrett asked.

"Yes," Edwards said.

Garrett said, "Okay," and went down to Personnel to resign. Edwards' phone call had also enraged the other members of the Illustrations Division. All of them had been trying to update the design of the Magazine, to open up the layouts, to use some white space, and Edwards hadn't let them. "Suddenly," Garrett recalls, "here was an outsider named Howard Paine who was going to be allowed to do it!"

When Edwards returned, he summoned the entire Illustrations staff to his office for a meeting with Merle Severy, Howard Paine, and a feltboard. Paine began to instruct the Illustrations Editors on how to lay out the Magazine pages.

"Toppy was a fairly small man, and he sat behind this huge desk," Garrett remembers. "And here was Howard Paine, nicest guy in the world, who'd been brought in with a feltboard to tell us how to lay out pictures. You could just cut the tension with a knife."

Paine, new to the *Geographic* and unaware of the conflicts within the Illustrations Division, was only trying to do what he had been told. Staff members who, like Breeden, had been doing layouts and suggesting the very changes Paine was proposing, felt they hadn't been heard, resented it, and made their feelings known.

333

"Even as the new head-quarters opened [in 1964]," Melville Grosvenor later recalled, "our 40-year-old membership records building in another section of Washington was bulging at the seams." In 1965, the Board of Trustees authorized the purchase of a hundred-acre site near Gaithersburg, Maryland, for the construction of new Membership Center Building.

A few days before the ground-breaking, Melville went out to the site with Boris V. Timchenko, the landscape architect. Disturbed by the planned location of the building in relation to the eleven-acre spring-fed lake and the rest of the terrain, MBG asked Timchenko, "Will the lake be used to best advantage?"

"[Not] the way the building is staked out now," the landscape architect replied.

"Then move the building," Melville said.

Timchenko realigned the stakes, literally turning the 420-foot building twenty-five degrees on its axis. The architects worked in a frenzy to finish revised drawings before the giant earth-moving machines arrived.

MCB—as the new Membership Center Building's name inevitably came to be abridged—opened in 1968 housing more than 1,100 employees and two giant computers to help keep track of the Society's nearly eleven million members in 170 of the world's 174 nations and to maintain all phases of communication with them.

Operations at MCB fall under the direction of Society Executive Vice President Owen R. Anderson, whose firm supervisory control led editorial wags to dub the Gaithersburg center "Andersonville."

"We were pretty well regimented in the membership fulfillment operation compared with the editorial world," Ander-son laughingly admits.

A certain amount of regimentation could be expected of an organization that takes care of the complete membership operation. The membership files are kept at MCB; its staff copes with membership renewals, the mailing of bills, the receipt of all remittances. "And since we have the files, we're responsible for addressing all the promotion pieces, all the billing operations, etc., for *all* the magazines and books," Anderson says. "Poor service is a great problem in various fulfillment houses. If you're not getting your magazine to the members, people will get disgruntled and they won't want it."

In 1986 alone, MCB received 21,595,224 pieces of mail, an average of 85,695 pieces of mail *per day*! Even though a largely automated computer operation provides immediate answers to many of the members' inquiries, many prefer instead to telephone, so in addition to the vast volume of mail, the Center receives an average 1,209 calls a day.

Anderson suggests that "maybe part of the National Geographic Society's high renewal rate [an astounding eighty-six percent in 1986] is due to the service that MCB offers."

On a "big day" more than half a million pieces of mail have arrived at MCB. The heaviest mail day is generally a result of the summer remittance operation mailing. "We send out a promotion called a voluntary summer remittance plan six months in advance," Anderson explains. "Memberships expire in December, and we ask the members to renew six months in advance so we can hold down renewal costs. As a result almost fifty percent of the members renew at that time. Therefore, when this huge mailing goes out in June a peak mail hits us the last of June or early July." In one day in July 1986 582,614 pieces of mail reached MCB.

Melville pushed for perfection and innovation in photography and showed that he was willing to pay for it by tripling the photographic budget. At Melville's direction, Illustrations Editor Wilburn increased the size of photographs printed in the Magazine and initiated the practice of having every article begin with a double-page picture. And each issue contained as much color as possible.

As dramatic as the changes were inside the Magazine, the outside was due for changes, too. Melville had grown tired of looking at the Magazine's same old conservative covers. So one day he asked several of his associates—among them his son Gilbert M. Grosvenor—to come to his office. On his desk MBG had a big pile of *Geographics*. As soon as the door was closed he picked up the Magazines and threw them on the floor, face up. "For a moment we wondered what was wrong with the Editor," Ted Vosburgh recalled. "Then he challenged us. 'Look at those Magazines,' he said, 'and tell me which is the latest issue.' Nobody could.

" 'You see!' declared Melville triumphantly. 'They all look alike.'

"Then he produced a dozen Magazines on which striking color photographs had been pasted," Vosburgh's recollection continues.

" 'Now look at these,' he said, holding up one with a picture of a geisha on the cover. 'If you saw this on a coffee table in a friend's home, you'd think, oh yes, there's last month's *Geographic* with a story on Japan. Or you'd think, I haven't seen that one yet; it must be the new issue.'

" 'Hereafter,' declared the Editor, almost belligerently, 'there's going to be a color picture on the cover.' "

A photograph of the new forty-nine-star American flag appeared on the cover of the July 1959 issue; there was no photograph in August; in September a small Navy jet fighter appeared, and color pictures have been on the cover of the *Geographic* ever since.

The Society next changed printing plants and processes. When Melville took over the Magazine, he wrote, "stood at a crossroads. With a rising membership of 2,175,000, we faced the fact that two and a half million would be the most that could practicably be printed by the method then in use. No longer could we hope to meet the needs of our members with presses that printed one sheet at a time, stacked the sheets, waited for the ink to dry, then printed the other side."

Thomas W. McKnew, then Executive Vice President of the Society and Secretary of a special Printing Methods Committee, and other members of the Committee debated whether to continue printing in Washington or to change processes and go elsewhere. They decided a move from Washington was the only solution. McKnew supervised moving the printing out of Washington, where it had been (with the exception of a brief period in 1901 when it had been printed in New York), taking it to R. R. Donnelley & Sons' high-speed color presses in Chicago, where, as MBG noted, "instead of the slow inserting of sheets, there would be a continuous web of paper running off a roll and through the presses at a rate of 1,200 feet a minute. Inks would be 'heat-set' (dried instantly) as the web passed over a hot drum....

"Although enormously complicated, the transfer of our printing to Chicago was carried out without a hitch, and by mid-1960 the move was complete. No longer would we have to limit our color illustrations to a few sections of 4, 8, or 16 pages. Now we could have an all-color magazine—color photographs on every page—and press capacity to meet every foreseeable need."

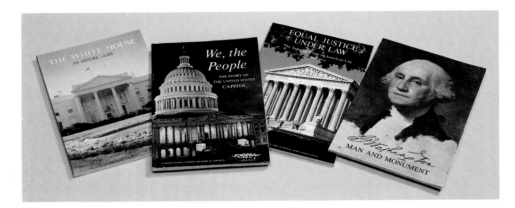

"A beautiful book," President John F. Kennedy commented when MBG handed him a copy of The White House: An Historic Guide, *produced by the Society at the request of the First Lady. The White House guide was first in a series of public service books prepared on such topics as the Capitol, the Supreme Court, the Washington Monument, and Presidents. More recently,* Liberty *has generated more than $4 million for the Statue of Liberty Foundation.*

the White House book, the Capitol's *We, the People; Equal Justice Under Law* on the Supreme Court; *G. Washington, Man and Monument*; and a book on the Presidents. All of these books were done as a public service by the Geographic (and a significantly expensive one), but it finally got to be too much. Breeden wrote a confidential memo to Melville Grosvenor suggesting, in effect, that the National Geographic should be publishing these small books "not just for others," but for itself and that a Department of Special Services be formed to do them. Breeden's memo continued:

> With a staff you could count on one hand, I am sure I could produce at least three such books a year. The Society, I estimate, could net $250,000 on its books and many times over this amount on free publicity on public service books.
>
> All of this would be done apart from our present Book Service, which already has an expanded program.

Breeden insisted in his memo that such a department "would not involve hiring new personnel" and concluded:

> When you stop to think about it, a Department of Special Services and a small book program is not anything new for the Geographic. We've been doing it for two years!

Melville called Breeden into his office and asked, "But Bob, you wouldn't want to leave the Magazine, would you?"

"Well no, not really," Breeden said, "but I would like to get to the point where I would not have to spend so many hours down here and could be with my family more."

Melville said he would think about it. Melvin Payne, President of the Society, appointed a task force to study the feasibility of publishing a series of low-cost books. The committee came back with a positive report: the Society could publish annually four high-quality, color-illustrated books averaging 200 pages each. With relatively low promotional costs the members could have them at a reasonable price; moreover, test mailings proved conclusively that the members would buy such books.

In 1965, the Special Publications Division was born. (Twenty years later, as a result of the creation of many new products, Breeden's original staff that "you could count on one hand" had grown so large it practically needed a small building of its own.)

By then Melville had also moved the Society into television—a medium his father had avoided, but an inevitable outgrowth of the Society's im-

SPECIAL PUBLICATIONS

"Why don't you print these articles as a separate book? My son used them for his homework and got an A." Letters such as this from members played a part in Melville Grosvenor's decision to launch the Special Publications Division in 1965 with Robert L. Breeden as its chief.

"An outgrowth of the public service books about the White House, the Capitol, and the Supreme Court, Special Pubs were intended to be small, magazine-page-size books," Breeden points out, "not the large format type of books done by Book Service.

"Melville had a great deal of respect for Merle Severy who was then chief of Book Service. One day Melville asked me to come in, and he said, 'Bob, I know you're going to be doing these books. Do you think they'll interfere with Book Service?'

"I told him I didn't think there would be any problem at all, and I asked, 'Would you like for me to go talk with Merle about this?'

"He grinned, obviously relieved, and asked, 'Bob, would you do that?'

"I went to see Merle," Breeden said, "and he was, of course, confident these small books wouldn't hurt the big ones. He saw no problem with it—although, I will have to say, there certainly developed a very strong feeling of competition between the two book services."

Special Publications and School Services, now under Director Donald J. Crump, publishes books that are generally more narrow-focused and tightly defined than Book Service's large-format "encyclopedic" books.

Special Pubs quickly moved into publishing books on a wide variety of popular topics such as U. S. history, wildlife, earth sciences, undersea and space developments, and New World

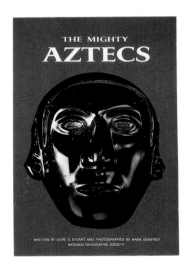

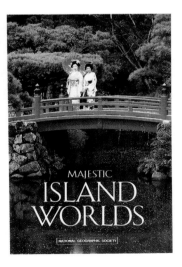

archeology—some of which were big enough to further blur to an outsider the already fuzzy distinction between Book Service and Special Pubs.

There is one distinction, however, that any publisher would envy. From an original core of 28,000, there are now more than 200,000 readers who purchase each Special Pubs volume without even seeing the announcement of the year's four new titles. "Forever Pubs," as these loyal members are known, helped push sales of Special Pubs' now eighty-seven titles to more than 34,000,000 by the end of 1986.

345

mensely popular lecture* series, which, since 1888, had thrilled Society members, first with lantern slides and later with color films. As Melville wrote in 1970:

> Many early members saw the North Pole meet the South Pole in 1913 when Robert E. Peary introduced Roald Amundsen; both described their discoveries.
>
> Many listened spellbound to Wilbur Wright telling of the birth of powered aviation. Later audiences rode vicariously with Richard E. Byrd on his pioneer flights over the Poles, ascended with balloonists Albert Stevens and Orvil Anderson into the stratosphere, took the first successful deep-ocean dive with William Beebe in his bathysphere.
>
> In the fifties and sixties, we presented other dramatic film lectures by modern trailblazers who devoted, and often gambled their lives to win new geographic knowledge: Sir Edmund Hillary, who, with Sherpa guide Tenzing Norgay, first reached the top of Mt. Everest; Commander [James F.] Calvert, who surfaced his atomic submarine *Skate* at the North Pole; Captain Cousteau and Dr. Leakey....
>
> The popularity of our lectures encouraged us to feel that a far wider audience awaited the color films that the Society's experience and talent could produce.

Perhaps even more encouraging than the lectures was the guest appearance Melville made with Luis Marden in January 1958 on NBC's television program "Omnibus." Marden, the previous year, had found, while diving off Pitcairn Island in the South Pacific, the remains of Captain William Bligh's ship H.M.S. *Bounty*, burned and sunk by mutineers 167 years before. Marden's discovery had made world headlines, and a Society lecture film, *The Bones of the Bounty*, was so successful that Melville began to believe the Society should be producing its own television shows.

In 1961, a documentary film department was organized by the Society's first Director of Television, Robert C. Doyle, who had the responsibility of producing four TV documentaries a year—and coming up with outside commercial sponsorship for the films.

In 1963, funds were made available to film the three-team assault on Mount Everest by Americans, one of whom was Barry C. Bishop, National Geographic staff geographer. This expedition, partially sponsored by the Society, was, in addition to being the first to ascend the summit by the West Ridge, the first ever on which motion pictures were taken from the peak:

> "The wind whipped and tore at us as we perched precariously on the earth's highest pinnacle," wrote an expedition member of how he and his teammate Luther (Lute) Jerstad made the film. "The American flag chattered in the gusts....Lute stuck his ice ax in the hard snow, anchored a motion-picture camera to its head...the ax shuddered in the wind. Lute's silk-gloved fingers began to freeze as he turned the camera's metal crank...."

The color motion-picture footage was edited and assembled; expedition member James Ramsey Ullman wrote the script. Encyclopaedia Britannica and Aetna Casualty Insurance agreed to sponsor it; David L. Wolper produced

A National Geographic Society lecture was scheduled the evening of November 22, 1963. That afternoon President John F. Kennedy was shot and killed in Dallas, Texas. Several Geographic staff members were sent to Constitution Hall to turn away Society members who might not have heard that the lecture was cancelled. An elderly couple, intercepted on their way to the hall, were told there would not be a lecture that night because the President had been assassinated. Shocked by the news, one of them asked, "Our Dr. Grosvenor?"

LEAKEY AND PROTÉGÉES:

Among the Magazine's "stars" who became television celebrities were several recipients of financial support from the Society's Committee for Research and Exploration such as the Leakeys ("The Legacy of L.S.B. Leakey," broadcast in 1978), Jane Goodall ("Miss Goodall and the Wild Chimpanzees," 1965), Dian Fossey ("Gorilla," 1981), and Dr. Biruté M.F. Galdikas (with Dian Fossey in "Search for the Great Apes," 1976).

Since 1959, the year Dr. and Mrs. Louis S. B. Leakey discovered the 1.75-million-year-old skull from a manlike creature they called *Zinjanthropus*, the Society supported their work in East Africa. In five decades of unearthing bones of hominids and other animals in Tanzania's Olduvai Gorge, the late paleoanthropologist Louis Leakey greatly expanded the record of early man. In the picture *near right top* Louis and his son, Richard, study the fossil skull of a man- and ape-like creature.

Leakey believed that by studying the great apes, insight could be gained into the behavior of early man. As a result, a direct link exists between the Leakeys' work and that of Jane Goodall *(near right bottom)*, Dian Fossey *(far right top)*, and Biruté Galdikas *(far right bottom)*—all Leakey protégées.

Beginning in July 1960, when Jane Goodall (shown here with Research and Exploration Committee members Leonard Carmichael, Melvin Payne, and T. Dale Stewart) began to live among the chimpanzees of Tanzania's Gombe Stream National Park, Society grants have helped support her continuing study of their behavior in the wild—she discovered that usually sociable chimpanzees can, on occasion, become killers and cannibals. She proved that they fashion and use tools—an observation of ob-

GOODALL, FOSSEY, AND GALDIKAS

vious importance for the scientific world. "Tool using always used to be considered a hallmark of the human species," Jane Goodall later said.

In December 1985 the Society—and the world—was shocked and saddened by the brutal murder of Dian Fossey in the forested mountains of Rwanda. She had made her home there since 1967, when she began her long-term study of the mountain gorilla. Fossey's years of painstaking observation of these, the largest of the great apes, helped change our perception of this endangered species from that of a fearsome jungle giant to that of a shy and unaggressive fellow creature.

Anthropologist Biruté Galdikas, who raised young orangutans at her camp in the Tanjung Puting Reserve study area in the Bornean rain forest, has also spent years trying to protect an endangered primate species.

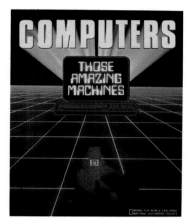

BOOKS FOR CHILDREN

The Society's children's book program began in 1972 with publication of the first set of Books for Young Explorers, a series designed for children four through eight years old.

The inspiration behind the series was then *National Geographic* Editor Gilbert M. Grosvenor, who was looking for non-fiction books designed for durability, illustrated with quality color photographs, and of interest to both the child listener and the parent reading aloud— books that he could share with his own young son. Books for Young Explorers were developed by the Special Publications Division under the leadership of Robert L. Breeden and his associates Donald J. Crump and Philip B. Silcott. Their goal was to stimulate in young children a love of reading by making books with texts that children themselves could read and that would sustain the interest of young listeners. The staff, working with educators and librarians, scientists and children's book authors, produced the first of the series of thirty-two-page books: *Dinosaurs, Dogs Working for People, Lion Cubs: Growing Up in the Wild,* and *Treasures in the Sea.* Packaged in sets of four, the Books for Young Explorers series are offered annually to Society members in time for Christmas.

In school and at home, the opinions of children in the four to eight age group were solicited in the selection of titles. Under the guidance of a reading specialist,

texts were tested on children to help set an appropriate readability level. Children were also shown photographic layouts to determine if they had any difficulty in "reading" the pictures.

In 1978, however, Books for Young Explorers were temporarily "put on hold" when the demographic trend of lower birth rates resulted in a lower demand from members. Three years later, in 1981, the program was reinstated. And the press run for its four-book set that year was 200,000 copies. By 1986, with the publication of Set 13—*Baby Bears and How They Grow, Saving Our Animal Friends, Animals That Live in Trees,* and *Animals and Their Hiding Places*—the press run had jumped to 410,000 copies. By the spring of 1987, more than twenty-one million individual Books for Young Explorers were in print.

In the late 1970s, the Society turned its attention to slightly older readers. Children who had avidly read Books for Young Explorers were growing up; and it was decided that the children's book program should grow up with them. The result was a series of Books for World Explorers for children ages eight to thirteen designed to be both educational and fun. The first book, *Secrets From the Past,* rolled off the press in October 1979, and amazingly—as in *Amazing Animals of the Sea, Amazing Mysteries of the World, Amazing Animals of Australia,* and *Computers: Those Amazing Machines*—one 104-page book after another has followed every three months since then.

The most recent children's book venture has been the Action Book. Each "pop-up book" contains twelve pages with dimensional and moving parts. Ingenious paper engineering enables a butterfly to take wing in one book, while monkeys dangle from three-dimensional trees in another. Introduced in 1985, the new program received instant acclaim.

it, and on the evening of September 10, 1965, *Americans on Everest*, narrated by Orson Welles, was seen on television.

This was no blurry, strung-together sequence of still pictures showing distant specks clinging to the side of the world's tallest mountain. It was superb close-up color motion-picture photography of the expedition members' torturous struggle against mind- and bone-chilling 20° below zero temperatures and 60 mph winds, against collapsing ice walls and treacherous snow cornices, against numbing fatigue and oxygen deprivation. It was about courage and determination, risk and achievement, and it took its millions of viewers along with Barry Bishop (who had sworn to himself: "If you have to crawl on hands and knees you're going to get there") up 29,028 feet to Everest's summit.

The day after *Americans on Everest* was shown, an ecstatic CBS reported to the Society that the film had received the highest ratings of any documentary ever telecast. Melville Grosvenor's "far wider audience" had been reached; and a formidable new era of increasing and diffusing geographic knowledge had begun.

During Melville Grosvenor's decade at the helm, the Society turned out one stunning documentary after another. *Americans on Everest* was followed by *Miss Goodall and the Wild Chimpanzees*, *Dr. Leakey and the Dawn of Man*, *The World of Jacques-Yves Cousteau*. The Magazine's "stars" became television stars. And then, in 1968, the Geographic special *Amazon* made television history when its lush river and jungle scenes were watched by thirty-five million people. It was the first television documentary to top all other shows in a two-week rating period.

Under Melville's leadership, massive new buildings rose to house the Society. He commissioned one of America's best-known architects to create a new headquarters to be linked with the older headquarters by a tunnel beneath a magnolia-shaded parking lot—and paid for it in cash. "The concrete capstone of Grosvenor's contributions," the *Washington Post* reported on September 13, 1974, "is represented by the white marble headquarters building at 17th and M Streets, NW, designed by Edward Durell Stone. It is proof that modern architecture can have grace and beauty."

The new headquarters was the first Washington building designed by Stone. On January 18, 1964, President Lyndon B. Johnson dedicated the gleaming, marble-clad ten-story building, saying, "Today in this house of exploration, let us invite exploration by all nations, for all nations." President Johnson was an appropriate choice to have dedicated the building. He had once told Melville, "My mother brought me up with the Bible in my right hand and the *Geographic* in my left."

With color photographs on the cover, vivid all-color Magazines, new printing techniques, expanded support of research and exploration, the advance into television and book publishing, Melville Grosvenor had taken what many in the senior echelons of the Society considered a "fussy, stagnant empire" and directed it through a decade of exciting, explosive expansion.

"However," as *The New York Times* noted, "Dr. Grosvenor did not dramatically modify the magazine's traditional tone of gentlemanly detachment from the ugliness, misery and strife in the world."

Publishing, outside the Society, continued to deride the Magazine's see-no-evil attitude. Calling the National Geographic Society "the least exclusive, farthest flung and most improbable nonprofit publishing corporation in the world," *Time* magazine in a June 15, 1959, article, characterized Gilbert H.

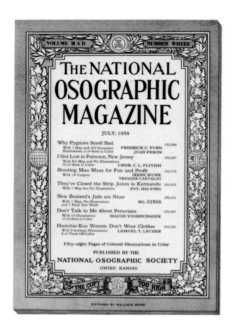

Look again. At first glance, Mad magazine's 1958 National Osographic Magazine *so mimics the* National Geographic *style that it risks being passed by. However, Mad's parody lead story,* "Why Pygmies Smell Bad," *inadvertently foreshadowed the* Geographic's *September 1986 article* "The Intimate Sense of Smell," *with its startling photograph of laboratory-jacketed women sniffing bare-chested men's armpits.*

Grosvenor's "I was always taught not to criticize other people" attitude as being the basis for the "unrealistic hue to the *Geographic*'s rose-colored world."

The National Geographic "thrives on a policy of daring serenity and a 'dear Aunt Sally style,' as staff members refer to it," *Newsweek* wrote in its November 11, 1963, issue, remarking on the Society's seventy-fifth anniversary in that year. "The world of National Geographic is usually a sunlit Kodachrome world of altruistic human achievement in settings of natural beauty, a world without commercial blemish or political disturbance, even, it sometimes seems, a world without germs or sin."

Melville Grosvenor's response to those criticisms was always to admit they were true, but, as he told one reporter, "We've always tried not to point out the sores. What the hell, there's so much wonderful stuff in the world, why get into the sordid too much? I mean, that's not our job."

It was with that attitude in mind that three years after Melville Grosvenor's resignation, *The New York Times Magazine* titled its piece on Gilbert M. Grosvenor's accession to the editorship "With the National Geographic On Its Endless, Cloudless Voyage." For *Esquire*'s "Two Cheers for the Geographic," Anne Chamberlin wrote, "The Magazine has mastered the art of admitting there are bad smells but not dwelling on them."

Even *Mad* magazine took on the *Geographic* in a 1958 parody called *The National Osographic Magazine* that contained such lead articles as "Why Pygmies Smell Bad" and "Don't Talk to Me About Peruvians" and a piece called "Africa is for the Birds," which said:

> Far up the trail, I could make out the form of a tall princely Buktuktu, his k'kkkaty glistening in the sunlight. Obviously, the Jdu-Jdu drums had heralded our arrival and he was a royal welcoming committee.
>
> He came forward with a smile that disclosed the sharply filed teeth of the Gwam'mbmba aristocracy. He bowed low, showing us his wumbt'tu, and I shielded Evelyn from the sight as best I could.

Chamberlin, in *Esquire*, rose to the *Geographic*'s defense, quoting one devotee: "Laughing at the *National Geographic* is like laughing at Harvard. No matter how hearty and well-deserved the laughter, it is still a great institution."

Had it not been, the Society might not have so readily withstood the chaos within its Illustrations Division and what Melville's son Gilbert M. Grosvenor would refer to as the "meandering oxbows of communications" and decisions "dependent upon who was the last person to get to MBG and his enthusiasm." And just as the Society had withstood the chaos within, it withstood the chaos without: the troubled 1960s—that decade of brutal and heartrending political assassinations and imprisonments, of escalating "protective reaction" raids against Southeast Asian villagers, that decade of racial and generational polarization which culminated so despicably in senseless campus killings and in mind-bending and life-ending experimentation with drugs, that decade of monolithic megacorporational indifference toward the environmental and ecological havoc they had wrought, that decade of Presidential and Congressional chicanery, that decade of alarming and confounding economic and spiritual crises....

The *Geographic* was able to withstand the storms primarily because of the leadership of Melville Bell Grosvenor: the right man, in the right place, at the right time.

On February 4, 1966, Gilbert Hovey Grosvenor, ninety years old, lay down for an afternoon nap at his Baddeck summer home. He had spent his first Christmas without his beloved wife and companion of so many years. Elsie May Bell Grosvenor, First Lady of the Geographic, had died the day after Christmas, 1964.

Dr. Grosvenor had grown increasingly frail as the New Year 1966 had commenced and, knowing the end was near, his family had gathered around him to say good-bye. Just before his nap that February afternoon, a daughter heard Dr. Grosvenor mention a recurring dream, one in which he was either just setting out on a voyage, or returning to port.

Looking back on his "long and happy tenure" as Editor of the Magazine and President of the Society, he had written, "Those golden years of my editorship bring to mind a fragment from Tennyson's beautiful poem *Ulysses*,"

> *For always roaming with a hungry heart,*
> *Much have I seen and known—cities of men*
> *And manners, climates, councils, governments.*

Gilbert Hovey Grosvenor never awoke from that nap.

That evening, President Lyndon B. Johnson and Mrs. Johnson telephoned their condolences, and the next day sent the following wire to Melville:

> As the Nation grieves the loss of your father, inquiring minds everywhere grieve the loss of a leader. Through words and pictures and through his own unswerving dedication, Gilbert Grosvenor opened the wonders of the world we live in to three generations of Americans. No mountain was too high, no sea too deep, no climate too forbidding for the teams of the National Geographic Society.
>
> If a great national power has an obligation to know and to understand the nature of the world around it, then it can truly be said that Gilbert Grosvenor played a vital role in America's coming of age.

More tributes, from former Presidents and other Chiefs of State, poured in, but among the most touching was the memory of a Society staffer who recalled that as "a shy cub from New England" he had been invited to spend a weekend with the Grosvenor family and their guests at their Florida winter home. As Vice President and Associate Editor Frederick G. Vosburgh wrote in his October 1966 *National Geographic* tribute to Gilbert Hovey Grosvenor:

> White linen suits were in style then and, on the advice of friends, he had brought one. But nothing had been said about white shoes, and when he went down to dinner he saw to his horror that of all the men present he alone was wearing black shoes. He had no others; there was nothing he could do in his embarrassment but try to lose himself among the guests.
>
> In a few minutes Dr. Grosvenor quietly excused himself and disappeared upstairs, to return shortly. He was wearing black shoes.

In 1967, one year after his father's death, Melville Bell Grosvenor, age sixty-five, fulfilled his vow not to deny his successors the opportunity to lead that had for so long been denied him. He stepped down from active editorship. Frederick G. Vosburgh was appointed Editor to replace him—a position that, like the editorship of John Oliver La Gorce, would serve as an interregnum between Grosvenors. Gilbert M. Grosvenor would succeed Vosburgh in 1971.

Melville Grosvenor's turbulent decade had been one of unquestioned success. While major mass-market magazines such as *Life*, *Saturday Evening Post*, and *Colliers* were folding all around him, the *Geographic*'s revered skipper had steered the Society into the twentieth century—and not a moment too soon.

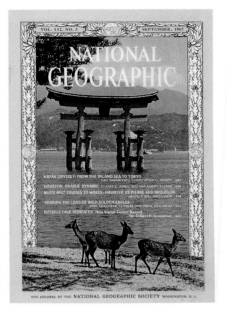

In 1967, at the close of Melville Grosvenor's decade as Editor, membership had more than doubled from 2,178,040, at the end of 1957, to 5,607,457.

"The Choice Is the Universe —or Nothing"

"There is no way back into the past: the choice, as [H.G.] Wells once said, is the Universe—or nothing. Though men and civilizations may yearn for rest, for the Elysian dream of the Lotus Eaters, that is a desire that merges imperceptibly into death. The challenge of the great spaces between the worlds is a stupendous one, but if we fail to meet it, the story of our race will be drawing to its close. Humanity will have turned its back upon the still untrodden heights and will be descending again the long slope that stretches, across a thousand million years of time, down to the shores of the primeval sea."

—From Arthur C. Clarke, *Interplanetary Flight: An Introduction to Astronautics*, as quoted by Carl Sagan in his article "Mars: A New World to Explore," in the December 1967 Magazine

Above: *The first* Explorer *balloon tugs at its tethers prior to its near disastrous July 28, 1934, ascent.*

Opposite: *November 11, 1935. Wearing football helmets borrowed from a high school squad, Capt. Orvil A. Anderson (left) and Capt. Albert W. Stevens (right) pause outside the gondola of the stratosphere balloon* Explorer II *before their ascent (sponsored by the Society and the U.S. Army Air Corps). They reached 72,395 feet—a record that stood for twenty-one years.*

Preceding spread: *Designed to bridge the gap between manned flight in the atmosphere and manned flight in space, the X-15 rocket plane thunders at five times the speed of sound on its April 30, 1962, run, carrying test pilot Joseph A. Walker to a record altitude of 246,700 feet—above 99.996 percent of the earth's atmosphere.*

Since its inception, the National Geographic Society has been in the forefront of those supporting aviation and space exploration. In 1911, at a time when American interest in aviation seemed to be faltering, Wilbur Wright took advantage of his opportunity as speaker at a Society banquet to warn the membership and President Taft, the Society's guest, that "the leading nations of the earth are taking up the subject, our own nation being the first of all to begin it. But unfortunately, there seems to be some hesitation at present."

In 1914, Alexander Graham Bell, who had sketched a rocket plane in 1893, predicted, "...heavier-than-air machines...of a different construction from anything yet conceived of, will be driven over the earth's surface at enormous velocity, hundreds of miles an hour, by new methods of propulsion....Think of the enormous energy locked up in high explosives! What if we could control that energy and utilize it in some form of projectile flight!"

Airship pioneers Hugo Eckener, Amelia Earhart, and Charles Lindbergh each lectured before the Society. So did stratosphere balloonists Auguste Piccard and Albert W. Stevens, to whom the altitude records then belonged.

The March 1933 *Geographic* carried Piccard's account, "Ballooning in the Stratosphere: Two Balloon Ascents to Ten-Mile Altitudes Presage New Mode of Aërial Travel," and told of his record-breaking ascents in hydrogen-filled balloons to altitudes of 51,775 feet on May 27, 1931, and to 53,152.8 feet on August 18, 1932. "The stratosphere is the superhighway of future intercontinental transport," Piccard proclaimed.

In October 1934, the *Geographic* contained "Exploring the Stratosphere," Capt. Albert W. Stevens' account of the National Geographic Society–U.S.

Man has already probed at the moon with some 45 spacecraft bearing names like Luna and Zond, Ranger, Surveyor, and Orbiter. From afar we have poked and scratched its surface, hammered on its rocks, assayed its chemistry, measured its temperatures. We have tested it with radio waves, the exhaust of rocket engines, and magnets. We have photographed from close up all but the merest smidgen of its tortured face.

And now, as this is written, a few chosen men, astronauts and cosmonauts, train with monastic zeal for the fantastic attempt that will bring alive the tales of Jules Verne and H.G. Wells.

The list of *Geographic* manned spaceflight articles is a condensed history of this country's space program en route to the moon. The first manned Mercury launch atop a Redstone rocket was covered in "The Flight of *Freedom 7*," by Carmault B. Jackson, Jr., and "The Pilot's Story: Astronaut Shepard's Firsthand Account of His Flight," which appeared in September 1961, four months after Alan B. Shepard, Jr., became the first American to ride a pure rocket into space. Shepard's launch was followed by Gus Grissom's in *Liberty Bell 7*, the last launch atop a Redstone rocket. Now that the Mercury capsule had been proven safe, the next stage of manned flight, atop the more powerful Atlas booster, was to test the performance of pilots in a more extended weightless condition. Robert B. Voas' "John Glenn's Three Orbits in *Friendship 7*: A Minute-by-Minute Account of America's First Orbital Space Flight" covered this stage. Voas was the Training Officer of Project Mercury; his article appeared in June 1962, four months after Glenn's launch, and recalls those pre-man-on-the-moon days when every space flight was breaking new ground. It also reminds us that such flights were dangerous—a lesson reinforced when the *Challenger* space shuttle exploded in January 1986.

Reading Voas' article today, one sees that even with Glenn's flight there were indications that NASA felt there were certain things it was better for the astronauts not to know. At the end of Glenn's first of three earth orbits, as Voas wrote, "a radio signal from the spacecraft indicated that the landing bag, which would act as a cushion when the capsule hit the water, had been deployed prematurely. If this signal proved valid, it would mean that the heat shield, which is attached to the landing bag, had also come free and would not protect the spacecraft from the fiery heat of re-entry." In other words, the capsule's heat shield would have sheared off during re-entry, and *Friendship 7*, with Glenn inside it, would have incinerated in seconds.

Glenn's first indication that there might be a problem occurred at 02:26:36 [2 hours, 26 minutes, and 36 seconds] into the flight, when capsule communicator Gordon Cooper in Muchea, Australia, asked Glenn, *"Friendship 7, will you confirm the landing bag switch is in the off position?"*

Voas' piece continues:

> *Affirmative,* Glenn answers. *Landing bag switch is in the center off position.*
>
> Cooper asks: *You haven't had any banging noises or anything of this type?*
>
> *Negative.*

Right: *With one solar panel lost en route to orbit, 100-ton Skylab orbits silently 270 miles above the cloud-shrouded earth.*

Overleaf: *The space shuttle* Challenger, *inverted high above Baja California in 1984, launches a satellite for testing materials in space.*

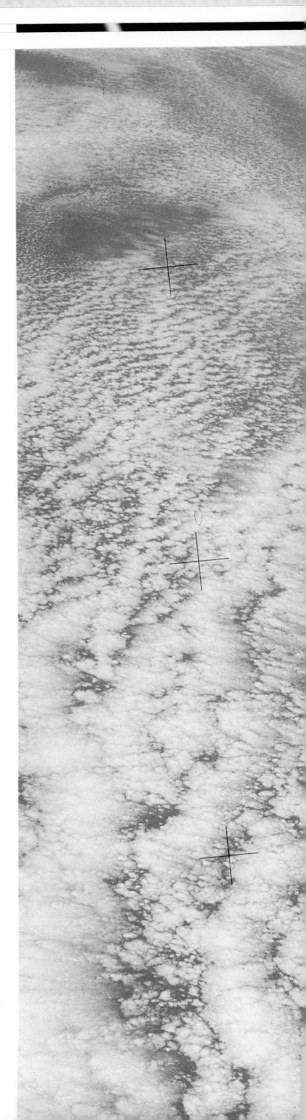

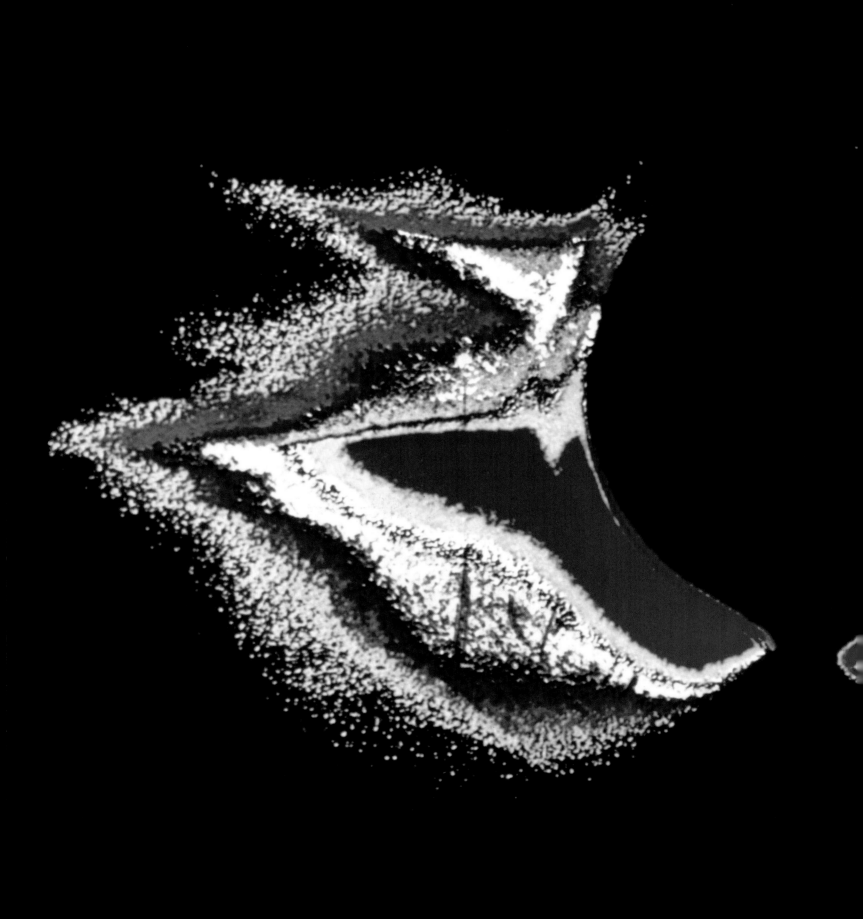

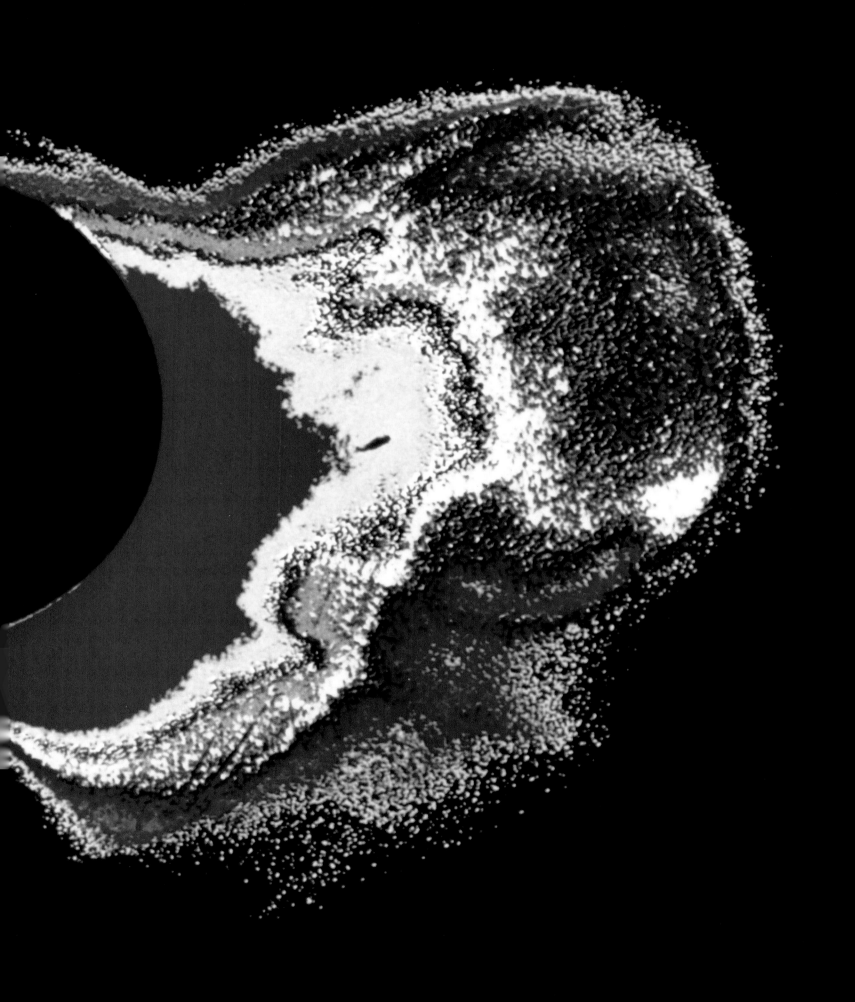

Above: *The Viking 2 lander touched down on Mars' Plains of Utopia in 1976, and its cameras and sensors commenced gathering data on the Red Planet's weather, atmosphere, chemistry, and biology.*

Opposite: *A bispectral mosaic made up from Viking Orbiter I images of Mars covers nearly an entire hemisphere of that planet.*

Preceding spread: *The sun's fiery corona glows in this color-coded photograph taken from the Skylab space station.*

Nearly four hours into the flight the autopilot is behaving erratically and Glenn bypasses it to take control of the spacecraft himself. At 04:38:25 into the flight the Texas capsule communicator in Corpus Christi identifies itself and tells Glenn:

> *We are recommending that you leave the retropackage on through the entire re-entry....*
> *This is Friendship 7. What is the reason for this? Do you have any reason?*
> *Not at this time. This is the judgment of Cape Flight.*

Glenn has still not been told that NASA is worried his heat shield has slipped. Glenn is busy bringing the nose of the Mercury capsule up until instruments indicate he is flying straight and level with the earth and ready for re-entry. Robert B. Voas' narration continues:

04:40:23: *Friendship 7, this is Cape...Recommend you...retract the [peri]scope manually.*
Roger. Retracting scope manually.
While you're doing that [Cape tells Glenn], *we are not sure whether your landing bag has deployed. We feel that it is possible to re-enter with the retropackage on. We see no difficulty at this time in that type of re-entry.*
During re-entry the heat shield, as its name implies, protects the pilot from the friction-heated air that slams against the capsule with a force of 8 g's. [Eight times gravity] The shock wave not three feet from his back incandesces with a temperature nearly five times that of the sun's surface.
04:42:52: *Seven, this is Cape....We recommend you....*
Shepard's voice fades away as the communications blackout begins. Glenn wonders what his message was.
Manually he starts the capsule rolling. Like a rifle bullet, the capsule must revolve slowly during re-entry for maximum accuracy in hitting the landing area.
Suddenly he hears a report; one of the stainless-steel retropack straps is hanging directly in front of the window.
This is Friendship 7. I think the pack just let go. His message goes unheard.
The needles on the indicators begin to move back and forth slightly. Glenn counters with the control stick to keep the capsule from oscillating too much.
Outside the window he sees an orange glow. Its brilliance grows.
Now the orange color intensifies. Suddenly large flaming pieces of metal come rushing back past the window. What can they be? He thought the retropack was gone. For a moment he feels that the capsule itself must be burning and breaking up. Deceleration holds him, pressing him back into the seat, or he would involuntarily rise up, expecting at any moment to feel the first warmth as the heat burns through the capsule to his back. But it doesn't come.
He keeps moving the control handle, damping oscillation. He peers out through the window from the center of a fireball. All around him glows the brilliant orange color. Behind, visible through the center of the window, is a bright yellow circle. He sees that it is the long trail of flowing ablation material from the heat shield, stretching out behind him and flowing together.
04:43:39: *This is Friendship 7. A real fireball outside.*
04:47:22: The fireball is fading. He hears the Cape calling, slightly garbled, *How are you doing?* He answers, *Oh, pretty good.*

Glenn splashed down at 04:55:24. Not quite nine and a half minutes later the U.S. Navy destroyer *Noa* began hoisting Glenn and his capsule on board.

The Apollo program ended in December 1972 with the return of Apollo 17 and the last of the twelve American astronauts who had walked on the moon and brought back 843 pounds of rocks. Even while the Apollo program was underway unmanned spacecraft had been sent out to explore the planets. Mariner 9, the first spacecraft to survey the planet Mars from orbit had been launched in May 1971 and revealed a Martian landscape cut by a 20,000-foot-deep, up to 150-mile-wide equatorial canyon stretching nearly a fifth of the way around the red planet, and massive volcanoes—among them the nearly 15-mile-high *Olympus Mons*, which towers more than 50,000 feet above Everest. Pioneer 10, the first spacecraft to visit the outer planets, was launched in March 1972. In January 1977 the Magazine's cover was a photograph taken from a Viking lander *on Mars*! Mariner 10's voyages to Mercury and Venus were chronicled in June 1975. Four and a half years later, the January 1980 Magazine contained the Voyager spacecraft's detailed photographs of "Jupiter's Dazzling Realm"; July 1981 carried Voyager's photographs of Saturn; and the August 1986 issue, "Uranus: Voyager Visits a Dark Planet."

As manned and unmanned spacecraft reach farther and farther out, mankind's knowledge of the universe expands with them. But there will always be those who would suggest that the lives lost and the monies spent in exploration might have been better used. Journalist and explorer Walter Wellman's response to those who questioned a previous century's efforts to attain an equally debatable goal, is as relevant to manned space flight to Mars today as it was to that former "most cherished of all geographical prizes." In the December 1899 *National Geographic Magazine* Wellman wrote:

> We may have differences of opinion as to the value of reaching the Pole. If we apply the utilitarian test, it is of small moment; but so is a poem. And what is polar exploration but an epic of endeavor, in which all sordidness is left behind, and in which a man, knowing the risks and the chances of failure, ventures his life and his all in a combat against the forces of ignorance? For I deem it beneath the dignity of man, having once set out to reach that mathematical point which marks the northern termination of the axis of our earth, which stands as a sign of his failure to dominate those millions of square miles of unknown country, to give it up because the night is dark and the road is long. He will not give it up. The polar explorer typifies that outdoor spirit of the race which has led conquering man across all seas and through all lands, of that thirst for knowing all that is to be known, which has led him to the depths of the ocean, to the tops of mountains, to dig in musty caves, to analyze the rays of light from distant worlds, to delve in the geologic records of past times. It will carry him to the North Pole, too, and that before many years shall have passed. Any one who supposes anything else of man doesn't know man. His acquaintance with human nature— with the nature of the adventurous races of our zone and times—is limited.

Anyone who supposes that the National Geographic Society will not continue to report man's explorations of space with the same attention it has paid exploration of our own planet for the past one hundred years, doesn't know the Geographic.

▶

James Hervat's painting from the January 1985 article "The Planets: Between Fire and Ice" depicts the Galileo probe, originally sched- *uled to have orbited Jupiter in 1988 where it would have released scientific instruments designed to help understand that planet's atmosphere.*

"Holding Up the Torch, Not Applying It"

"The Geographic's way is to hold up the torch, not to apply it."

—Frederick G. Vosburgh, Editor, *National Geographic Magazine*, 1967–1970

"He is one of the great editors of our time. No magazine has ever had a steadier, more reliable helmsman than Ted Vosburgh. This ship will miss his hand on the tiller, although I know the crew he has gotten together will do a great job."

—Melville Bell Grosvenor, on Ted Vosburgh's retirement in 1970

Preceding spread: *"The seal of the Society shall consist of... the western hemisphere, from 0° to 180° west from Greenwich, with the legend 'National Geographic Society' above and 'Incorporated A.D. 1888' below, as in the design herewith." —From Article IX of the by-laws of the National Geographic Society, adopted April 17, 1896.*

The bronze seal shown here is approximately seven feet in diameter and gleams in the marble floor of Explorers Hall. It and its twin were laid at the main entrances to the Society's Edward Durell Stone–designed headquarters in 1964 when the building was completed.

On August 1, 1967, ten years after assuming the positions of Editor of the Magazine and President of the Society, Melville Bell Grosvenor retired from both offices to become Chairman of the Board of Trustees and accepted appointment to the newly created position of Editor-in-Chief.

Despite MBG's opposition, the offices of Editor and President, which had been combined at Gilbert H. Grosvenor's insistence in 1920, were separated again—this time at the insistence of the Trustees, who felt that the organization had grown too big to be run by one man. Splitting the two offices, they believed, would enable the Editor to concentrate on running the Magazine and the President to direct his attention to the business of the Society.

Dr. Melvin M. Payne was elected Society President. He had started thirty-five years earlier as a secretary to the Society's then Assistant Secretary Thomas McKnew and had worked his way up through the ranks.

Frederick G. (Ted) Vosburgh, a Vice President and Associate Editor, the number two man under MBG on the Magazine, was appointed Editor—only its eighth since the Society's founding and the fourth in this century.

Robert E. Doyle, a Vice President and Associate Secretary, became Secretary, and Gilbert Melville Grosvenor was moved up from his former position as a Vice President and Senior Assistant Editor of the Magazine to become, along with Franc Shor, one of the Magazine's two Associate Editors.

At a staff meeting held before the formal appointment, Melville Grosvenor explained that separating the offices of President and Editor would "give others up and down the line a chance to grow and develop, and will help keep the Society alive and vibrant and in the hands of young, imaginative people, as it should be."

But Ted Vosburgh, into whose hands the Magazine had been placed, was only three years younger than Melville.

Vosburgh had joined the *Geographic* in 1933, spent eighteen years on the staff before becoming an Assistant Editor, and another five before becoming

Senior Assistant Editor in 1956. The following year, Melville's first act upon being named Editor had been to appoint Vosburgh his Associate Editor.

When Vosburgh became Editor ten years later, in 1967, he was already sixty-three years old. His reputation among staff members was for inflexibility and conservatism, rather than for imagination.

Melville was the one with the imagination, the big ideas, the broad strokes. Vosburgh was responsible for keeping MBG's excesses in check. "MBG was the first to say he could not have run the Magazine without Ted Vosburgh," Melville's son Gil is quick to point out. "Ted was his right-hand man. When MBG took off for a couple of months at a time, it was FGV who stayed home and picked up the pieces and put the Magazine together and made damn sure the Magazine was accurate and factual and came out—if not on time, at least that it came out."

Vosburgh was the "stickler for accuracy," the man who would remain late night after night working over the proofs. On one occasion, while the July 1964 issue was being printed, Vosburgh had the presses stopped when he discovered the engravers had eliminated a restrictive comma from a sentence in Peter T. White's "The World in New York City." At a cost of $30,000, Vosburgh had the comma restored and with it the *Geographic*'s reputation for accuracy.*

Vosburgh's caution as an Associate Editor was not necessarily an advantage as Editor. Although now Senior Associate Editor Joseph Judge observed that "under Vosburgh words like 'threatened,' 'polluted,' and 'imperiled' began appearing in the Magazine's titles with regularity," Vosburgh had to be talked into doing those stories. "He would have been the one to avoid that sort of topic very carefully," Edwards Park explained, "because showing the bad side of things, he felt, wasn't our job. Our job was to show the good side of things."

*The sentence had read: "Just the two boroughs on Long Island, Brooklyn and Queens, house 4,660,000 people more than either Chicago or Los Angeles." The $30,000 comma was inserted after "people."

Publication of that piece marked the Magazine's return to journalistic advocacy, a practice it had all but abandoned after 1916, when the National Geographic Society guided by Gilbert H. Grosvenor, responded to Congress' request for additional financial support with a significant monetary contribution to ensure the survival of California's majestic redwoods in the Giant Forest of Sequoia National Park.

Vosburgh's philosophy, expressed in his phrase "The *Geographic*'s way is to hold up the torch, not to apply it," was to present the facts about a problem and to let the readership decide what, if anything, to do about it. In his October 1967 "Threatened Glories of Everglades National Park," for example, he toured the drought-stricken Everglades, pointing out without editorializing that the diversion of Lake Okeechobee's waters, which previously had flowed southward into the Everglades en route to the sea, posed a threat to the Everglades' ecosystem. Nowhere in the piece did Vosburgh suggest the solution; but because of the way he had presented his facts, he didn't have to.

Frederick G. Vosburgh retired as Editor in October 1970. He was succeeded by thirty-nine-year-old Gilbert Melville Grosvenor.

Like John Oliver La Gorce's appointment, Ted Vosburgh's tenure was perceived by many as merely an interregnum between Grosvenors. But despite the fact that Gil Grosvenor's father, Melville Bell Grosvenor, his grandfather Gilbert Hovey Grosvenor, his great-grandfather Alexander Graham Bell, and his great-great-grandfather Gardiner Greene Hubbard had led the Society before him, there is nothing in the Society's charter that says a Grosvenor has to head—or even be hired by—the National Geographic.

Gil Grosvenor's ascendancy was less a *fait accompli* than one might think. As one senior staff member said, "When Melville retired he made Ted Vosburgh Editor and Mel Payne President with, I think, the understanding that Ted would stay on for three or four years and then Gil would be made Editor and that was the way it was going to be. But there was some resentment."

Gilbert M. Grosvenor had never intended to join the *Geographic*; his plans centered on his being a pre-medical student until, during the summer between his junior and senior years at Yale University, he went to the Netherlands as part of an international work force that was rebuilding dikes ravaged by that previous spring's disastrous floods. "I took a camera along," he has said, "and I guess that's when I was bitten by the bug."

By 1954, Gil Grosvenor had graduated from Yale and was hired by John Oliver La Gorce. With the exception of two years' military duty with the Army's Psychological Warfare Service, Gil Grosvenor has worked at the *Geographic* ever since.

During the next fifteen years GMG—as, of course, he would become known—wrote and/or photographed articles on Bali, Ceylon, the Italian Riviera, Copenhagen, Monaco, "Yugoslavia's Window on the Adriatic," the flight of the *Silver Dart*, a reproduction of Canada's first airplane (the original of which had been built by his great-grandfather Alexander Graham Bell and his fellow members of the Aerial Experiment Association), and President Dwight D. Eisenhower's 1960 visit to Asia, for which he won a first prize award in the nineteenth annual News Pictures of the Year competition.

Soon after GMG came to the *Geographic* he commenced a two-year apprenticeship in the administration, serving with the Secretary, the Treasurer, the membership-fulfillment section, and the correspondence office. He then returned to the editorial side of the Magazine with, as then Society President Melvin Payne said, "a real knowledge of how the magazine relates to our millions of readers." However, to Mel Payne mere possession of that knowledge did not mean that Gil Grosvenor was necessarily qualified to become Editor. Twenty years older than Gil Grosvenor, Payne "was working at the *Geographic,* doing responsible work," he said, "while Gil was still in school."

"Payne thought Gil was an upstart...," one Senior Editor said. "I think he resented Gil as a kid who had had it all his way, the 'silver spoon,' every door open to him, and he just walked into the job."

Doors had not opened easily for Melvin Payne. He was born the son of a railroad freight conductor on May 23, 1911, and grew up in a poor section of Washington, D.C. Orphaned at ten, he was reared by an uncle and aunt and contributed to his keep through earnings from a newspaper route and, later, by writing features for the New York *Sun*. Still later, while working during the day, he attended the National University Law School (now part of George Washington University) at night. In 1932, shortly after he had begun working for Thomas McKnew, Payne transferred to Southeastern University, where he continued to attend night school until he had obtained his law degree. In 1958, Payne had been elected to the post of Vice President serving as Associate Secretary in charge of administration; later that same year he was elected to the Board of Trustees. From that point on, Payne's rise in the hierarchy had been swift, and when Melville retired in 1967, Payne was the Society's newly elected President. He had come up the hard way and was very proud of that.

When the Board announced the appointment of Gil Grosvenor as the Magazine's ninth Editor, Mel Payne called Gil into his office. "He told me he was not in favor of it," Gil said, "but that was the way the Board went and he'd

AWARD-WINNING TV

Because of the success of the Society's lecture film *Bones of the Bounty*, shown on NBC's television program *Omnibus* in January 1958, Melville Grosvenor came to believe the Society should be producing its own television shows. And in 1961 a documentary film department was organized under Robert C. Doyle—"T. V. Doyle," as he was known, to distinguish him from then Vice President and Associate Secretary of the Society Robert E. Doyle.

Doyle was given the responsibility of producing four TV documentaries a year; and without any network commitment to show the films, the Society plunged ahead, confident that a market existed for documentaries made to the Geographic's own high standards. But it was not until the Society joined with David Wolper in the mid-1960s that its television productions began to be aired.

The Society's first documentary, *Americans on Everest*, was already in production. Broadcast on September 10, 1965, by CBS, it made television history. Narrated by Orson Welles and sponsored by Encyclopaedia Britannica and Aetna Casualty Insurance, this Geographic Special on the three-team assault of Mt. Everest by Americans—one of whom was National Geographic staffer Barry C. Bishop—received the highest rating of any documentary until then telecast. Although Wolper had nothing to do with the creation of this film, he was given sole credit as producer.

Americans on Everest was followed by *Miss Goodall and the Wild Chimpanzees:*

VIDEO: *Jane Goodall in small boat on Lake Tanganyika. In background, mountains at Gombe in the East African nation of Tanzania (formerly Tanganyika).*

AUDIO: Voice Over (Jane Goodall): "When I first arrived at the

Gombe Stream Reserve, I felt that at long last my childhood ambition was being realized. But when I looked at the wild and rugged mountains where the chimpanzees lived, I knew that my task was not going to be easy."

VIDEO: *Jane in boat. 2 chimps play. Jane observes.*

AUDIO: V.O. (Jane Goodall): "The chimps very gradually came to realize that I was not dangerous after all. I shall never forget the day after about 18 months when, for the first time..."

VIDEO: *Chimp group.*

AUDIO: V.O. (Jane Goodall): "...a small group allowed me to approach and be near them. Finally I had been accepted....it was one of the proudest and most exciting moments of my whole life."

VIDEO: *Jane with notebook near chimps.*

AUDIO: V.O. (Alexander Scourby): "Chimpanzees are as distinct from one another as are human beings, and Jane gave them names..."

VIDEO: *Chimpanzee "Flo."*

AUDIO: V.O. (Alexander Scourby): "...as she came to recognize them. Old Flo, with her bulbous nose and ragged ears, is matriarch of the family Jane would come to know best..."

Opposite: *Top row, left,* Americans on Everest; *right,* The World of Jacques-Yves Cousteau. *Middle row, left,* Rain Forest; *right,* Journey to the Outer Limits. *Bottom row, left,* The Incredible Machine; *right,* The Sharks. Left: Filming the Impossible. Below: Himalayan River Run.

Next came *Dr. Leakey and the Dawn of Man* and *The World of Jacques-Yves Cousteau.* And in 1968 the Society made television history again when its special *Amazon* was watched by over thirty-five million people and became the first television documentary to top all other shows in a two-week rating period.

In 1975 National Geographic Specials entered into partnership with WQED/Pittsburgh, supported by a Gulf Oil Corporation grant, to produce documentary programs for Public Television. Their success can be measured by the statistics: By 1986 nine out of the top thirteen most-watched shows on PBS were National Geographic Specials (with *The Sharks, Land of the Tiger, The Incredible Machine,* and *Great Moments With National Geographic* ranking one, two, three, and four).

385

"The U.S. should take the first step toward friendship," Fidel Castro (above) told Fred Ward, author of the controversial January 1977 "Inside Cuba Today" article. "We are certainly interested in improving relations. Since the U.S. practices the cold war with only a few small countries... the moral seems to be, it is a problem of size."

Publication of Ward's article distressed many conservative Trustees and members.

lem,' like a church picnic going down to the beach for the day. It just didn't fit the Geographic mode in terms of our past. It was in very poor taste."

On March 8, 1977, the National Geographic Special *The Volga* aired on television. It later won both the Television Critics Circle Award and a Council on International Non-Theatrical Events (CINE) Golden Eagle Award. It also attracted the attention of Accuracy in Media (AIM), which in its newsletter that month published "The Geographic's Flawed Picture," an article attacking both the Cuba piece and the *Volga* TV show:

> The National Geographic Society is famous for its accurate maps and lovely photographs. However, it now seems to be in danger of acquiring a new reputation—that of purveyor of inaccurate and distorted information about Communist countries such as Cuba and the U.S.S.R....

AIM took exception to *The Volga* because actor E. G. Marshall, who narrated the special, had pointed out that there had been no censorship of the film they had taken. AIM complained, "There was no need for that. Like Ward's Cuba pictures, what was shown was virtually all flattering."

The Accuracy in Media piece went on to quote excerpts from the six-page single-spaced letter AIM chairman Reed Irvine had sent Gil Grosvenor "citing numerous serious errors and omissions in the Ward article" and stated that Irvine had "asked that appropriate corrections be made by The National Geographic Magazine."

The corrections were not forthcoming, but confrontation with conservative Society Board members was.

At the Trustees meeting held on March 19, 1977, a divisive split made its first appearance before the Board—a split so serious that reports of it eventually escaped the boardroom's secrecy-cloaked deliberations and ended up on the front pages of newspapers across the land.

As the Trustees* assembled, Chairman of the Board Melvin M. Payne, upset by controversy created by the Cuba and Harlem articles, suggested that a committee be established to examine whether or not the editorial policy of the Magazine was changing direction.

Gil Grosvenor perceived Payne's proposed editorial policy committee as nothing more than an "oversight committee to throttle the Editor," a means by which the Chairman could gain editorial control. And he swiftly responded by insisting before the assembled Board of Trustees that the editorial policy had not deviated from its "89-year tradition of factual accuracy, timeliness, objectivity."

"The *Magazine* is not changing, the *world* is changing," Gil said, adding that MBG and Ted Vosburgh had both recognized that the Magazine would be doomed if it did not reflect the changing times. That was why, during their terms as Editor, sometimes controversial and critical articles had appeared on the Berlin Wall, the Berlin Airlift, the Hungarian Revolution, the Soviet Union, Vietnam, and South Africa—topics which, Gil said, under his grandfather's guiding principles would have been avoided.

"No great magazine has ever been created or maintained by a small committee," Gil insisted, adding that although he welcomed and relied upon "the Board's *collective* guidance and wisdom," he would be "terribly disappointed" if any of the Board were willing to delegate that responsibility to anyone else.

Dr. Payne reiterated his feeling that because of the concern expressed by several Trustees as to the direction in which the Magazine was going, there did need to be a discussion with the Board.

Former Editor Ted Vosburgh was so offended at the suggestion of any such editorial policy committee that to demonstrate support for Gil Grosvenor he proposed the motion "That the Board hereby expresses its confidence in the Editor and commends him."

Vosburgh's motion was voted and unanimously accepted.

For the time being, the idea of an "oversight committee" had been shunted aside.

The Magazine's April issue, the following month, contained Peter T. White's "One Canada or Two," an examination of the Quebec separatist movement. That article prompted a letter to Mel Payne from David Lank, the son of a former President of the Du Pont Company of Canada, an old friend of Trustee Crawford H. Greenewalt's. David Lank, a Canadian citizen and Society member, wrote that the piece was outrageous, that there was no such problem in Quebec, and that it was just going to stir people up over nothing.

On April 18, Trustee Greenewalt—already upset over the Castro-Cuba piece—wrote to Mel Payne:

> ...There seems to have been a rash of adverse comment on recent articles in the GEOGRAPHIC, particularly those pertaining to Cuba, the Volga, and the Quebec separatism question....I wonder...if it might not be timely to consider articles of this kind as a matter of policy....
>
> I'm inclined to believe that a rather full discussion at the Board level might be useful, and perhaps this could be based upon a written presentation by Gil Grosvenor or whoever else you think appropriate....

Greenewalt's letter gave Payne the excuse he needed at the May 12 Executive Committee meeting to raise the editorial policy committee issue again. As a result of the various complaints, Payne stated he felt it appropriate to appoint an ad hoc committee to study the controversy, review the mail the Society had received, discuss the problem with the senior officers for background, and prepare a report for the Board.

And then, when on the heels of the Cuba, Harlem, and Quebec articles, the Magazine's June issue containing "South Africa's Lonely Ordeal" angered not only the South African government, but conservative readers and some of the older Trustees as well, it must have seemed to Mel Payne to be the last straw.

"South Africa's Lonely Ordeal" contained a text by Senior Editorial Staff Writer William S. Ellis that devoted considerable attention to the impact of apartheid on blacks; it was accompanied by James P. Blair's unsentimental photographs of a black child's pathetic grave marked only by the infant's cherished white doll and a wood-and-cardboard cross, and of red-and-white gingham-clothed black maids holding a wealthy white couple's nightgowned children.

The South African Department of Information took out a large advertisement headlined "Here are some of the facts on South Africa that *National Geographic Magazine* withheld in its maiden attempt to enter the realm of advocacy reporting" and accused the *Geographic* of "anti-white racism" and serious omissions of fact.

At the June 9 Board of Trustees meeting, Mel Payne drew the Board's attention to the advertisement, reviewed the criticism generated by AIM's campaign, which had resulted in "an unusually large volume of critical mail" and "a degree of uneasiness among several Trustees," and concluded that because of these and other factors it had "seemed appropriate to take some action at the Board level to determine whether or not the charges are justified." That is why, Payne continued, at the Executive Committee meeting he had appointed an ad hoc committee "to review the situation."

Mel Payne asked for the Board's approval of the ad hoc committee, and Thomas W. McKnew moved that: The Chairman's action in appointing an ad hoc committee to study criticisms directed toward our publication of articles on Cuba and South Africa (as well as our film on the Volga River) be approved. McKnew's motion was brought to a vote and approved by a majority of the Board. Melville Grosvenor, Gil, and Ted Vosburgh clearly were not pleased.

"We *knew* we would have trouble over the South Africa article," Melville said impatiently. "We should not have to come to the Board every time there is an article like this. It is the re-spon-si-bi-lity of the *Editor*," he said, angrily tapping the top of the Board table before him. "If the Editor does not do his job, the Board can fire him. I don't believe *I* would serve as Editor with a committee like this looking over my shoulder...."

"The Magazine continues to be beautiful and interesting and informative," Mel Payne said, "*but* the question raised by all this furor is whether or not there is creeping into the Magazine some element that is *not properly a part of the National Geographic Society's mission*."

The first ad hoc committee meeting was scheduled for a little over two weeks later, on June 27 at 10 in the morning. By this time morale among the Magazine staff was low. Decisions were not being made. Work was not getting done. One Senior Editor complained that Gil was postponing everything "to keep a low profile."

But if the Magazine was in a turmoil, the rest of the Society was functioning normally.

Its 78,000-volume reference library remained open to the public. Its lectures and films continued to be well attended. Its Educational Media division, headed by Robert Breeden, was sending its filmstrips, multimedia learning kits, posters, and games to the schools. *World* magazine, Gil's updated version of the *School Bulletin* continued to be eagerly read by children.

Book Service, now under Jules B. Billard, was working on *Ancient Egypt*; a revision of *Everyday Life in Bible Times* was being published, as was *Visiting Our Past: America's Historylands*. Robert Breeden's Special Publications Division was providing books on subjects ranging from *The Mysterious Maya* to *Nature's Healing Arts*.

In the meantime, the Television Division was busy with *The Legacy of*

Tim Menees' June 3, 1976, "Word-smith" comic strip lampooning a National Geographic assignment on Harlem anticipated by eight months Frank Hercules' "To Live in Harlem..." article that appeared in the February 1977 issue on the heels of the Cuba piece. The above photograph from that article was captioned: "Outsiders may call it a ghetto, yet to half a million Harlemites it is home, the best-known black community in the Western world. In the heart of New York City, children play on West 138th Street, where traffic is banned for a Memorial Day block party."

The Harlem piece also worried many conservatives.

L.S.B. Leakey. Two years before, the Division had switched from the commercial networks to Public Television; and their PBS premiere, *The Incredible Machine,* had earned the highest audience ratings in Public Television history and was the first Public Television show to score higher ratings than the commercial networks in some major markets.

The Geographic's News Service was continuing to supply feature stories relating to specific Magazine articles and discoveries of Society research grantees to well over a thousand newspapers and periodicals.

"Sign of the times: Paint sprayed by Francophones blots English from a bilingual stop sign in front of a church in Sainte-Anne-de-la-Pérade. Bilingual labels, initiated to ease language tensions, satisfy neither English- nor French-speaking Canadians. Both prefer their own language exclusively. French culture, which once rallied around the Roman Catholic Church and rural life, has survived today's urbanization and weakening of religious influence. Calls for independence continue to mount."—From Peter T. White's article "One Canada—or Two?" in the April 1977 issue

This, too, was perceived as dipping into political waters.

But despite the fact that the tempest brewing within the Magazine over the ad hoc committee had little impact on the day-to-day operations of the Society as a whole, it is still important for several reasons.

First of all, the Magazine is the Society's flagship; to its membership the Society *is* the familiar yellow-bordered Magazine. As Melvin Payne observed to his fellow Trustees, "We are known throughout the world by our Magazine, and what the Magazine says is what the National Geographic Society says."

Second, just as "Black Friday" twenty years earlier had marked a revolution within the Illustrations Division that set the photographers and picture editors free from certain constraints, the struggle for editorial integrity brought on by the Chairman of the Board's ad hoc committee served to ensure the freedom of the Magazine from outside interference.

Third, the story of the ad hoc committee provides a rare insight not only into the operations and relationship of the Society and its Trustees, but also into how the Society perceives itself.

At 10 o'clock in the morning on June 27, 1977, the committee met. The group consisted of its chairman, Lloyd H. Elliott, Melvin M. Payne, Robert E. Doyle, and Gilbert M. Grosvenor; Trustees Crawford H. Greenewalt, James E. Webb, and Louis B. Wright; and Geographic Associate Secretaries Leonard J. Grant and Edwin W. Snider.

Elliott called the meeting to order and stated, "The purpose of our committee, is 'to investigate the question of whether there has been any significant change in the editorial policy of the Society's official journal, and, if so, whether such changes meet with the Board's approval.' "

Payne reviewed why, because of the AIM letters, the threatened resignation of members, the "relentless" efforts of the South African Embassy to embarrass the Society, he had "thought it was essential to have the Board look at the criticisms."

Gil Grosvenor responded by dismissing the AIM director as a right-winger whose financial support came from an industry that had "never forgiven us for not publicly condemning our statement about DDT and its effect on birds' eggs" (in the March 1974 article "Can the Cooper's Hawk Survive?").

Gil also discounted the significance of the letters and the South African government's advertisements and said, "You cannot run a 'hearts and flowers' story from South Africa when you get daily television news about Soweto." Payne noted that the Cuba piece had produced 105 letters, whereas an average story such as the one on Mars had produced only 30. "The point is," Gil said, "we are trying to talk about the significance of the level of criticism, where it is coming from and what is motivating it."

Elliott interrupted. "The point we are considering is, 'has there been a change in editorial content, policy, or subject matter?'... The point is whether the criticism reflects any change."

"*We* don't claim that we are changing," Gil said. "The *advertising* department said in some ads that we were changing."

"In your statement prepared for the Board, you said the Magazine has to change," Elliott said.

Gil pointed out that he was talking about "evolutionary" change in layout and so forth. "It is not a change in subject matter."

Former NASA administrator James Webb asked about the genesis of the South Africa article.

"We had not published anything on it in many years," Gil said. "We felt it was time to publish a 'country story' on South Africa...it was important for our members to see an article on South Africa. We did not go in with the idea of doing a hatchet job on South Africa, but a balanced article. If we missed, we missed. If it is policy of the Board, we can cloud over political questions in a country."

"My objection," Louis Wright said, "was that [the author of the South Africa article] did not take the historical point of view but rather the contemporary American view. It is the 'missionary' instinct which is difficult for Americans to overcome.... To sum up, the desirable thing for the *Geographic* is to do what it can do best. State precisely what the current situation is, but you don't take sides; you don't even quote people on either side....The traditional *Geographic* position is historic background, geographical discussion, scientific analysis of discoveries...."

James Webb asked if it was felt that there was a need for an oversight committee.

"The Editor should be able to control the Magazine," Gil said firmly. "You cannot have a committee run editorial content. Either you like the way we have been running it or you don't; then you say change it, or if you don't, get a new Editor."

"We have been under fire from organizations that would like to see us taxed," Wright cautioned. "That is a problem if you go political."

"I don't want to go political," Gil said. "There is no input from me or anybody on this staff to go political."

"I agree with Gil that you can't have an editorial committee breathing down the neck of the Editor," Wright said. "That is not the purpose of this committee or any other committee. On the other hand, the Trustees have a responsibility to see that the policy is one that is not changed unwittingly. That is, I think, what this is all about, the fear there is unwitting change in editorial policy which the Trustees have a right to be concerned about and pass judgment on."

Suddenly, to Gil's surprise, Crawford Greenewalt said, "...it is untenable that the Board should have a committee to exercise any continuing control over the contents of a magazine. You ask the Editor to run the show, and if there is a particular situation on which the Board can give advice, it should. My feeling is...the Geographic should stay away from [those areas that are so emotionally charged] that an objective piece cannot be written....I gather Gil is not too upset with that kind of amendment to existing policy. Let him write it up and come to us to hammer it out, and then we have no problem with the Board."

Elliott agreed, "...give us that statement about a week before the next meeting so that we can digest it a bit and have suggestions and then put a piece of paper together around the table."

The second meeting of the ad hoc committee was set for Thursday, August 11, at 2:00 P.M. after the Executive Committee meeting and luncheon.

One month later reports of the internal struggle began to creep into public print. "CHANGE AT THE GEOGRAPHIC" was the front-page headline in the July 17 *Washington Post*. The subhead was "Magazine's New Look Stirs Dispute." The story carried over into the inside of the newspaper's first section where it was considered important enough to be given half a page with the head "Geographic Faces Problem of Portraying Harsh Reality." Wrote *Post* staff writer Kathy Sawyer:

The dispute goes to the basic question of how boldly the society, with its tradition of Victorian delicacy, will pick its way through a global landscape where life's harsher realities, as one staff writer put it, often "leap right out at you."

Gil Grosvenor, according to Kathy Sawyer, saw it differently:

> In his book-lined office last week, Grosvenor talked with the air of a man caught in a delicate web he was loath to tear. He minimized the so-called "public reaction" noting that the "40 or 50 letters we get on a sensitive story" compared with the magazine's total readership are like walking once around the Geographic headquarters on 17th Street "and then walking to the moon."

In a nice touch, the reporter then added: "With typical Geographic attention to detail, [Grosvenor] had the society's research department check that out and later amended it to 'twice around the headquarters.' "

The following month, on August 5, the *Los Angeles Times* published a long piece headlined "Geographic: From Upbeat to Realism," which contained the following observation: "Even more startling [than the new candor of the *Geographic*'s articles] is the unseemly squabble within the genteel Geographic itself...."

The second meeting of the ad hoc committee took place not quite a week after the *Times* piece appeared.

Gil Grosvenor passed around the table the draft editorial policy statement the Committee had requested at the last meeting.

The committee members argued a bit over the wording, then Gil excused himself from the meeting to incorporate their suggestions. Together with then Senior Assistant Editor Joe Judge, Gil hammered out a revised version in about fifteen minutes, then returned to the committee to read the statement now titled "Reaffirmation of Editorial Policy at the National Geographic Society":

The mission of the Magazine is to increase and diffuse geographic knowledge. Geography is defined in a broad sense: the description of land, sea and universe; the interrelationship of man with the flora and fauna of earth; and the historical, cultural, scientific, governmental and social background of people.

The Magazine strives to present timely, accurate, factual, objective material in an unbiased presentation. Advocacy journalism is rejected.

As times and tastes change, the Magazine slowly evolves its style, format, and subject matter to reflect that change without altering the fundamental policies above.

Excellence of presentation—accuracy, technical superiority in printing and photo reproduction, and clarity of meaning—remain traditional goals against which each article is measured.

Mel Payne felt that the statement was so brief that he was not sure it adequately covered the subject.

William McChesney Martin disagreed; he thought the advantage of a short statement was that it left the Editor more flexibility.

After a brief discussion the committee agreed that the statement should be published in the Magazine.

A motion to accept tentatively the "Reaffirmation of Editorial Policy" as worked out by Gil Grosvenor was adopted without objection; it was, however, to be brought for final approval to the third and final meeting of the ad hoc committee scheduled for 11 o'clock in the morning before the September 8 meeting of the Board of Trustees. "It is my understanding," Committee Chair-

man Lloyd Elliott said, "that with our report the committee will recommend its own demise."

The meeting adjourned at 3:50 P.M.

Advance copies of the September 12, 1977, issue of *Newsweek* were already on newsstands the day before the final ad hoc committee meeting was held. Inside was an article titled "The Geographic Faces Life," with photographs of Gil Grosvenor and the controversial Harlem advertisement.

"In any other magazine," wrote *Newsweek*, "the articles on apartheid in South Africa, Cuba under Castro and life in Harlem would be considered tame—if not belated—attempts to report the issues of the day....But in a publication founded on the principle of avoiding matters of a 'partisan and controversial' nature, the stories have produced an unprecedented dispute over the Geographic's editorial direction between the magazine's earnest, socially conscious editor and its archconservative chairman of the board."

At 11 o'clock, Thursday morning, September 8, 1977, the final ad hoc committee meeting was called to order.

Gil Grosvenor passed out the reworked statement along with a proposed Editor's page commenting on editorial policy. He said he hoped our members would understand it and that the press would not pick up on it.

Mel Payne stated that all the newspaper publicity had emphasized and distorted "the so-called schism." To establish the fact that the schism did not exist, to show that there was unanimity in the organization, he insisted "the

"A life apart is endured by millions of black women, such as these in a Transkei village. The only man in the house is their retired father, left; their miner husbands live far away. The men send home a meager $12 a month. When they return—once a year—to the family hearth, they often find sadness as well as warmth...."

Following articles on Cuba, Harlem, and Quebec, William S. Ellis' June 1977 article, "South Africa's Lonely Ordeal," containing the above photograph and caption, proved the last straw for those conservative Trustees already concerned over the Magazine's direction under Editor Gilbert M. Grosvenor.

397

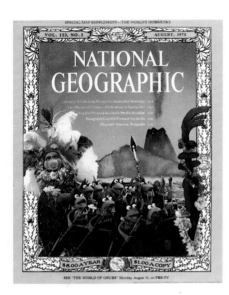

"*IMAGINE BEING TOLD of a handful of lush tropical islands, peopled by handsome and hospitable natives, and ruled over by a wise and beautiful queen,*" begins the text for this 1981 "Miss Piggy Cover Girl Fantasy Calendar" parody of the Geographic. "*Surely, you would protest, such places don't exist outside of fairy tales! And yet, as visitors to the verdant Pacific islands of Boara-Boara, Porku-Porku, and Rana-Kermi discover, this magical place does exist. And so does its storybook monarch, Queen Wahinipikki I, a lovely and sophisticated graduate of the Sorbonne and the London School of Economics, whom island legend says is descended from the sun and the moon and has the stars for cousins....*"

statement should be signed by the Board, the President, and the Editor. I hope that would heal the problem."

Gil suggested reinstituting the "President's Message" column. "It could include the reaffirmation of policy, bring in some of the other things we are doing, and we could run it in the December issue."

Greenewalt thought that to hide it in the President's Message would be a mistake. "The way to avoid any suggestion of internal disagreement," he said, "is to have the Chairman of the Board sign the statement for the Board along with the President and the Editor...."

Martin agreed. "I would take Mr. Grosvenor's statement and have it in the Editor's column," he said, "and have a separate reaffirmation of editorial policy to be signed by the Chairman, the President and the Editor."

Louis Wright agreed too, and pointed out that having the separate statement "would take the wind out of the sails of the critics. We would have gone on record in the Magazine on agreement."

Crawford Greenewalt introduced the motion that Gil Grosvenor "print the reaffirmation of policy statement in a box on the Editorial page and have it signed by the Chairman, President, and Editor."

The motion was unanimously carried. Gil Grosvenor had won the first round. The second round began with Lloyd Elliott asking, "Does the Committee wish to do anything in saying to the Editor we believe certain articles have not quite lived up to the editorial policy of the magazine, or do we want to advise the Editor that this Committee finds no reason for the publicity which has been given to the magazine, or to let the 'hot potato' drop?

"I think it would be beating a dead dog if we do anything but present this statement of reaffirmation," Greenewalt said. "I don't think we need to say anything else....just say here is our policy and we'll adhere to it as well as we can...."

Since there did not seem to be any disagreement, Elliott said, "Our report then is that 'We find no evidence of any intentional change in policy and we reaffirm the policy and commit ourselves to following it.' "

The committee was in agreement and the meeting was adjourned at 12:15.

An hour and forty-five minutes later the same seven committee members were gathered together again to attend the meeting of the National Geographic Society's Board of Trustees meeting. After all the Society officers' reports and other business had been done away with Lloyd Elliott delivered his report as chairman of the ad hoc committee for editorial policy, and presented copies of the "A Reaffirmation of the Editorial Policy of the National Geographic Magazine" statement that it was the committee's recommendation that the statement be printed in an appropriate box on the Editor's page of the Magazine to be signed by the Chairman, the President, and the Editor; and that the Editor may make reference to the statement in his own column as he wishes.

There then followed a discussion of the "Reaffirmation" statement and a short time later, the "Reaffirmation of Editorial Policy" statement was voted on and unanimously adopted. Vosburgh, Melville and Gil Grosvenor exchanged satisfied glances.

The Trustees voted to commend the ad hoc committee and particularly its chairman Elliott, and then Trustee Chairman Melvin Payne declared, "The Ad Hoc Committee is now dissolved."

Vosburgh leaned forward and asked, "Mr. Chairman, does that mean the idea of *any kind* of internal editorial oversight committee has been abandoned?"

Mel Payne assured Vosburgh it did.

The Trustees moved on to further business. Gil Grosvenor reported on future issues, that the December issue would have a supplement map and articles on the history of the New World, St. Brendan's voyage, the weather of 1977, Japan's inland sea, and…bowerbirds. The National Geographic Society had returned to business as usual—or almost as usual.

What resolution of the controversy had brought about was a vindication of the *Geographic*'s Editors and the Magazine's continuing evolution.

"I think one of the problems we have at the *Geographic*—or maybe," Gil Grosvenor said, "it's a blessing—is that we're a very conservative organization. We change slowly. There are some people who don't want us to change at all. Fortunately, they don't have much of a following. Basically, some people don't like the way the world is changing, and they want *something* to stay the way it is. They want *us* to stay the same. But we can't stand still. I'm convinced that unless you constantly evolve a publication, you're in trouble. And I also think if you make revolutionary changes, you're in trouble—or you make them because you're *already* in trouble. The *Geographic* has been fortunate in its leadership because the people that have come in, have come in time to make the changes."

On the Editor's page of the January 1978 issue, the following statement appeared over Gilbert M. Grosvenor's signature:

> …as journalists committed to objective, impartial reporting of what we can report, we accept the opportunity to reflect our times, realizing that only history can tell the full story.
>
> We often feel pressure to change that policy from those who would have journalism bear a message—their message. To some people, failure to denounce is the same as silent praise, and objective statement of fact amounts to advocacy—if fact fails to coincide with prejudice.
>
> But these voices from distant right and far left only serve to remind us to steer a course that avoids those biased and dangerous extremes of mind. Last year's record increase in new Society members, coupled with a high renewal rate, seems ample proof our course is sound.
>
> We will continue to travel the world unencumbered by ideology, to go along on a young man's walk across America, to peer into Loch Ness, and to fly to Mars and beyond. As the world goes its way, we will record it, accurately and clearly. This anniversary year is an appropriate time for us to reaffirm the principles that have served your Society so well.

The "Reaffirmation of Editorial Policy" statement approved by the ad hoc committee appeared directly below. It was signed:

| Melvin M. Payne | Robert E. Doyle | Gilbert M. Grosvenor |
| Chairman of the Board | President | Editor |

The rumblings stilled; the crisis had passed. Three years later Editor Gilbert M. Grosvenor would reluctantly give up what he called "the best job in the world" to replace Robert E. Doyle, who was stepping down as President of the Society. During Gil's decade as Editor, membership had increased from 6,402,674 to 10,771,886 despite a nearly twenty-seven percent increase in dues.

And as the decade of the 1980s commenced with a vacancy opening up in the office of Editor, for the first time in this century there wasn't another Grosvenor waiting in the wings.

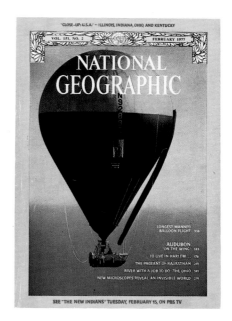

Ed Yost's "The Longest Manned Balloon Flight" [in the Silver Fox] *was the cover story for the February 1977* Geographic. *By the end of 1977 circulation of the Magazine had reached 9,756,312.*

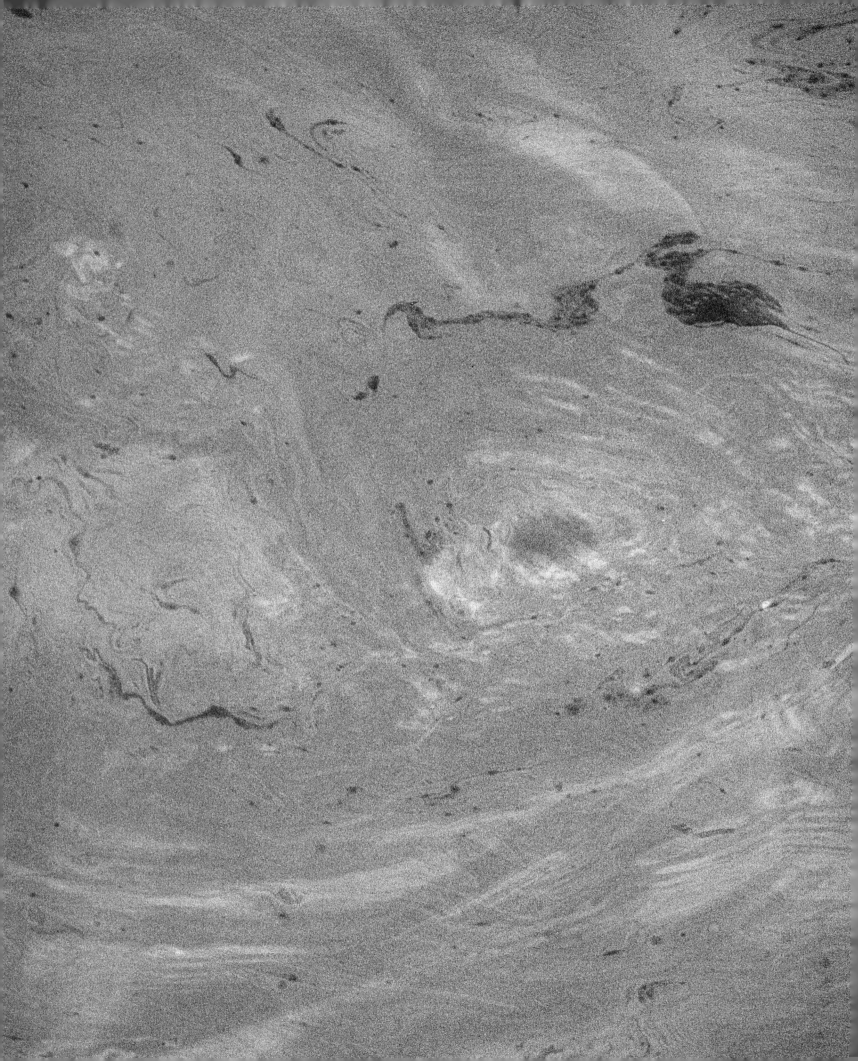

"Riders on the Earth Together"

"To see the earth as it truly is, small and blue and beautiful in that eternal silence where it floats, is to see ourselves as riders on the earth together, brothers on that bright loveliness in the eternal cold—brothers who know now they are truly brothers."

—Archibald MacLeish in *The New York Times*, December 25, 1968; partially quoted in the Editor's Note introducing Gordon Young's December 1970 *National Geographic* article, "Pollution, Threat to Man's Only Home"

The photograph that opens this chapter, a western grebe covered with a fatal coat of oil, appeared on the cover of the December 1970 *National Geographic*—the last issue edited by Frederick G. Vosburgh before his retirement. It was one he could take pride in.

Beneath the grebe on the cover was the issue's announced theme, "Our Ecological Crisis," with the subthemes "Pollution, Threat to Man's Only Home," "The World—And How We Abuse It," and "The Fragile Beauty All About Us."

The lead article contained photographer James P. Blair's grim, unromantic photographs of pollution-belching smokestacks, trash-infested New York alleyways, and Ohio's blackened Cuyahoga River "so covered with oil and debris that in July 1969 the river caught fire here in Cleveland's factory area, damaging two railroad bridges."

Gordon Young's somber text accompanying Blair's photographs began:

> We are astronauts—all of us. We ride a spaceship called Earth on its endless journey around the sun. This ship of ours is blessed with life-support systems so ingenious that they are self-renewing, so massive that they can supply the needs of billions.
>
> But for centuries we have taken them for granted, considering their capacity limitless. At last we have begun to monitor the systems, and the findings are deeply disturbing.
>
> Scientists and government officials of the United States and other countries agree that we are in trouble. Unless we stop abusing our vital life-support systems, they will fail. We must maintain them, or pay the penalty. The penalty is death.

Writer Gordon Young visited smog-bound Los Angeles (with its "witches' brew of pollutants, spewed primarily by automobiles"), Tokyo (where traffic policemen "pause regularly to breathe oxygen" and "pedestrians seek the same relief from vending machines"), Essen, Germany (where a formerly bright steel square exposed to the Ruhr's smog "for only two months, was chocolate brown and deeply corroded"). He took some comfort in London's victory over its killer fogs, the worst of which "settled over London on December 5, 1952. For four consecutive days the city's normal daily death rate of 300

Opposite: *Brig. Gen. William Mitchell (left) poses with the tiger he shot less than two miles from the palace of the Maharaja of Surguja (right), his host. "He was a beautiful creature, about 14 years old, 10 feet 4 inches between pegs," Gen. Billy Mitchell wrote in "Tiger-Hunting in India," for the November 1924 Geographic. "His paws, one blow of which could fell the largest buffalo, were as big around as the largest soup plate....He was the biggest tiger that I have ever seen."*

Preceding spread: *The blowout of an offshore oil well near Santa Barbara, California, in early 1969 created the slick through which this doomed, oil-coated western grebe swam in this photograph for the cover of the December 1970 issue.*

Above: *"Big Bruno, 800 pounds of muscle and claw, lies powerless from drugs as the team takes a blood sample. Red collar holds the radio that enabled the Craigheads to track No. 14 over some of the most heavily timbered and rugged country in Yellowstone. 'We followed this grizzly day and night,' Frank reported, 'and slept wherever darkness overtook us.'"*

As of August 1966, when this photograph from the Craigheads' "Trailing Yellowstone's Grizzlies by Radio" article appeared, the Society had contributed nine grants through its Committee for Research and Exploration to the seven-year grizzly research project then being conducted by the Craighead brothers. Since then, the brothers have received an additional nineteen grants from the Society for research on grizzly bears.

Opposite: *Like a worried mother on tiptoes, a female Alaskan grizzly rises up on her hind legs in an attempt to better locate her straying cubs.* —From "'Grizz'—Of Men and the Great Bear" in the February 1986 issue

for a fledgling cause called conservation— …enriched the public domain by approximately 230 million acres…quadrupled the existing forest reserves and proclaimed the first federal wildlife refuges, more than 50 of them. The number of national parks doubled; the first 18 national monuments came into being. The U.S. Reclamation Service was inaugurated to irrigate about three million acres in the arid West, and tens of millions of mineral-bearing acres also fell under Roosevelt's cloak.

"I hate a man who would skin the land," he bristled. He railed against corporate "timber thieves," and argued that "a live deer in the woods will attract…ten times the money that could be obtained for the deer's dead carcass." Again and again he preached, "Conservation of our natural resources is the most weighty question now before the people of the United States."

It may be hard to reconcile this conservationist Roosevelt with the T.R. who, shortly after leaving the Presidency, embarked on a hunting trip that was so thoroughly reported in the Magazine that between March 1909 and November 1910 four articles on it appeared. But his friend John Burroughs, the ardent naturalist who was instrumental in urging Roosevelt to establish wildlife refuges, was not disturbed by the President's hunting trips. "Such a hunter as Roosevelt," he wrote, "is as far removed from the game-butcher as day is from night."

Hunting did not seem at odds with loving nature. Eliza Ruhamah Scidmore wrote "The Greatest Hunt in the World" for the December 1906 issue; the Carl E. Akeley trophies described in the August 1912 article "Elephant Hunting in Equatorial Africa With Rifle and Camera" are still one of the American Museum of Natural History's major exhibits. Brig. Gen. William Mitchell went "Tiger-Hunting in India" for the *Geographic*'s November 1924 issue and photographs displayed his bag. But sixty years later, when the more conservation-minded *National Geographic* went tiger hunting again in "Tiger! Lord of the Indian Jungle" by Stanley Breeden, with photographs by Belinda Wright, there was a familiar opening but a new thrust:

> We set off at sunrise on this winter morning in central India, once again riding Pawan Mala, an old and venerable elephant. Out on the meadows the swamp deer stags are rutting. A tiger roars in the distance, a good omen.
>
> Mahavir, the mahout, steers the elephant toward the tiger's stirring sound. We soon find fresh tiger footprints along a sandy ravine, or nullah— the broad strong pugs of a male. They lead us into dense forest.
>
> We are on the right track; we can smell where the tiger has sprayed a bush to mark his territory. Belinda, my wife, sees the tiger first, an awesome vision in fiery orange and black stripes gliding through the green bamboo tracery. Ignoring us he walks on and on. We are alongside him now, about 30 feet distant. Once or twice he glances at us and snarls, pale yellow-green eyes burning.
>
> Suddenly the tiger stops in his tracks….

The Breedens shoot; the result—thousands of feet of film and the January 1985 National Geographic Special *Land of the Tiger*, which became the third-highest-rated evening program ever shown on public television.

"Ours has been a ten-year affair with the tiger," Stanley Breeden wrote, "a quest that lured us back again and again to the Indian jungles." The Breedens had been photographers nine years earlier for "India Struggles to Save Her

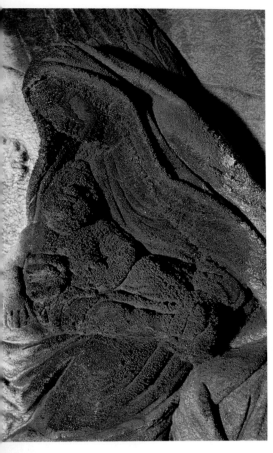

Above: "*Stone cancer spreads across a marble Madonna carved about 1650 beneath a buttress of the Cathedral of Milan. Here in Italy's industrial center, as in many world cities, the burning of high-sulphur coal and oil generates sulphur oxides. Deposited on stone, they combine with rain water to form sulphuric acid. The highly reactive fluid produces a chemical change in the stone, eventually disintegrating it under prolonged exposure. The acid has not remained long enough on the lighter areas to damage them severely. Such destruction threatens many of man's noblest monuments, from the gargoyles of Notre Dame de Paris to the Lincoln Memorial.*"—From "Pollution, Threat to Man's Only Home" in the December 1970 issue

Opposite: *Man is both culprit and victim of the pollution clouding St. Louis' air.*—From "Acid Rain: How Great a Menace?" in the November 1981 issue

curare-like drug was not strong enough and a bear would sputter into consciousness while they were leaning over it.

In this article, titled "Knocking Out Grizzly Bears for Their Own Good," Frank Craighead asked:

> But what good is a grizzly? Why spend such time and research money to save an animal?...John's 12-year-old daughter [answered], "We want to save the grizzly because when he's gone, he's gone forever, and we can't make another one."
>
> Here was the simple answer.
>
> No animal species other than man has ever been known to exterminate another. But man's list is long. Do we possess the right to annihilate a fellow creature?

It was not a question that much troubled the Society during its formative years. Between September 1907 and April 1909 five bear-hunting articles appeared—in the same period a Remington Autoloading Rifle advertisement, titled "The Right of Way," depicted a surprised hunter and a snarling, bloodthirsty grizzly confronting each other on a narrow mountain ledge. The truth is that "since 1900 only 14 people have been killed by grizzlies in the lower 48 states," and those fatalities were primarily the result of hungry bears lured into campsites by garbage. Since the advent of the repeating rifle, however, the bears have stood little chance. In his February 1986 article, " 'Grizz'—Of Men and the Great Bear," Douglas H. Chadwick noted that "tens of thousands of the great bears [lived] south of Canada as late as 1850. Only 600 to 900 remain there now....Standing sheeplike, shoulder to shoulder, the current lower 48 grizzly flock wouldn't cover half an acre."

For the past two decades, the Society has focused its attention on whales. Articles have appeared on sperm whales, blue whales, humpbacks, killer whales, false killer whales, narwhals, gray whales, right whales, white whales; 10.1 million copies of the recording "Song of the Humpback Whale" were bound into the January 1979 issue; two children's books on whales have been published; and the Society's 1978 television documentary *The Great Whales* won an Emmy Award for Outstanding International Programming.

Gilbert M. Grosvenor, in a December 1976 *Geographic* editorial remarking on the international controversy surrounding efforts to halt the killing of whales and the imposition of International Whaling Commission quotas, wrote:

> On one thing, all seem agreed. The natural legions of whales have been dealt a devastating blow in the past century, under impact of the explosive harpoon and the fast catcher boat. The blue whale, like the American buffalo, nearly became extinct. No one can tell if those that remain can restore their numbers....no one...can escape the conclusion that the whale has become a symbol for a way of thinking about our planet and its creatures, and in that, at least, there is hope of a better day for both whales and men.

The "better day" has not come for the 161 members of the eleven families who lived on Bikini Atoll, no matter how patiently they have waited. As staff writer William S. Ellis reported in June 1986:

> Nearly 40 years had passed since that Sunday in 1946 when Commodore Ben Wyatt of the United States Navy met with them after church services to say that their island was needed for a project that would benefit mankind. He implied that an authority higher than any on earth would be pleased if they decided to cooperate.

416

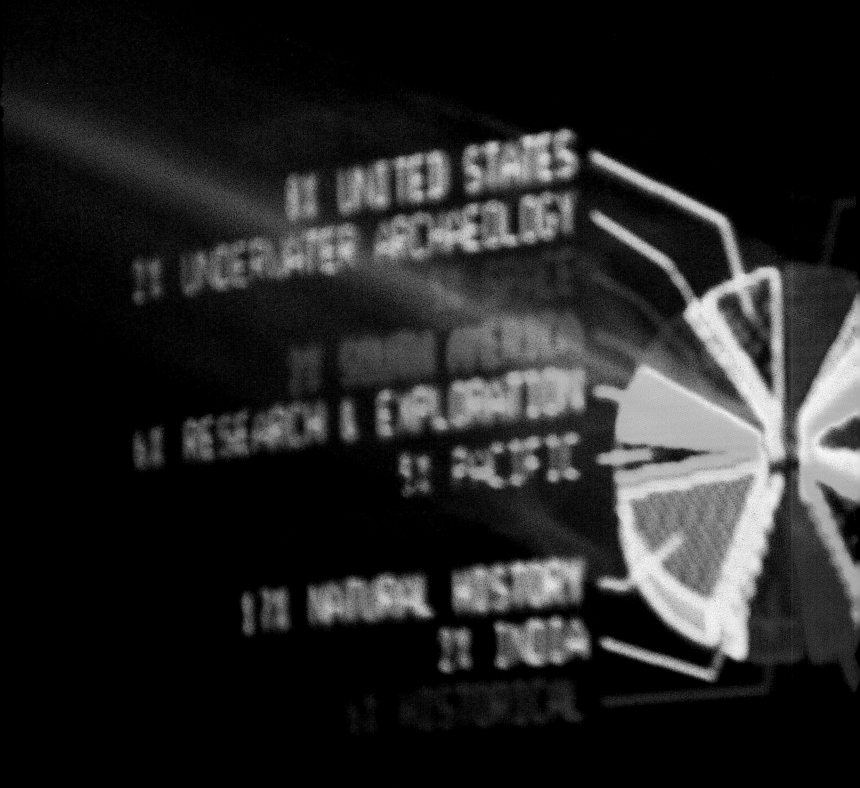

"Broadening the Outreach"

"There absolutely will be no radical or visible changes in the magazine. It's like being given control of apple pie and motherhood; you don't fool around with it."

—Wilbur E. Garrett, upon his appointment as the seventh Editor of the *National Geographic,* July 10, 1980

"I would hope that at our 200th anniversary, somebody will look back and say, 'Hey, you know, those people between the first and second hundred, they really broadened the outreach of the National Geographic Society!'"

—Gilbert M. Grosvenor

Preceding spread: *Shown on the display screen and a computer in the Society's new "Control Center" is a listing of the Magazine's 1986 stories by subject and area. An almost endless variety of screen display, reports, and even graphic representations can be generated from the same data. This center commenced operation in the spring of 1987, replacing the one Gilbert M. Grosvenor had "built in his basement" more than twenty years before.*

On June 27, 1977, when Dr. Melvin M. Payne, had told his fellow Trustees at the ad hoc committee meeting, "We are known throughout the world by our Magazine, and what the Magazine says is what the National Geographic Society says," his observation, even then, was only partially correct, for the Society was beginning to speak with other voices.

Perhaps twenty-five years ago the Society was, to an outsider, just the familiar yellow-bordered *National Geographic* mailed out to the Society's then 3.5 million members. To outsiders today, however, to the Society's 10.6 million members, to the Magazine's estimated 30 to 50 million readers, to the millions and millions who have watched its television specials, the National Geographic has evolved into something much, much more. And at the root of that expansion has been Gilbert M. Grosvenor's determination to make up for having to give up the Editorship of the Magazine in 1980 to become President of the Society because the ailing incumbent, Robert E. Doyle, was retiring.

Just two years before, Gil and Bob Doyle had directed the second major move of the Magazine to a new printer—and a totally different printing process. After eighteen years of printing by the letterpress method in Chicago, the Magazine was moved to a new plant in Corinth, Mississippi, where it was produced by the gravure process. As Gil Grosvenor told members in the November 1977 Editor's page, it was "the biggest technical change-over in the history of your Magazine."

When Gil Grosvenor resigned as Editor, the front-runners to fill the vacancy were Wilbur E. Garrett, Joseph Judge, and Robert L. Breeden. Both Bill Garrett and Joe Judge were Associate Editors of the Magazine. Garrett was in charge of illustrations and Judge in charge of text.

And although Bob Breeden's title was Senior Assistant Editor, his area was Related Educational Services of the Society—Special Publications and School Services. So Breeden had not, in reality, been with the Magazine since

he was asked by Melville Grosvenor to do the picture editing and layout for the White House book eighteen years before.

Because of Breeden's astounding success with the Special Publications Division, and the Society's natural reluctance to tamper with something obviously working so well, the search for Editor narrowed down to Garrett and Judge.

Garrett had joined the staff as a picture editor in 1954. He had progressed from Associate Illustrations Editor to Senior Assistant Editor and then to Associate Editor under Gil Grosvenor. Along the way Garrett had photographed, and sometimes written, almost two dozen articles, many of them reflecting his abiding interest in Southeast Asia, the preservation of antiquities—and his willingness to take risks.

In 1961, Garrett was in Laos with a U.S. Army Special Forces team and its captain, Walter Moon. Unknown to them all, they were surrounded by Pathet Laos. "It was during the monsoon season, and we couldn't get the wounded out or the supplies in because it was pouring rain," Garrett remembers:

> I lived in one of those little shacks upon sticks with Walter Moon and some of his people. Finally, one rainy day, the big helicopters got in through the

The supertanker Amoco Cadiz *foundered off the coast of Brittany in March 1978, broken-backed and gushing sixty-nine million gallons of crude oil into the sea. The ship was photographed for staff writer Noel Grove's July 1978 article, "Superspill: Black Day for Brittany," by Martin Rogers, sitting in the open door of a French military helicopter crowded with other photographers. "It was impossible for me to get up," Rogers later wrote. "I just kept shooting. I nearly got pushed out. But I had plenty of time to work the situation. I used at least three cameras."*

TRAVELING WITH NGS

"Travel is an extremely important part of one's geographic education," Gil Grosvenor said in 1986. "There is no substitute for being in a place and experiencing it yourself, the sights, the sounds, the feelings, the conversations...."

For one hundred years *National Geographic* readers explored the world through the pages of the Magazine; but during the past decade, as the *National Geographic* has continued to evolve, its editorial direction has taken it further away from its traditional travel piece. Still, readers of the Magazine, glimpsing the faraway lands portrayed in its pages, frequently found their appetites whetted enough to request information on places *they* could visit themselves—without sled dogs, Sherpas, or the need of a Citroën-type half-track vehicle. The Society's response was *Traveler*, launched in 1984—its first new magazine for adults since the *National Geographic* commenced publication in 1888.

With subscribers now approaching one million, *Traveler* differs in several significant ways from its parent publication. It is news-magazine size and focuses primarily on the more accessible places American travelers like to

visit. Seventy percent of the features are on destinations in the United States or Canada; the remainder are on favorite destinations in Europe, the Pacific, and the Caribbean. Articles emphasize what a particular location is really like, how to get there, and, once there, what a visitor is likely to find.

Traveler features articles on national parks, historic places, cities, specialized museums, regional crafts and cooking, vacation sites, quiet weekend retreats. "We have a huge responsibility to give our readers accurate, readable information that will broaden their experience and stimulate their minds—whether we're examining history in Williamsburg or Salzburg, a particular culture in Rajasthan or Cajun country, or the natural science of polar bear watching in Canada or bird-watching in Arizona," says editor Joan Tapper.

The magazine's photography, in the National Geographic tradition, is colorful, spectacular, and has already won awards. And with *Traveler*'s emphasis on good prose, it has attracted such freelance authors as biographer Edmund Morris, novelists Edward Abbey and Christopher Buckley, and travel writers Kate Simon and William Least Heat-Moon.

Traveler has always provided listings telling readers how to get there, what to see, and where to stay and eat. But recently, the magazine's extensive service information has included American Automobile Association (AAA) recommendations.

Subscribers have responded enthusiastically—perhaps because the Society's award-winning magazine *Traveler* recognizes that the most educational experience of traveling is in exposing minds to the unfamiliar. "Our destination is never a place, but a new way of looking at things," Henry Miller once said. *Traveler* aims to help its readers find that new way.

two heads: you have one person over there sending out a Magazine to 10½ million people—30 million readers—that the President has nothing to do with; and you have a President over here who's basically involved in running the Society, responsible for the books, for the educational products, but with no responsibility to the Magazine whatsoever. I feel it's very awkward, and I'm stuck with it. It's here to stay."

The appointment of the new Editor was announced on July 10, 1980. "There absolutely will be no radical or visible changes in the magazine," the *Washington Post* reported Garrett as saying. "It's like being given control of apple pie and motherhood; you don't fool around with it."

The following year, 1981, was the year that fifty-two American hostages held in the Iran embassy were freed, that Ronald Reagan took the oath as the fortieth President and escaped an assassination attempt that wounded him, his press secretary, and two others. It was the year the space shuttle *Columbia* completed its first successful test flight, Pope John Paul II was wounded by a gunman in the Vatican Square, that Charles, Prince of Wales, and Lady Diana Spencer were married, and that President Anwar Sadat of Egypt was assassinated. At the end of 1981, Gil Grosvenor took advantage of his new position as President of the Society to publish in the Magazine his "Report to the Members: It's Been a Banner Year!," a piece in which he determinedly expressed his—and the Society's—broadening interests.

The report was occasioned by the ground-breaking for the new multi-million-dollar headquarters building designed by Skidmore, Owings & Merrill architect David Childs that was to be built on the parking lot between the Society's older buildings on 16th Street N.W. and the Edward Durell Stone building on 17th Street.

"As I stood with the ceremonial shovel in hand, many memories—and hopes—crowded my mind," Gil Grosvenor wrote. "...Having relinquished my ten-year stewardship as Editor of the magazine for that of President of the Society 16 months ago, I view our mission with slightly different eyes, taking in the widening horizon of our many educational activities. What I see excites me and I wish to share with you some of the highlights of this year at National Geographic."

Gil marked the growth of the Society: "10,850,000 members in more than 180 countries...more than a third larger today than it was ten years ago"; the burgeoning staff which necessitated the new building; and the success of the television specials—"Carried by nine out of ten PBS stations, the Specials make up nearly half of the 25 top-rated PBS telecasts. Last year's series won not only four Emmys, TV's highest honor, but also a George Foster Peabody Award for 'unsurpassed excellence in documentaries.' "

"...To keep one of our most praised publications up-to-date," Grosvenor continued, "we published a completely revised and enlarged fifth edition of the *National Geographic Atlas of the World* in October. The new atlas places the earth in a galactic context. There are charts of the solar system, the visible stars, maps of the ocean floors and of the moon, and illustrations of the atmosphere, magnetosphere, plate tectonics, and climate...."

That fifth edition of the *Atlas* was not so popular as were its previous editions because all elevations and measurements were given in metric terms, prompting the sort of outcry the Geographic has come to expect ever since

First experimented with in the mid-1970s, the international publications program fully developed in the early and mid-1980s under the direction of Senior Vice President Robert L. Breeden and the coordination of William R. Gray. Under this program, publishers from other countries license the right to produce certain of the Society's books and magazines in languages other than English. Thus the Society broadens the fulfillment of its mission.

For example, the Society's 1986 large-format book The Incredible Machine *will appear in French, German, Italian, Japanese, Swedish, Finnish, and Dutch; the Society's Action ("pop-up") Books have appeared in five languages. And in June 1987, an Italian version of* Traveler *was launched by the Touring Club Italiano in Milan.*

JOURNAL OF RESEARCH

In 1890 the National Geographic Society awarded its first grant to a professional scientist in support of a field research project. The recipient was a geologist and Society founder, Israel C. Russell, of the United States Geological Survey, who was given the grant to explore the region of Mount St. Elias, Alaska. Since then, the Society has supported more than 3,000 research projects, 239 in 1986 alone.

Grant applications are subjected to peer review and subsequent consideration by the Society's prestigious Committee for Research and Exploration. Grantees are required to file preliminary and final reports on their research results. Final reports—retrospective to the first—were published, starting in 1968, in twenty-one hard-bound volumes called *National Geographic Society Research Reports*. In 1985, that series was replaced by a new quarterly scientific journal, *National Geographic Research*, edited by Harm J. de Blij, Professor of Geography at the University of Miami, member of the Society's Committee for Research and Exploration, and author of more than 25 books.

Many articles published in *National Geographic Research* are based on projects supported by research grants from the Society; however, any qualified scientist may submit a manuscript for possible publication.

Alexander Graham Bell's argument for the adoption of the metric system appeared in the Magazine seventy-five years before. The sixth edition of the *Atlas*, now in production, will retain metrics, but will also contain key measurements in inches and feet.

The Cartographic Division, responsible for all the Society's globes, atlases, maps, and supplements, is headed by John B. Garver, a former West Point professor. Garver is listed on the Magazine's masthead as a Senior Assistant Editor since, in the complex organization of the Society, the Cartographic Division falls under the direction of Wilbur E. Garrett as Editor of the Magazine.

Grosvenor's report also mentioned that "Our Special Publications and School Services Division produced 15 new books, 10 of them for children. All together, Society members received nearly four and a half million of these publications...."

The fact is the Society's books sell in such vast numbers that even an author of a book making *The New York Times Book Review*'s best-seller list would be green with envy. For example, the Book Service Division's *We Americans*, a lavishly illustrated, large-format, 456-page volume published in time for America's Bicentennial, sold more than one million copies. *Fifty States, Our World*, and *Our Universe*, the three-book set of children's atlases, have sold nearly two million copies. The Society is so conditioned by the remarkable sales records of its publications, that books which test out as selling under 150,000 copies are, as a rule, not even done.

"Our costs are between four and five million dollars to produce a book," explains Book Service Director Charles O. Hyman. "And to get that money back we've got to sell a lot of books. Break even is between 150,000 and 200,000....Our subject matter is fairly broad," Hyman said. "We don't just do 'Rivers of the United States,' we do 'Rivers of the World.' We also try to be a bit more encyclopedic, more comprehensive in our coverage, and make it more of a reference book."

Because of this, Book Service publishes books such as *Journey into China*; *Lost Empires*; *Living Tribes*; *Images of the World*; *The Adventure of Archaeology*; *Everyday Life in Bible Times*. Book Service Director Chuck Hyman reports to Bob Breeden.

Special Publications and School Services, under its Director, Donald J. Crump, publishes books that are generally more narrow-focused and tightly defined than the Book Service "encyclopedias." Established in 1965 as an outgrowth of the public service books, the Special Publications Division has grown in scope over the years to include books tailored to specific age groups and categories. For example, "Books for Young Explorers," begun in 1972, the series that carries books like *Baby Birds and How They Grow, Wonders of the Desert World, Animals That Live in the Sea*, and so forth, are designed for children four through eight years old. "Young Explorers" leads to "Books for World Explorers," started in 1977, a series with books like *Your Wonderful Body!*, *Amazing Mysteries of the World, Far-out Facts*, which are designed for children ages eight through twelve.

At 7 A.M. on April 12, 1981, the space shuttle Columbia *lifted off from Cape Canaveral on its maiden flight, returning Americans to space after a six-year absence. This photograph accompanied the October 1981 article "Columbia's Astronauts' Own Story."*

In "The Temples of Angkor: Will They Survive?"—his introduction to the Magazine's May 1982 coverage of Kampuchea's magnificent, eight-century-old religious complex at Angkor Wat—Geographic Editor Wilbur E. Garrett discussed his return to what had been Cambodia. "It was my first visit since 1968, when Prince Sihanouk's government still maintained a tenuous neutrality in war-ravaged Southeast Asia. That year a surplus of rice was harvested. At Angkor Wat a ballet company danced with the delicacy and grace of living apsaras, to the enjoyment of thousands of tourists. The countryside was green with life.

"What I now saw," Garrett continued, "were mass graves, barren fields, and a people trying to return from hell on earth. Only children—and only a few—were dancing."

What Garrett's photographs made evident was that not all the war's victims had been of flesh and blood, that even the temples' sculptures had been wounded.

Children who have outgrown the "World Explorer" books are then ready for the Special Publications Division's regular volumes, which the Division began publishing for the adult general membership in the mid-1960s. This series contains such popular staples as *America's Magnificent Mountains, America's Majestic Canyons, America's Seashore Wonderlands.** Special Publications Director Don Crump comes under the direction of Bob Breeden—the man he has worked with since they produced the White House Guide together in 1962.

In the same manner, children given subscriptions to *National Geographic World*, the Society's magazine for children ages eight to twelve, are expected, in time, to receive membership subscriptions to the *National Geographic*.

Gil Grosvenor's "It's Been a Banner Year" report continued: "...Countless school-age children have already been introduced to National Geographic educational materials through more than two million filmstrips so far distributed. Or perhaps they have learned about life in a pond, solar energy, or Ice Age hunters from multimedia kits prepared by our Educational Media staff, or watched a film about dinosaurs or the life of a wheat farmer...."

The report to the members further stated that the Society had given out 2.5 million dollars in grants that year to "help continue the essential discourse of research." The largest grant went to a new sky survey of the northern heavens which would probe "twice as far into space as the first survey in the 1950s." Other grants went to the archeological digs at Aphrodisias, a study of African elephant behavior and ecology, and an attempt to radio-track in the Himalayas the "elusive snow leopard, about which so little is yet known." In a conclusion that echoed Ishbel Ross' observation that membership in the Society made it possible for "the janitor, plumber, and loneliest lighthouse keeper [to] share with kings and scientists the fun of sending an expedition to Peru or an explorer to the South Pole," Gil wrote:

> These far-flung projects are the direct result of your membership in the Society and your encouragement of others to join. Each month thousands of you recommend friends by using the membership form in the front of the magazine. With the same vigor and dedication that have made the Society a unique institution for nine decades, the staff of the Geographic—and the scientists it helps support—will continue to push at the frontiers of man's knowledge of earth, sea, and sky. As a partner in these endeavors, you have good reason to feel proud.

The August 1982 issue carried the report that on April 22, 1982, Melville Bell Grosvenor had died. Bart McDowell, in writing the *Geographic*'s fond, remembrance-filled farewell, recalled:

> Once the Skipper wanted more space for a *White Mist* [MBG's yacht] story. "We need at least 55 pages," he told his friend Ted Vosburgh, MBG's successor as Editor.
> Ted objected. He knew that Mel, like most photographers, was too en-

---

**Titles with words such as "Wonderful," "Amazing," "Marvels," "Mysteries," "Splendors," "Primitive," "Adventure" and books about "America" consistently test high. So a wag at the Geographic fed various mainstays into a computer to determine what other potential best-selling titles might be. Among the hundreds of suggestions were "Marvels of the Primitive Adventure," "Isles of Sunset Paradise," "Our Mysterious Mountains," and the absolutely guaranteed, sure-fire, best-seller of all time: "America's America!"*

thusiastic about his own pictures. "That's more space than we're giving the whole solar system."

"Yes," said MBG, "but there are no *people* out there." The solar system was moved to another month.

I worked closely with the Skipper on his own stories....He loved italics and exclamation points ("Sable! Sable Island!"). I argued the virtues of understatement and finally held him to 15 exclamation points in one article. But next time around he whoopingly subverted me and used at least 40....

With his wife, Anne, at his side, he was an inveterate traveler, climbing over archaeological digs, fording forest streams, filling his pockets with notes....When President Lyndon Johnson asked him to attend the coronation of the King of Tonga, Mel Grosvenor wore striped trousers, cutaway—and a Leica camera hidden inside his silk hat; he thus made for history the only photograph of the moment of coronation....

He was, as so many friends remarked, a gentleman of the old school. And his death, on April 22 at age 80, was as gentle as the man himself. He simply went to sleep. His grave, beneath the pink bracts of a dogwood tree, was wet with a soft April rain. Sou'wester weather.

Bill Garrett said it for all of us who knew "this great, lovable man: His impact will be felt as long as there is a *Geographic*."

We wish our friend a brisk breeze for his far horizon!

Many of the *Geographic* staff consider Garrett to have inherited Melville Grosvenor's finger on the reader's pulse. "Garrett was very close to Melville," McDowell said. "He had a lot of Melville's own instinctive responses to pictures. He and Melville communicated in a terrific nonverbal way."

One long-time staffer went on to say, "Melville was perfectly willing to be the only one in the room with an opinion, and that's the one that prevailed. He didn't find this strange at all. I think Gil is more thoughtful and sensitive to other people's ideas, and sometimes hides behind a thicket of numerals to protect opinions he already has."

This same staffer feels Gil is remarkably like his father: "A kind of 'closet romantic' in a way. On the surface you don't get this from Gil. He doesn't express it the same way his father did—Melville whooped, and all his emotions were right there on the front burner; Gil inhibits his displays—but they're there. Gil really is a romantic."

Clearly the same fires that burned in Melville to move the Society into other fields burn in his son Gil. And, like his father, Gil has acted on his impulses.

On June 19, 1984, President Ronald Reagan dedicated the just-completed headquarters building on M Street, saying, "In a world that sometimes seems to have grown sated with all it knows, you still discover. You fund expeditions, you help researchers, you encourage impossible dreams—then you share the results with all the Society's members."

Earlier, as he looked around the vast new building, the President of the United States had joked, "I guess you have trouble storing your old *National Geographic*s, too."

In "Our Society Opens New Doors," the Magazine's piece marking the dedication of the new M Street building, Gil Grosvenor responded, "Mr. President, rather than needing a space to store our past, we needed a space to house our future."

The six sheep that this Peruvian shepherd boy had been tending for his family had just been struck and killed by a taxi when photographer William Albert Allard happened by and took this photograph. Allard's photograph, showing the young shepherd's grief-stricken face and the terrible desolation the boy felt, appeared in the March 1982 issue accompanying Harvey Arden's article "The Two Souls of Peru."

Five months later Bill Garrett reported in his Editor's page that members had "spontaneously contributed more than $4,000 to replace the sheep [and that] through CARE in Peru, the boy, Eduardo Condor Ramos, was found, and Assistant Executive Director Ronald Burkard presented him with six new animals.... Eduardo, incredulous, broke into tears again and said, 'God will pay you.'"

Pointing out that it was "only 16 years to year 2000, and a briefer four years" to the Society's centennial, Gil's report continued:

> It is our hope that the study and science of geography will make strides in the decades ahead. We have a major commitment to this goal....
>
> The newest building, 1600 M Street N.W., will enable us to experiment with and develop educational programming utilizing the laser disk, direct broadcasting, cable networks, and technologies not yet developed. We will be able to reach directly into members' homes and classrooms of the world with printed and broadcast material....
>
> It is an exciting prospect, and especially so in the light of the many challenges, essentially geographic in nature, that confront us—how to obtain clear skies and clear streams, protect wilderness and forests where genetic pools of life are safe, while still making progress in the increase of living standards for a rapidly, in places alarmingly, growing world population.
>
> Starting with the small but elegant Hubbard Memorial Hall on a corner of our Washington complex, the Society has grown continuously over the years as it responded to the changing world. Now our headquarters is complete, our sails are trimmed, and our course is set with confidence.

And as an example of that confidence Gil Grosvenor had already launched *Traveler*, the Society's first new magazine for adults since its founding in 1888.

The steadily evolving yellow-bordered *National Geographic*, Gil felt, had been moving away from the traditional geography travel piece, and *Traveler* was designed to fill that gap. "We know our membership is deep into travel and geography," Gil said, "and since travel is a significant part of one's geographic

EDUCATIONAL MEDIA: HELPING CHILDREN LEARN

In 1972, the Special Publications Division's Filmstrips Department's first catalogue offered thirty-four filmstrips for grades 5–12; by 1987, the Society had printed and delivered more than two million copies of nearly 450 filmstrips, which are now seen by millions of schoolchildren in grades K–12 each year.

Although filmstrips are still the cornerstone of the Society's efforts to meet the audiovisual needs of K–12 teachers, by the late 1970s and early 1980s the Society's educational programs had diversified rapidly both in media and range of subject matter. Captioned filmstrips for the hearing impaired were developed in the 1970s. So were Wonders of Learning Kits—a series of multimedia reading programs designed to teach science and social studies concepts while improving reading and listening skills. And a new teaching medium, Participatory Filmstrips

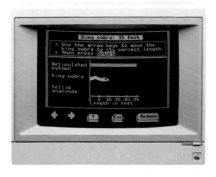

Computers in Your Life

called "Look, Listen, Explore," was designed for children in grades K–2.

After extensive testing with teachers and students, new multimedia kits that included computer software—in addition to filmstrips, color-illustrated booklets, and activity sheets— were developed in 1984. And the following year full-scale production began on the Society's first computer software designed to build skills in geography and other related subjects. By then the dramatic increase in the number and diversity of materials being produced by the department led to its restructuring, also in 1985, as the Educational Media Division with George A. Peterson as its Director.

Now interactive videodiscs are under development for schools. (The Division's first research project, *Whales*, scored so highly in field tests it has already been released for general distribution.) The videodisc's principal advantage is that the disc player's laser reader permits virtually instantaneous access to any part of the videodisc. The Educational Media Division is developing an interactive videodisc and computer project to teach geography. This technology will permit students and teachers to program their own lessons and to have access to a storehouse of information literally at their fingertips.

An exciting program called National Geographic Kids Network has been developed by the Division in collaboration with the Technical Education Research Centers of Cambridge, Massachusetts. Students across the country, using classroom activity kits and computer software produced by the Society, will be able to share data and compare geographic trends from common experiments via telecommunications. The National Geographic Kids Network is par-

tially funded by a 2.2 million-dollar grant from the National Science Foundation in addition to a matching 2.5 million-dollar contribution from the National Geographic Society.

In 1985, the Society embarked on a major program to improve geography education. Pilot projects were started by the Educational Media Division at Alice Deal Junior High School in Washington, D.C., and at Audubon Junior High School in Los Angeles, California, where social studies and science teachers experimented with a variety of ways to improve geography teaching methods and materials. The Division also administers the Society's Summer Geography Institutes, a network of regional Geography Alliances, and other related programs to encourage support for local and nationwide efforts to improve geography education.

In 1888 one of the aims of the Society was stated as giving "due prominence...to the educational aspects of geographic matters." The Educational Media Division is fulfilling that aim.

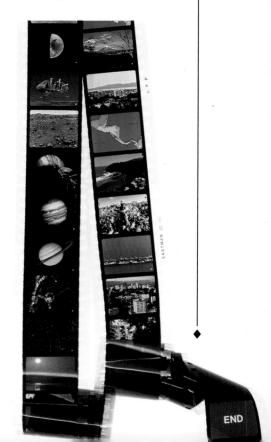

education, I feel travel is an important part of our obligation to the members. *Traveler* is still young; it's experiencing growing pains just as the parent magazine did. We're still evolving it to meet the needs of the readers."

Despite its youth, *Traveler,* under Editor Joan Tapper, has already published such fine pieces as Edward Abbey's "Big Bend: Desert Rough and Tumble," Ken Brower's "Gaspé: Quebec's Wild Peninsula," Steve Hall's "Baseball Scrapbook: Cooperstown's Hall of Fame and Museum," and Rob Schultheis' "Yellowstone: Wonderland at Zero Degrees." *Traveler* comes under the direction of Bob Breeden.

And that same year he announced he was starting yet another magazine: *National Geographic Research*, a scientific journal designed primarily as a publishing forum for the results of Society-funded research.

Ironically, seventy-six years earlier, the Geographic's Board of Trustees had passed a resolution calling for the Society to "undertake the publication of a technical journal to be separate from the *National Geographic Magazine.*" But that direction faded when the Society, guided by Gilbert Hovey Grosvenor, continued to concentrate on popular geography.

Until *National Geographic Research,* summaries of grant recipients' findings appeared in the Society's annual *Research Reports*—"a ledger of stiff, dry tracts," wrote Leonard Krishtalka, the Carnegie Museum's Associate Curator in the Section of Vertebrate Fossils, "devoid of maps or photographs."

"Not so *National Geographic Research,*" Krishtalka continued in his glowing review (in the September 25, 1986, issue of *Nature*) of the Society's newest magazine:

> [It is] the handsomest, most elegant professional scientific journal known to me…and it finally puts the lie to Darwin's axiom that if it's handsome, it's art; if it's science, it's dull….

National Geographic Research has already published articles on archeology, biogeography, botany, ecology, entomology, ethology, geology, historical geography, palynology, urban anthropology, vertebrate paleontology and zoology. One "unusually lucid" bit of writing from this last was Wesley W. Weathers' "Thermal Significance of Courtship Display in the Blue-black Grassquit (*Volantinia jacarina*)," which contained the following "science in the flesh" observation:

> One of the most common of a dozen or so species of small, lowland, Neotropical seed-eaters, the blue-black grassquit is remarkable…for the male's peculiar aerial display. Displaying males vault about 0.4 m into the air, emit an explosive buzzy *Dzee-we* call, and then return to the original perch. This behaviour is notable for its frequency (as many as 20 displays a minute) and because it is performed from an exposed perch, often in direct sunlight. By displaying in direct sunlight, male grassquits subject themselves to substantial heat stress. Indeed they often pant with their mouths open while displaying.

Weathers' piece begs for the kind of tongue-in-cheek response George B. Schaller's December 1981 "Pandas in the Wild" *Geographic* article inspired.

Writing of the fresh bamboo shoot diet and mating habits of pandas, Schaller had noted, "I observed [the male panda] mount her 48 times in three hours"—an observation that prompted one astonished reader to write: "Pandas—48 times in 3 hours? 180 divided by 48 = 3.75 minutes per cycle. No

Senior Associate Editor Joseph Judge's press conference on Samana Cay as the true landfall of Christopher Columbus in the New World was the most successful in the Society's history: A total of 1,016 newspapers and magazines with a combined circulation of 88,088,437 ran the story. It was on the front page of 177 newspapers and featured in all major television networks' news.

The press conference was orchestrated by one of the Society's oldest divisions: News Service—the Society's "public voice." It reaches millions of readers through the 1,500 newspapers and periodicals whose editors receive this free service from the Society, and millions of listeners through the 250 or so radio stations that regularly broadcast "Horizon" over the Associated Press network.

News Service Director is Paul Sampson.

("The Indomitable Cockroach," January 1981; "The Fascinating World of Trash," April 1983).

One of the most exciting pieces from this period was Garrett's own that appeared in the August 1984 issue. The Editor was on board a Guatemalan helicopter flying to the dramatic opening of an ancient Maya tomb that had, he wrote, "all the makings of a childhood fantasy. An ancient city lost under the green canopy of a remote jungle. Vines and roots snaking over temples and pyramids. And, beneath it all, an undiscovered tomb containing the art of a vanished civilization and the skeletal remains of a long-dead nobleman lying in undisturbed repose."

En route, the confused Guatemalan helicopter pilot—who had already landed four times in Mexico and Belize to ask directions—ran out of fuel over the jungle; the helicopter sheared off the tops of five trees on its way down. Garrett and the others in his party spent an uneasy night in the jungle, listening for guerrillas, before they were located by a second helicopter and supplied with chain saws so they could clear a landing pad and be lifted out.

Eventually Garrett reached the site of the Maya tomb—"the first to be officially reported in Guatemala in 20 years"—and recounted for the *Geographic* how the tomb had been found untouched since it had been "sealed by the Maya 1,500 years ago" in the Río Azul region of northern Guatemala:

> From the time of the fall of Rome the tomb had lain undisturbed. Even food and drink left for the deceased remained—now only powdery residue in ceramic pots and plates.
>
> For reasons still unknown, the site and the Maya culture had faded away by the tenth century. Under cover of the jungle the city—now known as Río Azul—lay for a thousand years as a vast mausoleum protecting the artifacts of the once bustling society. Palaces, homes, and pyramids of the early Classic period (A.D. 250–600) ever so slowly slumped into piles of rubble under the relentless wash of tropical rains and the insidious pushing and shoving of tree roots. As the green canopy grew over fields, canals, and plazas, only the occasional Indian chicle collector, armed with nothing more devastating than his machete, disturbed the tangle of vines and branches....

But under Garrett the Magazine has also gone into areas of advocacy journalism that would have been at odds with the sentiments of the members of the 1977 ad hoc committee. Among the more noteworthy pieces have been "Wild Cargo: the Business of Smuggling Animals" (March 1981), "Acid Rain—How Great a Menace?" (November 1981), "The Temples of Angkor" (May 1982), [this with photographs by Wilbur E. Garrett*], "Tropical Rain Forest: Nature's Dwindling Treasures" (January 1983), and "Escape From Slavery: The Underground Railroad" (July 1984), with Charles L. Blockson's moving text:

> "My father—your great-grandfather, James Blockson—was a slave over in Delaware," Grandfather said, "but as a teenager he ran away underground and escaped to Canada." Grandfather knew little more than these

---

*Garrett's "visa" for Cambodia consisted of a handwritten note torn out of a spiral notebook. He was one of the first outside journalists to reach Phnom Penh after the holocaust there and witnessed the opening of a mass grave containing more than 6,000 bodies, some with skulls still blindfolded and arms still bound by wire. The elaborate temple complex at Angkor, virtually closed to outsiders for more than a decade, had so sadly deteriorated that Garrett produced an exhibit sponsored by UNESCO which was sent to many countries in an effort to inform the world of what was happening.

PUTTING GEOGRAPHY BACK INTO AMERICA'S CLASSROOMS

"The most important thing you can do is validate teachers," Dr. Floretta McKenzie, Superintendent of the District of Columbia Public Schools and Society Trustee told Gilbert M. Grosvenor at a meeting held to discuss ways to improve geographic education in America. "Tell them they are important and that geography is important." Thus began the Geography Education Program, the Society's campaign to revitalize study of what many consider the "mother of all discipline," and what Gil's grandfather Gilbert Hovey Grosvenor realized the public regarded as "the dullest of subjects, something to inflict on schoolboys and to avoid later in life."

And yet if in recent years geography as a course of study has been inflicted at all on schoolboys and schoolgirls, it has clearly not taken hold! Consider these statistics from a recent CBS news survey: 25 percent of high school seniors in Dallas, Texas, could not identify the country that borders the United States on the south, and 63 percent of their Minneapolis–St. Paul, Minnesota, counterparts could not name the seven continents. And a statistic Gil Grosvenor finds particularly unnerving: 95 percent of the incoming freshmen at an Indiana college could not even locate Vietnam on a map!

The Geography Education Program's aim is "to elevate the status and effectiveness of geographic education," by helping to enhance geography teaching methods and materials, by developing a nationwide teacher support network, and by conducting a public awareness campaign to draw attention to geography and to recruit allies among the public, corporate, and foundation sectors.

The Society has created a network of regional Geographic

Alliances—groups of teachers, administrators, and college geographers who meet to exchange and develop teaching strategies and materials, and to discuss ways to upgrade geography curricula. These alliances will number twenty-two by 1988.

Groups of five to seven topnotch teachers, recruited from each alliance, are brought to Society headquarters each July to attend a four-week Summer Geography Institute—inaugurated by the Society in 1986—before returning to their home alliances to share what they have learned and to help organize regional institutes for the benefit of their colleagues. "The ideas you are giving us are causing light bulbs to go on in our heads," one teacher wrote of her 1986 Summer Institute.

Governor Gerald Baliles of Virginia declared his stance on the need for improved geographic education: "We no longer do an effective job of teaching geography, when we teach it at all." He backed his words with a $50,000 pledge in support of alliance activities in his state. Several more governors have committed state funds for alliance-run institutes, curriculum conferences, and other professional development activities.

The Society, for the first time in its 100-year history, has also begun to seek foundation and corporate co-sponsors to provide funding and other forms of support for geographic education activities.

In re-dedicating the energies of the Society to the restoration of geography in America's schools, Gilbert M. Grosvenor is determined to fulfill the pledge of its founders "to increase and diffuse geographical knowledge."

448

bare details about his father's flight to freedom, for James Blockson, like tens of thousands of other black slaves who fled north along its invisible rails and hid in clandestine stations in the years before the Civil War, kept the secrets of the Underground Railroad locked in his heart until he died....

Under Garrett the Magazine also published "The Poppy" (February 1985), "Storing Up Trouble...Hazardous Waste" (March 1985), and "Vietnam Memorial," which ran in the May 1985 issue.

As part of the "Vietnam Veterans Memorial" coverage there appeared Joel L. Swerdlow's "To Heal a Nation," one of the most moving pieces ever to be printed in the Magazine. It contained this passage on the impact the Vietnam Memorial's stark, name-filled, shining black granite panels have on viewers seeing them for the first time:

> ...for an unbroken stream of months and years, millions of Americans have come and experienced that frozen moment.
>
> The names have a power, a life, all their own. Even on the coldest days, sunlight makes them warm to the touch. Young men put into the earth, rising out of the earth. You can feel their blood flowing again.
>
> Everyone, including those who knew no one who served in Vietnam, seems to touch the stone. Lips say a name over and over, and then stretch up to kiss it. Fingertips trace letters.
>
> Perhaps by touching, people renew their faith in love and in life; or perhaps they better understand sacrifice and sorrow.
>
> "We're with you," they say. "We will never forget."

Three months later Garrett's editorial page opened:

> "I wept...." "My husband cried...." "The pages were wet with my tears...." "I was crying and didn't know why...." "It was the first time I cried over this war, and it felt good."
>
> So wrote five members. They symbolize the hundreds who felt compelled to respond to the articles about the Vietnam Veterans Memorial in our May issue. The reader response may eventually be the largest in our magazine's history; there is no question that it is already the most intensely personal.

Among those who responded was the widow of Walter H. Moon, the Special Forces Army captain Garrett had last seen alive in Laos in 1961 ordering a reluctant helicopter pilot to get Garrett "out of here *now*!"

"My son...was thrilled by your Editor's column, where you said you had looked for his father's name. He was eight and my daughter four when Walt left. Though they don't remember him as well as they would like to, they loved him and are very proud of him," she wrote.

The November 1985 Magazine with its stunning holographic cover image of Africa's one- to two-million-year-old Taung child contained "The Search for Our Ancestors," a comprehensive article on fossil discoveries of prehistoric man around the world. Publication of that article led, as expected, to an outcry from creationists. A Lubbock, Texas, man wrote:

> The theory of evolution is probably the biggest hoax ever foisted on intelligent people. Even though it is widely accepted theory, it is held mostly by those who have already rejected a belief in God. I cancel my subscription.

And a man from Angleton, Texas, complained:

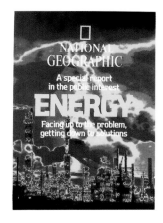

Early in 1981 the National Geographic Society released a special 115-page supplement to the Magazine reporting on the outlook for energy resources and technologies. Prepared during the Editorship of Gil Grosvenor under the direction of Geographic *Science Editor Kenneth Weaver, the report was titled "Special Report on Energy."*

In a pre-publication announcement of the energy special newly elected Editor Wilbur Garrett reported, "This edition will carry no advertising. All costs will be borne by the Society as a service to you the members."

Costs in staff effort were high enough to make "We Survived the Energy Issue" a popular T-shirt among those assigned to the project.

"Psst! Want to buy some National Geographic centerfolds?"

accepting an award from an honor society for professionals in education which recognized the National Geographic Society as "Educator of the Year" for its role as "a vital force in the continuous education of mankind."

Citing the appalling results of a questionnaire on geography given to 2,200 North Carolina college students (only 27 percent could name in what countries the Amazon River was mainly found and in what country the city of Manila was located, only 7 percent could name three of the thirty countries between the Sahara and South Africa, and 69 percent could not even name one!), Gil Grosvenor had written:

> How this coming generation will make any sense of a world increasingly tied together by communications, transportation, trade, and international relations, I cannot imagine....
>
> When I accepted our Society's award as "Educator of the Year," I said it would be better given for "Non-educator," considering the low state of geography in our schools. I reaffirmed my personal commitment, as well as the Society's, to help improve the education of our citizenry in geography.
>
> Mine is not an idle promise. We are increasing our efforts in developing learning materials for schools, and we are exploring joint efforts with others in the private sector. You will hear more from me on the subject of geographic education, and I would like to hear more from you. I am angry; I am embarrassed; I am determined.

Fifteen months after that President's column appeared, *Newsweek* was able to report that "Having reached a nadir, there are now signs that geography studies may be starting the long climb up." Continued the September 1, 1986, *Newsweek*:

> Much credit belongs to the National Geographic Society (NGS), which has budgeted $4 million to improve geographic education. At the NGS's recently concluded Summer Geography Institute, 50 high-school instructors from around the country gathered in Washington, D.C., to learn how to teach the subject more effectively; as part of the deal, they agreed to give at least three geographic methods workshops to colleagues back home. The society is also cosponsoring school-year pilot programs in Washington and Los Angeles. A few states, including South Dakota and California, have implemented geography requirements for graduation. Clearly, geography is finding its way back onto the map. Now it's up to teachers to make sure students can read it.

"You *can* make geography exciting," Gil Grosvenor says.

> I'm very excited about this program. I spend a helluva lot of my time on it. I feel it's important, that we can perform a service for this country, a service for the Society, and that we can materially influence the education, the geographic awareness of the average American—particularly as he or she goes through the school system.
>
> "Geography" is more than just place, location, the inner relationships between flora and fauna on this planet earth. Geography in a very broad sense is human and environmental issues, it's movement, it's regional influences. You're dealing with climate, with agriculture, with such things as desertification, soil, acid rain....Without geography you're going to have, at best, a two dimensional outlook on life. Geography permeates every aspect of our life. Pick up a newspaper and every single day you'll see how geography plays a dominant role in giving you a third dimension on life.

Geography *drives* history. Unless you've been to the Pass of Thermopylae you haven't the faintest idea what happened there. But the Battle of Thermopylae could only have happened at Thermopylae. Geography drove that battle. Even today geography is driving history. Look at Afghanistan: the Russians are in Afghanistan for geography. They're looking for routes to the sea, for routes down through the Himalayas, for routes to oil. They're not in Afghanistan just to expand their territories. Geographical-political implications are what's driving them! It's what drove us into Vietnam, and I submit to you that if our leaders had *really* been informed on the geography of Southeast Asia, we never would have been in a war there.

What disturbs me, is that 95 percent of the incoming freshmen at a pretty good Indiana college couldn't locate Vietnam on a map! What this tells me is that the next generation hasn't learned a damn thing about the disaster this government participated in in Southeast Asia. Not a damn thing. And that's scary. I feel it's going to be even more critical in the years ahead for a citizen to have a balanced knowledge of the planet earth. It all makes sense. What is frightening to me is why were we asleep for so long? Why did we watch geography go down the chute without really realizing it? It really is important.

What about the future?

I would hope that as time progresses the average member will perceive us as a Society above and beyond a magazine, that they will see us as a Society dedicated to the increase and diffusion of geographic knowledge across an entire age spectrum, and utilizing as many different media of communication as is possible: the printed medium, electronic communications—electronic communications, I think, are going to dramatically increase.

The day may come, 30 or 40 years down the line, when it might become prohibitively expensive to send the Magazine out in print; the day may come when the Editor will produce a thirty-page guide to what is on the "menu" for this particular month and the member will get a laser-video disc with 56,000 images on it, and maybe that guide is what will motivate the "reader" to get into this month's menu. I don't think we will reduce our Magazine, but I do think we're headed in the direction of *complementing* the Magazine, of adding to it, making it more useful and enjoyable.

"I would hope that at our 200th anniversary," said this great-grandson of Alexander Graham Bell, "somebody will look back and say, 'Hey, you know, those people between the first and second hundred, they really broadened the outreach of the National Geographic Society! It became an even more important international educational institution for the increase and diffusion of geographic knowledge.'"

There are currently almost eleven million members scattered all over this planet—in the Americas from Argentina to Venezuela; in Africa from Algeria to Zimbabwe; in Asia from Afghanistan to the two Yemens; in Australasia from Australia to New Zealand; in the Atlantic Ocean from Ascension Island to St. Pierre and Miquelon; in Europe from Andorra to Yugoslavia; in the Mediterranean from Corsica to Malta; in the Pacific from Fiji to Western Samoa; in the Indian Ocean from Mauritius to the Seychelles; in the British Isles from the Channel Islands to Wales—nearly eleven million members who have no doubt whatsoever that in the year 2088 the National Geographic Society will still be around.

The March 1984 issue carried the first hologram cover, an eagle. The holographic portrait of the skull of Africa's "Taung child" appeared in November 1985.

By the end of the Society's ninety-eighth year, circulation was 10,764,998 with membership in 170 of the world's 174 nations.

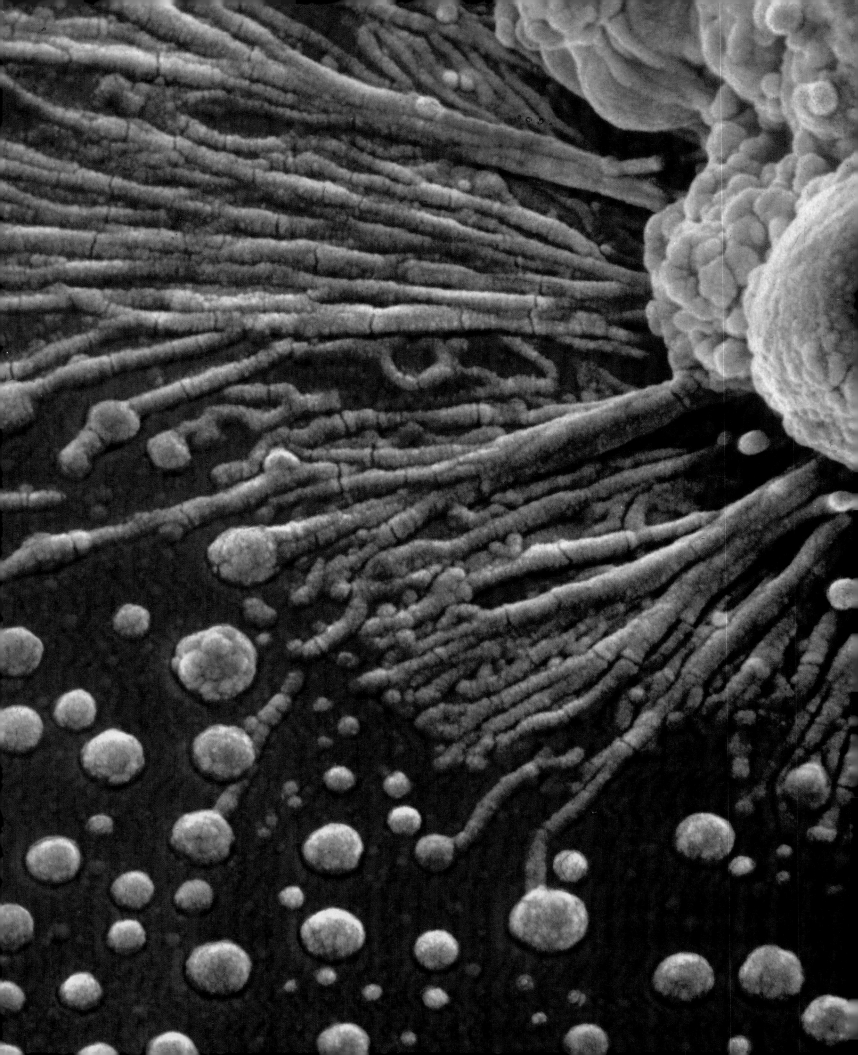

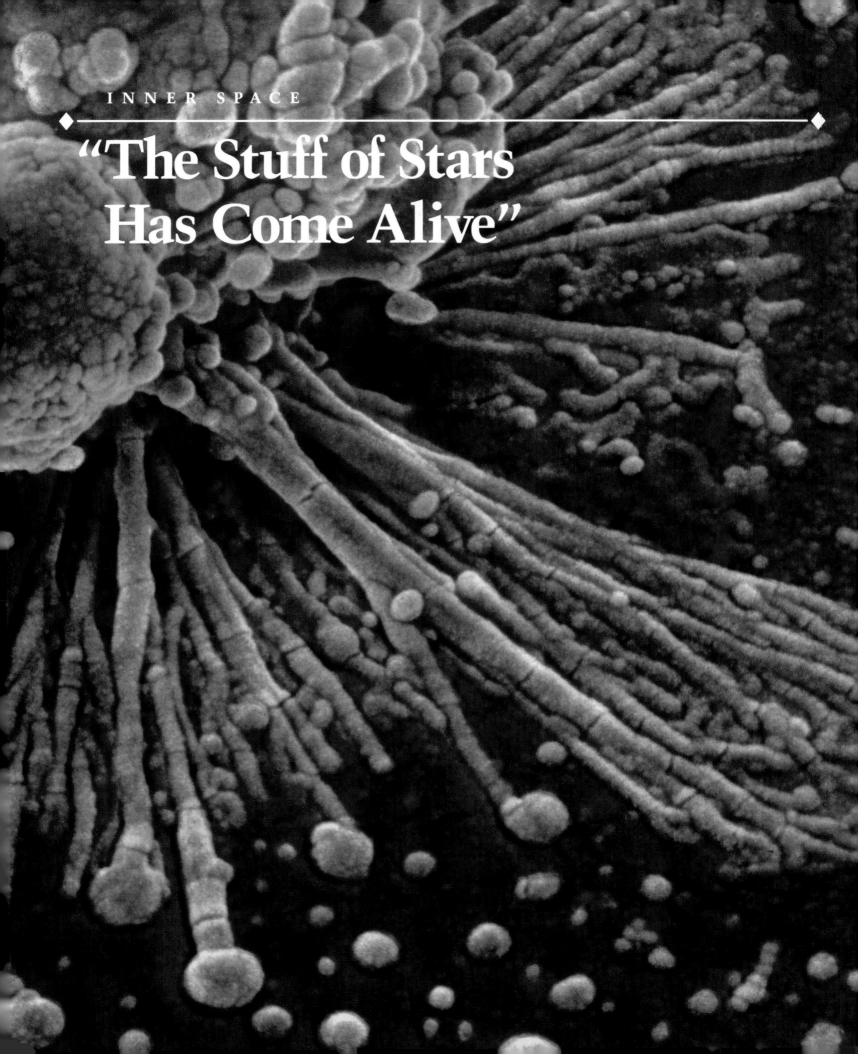

"The Stuff of Stars Has Come Alive"

Just as scientists with devices—optical and otherwise—are trying to look deeper and deeper into outer space, scientists elsewhere—also with devices, optical and otherwise—are trying to look deeper and deeper into inner space. Paradoxically, as Susan Schiefelbein writes in the National Geographic Society's striking book *The Incredible Machine*, what these scientists are finding is that:

> Within our bodies course the same elements that flame in the stars. Whether the story of life is told by a theologian who believes that creation was an act of God, or by a scientist who theorizes that it was a consequence of chemistry and physics, the result is the same: The stuff of stars has come alive. Inanimate chemicals have turned to living things that swallow, breathe, bud, blossom, think, dream.

How did that happen? What caused the "Big Bang"? Out of what did vast swirling clouds of hydrogen and helium collect together into huge clumps? Why were these riven by nuclear explosions as atom blasted into atom until, burning star bright, they burst yet again to fling even more and different combinations of atoms throughout space?

And how, out of all that nuclear debris, did the hot ball of gases we call our Sun form and burn at exactly the right temperature so that bits and chunks of matter, collecting together to become our infant planet earth, would bubble and seethe, cool and harden, wrinkle and fracture, and bathe its wounds until primordial oceans formed?

And how over those billions of years in that oceanic chemical caldron did molecules fuse into chains that mixed and mingled in such astonishing, infinite variety that suddenly somehow—because of ultraviolet light? heat? lightning?—one of those chains became unlike any other? And what made it so utterly different was that it was *alive*!

As National Book Award winner Dr. Lewis Thomas writes in his Foreword to *The Incredible Machine*, how that happened remains

> ...the greatest puzzle of all, even something of an embarrassment. Somehow or other, everything around us today—all animals, ourselves, all plants, everything alive—can trace its ancestry back to the first manifestation of life, approximately 3.5 billion years ago. That first form of life was, if we read the paleontological record right, a single bacterial cell, our Ur-ancestor, whose progeny gave rise to what we now call the natural world. The genetic code of that first cell was replicated in all the cells that occupied the Earth for the next 2 billion years, and then the code was

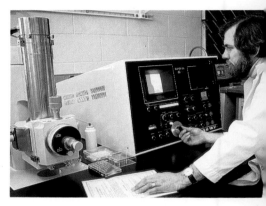

Just as the Society has reported the exploration of outer space, it has chronicled the exploration of inner space, choosing the best images technology can provide of this largely invisible world.

Above: A technician adjusts a scanning electron microscope capable of magnifying thousands of times— it makes a human hair look like a tree limb.

Opposite: David Fairchild and his wife prepare "Long Tom," the twelve-foot camera with which he photographed his 1913 "monster" pictures—ordinary insects enlarged up to twenty times—that appeared in the 1914 Society publication The Book of Monsters. *Capturing the insect's image on a 5 x 7 photographic plate requiring a one-minute exposure, though laborious, was easy compared with getting the creature to stand still.*

Preceding spread: "Scanning electron microscope shows a macrophage, a human defense cell, seeking to engulf droplets of oil." Magnified 18,000 times.—From the June 1986 issue

passed along to nucleated cells when they evolved, then to the earliest multicellular forms, then to the vertebrates some 600 million years ago, and then to our human forebears. The events that [have taken] life all the way from a solitary microbial cell to the convolutions of the human brain and the self-consciousness of the human mind, should be sweeping us off our feet in amazement.

We *are* amazed, of course; and it is an amazement that is in no way diminished as we develop devices and technology with which to see yet deeper, to peel back layers of the mystery, only to discover even greater mysteries still. We are at the edge of a frontier of discovery that boggles the mind; we are peering at the threshold of creation itself. How can we not approach it with wonder?

In 1913, when Department of Agriculture botanist David Fairchild began experimenting with long-lens cameras to capture close-up views of insects, his photographs were so stunning for that era that they were published in a May 1913 *Geographic* article, "The Monsters of Our Back Yards," and later as one of the Society's earliest books, *Book of Monsters*. Fairchild (Gilbert Hovey Grosvenor's brother-in-law) was a scientist first and a photographer second; but science and photography have been linked ever since Louis Daguerre's discovery in the 1830s that a real image could be fixed. Striking though they may have been, Fairchild's photographs were still only close-ups—close-ups of the *exteriors* of life forms already visible to the naked eye.

Two and a half centuries before Fairchild's experiments, Anton van Leeuwenhoek, an unschooled Dutchman, had, even with his crude instruments, been able to see and sketch protozoa and bacteria. But even now the best optical microscopes are limited, as were Fairchild's camera and van Leeuwenhoek's primitive microscope, to objects visible within the wavelengths of light. They can magnify no more than 2,000 times. That is, they can focus on objects no smaller than 1/125,000 of an inch—or 2,000 angstroms.

But with the electron microscope, then Senior Assistant Editor Kenneth Weaver wrote in "Electronic Voyage Through an Invisible World," for the February 1977 *Geographic*, "scientists have opened up a whole new realm of atoms and molecules, a world man has never seen before. Just as today's largest telescopes take us into the bizarre universe of quasars and black holes, so the electron microscope takes us into the Alice-in-Wonderland world of inner space. What we see there is sometimes hauntingly beautiful, sometimes awesome, and frequently of supreme significance."

As Weaver points out, the best electron microscope at that time could:

> magnify an incredible twenty million times, with a resolution on the order of two angstroms. And even the individual atom, which has a diameter of only about one angstrom (about four-billionths of an inch), can be photographed in the same way that an invisible mote of dust can be "seen" by the light scattered when the mote floats through a bright beam of sunlight. These angstrom-wide atoms are so small that nearly a million of them lined up side by side, would fit into the thickness of this sheet of paper.

◄ ────────────────────────────────

Sixty-four years after Fairchild's long-lensed experiment, a scanning electronic microscope in 1977 catches a quarter-inch-long velvety tree ant at its bath, capturing the insect, here magnified eighty times, in the act of cleaning its antenna with a foot.

The word "atom," from the ancient Greek, means, literally, "uncuttable." In his wonderfully lucid 1985 Magazine article "Worlds Within the Atom," author John Boslough both explains the derivation of the word and, like Weaver, attempts to help us comprehend its minuscule angstrom-wide size:

> Some 2,300 years ago the Greek philosophers Democritus and Leucippus proposed that if you cut an object, such as a loaf of bread, in half, and then in half again and again until you could do it no longer, you would reach the ultimate building block. They called it an atom.
>
> The atom is infinitesimal. Your every breath holds a trillion trillion atoms. And because atoms in the everyday world we inhabit are virtually indestructible, the air you suck into your lungs may include an atom or two gasped out by Democritus with his dying breath.
>
> To grasp the scale of the atom and the world within, look at a letter "i" on this page. Magnify its dot a million times with an electron microscope, and you would see an array of a million ink molecules. This is the domain of the chemist. Look closely at one ink molecule and you would see a fuzzy image of the largest atoms that compose it.
>
> Whether by eye, camera, or microscope, no one has ever seen the internal structure of an atom: Minute as atoms are, they consist of still tinier subatomic particles. Protons, carrying a positive electric charge, and electrically neutral particles called neutrons cluster within the atom's central region, or nucleus—one hundred-thousandth the diameter of the atom. Nuclear physicists work at this level of matter.

And what nuclear physicists are working at is "cutting the uncuttable." They are smashing the atom. Ironically, as Boslough points out, "exploring the smallest things in the universe requires the largest machines on earth": Machines such as Stanford University's two-mile-long linear accelerator near Palo Alto, California, which fires negatively charged electrons at atomic nuclei, and the more than four-mile-long European Laboratory for Particle Physics (CERN) near Geneva, Switzerland, which fires the heavier protons that cause more collisions. (Still, as one *Geographic* staffer noted, "To hit an atom's nucleus with a charged particle is something like playing pool in the dark on a table as big as Texas.")

There are already ten large accelerator centers in existence in the United States, Japan, Europe, and the U.S.S.R.; but they will all be dwarfed by the fifty-two-mile-long accelerator proposed to be built in the 1990s in the U.S.

In his "Worlds Within the Atom" author John Boslough interviewed the Fermi Laboratory director Dr. Leon Lederman and wrote:

> Using the CERN accelerator like an immense microscope, physicists are probing the structure of the atom, an inner cosmos of subatomic particles as remote from our daily experience as the farthest reaches of space. Yet that structure may hold an explanation of how the universe was born.
>
> During the past 50 years scientists exploring the atom's interior have solved many age-old mysteries of matter and energy. This new knowledge has brought us lasers, computers, transistors, space travel, and nuclear energy for weapons and power.

Magnified 10,000 times and opened up for an inside view, human cells display the nuclei as large yellow spheres, mitochondria colored red, *ribosomes as pale dots; throughout runs the ropelike maze called the endoplasmic reticulum.—From* The Incredible Machine

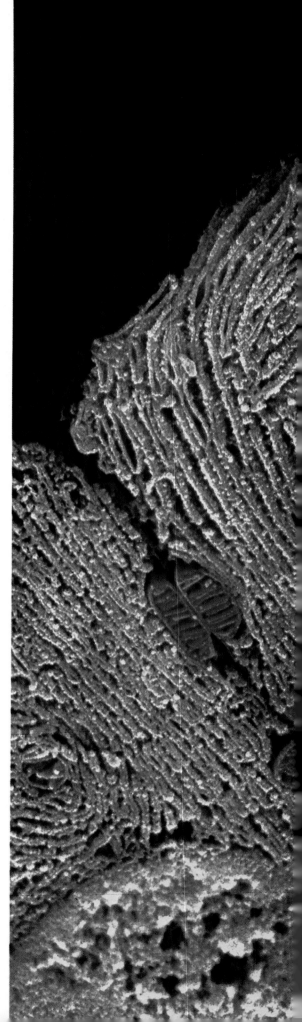

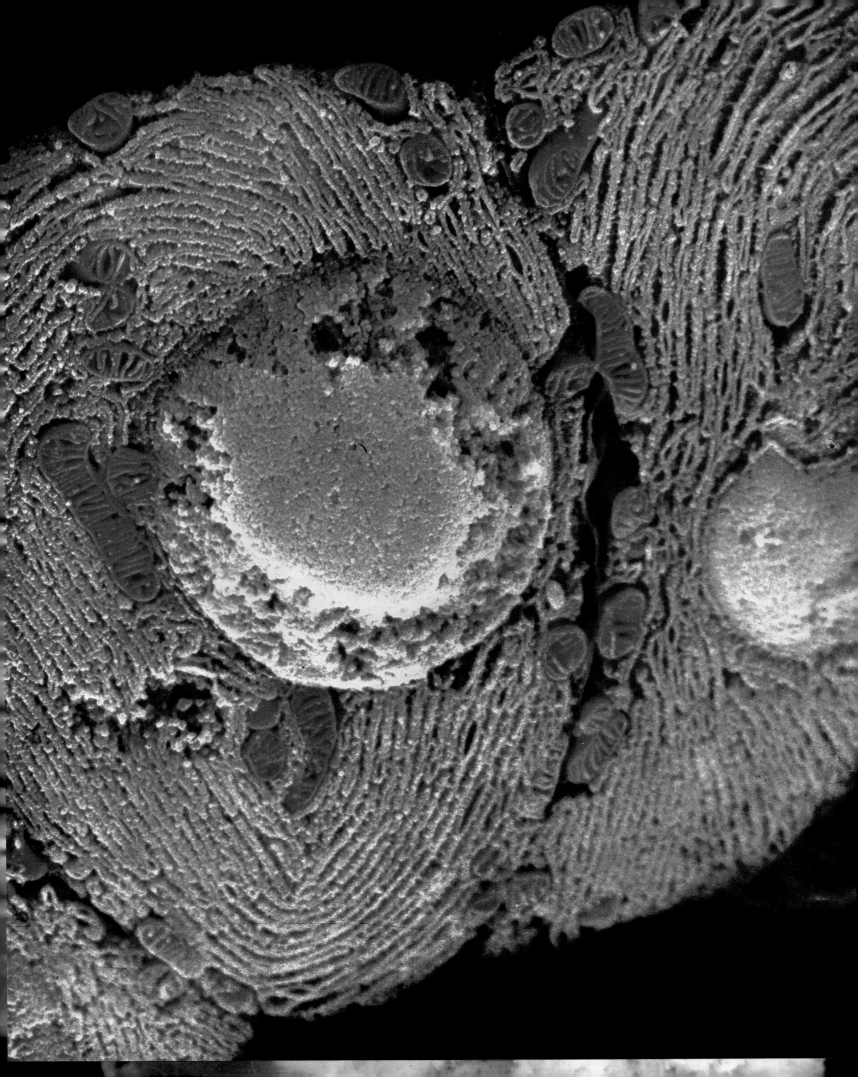

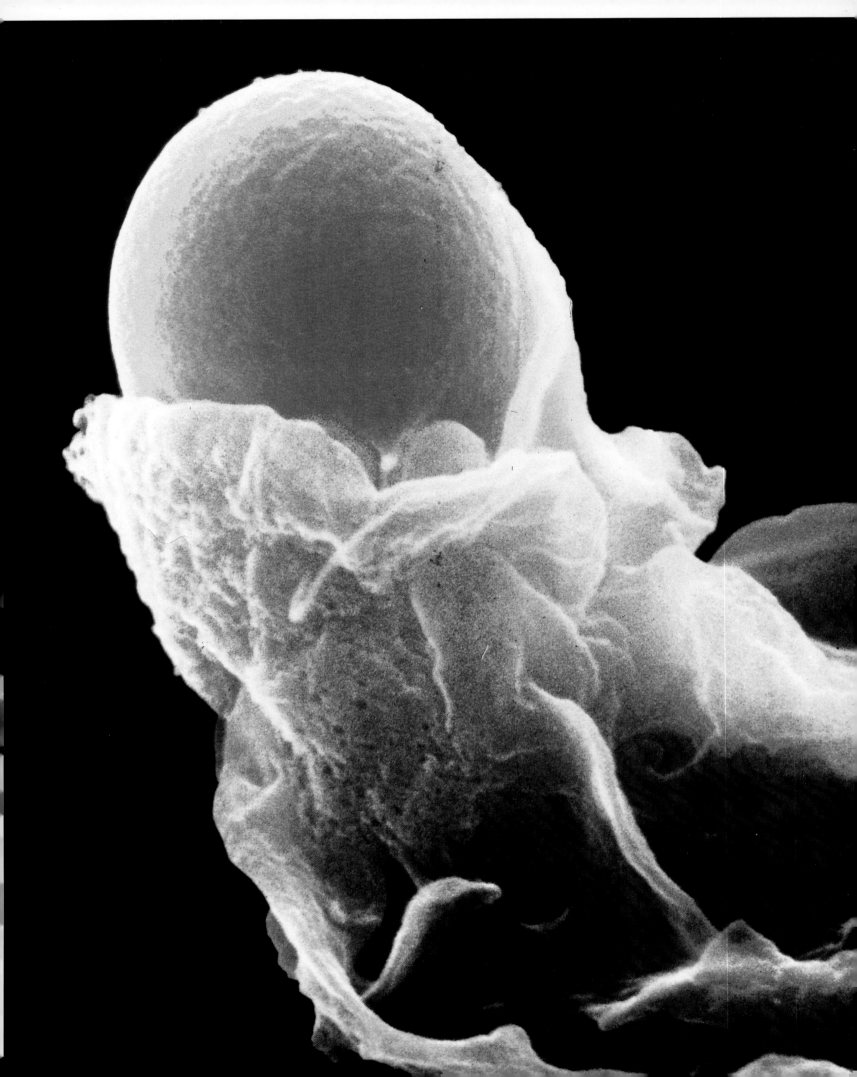

And yet in 1881 researchers studying starfish and sea urchin eggs had discovered nuclein, threadlike hereditary material that merged when egg and sperm ("DNA with a tail," Gore called it) were joined. Those researchers had unknowingly also discovered the manner in which human reproduction occurs and that life for us begins not, as had been thought for centuries, with a microscopic human being tucked into a minuscule egg, but, as Susan Schiefelbein wrote in *The Incredible Machine*, as a "fragile thread spun of chemical memory."

We have learned a great deal since 1881, as she explains:

> We know the code by which these gossamer filaments send their messages. Heredity is written on a chemical ribbon that twists like a spiral staircase, the steps built of four chemical bases attached to chains of sugars and phosphates—DNA....Thousands of these steps make up a single gene. Tens of thousands of genes, arranged along structures called chromosomes, transmit the instructions for existence, dictating eye color, hair texture, vulnerability to disease, perhaps even stuttering and altruism.
>
> Some six billion steps of DNA in a single cell record one life's blueprint. This DNA plan for a single human life can be stretched six feet, yet it is coiled in a repository just 1/2500 of an inch in diameter—the cell's nucleus.

And, as noted elsewhere in *The Incredible Machine:*

> The DNA molecule is a miracle of organization, structured like a twisted ladder....Elegant in structure,* DNA is also vibrant. Any still portrait of this molecule conveys only part of its nature, for motion characterizes the rest. DNA bends and twists a billion times a second while its ladder sides "breathe" in and out. This dance likely arises as DNA engages in its two key roles: to direct the creation of protein and to duplicate itself.

The creation of protein is essential to the cell and to ourselves. Although when we think of protein we tend to think of it as a specific value to be sought after in certain foods, protein is actually the name for the countless variety of chemical compounds which, when broken down, provide our cells with the nutrients needed to produce more protein. Hormones like insulin, which controls energy use, are proteins; collagen, which builds skin, is a protein; hemoglobin, which supplies oxygen, is, too; the dozens of different enzymes are proteins; as are the various structural components from which cells are built.

When cells divide, the necessary instructions for duplicating their own proteins come through the DNA in their genes. Moreover, Rick Gore wrote:

> [Scientists] have found that virtually every cell contains the entire repertoire of genes for that plant or animal. One cell in my toe, say, has all the data in its DNA for making another man physically identical to me. That many instructions, if written out, would fill a thousand 600-page books. The unique experiences of our lives, of course, make us more than a product of our genes. Yet it is our DNA that sets the basic physical limits of what we can or cannot become.

The fact remains that we are all different—even identical twins have multiple differences in palm and fingerprints and markings of their irises—but we share a common entrance into this world; and the mystery and the miracle

The first descriptions of the structure of DNA appeared in a one-page scientific paper published by James D. Watson and Francis Crick in 1953. In it they drew the scientific community's attention to this molecule with "novel features which are of considerable biological interest."

Opposite: *National Geographic authors have always enjoyed the "a-million-ink-molecules-are-contained-in-the-dot-at-the-top-of-this-'i' " assists at visualization; Rick Gore is no exception. In his September 1976 article "The Awesome Worlds Within A Cell," Gore wrote, "Our blood holds twenty trillion red blood cells; thirty thousand would fit in this one O."*

Beginning life deep in the bone marrow, a red blood cell divides and fills with hemoglobin. In six days the cell enters the bloodstream. At about 120 days, it begins to expire. "One theory," it was noted in The Incredible Machine, *"holds that the cell, without a nucleus to renew old parts, depletes its inner resources. Its outer membrane may also wear out, like tread on an old tire, from thousands of trips through the bloodstream. A macrophage, the white blood cell responsible for cleanup, senses that the time has come. Catching the aging cell in its embrace, the macrophage engulfs and digests it." (Magnification 10,000 times.)*

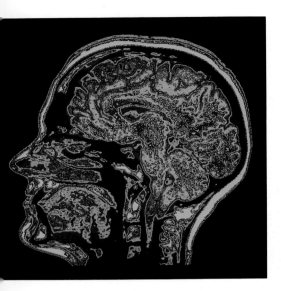

Above: *"A color-enhanced profile made by magnetic resonance imaging (MRI) shows a herniating finger of tissue from a brain slumping into the base of the skull. Frequently used to view soft tissue such as the brain's, MRI machines do not use X rays to penetrate the body but instead employ a combination of radio waves and a strong magnetic field."*—From *"Medicine's New Vision," January 1987 issue*

Opposite: *"Ghostly in the dark, a normal face seems otherworldly when viewed by an MRI scanner. The eerie forehead, eyebrows, cheeks, nose, and lips appear brightest because water density is higher than in other tissues. MRI reflects water because it focuses on the behavior of hydrogen atoms in water molecules....Teeth and bones, which contain little water, do not appear at all in MRI...."*—From *"Medicine's New Vision," January 1987 issue*

both start at our beginnings. As Schiefelbein wrote in her *Incredible Machine* chapter "Beginning the Journey":

> The newborn baby embodies innocence, yet conceals the most taunting of all riddles: the generation of human life. The story begins with sperm and egg as they combine to form a single cell. Sheltered in the mother's womb, the cell multiplies. Soon there are hundreds of different cells able to make some 50,000 different proteins to control the work of all our cells....
>
> Before long, the groups of cells are gathering into layers, then into sheets and tubes, sliding into the proper places at the proper times, forming an eye exactly where an eye should be, the pancreas where the pancreas belongs. The order of appearance is precise, with structures like veins and nerves appearing just in time to support the organs that will soon require them. In four weeks the progeny of the first cell have shaped a tiny beating heart; in only three months they are summoning reflex responses from a developing brain.
>
> Nothing more than specks of chemicals animate these nascent cells as they divide. Yet in just nine months, some twenty-five trillion living cells will emerge together from the womb; together they will jump and run and dance; sing, weep, imagine, and dream.
>
> A single cell engenders a multitude of others, but the multitude acts as an entity, as a community. The appearance of life in the womb, like the appearance of life on Earth, cannot be completely explained, even by our burgeoning scientific knowledge. Biologists have identified the sequence of reproductive events; yet they know merely *what* happens. They do not know yet exactly *how* or *why*.

And once we are born, our bodies must wage battle against a host of enemies mounting attacks without and within our bodies every sleeping and waking moment for the rest of our lives.

"The combatants are too tiny to see," Peter Jaret wrote in "Our Immune System: The Wars Within" for the June 1986 Magazine. "Some, like the infamous virus that causes AIDS, or acquired immune deficiency syndrome, are so small that 230 million would fit on the period at the end of this sentence."

The instruments that made surveillance of these wars within us possible were unavailable twenty-five years ago. The field of immunology, the study of the immune system, depended more on the science of deduction than on the science of medicine. But with the advent of the electron microscope and more sophisticated laboratory techniques, guesswork gave way to exploration and discovery of the strategies and counter-strategies of both our body's defenders and its foes. During this past decade, immunology has moved out of the backwaters of medicine and into the forefront as diseases such as AIDS have created the kinds of crises medicine mobilizes against.

"Some bacteria, such as the familiar streptococci and staphylococci, continuously swarm in legions over our skin and membranes, seeking access that can cause sore throats or boils," Jaret wrote. "Or consider the bacterium *Clostridium botulinum*, the cause of botulism. This single cell can release a toxin so potent that four hundred-thousandths of an ounce would be enough to kill a million laboratory guinea pigs."

However, of all the body's enemies, Jaret points out, both "the simplest and the most devious" is the virus:

> A virus is a protein-coated bundle of genes containing instructions for making identical copies of itself. Pure information. Because it lacks the basic machinery for reproduction, a virus is not, strictly speaking, even alive.

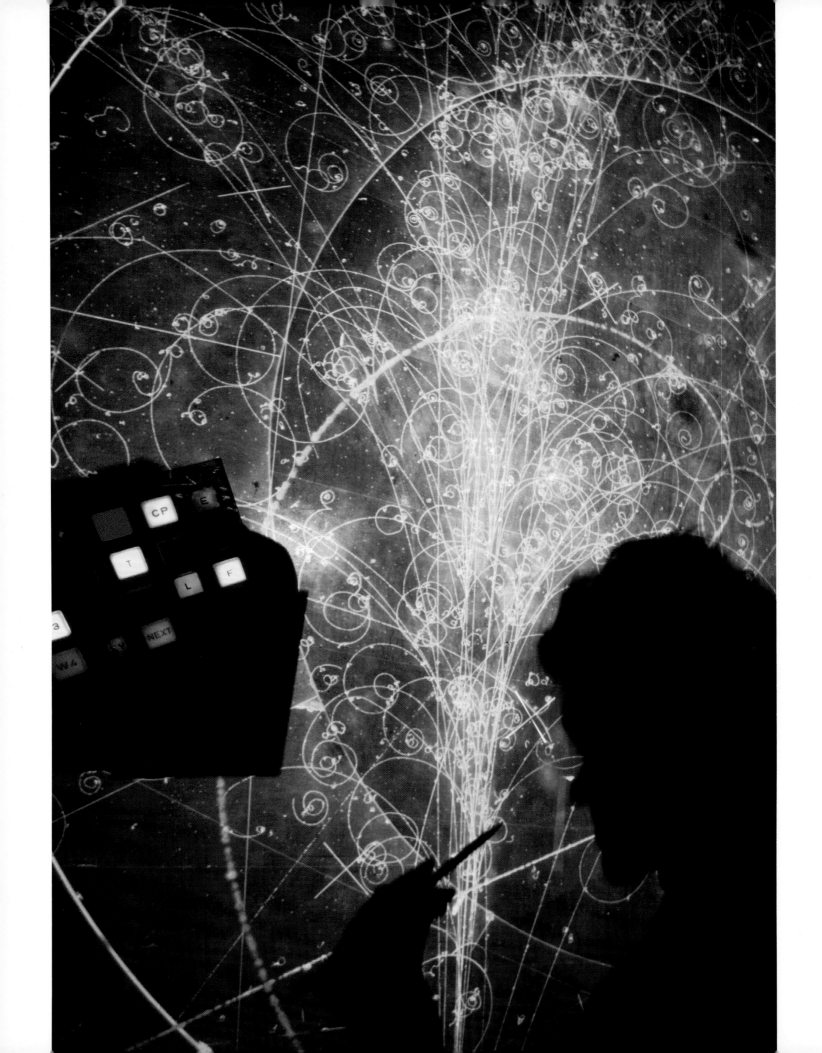

But when a virus slips inside one of our cells, that bundle of genetic information works like our cell's DNA, issuing its own instructions. The cell becomes a virus factory, producing near identical viruses. Eventually they may rupture the cell, killing it. Viral clones fan out to invade nearby cells.

"Keep in mind that a virus can create thousands of copies of itself within a single infected cell," immunologist Steven B. Mizel of Wake Forest University's Bowman Gray School of Medicine told Jaret. "Invading bacteria can double their numbers every 20 minutes. At first the odds are always on the side of the invader."

As Peter Jaret embarked on this piece he found himself at Purdue University with a sore throat, runny nose, and he was sneezing. Biologist Michael Rossmann identified the enemy battling him as "Rhinovirus 14, one of the causes of the common cold."

Jaret used his own illness as the device with which to attack the story. Taking comfort in knowing that "of the one hundred trillion cells that make up my body, one in every hundred is there to defend me," Jaret explained they were the white blood cells "that are born in the bone marrow. When they emerge, they form the three distinct regiments of warriors—the phagocytes and two kinds of lymphocytes, the T cells and B cells. Each," he pointed out, "has its own strategies of defense."

As recently as the mid-1960s it would have been impossible for Jaret to have written that piece. It wasn't until the late 1950s that immunologists began to comprehend how antibodies were produced. That there was a difference between T cells and B cells came clear only in the 1960s. Macrophages are still not completely understood. "Indeed," Jaret points out, "had AIDS struck twenty years ago, we would have been utterly baffled by it."

Among the medical advances examined in the Society's publications and films, none have been more astounding, perhaps, than those made in diagnostic medicine. Although German physicist Wilhelm Konrad Roentgen made the first X ray in 1895, and doctors were quick to see its benefit in diagnosing fractures, veteran writer for the *Geographic* Howard Sochurek points out that the "recent advances made in imaging technology, or 'machine vision,' [which] enable doctors to see inside the body without the trauma of exploratory surgery, [have resulted in] more progress [being] made in diagnostic medicine in the past 15 years than in the entire previous history of medicine."

Among the new machines and techniques Howard Sochurek discussed in "Medicine's New Vision" for the January 1987 *Geographic* was magnetic resonance imaging (MRI), which does not use X rays but rather a combination of radio waves and a strong magnetic field to produce views of soft tissue such as that of the brain.

Sochurek called MRI "an area of excitement and explosive growth. This seeing machine may prove to be as great a tool to modern medicine as the X ray....

"Magnetic resonance imaging relies on the principle that hydrogen atoms, when subjected to a magnetic field, line up like so many soldiers," Sochurek explained. "If a radio frequency is aimed at these atoms, it changes the alignment of their nuclei. When the radio waves are turned off, the nuclei realign themselves, transmitting a small electric signal. And since the body is primarily composed of hydrogen atoms, an image can be generated from the returning pulses, showing tissue and bone marrow as never seen before."

Opposite: *"Particle-track pyrotechnics from a bubble-chamber detector flash on a screen at CERN [the European Laboratory for Particle Physics near Geneva, Switzerland]. Debris from subatomic collisions leave distinctive wakes. For instance, electrons and positrons spiral tightly in opposite directions. Computers now sort through such jungles of tracks to pinpoint results significant to experimenters."—From "Worlds Within the Atom," May 1985 issue*

We have taken great strides forward. . . . I will step down as president with the same bullish confidence about the Society's future as when I began my career in June 1954. . . . The Society—and all of you—will flourish.

—Gilbert M. Grosvenor, Chairman, Board of Trustees, National Geographic Society

On Thursday evening, November 17, 1988, the National Geographic Society capped its yearlong celebration of its hundredth anniversary with an elegant black-tie dinner in the ballroom of the Sheraton Washington Hotel attended by 1,400 Society officers and employees, in addition to friends, members of Congress and the Cabinet, senior government officials, and representatives of the diplomatic community. Centennial Awards—delicate, engraved crystal globes atop crystal pedestals—were presented to fifteen of the Society's "Pioneers of Discovery." Present also for the predinner festivities was then President-elect George Bush, to whom Society President and Chairman of the Board of Trustees Gilbert M. Grosvenor promised a lifetime National Geographic Society membership (so he wouldn't have to "pilfer" his wife's copy of the Magazine), then added, "And sir, don't worry. I'll take care of your address change." Bush responded with a recollection of a personal advertisement he had come upon in the *Denver Post:* "Sheila, please return my *National Geographic* collection; you can keep the engagement ring."

If the opening remarks of the President of the National Geographic Society and the President-elect of the United States were lighthearted, both presidents, reported the next day's *Washington Post,* "had serious things to say about the fragility of our Earth and the need to educate people everywhere on the subject, as the *Geographic* has been doing for 100 years."

A crystal globe similar to the ones presented to each of the honorees appeared on the golden holographic cover of the Magazine's December issue. There, over the question, "As we begin our second century . . . can man save this fragile earth?" the three-dimensional globe is seen breaking into pieces.

"On our holographic cover an elegant crystal earth shatters after being hit by a bullet," *Geographic* Editor Wilbur E. (Bill) Garrett explained. He went on to sound the warning, "True, human destruction of the real planet moves slower than a bullet, but unless we change our ways, the result will be just as shattering."

As this history's earlier "Riders on the Earth Together" chapter makes clear, the threat of an environmental apocalypse was not a new issue seized upon by the Society. But the energy with which Society President and Chair-

Preceding spread: *On June 20, 1996, the National Geographic Society launched its first online presence on the World Wide Web. The Society's Web address is www.nationalgeographic.com.*

man Gilbert M. Grosvenor focused the attention of the membership on the problem was new. "The National Geographic Society began its first century with a determination to better understand the world," Grosvenor wrote in that December issue. "We have begun our second with the same determination but with an added imperative: to encourage a better stewardship of the planet. . . .

"The responsibility lies squarely with us," Grosvenor wrote and concluded with the question, "Will future generations praise our foresight or look back in anger and dismay at what we had, and what we lost forever?"

By 1988 membership in the National Geographic Society had reached 10.5 million, among them then President Ronald Reagan, General Secretary Mikhail Gorbachev, Queen Sirikit of Thailand, King Hussein of Jordan, Lech Walesa of Poland, and Woody Allen of New York. The vast majority of members—92 percent—lived, of course, in English-speaking countries: some 80 percent in the United States, another 12 percent in Canada, the British Isles, Australia, and New Zealand. And during the Centennial year many of the more than 15,000 letters written to the Magazine included congratulations on the Society's birthday. Typical correspondence spoke of the writers' long association with the Society and what the Magazine had meant to them and to their families. And as was to be expected, 113 formerly loyal members resigned when Bill Garrett in his October 1988 essay "Where Did We Come From?" referred to God's having created "first a man and then a woman in the Garden of Eden" as a Judeo-Christian "creation myth." But not even the Society's continuing pro-evolution stance could have been responsible for the drop of more than 1.5 million members that has occurred between 1988 and 1997. Such a reduction in membership can be attributed to many factors, including a mem-

At the Society's 100th anniversary celebration black-tie dinner at the Sheraton Washington Hotel, Centennial Awards were presented to Mount Everest conqueror Sir Edmund Hillary, undersea explorer Jacques-Yves Cousteau, primatologist Jane Goodall, anthropologists Mary and Richard Leakey, bioecologists John and Frank Craighead, former astronaut Senator John Glenn, photographic inventor Harold "Doc" Edgerton, underwater archeologist George Bass, mountain mappers Bradford and Barbara Washburn, archeologist Kenan T. Erim, deep-sea explorer Robert Ballard, and travel lecturer Thayer Soule. Control of the evening was almost lost when, during a break, guests sought to climb the dais to gather autographs from the Society's heroes.

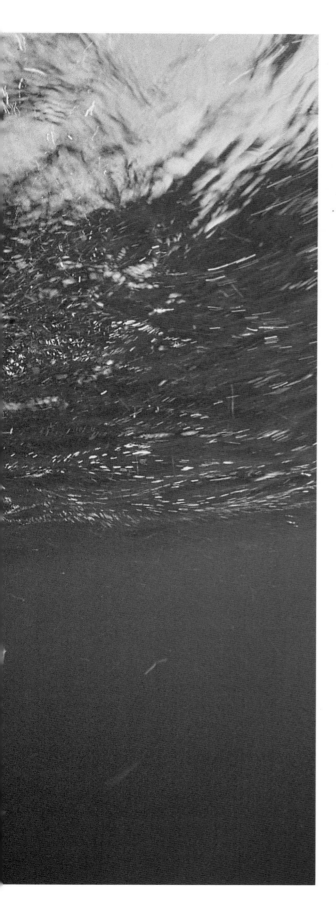

Above: *Freelance photographer Bill Curtsinger, wearing a stainless steel mesh suit, slipped into a plastic "shark scooter" while photographing in Bikini Lagoon for the January 1995 article "Close Encounters With the Gray Reef Shark." Just how close that encounter was did not become clear until dive companion Eric Hiner's photograph was developed. "The eerie thing," wrote Curtsinger, who had survived a shark attack in 1973, "is that I didn't know that a gray reef shark had sneaked up below me until I saw this picture."*

Left: *Curtsinger's story on gray reef sharks centered on the waters of Bikini Atoll, a former nuclear test site in the Pacific Ocean. Several of his pictures there were made with a special underwater remote-control camera, which has attracted the sharks' attention here.*

bership price increase and the increasingly fierce competition for readers' time. The decline coincided with a dramatic drop in staff morale due to the long-standing turf wars within the Society. Chief among these battles was the conflict between the Society's President, Gilbert M. Grosvenor, and the Magazine's Editor, Wilbur E. Garrett.

Perhaps the seeds of this conflict were planted in the Geographic's earliest days: Gil's grandfather, Gilbert Hovey Grosvenor, had felt that from his April 1, 1899, appointment as Assistant Editor and throughout the twenty-one years thereafter, his autonomy was threatened by the various Society Presidents who had their own ideas on what the Editor should and should not publish. This conflict was only resolved in 1920 when, at GHG's insistence, the offices of Editor of the Magazine and President of the Society were combined. For the next forty-seven years the individual holding the titles of President and of Editor remained one and the same. It was not until 1967, when Melville Bell Grosvenor retired from both offices to become Chairman of the Board of Trustees, that the Board insisted the two offices be separated again so the Editor might concentrate on running the Magazine and the President could focus on the business of the Society. At that time Frederick G. (Ted) Vosburgh was appointed Editor and Melvin M. Payne was elected President of the Society. Three years later, in October 1970, Vosburgh retired and Gilbert M. Grosvenor was made Editor. Gil remained in that position until July 1980, when he was elected President. Because the Board of Trustees had previously established the division of the two offices, Gil resigned from what he referred to as "the best job in the world" to take over as President of the National Geographic Society. Bill Garrett replaced Gil Grosvenor as Editor.

Both Garrett and Grosvenor had joined the Society at roughly the same time in 1954. They became close friends, and even took vacations together. But their friendship seemingly came to an end on the day Garrett was named Editor. From that day on, according to Garrett, their relationship was never the same. Nine years and eight months later, on April 16, 1990, when Gil Grosvenor called Bill Garrett into his office to notify him that he was fired, only Garrett himself seemed to have been taken by surprise. "One minute he was hustling across the National Geographic Society's executive suite to the office of the president and chairman, Gilbert M. Grosvenor, his colleague and friend of 35 years, for a seemingly routine Monday afternoon huddle," Charles Trueheart reported in the *Washington Post*. "Less than 30 minutes later," Trueheart continued, "Garrett was leaving the 17th Street headquarters for the last time."

Gil Grosvenor selected William Graves as the new Editor, an appointment that came as a surprise to the staff. As the Magazine's former senior assistant editor for expeditions, he had spent most of his long career writing and editing text, turning often turgid accounts by expedition leaders into readable prose.

News of Garrett's departure and Graves's appointment to replace him appeared in major national newspapers and magazines, the press services, and foreign journals. The reasons given for Garrett's departure were "a policy dispute," "different publishing philosophies," "the inevitable outcome of long-brewing battles over finances, cutbacks and other differences of opinion," "a slow but inevitable collision course over the editor's single-minded efforts to adapt the 102-year-old magazine to a changing, and younger, readership," "personality conflicts," and this dazzling understatement: "President Gilbert Grosvenor and Garrett grew apart."

Bill Graves remained Editor of the Magazine for the next four years and eight months—one of the most emotionally draining times *Geographic* staff members had ever passed through. One senior staffer said that Graves was "a loose cannon, you didn't know where he was going to explode next. Usually it was in your face. Graves damaged people. I don't know if it was intentional, but he could really destroy a certain part of your soul."

And yet, under Graves, the Magazine was getting good reviews—even from the *Washington Post*'s Charles Trueheart, whose earlier reporting of the intimate details of Garrett's firing had caused such dismay at Society headquarters. "Many worried that the *National Geographic* would retreat from covering the real world after the fiery Wilbur Garrett was fired 18 months ago and the mild-mannered William Graves was brought in to replace him," Trueheart wrote. He continued: "Graves and his evolving senior staff have been publishing more tightly edited and creatively imagined issues than ever. . . . In the August issue, at what constitutes lightning speed for *National Geographic*, the magazine presented a portfolio of scenes of destruction from the Persian Gulf, a black scar on the planet. Also in that issue, a new and improved map of Pierre L'Enfant's Washington, D.C., by the technological wizards in the cartographic department. In July the magazine profiled the Wyeth family and published a retrospective on the Blitz. This is not your father's Oldsmobile."

The *Geographic* continued to publish striking stories. But sustaining the artistic atmosphere necessary to come out with topnotch writing and photography wasn't always easy. "There was a certain climate of fear that had seized this place," one senior staffer recalls.

Still, Graves defenders do exist. And that same senior staffer also remembers that, "with Graves there was an energy and a flamboyance, probably a sense deep down of love on his part for the institution." And Charles McCarry warns that one shouldn't be too harsh on the former Editor: "Graves was highly intelligent, the smartest person at the Magazine next to Garrett, and very sophisticated, but he kept all that under cover. He chewed out people who should have been chewed out years ago." It fell to Graves to get rid of the deadwood after the firing of an Editor who, because of his treatment, had now become a revered figure.

Bill Graves retired in December 1994, and the January 1995 issue was the first showing that Associate Editor William L. Allen had been appointed Editor.

"Bill Allen's the perfect man for the job right now," says Elizabeth A. Moize, who has been with the Magazine longer than anyone else: thirty-seven years, a third of the Society's history. She came in when Melville was Editor, continued to serve through Ted Vosburgh, Gil Grosvenor, Bill Garrett, Bill Graves, and is now, with Robert M. Poole, one of the two associate editors directly under Allen. "He is aware technically," she says. "He is open to new ideas. He has generated some changes in the Magazine which I think are in keeping with our tradition, but are making it more lively, and our readers have responded with approval."

"There have been a number of people who have called in and said the one thing they really like is the increased number of editorial pages in the Maga-

481

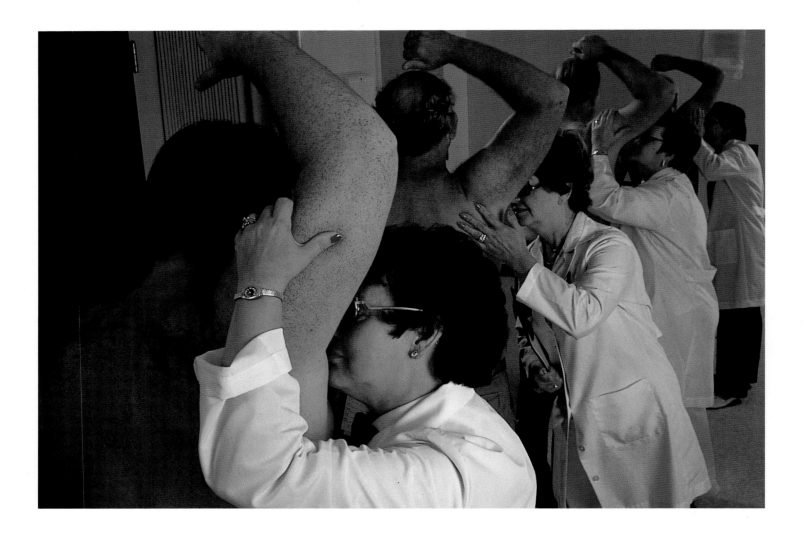

This photograph of odor judges testing the effectiveness of underarm deodorant appeared in Boyd Gibbons's fascinating September 1986 article "The Intimate Sense of Smell." Included in the issue was a scratch and smell survey that asked members to conduct their own tests. The response was overwhelming. Then Editor Bill Garrett recalled, "It was the greatest collection ever of scientific data on the human sense of smell." Results of the survey, published a year later, revealed, among other things, that about two-thirds of the respondents had suffered a loss of smell at one time or another and that 1 percent of them couldn't smell at all.

zine," Bill Allen said. "The fact is, the number of editorial pages is exactly the same. The difference is that we are providing more titles in the Magazine, a greater variety of articles to increase the likelihood that every member is going to find something that they have a more-than-ordinary interest in." It is Allen's contention that if a reader can find at least one article in every issue that appeals to his heart or soul or mind, then the *Geographic* has been a success in that reader's mind. "And if you're doing seven articles per issue rather than five, you're able to increase the odds by 40 percent that you're going to snag a reader with something that is of passionate interest to that person."

Graves's interests were expeditions—adventure and discovery. Science is one of Allen's primary interests, and it has always been explained in the *Geographic* on an accessible level better than anywhere else. "I'm committed to doing that even more in the future," Allen says. "I feel an obligation to explain the scientific method, the scientific process, and to give people the background so that they are able to separate science from pseudoscience."

Graves, and Garrett before him, were reactive, instinctive editors. Somebody would come in with a story idea and those editors would say, "Yeah, let's do it." Bill Allen is more deliberate, reflective, systematic. Bill Allen is also "a great delegator," Moize said. "He solicits everyone's opinions."

Although Garrett's departure and Graves's unnerving outbursts caused deep wounds, they have begun to heal. And so it is the downsizing, the reduction of staff to make a more cost-efficient organization, that will probably emerge as the most traumatic experience for members of the staff during the last decade. In 1990 there were approximately 2,800 employees at the Society; by 1995 that figure had dropped to 1,600.

Between April 1990, when Garrett left, and December 1991, a large number of senior people resigned, retired, or were encouraged to leave. Suddenly, after generations of very senior hierarchical leadership, new openings existed, but, especially on the business side, the openings were being filled from outside the Society, something that had rarely happened before. In September 1990, Special Publications and Book Service were combined, *Traveler* and *World* were placed under the same corporate umbrella, and more than 200 middle- and lower-level personnel in those departments were offered tempting severance packages. "To many Society employees," Howard Means reported in his December 1990 *Washingtonian* article, "it appeared that the purge of the *Geographic* generals was working its way well into the ranks."

The Society is not immune to outside forces; there was a visible erosion of membership, a falloff in book sales and mailings. Direct mail had traditionally

"From the leaves of a South American shrub comes a substance with immense power to stimulate pleasure, to generate wealth—and sometimes to kill." So reads a caption in "Coca: An Ancient Indian Herb Turns Deadly," Peter T. White's outstanding January 1989 report on the shadowy world of growers, dealers, and users of this illicit drug.

483

During the filming of the National Geographic Special "Baka. People of the Forest," the four-year-cld "star" of the show, Ali, assumes the role of cameraman, imitating the stance of producer/cinematographer Phil Agland. Ali's people, the Baka Pygmies of Cameroon, who live in the rich rain forest and are dependent on an intimate knowledge of forest resources, were the subjects of this engaging documentary.

Reg Murphy went to work quickly. In a memo dated a week after Gil's appointing him to carry out a comprehensive review of operations, Murphy announced a variety of cuts, mostly in staff amenities. "This process is not enjoyable," Murphy's memo concluded, "but it is critically important if we are to wring out unnecessary costs so we can get ready for the future." By these measures, Murphy hoped to save the Society more than $1 million a year.

At the end of July, Gil announced that effective August 13, NGT, Inc. (National Geographic Television) would "legally become a taxable subsidiary company" of the Society. "I view the new company as an exciting evolution in the Society's history," Gil's memo to the staff continued. "NGT will allow us to explore new technologies, distribution networks, and joint ventures more freely, at the same time ensuring that Television activities will not adversely impact the Society's continuing status as a nonprofit organization recognized as tax-exempt under IRS guidelines."

On January 18, 1996, the Society's Board of Trustees announced that effective May 1, Reg Murphy had been elected President and Chief Executive Officer to succeed Gil Grosvenor upon his retirement from those positions. In February, English left the Society to become president of a new operating unit at the Discovery Channel. Gil remains Chairman of the Board of the National Geographic Society, but on May 1, 1996, he determinedly withdrew from the day-to-day operations of the organization to give the new President space.

Gil, like his father before him, pushed the Society into new areas. It was Gil who thrust it into the electronic age, who created the Education Foundation with a $40 million commitment to geography, who spun off Television as a wholly-owned, taxable subsidiary, and who created National Geographic Ventures so that the Society could have other wholly-owned subsidiaries that would take some of the restraints off its programs and protect its nonprofit status.

Robert E. Dulli, the Society's Assistant Vice President and Director of the Geography Education Division, has run Gil's Geography Education Program for seven years and was an assistant in education to Gil for three. "What has happened is very exciting. We are changing the landscape of American education! What you have to remember is that ten years ago geography was barely in the schools. In most schools it didn't exist. We are talking about a discipline that had virtually disappeared and we are putting it back school by school. We are affecting what is going on countrywide. This is one of the most remarkable feats the Society has ever accomplished."

The Society's geography education campaign, now in its second decade, has invested $85 million, and it is making a difference. The results of a 1994 National Assessment of Educational Progress (NAEP) test given to 19,000 fourth-, eighth-, and twelfth-grade students indicated that 70 percent in those three grades were at or above the "basic" level with a partial mastery of geography. About one-fourth of the students tested at or above the "proficient" level, and 2 to 4 percent reached the "advanced," or superior performance level.

The last major survey to assess adult geographic knowledge was conducted by the Gallup Organization in 1988 and 1989. Commissioned by the National Geographic Society, the survey tested more than 12,000 adults in Canada, France, Italy, Japan, Mexico, the former Soviet Union, Sweden, the United Kingdom, the United States, and West Germany. Adults in each coun-

The Bridges of Madison County, Robert James Waller's sappy, megahit novel about the love affair between Iowa housewife Francesca Johnson and a *National Geographic* photographer named Robert Kincaid, was published in 1992. The movie based on the book, starring Clint Eastwood and Meryl Streep, was released in 1995. By that time the Society had already received hundreds of letters and phone calls from devotees of the book seeking to speak with the fictional Robert Kincaid, or to obtain copies of the issue containing Kincaid's alleged photos of Madison County bridges. Editor Bill Allen was confronted by one furious moviegoer who told him she had always trusted the *Geographic* until this conspiracy to hide Kincaid's existence. So many inquiries came in about Kincaid that the Society was forced to create a form letter in response.

The Magazine was inspired to set the record straight. "Reel to Real," senior writer Cathy Newman's whimsical August 1995 article, opened, "So there's this guy, Robert Kincaid. Photographer. Drives a pickup truck. Plays guitar. Doesn't eat meat but smokes Camels. Goes out to Iowa to shoot the covered bridges of Madison County for *National Geographic* magazine. Romances a farmer's wife. Loves her. Leaves her. . . . Is that how it is with our photographers on assignment?" Newman asks, and answers, "Hardly."

In the book, Kincaid climbs a tree and scrapes his arm, but according to Newman, Kincaid got off easy. "Tell that one to Steve McCurry, who was flying in a small plane that flipped into an alpine lake in Yugoslavia," Newman wrote:

> The pilot swam away unscathed, leaving McCurry submerged upside down in freezing water. McCurry managed to squeeze under the buckled strap and escape. He suffered a detached retina.

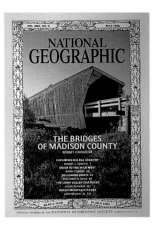

There was the time Joe Scherschel fended off hippos with a paddle on the Nile, Loren McIntyre was jailed in Venezuela, Dean Conger was placed under house arrest in Damascus, a Bedouin chief nearly abducted Jodi Cobb in Jordan (colleague Tom Abercrombie ransomed her for a fistful of dinars), a gorilla tossed Michael "Nick" Nichols down a hill in Rwanda ("I felt this big hand on my shoulder. . . .")

Or the time Chris Johns was singed by lava in Zaire, Sam Abell was mugged in Dublin, George Steinmetz nearly lost his vision to a *loa loa* worm that infected his eye in central Africa . . . David Doubilet was chased by a great white shark, Bill Curtsinger was mauled by a gray reef shark, George Mobley was bitten by a penguin.

And whereas, as Newman pointed out, Kincaid took on assignment three cameras, some accessories, and 200 rolls of film, deepwater photographer Emory Kristof "shipped 15 tons of equipment . . . to Lake Baikal, in Siberia, for a 1992 story. The shipment, 171 crates, included a satellite dish ('we had our own country code,' he recalls), a complete color lab, a rubber boat, two remotely operated vehicles for photographing deep-sea vents in the lake, and a diesel generator." His one million dollars' worth of equipment resulted in six photographs being published.

Six out of how many? As Leah Bendavid-Val reported in *National Geographic: The Photographs*, "Depending on the assignment, photographers can come back with 600 to 800 rolls of film—about 20,000 to 30,000 frames. But the pictures are not of 20,000 different subjects. Photographers think ahead to the editing process, which reduces the number of pictures to a single slide tray—80 slots. Many photographers say they shoot for the tray. They want to create a tray so perfect that a picture editor will find it nearly impossible to go from 80 to the 30 selected for publication."

Above: Geographic *photographers on assignment. Clockwise from top: Clint Eastwood as Robert Kincaid, Steve McCurry with assistant, and David Alan Harvey. The mock cover for May 1966 was done at the* Geographic *for the movie.*

1996 National Geography Bee winner, seventh-grader Seyi Fayanju, 12, of Verona, New Jersey, with Alex Trebek, host of TV's popular quiz show Jeopardy. He correctly answered "Andorra" to the question: "Name the European co-principality whose heads of state are the president of France and the bishop of Urgel." Fayanju's response won him a $25,000 college scholarship and an all expenses paid 10-day vacation for himself and his family.

Above, right: To better coordinate cooperation among the Society's divisions, the Executive Management Council meets every workday morning in Reg Murphy's office. Members of the group are (from left to right): Dale Petroskey, Senior V.P., Public Service; John Fahey, Executive Vice President and Chief Operating Officer; Bill Allen, Editor, National Geographic; Sandra Gill, Senior V.P., Administration; Reg Murphy, President and CEO, National Geographic Society; Chris Liedel, V.P., Strategic Planning; Tim Kelly, President, NGT, Inc.(National Geographic Television); Gene Ferrone, Senior V.P., Member Services; Nina Hoffman, Senior V.P., Publications; Suzanne Dupré, V.P., Corporate Counsel and Secretary; Bob Sims, Senior V.P., Magazine Publishing and Communications.

try were asked to locate Central America, the Pacific Ocean, the Persian Gulf, and thirteen selected countries on an unmarked world map. One in seven Americans could not identify the United States! One in four Americans could not locate the Pacific Ocean. The United States test scores were higher only than Italy's and Mexico's, and Americans in the 18-to-24-year-old group finished last.

The Society's long-term campaign to improve geography education today includes the National Geographic Society Education Foundation, established on the Society's Centennial in January 1988 with an initial $20 million grant and a $20 million pledge to match outside contributions. Today, the fund stands at more than $70 million, and grants some $3 million annually to help finance the Geographic Alliance Network. The alliances are composed of professional geographers, officials at state departments of education, and tens of thousands of K–12 teachers in every state, the District of Columbia, Puerto Rico, and Canada. The Society also provides funds to support professional development opportunities for teachers and the creation of exciting geography programs and products for teachers, students, and parents.

By 1997, 1,400 teachers had passed through the Society's Summer Geography Programs and more than 10,000 teachers had trained in geography teaching strategies at their state alliances. The alliance network is modeled after an alliance established by Professor Christopher (Kit) Salter and colleagues at UCLA in 1983.

"What's really significant about this is that we have almost 12,000 teachers who have been through an institute either here in Washington or out in the states who are now part of this alliance network," Robert Dulli explained. "We now have a really strong corps of teachers who understand what geography is, what its potential is in the classroom, and how much of what they already teach can fit into a geography curriculum relevant to their students' lives. And they get very excited about that! We call them 'Geo-Evangelists,' and they go back to their schools and communities and are ready to work hard for their state geo-

Above, left: *In July 1994 the Society signed an agreement with Nikkei Business Publications to publish the Magazine in Japanese, the first non-English local-language edition. Nikkei, the only Japanese publisher offering magazines through subscription, makes it possible for the Magazine to continue its tradition of being member-supported.*

Above: *In Japan working on "Tokyo: A Profile of Success," which was published in the November 1986 issue of the Magazine, William Graves, who was then Senior Assistant Editor, shares a laugh with Gil Grosvenor, who tries on a pair of boots in a street bazaar.*

graphic alliances, Gil Grosvenor, the National Geographic Society, and the discipline of geography."

The Geographic Alliance Network is unique in American education. The alliances work toward curriculum and assessment reform at all levels of the educational system, create much-needed geography support materials, and conduct professional development opportunities for teachers. Since 1986, they have raised more than $15 million from public sources, and close to $5 million from private sources for geography education. There is nothing like the alliance network in any other discipline. From 30,000 alliance members in 1989, there are now 150,000 members across the country, 85 to 90 percent of whom are teachers. What this means is that in virtually every state there are alliance members involved in state and local geography education reform.

Currently, the national trend in curriculum and assessment reform is toward setting high standards. The National Geography Standards, called *Geography for Life*, were published in 1994 as a joint project of the Society, the Association of American Geographers, the National Council for Geographic Education, and the American Geographic Society. They have had wide acceptance across the country and are being used as a model for building state and local geography standards.

"The College Board has just approved an advanced placement test on geography," Dulli continued, "and once again that all started because Gil Grosvenor called them up and said, 'Can we meet and talk about geography?' And basically when that meeting happened, they said 'Yes, we just haven't considered it.' Now don't get me wrong, it took about three years of hard work on the part of a lot of people to really push it through and get it to the point where the College Board would accept it. But it all started with that phone call. In ten years we have taken the discipline from where it was lost to being on the map. And I think in another ten years, when people think of education, they will also think geography. They used to think that back in the 1920s, and we will put it there again."

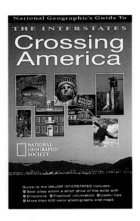

In September 1990, Special Publications and Book Service were combined into one Book Division, under the direction of Vice President William R. Gray. The Division's large-format, lavishly illustrated books are among its most recognizable publications, although since 1955 the Society's ever-expanding book program has produced a library of adult and children's books, board games, activity kits, and calendars. In 1993, the Society signed a contract with Random House to distribute Society publications for the first time to the book trade. In 1995, Book-of-the-Month Club began offering Society books to its members. The Company We Keep: America's Endangered Species *(top), the first Society book developed expressly for the trade, explores the diverse and threatened worlds of more than 950 endangered plant and animal species.* Crossing America: National Geographic's Guide to the Interstates *(bottom), also available in the trade, covers attractions along 30 major highways. This handy 352-page softcover guidebook has sold 325,000 copies.*

For the past eight years the Society has sponsored the National Geography Bee in grades four through eight, during which students are tested about the earth and everything in it. According to Gil Grosvenor, five million students participated in the 1996 school bees. "Therefore," as he said in his opening remarks at the televised finals, "each one of these ten youngsters on stage represents 500,000 youngsters who competed." And then, succumbing to the kind of image the Geographic loves best, he added, "That's five Rose Bowls filled to capacity."

As exciting as the Society's various programs promise to be for the teaching of geography, the electronic age will prove even more promising. Larry Lux joined the Society in 1995; he is the Vice President of National Geographic Interactive, a new division designed to produce consumer- and education-based CD-ROMs, to run the Society's Web site, its Interactive TV, and, as he put it, "whatever else comes down the media pike." Lux has seen the future, and although the Magazine staff is apprehensive that it may not be print, Lux does not see a conflict. "There are some people who feel National Geographic Interactive is a threat to the subscription base of the Magazine, but I think it's just the opposite. It is a way of getting a whole new group of people involved in what the Magazine does, and to bring what the Magazine does to them. It's also a way to increase television viewership. So the people who do understand the new medium are behind it."

A decade from now, Lux suggests, his division will become the National Geographic Society in the minds of most onlookers. "People will always take magazines," he said, "but if you assume the average age of our members is fifty-four at this point and it's been continuing to age, we'd like to help change that; and we think that by getting into this younger group of Web users demographically, we will. The new generation has become computer literate before they become book literate. And that's going to cause a fundamental change in behavior."

The Magazine has always appealed to the older generation; its members have, as Gil Grosvenor admits, been "graying with the population;" and its readers, Reg Murphy concedes, "always will be older." The Magazine, he said, "is an empty-nester kind of publication."

What troubles Murphy, he said, is that "we have the six-to-fourteen-year-old kids whom we have lots of products for, and then from forty-five to infinity, we have products for them. What we have to fill in here is this gap between age fourteen, when they would typically be through with *World*, to the time when their children are in or through with college and they have more time to think about where they would like to go, or what they'd like to explore. If they're not going to go themselves, then they would like to know about it and think about it. So what do you do to fill in the gap? You do Interactive," Murphy continued. "You do television specials. We've just signed a deal to do some movies. You keep *Traveler* and you keep it growing. You can look at that gap as a great big chasm, or you can look at it as a big opportunity. I look at it as a huge opportunity. And if we can fill out the rest of this product line so that the National Geographic Society will be accessible to all ages, we will have a continuity of membership that will make life easier for my successors."

Reg Murphy, the Society's first President who did not rise up through its ranks, inculcated with the organization's history and lore, views his having been an outsider as an advantage. "I'm glad that I had other experiences," he said, "because the way the communications business is changing requires the same kind of change here that it requires in lots of other places. If we're going to continue to attract and retain new members and then please them with what we do, we're going to have to adapt.

"Because of its scholastic background," he continued, "this organization thought of itself as a collection of colleges, with deans of each of the colleges, and they were intellectual places, where people cared a great deal about how they maintained quality—and about how they maintained absolute control." Now, at nine o'clock every workday morning, all the major department heads meet in Reg Murphy's office, where, the Society's new President says, "we talk about whatever there is, so everybody will begin to know what the other groups are up to so that if there's a possibility of combining assignments we will do that."

With the emphasis within the Society shifting toward the electronic mediums, members of the Magazine staff worry they are losing their status as the Society's flagship, and, instead, are being considered merely another money-maker, part of the product line. Unquestionably, the absolute power of the Editor has diminished, but the Magazine remains the Society's major income producer and a national institution. It is special. Still, there's a general feeling through the organization that the change is not over, that more senior people in various areas may be brought in from the outside by Reg Murphy, and that there will probably be some more moves toward downsizing in areas that may not have been as focused on as others.

Among the senior people Reg Murphy brought in is Nina Hoffman. She came to the Society from New York publishing and is now a Senior Vice President overseeing the Society's books. But she is also focusing very heavily on greater development of material for the schools. "In every eco-trend report that's come out," Hoffman said, "National Geographic material is number one in the schools. It still has the authority and purity that if some book, map, curriculum unit, has the National Geographic Society name, it's the seal of approval. And I don't think we have really taken full advantage yet of the educational possibilities. There should be National Geographic textbooks. There should be National Geographic supplemental material. There are areas that should be developed that aren't. National Geographic should be the number one line in travel books, and yet they've just now launched travel programs. Things that everyone associates with the National Geographic and thinks them to be the leader with, they are. But it's more in mystique and lore than in actual materials, all having been done through the Magazine."

In a *Washington Post* article of April 15, 1996, on the changes anticipated under the new management, former Chairman, President, and CEO of Time Life, Inc., John M. Fahey, now Executive Vice President and Chief Operating Officer of the National Geographic Society, was quoted on his and Nina Hoffman's recruitment by Reg Murphy. "Reg was looking for people with a perspective outside the Society," Fahey said. "There's a faction here that just wishes things were the way they were 20 years ago. But consumers have changed, the competition is more acute. We've reached a point where we need to be more aggressive."

One suspects GHG would approve.

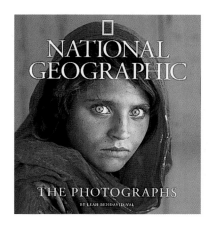

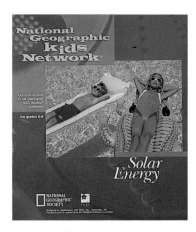

National Geographic: The Photographs *(top), the phenomenally successful collection of pictures published in 1994, has sold 300,000 copies. Insiders refer to the Afghan girl on the cover as "the Society's Mona Lisa."* Solar Energy *(bottom), is one of the many units that are a part of National Geographic Kids Network, a telecommunications-based curriculum that supports the National Standards for Geography, Science, and Math. Using the NGS Works™ software and the Internet, students gather data, share their findings with other students around the world, and analyze their results. With the help of independent scientists, students study real-world topics of global significance.*

The New Generation

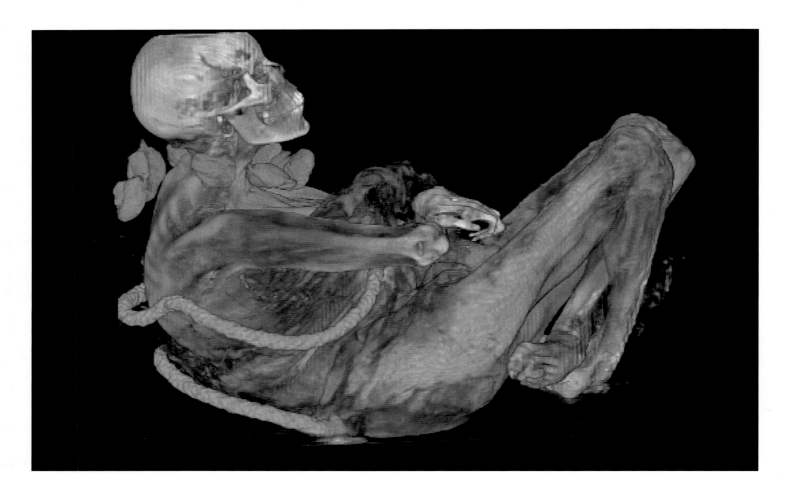

On September 11, 1995, George Stuart was in his office in the Society's M Street building when the telephone rang. "It was a little after three and it was Johan Reinhard," Stuart recalled. "Joe said, 'We've just come off the mountain and we have an incredible situation here. We've found the frozen body of a young girl probably from Inca times, maybe 500 years old, and we've got to get a freezer for it and then get back up there.' They had rushed down, in effect, to save the frozen body, and they needed to get right back up the mountain to investigate the context of the find—the shrine, the remains that might still be on the ground, other shrine sites—before looters overran the area.

"Anyway," Stuart continued, "Joe needed money for himself and his Peruvian colleagues and they needed money that afternoon! Well, we all knew he was trustworthy. In addition, Joe's project had it all: It was good science—a discovery that had the obvious potential to add considerably to our knowledge. And so we sent money that afternoon—wired it to the account of one of the Peruvian archeologists in Arequipa, which allowed them to mount an expedition to go back up there immediately to do the essential surface survey of the area seriously."

Two years earlier Ampato's summit ridge had been covered with ice thirty feet across; now, as Johan Reinhard and Miguel Zárate battled the mountain, the ridge was barely three feet wide. The dark volcanic ash settling on the summit had absorbed the sun's heat and the snow and ice had melted, causing the ridge to collapse. While Reinhard paused on their climb to take notes, Zárate went on ahead and then, as Reinhard wrote,

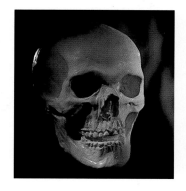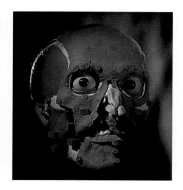

> I heard a whistle and saw his ice ax raised in the air. When I reached him, he pointed to a tiny fan of reddish feathers protruding from a nearby slope. We both knew instantly that they were part of a headdress of the sort found on Inca ceremonial statuettes.

Reinhard secured Zárate with a rope and the Peruvian worked his way down the steep slope until he could reach the feathers. They were in almost perfect condition, an indication that they had only briefly been exposed to the elements. In all, they found three classic Inca figurines wearing textiles and feather headdresses. One was made of gold, another of silver, and the third of the rare, red and white spondylus shell that the Inca considered as valuable as gold. The figurines had been buried facing the highest point of Ampato's summit and, looking around, Reinhard spotted at the head of two gullies some large stones that appeared to have formed the corner of an Inca ceremonial platform. Beneath the cornerstones the gullies dropped some 200 feet to a maze of ice pinnacles in the crater below. In an effort to discover if the rest of the ceremonial platform and additional objects might have tumbled farther down, Reinhard wrapped two rocks in yellow plastic and tossed them down the gullies; the stones dropped out of sight. Descending the ridge after them, Reinhard and Zárate located one of the yellow plastic-wrapped rocks and not far beyond it, on an icy outcrop, what appeared to be the cloth bundle of a mummy.

Reinhard had climbed more than a hundred Andean peaks in the previous fifteen years and conducted various high-altitude archeological excavations but had never found a mummy bundle like this on a mountain. The mummy was "on top of a piece of ice like a pedestal," Reinhard later said. "The body had shielded the ice beneath it from the sun and it was amazing! The ice had melted around it and it was just laying there like a gift." Working carefully with his ice ax so as not to ruin the textiles wrapped around the body, Zárate freed the mummy from its icy pedestal and turned it on its side for a better grip. That was when they found themselves looking into the dried-out face of an Inca girl sacrificed at roughly the time Columbus was "discovering" America.

Based on the condition of her face, Reinhard assumed that the girl's body was dessicated as well, so "when we tried to lift her," Reinhard continued, "we never thought she would be as heavy as she was. The weight meant that her body was frozen and as soon as I knew *that*, it was like a shock just went through my body because *then* I knew it was the first frozen female Inca ever found! And it had potential for being one of the best pre-Columbian mummies in terms of preservation of internal organs."

Reinhard did not dare leave the mummy on Ampato, where the sun and volcanic ash would wreak further havoc on her body, and he had to get her down

Preserved in his icy tomb for 5,000 years, the body of a 5'2" tall Copper Age man in his forties was discovered by a German couple hiking near the border between Austria and Italy. Reconstructed by John Gurche, an anthropologically trained artist, for the June 1993 issue of National Geographic, *the Iceman appears in a bust modeled from forensic data to suggest how the ancient traveler might have looked in life.*

"*Burdened by tons of topsoil, Mada-gascar's raveling Betsiboka River struggles to reach the blue waters of the Indian Ocean,*" begins the caption for this photograph taken with a handheld camera from the Discovery space shuttle in 1984. This image ran in the November 1996 Magazine; it and many others can be found in the Book Division's handsome 1996 *volume* Orbit: NASA Astronauts Photograph the Earth.

in absolute secrecy before looters, learning of the find, could pillage the site. Additional impetus, of course, was the concern that any day a heavy snowfall could bury the summit, thus rendering further exploration difficult. But if his first priority was to get the mummy down, Reinhard's second priority was to prevent her from even slightly thawing.

Wrapping the heavy mummy in a plastic sheet, Reinhard then fitted her wrapped-up feet into the bottom pouch of his backpack, lashed the mummy to the pack, and started down the icy mountain with Zárate leading the way. Time after time Reinhard slipped and fell, but always managed to fall to the side to avoid injuring his precious cargo. And time after time Zárate asked Reinhard to leave the mummy behind, not, as Reinhard had thought, so much out of concern for his well-being, but rather, as Zárate later explained, "If you'd fallen on me with that load, we'd both have been swept down the mountain."

After dusk, with their headlamps providing little light, Reinhard finally agreed to leave the mummy wedged safely between two ice pinnacles for the night. Two hours later the exhausted climbers reached their 19,200-foot-high camp and crawled into their sleeping bags.

The next morning, Reinhard sent Zárate with their gear 3,000 feet farther down to the base camp to make sure their burro driver would be waiting, then Reinhard climbed back up for the mummy. By the time he had returned to the high camp with the mummy, Zárate had rendezvoused with the burro driver and come back up. That night they camped at 15,300 feet, and at dawn they loaded the mummy onto the burro and commenced a daylong trek to the village of Cabanaconde. That night they slid the mummy onto the undercarriage baggage rack of the 11 P.M. overnight bus to Arequipa. Reinhard later wrote:

> We decided to split up: Theft is always a possibility on a night bus, and we were both too tired to stay awake. Miguel, who lives in Arequipa, went ahead with the mummy, and I stayed behind with the artifacts.
> By 9 A.M.—64 hours after we began our descent from the summit of Ampato—the mummy was in a freezer. That evening when I got to Arequipa, I immediately asked José Antonio Chávez, dean of the archaeology department at Catholic University, how much thawing had occurred. 'There was still ice on her outer textile when we put her in the freezer,' José said, and I felt the tension drain out of me.

Chávez and Reinhard, codirectors of the High Altitude Sanctuaries of the Southern Andes Project, immediately concentrated on assembling a full-scale archeological expedition to return to Ampato. Within a month, Reinhard wrote, "thanks to speedy issuance of an archeological permit by Peru's National Institute of Culture and grants from the National Geographic Society," they were back on the mountain. Accompanying them was a photographer on assignment for the Magazine and National Geographic Television producer Amy Wray, the first woman known to climb Nevado Ampato (and live to tell the tale) and her film crew. They were in place to film the discovery at 19,200 feet of the lightning-ravaged remains of two more Inca children in sacrificial burials about twenty feet apart. But the big story remained the initial recovery of the young girl's body one month before. Mummified corpses of other Inca sacrifices have been found over the years; and in 1991 the freeze-dried body of a 5,000-year-old man was recovered in the Alps. His story was chronicled in David Roberts's June 1993 story "The Iceman: Lone Voyager from the Copper Age." But none of these bodies appears to be as remarkably preserved as the Inca girl Reinhard and Zárate had just brought down.

Opposite: *"Going down the rope required Zen concentration," said Eric Valli, here beginning a cliff descent to photograph Nepali honey hunter Mani Lal at work. "There were so many bees I was afraid I might freak out. But I knew if I did, I would be dead. So I took a deep breath and relaxed. Getting stung would be better than finding myself at the bottom of the cliff." Valli's experiences in Nepal were shared by Diane Summers, who endured equally the trials of four years of work that resulted in their photographs and text for "Honey Hunters of Nepal," published in the November 1988 issue of the Magazine. The photographs won a first prize in the 1988 World Press Photo Foundation competition.*

"Each year Americans replace 135,000 hips, 110,000 knees, and tens of thousands of other body parts—at an estimated cost of two billion dollars," explained the caption for this December 1989 illustration of the extraordinary prosthetic devices now available to be implanted or attached to our "wet, hot, salty, and ever in motion" bodies.

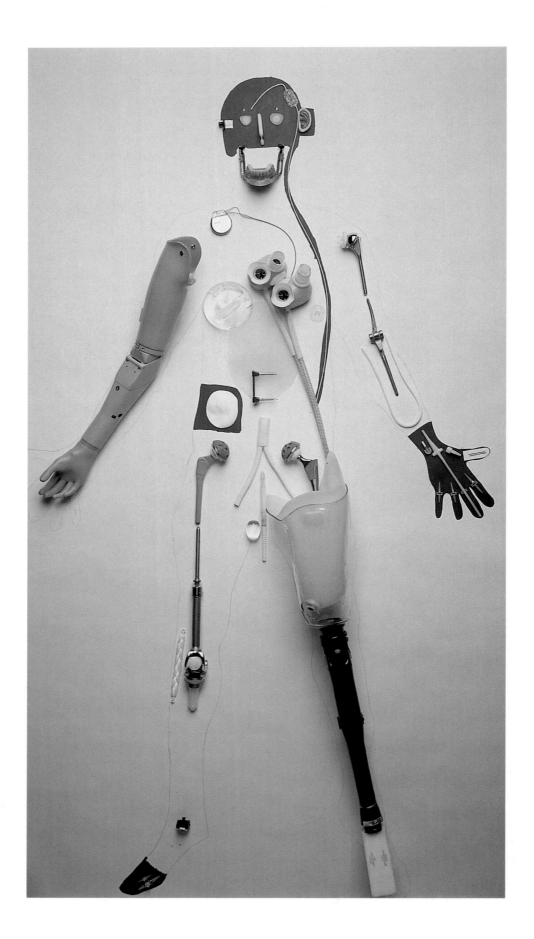

"Valuable beyond price, fragile beyond measure," the narrator of the *Explorer* television show proclaims. "It is a frozen piece of history, a treasure from the past. A mummy. A girl. She may be the closest thing to a living Inca modern science will ever see. She is known as the 'Ampato Maiden.' And she met her end on a remote mountaintop. A sacrifice to the gods."

The film was just one of the Society's efforts to exploit and coordinate coverage of the discovery—although exploit is hardly the appropriate word in light of the media frenzy that accompanied announcement of the mummy's recovery. Eagerness to get a picture and competition between various nations' press photographers and film crews to cover the story precipitated a shoving match in the Society's staid headquarters when on May 21, 1996, the Ampato Maiden went on display in her Carrier Corporation's donated, specially designed, glass-walled refrigerated case in Explorers Hall. The exhibit, inaugurated by Peru's President Alberto Fujimori accompanied by First Lady Hillary Rodham Clinton, opened right after a press conference in Grosvenor Auditorium at which the big news story was the results of the CT scans and needle biopsies of the mummy. These tests, performed earlier at Johns Hopkins Hospital, showed the Ampato Maiden had died not by suffocation as Reinhard had thought, but rather by a sharp blow to her right temple; furthermore, she had eaten a meal of vegetables six to eight hours before her death.

"We had hoped the biopsies would also provide cell nuclei containing DNA," Reinhard subsequently reported in his January 1997 Magazine follow-up article,

> making it possible to trace the ice maiden's maternal and paternal lines of descent and perhaps even to locate her living relatives. But all the nuclei had dissolved, which suggests that her body did not freeze immediately after she died. Our hopes for establishing genetic links now rest with mitochondrial DNA isolated from her heart, skin, and muscle tissue by scientists at the Institute for Genomic Research in Rockville, Maryland. Mitochondrial DNA, found outside the nucleus, is passed down only on the female side.

A caption accompanying the scans reported, "What the scans did not uncover is also important: Neither bones nor teeth show signs of disease or malnutrition. The Inca chose a perfectly healthy girl—about 14 years old and four feet ten inches tall—as a gift to their gods."

In addition to Magazine articles, an *Explorer* television show, and an exhibit in Explorers Hall, coverage of the Ampato Maiden included reporting on the Society's Web site and in *World* magazine.

And just as there was a new emerging attitude of cooperation between the various Society divisions, a new attitude toward adventure and exploration was emerging among its younger photographers. Two of them, George Steinmetz and Michael "Nick" Nichols—hard though it is to believe—were recently able to explore areas so remote in Steinmetz's case, no outsiders had been seen there. And in Nick Nichols's case, a site so remote it was possible that no humans at all had been seen: deep in one of the most significant tropical forest preserves in the world—the Republic of Congo's recently created Nouabalé-Ndoki National Park, an area of nearly a million acres.

Frequent Society contributor Douglas H. Chadwick, a wildlife biologist of consummate writing talent, accompanied Nichols into the national park, and Chadwick's opening paragraphs seem almost a parody of earlier *Geographic* adventure reporting:

To reach this place, our expedition had traveled up one of the Congo River's main tributaries, the Sangha, to the little village of Bomassa, just three miles from the southern tip of the Central African Republic. From there we turned east, crossing overland to the river called Ndoki, and poled dugout canoes up its sunless channels of black water. White lilies lit the way. We began marching through this low-lying part of the Congo Basin after that, sometimes south and sometimes east and too often through hip-deep marshes of muck, leeches, tsetse flies, and dwarf crocodiles. By now we were beyond even the nearest Pygmy hunting territories, probing truly unknown country. I was tired. We were all tired, and it was taking a toll. . . .

Our expedition was to examine a section of the park's southern boundary, then forge on to tributaries of the Oubangui, and the swamp known as Likouala aux Herbes, which begins 50 miles southeast of Bomassa. Rumors say this vast marsh is the home of *mokélé-mbembé*, the legendary Congo Basin dinosaur.

They never saw a *mokélé-mbembé*, but they did see "more than a dozen chimpanzees," Chadwick wrote, "that had almost surely never seen a human being in their lives." An American ecologist guiding the team, J. Michael Fay, was able to imitate the "nasal yowls" of an antelope called a duiker, and the chimps "had come from all sides on the ground, probably intent on catching a duiker to eat." Chadwick reported,

As soon as they made out our still forms through the foliage, they screamed again and leaped into the trees. There, led by a big, grizzled male, they began an even wilder display, yelling, baring their teeth, hurling sticks with fair accuracy—and urinating with equally unsettling aim. Yet within minutes several members of the group were starting to alternate such threats with soft, questioning *hoo*'s.

Everywhere we looked, eyes built by genes practically identical to ours stared back. Behind those eyes, I felt sure, were minds overcome by the same astonishment we felt. . . .

An hour or so after first contact, most of the chimps continued to stare without letup, now and then hugging one another. 'For reassurance,' Nick whispered. The big male turned to lie on his back atop a thick liana, where he began to rock slowly as if settled into a hammock, occasionally sneaking a peek over his shoulder. A small male of perhaps six or seven years of age clambered down to perch no more than 20 feet from us, glancing from face to human face. He widened his eyes; we widened ours. He hooed. We hooed back, and he responded with another hoo right away. We carried on the same conversation with several different animals. We even mimicked the chimps unconsciously, scratching our sides and waving our hands past our faces, for the insects had begun to swarm our primate parley.

"It's easy to talk about first contact," Nick Nichols said sometime after his return from Ndoki, "but is it really? How the hell do you know? And one of the ways we thought to verify it was to just try to find the same group the next day, or two or three days later. And when we did that, they never paid any attention to us except for one or two quick looks from the tops of trees and then they went on about their business of hunting or foraging or whatever, because they had satisfied this curiosity the first day and they were, in effect, saying, 'Okay, we know about this thing now, let's keep going.' There wasn't even a smattering of the same intensity the second visit as there was the first. So I think it really was a first contact, or the first contact within ten years or five years or within the collective memory of the group."

Despite having spent more than ten years in Asia and Africa photographing the great apes, Nichols insists he is still learning how to be a wildlife photographer and the real test, he said of his journey to Ndoki, was to try to get pictures of wild animals that were somewhat artistic and did them justice. Asked what photograph does a wild animal justice, Nichols replied, "It's when you give them their *dignity*. So much wildlife photography takes that away when we capture them or put them in enclosures to photograph them. It's something about trying to find their *spirit*. My whole thing is to try to make the photograph a little more edgy and weird in the sense of the surreal, because I think that world really is. Especially Ndoki. It was such a dark and forbidding place that humans just have no business being there. And I wanted that feel to my pictures. I see a lot of photographers who just say, 'Let's get this on film as a portrait of the face of this tiger,' but it tells you nothing about the tiger. I want the tiger to scream at you that '*I'm the wildest thing there is and I deserve to be left alone!*'"

There are those scientists who said that if the Ndoki is really as untouched as Chadwick, Nichols, and the rest said, then didn't Ndoki, too, wild as it is, deserve to be left alone? Nichols's response is that it's "sort of a fantasy to think that it's going to stay that way. Don't forget that the chain saws and the bulldozers are just minutes away."

Photographer George Steinmetz was brought up in Beverly Hills and has been arrested twice in Africa for spying, the first time in Burkina Faso, north of Ghana. "I was impetuous, if not a bit imprudent," he explained. "I was taking pictures of people smuggling things across the border, which I wasn't supposed to be doing." His second arrest was in Cameroon, "basically because I didn't have a camera permit," he said. "The cops were kind of corrupt." He has had two cases of malaria, almost lost his eyesight to a *loa loa* worm, and dropped out of Stanford long enough to hitchhike across seventeen African countries in eighteen months before returning to graduate with a degree in geophysics.

"I was eating a lunch of tinned biscuits and tea when a shrill cry rose from

Following spread: *In the fall of 1996 Arctic explorer Will Steger became the first explorer-in-residence of the Society, which permitted him to exchange ideas and share his perspective as an explorer and educator with staff members, an important means, he later said, "to make vital the mission of the Society." In January of that year, the Magazine had published "Dispatches from the Arctic Ocean," a stirring account of his previous year's trek across the Arctic Ocean, with a five-day stopover at the North Pole. Battling blizzards, cold, shifting ice, and open water leads, Steger's team of American, Japanese, Russian, Danish, and British explorers, acting to draw attention to the Arctic environment as a single ecosystem, encountered considerable beauty and extreme danger. The caption for the photograph on the following pages documents one episode: "The sled was going down. If the dogs couldn't save it, our journey from Russia to Canada would be finished only halfway across the Arctic Ocean. This time we were lucky. Our huskies were strong and we pushed on."*

505

the far side of the clearing," his February 1996 Magazine essay on two remote tribes living in Irian Jaya, the Indonesia side of New Guinea, began:

> I glanced up just as two naked men burst into view and came dashing toward us, fitting large barbed arrows to their bows. Our porters halted them, bows drawn, just yards away. Angry words flew, then quieted as my interpreter offered them gifts and greetings. I soon learned that they were father and son, that we were the first outsiders they had ever seen, and that they had intended to kill us. This was my introduction to the tree-dwelling Kombai people of Irian Jaya.
>
> Two years later I was back, slogging through a swampy 600-square-mile tract of forest inhabited by perhaps 3,000 Korowai, one of Irian Jaya's 250 indigenous tribes. The Korowai are neighbors of the Kombai. The two peoples' material culture, including tree houses, is nearly identical, but their languages are very different. Both cultures are endangered as Indonesia continues its efforts to settle the Irian Jaya backcountry. I had returned to document their lives before they were changed forever.

"The way we came to that area," Steinmetz later recalled, "was that writer Tom O'Neill wanted to find the place that was the most untouched. And when we went in there I just thought we were too late, that the time to have been there was in the 1940s or '50s or '60s. There was a lot of talk from the porters about cannibalism, about these people being naked, that they had nothing but stone tools, and I thought, 'Yeah, yeah, yeah, I'll believe it when I see it,' and then these guys come running out of the forest trying to kill us with bows and arrows and *it was real!* These guys were trying to kill us because they believed we were *ghosts!* And that made me a believer."

Steinmetz, too, has been asked why he didn't just leave the Korowai alone, and he admitted he had some misgivings about being there. "Virtually all the cultures in New Guinea have been changed by contact," he said, "and it was inevitable that these people were going to be contacted and changed, too. Outside the huge gold mine in the Sudirman Mountains of the central highlands I overheard one miner say of another, more native miner, 'That guy's more bone-in-the-nose than I am!' Both were only a generation or two away from their first contact with whites. And with the Korowai, I just wanted to make a document of what their life was like so that later, when they had changed, they could come back and look at what their lives once were. I wanted to make some sort of document for them so they could *find* their way back."

The problem, Steinmetz said, was that he couldn't photograph the way the Korowai were before he got there; he could only photograph the impact his presence had on them. "All they wanted to do was stare at whitey," Steinmetz recalled. "It was just so *weird* for them. They weren't sure who I was. Something from the spirit world. They call clothing 'spirit skin,' a steel tool might be a 'spirit ax.' I wanted to get some of the porters away so the Korowai would relax—but not so many that we would get attacked. We'd get down to ten people and still they'd just be staring at us. We were spending a week in their clan territory waiting to see these people do whatever they'd do. We'd say, 'What are you doing today?' And they'd just look at us, watch us. So I'd say, 'What are you thinking?' And they'd say, 'What do you mean what are we thinking? *You* are here!'

"It was kind of like a Martian ship landing in your backyard," Steinmetz continued, "and all these green guys come out in gold suits and say, 'Just act natural. We want to walk about your house and take pictures of you.' And you

don't know what a picture is; you don't have any police to call. So you're just going to want to sit there with your bow and arrow ready and watch the whole time."

Steinmetz would climb a tree and hope from that vantage point he could catch some natural shots of Korowai home life. "I'd hang out in this tree for a couple of hours until my legs were turning blue and they'd just be sitting there watching me," he said. "I finally realized the thing to do was to go up the tree in the dark. So I'd climb up at five in the morning and they'd wake up and go, 'Oh, that crazy whacker's out in the trees again!' But that was the game: to try to get them bored enough to go about their natural business. Granted it's a foreign situation, but you can guess how natural somebody's being. It's early in the morning; they're kind of rubbing their eyes, and either they're looking at you or they go deal with their screaming kid. Whatever. They may seem natural to me, but I can't really be sure."

"What's different about us in the 1990s and when Joseph Rock was running around in the 1920s," Nick Nichols said, "is that we're so sensitized because of television and because you can travel the globe in five minutes. When George Steinmetz and I go out there and bring back these stories, we *want* there to be a Ndoki, a 'bone-in-the-nose' people. It's an intense desire and I think that's why the exploration part of the Geographic is so important in the public mind. But if we find them then I feel we have this tremendous moral obligation to protect them. That's the difference. Before, there was no moral obligation. You were out exploring for the sake of it, to bring back new knowledge. Now, sometimes when we're exploring, as soon as we find it we say, 'We have to build a wall around this! We've got to protect it!' And the Geographic's role in publicizing such concerns to this huge readership that we have is invaluable. That's why I've decided to do just this: the 'Geographic thing.' I feel an obligation to make a lot of noise about this stuff and the Geographic gives me a perfect vehicle for it. I just hope we don't evolve to the point where we are just a corporation where the bottom line is all that's important."

Dale Petroskey is the Society's new Senior Vice President, Public Service. Before he came in 1988 as Director of Public Affairs, his life had been in Washington politics. Now, in addition to being in charge of the Geography Education Program, the Geography Bee, the Education Foundation, and Explorers Hall, Petroskey oversees the Committee for Research and Exploration, and, as a Senior Vice President, he is a member of the Executive Management Council and clearly part of the new corporate structure. What he says about the future of research and exploration reflects current management's thinking.

"Reg Murphy has started a $5 million endowment for Research and Exploration," Petroskey said. "His goal is to give more money to Research and Exploration next year than this year and on into the future. Every year the first 5 percent of that $5 million endowment will go toward the following things: a $100,000 tax-free, no-strings-attached prize to the person or persons we believe epitomizes 'the increase and diffusion of geographic knowledge'; $50,000 for George Stuart to award to as many as five grantees to help further their scientific work—it could be $10,000 here, $5,000 there—it will go to people who have received grants from us in the past. We've also instituted the explorer-in-residence program; Will Steger was our first, Johan Reinhard our second. The average Research and Exploration grant has been $15,300 and about 75 percent

Opposite: Houses of Irian Jaya's Kombai and Korowai people are built as high as 150 feet—"to see the birds and the mountains and to keep sorcerers from climbing my stairs," explained one Korowai tribesman to contract photographer George Steinmetz.—From "Irian Jaya's People of the Trees," in the February 1996 issue

511

A playful polar bear juggles a tire that it had wrested away from another bear. Such spontaneous behavior occurs among mammals and many bird species and was the subject of "Animals at Play," one of the five most popular Magazine stories in 1994, according to member surveys. "I was laughing so hard my vehicle shook," reported Norbert Rosing, who made this photograph.

In the Peary collection at the National Archives in Washington, D.C., are stored tools of the trade for an Arctic explorer in 1909: a bottle of mercury used in creating an artificial horizon when ice ridges blocked the view; the pan into which the mercury was poured; Peary's three watch-type chronometers, whose serial numbers one astronomer mistook for Peary's compass readings; and a sextant with eyepieces.

The controversy over whether or not Peary reached the North Pole refuses to die in part because of gaps in his documentation and because of his abrasive personality. The Society, however, supported by a recent reexamination of all the evidence, holds with its original conclusion that Peary did indeed reach the Pole.

of our budget will continue to be in these small grants. But for the first time we're going to have 'super grants' of $60,000 for at least five high-impact scientific research projects that will allow us to do more high-profile fieldwork which, in turn, could provide more editorial material for us and be attractive to additional donors. We'd like to pick a big project—coral reefs, maybe, or Olmec archeology—and say, 'Okay, send us a proposal that's worthy of a big grant.' And then we can interest an individual or an organization to augment that funding.

"Research and Exploration, of course, are the underpinnings of the Society," Petroskey continued. "They provide us with the great stories to tell in the Magazine, on television, in books, on the Web site, in the classroom. We have rarely in any formal or systematic way had a lecture program where people go outside of Washington and talk about the excitement of what they do. Johan Reinhard, for example, would be a huge hit if we took him out to Washington State or Colorado. People would be talking about that for weeks. So would Paul Sereno on the new dinosaur finds. Or there could be Bob Ballard, Will Steger, or Todd Skinner, who free climbed the sheer 3,000-foot vertical rise of Pakistan's Trango Tower to its peak at 20,469 feet. There are photographers like Nichols and Stein-

metz. Then there is Maurice Hornocker on Siberian tigers, naturalist-cinematographers Beverly and Dereck Joubert, who have lived with the lions of Botswana for fourteen years. There are Tim Laman and Cheryl Knott, another husband and wife team. He has a Ph.D. from Harvard in rain forest ecology; she's getting her Ph.D. in anthropology and is studying orangutans. They're working in Borneo right now. Any or all of them could be the new heroes, the new Leakeys and Goodalls and Hillarys. And so one of my responsibilities now is to help find these guys and then turn them into the great storytellers of the future for us so that people identify them with the National Geographic Society. The $100,000 prize, the discretionary money for George Stuart, the 'super grants,' the explorer-in-residence program are going to allow people to do big projects with us now. And the prospect of attracting people to increase the size of those super grants through the Development Office and the Grosvenor Council, that special group of people who donate $1,000 or more per year for five years, is not only very exciting, it guarantees the continuation and expansion of the sort of research and exploration that made the Society famous."

Paul Sereno, associate professor of paleontology and evolution at the University of Chicago, braces himself on a sandstone cliff in Morocco in 120-degree heat to uncover the grooved teeth of a Carcharodontosaurus, *among the largest land predators ever found. Sereno and his team have found "compelling evidence that Africa's dinosaurs evolved along divergent paths from those elsewhere on earth."—From "Africa's Dinosaur Castaways," in the June 1996 issue*

It could kill man-size prey in a single bite. Carcharodontosaurus—its 90-million-year-old skull reconstructed here—is the most remarkable of new finds excavated in the Sahara. Its name means "shark-toothed reptile," a reference to its bladelike teeth, the sides of which contained a series of grooves, whose purpose is unknown.

Acknowledgments

With a book such as this, it is difficult to know where to begin acknowledging one's debts. In my mind, individuals deserving precedence jostle one another like an after-theater crowd searching for taxis. Certainly, the willingness of Gilbert M. Grosvenor, President and Chairman of the Board of the National Geographic Society, to go outside the Society and choose an independent publisher of its centennial history might justify putting him at the head of the list. But since it was Paul Gottlieb, President and Publisher of Harry N. Abrams, Inc., who persuaded Gil Grosvenor that Abrams was the right organization to produce such a book and then selected me to write the text, should not his name with equal justice—and a flagon of prudence—take priority?

Robert L. Breeden, the National Geographic Society's Senior Vice President, Publications and Educational Media, has been a friend indeed. Generous with both time and advice, Bob Breeden always stepped in at the appropriate moment with the necessary energy, perspective, and experience to knit the Abrams and Society teams together when differing publishing methods threatened to unravel the project's seams. (Bob Breeden's line "The dark at the end of the tunnel is what we're finally seeing" will long be remembered.)

The enthusiastic cooperation of members of the *National Geographic* staff was amazing to this outsider. Gilbert M. Grosvenor, despite his busy schedule, sat through interview after interview, was unswervingly frank in his answers, and unhesitatingly provided supporting documents. Editor Wilbur E. Garrett, despite deadlines and staff meetings, always found time to answer questions and give advice. Senior Associate Editor Joseph Judge, writer, raconteur, and lunch companion without equal, I shall sorely miss. Associate Editor Thomas R. Smith, Senior Assistant Editors William Graves, Carolyn Bennett Patterson (ret.), Edward J. Linehan, Samuel W. Matthews, O. Louis Mazzatenta, Charles McCarry, Elizabeth A. Moize, Howard E. Paine, Mary G. Smith—thank you all for your patient, informative, and, in many cases, hilarious interviews and reminiscences.

I could not have written the sections covering the development of color photography at the Society without the counsel and advice of *Geographic* Senior Writer Priit J. Vesilind and his generous sharing of his Master's thesis. Priit deserves a special credit line here of his own.

Assistant Editors Kent Britt, Rick Gore, Bart McDowell, Merle Severy, Senior Writers Thomas J. Abercrombie, William S. Ellis, Peter T. White, and Senior Editorial Staff members Boyd Gibbons and David Jeffery—I am grateful to you as well. Photographers Dean Conger, David Alan Harvey, George F. Mobley, Steve Raymer, Robert F. Sisson, and Director of Layout Robert W. Madden, each of you is worth a thousand words—or is it ten thousand? Senior Assistant Editor John B. Garver, Jr., and his Cartography Division helped me find my way.

In daily dealings with this book, Senior Assistant Editor and Book Service director Charles O. Hyman was our friend and benefactor. Never one to let my words stand in the way of a good picture, Chuck eased us over some rough spots. Senior Assistant Editor and Special Publications Director Donald J. Crump was a major source for the early days of Special Pubs; Director of Educational Media George Peterson taught me much—and not just about the life cycle of the frog. Ralph Gray, former School Service Chief, and Executive Assistant William Gray—father and son—a special thanks to the two of you. Joan Tapper, editor of *Traveler*, and Director of Publications Art John D. Garst were giving of their time and friendship. Associate Director Tim T. Kelly was helpful about the Society's television and films, and Susanne K. Dupré, the Society's Corporate Counsel, was open and, parenthetically, informative about the Society's efforts to protect its nonprofit-organization tax-exempt status.

Library Director Susan Fifer Canby and Reference Librarian Carolyn Locke helped me find the sources, and Ted Wojtaskik came up with exactly the right correspondence. News Service's Boris Weintraub—though in a fur-lined foxhole—showed a newspaperman's heart. And Everest conqueror and now Vice Chairman, Committee for Research and Exploration, Barry C. Bishop proved "When one can no longer see, one can at least still know."

The crusty former Senior Assistant Editor, Photography, Robert E. Gilka (in whose office had lain a pillow needlepointed, "Wipe your Knees Before Entering") was a pleasure to talk with—if for no other reason than his line about Gil Grosvenor: "He's east, east, east, east—a Yale man. You don't get much more eastern unless you go out swimming." I am grateful to retired *Geographic* photographer Volkmar K. Wentzel and to Edwards Park, editor of the Society's 75th-anniversary book, *Great Adventures,* and, later, of *Smithsonian;* both of them were good enough to come in to talk. And former *Geographic* Editor and Society Trustee Frederick G. Vosburgh was extremely kind in submitting to lengthy telephone interviews.

Former Chairman of the Board Melvin M. Payne, Vice Chairman Owen R. Anderson, Chairman Emeritus Thomas W. McKnew, and Society Vice President Leonard J. Grant assisted me in understanding both the mood and the history of the Society's earlier decades. And it was a special honor and delight to spend as much time as I did with the Society's legendary Luis Marden.

I am grateful as well to Society Vice President Danforth P. Fales and to Dorothy (Dori) Jacobson, both of Publications and Educational Media. Their friendship and encouragement meant a great deal to me.

Abrams' Senior Editor Edith M. Pavese's tireless good humor and supportive efforts daily saw this book through. Edith, what a pleasure it has been to work with you again!

I felt that same pleasure working with this book's Art Director, Samuel N. Antupit, whose work I have admired ever since we were together at *Monocle* more than twenty-five years ago.

Thanks also to Maria Miller, who, with patient good nature, coordinated the various aspects of design and production. And to Gertrud Brehme, who organized the sometimes conflicting demands of the production and technical teams.

Illustrations Editor Anne D. Kobor's experience was invaluable. It was she and Illustrations Researcher Brooke Kane who searched for, found, and assembled all the pictures for this book—though not without the help of Leah Roberts, Linda Rinkinen, Bill Bonner, Eudora (Dori) Babyak, and Elizabeth Leader.

Edith, Sam, Maria, Anne, and Brooke, this is your book, too.

Finally, if the National Geographic Society deserves its reputation for accuracy and thoroughness—and, believe me, it does—it is due to its researchers, who tirelessly track down sources and confirm facts. I was fortunate to have had researcher Tee Loftin save me much anguish and hardship on my various literary journeys to the Poles. I thank her, and I thank, too, researcher Tori Garrett Connors, who joined this project at midpoint and spent many overtime hours seeing it through.

But there is no one to whom I stand in greater debt than Sallie M. Greenwood, the researcher assigned by the Society from the beginning of the project to ensure the accuracy of the first edition's text. When in 1996 it was decided to update that edition Sallie was no longer with the Society. Working with me instead was Victoria Cooper, whose research skills were equaled only by her good humor and patience. Illustrations Editor Thomas B. Powell III's keen eye and wry wit, too, were a godsend.

William R. Gray, now the Vice President and Director of the Society's Book Division, worked hard to ensure that my text reflected as much of the Geographic's past ten years as the Society felt was important. Thanks, Will. And thank you Barbara A. Payne, Bob Madden, Johan Reinhard, George Steinmetz, Cathy Newman, Charles Kogod, Leah Bendavid-Val, and all who contributed to my good humor in Washington.

And finally, a very special thanks to Abrams' Director of Special Projects Robert Morton, my editor on this edition and friend. Aware that all writings are a compromise, some more delicate than others, Bob's quiet diplomacy constantly smoothed the road between the rocks and hard places.

C.D.B. Bryan
Guilford, Connecticut

Bibliography

Beebe, William. *Half Mile Down*. New York: Harcourt, Brace, and Company, 1934.

Bruce, Robert V. *Bell: Alexander Graham Bell and the Conquest of Solitude*. Boston: Little, Brown and Company, 1973.

Buckley, Tom. "With the National Geographic on Its Endless, Cloudless Voyage." *New York Times Magazine*, September 6, 1970.

Chamberlin, Anne. "Two Cheers for the National Geographic." *Esquire*, December 1963.

"Change at the *Geographic*." *Washington Post*, July 17, 1977.

Chock, Alvin K. "J. F. Rock, 1884–1962." *Hawaiian Botanical Society Newsletter*, January 1963.

"Climbing Mount Everest Is Work for Supermen." *New York Times*, March 18, 1923.

Conaway, James. "Inside the Geographic." *Washington Post*, December 18, 19, 20, 1984.

Cornell, James. *The Great International Disaster Book*. New York: Charles Scribners' Sons, 1982.

Eber, Dorothy Harley. *Genius at Work: Images of Alexander Graham Bell*. New York: The Viking Press, 1982.

"Footnote to Geography." *The New York Times* editorial, July 26, 1942.

Frazier, Kendrick. *The Violent Face of Nature: Severe Phenomena and Natural Disasters*. New York: William Morrow and Co., Inc., 1979.

Garrett, W. E. "The Magazine Today." National Geographic Index, 1947–1983.

_____. "National Geographic: The Magazine That Taught Us How to Use Pictures...and Color." *Photojournalism: Principles and Practices* (2nd ed.). Clifton C. Edom, ed. Dubuque, Iowa: Wm. C. Brown Company, 1980.

"The Geographic Faces Life." *Newsweek*, September 12, 1977.

"Geographic from Upbeat to Realism." *Los Angeles Times*, August 5, 1977.

"Geographic Moves, Like a Glacier." *San Francisco Examiner*, September 25, 1977.

"Geographic Society Raid Drill Empties Building in 3 Minutes." *Washington Star*, February 15, 1942.

"The Geographic's Flawed Picture." *Accuracy in Media*, vol. VI, no. 6 (March 1977).

Great Adventures with National Geographic. Washington, D.C.: National Geographic Society, 1963.

Grosvenor, Gilbert H. "Earth, Sea, and Sky: Twenty Years of Exploration by the National Geographic Society." *The Scientific Monthly*, May 1954.

_____. "First Lady of the National Geographic." *National Geographic Magazine*, July 1965.

_____. *The National Geographic Society and Its Magazine: A History*. Washington, D.C.: National Geographic Society, 1957.

_____. "The Romance of the Geographic." *National Geographic Magazine*, October 1963.

_____. Speech at *U.S. Camera* Achievement Awards Dinner, November 6, 1951.

Grosvenor, Melville Bell. "Bringing the World to Your Fingertips." Washington, D.C.: National Geographic Society, 1970.

_____. "Editor's Note." *National Geographic Magazine*, October 1963.

Grun, Bernard. *The Timetables of History: A Horizontal Linkage of People and Events*. New York: Simon and Schuster, 1975.

Hart, Scott. "Whole Earth Monthly: The Power and the Glory of Being the National Geographic." *Washington Star-News*, September 23, 1973.

Hellman, Geoffrey T. "Geography Unshackled." *The New Yorker*, September 25, October 2, October 9, 1943.

Hoffer, William. "All the World's a Page." *Regardies*, March 1986.

Huntford, Roland. *The Last Place on Earth*. New York: Atheneum, 1986.

_____. *Scott and Amundsen*. London and Toronto: Hodder and Stoughton, 1979.

Images of the World: Photography at the National Geographic. Washington, D.C.: National Geographic Society, 1981.

Kirwan, L. P. *A History of Polar Exploration*. New York: Norton and Company, Inc., 1959.

LaGorce, John Oliver. *The Story of the Geographic*. Washington, D.C.: National Geographic Society, 1915.

"Maps of a Changing World." *The New York Times* editorial, January 15, 1945.

Marden, Luis. Tribute to Melville Bell Grosvenor. Address delivered at the Cosmos Club, Washington, D.C., May 1979.

McGee, W. J. "Fifty Years of American Science." *Atlantic Monthly*, September 1898.

Mott, Frank L. *A History of American Magazines, 1885–1905, vols. I–V*.

Cambridge, Massachusetts: Harvard University Press, 1930–1968.

Mowat, Farley. *The Polar Passion: The Quest for the North Pole*. Boston: Little, Brown and Company, 1967.

"The 'Mystery' Army of World War II." *Trading Post*, March–April 1956.

National Geographic Index, 1888–1946. Washington, D.C.: National Geographic Society, 1967.

National Geographic Index, 1947–1983. Washington, D.C.: National Geographic Society, 1984.

"National Geographic Photographers: The Gang That Better Shoot Straight." *Potomac (The Washington Post)*, July 7, 1974.

"National Geographic Still Poking Its Lens Around the World." *Chicago Tribune*, Tempo Section, September 12, 1977.

Oehser, Paul H., ed. *National Geographic Society Research Reports, 1890–1954*. Washington, D.C.: National Geographic Society, 1975.

"One of the Grosvenor Twins of Amherst to Wed the Bell Telephone Millions." *Boston Sunday Post*, October 7, 1900.

Payne, Melvin M. "The Geographic Society at 75." *Washington Star*, January 27, 1963.

_____. "75 Years Expanding Earth, Sea and Sky." *National Geographic Magazine*, January 1963.

"Rose-Colored Geography." *Time*, June 15, 1959.

Ross, Ishbel. "Geography, Inc." *Scribner's*, June 1938.

Sullivan, Wilson. "National Geographic: 'The Whole World Inside.'" *Saturday Review*, March 14, 1964.

Sutton, S. B. *In China's Border Provinces: The Turbulent Career of Joseph Rock, Botanist-Explorer*. New York: Hastings House, 1974.

This Fabulous Century: 1920–1930. New York: Time-Life Books, 1968.

Vesilind, Priit Juho. "National Geographic and Color Photography." Unpublished Master's thesis in Journalism, Syracuse University, December 1977.

Vosburgh, Frederick G. "To Gilbert Grosvenor: A Monument 25 Miles High." *National Geographic Magazine*, October 1966.

"What National Geographic Can Teach You." *35mm Photography*, Spring 1970.

Index

Credits

ILLUSTRATIONS CREDITS

Note. The following abbreviations are used in this list: (t) top, (c) center, (b) bottom, (l) left, (r) right; NGP National Geographic Photographer, NGS National Geographic Staff.

1 Thomas Ives. 2, 3 Jen and Des Bartlett. 4, 5 Steve Raymer, NGP. 6, 7 David Austen. 8, 9 Merlin D. Tuttle. 10, 11 Thomas J. Abercrombie, NGS. 12, 13 Nicholas DeVore III. 14, 15 David Doubilet. 16, 17 Gordon W. Gahan. 18 Charles O'Rear.

22, 23 Painting by Stanley Meltzoff for *National Geographic*. 26 Peter Bissett. 28 John K. Hillers, Smithsonian Institution. 29 Culver Pictures, Inc. 32 Painting by Paul Calle for *National Geographic*. 34, 35 Kokusho Kankokai, Inc. 38–45 Gilbert H. Grosvenor Collection, Library of Congress. 46 Library of Congress. 47 Gilbert H. Grosvenor Collection, Library of Congress.

50, 51 Will Steger. 52–59 Robert E. Peary Collection, National Geographic Society. 60, 61 Naomi Uemura. 62(1) From Richard E. Byrd. 62, 63 Painting by N.C. Wyeth for *National Geographic*. 64, 65 Jannick Schou. 67 Herbert G. Ponting. 68, 69 Byrd Antarctic Expedition. 70, 71 Charles Swithinbank. 72(1) Paul A. Siple. 72, 73 Thomas J. Abercrombie, NGS. 73(r) William R. Curtsinger. 74, 75 David Pratt. 76, 77 George Lowe, Royal Geographical Society, London. 78 Paul A. Siple. 79 Robert Benson.

80–87 Gilbert H. Grosvenor Collection, Library of Congress. 88(t) C.W. Blackburne. 88(b) Painting by Paul Calle for *National Geographic*. 89 Dean C. Worcester. 90 John Oliver LaGorce. 91 Fred J. Maroon. 92 Tsybikoff and Norzunoff. 93 Joseph D. Lavenburg NGP. 94 Robert S. Oakes.

96, 97 Maurice and Katia Krafft. 98 From Morris J. Elsing. 100, 101 Gary Rosenquist, Earth Images. 102 National Earth Satellite Service, NOAA. 103 Laboratory for Atmospheric and Space Physics, University of Chicago. 104, 105 Guillermo Aldana E. 106, 107 John LeBaron Collection. 108, 109 Winfield Parks. 110, 111 Guillermo Aldana E. 112,113 Annie Griffiths. 114, 115 Steve Raymer, NGP.

116, 117 Grace Adams, Gilbert H. Grosvenor Collection, Library of Congress. 120 From F. P. Sargent. 122, 123 George Shiras III. 125 Thomas Barbour. 126, 127 William W. Chapin. 128, 129 Charles Martin. 130 Wallis W. Nutting, Gilbert H. Grosvenor Collection, Library of Congress. 131 Gilbert H. Grosvenor. 132(t) A.R. Moore. 132(b) Horace Albright, Gilbert H. Grosvenor Collection, Library of Congress. 133 Franklin Price Knott. 134(tl) American Red Cross. 134(tr) From Harriet Chalmers Adams. 134(b) Christina Krysto.

136, 137 Edwards Park. 138 Paul Bestor. 139 E.C. Erdis. 140, 141 Loren McIntyre. 142–144 Richard H. Stewart. 145 Farrell Grehan. 146, 147 Bates Littlehales, NGP. 149 Paintings by H.M. Herget for *National Geographic*. 150–153 David Brill. 154, 155 O. Louis Mazzatenta, NGS. 156 David Brill. 157 Adam Woolfitt. 159 Chinese photographer.

165 Frank J. Magee. 167 Benjamin A. Stewart. 168 Franklin Price Knott. 169 M. Stephane Passet. 170 Maynard Owen Williams. 171 Charles Martin and W.H. Longley. 172(t) Keystone View Company. 172(b) Wide World Photos. 174 Drawing by Carl Rose; © 1934, 1962 *The New Yorker*, Inc.

176–182 Maynard Owen Williams. 184, 185 Drawings by Alexandre Iacovleff. 186, 187 Joseph F. Rock. 188, 189(1) Jodi Cobb, NGP. 189(r), 190, 191 Joseph F. Rock. 192, 193 United Press International, Bettmann Newsphotos. 195 Robin L. Graham. 196 Cotton Coulson, Brendan Archive. 198, 199 Carlo Mauri.

200–204 B. Anthony Stewart. 205 Henri de Monfreid. 206(tl), 206(cl) Charles Martin. 206(tr) Franklin Price Knott. 206(b) Melville Bell Grosvenor. 207(tl) Hans Hildenbrand. 207(tc) Charles Martin. 207(tr) B. Anthony Stewart. 207(bl) W. Robert Moore. 207(br) Eastman Kodak Company. 208 Victor R. Boswell, Jr., NGP. 209 W. Robert Moore. 210, 211 Alan J. Villiers. 212, 213 American Museum of Natural History. 214 Keystone View Company. 215 Wide World Photos. 216, 217 Arthur A. Allen. 218 Drawing by Gaar Williams; Reprinted by permission: Tribune Media Services.

220, 221 Robert B. Goodman. 222 David Knudsen, from William Beebe. 224, 225 Paintings by Else Bostelmann. 226, 227 Luis Marden. 228, 229 David Doubilet. 230, 231 Jonathan S. Blair. 232, 233 William R. Curtsinger. 234(1) David Doubilet. 234, 235 Anne L. Doubilet. 235(r) David Doubilet. 236, 237 Emory Kristoff, NGP. 238 Al Giddings, Ocean Images. 239 Emory Kristoff and Alvin M. Chandler, both NGS. 240, 241 Painting by Pierre Mion for *National Geographic*.

242–245 U.S. Navy. 247 Paintings by Thornton Oakley for *National Geographic*. 249(r) United Press International, Bettmann Newsphotos. 251(tl) U.S. Navy. 251(bl) United Press International, Bettmann Newsphotos. 251(r) George De Zayas. 253 U.S. Navy. 253(b) B. Anthony Stewart. 255 British Ministry of Information. 256(t) U.S. Navy. 258 Carl R. Markwith. 260(t) Robert S. Oakes. 260(b) Drawing by Selz; © 1943, 1971 *The New Yorker, Inc.*

262, 263 Wally McNamee. 264 Drawing by Lucien Jones. 265 Brown Brothers. 266 © Times Newspapers Ltd. London. 267 Solo Syndication & Literary Agency. 268, 269 Painting by Lt. William F. Draper, U.S. Navy. 270, 271 Howard Sochurek. 273 Gordon W. Gahan. 274 Robert Azzi. 276 Michael Coyne, The Image Bank. 278, 279 Wilbur E. Garrett, NGS. 280, 281 Michael S. Wilson. 282, 283 James Nachtwey. 284, 285 Steve McCurry.

286, 287 J.R. Eyerman, *Life* © 1958 Time, Inc. 290(1) Wide World Photos. 290(r) Fred J. Maroon. 291 Culver Pictures, Inc. 293 By Edgerton, Germeshausen and Grier, Inc. for the U.S. Atomic Energy Commission. 293(r) U.S. Army. 295 Robert E Sisson, NGP. 296(t) Willard R. Culver. 296(b) Andrew H. Brown. 298 B. Anthony Stewart. 299 Andrew H. Brown. 300(t) Leet Brothers. 300(b) Clifton Adams. 301 Luis Marden. 303 J. Baylor Roberts.

306, 307 Samuel Silverstein. 308 U.S. Geological Survey. 310, 311 Bradford Washburn. 313 Galen Rowell. 314, 315 Bradford Washburn. 316 Barry C. Bishop, NGS. 317 Luther G. Jerstad. 318, 319

Nicholas De Vore III. 320, 321 Vera Komarkova. 323 John Roskelley, Photo Researchers. 324(l) Nena Holguin. 324, 325 Reinhold Messner. 326, 327 Galen Rowell.

328, 329 Bates Littlehales, NGP. 331 W. Robert Moore. 332 Joseph D. Lavenburg, NGP. 335 Victor R. Boswell, Jr., NGP. 336 Joseph D. Lavenburg, NGP. 338 B. Anthony Stewart. 339(tl&b) Luis Marden. 339(tr) Wilbur E. Garrett, NGS. 340(t) James L. Stanfield, NGP. 340(b) Joseph H. Bailey, NGP. 342(t) Thomas J. Abercrombie, NGS. 342(b) Volkmar Wentzel. 343 Harald Schultz. 344(tl) Winfield Parks. 344(tr&c), 345 Victor R. Boswell, Jr., NGP. 347 (tl) Gordon W. Gahan. 347 (tr) Baron Hugo Van Lawick. 347 (bl) Rod Brindamour. 347 (br) Robert M. Campbell. 348 Joseph D. Lavenburg, NGP. 350 *Mad* magazine © 1958 by E.C. Publications, Inc.

352, 353 Dean Conger for NASA. 354, 355 Richard H. Stewart. 356, 357 Painting by Tom Lovell for *National Geographic*. 358 Henry Burroughs, Wide World Photos. 359 Doug Martin. 360, 361 James A. McDivitt, NASA. 362, 363 E.C. Cernan, NASA. 364, 365 NASA. 366, 367 Scene from the IMAX®/ OMNIMAX® Film "The Dream Is Alive" © Smithsonian Institution and Lockheed Corporation 1985. 368, 369 NASA. 370, 371 U.S. Geological Survey, Flagstaff, Arizona. 372, 373 NASA. 374, 375 Painting by James Hervat for *National Geographic*.

376, 377 James L. Amos, NGP. 379 James L. Stanfield, NGP. 380, 381 James P. Blair, NGP. 382 Mate Mestrovic. 384(tl) Barry C. Bishop, NGS. 384(cl) Carol Hughes. 384(bl) Joseph H. Bailey, NGP. 384(tr) Daniel Tomasi, the Cousteau Society. 384(cr) Jonathan Wright. 384(br) David Doubilet. 385(l) Edgar Boyles. 385(r) Mick Coyne. 386(l) Victor R. Boswell, Jr., NGP. 386(r) Foster Wiley. 387 Bianca Lavies, NGP. 388(t) Joseph H. Bailey, NGP. 388(b) Joseph D. Lavenburg, NGP. 389 Victor R. Boswell, Jr., NGP. 390 Fred Ward, Black Star. 393(t) Leroy Woodson, Wheeler Pictures. 393(b) WORD-SMITH by Tim Menees. © 1976 Universal Press Syndicate. Reprinted by permission. 394 Winfield Parks. 397 James P. Blair, NGP. 398 © 1980 Henson Associates, Inc. Reprinted by permission.

400, 401 Bruce Dale, NGP. 402 From Brigadier General William Mitchell. 404, 405 Belinda Wright. 406, 407 Oria and Iain Douglas-Hamilton. 408 Frank and John Craighead. 409 Pat Powell. 410, 411 Al Giddings, Ocean Images. 412, 413 Glenn W. Elison. 414 U.S. Air Force. 415

Robert S. Dyer, Environmental Protection Agency. 416 James P. Blair, NGP. 417 Ted Spiegel, Black Star. 418, 419 Dewitt Jones. 420 James P. Blair, NGP. 421 Walter Meayers Edwards. 422, 423(1) Fred Ward, Black Star. 423(r) James P. Blair, NGP. 424, 425 Steven C. Wilson, Entheos.

426, 427 James L. Amos, NGP. 429 Martin Rogers. 430 Pat Lanza Field, NGS. 431 Painting by Ned M. Seidler for *National Geographic*. 432 Joseph D. Lavenburg, NGP. 433 Victor R. Boswell, Jr., NGP. 434 Robert S. Oakes. 435 Jon Schneeberger, Ted Johnson, Jr., and Anthony Peritore, all NGS. 436 Wilbur E. Garrett, NGS. 439 William Albert Allard. 440, 441 Claude E. Petrone, NGS. 442 Joseph D. Lavenburg, NGP. 443 Joseph H. Bailey, NGP. 444 Lowell Georgia. 447 Steve McCurry. 448 Joseph H. Bailey, NGP. 451 James L. Amos, NGP. 452 GRIN AND BEAR IT by Lichty and Wagner © 1982 Field Enterprises, Inc. by permission of North American Syndicate, Inc.

454, 455 Boehringer Ingelheim International GmbH. 456 David Fairchild. 457 Phillip Degginger, Bruce Coleman, Inc. 458, 459 David Scharf. 460–464 Lennart Nilsson. 466 Mallinckrodt Institute of Radiology, St. Louis. 467 Howard Sochurek. 468–471 Kevin Fleming. 472, 473 National Optical Astronomy Observatories, Arizona.

474, 475 Stephen G. St. John. 477 Lydia Mychiliuk Suchy. 478–479 Bill Curtsinger. 479 Eric Hiner. 482 Louie Psihoyos. 483 José Azel. 485(t) Steve Raymer. 485(b) George Steinmetz. 486 Lisa Silcock/DJA River Films. 487(tc) Ken Regan/Camera 5. 487(tr) Steve McCurry. 487(b) David E. Hornback. 488(tl) Mark Thiessen. 488(tr) James L. Stanfield. 489(tr) David Alan Harvey.

492, 493 Stephen Alvarez. 494 Johan Reinhard. 496 Johns Hopkins Hospital. 497 Kenneth Garrett. 498, 499 Original photograph courtesy of NASA. Printed from digital image © 1996 CORBIS. 500 Eric Valli and Diane Summers. 502 Ted Tamburo. 504 Joseph McNally/Superimposed brain image by Bassem Mora and George Carman. 506, 507 Gordon Wiltsie. 509(t&b) Michael Nichols, NGP. 510 George Steinmetz. 512, 513 Norbert Rosing. 514 Victor R. Boswell, Jr. 515 Hans Larsson. 516, 517 Louie Psihoyos.

TEXT CREDITS

Grateful acknowledgment is made for permission to quote from the following:

William Beebe, *Half Mile Down*, published by Harcourt Brace, 1934. Rights reserved

by Meredith Corporation, New York.

Tom Buckley, "With the National Geographic on Its Endless, Cloudless Voyage," September 6, 1970, Copyright © The New York Times.

Arthur C. Clarke, *Interplanetary Flight: An Introduction to Astronautics*, 1960. By permission of the author and the author's agents, Scott Meredith Literary Agency, Inc.

Michael Collins, *Carrying the Fire*, copyright © 1974 Michael Collins. By permission of the publishers, Farrar, Straus and Giroux, Inc.

C. Day-Lewis, "Transitional Poem" from *Collected Poems 1929–1933*, published by The Hogarth Press, 1938.

Kendrick Frazier, *The Violent Face of Nature: Severe Phenomena and Natural Disasters*, published by William Morrow & Company, Inc., 1979. By permission of William Morrow & Company, Inc., and Harold Matson Company, Inc.

Bernard Grun, *The Timetables of History: A Horizontal Linkage of People and Events*, copyright © 1975, 1979 Simon & Schuster, Inc. (A Touchstone Book).

Geoffrey T. Hellman, "Geography Unshackled," September 25, October 2, and October 9, 1943, published by *The New Yorker*. Included here by permission of Special Collections, New York University.

Tom Holzel and Audrey Salkeld, *First on Everest: The Mystery of Mallory and Irvine*, published by Henry Holt and Company, Inc., 1986.

Roland Huntford, *Scott and Amundsen*, published by Hodder & Stoughton, London and Toronto, 1979.

Roland Huntford, *The Last Place on Earth*, published by Atheneum, 1986.

Rudyard Kipling, *The Explorer*, © 1940 Elsie Kipling Bambridge, published by Doubleday & Co., Inc.

Archibald MacLeish, "A Reflection: Riders on Earth Together, Brothers in Eternal Cold," December 25, 1968, copyright © *The New York Times*.

Frank Luther Mott, A *History of American Magazines, 1885–1905*, published by The Belknap Press, Harvard University Press, 1930–1968.

New York Times editorial, "Footnote to Geography," July 26, 1942, copyright © *The New York Times*.

New York Times editorial, "Maps of a Changing World," January 15, 1945, copyright © *The New York Times*.

Time-Life Books Editors, *This Fabulous Century: 1920–1930*, copyright © 1968 Time-Life Books Inc.

Washington Star feature article, Sunday Section, February 5, 1942. All rights reserved.